This is a full-scale study of prices in medieval Scotland, *c*. 1260–1542, which includes detailed discussions of coinage, and weights and measures. Nearly 6,000 prices are listed individually, average prices are calculated for each commodity, and for groups of commodities such as cereals and livestock. Scots prices are compared with English, and the significance of the data for the economic history of medieval Scotland is analysed fully.

This is the only full study to have been undertaken on Scots medieval prices, and there is no comparable work on Scottish medieval economic history in print.

Changing values in medieval Scotland

Changing values in medieval Scotland

A study of prices, money, and weights and measures

Elizabeth Gemmill and Nicholas Mayhew

CAMBRIDGE UNIVERSITY PRESS
Cambridge, New York, Melbourne, Madrid, Cape Town, Singapore, São Paulo

Cambridge University Press
The Edinburgh Building, Cambridge CB2 2RU, UK

Published in the United States of America by Cambridge University Press, New York

www.cambridge.org
Information on this title: www.cambridge.org/9780521473859

First published 1995
This digitally printed first paperback version 2006

A catalogue record for this publication is available from the British Library

Library of Congress Cataloguing in Publication data

Gemmill, Elizabeth.
Changing values in medieval Scotland: a study of prices, money, and weights
and measures / Elizabeth Gemmill and Nicholas Mayhew.
p. cm.
Includes bibliographical references and index.
ISBN 0 521 47385 3
1. Prices – Scotland – History. 2. Money – Scotland – History.
3. Weights and measures – Scotland – History. 4. Scotland – History – 1057–
1603. I. Mayhew, N. J. II. Title.
HB235.S4G46 1995
332.4′9411′0902–dc20 94-5287 CIP

ISBN-13 978-0-521-47385-9 hardback
ISBN-10 0-521-47385-3 hardback

ISBN-13 978-0-521-02709-0 paperback
ISBN-10 0-521-02709-8 paperback

Contents

Figures

Tables

Preface

When preparing a catalogue of the Scottish coins in the Ashmolean Museum, I quickly discovered the need for a book on Scots medieval prices. No such study then existed,[1] so I set out to provide one. In so far as I have made any progress at all towards that goal, it is largely due to the help that I have received along the way. The earliest assistance came from the Pitlochry Colloquium for Scottish Medieval and Renaissance Studies, who adopted this research as one of their Economic History Projects, and from the University of Glasgow who elected me to a Newlands Visiting Fellowship. It soon became apparent that part-time and voluntary work was unlikely to make much impact on the task, but in 1986 the University of Oxford awarded me a one-year grant which permitted the appointment of Dr Elizabeth Gemmill (then Davies) as research assistant. On the basis of the work prepared in that first year, we were able to win two further years' funding from the Economic and Social Research Council. This essential support permitted the collection and analysis of a large body of data. Dr Gemmill worked from the first with a degree of enthusiasm and palaeographic expertise which quickly transformed her role from that of research assistant to one of co-author. Moreover, she has sustained that commitment, unpaid, throughout the four subsequent years which it has taken us to complete our task.

While research grants permitted the employment of Dr Gemmill, my own involvement in this project was only made possible by the support of my own institution, the Ashmolean Museum, Oxford. For this I am grateful, above all, to my head of department, Michael Metcalf, whose understanding of the wider relevance of numismatics enabled him to encourage me in studies on the fringes of the principal area of my

[1] Though Alexander Grant, *Independence and Nationhood: Scotland 1306–1469* (London, 1984), and Alexander W.K. Stevenson, 'Trade between Scotland and the Low Countries in the Late Middle Ages' (unpublished PhD thesis, University of Aberdeen, 1982) have now both published short tables of prices which serve to illustrate the importance of the subject.

museum responsibilities. It is a pleasure to record my debt to him, and to be able to celebrate the continuing tradition of liberal scholarship in Oxford, at a time when it is so much under threat elsewhere. My debt to Scottish scholars, alive and dead, will be apparent to anyone reading this book, but I should particularly thank Professor G.W.S. Barrow for early encouragement, and Dr Alexander Grant, Dr David Ditchburn, Dr Grant Simpson, and Dr Alexander Stevenson who all read at least part of it in draft.

A general review of price trends in Scotland from the thirteenth to the sixteenth century appears in Chapter 1. This attempts to summarize, in its broadest outlines, a picture actually made up of thousands of separate transactions, which have been individually recorded and analysed. In addition to the collection of price data, the combing of so much medieval Scottish material has generated a number of by-products. In searching the incomparable Aberdeen archives for prices, Dr Gemmill has also accumulated evidence for a broader-based discussion of the economic life of the medieval burgh which appears as Chapter 2. Chapters 3 and 4, on weights and measures and the coinage, are essential pieces of apparatus for the study of prices. Chapter 5 lists the prices commodity by commodity. In Chapter 6 by way of conclusion, I have offered an interpretation of some of the larger trends influencing the Scottish economy. This is not a one chapter economic history of medieval Scotland, but an attempt to apply the price evidence, summarized in Chapter 1, to illustrate its wider meaning for the history of the period. Micro-economics can hardly become more detailed than to examine the individual transactions in the way that we have done, yet the overall price evidence is, of course, a crucial macro-economic indicator. It has to be admitted that while the first five chapters of this book attempt objective description, the last chapter is much more in the nature of speculative discussion. It may be anticipated that this last interpretative chapter will stand the test of time less well than the earlier factual sections, but this awareness cannot excuse us from the task of trying to make sense of the evidence we have collected.

This book appears as the work of joint authors. We have both read it all and subscribe to it all. However, some indication of the division of labour and responsibility is appropriate. Dr Gemmill performed the lion's share of the data collection.[2] She has also written Chapter 2 on Aberdeen, with the exception of the sections on bread and ale. Chapter 3 on weights and measures is entirely her work. I have directed the

[2] Dr Margaret O'Hara also worked on the project for the final two months of funded research, after Dr Gemmill took up her post in the Department of Medieval History, at the University of Glasgow.

project and assumed responsibility for the administration of the two research grants mentioned above. The work could not have been attempted without this support from the University of Oxford and the Economic and Social Research Council. I have written the Introduction and Chapters 1, 4, 5, and 6, although Chapter 5 on the prices of individual commodities was heavily dependent on Dr Gemmill's collection of data and rigorous eye for detail.

N.J.M.

Abbreviations

Aberdeen Charters	P.J. Anderson (ed.), *Charters and Other Writs Illustrating the History of the Royal Burgh of Aberdeen* (Aberdeen, 1890)
ACR	Aberdeen Council Registers
ADG	Aberdeen Dean of Guild Accounts
ALA	Thomas Thomson (ed.), *The Acts of the Lords Auditors of Causes and Complaints*, Record Commission (Edinburgh, 1839)
ALC	Thomas Thomson (ed.), *Acta Dominorum Concilii: The Acts of the Lords of Council in Civil Causes*, Record Commission (Edinburgh, 1839)
ALCPA	R.K. Hannay (ed.), *Acts of the Lords of Council in Public Affairs 1501–1554* (Edinburgh, 1932)
Ancient Laws	Cosmo Innes (ed.), *Ancient Laws and Customs of the Burghs of Scotland I* A.D. 1124–1424, *SBRS* (1868)
APS	T. Thomson and C. Innes (eds.), *Acts of the Parliaments of Scotland*, I–V (Edinburgh, 1814–75)
BAR	British Archaeological Reports
BNJ	*British Numismatic Journal*
'Burgh Laws'	'Leges Burgorum', in *Ancient Laws*, pp. 4–58
CDS	Joseph Bain (ed.), *Calendar of Documents relating to Scotland Preserved in Her Majesty's Public Record Office, London* (Edinburgh, 4 vols., 1881–8). Grant G. Simpson and James D. Galbraith (eds.), *Calendar of Documents relating to Scotland Preserved in the Public Record Office and the British Library, V* (Supplementary AD 1108–1516), SRO (Edinburgh, 1986)
Cochran-Patrick	R.W. Cochran-Patrick (ed.), *Records of the Coinage of Scotland* (Edinburgh, 2 vols, 1876)

Coinage in Medieval Scotland	D.M. Metcalf (ed.), *Coinage in Medieval Scotland (1100–1600)*, BAR, 45 (Oxford, 1977)
CP	Coldingham Prior
CS	Coldingham Sacrist
DB	Durham Bursar
DHS	Joseph Stevenson (ed.), *Documents Illustrative of the History of Scotland from the Death of King Alexander the Third to the Accession of Robert Bruce, 1286–1306* (HMSO, Edinburgh, 2 vols., 1870)
DPS	Durham Proctor of Scotland
EcHR	*Economic History Review*
ER	John Stuart and others, *Rotuli Scaccarii regum Scotorum. The Exchequer Rolls of Scotland,* I–XVII, 1264–1542 (HMSO, Edinburgh, 1878–97)
HBJV	(Household Book of James V) J.H. and J. MacKenzie and R. Graham (eds.), 'Excerpta e libris domicitii domini Jacobi Quinti Regis Scotorum. MDXXV–MDXXXII' Bannatyne Club, 54 (Edinburgh, 1836)
HI	Holy Island
HMS	Historical Manuscripts Commission
MLWL	R.E. Latham, *Revised Medieval Latin Word-List from British and Irish Sources* (London, 1965)
NC	*Numismatic Chronicle*
PRO	Public Record Office
PSAS	*Proceedings of the Society of Antiquaries of Scotland*
SBRS	*Scottish Burgh Records Society*
SCBF	W. Croft Dickinson (ed.), *The Sheriff Court Book of Fife 1515–22,* SHS, 3rd ser., 12 (1928)
SCBI	*Sylloge of Coins of the British Isles., XXXV: Scottish Coins,* J.D. Bateson and N.J. Mayhew (Oxford, 1987)
SHR	*Scottish Historical Review*
SHS	Scottish History Society
SMT	M. Lynch, M. Spearman, and G. Stell (eds.), *The Scottish Medieval Town* (Edinburgh, 1988)
SRO	Scottish Record Office
SS	Surtees Society
SSG	Surtees Society Glossary (the Glossary of terms

used in account rolls of obedientiaries of Durham Cathedral Priory made by Canon Fowler in volume III of his extracts from obedientiary accounts: SS, 103 (1901), pp. 889–989)

TA	Thomas Dickson (ed. of I) and Sir James Balfour Paul (ed. of II–VII), *Compota Thesaurariorum regum Scotorum. Accounts of the Lord High Treasurer of Scotland*, I–VII, 1473–1541 (HMSO, Edinburgh, 1877–1907)

Weights and measures

b.	boll
c.	chaldron (= celdra)
cod.	codrus
cog.	cogall
d.	dicker
dol.	tun (= doleum)
f.	firlot
g.	groot
h.	hide
lag.	gallon (= lagena)
l.	last
lb	pound (= libra)
LH	long hundred
pet.	stone (= petra)
pond.	weight, pound (= pondus)
qr	quarter
SH	short hundred

Introduction

It is now well over a century since the appearance of Thorold Rogers' great study of English prices and wages, and fifty years since Beveridge was diverted from his study of price history to devote himself to his more famous Report.[1] Why, then, has there been no similar price history for Scotland?[2] The chief deterrent to such work has been the absence of sufficient data. While English historians are blessed with one of the largest body of surviving contemporary records in Europe, medieval Scottish documents are rare, and documents containing prices especially so. English price historians can reject large bodies of evidence, choosing instead only the best series of most reliable and comparable material, while the Scottish price historian seems in contrast often to be grasping at straws. Whereas the English evidence permits the calculation of mean prices and even of means of means, in Scotland there are often periods of years at a time for some commodities which have failed to yield a single price. The task had not been attempted in the past quite simply because it did not seem feasible. The rules drawn up by the International Scientific Committee on Price History in 1930 called for data to be collected only from a single city or limited area, with each commodity series drawn from the same set of records for the whole of the period studied.[3] Within the terms of this council of perfection, no Scottish medieval price history can ever be written.

[1] J.E. Thorold Rogers, *A History of Agriculture and Prices in England, 1259–1793* (Oxford, 7 vols., 1866–1902). W.H. Beveridge, *Prices and Wages in England from the 12th to the 19th Century* (London and New York, 1939). More recently, of course, this field has been dominated by the work of David Farmer, culminating in his contributions to the *Agrarian History of England and Wales*, II, ed. H.E. Hallam (Cambridge, 1988), pp. 716–817, and III, ed. Edward Miller (Cambridge, 1991), pp. 431–525.

[2] As I write T.C. Smout's study of prices in early modern Scotland approaches publication: Alexander Gibson and Christopher Smout, *Prices, Food and Wages in Scotland, 1550–1780* (Cambridge, 1994).

[3] Summarized by Ingrid Hammarström, 'The Price Revolution of the Sixteenth Century: Some Swedish Evidence', *Scandinavian Economic History Review* (5), 1957, 118–54, reprinted in Peter H. Ramsey (ed.), *The Price Revolution in Sixteenth-Century England* (London, 1971).

Nevertheless, it was an English analogy which led me to explore a different approach. David Farmer's brief study of prices in Angevin England,[4] though lacking the massive authority of his work on later periods because of the scarcity of early data, caught my interest because it showed that important developments could sometimes be revealed, at least in outline, by even a few shreds of evidence. Accordingly, I determined to set about collecting such Scottish price evidence as I could find. I believe that the material collected here does provide enough of the picture for the major trends in Scottish medieval price movements to be discernible.

We have, however, encountered a number of major problems, and it would be foolish to underestimate them. Weights and measures caused numerous difficulties. They changed over time, and they also varied from place to place, making it difficult to be sure that we were able to compare units of equal size. The chapter on weights and measures prepared by Dr Gemmill goes some way towards clarifying and quantifying this problem, though not to eradicate it, and it is hoped that this chapter will be a useful contribution to the study of weights and measures in Scotland. Our general approach to complications of this type has been to collect the data as a first step towards increasing our knowledge and understanding of the difficulty, rather than to use the problem as an excuse to do nothing. In the same way I have devoted a chapter to the question of currency, a subject which is obviously of crucial importance for the study of prices. Both these two chapters have had to deal with somewhat technical subjects in considerable detail. Adam Smith once remarked, 'I am always willing to run some hazard of being tedious in order to be sure that I am perspicuous'[5] but immersed in the mass of numismatic and metrological minutiae there is some danger of tedium without its counter-balancing compensations. Less patient readers may prefer to take these sections on trust.

A further problem concerns the various different kinds of price quotation which we have encountered. Where the data permit, price historians rightly prefer to restrict their enquiry to prices of a single type; for example sale prices from one particular type of account. As has already been observed, we have had to make do with any kind of price quotation we can find, despite the distortions which this may sometimes entail. Thus in royal accounts purchases tend to give rather

[4] D.L. Farmer, 'Some Price Fluctuations in Angevin England', *EcHR*, 2nd ser. 9 (1956), 34–43.

[5] Adam Smith, *The Wealth of Nations* (London, 1977), p. 25.

high prices,[6] while sales are often on the low side, yet we have had to use whatever material we can find. In any case, since one man's sale is another's purchase, our view of any transaction depends on whether the buyer's or seller's accounts survive. Moreover, sales mentioned in all kinds of accounts are sometimes little more than accounting devices. 'Sales' in the *Exchequer Rolls* could be genuine market transactions, or a money valuation set on items listed in the charge side of the account, or a commutation of a render in kind.

This brings us to the vexed problem of valuations. The significance of accounting valuations for the price historian is likely to be highly variable. Sometimes such information can give an accurate reflection of likely average prices at any given time, possibly providing a more accurate guide than some genuine transactions which might have been distorted by particular circumstances. On other occasions valuations which have clearly become outdated continue to be applied years later.[7] One interesting barley price illustrates something of this: the price offered attempts to indicate the average price over a number of years – 'ilk yeir to mend uthir' – but the whole case hinges on the question of whether certain rents are too low because of valuations set long before.[8] Our general policy has been to try to accumulate enough instances to begin to be able to distinguish reliable valuations from fossilized ones. However, legal valuations also raise different problems from accounting valuations. The values of goods claimed in court often seem somewhat inflated, while the awards made by the courts sometimes look more moderate,[9] so one needs to be aware of the particular circumstance when evaluating the evidence. However, assize valuations raise still other issues. These local government attempts at price control were essentially designed to hold prices down to reasonable levels in time of scarcity, and to regulate the profits of craftsmen. Most importantly they concerned the price of bread and ale in the burghs, and the prices they ordained for these commodities though generally reliable may tend to flatten out the extremes of glut and dearth. Yet in fixing

[6] *APS* II.7 shows James I's attempt to restrict prices paid by the court to the levels which had prevailed ten days before their arrival.

[7] See, for example, the Exchequer valuations of marts. Below, pp. 232–3, and Athol Murray, 'The Exchequer and Crown Revenue of Scotland 1437–1542' (unpublished PhD thesis, University of Edinburgh, 1961), pp. 83–6.

[8] *ALCPA*, p. 519.

[9] See *SCBF*. Dickinson's note on procedure shows that if spuilzie were proved the valuation was determined by the oath of the pursuer, although the sheriff did have the power to moderate either the quantity or the price claimed, in a procedure known as the taxation of the oath. For the contrast between claims and subsequent awards, see wheat 213–14, 245, 255–6, 262–3, malt 202, oats 80, 126, meal 187, cows 47, 60.

bread prices, the assize often mentions the price of wheat, and this quotation is more likely to be impartially reported. The same observation may be made regarding ale, and barley and malt prices. Obviously the use of prices of various different kinds from various different sources is not straightforward. In order to keep this issue in the reader's mind, individual prices are here published with a letter code giving some indication of the type of price involved.[10] However, such summary classification of sometimes quite complicated transactions can only provide the crudest of indications.

Further difficulties arise from the comparison of prices from a variety of different locations in Scotland. Regional variations in weights and measures have already been mentioned, but price variation across the country was also a result of varied climatic conditions, local specializations, or the effects of war or plague which could sometimes be restricted to limited areas. Unfortunately the evidence at our disposal for the whole of Scotland is too limited to permit us to break it into its appropriate regions, but there can be no doubt that regional price variation will have affected the national picture.

In addition to these major problems we should draw attention to some of the lesser factors which will no doubt have contributed some inaccuracies. The giving of charity, i.e. generous measure, is discussed more fully in the weights and measures chapter. Long and short hundreds can confuse calculations. Although there is some consistency of practice within each commodity, livestock and fish being particularly prone to the use of the long hundred of 120, this can by no means always be assumed. Cloth transactions especially may well involve the use of both long and short hundreds. Accordingly where there is any ambiguity we have calculated unit prices for all commodities on both a 100 and 120 base; where this calculation yields a round number, it may usually be regarded as evidence for the particular hundred in use.

The dating of our evidence is often somewhat uncertain. Accounts often span more than a single year, and it has been our practice consistently to list prices under the earliest possible date, which will usually have been the year of the harvest in question. Thus prices in the account year 1328–9 are listed as 1328, if there are no other definite indications. This policy sometimes has unfortunate effects: for example some high 1481 prices probably properly belong to the notoriously difficult year 1482, but the advantages of following a consistent policy seem in this instance paramount. In addition it needs to be recognized that the dating of legal cases is often particularly difficult since the

[10] The key to the letter code appears in Chapter 5, p. 150.

disputed transaction and the law suit arising from it are often years apart. Even when both dates are known it is not always apparent to which year any valuations in the case relate. Finally on the question of dating, it should be noted that all dates have been converted as necessary to modern years commencing on 1 January.

Carriage costs sometimes affect prices, and though they can be allowed for when explicitly mentioned in the original source, they must usually have been included in the given price without any explicit reference. Variable quality will also have affected prices markedly. The Aberdeen courts talk continually of goods of sufficient merchant quality, and often accounts will explain a particularly low price by reference to poor quality. However, most price quotations make no explicit mention of the condition of the goods concerned. The reality is that a wide variety of goods will have been involved, and stinking fish will not always have been distinguished from sweet, nor fattened beef from tough old oxen. Finally one has to recognize that clerical and arithmetical errors, both medieval and modern, will have crept in, and that where the total volume of evidence is as slim as it is in Scotland the consequences of such errors will be correspondingly great. For example, the oatmeal price from Little Cumbray exceptionally occurs as 22s. per celdra instead of 32s.[11] In this case the details of total price and quantity make the error clear, but some other errors will certainly have slipped through unnoticed.

Further sensible reasons why this project should never have been undertaken could be discussed at length, but perhaps enough has been said to establish that few students are more aware of these problems than those who have grappled with them. However, despite the difficulties, it is our conviction that this project has been worthwhile. Despite all the factors tending to blur and distort our vision, the resultant picture has a degree of plausibility, in relation to English prices and to what else we know of Scottish medieval economic history, sufficient to render these results credible.

It may be helpful to say a few words here about the presentation of the data. In Chapter 5 there appear lists of unit prices for each commodity arranged by year, often running to several hundred prices. There is also a summary table for each commodity arranging the material to give a mean price for each of a series of time periods from the thirteenth century to 1542 (the death of James V). From the 1460s these time periods are straightforward decades, but before then the

[11] *ER* V. 288, 332.

evidence did not survive with sufficient consistency to permit the calculation of decennial means. The time periods A to I were devised to permit some sort of comparison between commodities over the first part of our period. These periods are dated as follows:

A – thirteenth century
B – 1300 to late 1330s
C – late 1330s to 1340s
D – 1350–67
E – 1367–97
F – 1398–1414
G – The Hume Will of 1424
H – 1430s to 1443
I – mid-1440s to 1459

No great claims are being made for the exact figures produced by the calculation of means. They could be recalculated on the basis of slightly different assumptions to produce slightly different results, though the overall picture would not be much changed. Thus all that has been possible is an incomplete outline sketch. It is especially important to remember this when using these mean prices. These figures are not facts, but the result of a series of judgements, selections and interpretations which we have made to render the material more manageable. We believe these conclusions to be valid, but we recognize that scholars will wish to make their own assessments as well. This is made possible by the lists of unit prices. These are published here in summary form only, but it should be enough to give some indication of the hard evidence behind the mean prices and trends which we have calculated. Interested scholars may also make application to the ESRC data archive for access to our complete data base, which contains further information about each price quotation, together with details of additional transactions not capable of yielding the simple unit prices required for the price lists. It is on this complete data base that our calculations have been founded.

The summary table also provides the results of calculations made to convert the mean Scottish currency price to a sterling equivalent. This is necessary in order to strip out the direct effects of the depreciation of the Scots currency. A more usual procedure would have been to calculate pure silver prices, but this approach has the disadvantage of failing to recognize the changes taking place in the later middle ages right across Europe in the value of silver. The sterling equivalent calculation makes some concessions to the rising value of silver, while still providing a reliable yard-stick. This procedure is discussed more fully below.[12] Finally these sterling equivalent prices are indexed on the base period B–C (1300–40s) to facilitate comparison of price trends between commodities, and with Farmer's indices of English prices. Composite indices of Scots cereal and livestock prices have been compiled for comparison with Farmer's English indices, and these appear in Chapter 1.

This book is about medieval Scotland, but neither of the authors is Scots. We can only apologize for the errors from which a Scottish upbringing would have saved us, most particularly in the matter of place-names. It has been our practice to modernize names where we have been able to identify them, leaving those not known to us in the original. Shortly before his death the late Professor Ian Cowan generously agreed to help us with this; we can only ask our Scottish readers to treat our ignorance with the good-humoured indulgence which he would have brought to our problem.

For those readers who are not Scottish, or not familiar with some of the terms, especially those employed as units of weight or measure, it should be pointed out that a glossary appears on pp. 382–409 containing a full explanation of such terms. Those most commonly encountered are the chaldron (celdra), the boll and the firlot, all units of volume usually employed in measuring grain. These terms have often been abbreviated to c., b., and f.: thus the expression 10d.b. stands for 10d. per boll. All sums of money are in Scots currency unless otherwise stated. Before 1367 this is indistinguishable from sterling, but after that date English or sterling money is specifically so designated. Equally Flemish money is often distinguished by the abbreviation g. for groot, while French coin occurs either as sous and denier tournois (s.d.t.) or as francs.

In all we have assembled almost 6,000 prices for twenty-four commodities dating from the thirteenth century to 1542. So meagre an offering cannot be judged by the standards of English, or of early modern, price history. Nevertheless, it is our contention that even so modest a collection does add something to our understanding of medieval Scottish history.

[12] See Chapter 4, pp. 137–40 below.

1 Price trends in medieval Scotland

Scotland is half the size of England and Wales, but because of its relief, soil and climate, the area of Scottish arable and good pasture land is only about a fifth or sixth the size of England's.[1] Rough grazing in Scotland is three times as plentiful as arable land, ensuring a pastoral bias in its agriculture and economy which has left its mark on Scottish prices. Scotland was always a country 'more gevin to store of bestiall than ony production of cornys'[2], making grain correspondingly dear there and livestock cheap. Geographical factors also encouraged the consumption and even the export of fish.

Estimates of the population supported on this land have varied widely, from about a million to less than half that, but the most recent work on English population, estimates of which have also fluctuated widely, now suggest that the larger figures look the more reliable.[3] A figure of

[1] These introductory remarks owe much to the essays on the Scottish economy in Alexander Grant, *Independence and Nationhood: Scotland 1306–1469* (London, 1984), pp. 61–88, and Ranald Nicholson, *Scotland: The Later Middle Ages* (Edinburgh, 1978), pp. 1–26. For the physical geography of Scotland see Peter McNeill and Ranald Nicholson (eds), *An Historical Atlas of Scotland c.400–c.1600* (St Andrews, 1975), maps 1 and 2 and text 1. See also *Agricultural Statistics United Kingdom 1988* (HMSO, 1990). The figures for land use in the 1980s may be summarized, in millions of hectares, as follows:

	Total agricultural land	Arable	Pasture	Rough grazing
England	9.9	5.3	3.1	1.2
Scotland	6.0	1.1	0.6	4.1

[2] A sixteenth-century observation cited by Nicholson, *Scotland*, p. 4.

[3] For example, John Hatcher, *Plague, Population, and the English Economy 1348–1530* (London, 1977), pp. 13, 68, and for the most up-to-date statement by a demographic specialist, R. Smith, 'Demographic Developments in Rural England, 1300–48: A Survey', in B.M.S. Campbell (ed.), *Before the Black Death: Studies in the Crisis of the Early Fourteenth Century* (Manchester, 1991), pp. 25–78. Estimates of English urban populations are also under-going a process of marked upward revision. See D. Keene, 'A New Study of London before the Great Fire', *Urban History Yearbook* (1984), p.

about 6 million for England now commands widespread respect, if not universal agreement, and that in turn might imply about a million for Scotland.

The six to one ratio with England recurs with disconcerting frequency, but the upper population estimate for medieval Scotland is also supported by what we know of early eighteenth-century Scottish population totals. In England and very probably in Scotland too, it was not until after 1700 that population recovered to the levels achieved before the Black Death, so the figure of 1.1 million for Scotland in 1707 has implications for medievalists. The eighteenth-century data[4] also show that this population was much more evenly distributed across the whole country before the clearances and industrialization, and this is borne out by the 1366 valuations which were higher for the land north of the Forth than for that south of it. A similar mental adjustment needs to be made in favour of the west, which was probably more densely settled than the distribution of urban settlements, which is strongly eastern in character, would suggest.[5]

The Scottish medieval urban population is usually guessed to have been about 10% of the total, a figure reached in England by the eleventh century. Very little work has so far been done on this topic, but an urban population of some hundred thousand people living in about fifty burghs *c.* 1300 would give an average of 2,000, with most of the burghs falling well below that figure. Such evidence as we possess from burgess lists, tax rolls, or estimates of house and burgage plot numbers has led a leading student of fourteenth-century Scottish urban life to speak of most burgh populations in hundreds rather than thousands.[6] Scottish lists of burgesses and tax payers need to be treated with great caution, as they seem to require larger multipliers than corresponding English lists. Edinburgh certainly exceeded 12,000, plus the suburbs and Leith and Canongate, in the later sixteenth century, despite a 1583 tax roll listing only 1,245 payers.[7] On this reckoning the top ten medieval Scottish burghs may have ranged from as much as 10,000 down to

20; D. Keene, *Survey of Medieval Winchester* (Oxford, 1985), I, pp. 367–8; E. Rutledge, 'Immigration and Population Growth in Early Fourteenth-Century Norwich: Evidence from the Tithing Roll', *Urban History Yearbook* (1988), p. 27.

[4] Grant, *Independence and Nationhood*, pp. 72–3.

[5] G.W.S. Barrow, 'The Sources for the History of the Highlands in the Middle Ages', in Loraine Maclean (ed.), *The Middle Ages in the Highlands* (Inverness, 1981), pp. 11–22.

[6] Elizabeth Ewan, *Townlife in Fourteenth-Century Scotland* (Edinburgh, 1990), p. 5.

[7] *SMT*, p. 12. See also Michael Lynch, 'The Social and Economic Structure of the Larger Towns, 1450–1600', in *SMT*, p. 285 n. 82, for a summary of evidence and opinion relating to sixteenth-century Scottish urban populations.

something under 5,000 inhabitants, compared with recent estimates for London of 80,000, Norwich of 25,000, Winchester of 10,000, and Dublin of 11,000.[8]

Whatever the size of the Scottish burgh, it seems probable that town life and international trade occupy a larger place in this study than they did in reality. Elsewhere I have estimated England's buoyant exports *c.* 1300 at as little as 4% of GNP[9], and it seems unlikely that the corresponding Scottish figure was greater. The core of the Scottish economy was built up of thousands of men and women eking a living from the land. This truth notwithstanding, the survival of export data and the Aberdeen council records have guaranteed towns and foreign trade a larger than life role in this study. Yet rural evidence is not totally absent. The *Exchequer Rolls* provide much information about the remoter royal estates, as well as about high life at court, while the legal records of the Lords Auditors and of the Lords of Council are a (largely unexplored) mine of information on fifteenth-century agriculture and rural life. These sources show plainly that in the country as well as in the town a market was in operation drawing supply and demand into equilibrium through the mechanisms of money and adjustable prices. This is not to suggest that we do not meet barter, or fossilized, prices, for both these phenomena are met frequently. But it is equally true that ancient prices were recognized and understood as such, while transactions in kind were usually valued, and often actually carried out, in coin. Although no medieval market can be called free, market forces were operating strongly as the movement of prices demonstrates. Even in the highlands, where the sources are lacking, evidence of medieval fairs and markets survives[10] as a witness to the extent of internal trade, carried on independently of the burghs. Equally medieval coins have been found all over Scotland, both north and south, and in town and country.[11] This evidence, which has been increasingly commonly found

[8] See n. 3, and for Dublin, J.C. Russell, *Medieval Regions and their Cities* (Newton Abbot, 1972), pp. 136–7.

[9] N.J. Mayhew, 'Modelling Medieval Monetisation' in B.M.S. Campbell and R.H. Britnell (eds.), *A Commercialising Economy* (Manchester, 1995) forthcoming.

[10] Barrow, 'Highlands'.

[11] D.M. Metcalf, 'The Evidence of Scottish Coin Hoards for Monetary History, 1100–1600', in *Coinage in Medieval Scotland*, pp. 1–60. For single finds see J.D. Bateson, 'Roman and Medieval Coins Found in Scotland, to 1987', *PSAS*, 119 (1989), 165–88, which also usefully up-dates Metcalf's paper. Metal detectors and much more careful archaeological excavation have dramatically extended our knowledge since 1977. This point is most vividly illustrated in J.D. Bateson, *Coin Finds from Cromarty* (Cromarty, 1993). This evidence for medieval monetization is all the more telling because of the remoteness of such sites from the usual centres of trade, such as Berwick, Edinburgh, Perth, and Aberdeen. Similar evidence is emerging from Llanfaes, on Anglesey (information kindly supplied by Edward Besly of the National Museum

in the last decade or so, now argues strongly for a widely monetized society by the thirteenth century similar to that long recognized in England.

Thus the discussion of prices needs to be set in the context of a largely rural and pastoral society, which nevertheless contained significant urban and arable elements. Clannish and feudal features existed side by side with cash trading and money lending. The prices which emerge necessarily reflect the society which gave rise to them. In the rest of this chapter some of the principal price trends evident in Scotland from the thirteenth to the sixteenth century will be outlined. Much of the supporting evidence for this outline lies in the succeeding chapters, but an overview of the price evidence at this stage may help to distinguish the wood from the trees.

Monetary changes[12] had an obvious importance for prices expressed in monetary terms, so this discussion will distinguish first, prices before 1367, expressed in sterling, the common Anglo-Scottish currency, and secondly, after that date, when 'the usual money of Scotland' became increasingly distinct.

Before 1367

The early evidence for the price trends of the separate commodities gives a very patchy impression.[13] Before the fifteenth century only a few commodities have enough prices to enable us to draw firm conclusions about price trends, while some other series have so little data that they give us no clear impression at all. However, taking all commodities together, it will be seen that the very vague indications given by separate commodities do, to a considerable extent, confirm and reinforce one another. For example, on one of the simplest points, it is apparent that a large number of commodities showed a rise in prices in the fourteenth century over their levels in the second half of the thirteenth century. We may note such a jump in prices for wheat,

of Wales), while the historical evidence for a cash economy in Wales has recently been discussed by Carr and Pratt. A.D. Carr, 'The Medieval Cantref of Rhos', *Transactions of the Denbighshire Historical Society*, 41 (1992), 7–24, and 'A Debatable land: Arwystli in the Middle Ages', *Montgomeryshire Collections*, 80 (1992), 39–54. D. Pratt, 'Fourteenth-Century Marford and Hoseley: A Maerdref in Transition', *Transactions of the Denbighshire Historical Society*, 41 (1992), 25–69. For the monetary resources of fourteenth-century Cumberland drawn into Scotland, see C. McNamee, 'Buying off Robert Bruce: An Account of Moneys Paid to the Scots by Cumberland Communities in 1313–4', *Transactions of the Cumberland and Westmorland Antiquarian and Archaeological Society*, 92 (1992), 77–89.

[12] For a detailed discussion of currency matters, see Chapter 4 below.

[13] For prices of individual commodities, see Chapter 5 below.

oatmeal, oxen, cows, sheep, salt, wool, and wine. And since this trend is clear for all these commodities, it is likely that the less conclusive evidence for the same trend shown by malt, oats, and hides is giving us the same message. Indeed, such is the accumulated weight of the evidence that it seems reasonably certain that there was a rise in price between thirteenth- and fourteenth-century levels for all commodities.[14]

Unfortunately lack of data prevents us from dating this rise in prices any more closely. Direct Scottish evidence for any commodity between 1304 and 1325 is extremely rare. It is clear that prices had jumped markedly by the late 1320s, but we are unable to say more precisely when it happened.[15] The evidence is better from the late 1320s – when all prices were high – to the 1340s when a number of commodities (for example, wheat, oats, marts, sheep, wool, and hides) provide some indication that there was a dip in prices. Very occasionally, it is also apparent that a particular year stands out as especially good or bad. The year 1288 saw unusually fine weather, producing a good harvest of wheat and oatmeal, and relatively easy production of salt, leading to lower prices for these commodities. On the other hand, 1330 was an expensive year. Importantly, these exceptionally good or bad years, the rising fourteenth-century prices, and the 1340s dip, all correspond to similar circumstances in England.

The comparison between Scottish and English prices is clearly worth making in detail.[16] Cereals were consistently dearer in Scotland than in England, but some other commodities, particularly livestock, were regularly cheaper in Scotland. This consistent tendency in the price evidence is nothing more than we might expect: it confirms everything we know about Anglo-Scottish trade, in which cereals were regularly imported into Scotland, while cattle were driven, or their meat barrelled, and shipped south.[17] For some commodities, especially wool and perhaps sheep, lower Scottish prices may be attributed to the poorer quality of the Scottish article, but for the most part the relative price structures north and south of the border result from the different agricultural

[14] However, the 1260s were not a dear decade in England, and it may be that if Scots prices had survived from the dearer 1270s, the rise in prices in the fourteenth century would probably appear less marked.

[15] Comparison with England, however, suggests a pretty reasonable guess. See below, pp. 15–16.

[16] See especially the comparative tables in Chapter 5.

[17] Cf. Smith, *The Wealth of Nations*, p. 67: 'Grain, the food of the common people, is dearer in Scotland than in England, whence Scotland receives almost every year very large supplies', and p. 135: 'It is not more than a century ago that in many parts of the highlands of Scotland, butcher's meat was as cheap or cheaper than even bread made of oatmeal.'

conditions which encouraged or discouraged particular types of farming. The physical geography of Scotland, then as now, did not promote the widespread cultivation of wheat which could be more easily had by importing it from England or Ireland. The same was true of all cereal cultivation, though the evidence perhaps suggests that English and Scots prices were closer to one another for barley, malt, and oats than for wheat. This may result from the possibility of cultivating barley and oats in harsher regions than was feasible for wheat, but this is perhaps reading too much into the evidence which is not clear-cut in any case. At all events, the journey of John de Rystone, riding from Scotland with the English king's horses in 1304, gives a very clear indication that the price of oats fell as he travelled south, clearly suggesting that even oats – the Scottish cereal *par excellence* – were more easily and more cheaply come by in England.[18] Apart from cereals, the relatively high price of wax in Scotland is perhaps also attributable to the less favourable climate. For goods which were imported by both Scotland and England, most obviously wine and salt, higher Scottish prices may well have been caused by the longer and more perilous distances travelled by merchants.[19]

On the other hand the relatively low Scottish prices of livestock and associated products, particularly wool and hides, reflect the pastoral bias of Scottish agriculture, and confirm those sources which inform us of major Scottish exports of cattle, hides, and wool. Equally, the comparatively low prices of fish in Scotland, most notably salmon, make perfect sense in terms of Scotland's natural advantages of coastline, river, and loch.

It is even possible to refine the picture further with a consideration of price levels at Durham. Tables have been compiled for individual commodities in Chapter 5 which compare Scottish prices with southern English and Durham prices. It is clear that for many of our commodities, prices at Durham tended to fall between the Scottish and the English levels, though there were significant exceptions to this: sheep, for example, were sometimes cheaper there than in Scotland while cattle were usually dearer. Since our English price series are, for the most part, dominated by the much more plentiful southern material, Durham's intermediate position in terms of price levels and in terms of the relative

[18] PRO E 101/98/33, extracted by Bain in *CDS* II, no. 1581, p. 410. See also below, pp. 189–90.

[19] Salt, of course, was also domestically produced in England and Scotland. See below, pp. 323–30.

importance of commodities, which was similar to that for Scotland, confirmed the perceived Scottish trends.[20]

It is reassuring that the evidence of Scottish prices compared with English should so clearly confirm what we know of Anglo-Scottish trade and the natural bias of northern agriculture. It both illustrates trade and farming patterns, and confirms the impressions formed from limited price data. Given that the evidence is so scarce, such confirmation from what we already know is useful.

Two conclusions follow. It is apparent that Scottish prices were not the same as English but that they did move in a fairly constant relationship to them. This is not to postulate a close correlation of annual averages or fluctuations, but it is to suggest that prices both north and south of the border do rise and fall together in a broadly discernible pattern. Though cereals were dearer in Scotland, and livestock cheaper, price movements in England and Scotland exhibit markedly similar trends. Secondly, and following from that, since Scottish prices followed a similar trend to English, an awareness of English price movements in fact provides a broad guide to likely developments in Scotland. This conclusion, based on a thorough survey of the available Scottish price evidence for the period has considerable implications for Scottish economic history. It means that despite the scarcity of direct data, the analogy with English prices permits us to gain an approximate indication of the probable behaviour of Scottish prices from the late twelfth to the mid-fourteenth century. Within this framework it seems likely that Durham prices, for some commodities at least, provide a better guide than the general English series. Lowland Scottish prices were probably in a similar relationship to Durham prices as Durham prices themselves were compared with those from farther south. Following Gras' idea of price regions operating at different levels within the same overall system, Scotland was simply another price region.[21]

Of course, Scotland herself no doubt contained several separate price regions, but at this date the evidence is simply insufficient to refine this point, except in so far as certain commodities were generally cheaper in natural centres of supply; Crail, for example, was a source of plentiful and cheap herring and salmon was cheap in Aberdeen. The important general point is that such evidence as we have for Scottish price trends – though not price levels – indicates that they were similar to those for which the evidence is so much more plentiful in England.

[20] For details of the Durham comparison, see the discussion in Chapter 5 under specific commodities.

[21] N.S.B. Gras, *The Evolution of the English Corn Market* (Cambridge, Mass., 1915).

Common price trends perhaps betoken shared economic developments. Since the evidence that we do have points to similar price trends in England and Scotland before 1367, it seems likely that Scotland, like England, may have shared in the quickening pace of economic life discerned by some scholars[22] as a European phenomenon from as early as the late twelfth century. A monetary take-off in the late twelfth century which helped to stimulate prices and economic activity may be seen as one of a number of ingredients – including, of course, demographic growth – which came together at this time, contributing to the great thirteenth-century boom. This boom, which extended into the first quarter of the fourteenth century, has been characterized as a commercial revolution for Europe as a whole. Since Scotland shared so many of the developments on which this commercial revolution was based – the growth in international trade, the foundation of Norman economic and governmental institutions, the booming money supply – and since what later evidence we have shows Scottish prices following the same buoyant trend as in England, it seems likely that Scotland also enjoyed the same general economic up-turn from the twelfth century.[23] Thus, though the Scottish prices which have survived suggest low thirteenth-century levels as the base for the fourteenth-century boom, the English comparison strongly suggests that the thirteenth-century Scottish levels were themselves an advance upon pre-existing prices.[24]

Similarly we may use the English analogy to date more closely the fourteenth-century leap in prices, which may have occurred in Scotland as it did in England in the second half of the first decade of the century. The most likely explanation for the English leap is an influx of bullion brought about by record receipts from the wool trade. Scotland may have shared in this boom, though the likely disruptive

[22] Most notably P. Spufford, *Money and its Use in Medieval Europe* (Cambridge, 1988).

[23] For Scottish money supply, see N.J. Mayhew, 'Money in Scotland in the Thirteenth Century', in *Coinage in Medieval Scotland*, pp. 85–102, recently amended in N.J. Mayhew, 'Alexander III – A Silver Age? An Essay in Scottish Medieval Economic History', in Norman H. Reid (ed.), *Scotland in the Reign of Alexander III 1249–1286* (Edinburgh, 1990).

[24] There are almost no Scottish prices available from before the 1260s. One early wool price – 40s. a sack, 1242, *CDS* I, no. 1594, p. 291 – looks low compared with wool prices from the end of the century, but probably itself represents a rise over early thirteenth-century levels. For rising rents, see below, p. 362. For the late twelfth-century European monetary and price boom, see Spufford, *Money and its Use*, and N.J. Mayhew, 'Frappes de monnaies et hausse des prix en Angleterre de 1180 à 1220', and P. Spufford, 'Le rôle de la monnaie dans la révolution commerciale du xiiie siècle', both in John Day (ed.), *Etudes d'Histoire Monétaire* (Lille, 1984), pp. 159–78 and 355–96.

effects of the war with England should not be underestimated.[25] At any rate, when prices next become plentiful in the 1320s they are high and remain buoyant well into the 1330s. Scotland presumably also experienced the famine levels of 1315–17, though no one would suggest that high prices then constituted any kind of boom.[26]

In Scotland, as in England, there is some evidence of a slight dip in prices shortly before the Plague. Malthusian explanations often advanced for England seem less probable for Scotland which most scholars have not thought crowded,[27] but monetary shortage and the impact of war on trade may well have affected England and Scotland alike, and may perhaps more easily provide a common explanation for a trend in prices which was shared in both countries. It should, however, be conceded that when demographic factors influenced prices in the larger dominant English market, Scots prices would also have been affected, even without corresponding population problems in Scotland.

The Black Death had a shattering impact right across Europe, but in the twenty years after its first appearance its effect on prices and wages in England was complex. Although overall demand probably fell more than production, English prices were generally buoyant well into the 1370s. As well as the rising price of scarce labour, this may reflect a plentiful *per capita* money supply.[28] There is surprisingly little direct evidence for the impact of the Black Death in Scotland, but comparisons with upland England or with Scandinavia are interesting;[29] there can be no doubt that Scottish population will also have fallen dramatically.

The economic effects of such a fall were no doubt complex, and the price evidence is scarce and difficult to interpret. Most of the problems relate to the behaviour of Scottish cereal prices. Wheat and malt prices

25 The only price we have from the critical period – that for cows in 1311 – is low.

26 We have some indication of famine at Berwick in 1315 and 1316, but this may be a result of siege conditions as much as of widespread harvest failure. *CDS* III, nos. 452, 470, and 486, pp. 84–5, 89–90, and 93.

27 On Scottish thirteenth-century population, see R.A. Dodgshon, 'Medieval Settlement and Colonization' in M.L. Parry and T.R. Slater (eds.), *The Making of the Scottish Countryside* (London and Montreal, 1980), p. 28, and A.A.M. Duncan, *Scotland: The Making of the Kingdom* (Edinburgh, 1975), p. 367.

28 English mint output was directly boosted by devaluation, a buoyant export trade (albeit something of an Indian summer), substantial ransom payments, and the introduction of gold coinage. Thus a growing money supply was available to a dramatically reduced population.

29 Mayhew, 'Alexander III', pp. 65–6. Though the argument here is flawed since evidence of mortality from upland benefices can only be an uncertain guide because of the prevalence of absentee clergy. Barbara E. Crawford, *The History of Dunbeath in the Medieval Period* (Dunbeath Preservation Trust, 1990), p. 6, however, makes the comparison with Norway, where she estimates mortality to have been at least one third of the population. See also below, p. 370.

rise sharply, following the English pattern, but barley prices appear to fall, while oats and oatmeal merely hold their own. It is tempting to surmise that oats and barley were more widely available in Scotland, and that it was the imported wheat price which was inflated, but high malt prices cast some doubt on this interpretation. Of course malt also was imported from England, but even so malt prices ought to have been broadly in line with barley prices, even for barley cultivated at home. One might also ask if the inflated wheat and malt prices reveal a shift in preference over the cheaper grains reflecting a new prosperity for the Scottish people. Yet this speculation is probably to place more weight on the few surviving prices than they will bear. A more critical approach to the surviving barley prices may provide a simpler explanation: the barley evidence especially looks curiously out of step with malt, and barley even looks cheap at this date relative to oats. Later prices suggest that the poorer grains did subsequently rise in price more in line with wheat, suggesting either that the barley price was slow to move after the plague, or, more probably, that the barley evidence at this date is anomalous.

Although the barley and to a lesser extent the oats prices do not appear to match the clear wheat evidence closely, post-Plague cereal prices, probably because of the high labour input and the relative scarcity of good corn land in Scotland, were more buoyant than livestock prices. There is little evidence to suggest that the Plague caused an immediate rise in the Scottish price of livestock. Nor does it seem that prices were any higher in the 1360s than they were in the 1350s. In this respect, the impact of the Plague on Scottish prices was a little different from its effect upon English ones. In England there was a slight rise in the price of some livestock from their 1340s levels after the Plague, but the real price rise occurred during the 1360s.[30] Even then, however, prices were much the same as they had been during the expensive years between 1311 and 1330.

That the price of Scottish cattle and sheep did not rise after the Plague should be seen in conjunction with the behaviour of wool and hide prices at that time. The suggestion that wool prices fell after the Plague is fairly strong, although it is also to be noted that prices seem to have been recovering towards the end of the 1360s. The post-Plague evidence for hides, though it is far less unequivocal, points to a decrease in prices there too, confirming the impression of stagnant prices of Scottish livestock in the post-Plague period. Unfortunately we have no real evidence at this date about the behaviour of other animal-derived

[30] See below, pp. 21–4, especially Farmer's livestock mean price.

products, such as wax and cheese, nor indeed for fish, another important Scottish export item.

The post-Plague prices of other commodities are fairly scant, but where the evidence is forthcoming it suggests that there was a price rise for salt, and possibly for coal, iron, and canvas. The increased costs of labour may have been important here.

Despite the somewhat equivocal nature of some of the Scottish price evidence at this time, any information about prices is of considerable importance for the interpretation of the 1366 tax assessment. This 1366 assessment is perhaps the most important single piece of data for Scotland's economy in the immediate post-Plague era.[31] It suggests a dramatic fall of almost half in the value of baronial and ecclesiastical revenues in 1366 compared with those indicated by the surviving thirteenth-century assessments.

One explanation which has been advanced suggests that it was the monetary value of those revenues which had fallen because of an acute shortage of money in Scotland.[32] In fact the monetary evidence does not support the suggestion,[33] and neither does the price data. Although the price evidence is not as clear-cut as we would like at this time, it certainly does not support the idea of a wholesale collapse in prices. The limited evidence for Scottish barley, wool and hide prices could be interpreted to suggest that 1360s prices for these commodities had fallen to about thirteenth-century levels, but it can hardly be maintained that they fell significantly below them. For most commodities post-Plague prices remained well above thirteenth-century levels, and that is enough to dispose of the thesis of monetary deflation as an explanation of the low levels of the 1366 assessment.[34] More generally, however, the evidence for Scottish prices immediately after the Plague is by no means as plentiful as we should like, and is too equivocal, especially in terms of grain prices, for simple explanation. The relative importance of conflicting factors probably varied from commodity to commodity, but in the broadest terms we may suggest that the price of the labour-intensive produce of the best-quality land seems to have been higher

[31] *APS* I. 498–501. For a discussion of the 1366 assessment and the thirteenth-century assessments, see below pp. 363–71, and Tout's introduction to W.N. Thompson and T.F. Tout (eds.), *Register of John de Halton*, Canterbury and York Society (London, 1913).

[32] Nicholson, *Scotland*, p. 175, and also in 'Scottish Monetary Problems in the Fourteenth and Fifteenth Centuries', in *Coinage in Medieval Scotland*, pp. 103–14.

[33] Mayhew, 'Alexander III', pp. 63–4, shows that money supply was buoyant then, and suggests that reduced population may have been a chief cause of the low 1366 assessment.

[34] It may be conceded, however, that we have no highland prices from this time, and it is here that the assessments were especially low.

in post-Plague Scotland, while that of more easily produced goods from the poorer land remained stable or even fell. This really means that Scottish cereals got more expensive, and Scottish livestock grew even cheaper.

Thus the Plague did not change the basic structure of prices in Scotland. Livestock was still relatively cheap in comparison with cereals, indeed perhaps in greater degree after than before the Plague. The commodities which were cheaper in England before the Plague remained so after it, and those which had been more expensive in England earlier also remained so later. Broadly speaking, the economic differences between England and Scotland did not diminish on account of the pestilence, rather they were accentuated by it. As the Black Death eased European land-hunger, marginal economies like Scotland's were probably disproportionately disadvantaged. It may be noted that while the prices of Scotland's exports were more or less static after the Plague, her imports were generally more expensive. In theory at least this should have stimulated Scottish domestic production as an alternative to importing, and promoted the price competitiveness of Scots exports. After 1367, Scottish debasement, working like a modern devaluation, should have magnified this import–export price contrast. But when the bottom fell out of the wool trade at the end of the fourteenth century this widening gap between the price of Scottish imports and her exports would become ever more critical. It remains to be considered whether debasement was the wrong strategy in a period of shrinking volume of international trade, or whether the later medieval recession would have been much worse in Scotland if sound money policies had been pursued.[35]

After 1367

When Scotland left the sterling area in 1367 the direct currency connection between prices north and south of the border was broken. The comparison between English and Scots prices therefore becomes much more difficult; simple tables comparing individual prices – never a very certain guide – become out of the question. However, some more general price comparison is possible as the data become more plentiful. Figures 1 and 2 illustrate very crude indices of Scottish cereal and livestock prices, from the thirteenth century to the 1530s. These are based on simple averages of such mean and currency-adjusted indexed prices as it has been possible to calculate for wheat, barley, malt, oats,

[35] See Chapter 6.

Table 1. *Crude Scottish price indexes*

Period	Livestock	Cereal
A	72.8	60.4
B–C	100.0	100.0
D–E	78.8	(104.4)
F	57.0	88.7
G	92.8	95.6
H	71.6	118.3
I	78.9	134.0
60s		
70s	70.5	134.1
80s		
90s	84.9	172.0
1500s	77.5	153.8
10s	69.7	152.2
20s	95.6	203.4
30s	83.7	180.7

Note: parentheses have been used to flag up calculations which are less securely based than others – either because they are based on a smaller amount of data, or because they involve certain, possibly questionable, assumptions.

and oatmeal, and for marts, oxen, cows, and sheep.[36] The data for Figures 1 and 2 appear in Table 1. Figures 3 and 4 are based on Farmer's index of prices 1330–1500 for cereals, and livestock, though this material has been recalculated in periods to permit comparison with the Scottish data.[37] The data represented in Figures 3 and 4 appear in Table 2. No 'basket of consumables' has been offered for Scotland, since comparison on the basis of the English basket would take no account of the different eating habits in the north, while comparison with a different Scottish basket would hardly be valid.[38]

It would be difficult to overstate the statistical and historical crudity of the calculations involved in Figures 1 and 2. If Farmer's original

[36] The principles governing the calculation of these mean and indexed prices for the individual commodities are discussed in the Introduction, pp. 5–7, and in Chapter 5.

[37] D.L. Farmer's contributions to the *Agrarian History of England and Wales*, II and III. We are most grateful to Dr Farmer for allowing us an early sight of his tables in advance of publication.

[38] Those wishing to pursue the question of a Scottish cost of living index might begin with a consideration of contemporary calculations of monks' portions. This was valued at £44 Scots at Kelso in 1551. At Coldingham in 1540 a presbyter professus was entitled to 8b. of wheat for bread, 13b. 3f. 1 peck of bere for ale, 27b. 2f. 2 peck of oats with which to buy flesh, 4b. 1f. 2 peck of oats to buy fish, and 8 merks for clothing. Using the values we have found current for the period 1530–42, this works out at a total of about £30. A commendator of Dunfermline after the Reformation

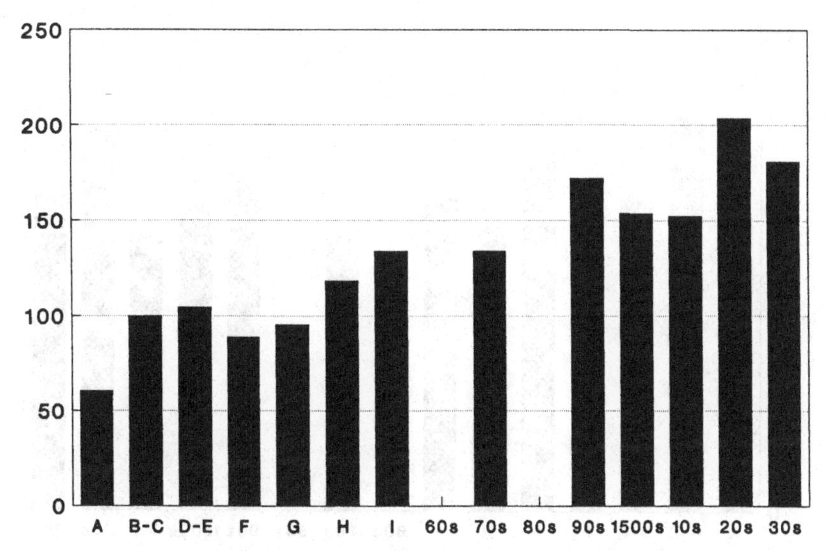

1 Crude Scottish cereal index (sterling equivalent)
For periods A–I, see Introduction, p. 6

index is an analytical tool which may be likened to a surgeon's scalpel, then the Scots index best resembles a very blunt instrument. If the one permits precise dissection and minute analysis, then the other can do no more than bludgeon the data into the simplest order. Nevertheless, the message resulting from this violent assault upon the historical evidence is, at its simplest, sufficiently clear-cut, and in sufficient contrast to the English graphs to excuse this method of attack. It suggests that while English livestock in the later middle ages equalled or somewhat exceeded its price in the base period 1330–46, Scots livestock never recovered the price levels of the base period and were often some thirty points below them. Conversely, English cereal prices often fell below their base period price, while Scottish cereal prices rose dramatically above theirs. By the end of our period, the Scots currency-adjusted price index for cereals was almost double that of the base period.

received £50 Scots for food, 20s. for coals, plus continued use of chamber and yard. *ALCPA*, p. lvi. All these men will have lived rather well. The food listed in the Coldingham agreement works out at something in the region of 7,500 kcal a day, far in excess of an individual's normal requirements. If this approach is to be pursued further, it would be necessary to collect other Scottish examples of less lavish maintenance agreements. Cf. Christopher Dyer, *Standards of Living in the Later Middle Ages: Social Change in England c. 1200–1520* (Cambridge, 1989), pp. 151–4, and Barbara Harvey, *Living and Dying in England 1100–1540: The Monastic Experience* (Oxford 1993), pp. 179–209.

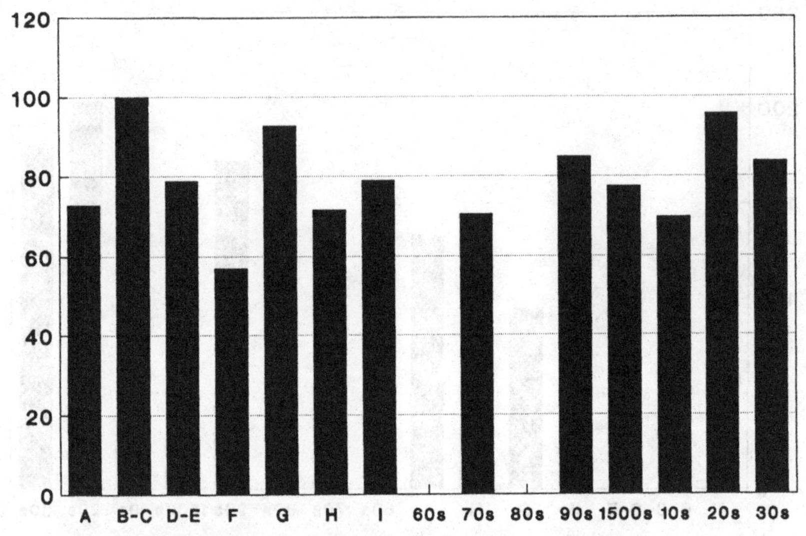

2 Crude Scottish livestock index (sterling equivalent)
For periods A–I, see Introduction, p. 6.

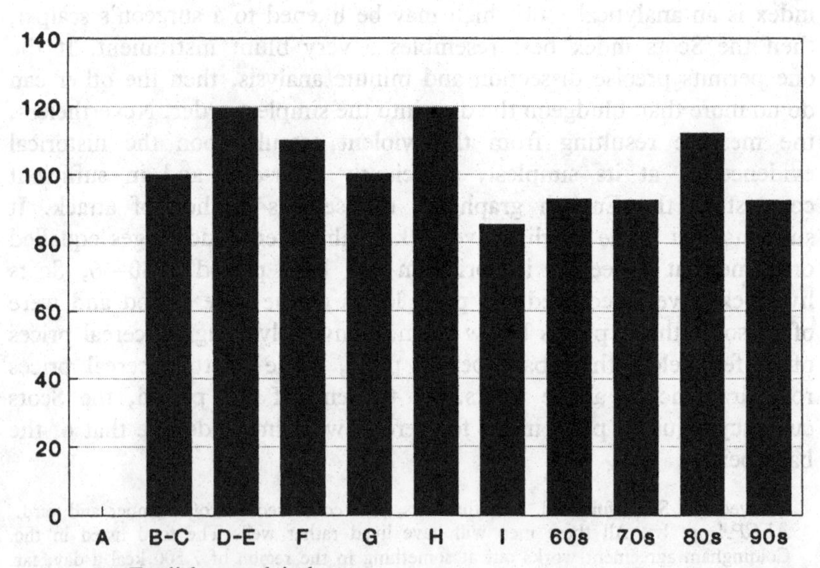

3 English cereal index
Source: data drawn from Farmer's annual tables in *Agrarian History of England and Wales*, III, and calculated in periods to permit comparison with Scots data.

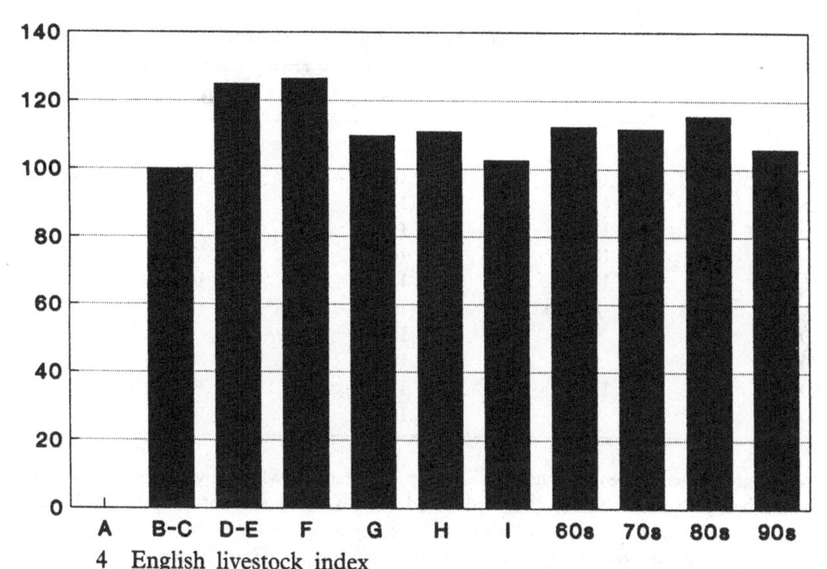

4 English livestock index
Source: data drawn from Farmer's annual tables in *Agrarian History of England and Wales*, III, and calculated in periods to permit comparison with Scots data.

A large part of this increase may perhaps be explained in terms of the gradual enlargement of Scottish capacity measures. We estimate below that the boll and firlot may have grown by something like 15% a century, suggesting a possible rise of about one third between the 1320s and the 1530s.[39] Yet even after allowing for this, cereals in Scotland still appear to have been rising in price in sterling equivalent terms through the later middle ages. This is probably to some extent a reflection of the scarcity of good arable land. Scottish livestock prices fared nothing like so well.

It is important to stress that the currency-adjusted prices which are the basis of the index have already been calculated to strip out the effects of Scots debasement, leaving the figures comparable with English currency prices. The principles underlying the adjustment of prices are discussed in Chapter 4 on currency below.[40] These are not converted to pure metal prices, because the value of gold and silver was itself rising at this time. Instead the process is designed to establish what

[39] See Chapter 3 below, pp. 95–6.
[40] Pp. 137–40. It is important to understand that both the Scots and the English indices are calculated on the basis of sterling or sterling-equivalent prices. This is not the same as the pure silver prices in which some European price series have been calculated.

Table 2. *English cereal, livestock, and basket indexes*

Period	Cereal	Livestock	Basket
A			
B–C	100.0	100.0	100.0
D–E	(119.5)	(124.8)	(117.7)
F	110.0	126.5	109.0
G	100.2	109.7	95.7
H	119.5	110.9	108.2
I	(85.45)	(102.6)	(81.4)
60s	92.9	112.4	87.9
70s	92.6	111.8	83.1
80s	112.1	115.5	101.1
90s	92.4	105.8	83.4

Note: parentheses have been used to flag up calculations which are less securely based than others – either because they are based on a smaller amount of data, or because they involve certain, possibly questionable, assumptions.
Source: data drawn from Farmer's annual tables in *Agrarian History of England and Wales*, III, and calculated in periods to permit comparison with Scots data.

any given Scottish mean price might be if expressed in contemporary sterling. This sterling-equivalent quotation is a useful guide to the international hard-currency value of Scottish imports and exports.[41] From 1367 the domestic Scots currency value of any commodity, i.e. the actual price, grew away from the international hard-currency value, and the opening up of this gap had important consequences.[42]

The currency-adjusted prices show that while Scots imports – chiefly cereals – rose strongly in price, Scots exports – livestock, hides, wool, and salmon – actually fell in sterling-equivalent terms. To this extent devaluation of the Scottish currency worked. It made her exports easier to sell abroad, while importing would have been discouraged by high prices. In theory at least this should have stimulated Scots domestic production as an alternative to importing, and promoted the price competitiveness of Scottish exports. How far this actually occurred is considered in the final concluding chapter of the book.

[41] It may be suggested that conversion to a Flemish or French price equivalent might as closely reflect Scottish trading interests. However, both the French and Flemish currencies experienced somewhat erratic careers, being at times notably weak and at others notably strong, which makes these coinages less suitable as a yard-stick than sterling.

[42] In the discussion of individual commodities which follows in Chapter 5, tables supply the mean actual prices and mean currency-adjusted prices for most commodities.

2 Prices in medieval Aberdeen

A special study of the circumstances in which trade was carried on in medieval Aberdeen is made possible by the survival of an almost continuous series of the Aberdeen Council Registers from 1398 until the end of the period with which we are concerned;[1] and it is because these records yield price material from one locality over a period of a century and a half that we have chosen to concentrate on the Aberdeen evidence, although we have also studied some of the printed records for Edinburgh and Ayr.[2]

Two of Aberdeen's special features were the prominence of its salmon trade and its comparatively northerly location. These were recognized by contemporaries as significant factors affecting the burgh's economic

[1] The Council Registers are housed in the Charter Room in the Town House at Aberdeen. There is a break in the material in the first volume between 1402 and 1405, and after the end of the period to 1414 covered in the second volume there is no further material until the beginning of the period covered by the fourth volume, 1434. The current archivist, Ms Judith Cripps, has undertaken a thorough search for the missing material for the intervening period at the request of the City of Aberdeen District Council's Licensing and General Purposes Committee. The results of these investigations are contained in the archivist's report to the committee made in 1981, which she has kindly made available to us. William Kennedy, in his *Annals of Aberdeen, from the Reign of King William the Lion* (London, 2 vols., 1818), p. 107, gives us a few prices for 1417 and 1433, which may have been taken from an unidentified manuscript of excerpts from the Council Register made after 1560, but we have treated these with considerable caution, since their provenance is uncertain and since most of them appear to duplicate groups of the prices we have found in the volumes which survive.

In addition to the Council Registers, we have consulted the following Dean of Guild Accounts at the Town House: Dean of Guild Accounts, 1452–3 (in the Guildry Accounts, 1453–1650) and 1470–1 (Acc. 1000/7; photocopy from Gordon of Gordonstoun MSS in Yale University Library). W.C. Dickinson has transcribed the material covering 1398 to 1400 as well as the court roll for 1317 and extracts from the registers from 1401 to 1407 in *Early Records of the Burgh of Aberdeen, 1317, 1398–1407*, SHS, 3rd ser., 49 (1957), and his substantial introduction is of great value for our understanding of these records and of royal burghs more generally. Further useful extracts from the Aberdeen records are printed in *Extracts from the Council Register of the Burgh of Aberdeen*, I: *1398–1570* ed. J. Stuart, Spalding Club, 12 (Aberdeen, 1844).

[2] *Extracts from the Records of the Burgh of Edinburgh.* AD *1403–1528*, ed. Sir James D. Marwick, *SBRS*, 2 (1869), and 'Ayr Burgh Accounts, 1428–9', ed. G.S. Pryde, *SHR*, 31 (1952), 139–46.

well-being. Thus the preservation of the burgh's reputation as an exporter of quality salmon was thought crucial;[3] it was also seen to be important to channel the trade in animal products through Aberdeen rather than allow it to drain to the more southerly burghs.[4] Those in Aberdeen capable of recognizing the town's economic strengths – above all salmon – and weaknesses – its remoteness – were also capable of applying the practices of other burghs in Aberdeen. Aberdonians who were merchants, commissioners to parliament, or members of embassies to foreign parts would have taken the opportunity offered by contact with their colleagues from other towns to learn and to take new ideas home with them. For example, when the provost, baillies, and council considered in January 1517 how they should set the assize of the twopenny loaf, they looked at the weight of wheat bread in Edinburgh, Dundee, Perth ('Sanctjohnistoun'), and elsewhere in Lothian and Angus, and then compared the quality of wheat in Lothian and Angus with that in the countryside around Aberdeen.[5]

Thus many of Aberdeen's market regulations were broadly in line with the prescriptions set out in earlier collections of laws for the government of the burghs, and other burghs also set out rules controlling the supply, quality, and price of foodstuffs.[6] For instance, Edinburgh like Aberdeen had a practice of purchasing imports for its inhabitants.[7] Of course each Scottish medieval town's social and economic structure and development were distinct,[8] but a special study of a particular burgh can help us to understand the mechanisms, purposes, and limitations of price controls more generally. Aberdeen, because of the quality of its early records, is an obvious choice for such a study.

Indeed, the volume of material from Aberdeen is so large that we have had to adopt a selective approach to the evidence with effect from the beginning of the eighth volume, which begins in 1501. We have from there on made increased use of marginal notes as a guide to entries likely to yield prices and information about the regulation of trade. There is as a result a greater concentration in our work in the sixteenth century on assize prices and prices involving infringements of price controls, because the marginal notes draw attention to such entries. It will be apparent from the series that we have where possible also

[3] See below, p. 105.
[4] See below, pp. 67–8.
[5] ACR IX.659.
[6] For a brief but useful study of market regulations in the burghs, with special reference to Selkirk, see Peter Symms, 'Market Regulation in the Early 16th-Century Burgh', *PSAS*, 118 (1988), 277–87.
[7] See below, pp. 72–6.
[8] Lynch, 'Social and Economic Structure', stresses the variety of experience from town to town.

extracted further prices, although a re-examination of the sixteenth-century volumes would probably reveal further evidence, particularly that occurring in law suits between individuals.

The Aberdeen Council Registers are the records of the sessions of the burgh courts, of which there were several kinds. The most frequent, and those with which townspeople would have been most familiar, were the baillies' courts. These were held every few days and dealt with a plentiful amount of varied business, but there were also the guild courts, which specialized in trade and commercial matters,[9] and the formal, thrice yearly head courts, of which the most important was the Michaelmas session. There are also the records of the royal chamberlain's ayre when it came to Aberdeen. The ayre dealt with pleas which could not be settled in the burgh's own courts, and oversaw the activities of the burgh officials and trade.[10]

The registers are much wider in scope than their role as court records might suggest; they cover the full range of the business with which the burgh government concerned itself. Granted, much of the officers' time was spent on dealing with offences and settling disputes. Cases involving damage to property and person, theft, debt, failure to make payment or deliver goods or services, rights to rent or goods of heirship, or surety agreements fill many of the pages in these records. But in addition the detailed supervision and direction of the social, economic, and political life of the burgh operated through its courts. We read of the appointment of burgh officials and of commissioners to parliament or embassies to foreign powers, of admissions to burgess-ship and guild fraternity, of contributions of taxes, customs, and propines (that is, customary gifts) to the king, of leases of burgh rents, fishings, stalls, and mills, and of the establishment of rules for craftsmen and merchants. More generally, the authorities provided for the well-being of the burgh's inhabitants, supervising matters such as sanitation, defence, and fire prevention. The registers also seem to have been used as a convenient place to record other information of importance to the burgh and its officials, for we also find lists of tax payers and of contributors to public works, copies of royal letters and charters, and the occasional account.

The wide range of business covered in the courts is reflected in the price evidence itself, which is of many different sorts. A category of special interest is the assize prices. Most Aberdeen prices for bread and

[9] The records of the guild courts were kept separately from 1441 to 1468, and are in ACR V ii, *passim.*

[10] For the business covered by the chamberlain in his ayre, see esp. 'Articuli Inquirendi', and 'Modus Procedendi', both in *Ancient Laws*, and W.C. Dickinson, 'A Chamberlain's Ayre in Aberdeen, 1399 x 1400', *SHR*, 33 (1954), 27–36.

candle are in the form of assizes, fixing the weight of the article that must be sold for a given price. The ale assizes are especially useful, for the assizes themselves, which stipulate the price per gallon, are complemented by sale prices involving infringement of the assize. There are also reports of jurors about the going price of grain in the market. These were used as the basis for the assizes for bread and ale, and we have important data on the market prices of wheat and malt for the early fifteenth century from this source. The procedure was changed in the middle of the century, however, so that the price of grain was no longer recorded when the assize itself was prescribed. We also have some assizes for mutton and lamb, some maximum prices for wool and hides, and some minimum prices for salt and iron.[11] Most of the Aberdeen data relating to other commodities are in the form of prices or valuations of goods which were the subject of actions between parties; of prices of goods offered to the king or nobles in propine or given for the purpose of financing public works; and of appraisals of items confiscated for paying off their owner's debts.

Procedure

The Aberdeen courts were not informal. Certain set procedures had to be followed in initiating cases, in bearing witness, and in making awards. But formality did not preclude candour on the part of suitors, witnesses, and officers, and it is often this candour which brings home to us the reality of the situations which brought men and women before those who dispensed justice and upheld the burgh laws. It also reminds us that the price data, like all historical evidence, derive essentially from human testimony, and are subject to uncertainty and even disagreement.

We learn, for example, at a very basic level, that the giving of evidence was not a thing done lightly. People recognized the seriousness of making a particular statement which was then regarded as authoritative in the eyes of the law. When Alexander Rede took on the role of master of the kirk work in 1496 he had it recorded that he could not warrant the account except by his own conscience because he could not write.[12] It was important for the court to record such reservations or uncertainties on the part of witnesses. Similar doubts were recorded by the merchants who were required to testify as to the price Tom Forman had negotiated for wheat purchased from John Smot of Edinburgh in 1447. They could not remember whether they had agreed on

[11] There are also maxima for skins, tar, and soap in the records but we have not constructed series for these commodities.
[12] ACR VII.704.

4s. (as Tom claimed) or 4s. 6d. the boll, although they do seem to have been sure that Tom had offered to pay for the wheat on the spot.[13] Making valuations was another form of bearing witness, and it was sometimes a matter in which personal honour and reputation were at stake. On 22 October 1484 Sym (Simon) of Gardin was convicted by assize for slandering and defaming John Colison, one of the baillies, having said that although he, Sym, and other meat appraisers had priced two carcases of beef for 18s. apiece John had written one of them as worth 16s. and the other 17s.; John said he would not have sustained this defamation for 500 marks.[14]

If a valuation of this sort, in which the valuers were supposed to be disinterested, could give rise to outrage, how much greater passion may have been aroused when vendors who were directly involved did not succeed in achieving the prices they wanted for their goods. For example, the fury felt by Gilbert Brabner's wife in November 1540 when she was amerced for selling 16d. ale was such that she threw away her brew rather than see it doled out at the market cross, even though she might have guessed that she would be fined again, and that the officers would be ordered to 'poind' (distrain) her for the value of that amount of ale, buy it, and then dole it out.[15] Indignation is also clear in the case between William Baudy and John Reaucht in 1538, in which Reaucht's excuse for not wishing to open his second, and deceitfully packed, barrel of salmon for inspection by Baudy's wife was reported verbatim. We have included this case in our appendix of documents because it illustrates some of the difficulties encountered by merchants who traded overseas, who bought and sold goods on trust, and who engaged the services of agents to act on their behalf.[16] It is of particular use for the study of prices to know that a barrel full of grilse fetched less on the French market than a barrel of salmon did; and it is of general use to know that there were a number of risks for overseas traders which may have had an impact on the prices of imports and exports in general.

The Aberdeen evidence brings home the point that the prices of the things people bought and sold had a real bearing on their financial well-being. The point is not a gratuitous one; nor is it sentimental. It is all too easy to lose sight of it because we are bound to isolate price figures from the circumstances which produced them in order to discern a pattern among them. There is, moreover, evidence to show that while

[13] ACR IV.498.
[14] ACR VI.884.
[15] ACR XVI.635.
[16] Below, Appendix of Documents, no. III, pp. 79–80.

contemporaries' sense of the broader significance of price trends might be uncertain, they knew only too well what difference prices made to themselves. For example, in the guild court on 25 April 1538 John Lorymer, a member of the guild, was convicted for infringing the burgh statutes by attempting to buy victuals from a Prussian ship both at sea and in port, and for saying openly and in front of divers persons that he did not wish to lose his own profit for the sake of the provost or baillies.[17] The candlemakers of Aberdeen were as a group aware of the importance of prices when they told the authorities plainly in 1520 that they might as well not bother to trade if they were to be made to sell candle at the assize price.[18] And the importance of price levels to the community as a whole is brought home to us above all in the efforts of the authorities themselves to control prices and to control the supply of goods to the burgh.

On 28 April 1503 Robert Walcar was amerced for slandering the alderman Alexander Menzeis 'sayande thar was nevere luk in his tyme and he fande the bole of meile at iiij^{or} s' he will leif it at xx^{ti} s' '.[19] Then, as now, people blamed the government when things were going badly, but the fact that the alderman was being held responsible for an actual or apparent price rise suggests people thought the burgh authorities had some sort of control over prices, and must lead us to explore how true this was. The most obvious influence the burgh authorities had on prices was when they set fixed maximum or minimum prices for goods bought and sold in Aberdeen. Most of the controls of this sort were in respect of household necessities supplied by burgh craftsmen, and it is worth considering these in some detail.

The assize of bread

The operation of the assize of bread in Aberdeen needs to be seen in the context both of the earlier medieval evidence which is of a general nature intended to apply broadly across Scotland, and in the light of the later evidence which is specific to other burghs, especially Edinburgh. The custom of regulating the price of bread in line with the price of wheat dates in Scotland apparently from the twelfth century.[20]

[17] ACR IV.132.
[18] See below, p. 56.
[19] ACR VIII.211.
[20] The significance of David's reforms was such that throughout the middle ages similar legislation rarely failed to claim its origins in the work of David I. It has been suggested that such a claim became an almost obligatory convention perhaps more securely rooted in custom than in fact. See Hector L. MacQueen and William J. Windram, 'Laws

In fact, as David I's assize of bread shows, it was the weight of the loaf rather than its price which fluctuated.[21] David's system was sophisticated enough to distinguish between different kinds of bread, and between the weight of bread when raw, when newly cooked, and when dry and therefore lighter, but this structure is only known to us from fourteenth-century copies. The version published in *APS* I.675–9, is taken from the Cromertie Manuscript, with the Ayr Manuscript printed as a footnote at p.50. The prices of wheat envisaged in these early fourteenth-century manuscripts – 10d. to 24d. per boll – accord well with what we know from other sources of the range of wheat prices at this time rather than earlier, so whatever the date of any original, it seems likely that the copiers substituted figures appropriate to their own time.

The editors of *APS* found the Ayr Manuscript 'so irreconcilable with any system of calculation, that it was not used for the text'. It starts and finishes with bread weights almost the same as those in the Cromertie Manuscript, and the intervening weights fall in a reasonably orderly manner, being fairly consistently about 50dwt higher than the Cromertie figures. Inconsistent irregularities may have arisen from copying errors; consistent variation may reflect local practice. Nevertheless, the Cromertie Manuscript does give greater detail about other types of bread, so it is convenient to work chiefly from this text printed in *APS* I.[22]

First the assize orders weights for raw dough (*pastus panis*), newly baked bread (*coctus*), and baked and dried bread (*coctus et siccatus*), appropriate for the ½d. wastel loaf. The wastel loaf was white and well bolted, that is sieved (*albus et bene bultatus*), but other types of loaf were also listed. The quachet loaf was of the same bolted flour, but had to weigh 2s. (i.e. 24dwt) more than the wastel, because the

and Courts in the Burghs', in *SMT*, p. 210. In what follows we shall continue to refer to David's assize without intending to imply thereby a twelfth-century date.

[21] The Scottish assize of bread is closely paralleled by the English system, see A.S.C. Ross 'The Assize of Bread' *EcHR* 2nd ser. 9 (1956), 332–42, and the references cited there. Assuming 4 bolls to the quarter, the English and Scots pricing systems are closely comparable. A Scots wheat price of 2s.b. gives 21 to 19 oz of bread in the ½d. loaf while 8s. a quarter gives 10.2 oz of bread in an English ¼d. loaf. In England, and as we shall see in Scotland, the earlier documents envisage a lower range of wheat prices, and the weights appropriate for a low wheat price quite quickly become impractical if simply extended in proportion for higher wheat prices. In England it looks as if the system had to be periodically revised when wheat prices moved outside the range originally envisaged (ibid., p. 341) and as we shall see the same sort of thing seems to have occurred in Scotland.

[22] Esp. pp. 677–8; p. 676 gives a bread assize for wheat at 10d. a boll; p. 679 is for 1d. loaf weights.

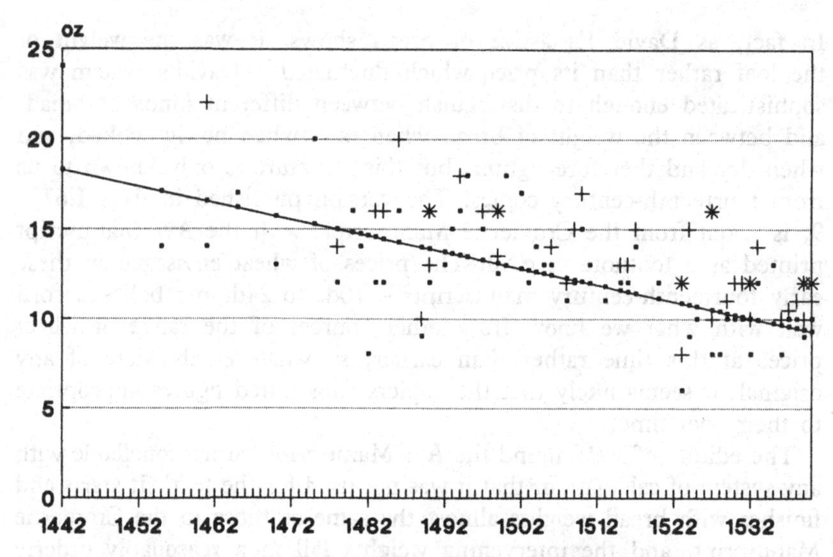

5 Weight of the wheat loaf (in ounces for 1d.)
The solid line is a linear regression of the legal weights.

quachet was fermented.[23] Simnel bread was of a higher quality than wastel, having been better bolted, and accordingly weighed 2s. less than the wastel. Mixed corn bread (*de blado mixto et de priori bultura*) weighed 1½ quachet loaves as did the whole wheat loaf (*panis integer de frumento*). *Panis de trayt*, and *de omni blado* were the lowest grades, weighing 2 quachets.[24]

One surprising area of ambiguity characterized all these assizes. Bread weights were adjusted for each 2d. step in the wheat price, but it was explicitly noted that the same weight applied for wheat prices 1d. above and below the given price. This in effect created an overlap, explicitly recommending, for example, both the 16d. weights and the 18d. weights when the wheat price stood at 17d. the boll. Given the care with which loaf weights were to be monitored, this curious vagueness raises some doubt about the clerks' familiarity with the system in practice.[25]

From the mid-fifteenth century we have a body of evidence for the Scottish assize in actual use in Aberdeen. Though the principles estab-

[23] 'quia fermentatus est'. In England it was called cocket bread or panis levatus. It is difficult to believe, however, that other types of bread were entirely unleavened.
[24] A similar list of the varieties of bread appears in *Ancient Laws*, appendix IV, p. 333.
[25] There are, however, some examples of latitude in the application of the assize at Aberdeen. The assize for rye bread given at Aberdeen in 1537 allowed some leeway according to the baker's conscience (ACR XII i.188); the Aberdeen assize for 1530 (ACR XIII.6) also suggests flexibility.

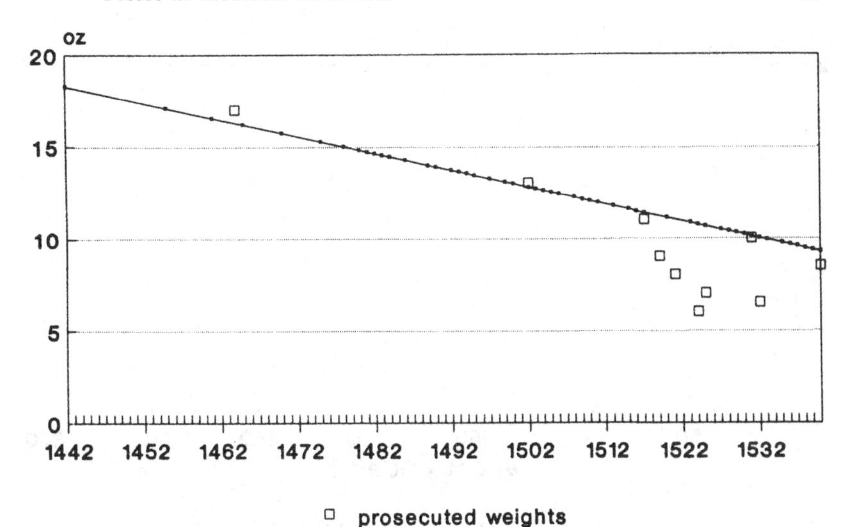

6 Weight of the wheat loaf: prosecutions (in ounces for 1d.)
The solid line is a linear regression of the legal weights.

lished by 'David's' assize still apply, the actual range of fourteenth-century wheat prices in the printed assize is much lower than those from Aberdeen beginning in 1442 which make up the series studied here.[26] Indeed, even in the hundred years studied here, 1442–1542, the weight of the penny loaf shows a marked fall, amounting of course to a rise in the price of bread (see Figure 5). This falling weight of the loaf is the corollary of the rising price of wheat over time. Apart from the crisis decade of the 1480s, a norm of around 15 ounces in the second half of the fifteenth century falls to around 10 ounces in the first half of the sixteenth century. As we would expect, the weight of loaves as recorded in prosecutions of bakers (Figure 6) usually falls fairly consistently below the trend line for legal loaves.

The clear trend over the period needs to be kept in mind when considering the weight of the loaf as plotted against the price of wheat. Figure 7 has been compiled using only those years with surviving Aberdeen information about both the weight of the loaf and the price of wheat.[27]

Because of the rising price of wheat over the period, and the corresponding falling weight of the penny loaf, the lower weights and higher

[26] Table 3, below, compares the *APS*, Aberdeen, and Edinburgh assizes.

[27] However, the wheat prices used are not only those mentioned in the assize of bread, nor are they necessarily from the same time within the year as the assize.

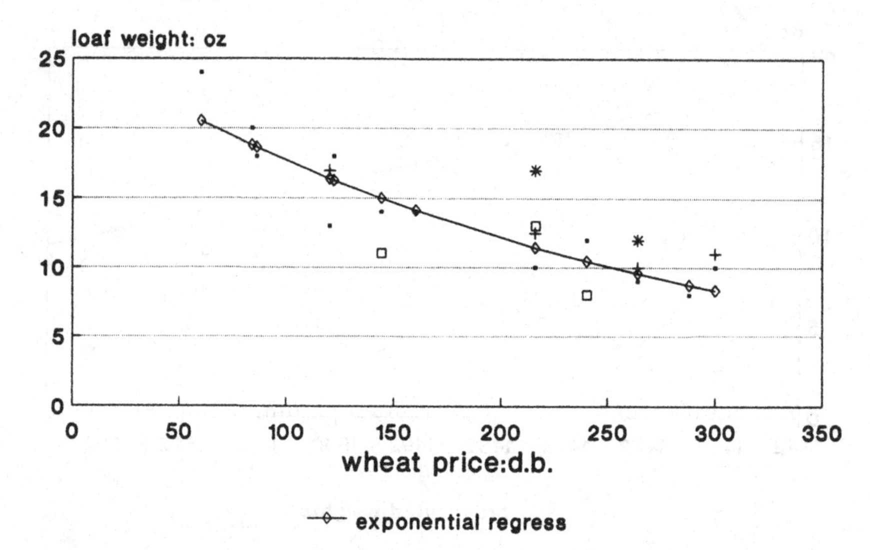

7 The assize of bread (Aberdeen) (loaf weight against wheat price)

wheat prices derive mostly from the sixteenth century. The steeper the curve, the more sensitively loaf weights are responding to changes in wheat price. As the price of wheat reaches higher levels, the weight of the loaf falls, but not as sharply as a similar size of wheat price change would have caused it to fall when wheat was cheaper.

It could be that in a period of inflation the Aberdeen burgh council were prepared to squeeze the bakers in order to alleviate the effects of high prices on the general public. We can test this suggestion by comparing the Aberdeen wheat price/loaf weight curve with that derived from the 1555 Privy Council policy laid down for the assize of bread, and applied with reasonable consistency in Edinburgh thereafter.[28] The Privy Council established that the boll of wheat should yield 140 pounds 2,240 ounces of good wheat bread. If x = the number of penny loaves from a boll of wheat, and y = the weight of the loaf in ounces, then the curve y = 2,240/x expresses the 1555 Privy Council ruling in a form in which it can be drawn on the graph and compared with practice in Aberdeen.[29] (Figure 8. In order for the baker to balance his books

[28] Gibson and Smout, *Prices, Food and Wages*; also *TA* IV. 488, provides early evidence for an allowance to a baker, of 6s.8d. for baking a chalder of birsket (mixed rye and wheat), and the same rate for 'sour bread'. But this has somewhat the look of a special contract between the crown and a baker.

[29] This is to leave on one side the question of whether the price of wheat referred to when setting the weight of the loaf included an allowance for the baker's costs and profits. Smout and Gibson believe it did, at any rate from the mid-sixteenth century

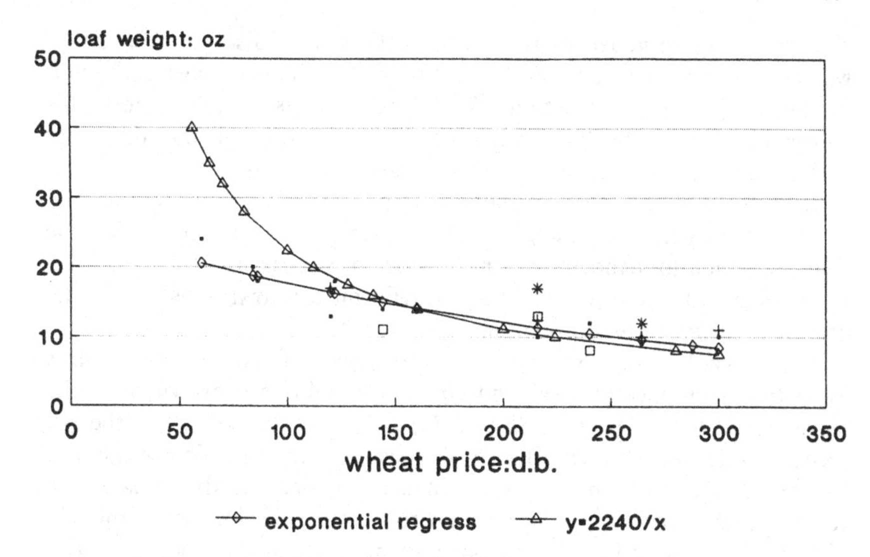

8 The assize of bread (Aberdeen and Edinburgh) (loaf weight against wheat price)

x, the number of penny loaves from the boll of wheat, must at least equal the price of wheat per boll.)

From this comparison the graph (Figure 8) shows that once the price of wheat exceeded about 200d.b. the Aberdeen authorities seem to have expected a heavier penny loaf than that demanded in Edinburgh under the Privy Council system. However, for a period of lower wheat prices (for example the fifteenth century), the Aberdeen curve demands lighter loaves for a given wheat price than would have been indicated by the y = 2,240/x formula.[30] It thus appears that in the sixteenth century the Aberdeen authorities may have still been operating a system designed for the lower prices of the later fifteenth century. In imposing this system after wheat prices regularly rose above 200d.b. they created genuine difficulties for the bakers. It may have been in recognition of similar difficulties that in the mid-sixteenth century the Privy Council

onwards. At Aberdeen before this date there is no evidence that it did, and an impression from the wording of the assize entries that it did not. Indeed, if anything, Aberdeen assize prices look low, e.g. January 1517 when the assize of bread mentions a wheat price of 144d.b. while another Aberdeen case in the same month sets it at 160d.b. In short, no bakers' allowance is ever mentioned in medieval Scotland, and in England where bakers' costs are sometimes calculated, no attempt is made to build the calculation into the price or weight. See also the assize of ale, p. 48.

[30] Similarly in Edinburgh, the assize demanded relatively light loaves for the times of lower wheat prices, 1495, 13.75 oz 1d. loaf, wheat at 132d.b.; 1528, 11½ oz 1d. loaf, wheat at 144d.b. (Gibson and Smout, *Prices, Food and Wages*).

instituted a more generous regime for bakers. It is also possible that it was at this time that it became usual to add the bakers' cost and profit margin to the 'price' of wheat. While the curve is relatively steep this allowance would not have been necessary because of the flexibility within the system, but as the curve moves out of the range of wheat prices originally envisaged, it flattens. This leaves less room for the loaf weight to respond to changing wheat prices, and less room for the baker in which to manoeuvre. On the whole it appears that the Aberdeen assize of bread did bear unusually heavily on the town's bakers in the first half of the sixteenth century.

Finally Table 3 sets out the simplified details of four separate assizes for comparison. Sections (a) and (b) in this table are drawn from the versions printed in *APS* I. Section (a) relates to the weight of the ½d. wastel, while Section (b) is for an unspecified 1d. loaf. The weights in (b) are roughly four times heavier than in (a) because they relate to a 1d. loaf rather than a ½d. loaf, and also because the loaf was probably of much coarser stuff. As we have seen, *panis de trayt* and *de omni blado* weighed two quachets, and slightly more than two wastel loaves. Given this assumption about quality, (a) and (b) are thus compatible. Section (c) presents in tabular form an analysis of the Aberdeen assize in practice, already discussed above, while Section (d) records the Edinburgh assize of 1555.

Column 4 in Table 3 is perhaps worthy of further comment. The minimum weight of bread per boll of wheat is simply column 2 × column 3, i.e. the loaf weight × the number of loaves required to cover the cost of a boll of wheat. This is the minimum weight of bread, since the baker will certainly have baked more to cover his other minor costs and to generate his profit. But as the minimum weight of bread rose it must have approached the maximum weight possible, squeezing the baker's margin. At this point the baker had to choose between going out of business or gradually reducing the quality of the loaf, in the belief that this might be less noticeable than an unauthorized weight reduction.

However, the regulation of bread weights and prices was only a part of the organizational framework designed by the burgh authorities to provide and safeguard a ready supply of bread for the town. The basic principles of the organization of the craft are clear enough, although two caveats need to be borne in mind. First, practices evolved over time, so that what was usual in the sixteenth century may not have been the norm in the fourteenth century; on the other hand new nomenclature did not always mean new practice. Thus the 'deacons' who appear in the sixteenth century may not in practice have been very different from the 'officers' or leading bakers mentioned at other

Table 3. *The assize of bread*

Wheat price (d.b.)	Loaf weight (oz)	No. of loaves required to cover cost of wheat	Minimum weight of bread per boll wheat (oz)
(a) Prescribed weight of ½d. wastel, baked and dry for given wheat prices.			
10	45.6	20	912.0
12	38.0	24	912.0
14	32.575	28	912.1
16	28.5	32	912.0
18	25.3375	36	912.15
20	22.8	40	912.0
22	20.7	44	910.8
24	19.0	48	912.0
(b) Prescribed weight of 1d. loaf, baked and dry, for given wheat prices			
24	76.05	24	1,825.2oz.
28	53.8, *recte* 65.14	28	1,506.4/1,823.92
32	63.4	32	2,028.8
36	56.8	36	2,044.8
40	50.0	40	2,000.0
44	45.6	44	2,006.4
48	36.8, *recte* 41.66/38	48	1,766.4/2,000.0/1,824.0
(c) Aberdeen practice for 1d.loaf (Aberdeen loaves were often weighed straight from the oven, not dry).			
60.0	24.0	60.0	1,440.0
84.0	20.0	84.0	1,680.0
85.71	18.0	85.71	1,542.78
120.0	17.0	120.0	2,040.0
120.0	14.0	120.0	1,680.0
120.0	13.0	120.0	1,560.0
144.0	14.0	144.0	2,016.0
160.0	14.0	160.0	2,240.0
216.0	10.0	216.0	2,160.0
216.0	12.5	216.0	2,700.0
240.0	12.0	240.0	2,880.0
264.0	9.0–10.0–12.0	264.0	2,376.0/2,640.0/3,168.0
288.0	8.0	288.0	2,304.0
(d) Edinburgh 1555			2,240

Sources: (a): *APS* I.676–8; (b): *APS* I. 679; (c): ACR

times.[31] The trade could only be effectively controlled by practised men who undertook the craft. The second caveat is that some regulations were imposed at times of particular scarcity and were not intended to be enforced permanently, although the temporary nature of the

[31] ACR XIV.23–4, 194, 285; XVI.19, 320. The term officers can, however, refer to the burgh serjeants.

arrangements may not have been explicitly stated. For example when it was enacted that from Martinmas 1444 bread was only to be sold in the booth under the Tollbooth[32] we may be sure that this was not a permanent rule applied constantly thereafter but a special measure designed to ensure open and equal distribution in a time of scarcity. Equally when in 1508 the town itself supplied bakers with wheat for distribution as bread to townsmen,[33] it seems clear that this was a special arrangement rather than normal practice.

Nevertheless, despite the danger of mistaking exceptional measures for customary procedures, the general assumptions and principles governing the trade stand out quite clearly. Bakers were freemen of the burgh,[34] and if unfree bakers did spring up they were listed and banned.[35] They were usually men, unlike the brewers who were more often women.[36] The numbers of bakers practising at any one time varied from about a dozen to as few as four.[37] The bakers so listed were senior responsible men with other staff working under them, though the underbakers impinge on the records only rarely.[38] The contracting bakers and their oven-masters were both responsible for all the bread from their oven, which had to be marked with distinguishing signs to enable their work to be identified.[39] These contracting bakers were present at the assize of bread and consented to bake bread on the terms fixed by the assize.[40] A baker who felt the assize was unjust could withdraw from the craft for the year[41] but failure to do so implied consent to the assize. On occasion the bakers assented only slowly and reluctantly,[42] or united in their opposition to the terms being imposed upon them,[43] though the burgh authorities especially resented such conspiracies and were likely to amerce any league of bakers[44] or even

[32] ACR V ii.686.
[33] ACR VIII.835.
[34] ACR V i.198.
[35] ACR VII.975.
[36] See ACR VI.747 for one woman; ACR X.170–1 has three women out of thirteen bakers.
[37] E.g. four bakers ACR VI.758; nine bakers ACR XIV.290; twelve bakers ACR V i.337; thirteen bakers ACR X.170–1.
[38] E.g. ACR VI.183, 758; X.170–1. See also *Ancient Laws*, appendix III, p. 318, and appendix IV, p. 333, where the staff appropriate for an oven were listed as no more than a master baker, two servants, and a lad. There may also have been a dominus, or owner of the oven, over them all.
[39] ACR V i.337; VI.758.
[40] E.g. ACR VIII.24, 404, 794, 900;XII i.256, 260.
[41] ACR VII.973.
[42] ACR XIV.290.
[43] ACR VI.912–13.
[44] ACR XI.496; ACR VIII.1020.

any 'murmuring' against the assize.[45] Groups of bakers, jointly contracting with the council to serve the town, were, however, welcomed and granted monopolies,[46] but if there was no such monopoly group operating, it seems that any baker who did not withdraw from the craft for a year implicitly accepted the assize and with it an obligation to serve the town. Failing to serve the town was an offence, being especially culpable if the baker had wheat or flour to hand, since refusal to bake then became effectively a strike against the assize. Failure to serve the town on the part of all the bakers at once smacked of conspiracy.[47] Prearranged fines were sometimes set for failure to serve the town.[48] Bakers might sometimes be obliged to buy flour or wheat so that they could be in a position to serve the town,[49] and on occasion listed bakers were granted a monopoly of the right to buy wheat,[50] though this was in the disastrous year 1482. Refusal to bake or otherwise infringing the assize often led to fines or even to expulsion from the craft for a year[51] and further punishment could follow for bakers who continued to bake after expulsion.[52] Bakers were also bound by all the other usual regulations controlling buying and selling. Thus the obligation to supply the town did not excuse bakers forestalling the burgh to buy wheat,[53] although the system did try to recognize fluctuations in the market, for example distinguishing between this year's wheat and last year's,[54] or encouraging bakers to come back to council if they had to buy new flour, so long as they did so before baking it.[55] The law governing sales of bread was particularly important for such a staple commodity; townsmen came first, Old Aberdonians[56] and 'outdwellers' only being served later, though they had to be sold bread of the same weight as that sold to townsmen. Within the town there was to be no favouritism, and sales were to be open with nothing kept back.[57]

[45] ACR VI.728. In the sixteenth century bakers were quite often amerced for 'diminishing' the assize. ACR VIII.637; X.27, 86; XIV.587, 589.
[46] ACR V i.337; X.170–1.
[47] ACR VI.920; VII.101; VIII.162–3, 483, 484, 512, 641, 893, 898, 996, 998, 1020, 1054, 1097, 1114; IX.8, 14, 19, 54, 62, 176, 185, 199; X.172; XV.222; XVI.10, 358.
[48] ACR VIII.68; XIV.607.
[49] ACR XVI.604, against the arrival of the king.
[50] ACR VI.758.
[51] ACR VI.746; X.321; XI.640; XII i.260.
[52] ACR XII i.296, 305.
[53] ACR VI.502, 527–8, 832; XIII.443; VIII.369 for a dispute between bakers involving 'overbuying' wheat.
[54] ACR XVI.358.
[55] ACR XIII.233, 243, 437.
[56] Old Aberdeen lay outside the burgh.
[57] For regulations affecting the sale of bread see ACR VI.823; VII.952; VIII.855; XII i.188, 205, 260.

Obviously weight was the central point of the assize of bread,[58] but apart from low weight bakers could be fined for selling bread unweighed or failing to notify the officers when bread was to be drawn from the ovens.[59] Finally, of course, bread might be of good weight but of insufficient quality.

As already noted above, King David's assize of bread recognized a number of varieties of bread of different qualities, and the Aberdeen records equally provide evidence for a range of different breads. We are probably safe in assuming that bread without further qualification or description was usually a wheat loaf of fairly coarse flour leavened by the yeasts naturally present in the flour but producing a fairly dry and solid loaf.

However, there were several variables affecting the finished product, namely the type of grain used, the fineness of the milling, the bolting or sieving of the flour, and the degree of leavening. Rye bread was considerably cheaper than wheat bread. Some, and probably most, of the rye was imported from the Baltic.[60] Oat bread or cakes were only rarely permitted,[61] such sales being more often expressly prohibited.[62] Selling oatcakes was repeatedly forbidden. The point of this ban on selling oat bread and cakes was that this was the staple food of the poor, prepared by themselves for themselves and not for resale. Oatmeal supplies were to be reserved for domestic needs only, and sold only in quantities appropriate to household – not retail – purposes. Indeed not only were merchants forbidden to buy meal in bulk, but they were also obliged to make such quantities as they might receive – for example in payment for other goods – immediately available in the market for others.[63] The rare exceptions to the ban on selling oatcakes or oat bread are an indication of especial difficulties in the grain market.

Most often, however, bread meant wheat bread. Scots wheat is often met in the records and was used for making bread[64] but much wheat was imported for bread from England and France. The different characteristics of these various wheats were evidently such that mixing flour of different wheats was strongly disapproved of.[65] Bakers bought both grain and flour as opportunity presented itself.[66] The grain would keep much

[58] For a good example of a range of poor weights and named offending bakers, see ACR XVI.545.
[59] ACR VIII.1140; XI.571; XII i.368.
[60] ACR VII.243 for a baker buying rye from an esterling.
[61] ACR VI.883; XII ii.553; XIV.543; XVI.650. For oatcakes, see also below, pp. 41–2.
[62] ACR XII ii.600; XIII.142, 233, 243, 439; XIV.39; XVI.645.
[63] ACR XII ii.600.
[64] E.g. ACR V i.428; VII.689 for an Aberdeen baker buying wheat from the Lord of Ogilvy.
[65] ACR VII.554, 785, 1066.
[66] ACR XIV.66.

better if adequately stored but had to be milled. The bakers were enjoined to keep the old statutes relating to the town's mills in 1508 and 1538, though we have no further clue as to how they might have been infringing them till 1541 when the town miller was ordered to make his mill work properly or the bakers would mill elsewhere without paying him his multure.[67] Of course, more finely ground flour would make finer, more expensive bread, so the bakers' involvement in the milling process was important. Nevertheless, we also meet bakers buying their flour ready milled in barrels,[68] and however finely the flour was milled, the bolting or sieving process was also critical to the nature of the bread produced. Distinctions were regularly drawn between the prices of bolted, dear, and unbolted, cheaper, bread; so 'greit', the 'outtakings' of wheat and rye, might be permitted in some bread but not in others, though when it was permitted the resulting loaves were always to be cheaper.[69] On occasion 'brunn' and 'clecc' were specifically forbidden but bran was also sold on its own[70] and used as animal feed, sometimes baked as horsebread. Thus when bakers were prosecuted, for evil or insufficient stuff, as they often were, it is sometimes difficult to know if the flour was irredeemably bad or merely of too poor quality for the type of bread required.[71]

Fowat and craknel were two of the dearer types of bread met in Aberdeen.[72] They were probably made of more finely bolted flour, but other variations in baking techniques may also have been involved. In particular very little seems to have been said about leavening except for references to some well-bolted rye bread which was additionally described as 'sourit', indicating a specially fermented or risen loaf.[73]

The quality of bread offered for sale was much less easily checked or objectively demonstrated than its weight, and despite prosecutions for evil stuff it seems probable that as the authorities demanded an ever larger weight of bread from the boll of wheat bakers may have protected their profit margin by a gradual coarsening of the loaf.

Oatcakes and meal

Wheaten bread supplied by the burgh's bakers was perhaps not exactly a luxury, but oatmeal products were certainly a cheaper farinaceous

[67] Multure, the miller's fee. ACR VIII.831; XII i.365; XVI.726.
[68] ACR VI.590.
[69] I.e. heavier, e.g. ACR XI.496; XII i.160.
[70] In 1521 at 32d.b., ACR X.321.
[71] Evil stuff: ACR VI.614; VII.406, 382, 587; VIII.63; XII i.367. Insufficient stuff: ACR VII.499; XI.292, 297, 362; XII i.378, 823–4; XVI.398.
[72] E.g. ACR VI.238 for a single assize showing the relative prices of bread, fowat, and craknel.
[73] ACR VIII.866; XII i.260.

alternative. It is likely that most people will have made their own porridge and oatcakes, and indeed the baking of oatcakes for sale was an activity prohibited for most of the period under study here.[74] There is, however, evidence to suggest it was allowed for a while at the end of the fifteenth century, at least in the 1480s, perhaps as a famine measure. On 4 October 1482 it was ruled that there were to be only two cake bakers in each quarter of the town, and that they were to bake cakes according to the price of victual.[75] On 8 October 1484 an assize of cake of 24 ounces per penny was made, though here no mention was made of a permitted number of bakers.[76] Both these instances suggest that the sale of oatcakes was permitted under the conditions specified. But this was only in the special circumstances of the 1480s; otherwise cake baking for sale was forbidden because if cake bakers had been free to bake in large quantities the supply of meal to others in the burgh would have been greatly lessened. Cake baking for sale was in practice very commonly associated with spoiling the market. Women convicted for buying more meal than they were allowed to do or otherwise spoiling the market were often cake bakers.[77] In the guild court of 8 October 1507 all cake bakers and hucksters were expelled from the market so that it might be properly kept.[78] Restrictions on the amount of meal women and others might buy and other ordinances about the purchase of grain were often made in conjunction with inhibitions against cake bakers, or were addressed specifically to them.[79]

Meat and fish

The authorities also exercised controls over the prices of meat and fish. That meat was consumed in considerable quantities in the burgh is suggested by the frequency with which regulations concerning its sale were made and indeed broken.[80] Nor does it seem to have been a luxury con-

[74] See esp. *Early Records of the Burgh of Aberdeen*, ed. Dickinson, pp. 142, 179, 211; ACR II.182; IV.33; V ii.722; VI.204; VIII.519; XI.359–60; XII ii.553; XIII.144, 233, 439.
[75] ACR VI.755.
[76] ACR VI.883.
[77] See esp. *Early Records of the Burgh of Aberdeen*, ed. Dickinson, pp. 41, 93, 122, 126; ACR II.83; VII.88; VIII.623, 816; X.368; XI.359–60; XVI.398, 615, and see XI.406.
[78] ACR VIII.754.
[79] Eg. ACR VII.34; VIII.518–19; XI.360; XIII.144. See also below, p. 63 and note 202.
[80] This observation is confirmed by the archaeological evidence which shows that large amounts of cattle and sheep were eaten. Pork bones seem significantly scarcer. See Lisbeth M. Thoms, 'Trial Excavation at St Ann's Lane, Perth', *PSAS*, 112 (1982), 437–57, and *Excavations in the Medieval Burgh of Aberdeen 1973–81*, ed. J.C. Murray,

fined to the wealthy, as is evidenced by an injunction made in 1494 that apprentices were not to wear knives except for carving their meat.[81] Moreover, in 1524 the fleshers were convicted for regrating the burgh and 'skaptyne' (scathing) the poor commons by selling dear mutton and lambs.[82] Both instances suggest that even quite lowly members of the burgh community could expect to eat meat on a regular basis.

The meat which the burgh's fleshers dealt in was mainly beef, mutton, and lamb, for when the particular kind of meat is specified in the regulations for the trade, it is nearly always these. No meat was supposed to be sold before it was appraised – valued – by specially appointed meat appraisers.[83] It was appraised by the carcase,[84] and must not be cut up before the appraisal had taken place.[85] The quality of the whole carcase seems to have been what was important rather than the relative value of particular cuts. This may suggest that it was not actually sold by the individual cut, although the evidence is not clear on this point. Sales by the carcase must have been frequent, especially for mutton, and particularly when the wealthier burgesses were buying, but sales in smaller quantities were demanded too, though they were not always welcomed by the fleshers. On 11 February 1511, for instance, one David Was was amerced for refusing to sell 'collapis' (slices) of mutton to gentlemen for their breakfast.[86] We are not told why he would not make the sale, but it may have been on account of the small quantity asked for. There is no solid evidence, however, to suggest that fleshers were regularly expected to sell in small quantities according to

(Edinburgh, 1982), pp. 229–38, both with bone reports by G.W.I. Hodgson and A. Jones. Also *Excavations in the Medieval Burgh of Perth 1979–1981*, ed. P. Holdsworth (Edinburgh, 1987), pp. 196–9, for the bone report by C. Smith and G.W.I. Hodgson. In smaller towns more sheep may have been eaten. See Piers Dixon, *Excavations in the Fishing Town of Eyemouth 1982–84* (Edinburgh, 1986), p. 84.

[81] ACR VII.506.

[82] ACR XI.458.

[83] ACR IV.33, 401; VI.755, 824; VII.972; VIII.485; VIII.508, 646, 708, 754, 854; IX.37, 574; XI.645. See also 'Burgh Laws', p. 31, clause lxiv; 'Fragmenta Collecta', p. 182, clause xliii; 'Articuli Inquirendi', p. 116, clause 20; 'Modus Procedendi', pp. 139–40, clauses vii–viii.

[84] E.g. ACR VI.884 and VII.972: on 23 July 1499 the alderman ordered the baillies to go with the appraisers every Saturday and at all other suitable times to the fleshers and cause all their flesh – beef and mutton – to be appraised. They were to write the price on every carcase and mutton 'bouk'. But cf. *Early Records of the Burgh of Aberdeen*, ed. Dickinson, p. 76, where it appears that an ox had been appraised by the quarter.

[85] E.g. 14 October 1475: John Lammyntoun was amerced for breaking meat before it was appraised (ACR VI.402); on 20 January 1484 it was ruled following a mutton assize that fleshers were to break no flesh until they warned the appraisers and until it was appraised: ACR VI.824.

[86] ACR VIII.1156.

customers' requirements, as were, for example, candlemakers and vendors of fish.

Alongside the appraisal arrangements went the assize of flesh, and it is interesting to note that while both lamb and mutton were very frequently subject to compulsory maximum prices, beef was never – according to the surviving evidence – subject to such a general assize. This may have been because the quality of beef varied so considerably that it was not feasible to set a single maximum price. (Even for mutton, allowances for such variation meant several assizes were sometimes given according to the quality of the meat.[87]) This meant that the appraisal of beef was particularly crucial (whereas with mutton, there was a fixed and public maximum price to provide some sort of overall check) and indeed sixteenth-century ordinances providing for appraisal often referred specifically to beef.[88]

Fleshers frequently broke the assize of mutton, or sold meat dearer than its appraised value, or sold it before appraisal. Another offence was the failure to supply the town with meat. Whether the frequency of such offences reflects genuine hardship in practising the trade within the bounds of the regulations is difficult to tell, because the sale of the meat was not the only factor involved. The assize prices refer to the prepared carcases, stripped of the animal's other marketable parts, that is, its wool, its skin or hide, and even its tallow and offal. These the flesher could sell to merchants and other craftsmen or women, although it was others who made the profit from refining or exporting such things because the flesher was not himself allowed to do so. Fleshers' wives were on at least one occasion, 9 October 1506, forbidden to make candle to sell.[89] It is not clear, however, how long this ruling was intended to last, and in 1518 Simon Fleschare's wife was amerced and forbidden the craft (of candlemaking) for a year for breaking the assize of candle, but not actually for making candle to sell.[90] Restrictions applied even to offal: on 4 June 1444 it was ruled that no flesher within or outside the burgh was to remove the kidneys (*neris*) or kidney fat (*nerecres*) from any mutton between Easter and Michaelmas.[91] And an

[87] E.g. Sheep, List 280, 282, 287, 301. Another way in which the assize acknowledged the different quality of meat was to stipulate the assize for the best mutton: Sheep, List 47, 104, 239, 265, 297. 'Fragmenta Collecta', p. 182, clause xliv, sets an assize of mutton for Berwick at different levels according to the time of year: 16d. between Easter and Pentecost; 12d. between Pentecost and the feast of St James (25 July); 10d. between St James' and Michaelmas (29 September); 8d. between Michaelmas and Easter.

[88] E.g. ACR VIII.485, 506, 508, 708, 854; IX.37, 574; XI.645.

[89] ACR VIII.614.

[90] ACR X.12.

[91] ACR V ii.680.

old rule was that fleshers were not supposed to be pastry cooks, possibly because of the doubtful nature of the contents of any pies they might make.[92] The most important restriction was, however, that fleshers, like other craftsmen, were not allowed to buy and sell as merchants unless they ceased to engage directly in their craft.[93] They were not, therefore, able themselves to export wool, skins, or hides. Fleshers were not the only craftsmen to be restricted in their economic opportunities by the age-old rule that they should renounce their craft if they wished to engage in higher status commerce, but for them it must have been an especially galling inhibition. Fleshers must generally have been men of some means, for the purchase of livestock for slaughter would have involved them in significant financial outlay. Certainly, at the end of the fifteenth century and in the opening years of the sixteenth we find a number of convictions of fleshers for the occupation of their craft and merchandise.[94]

We form an impression of genuine difficulty over practising the craft within the bounds of the regulations when large numbers of fleshers were involved in breaking the rules. On 19 February 1484 thirteen fleshers were amerced for breaking the assize of mutton, selling meat unappraised and dearer than it had been appraised, for treating customers unequally by concealing the price of meat after its appraisal, and for building up great stores of meat and selling from them against the law and statutes of the burgh.[95] On another occasion, 17 June 1486, nine men were amerced for breaking the price set by the appraisers on meat and selling unappraised meat.[96] Both these instances may have had something to do with the economic dislocation of the 1480s arising chiefly from the black money. The fleshers, who probably bought several animals at a time and therefore bought with silver and gold, will perhaps have had to accept payment in the king's copper money when they sold meat. If so they will have been especially hard hit by the currency

[92] 'Fragmenta Collecta', p. 182, clause xliii. 'Articuli Inquirendi', p. 119, clause 37, expresses worries about meat and fish pies, especially those which had passed their 'sell by' date: 'Item de cocis decoquentibus carnes in pane uel pisses minime sufficientes humano vsui uel eciam postquam talia tenuerint ultra debitum tempus ea alias recalefaciunt et vendunt in manifestam populi deceptionem.'

[93] The craftsmen explicitly excluded from the merchant guild were dyers, fleshers, and shoemakers; the Ayr manuscript version of the Burgh Laws also bars fishermen. See 'Burgh Laws', p. 46, clause xciv, 'Statuta Gilde', p. 78, clause xxx, 'Articuli Inquirendi', p. 125, clauses 75 and 76, 'Modus Procedendi', pp. 152–3, clause xxviii. See also ACR VII.709 and 716, VIII.326, and XII ii.558 and 561, and *APS* II.86 and 178.

[94] E.g. ACR VII.707, 717, 1001; X.9.

[95] ACR VI.829. 'Modus Procedendi' provided for enquiry into fleshers who made larders in great and sold from them in small quantities: p. 140, clause viii.

[96] ACR VI.963.

experiments of the 1480s. Certainly, a set of ordinances enacted on 11 July 1482, aimed against strikes by retailers of foodstuffs who did not wish to furnish the town with their products because they would only be paid in black money, had a clause for fleshers as well as for brewsters and bakers.[97] The first and third decades of the sixteenth century also saw large numbers of fleshers breaking the rules respecting their craft.[98] The placks of James IV and James V may also have contributed to retailers' difficulties at this time, although one might also have expected similar problems in the second decade.

An interesting development in the meat trade in the sixteenth century was that the authorities opened it up to unfree and country people, albeit temporarily. The timing of the experiment suggests it was related to fleshers' attempts to become involved in commerce, and to their unwillingness to comply with the town's regulations for their craft. It is also a parallel to the encouragement given in the sixteenth century to landmen to come and sell their victuals in the town.[99] On 11 August 1511 licence was given to anyone of the burgh or the land who so wished to bring all manner of flesh – beef, mutton, kid, lamb and veal – to the burgh and to break (butcher) and sell them in small and great (retail and wholesale) as they pleased wherever in the town they thought most expedient, on weekdays and Sundays in future. It was confirmed on the same day (which suggests the issues were connected) that no flesher dwelling within the burgh should occupy merchandise nor sail in merchandise without abjuring his craft.[100] On 12 January

[97] ACR VI.742.

[98] E.g. On 25 August 1505 ten fleshers were amerced for selling beef before it had been appraised, selling meat for an incompetent price to scathe the town, and selling meat dearer than it had been appraised (ACR VIII.484–5); on 19 April 1507 eight fleshers were amerced for want of meat to furnish the town and selling meat for more than it was worth (ACR VIII.684); on 18 July 1508 all burgh fleshers were amerced for not providing the town with beef, selling mutton dearer than was reasonable, and especially selling mutton before it had been considered by the good men of the town (ACR VIII.854); on 17 April 1509 ten fleshers were convicted for having no meat ready to serve the town and (with the exception of two of them) for selling it dearer than it was worth or appraised at (ACR VIII.946); on 29 June 1521 six fleshers were amerced for selling flesh and tallow dearer than statute (ACR X.329); on 20/2 June 1524 all fleshers were convicted for regrating the burgh and 'skaptyne' the poor commons in selling dear mutton and lambs (ACR XI.458); on 12/13 June 1525 five fleshers were amerced for regrating the town in selling lambs for 32d. and 28d. and buying them before they were presented to the market (ACR XI.589); on 6 November 1525 all the town fleshers were amerced (though this was superseded) for breaking the assize of mutton (ACR XI.645).

[99] See below, pp. 64–5.

[100] ACR IX.10. The licence was reiterated on 10 October, following an order to the fleshers to have flesh ready for sale; no beef must be sold before appraisal nor dearer than appraised.

1515 licence was given for a year to John Colisone, baxter, to sell all flesh, both beef and mutton, to buy it wherever he pleased, and to take any booth where he pleased and set up shop so long as he sold 'wedder bouk' and other flesh cheaper by 4d. than it was sold by the common fleshers.[101] The town was attempting, it seems, to break the monopoly enjoyed by fleshers on the supply of meat.

By 1529, however, the fleshers' privileges were to an extent reinstated. It seems that a compromise between the fleshers' legitimate rights, the town's interest in free supply, and reasonable competition from outsiders and the unfree was being hammered out. An ordinance of 16 April makes it clear that unfree fleshers were now only permitted to sell on certain days of the week: it was ordered that no fleshers within the burgh or outside it were to sell any flesh within the burgh except on market days except those who joined with the town's fleshers and paid their share of the fleshhouse mail and found sureties for their debts to the landward men to avoid the town's suffering for these. Seven fleshers were listed as having found sureties to that effect.[102] In June that year all unfree craftsmen were given licence to sell their wares every Wednesday and Saturday during the town's and the council's will,[103] and unfree fleshers were specifically included in this ruling. Further entries seem to show that only licensed fleshers could sell their meat other than on the two market days.[104]

The term flesher in medieval Aberdeen also referred to a supplier of fish, which was another important source of protein for the town, especially perhaps among the poorer elements. Aberdeen was renowned for its salmon fishings in the Don and the Dee, and added to this was the plentiful supply of sea fish off the Aberdeen coast. We read of keling (a type of cod, particularly the larger sort), ling, mullet (*mullones*), turbot, and shellfish such as oysters and mussels. The impression is that these sea fish dominated the domestic market, while salmon and the younger version, grilse, were generally exported abroad.

The authorities' control on profit from the sale of fish was not in the form of the conventional assize, but consisted instead of an upper limit of 1d. per shillingsworth as the fleshers' fee for cutting up and cleaning at least the larger 'great line' fish (salmon, keling, turbot, and presumably other larger varieties). For smaller fish their service would

[101] ACR IX.388.

[102] ACR XII ii.552. Included in the ordinance was an order that no flesher was to buy fish to break for himself and sell in small quantities to the town's common people and indwellers but was only to break the fish bought by others and take 1d. per shillingsworth for his work.

[103] ACR XII ii.601.

[104] E.g. ACR XVI.307 and 567; see also XII ii.732.

presumably not have been necessary in any case. This ruling is first met in 1441, when it applied specifically to turbot[105] but it was afterwards extended to cover all 'great line' fish, and indeed it seems fleshers were eventually not allowed to cut up and clean their own fish for resale but only to cut up and clean other people's for their fee.[106]

With fish, then, control on the flesher's profit was imposed in the first instance in the form of a fixed percentage of the value of the article. This is interesting, for the profit would in theory rise along with any rise in the price of fish. The position of the flesher as a marketer of his own fish was, however, eventually undermined and he seems to have become a hired refiner of other people's fish. Yet, his fee was still related to the value of the fish and was thereby protected. In this respect fleshers were, on the face of it at least, in a better position than bakers or brewers.

The assize of ale

King David's assize of ale, like that for bread, is known only from fourteenth-century copies, and the prices of malt envisaged in it, ranging from 6s. 8d. the chaldron to 40s. the chaldron, relate also to the later period.[107] It provides for 160 gallons of ale to be sold from each chalder of malt, which would apparently permit the brewing of two gallons of the best knight's ale for every one gallon of the lesser armiger's or servant's ale. This ambiguity about the quality of ale envisaged is compounded when the assize points out that though the brewster should *sell* 160 gallons per chalder (s)he should make a further thirty-two gallons from the same chalder from which to take the profit, either in ale, or in cash if it were sold. A brew of this strength (192 gallons per chalder) was called cervisia venalis or tavern ale.

It is important that this assize thus makes explicit the mechanism by which the brewster was to take his profit, for although the assize of bread is not clear in this way, it is argued above that a similar mechanism also controlled the baker's profit.

[105] ACR IV.252 (printed, *Extracts*, ed. Stuart, pp. 396–7): 23 August: 'Item that na fleschewar mak price na by to sel agayne ony turbote as said is bot as thai sall have for the brekyng of a turbote quhilk is botht within xij d' j d' and quhen it excedis xij d' ij d' quhil it cum to ij s' and swa furtht for ilke schilling j d' and he sal have nane othir eschetis bot al sal be brokin to the biaris.'

[106] See esp. ACR VI.237, 238, 755; VII.1035; VIII.198, 323; XI.66; XII ii.552; XIV.555; XVI.755.

[107] *APS* I, p. 675.

King William's assize of ale likewise survives only in a fourteenth-century copy with fourteenth-century malt prices (10s. the chaldron to 40s. the chaldron). However, William's ale must have been weaker since the prices it proposes were clearly calculated on the basis of selling 240 gallons for the cost of each chalder of malt.[108] Smout and Gibson have shown that ale of this strength was still the standard required type in the seventeenth century, suggesting that the quality of assize ale should have remained stable over centuries.[109] This was possible because the price of the gallon, rising from ½d. a gallon in the early fourteenth century to 16d. a gallon by the mid-sixteenth century, was essentially open-ended and could rise to reflect the rising price of malt.[110]

In theory, then, the quality of the ale was fixed but the price was variable. In practice, however, the assize often attempted to hold prices down, resulting in many cases no doubt in ale of variable quality. At Aberdeen ale which failed to pass the best quality controls was sometimes passed for sale, but at a lesser price.[111] Beer – i.e. ale with hops – was not often mentioned in the assize, but if it were, it cost slightly more.[112] Separate pricing of ales of different strengths also probably explains the arrangements for the pricing of ale made by free and unfree brewsters. Higher price ale was the preserve of free brewers, though sometimes there was provision for an overlap, the cheapest 'free' ale being priced equally with the dearest 'unfree' ale.[113] Given that unfree brewsters would not have been permitted to undercut free brewsters selling at the price prescribed for them, it seems certain that cheaper ale meant weaker ale.[114]

[108] When malt stands at 15s. c. the assize exceptionally, and probably erroneously, requires 270 gallons to be brewed from the chalder.

[109] Gibson and Smout, *Prices, Food and Wages* citing *APS* VI(1). 240, 29 July 1644; 15 gallons per boll = 240 gallons per celdra. All this compares reasonably well with what we know of ale in England. Barbara Harvey found the ale at Westminster Abbey to be about the strength of modern pale ale, a quarter of malt yielding 45 to 50 gallons. Dyer notes a range of strengths, giving 50 to 75 to 96 gallons per quarter. Harvey, *Living and Dying in England* p. 58. Dyer, *Standards of Living*, p. 58. Comparison of English and Scots capacity measures suggests 192 gallons per chalder is roughly equivalent to 48 gallons per quarter, while 240 gallons per chalder works out at about 60 gallons per quarter.

[110] Bread prices in contrast were tied to the conventional loaf prices ½d., 1d., and 2d.

[111] ACR VI.526 and 606 give three prices on each occasion according to quality.

[112] ACR V i.197, V ii.776, VI.113, VIII.959. See also *ER* VII.586; *TA* IV.304.

[113] ACR VII.1066, XV.222, XVI.10, 358. At times, however, unfree brewing was forbidden altogether, ACR VII.109.

[114] *Extracts*, ed. Stuart p. 9, gives a range of prices, differentiating between gild members, gild brewers, and others in 1442. ACR VI.698 seems to imply that unfree ale be cheaper and weaker. ACR VI.733 shows that the unfree status of the women clearly

The assize of ale must have been more difficult to enforce than that of bread. In the first place the quality of ale must have been more difficult to monitor objectively.[115] Secondly, brewing was carried on all over the town by scores of different brewsters, both free and unfree, and controlling so much dispersed activity must have been difficult. The numbers of brewsters amerced at a time sometimes came to over fifty,[116] so tasting on this scale was best reserved for Sundays when no other work would be expected of the serjeants and cunnars (ale-tasters).[117] In 1509 all the brewsters in Aberdeen were listed.[118] There are 153 names, of whom 29 are unfree. It seems that almost anyone could brew and sell ale. Exceptionally Andrew Wricht was excluded because he was a stallholder, but we do meet other brewsters with additional means of employment.[119] Women particularly often combined brewing with various means of making a small income. Thus Wricht's wife was permitted to brew, though she was amerced for overpricing.[120] Brewing was perhaps popular with women for a number of reasons; the work could be carried out at home, involved minimal overheads, and might have amounted to little more than an extension of a woman's brewing for her own family.[121] Servants sometimes appear as brewsters,[122] though it is not clear if they worked on their own account or as employees of more successful men.

Whatever the reason for the widespread involvement in brewing, the total numbers brewing were clearly large. The problem of controlling so much brewing may explain the attempt made in 1489 to prohibit all unfree brewing, and to restrict the dearest ale to four brewsters per quarter.[123] In the sixteenth century there was a marked shift towards administration of the assize on a quarter by quarter basis, but otherwise the attempt to restrict numbers of brewsters and to exclude the unfree seems to have been of only very temporary effect.

affects the price they could charge. For free and unfree prices generally, see ACR VI.238, VII.671, VIII.25, 163, 508, 753, 1016, XIV.7–8, 194, 286.

115 In the sixteenth century attempts were made to describe the required quality – gud, clyne, quhyt and stark (strong) being the terms used. ACR XIII.5, 77, 234, XIV.7–8. Earlier it had to be merely 'provable', or worth the set price.

116 ACR X.82–3, 207, XVI.616.

117 ACR VIII.484, 715, 798, IX.386.

118 ACR VIII.1205–9.

119 ACR II.194. An unfree pynour (docker) was amerced for breaking the assize, but it seems he was allowed to brew (ACR XI.339), and a 'maltman' was named among the unfree brewers of Futy, ACR VIII.1209.

120 ACR II.194. Women were often candlemakers and hucksters as well as brewers; see p. 54.

121 'Burgh Laws', pp. 30–1, assumes throughout that brewsters are women.

122 ACR XV.222.

123 ACR VII.109.

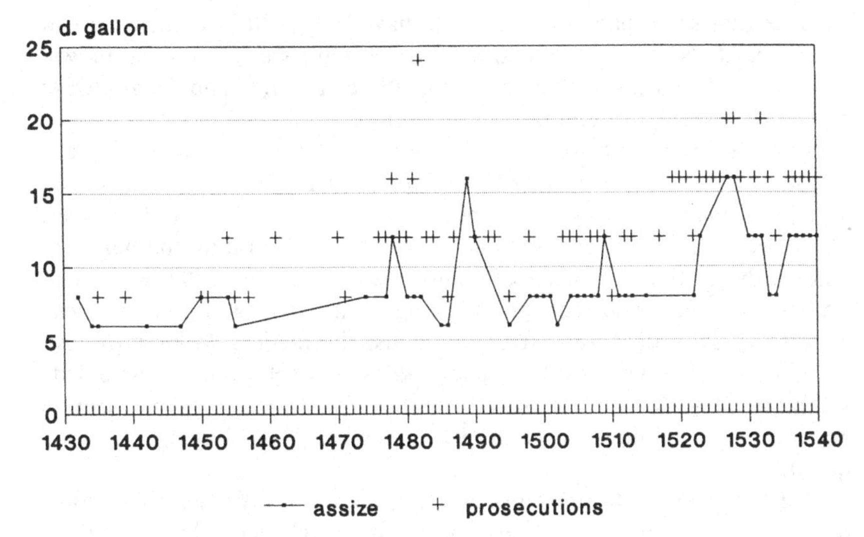

9 The assize of ale (Aberdeen)

The Aberdeen records are full of amercements of brewsters. Usually the offence is a simple one of charging more than the assize price. Figure 9 shows clearly how prosecutions run consistently above the assize price. However, occasionally a brewster might be fined for the more particular offence of selling her ale above the price at which it was set, which could have been below the general assize price if it were of lesser quality.[124] Obviously brewsters had a number of other tricks at their disposal, for which they might be fined when caught. False measures are surprisingly rare,[125] probably because customers would not be slow to complain, but one such case occurred in the notoriously difficult year 1482.[126] On another occasion one brewster was apprehended charging different prices for ale from the same barrel,[127] and another took away the set price from her door after it had been fixed by the officer.[128] Brewsters were fined for selling ale before it had been tasted and priced,[129] or for not attending the assize.[130] Equally, when brewsters were served written notice of the set price of their ale,[131] we may

[124] ACR VIII.388.
[125] See Chapter 3.
[126] ACR VI.736.
[127] ACR XI.220.
[128] ACR VIII.1028.
[129] ACR VIII.1077.
[130] ACR X.370–1, XII i.249, XIV.475, XV.522, XVI.633.
[131] ACR VIII.515.

surmise that some had claimed not to have been told how their ale had been priced. Nor need we assume that the fault was always the brewsters'; the officers themselves were sometimes fined,[132] and seem always to have operated throughout under oath.[133]

Naturally brewsters were also subject to all the more general regulations for buying and selling. They were meant to buy only a week's supply of malt at a time so as not to create a dearth,[134] and we read also of eight unfree alewives in the Grene quarter regrating the burgh.[135] The authorization of wholesale purchases of ale in 1504 was most unusual,[136] the important point being that such authorization was necessary, as a departure from more usual practice. More typically, there was a general requirement that sales be open, and even-handed, selling to all at the set price while supplies lasted without favouritism,[137] and no one spilling the market, presumably by buying in large quantities.[138]

The commoner infringements of the assize often involved prosecution of large groups, or of 'the brewsters of the burgh generally'.[139] Certain periods of mass prosecutions stand out particularly,[140] and some of these periods can be associated with particular harvest or monetary problems; others may simply have been the result of special judicial vigour.

When amercement becomes practically universal it might be thought that what we are looking at is more a system of licensing rather than the genuine punishment of offenders. This is not the case. The record sometimes observes that certain offenders were more obstinate than the rest,[141] or distinguishes first offenders.[142] Despite almost universal infringement, these were definitely perceived as offences to be punished, not licences to be bought. Sometimes fines were suspended pending good behaviour, clearly a procedure concerned with conduct rather

132 ACR X.36.
133 ACR VIII.753.
134 ACR IX.107.
135 ACR XVI.394.
136 ACR VIII.337.
137 ACR VI.736, XII ii.704.
138 ACR XIV.465.
139 ACR VIII.784; for amercements of all brewers see ACR VIII.1053–4, IX.270; for all free and all unfree brewers see ACR VIII.1077, 1126, 1139; for all the brewers of specific quarters see ACR IX.106, 270, XI.360–1.
140 E.g. 1478–9, 1482–3, 1495, 1507–8, 1510, 1512–13, 1519–24, 1527, 1531–4, 1538–40; many of these years were also difficult for the bakers and the fleshers.
141 ACR XI.401.
142 ACR XVI.633, 635.

than revenue generation.[143] Moreover, punishments were not always monetary, but might involve instead the destruction of equipment.[144]

However, widespread infringement of the assize does suggest that the prices set may often have been unrealistic. Certainly the other ordinary purchase prices recorded in this series look more in line with the prosecution price at Aberdeen than with the assize price. As Figure 9 shows, when the assize price was 6d., prosecutions were regular at 8d.; when the assize moved to 8d., many brewsters were already charging 12d.; and when the assize moved to 12d. at the end of our series, 16d. had already become normal on the open market. The range of prices cited by Symms from Edinburgh, Selkirk, and Peebles confirms the impression that the Aberdeen assize price was often set unrealistically low, though with quality being such a variable factor one cannot push this comparison much further.[145] The assize of ale was designed as a brake on inflation, to restrain unwarranted profits and to protect the interest of the community at large, and as such it was bound to drag its unwilling feet after the 'open market' price. Yet the difficulties such a policy was bound to cause the brewsters do not seem to have been as severe as those afflicting the bakers. The brewsters had only rarely to be reminded of their obligation to serve the town,[146] suggesting either that the authorities were less anxious about the supply of ale or that brewsters seldom found the terms of the assize so unreasonable as to drive them from the trade. Instead of giving up altogether, or threatening to do so, the brewsters probably found they could economize enough on the quality of their ale, without alienating their customers, to pay their fines when they fell due and to make enough profit to justify their labour. Admittedly, with so many brewsters operating, any boycott or strike would have been unlikely to succeed, yet the very fact that there were so many brewsters suggests that the assize never totally extinguished the profit in ale.

Candlemaking

Women were also prominent in the craft of candlemaking. This is clear from evidence of breaches of the assize and other offences in candlemak-

[143] ACR VII.160, VIII.757, X.370.

[144] *Extracts from the Records of the Burgh of Edinburgh.* AD *1403–1528*, p. 150. Symms, 'Market Regulation', 280, cites this case, and another from Peebles (*SBRS* (1910), 218–19).

[145] Symms, 'Market Regulation', 280.

[146] ACR VIII.508, IX.36.

ing, where it was most often women who were convicted.[147] On one occasion, moreover, the assize of candle was addressed to six women.[148] Candlemaking was a simple craft, but this is not to say it was unimportant. Especially in winter and in northern latitudes candles were a necessity. Tallow candles were what most people would have used. Wax was an expensive luxury, offered by the town as a propine to the king or visiting nobles, or by individual burgesses to 'the Holy Blood light' in St Nicholas' church as a customary penalty for their offences against the burgh laws.[149] Wax was the refined product, and most people will not have been able to afford it.

It was thus necessary to ensure an adequate supply of tallow for the purpose of candlemaking, and the burgh authorities regularly issued ordinances with the purpose of conserving it. In 1484, burgh fleshers were told to present in the market the tallow of the animals they had slain as well as the meat itself.[150] In the guild court held on 5 October 1442[151] neighbours were forbidden to buy tallow to send to Flanders or to 'tap' again; they were only to buy for their own use.[152] And in the guild court held on 7 November 1449 men were forbidden to buy more tallow than would suffice their own household or to make merchandise of it, that is, to trade in it at a profit. That which had been bought in the past (presumably in breach of this regulation) was to be handed over to the commons at its original purchase price.[153]

In the 1440s, then, it looks as though tallow, like grain throughout our period, was not a commodity to be trafficked in. It is possible in consequence that candlemaking was also forbidden at that time although this is not explicit. By the 1480s, however, candlemaking for sale was permissible, as is clear from the fact of the first surviving assize in 1482,[154] but the authorities' concern that the town's need for tallow be met is evident in rulings over the rest of our period which either forbade outside sales of tallow (and sometimes flesh) altogether or (from

[147] E.g. ACR VI.246 (five women); VIII.518 (three women); 625 (two women); 665 (three women and man in wife's name); 888 (four women); 894 (four women); X.12 (one woman); 21 (one woman); 30 (one woman); 242 (four women); XI.220 (one woman); XII i.76 (two women); and cf. X.11 (male offender) and XII i.104 (man and wife).

[148] ACR VII.908.

[149] The cult of the Holy Blood probably reflects the influence of Bruges: see *SMT*, p. 8.

[150] ACR VI.883.

[151] The date is given incorrectly in the text as Friday after Michaelmas, 5 September.

[152] ACR V ii.660.

[153] ACR V ii.745.

[154] List 1.

the 1520s) stipulated that the town's needs be met before any tallow were exported or sold to outsiders.[155]

Prices of candles were controlled by the assize of tallow[156] as well as the assize of candle. Candles had to be sold by weight rather than by the piece, though it was important too that they be available in various sizes.[157] The assizes of tallow and of candle and other rules respecting the craft were generally made in October and November, possibly in anticipation of Martinmas when large numbers of animals were slaughtered, and indeed with the onset of long winter nights when the need for candles would increase. The assize of tallow sometimes distinguished sheep and 'nolt' (beef) tallow, the latter being cheaper. This was perhaps because when melted down it lost more weight than did sheep fat.

It is difficult to tell how much profit the candlemakers were permitted to make, because the number of pounds to the stone of tallow is not clear;[158] nor do we know how much weight was lost in the melting of

[155] ACR VI.758, 882, and 935; VII. 355; VIII. 614 and 752; XII ii. 732; XIII.234; XIV.8; XV.235. Royal legislation also banned the export of tallow and, though less frequently, cattle: *APS*, II.7, 92, 174, 314, 378 and see also 346–7.

[156] We have not compiled a series of tallow prices as the entries are not frequent, but a list of tallow assize prices is given below.

Reference	Date	Assize (s. per stone)
ACR X.20	8 Nov. 1518	4s. (statement about assize made by flesher accused of breaking it) (Assize of candle made 11 Oct. 1518 to last until 1 Nov. 1518 4d. lb; thereafter 3d. lb: Candle List 30)
ACR XI.645	6 Nov. 1525	5s. sheep and nolt tallow 'ourhed' (assize of candle made same day 5d.lb: Candle List 31)
ACR XII i.66	5 Nov. 1526	5s. nolt; 6s. sheep
ACR XII ii.719–20	8 Nov. 1529	4s. nolt; 5s. sheep (statements about assize made when fleshers were amerced for infringing it)
ACR XII ii.732	14 Dec. 1529	4s.6d. nolt; 5s. sheep
ACR XIII.234	6 Oct. 1531	6s. sheep; 5s. nolt (candle assize made same day 6d. lb: Candle List 33)
ACR XIV.8	4 Oct. 1532	5s. sheep; 4s. nolt (candle assize made same day 6d. lb: Candle List 34)
ACR XV.235	23 Oct. 1536	5s.6d. sheep; 4s.6d. nolt

[157] ACR VIII.507, 614 and 1127; IX.36; and XI.645 (Candle List 16, 17, 22, 24, and 31).

[158] But see Glossary, under stone.

the tallow. We can, however, infer from rulings made in the candle assizes that an important factor determining the candlemakers' profit was the degree to which they were able to add to the weight of the finished product. That candles were to be well dried was one frequent stipulation; that the wicks were to be small and well dried was another.[159] That it was thought necessary to rule on the size or weight of the wicks would suggest that the material from which the wicks were made was cheaper than the tallow itself, so that the amount of wick in part determined the candlemakers' profit. In particular, on 11 October 1533 the candlemakers were licensed to sell the pound of made candle for 5d., on condition that the weight of the wicks for a whole stone of candle weighed only ½lb.[160]

Convictions for breaking the assize of candle or committing other offences are not infrequently met, although such instances (as with infringements of the assize of bread) only occasionally involve actual weights.[161] It seems in fact that candlemakers did not get into trouble as frequently as alewives did, but this may be only an indication that a smaller number of people were engaged in the craft. On one occasion, in 1518, the authorities recognized that times were hard for candlemakers and allowed them to sell at a higher price for a short period, but with the intention that afterwards the assize they thought was reasonable should be kept.[162] Yet, we have seen already that in October 1520 four women candlemakers encountered a harsh attitude when they protested against the charge of failing to keep the assize, saying they could not do so without damage to themselves, and that they would give up the craft before they kept it. The baillies for their part merely charged them to desist from candlemaking under penalty of 8s.[163]

This bland response on the part of the baillies was not in fact typical of the authorities' attitude. In general they wanted the candlemakers to produce, even if they did not allow them large profits. A number of the assizes enjoined the candlemakers to have candle ready to sell,[164] and on one occasion they were told to have candle ready to sell daily and nightly to all persons either in the burgh or in the hinterland.[165] Further, a statute for craftsmen enacted on 17 November 1497 in anticipation of a royal visit enjoined candlemakers, along with merchants

[159] See Chapter 5, p. 297.
[160] ACR XIV.286 (Candle List 36).
[161] Cf. ACR VIII.625 (Candle List 18).
[162] ACR X.9 (Candle List 30).
[163] ACR X.242.
[164] ACR VII.671, 762, 841, and 908; VIII.163, 753, and 1033; and IX.36 (Candle List 8, 9, 11, 12, 14, 19, 20, and 24).
[165] ACR IX.36 (Candle List 24).

and other craftsmen, to be well stocked with goods in order to supply the king and his lords.[166]

Although the assizes we have just discussed look like price controls on basic household necessities, in fact they were controls on the amount of profit craftsmen were permitted to make when they sold their goods in the burgh. In other words, they represented what was considered to be the fair price of the craftsman's labour added to the cost of his raw materials and equipment. The cost of those raw materials had to be taken into account by the authorities when setting the assize, and this is most obvious in the case of ale and bread, where in fact in the early part of our period we do not have assizes as such, but rather a report on the going price of grain which was used to determine the assizes. The price of candle was related to that of tallow, and the flesher's fee was related to the value of the fish. The authorities could not reduce the amount of profit beyond a certain point and, when the craftsman's profit was too small, he would naturally protest and even threaten to withdraw the supply of the manufactured article. The structure and level of prices in the burgh depended therefore to a great extent on the prices of primary produce.

The corn market

The authorities' control over the prices of primary produce was necessarily limited. There was, for instance, no assize of grain. Instead, its price was subject to negotiation between vendor and purchaser. Transactions were, however, subject to a number of strict regulations intended to ensure that they took place publicly and that it be clear how much produce was available and what demand there was for it. All the grain coming from the countryside had to be presented first to the market.[167]

[166] ACR VII.846.

[167] E.g. *Extracts*, ed. Stuart, p. 381; ACR I.196; IX.107 and 270. In these rulings the emphasis is on presentation in the market in the first instance, which left open the question of where the grain might be sold subsequently; but other rulings state explicitly that all transactions in grain must be in the market place. For instance, on 19 April 1445 it was ruled that no victual was to be sold or tapped in houses or anywhere except the market (ACR IV.401), while on 23 August 1441, in association with a limit on the amount of grain townspeople might purchase, it was ruled that if any neighbour had victual to sell he was to tap it not at home but in the market, 'playneli', on the market day: ACR IV.252 (printed, *Extracts*, ed. Stuart, p. 397). The meaning of some of the rulings made on 18 March 1401 does not emerge fully, because of damage to the manuscript, but it does seem clear that no one was supposed to buy malt except in the market, that anyone buying or having malt or meal in the countryside should not sell it in town except in the market, and that no one living in town should receive the malt or meal of countrymen unless it were presented to the market; nor should they receive it in their homes with the intention of selling it

Townspeople were not permitted to go into the country and buy up grain for resale in town,[168] and private measuring of grain also seems to have been forbidden.[169] In the latter part of the fifteenth century the grain market opened at either twelve or one o'clock in the afternoon, noon becoming established as the standard time in the sixteenth century.[170] The point of confining transactions to the market, and fixing the time at which it opened, was to ensure that those who needed to buy had a fair opportunity to do so.

The going price for victual (grain generally, especially barley and meal) on a particular market day seems to have been established on the basis of what most people were prepared to pay for it. That price then acquired authority as the correct price for grain until the next market day and as the basis for the assize of bread and ale.[171] The price of grain thus had an ongoing importance beyond its significance for the individual transaction. It must have been partly because of this that even the negotiations between vendor and purchaser were subject to certain rules. Individuals were not permitted, in order to secure a purchase, to offer the vendors a higher price than that which their neighbours were paying. On 19 December 1519 Robert Morisone was amerced for spoiling the market (spoiling or 'spilling' the market is a term very frequently met which could cover a variety of market offences) and buying meal for 10s. while the rest of his neighbours bought for 8s.[172] On 27 October 1530 two women were forbidden to buy either meal or malt in the market until the following Michaelmas because they had broken the market on the last market day by paying more

afterwards for more money: *Early Records of the Burgh of Aberdeen*, ed. Dickinson, p. 179.

168 E.g. *Early Records of the Burgh of Aberdeen*, ed. Dickinson, p. 179, and ACR IX.386 and see also XII i.154: on 7 May 1527 eleven women were amerced for measuring victuals outside town and buying them before they came to market, which caused 'sak dartht' to be within the town.

169 This is inferred from records of offences. For example: a man acquitted himself on 13 January 1400 of having made a market at home, buying and measuring meal or malt in his house with a common firlot (*Early Records of the Burgh of Aberdeen*, ed. Dickinson, p. 118); the wife of John de Abernethy was acquitted on 8 October 1408 of buying oats which came to her house in blankets and sheets, which was a sign that they were measured before they came to her house (ACR II.20). Retailing offences often recorded the use of peck and firlot: e.g. ACR X.15 and 16; XI.184–5 and 211. On 12 January 1532 all market spillers were summoned so that they could be forbidden to receive or measure any victuals in their houses or buy more than they needed for themselves (ACR XIII.326). For a good selection of offences against the various regulations governing the sale of grain, see ACR II.20–1.

170 ACR VI.500, 526, and 937; X.16 and 83; XI.211–12 and 288; XV.222–3 and 735 and XVI.29.

171 See p. 28.

172 ACR X.150.

for these than other neighbours would have done.[173] Another practice, that of interfering with a transaction which had already been agreed, by offering the vendor more than the original purchaser had done, was known as overbuying and was similarly forbidden. On 14 November 1399, for instance, one Walter Rede was accused in his wife's name of having spoilt the market by buying malt, meal, and oats for a higher price than his neighbours had offered through the earnest-money they had handed over to the vendors.[174] Earnest-money, 'erllys', 'arlis', or 'ayrllis', referred to the token sum given in advance by a purchaser to show his good faith. This was a way of agreeing the transaction, on the understanding that payment would be made later. But the danger was that others might be tempted in the meantime to overbuy the purchaser or, if the vendor had not taken the precaution of fixing the actual price he wished to get, he was open to efforts by the purchaser to reduce it. On 7 November 1485, it was laid down that buyers had to 'make price' (that is, negotiate and agree on a price) of the actual poke and sack they were buying. They could not simply promise to pay the highest price of the market.[175] On 14 November 1505 women were forbidden to buy meal in the market unless they made the price for it before they gave their earnest-money.[176] The order was repeated in 1513, with general application to all towndwellers, and with the addition that once the price had been made the buyer was to carry the victual away and not allow it to stand any longer in the market. No one was to give earnest-money on top of what their neighbours had given with the intent of overbuying them.[177] On 11 October 1533 a further ordinance forbade anyone in town to give an 'arle penny' to the 'vittell men' saying they would give them as much as the market price was on that day. They must instead agree on an actual figure.[178]

Thus while the authorities did not control the price of grain directly, they influenced the process by which the market price was reached to ensure that it reflected what the majority were willing to pay. In order that it should be determined fairly and should prevail, people were not allowed to hedge their bets or raise the going rate to secure their own purchases. At times, the authorities found it appropriate to restrict the privilege of negotiating prices to free people. On 29 October 1507

[173] ACR XIII.34.

[174] *Extracts*, ed. Stuart, p. 378 (*Early Records of the Burgh of Aberdeen*, ed. Dickinson, pp. 80 and 112). Rede was also accused of illegally retailing what he had bought in his house.

[175] ACR VI.937.

[176] ACR VIII.518.

[177] ACR IX.270.

[178] ACR XIV.286.

unfree people were forbidden to buy victual in the market or make price. They were to use the price that free people who bought had made.[179] Again, on 9 October 1536 unfreemen's wives were forbidden to come to market until the price of both meal and malt had been made. They were not to make prices but should use the going rate.[180] It should not surprise us that the unfree were restricted in this way, and in fact there are other occasions on which the unfree were forbidden to buy: on 6 October 1531 unfreemen's wives were barred from brewing or buying victuals in the common market until the council was further advised;[181] this order was repeated on 12 October with the additional restriction that unfreemen's wives were not to receive victuals in their houses.[182] On 22 March 1541 unfreemen's wives, along with their husbands and servants, were forbidden to sell bread, to brew or sell ale, or to tap or buy more meal, malt, fish or flesh than would sustain themselves, whether in the market or outside it.[183]

Such restrictions on the unfree may well have been associated with times of scarcity, for the town was on other occasions more flexible in its attitude towards the activities of the unfree. In particular, the unfree were generally allowed to brew ale for sale, although for a lower price than that permitted for free brewsters.[184] Scarcity possibly accounts for a particularly interesting enactment designed to limit the numbers of those involved in negotiating grain prices. On 13 October 1522 it was decided that eight women, two from each of the town's quarters, were to assemble every market day, some of them going to the meal market and the rest to the malt market. They were to meet with the landmen and make the price of both meal and malt, and no one else was to be seen in the market until this had been done.[185] It is not clear how long this experiment lasted, but the fact that such responsibility was given to women confirms the prominence of women as purchasers of malt and meal.

The initial sale of grain by countrymen in town was not the end of the story, for it is clear that townsmen retailed grain afterwards. Such trade operated under the most strict conditions. One restriction was on the sale of grain to outsiders, as it was felt that grain ought to be available first to townspeople, particularly in times of scarcity. On 30 October 1413 John Henry of the Grene quarter and his wife were

[179] ACR VIII.763.
[180] ACR XV.223.
[181] ACR XIII.234.
[182] ACR XIII.243–4.
[183] ACR XVI.763.
[184] See above, p. 49.
[185] ACR XI.187.

convicted by assize for the sale of meal to outsiders and for making dearth in the meal market.[186] On 7 June 1497 three men were amerced for putting meal in barrels and selling it to foreigners, while on 14 June a man was in trouble for selling a last of rye meal to foreigners.[187] On 17 April 1523 a statute laid down penalties for neighbours who forestalled the market in town or in the country by buying victuals in great and regrating in selling them to outlandmen. The statute was annotated as being made in times of scarcity.[188]

The purchase of grain in order to make a profit by selling it for more was explicitly forbidden,[189] as was selling dearer than the price of the preceding market day.[190] On 17 July 1532 a woman was amerced for selling meal dearer on weekdays than on the market day preceding, that is, at 24s. the boll when it went for 20s. on the previous market day.[191] On 8 May 1536 George Baxter was amerced for tapping meal in small for 10d. the peck, when meal was being sold at the same time in town for 9d. the peck.[192]

While tapping grain was on occasion explicitly forbidden,[193] the point seems to be that it was selling at a profit which was condemned,

[186] ACR II.194.

[187] ACR VII.813–14 and 815. Following the conviction of 14 June it was laid down that if the offender or any other inhabitant of the burgh were to sell or send victuals out of town he should pay ten marks (£6 13s. 4d.) to St Nicholas' work.

[188] ACR XI.277.

[189] E.g. *Early Records of the Burgh of Aberdeen*, ed. Dickinson, p. 179, and ACR V ii.757 and 789. The terms of all three enactments are interesting. The text of the (printed) ordinance of 18 March 1401 is damaged but the meaning is clear: 'Item nullus manens in burgo recipiat brasium vel farinam ruralium [*sed*] presentatur foro et [. . .] in domibus suis ad expectandum quod postea carius possint vendi sub dicta pena.' In the ruling of 9 October 1450, no man was to buy victual to sell dearer again and make merchandise of it; in that of 25 October 1455, no indweller of the burgh of any degree was to buy any victual to sell again 'for wynnyng' to thaim singular'ly'.

[190] E.g. ACR XIV.285, and XVI.359.

[191] ACR XIII.478.

[192] ACR XV.139. Other offenders against the principle of the just price and the authority of the market in determining it were Sandy Morisone, who on 22 October 1518 was amerced for regrating the burgh in 'selling and tappine furtht in smallis wit pecc' and firlot' on Sundays and holy days dearer than the common price of the market, and the women who on 24 November 1522 were amerced for regrating and scathing the poor commons in 'paccin' (tapping) meal in smalls with peck and firlot on market day and week day dearer than the prices of the market: ACR X.15 and XI.211.

[193] E.g. *Early Records of the Burgh of Aberdeen*, ed. Dickinson, p. 179. The register is damaged at this point, but the editor's text makes the meaning reasonably clear: 'In prima tenta xviii die mensis Marcii anno millesimo quadrigentesimo [. . .] quod nullus manens infra burgum emat farinam ad usum [. . .], propinet farinam, aut vendat laganas: eciam vendicio lagan[arum. . .] villam habitantibus prohibetur.' In February 1454 an ordinance forbade any man to buy any kind of victual in the market to tap again upon the town's neighbours (ACR V i.197), and later, on 7 June 1529, merchants and craftsmen within the burgh were forbidden to tap any meal in the burgh either in small or in great. They were to buy no more in the country in great than would

especially as it is clear on other occasions that the resale of grain was allowed so long as all the rules to ensure neighbours did not profit were followed. The resale of grain was permitted implicitly in certain orders concerning the duties payable on victual,[194] and also in enactments laying down strict conditions under which tappers were to operate. On 10 October 1522, for example, it had come to the attention of the authorities that there were sundry neighbours in the burgh who kept 'open gyrnale' and sold grain with peck and firlot in smalls both on market day and weekday to poor folk for more than it was sold at in the market. This, the authorities thought, caused great 'dartht' and 'heing' of the prices of victuals within the burgh. So they ruled that no townsman should tap any victuals in smalls unless he came first to the provost and baillies, told them he had such victuals to sell, and agreed with them on the price. Then the handbell man was to make known throughout the burgh who the vendor was and advertise his grain and its price.[195] The enactment was repeated on 24 November, with special reference to meal, with the stipulation that the agreed price was to be no higher than that of the previous market day. If the quantity of the victual were great this, and its whereabouts, were to be made known to the community by the handbell.[196]

Tapping, then, might be tolerated, but only under circumstances which brought benefit to the purchaser – by making grain available – rather than profit to the vendor. Of course, the kind of person who offended against the rules will have varied enormously, from the deliberate speculator who had means to buy up grain in bulk and to store it until it suited him to sell at a large profit, to the small-scale retailer seeking to eke out a precarious livelihood and occasionally falling foul of the laws. Andrew Durty, who was publicly asked on 17 April 1523 (the day when the statute about selling victual to outlandmen in time of scarcity was made) whether he had any victuals stored up ('girnellit')

meet their own household needs, and if any landman were to give them any meal in great in payment for their merchandise, and they intended to sell it, they were to present it to the market, on the market day, and sell it at the market price and no dearer: ACR XII ii.600.

[194] ACR XIV.555 and XVI.274.

[195] ACR XI.184–5. It was also decided on this day that every baillie, with his officer and four or five reputable witnesses, should pass through his quarter and seek out all unlawful neighbours and those who received the goods of their neighbours, such as corn, fuel, kail, fish, or any other stuff. Such persons were to be brought before the provost and council for punishment. The search was to be done quietly all on one day. It was also arranged that those who carried salmon or any other merchandise after nightfall should be banished from the town.

[196] ACR XI.211. On this day several women were amerced for regrating meal: see above, n. 192.

in great and whether he intended to sell them in the burgh at the market price, but who denied having any,[197] looks like an example of the former, and in quite a different league from the fifteen suspected market spoilers who a few days later were forbidden to come into the market to buy more victuals than would sustain themselves or to tap any in smalls – either on market day or other days – until they got fresh licence.[198] Indeed the authorities' favoured solution to the natural temptation to profit from the sale of grain was to prevent townspeople from buying more than they needed for themselves and their households in the first place. This was done in the autumn of 1438 (the worst year of the century right across Europe), when there was a very severe general shortage of foodstuffs. On 7 October it was ruled that only men were to buy meal in the market; that meal was to be measured with the half firlot as well as with the peck and half peck;[199] that no huckster should be in the burgh unless her husband were a free burgess; and that no meal buyer or any other burgess should buy more meal on one market day than would meet his reasonable household needs until the next market day. The ordinance also imposed restrictions on the purchase and sale of other staple foodstuffs.[200] A few years later, on 23 August 1441, it was ruled that no one was to buy more victual than they needed for their own house to tap again at dearth on the commons; if anyone had victual to sell they were to tap it not at home but in the market, 'playneli', on the market day.[201]

The ordinance of 1438 was made as a result of an emergency, and that of 1441 looks like an effort to curb undue profit and to ensure transactions took place openly. But from the latter part of the fifteenth century onwards, people were frequently forbidden to buy more than they needed for themselves. Sometimes, the restrictions applied to those obviously most likely to buy in bulk – cake bakers, hucksters, brewsters, notorious market spillers – even women in general.[202] Cake bakers and

[197] ACR XI.278.
[198] ACR XI.282.
[199] It is surprising that, in time of scarcity, the authorities were enjoining the use of the larger measure as well as the smaller ones. Perhaps it was felt that the availability of a measure of a different capacity would provide a check on the reliability of the others.
[200] ACR IV.143 (below, 'Appendix of documents', no. I).
[201] ACR IV.252 (printed, *Extracts*, ed. Stuart, p. 397).
[202] ACR VII.34 (23 October 1487: hucksters, cake bakers, and market spillers only to buy as much meal as would serve their own needs between market days); VIII.518–19 (14 November 1505: no woman to buy more meal than needed for herself and her household; no one to bake 'saile' cakes until permitted by authorities); IX.107 (16 June 1512: no brewster to buy more malt than one 'lad' per week, as much as might serve her for a week, and no meal buyers to buy more meal than needed for themselves); XI.288 (4 May 1523: statute for market spillers: several injunctions to

hucksters were expelled from the market on 8 October 1507, in order that the market should be kept.[203] Sometimes the wives of the burgh's four serjeants were made to set an example, often by use of the threat that if they bought more than they were allowed their husbands would be deprived of office.[204] The unfree and their associates were, as we have seen, restricted in both buying and selling in 1541.[205] But sometimes no one was allowed to buy more than they needed for themselves, and such general inhibitions may well have been associated with grain shortages.[206]

The attempts by the authorities to prevent people from buying more than they needed for themselves nearly all come from the sixteenth century, and may be seen as evidence of an increased demand for grain in the burgh. This theory is given added weight by evidence of the authorities actively encouraging, even forcing, vendors to make their grain available. A clause in the ruling of 14 November 1505 already referred to was that all landmen were to have their sacks ready open to sell to all who wished to buy victual by the boll, half boll, peck and half peck.[207] On 22 January 1509 a statute enacted for the common weal of the town and the landmen made it lawful for all persons who had victuals to sell to bring them to the market daily, to open their sacks and sell all day, though no purchases were to be made after three

victual buyers, including that they should not buy more victual than a 'laid' on one day until the whole town had been served); XIII.144 (29 April 1531: none of the burgh's cake bakers to bake more cakes than required for own household, and not to sell in town, nor to buy more meal on market day than needed for their house until the next market day, nor to buy anywhere else than the common market or before the due time of day); XIII.326 (12 January 1532: all market spillers in town to be forbidden to receive or measure any victuals in their houses or to buy more than needed); XIV.285 (11 October 1533: statute that anyone convicted three times for market spilling or for not paying the foreigners who sold their victuals in town would be expelled from the market for a year and from all buying and selling of bread and drink beyond what was necessary for themselves and their households).

203 ACR VIII.754.

204 E.g. ACR VIII.297 and 499; IX.261; and XVI.18.

205 See above, p. 60.

206 ACR VIII.202 (5 April 1503: associated with amercement of fifteen women for market spilling in buying meal and regrating of it again against the common ordinance; no one to buy more meal than would suffice themselves); and 763 (29 October 1507: no one to buy more than one 'laid' ' of victual on one day); IX.270 (7 October 1513: no one to buy more victuals than would suffice themselves between two market days); 386 (11 January 1515: no one to house or buy more victual than they needed for themselves); XIV.286 (11 October 1533: no one in town to buy more meal or malt than needed for own house until the next market day); XV.222–3: (9 October 1536: no one, free or unfree, to buy more victuals than needed for their household for a week); XVI.359 (13 October 1539: no one to take in more victual than needed for themselves and their household until the next market day).

207 ACR VIII.51.

o'clock.[208] On 17 January 1522, finally, the baillies ordered three malt-men to present all their malt to the market on the market day and sell it at the going rate. They were not to hold it to a dearth and scathe the poor commons.[209] The tone of the authorities' message might be peremptory or encouraging, but it was the same in each instance: 'Come and sell.' It coincides, broadly speaking, with other efforts on the part of the authorities to increase the supply of food available in the burgh, notably by buying up grain from abroad in bulk, and by encouraging landmen to bring other foodstuffs to town to sell.

Imports and exports

The principle that a fair price was what the majority were willing to pay is also evident in the authorities' price controls on exports and imports. It is interesting to note that although the authorities did not actively seek the power to establish price controls on grain, they did have the authority to control the prices paid for animal products intended for export from Aberdeen. Most controls in respect of prices of exports and imports date from the middle years of the fifteenth century; and while there may have been special concern over prices in that period, the apparent concentration is also owing to the fact we have a whole volume of records of the guild court, which specialized in trading and commercial matters, for the period 1441 to 1468.

The stipulations cover the prices of wool, skins, and hides,[210] though on one occasion, 27 April 1442, maximum prices were not only given for wool and woolskins, but also for 'schorlyngez', 'scaldynez', 'lentrin-war', and 'futfellez', possibly showing there was a significant demand for skins of lesser value.[211] The price regulations can also be informative about the quality of wools of different regions. The wools of Mar and Garioch were allowed higher prices than the wool of Buchan in ordinances of 17 June 1400 or 1409;[212] on 13 May 1445 the wool of Mar was again given a higher price.[213] Higher prices were also permitted when the vendors were persons of quality. In the same ordinance of

[208] ACR VIII.924.

[209] ACR XI.15.

[210] Hides List 28, 29, and Wool List 36–9, 41–2, 50–3, and see also the references given for Wool List 34 and 35.

[211] ACR V ii.654 (printed, *Extracts*, ed. Stuart, p. 397). 'Schorlyngez' were the skins of recently shorn sheep; 'scaldynez' were skins of low value; 'lentrinwar' was a type of lambskin; 'futfellez' were the skins of lambs which had died – fallen at the foot of the ewe – soon after birth.

[212] The rulings are apparently dated 1400 but occur in the manuscript among entries for 1409.

[213] ACR II.52 and V ii.702.

June 1410 it was forbidden to buy Buchan wool for more than 2s. except that of lords and free tenants, which must not be bought for more than 30d. – the price permitted for the wools of Mar and Garioch. But a ruling of a different sort, made in the guild court of 20 November 1467, shows more constraint towards the substantial landowner. It forbade merchants to encourage lords to buy wool from their husbandmen (unfree tenants) to be allowed in their mails.[214] The thinking behind this was perhaps to prevent lords from creating a monopoly on the supply of raw wool; but it is more difficult to see why merchants would have wished lords to buy up their tenants' wool, if lords were able to get higher prices. Perhaps merchants of substance found it more convenient to buy in bulk from a single vendor, even if they had to pay more.

Aberdeen's ability to enforce controls such as these depended in large measure on the success of the monopoly on export trade which it enjoyed in common with other 'cocket' burghs. It was not permitted to anyone to take goods outside the sheriffdom of Aberdeen to sell or export, without presenting them to the market in Aberdeen and paying the necessary customs.[215] Nor was it permitted to townspeople to go outside the town to buy up goods before they reached the burgh market.[216] To do these things was to forestall, and forestalling was an endemic problem for the Aberdeen authorities, bringing loss of revenue from tolls which had to be paid on goods entering the town; loss of trade in the burgh market; and loss of the equal opportunity for burgesses to buy, which was a fundamental principle on which so many of the burgh's regulations concerning trade were based.

Specific motives for forestalling varied. In times of dearth people will have been driven by hunger out of town to buy what little was available to feed themselves and their families. But at any time those who made their living by buying in order to sell by retail at a profit – regrators, also known as hucksters – will have been especially tempted to buy produce

[214] ACR VI.35.

[215] In October 1485 the council and guild brethren agreed that the provost should obtain a royal letter as authority to escheat all beef and tallow that was shipped or taken out of the burgh except for ship's store and men's victual; the letter should also forbid anyone dwelling in the sheriffdom of Aberdeen to take cattle or goods such as wool, hides, and skins to the Mounth: ACR VI.935. Royal letters issued in 1458, 1495, and 1511 gave the Aberdeen authorities the power to escheat wool, skins, and hides taken outside the sheriffdom of Aberdeen without payment of royal custom: ACR VI.568 (and also VII.544–5) (printed, *Aberdeen Charters*, pp. 29–30), VII.713 (printed, *Aberdeen Charters*, pp. 36–8), and IX.20 (printed, *Aberdeen Charters*, pp. 38–40). The 1511 commission also covered victual. See also 'Assise Willelmi Regis', p. 61, clause xl, and 'Fragmenta Collecta', p. 183, clause xlvi.

[216] ACR IV.33 and 'Burgh Laws', p. 35, clause lxxii.

before it reached the market. On 27 May 1519 the baillies ordered the town serjeants to escheat all the butter, cheese, and eggs they found in possession of ?Schorun[217] and the rest of the hucksters, whether they had bought these before they came to market or in market-time, because they were guilty of forestalling and regrating the market, by going out of town in the mornings, measuring the goods before they were presented to the market and keeping them to a dearth.[218]

But while it is certainly common to find forestallers of foodstuffs, far more frequent are the entries recording forestallers of wool, hides, and skins, that is, the valuable animal products which were refined by burgh craftsmen and exported abroad. The common practice of forestalling live animals – usually sheep and cows – was probably a result of the fact that their meat could be consumed in the burgh while the hides, skins, or wool could be exported, so that there was a double motive for the offence. Sometimes these forestalled articles were brought to Aberdeen for resale at a higher price, or for export, but a common problem for the authorities was the diversion of goods to the south. In a list of forestallers made after Michaelmas 1408 one 'filius Wilkyson' apud Achyustyuk' ', referred to as 'maximus foristallator', had been transporting his goods to the Mounth where he sold them or exported them by ship.[219] A statute of 15 November 1464 ordained that no free or unfree man was to take to the Mounth wool, hides, or skins to sell out of the freedom of the burgh, nor were they to buy any woollen cloth out of Dundee, Brechin, or any other place beyond the Mounth to sell again.[220] On 18 December 1511, William Quhit, a forestaller of wool, hides, and skins, who was also illegally involved in retailing imported commodities, had to give caution that he would not take any goods to Dundee or other places but would present them to the town and sell them to neighbours of the burgh.[221] On 2 August 1532 John Perke was amerced for sending his wethers to the Mounth to sell, without their having been presented to the king's market or paying the king's custom in Aberdeen, for forestalling in buying wool, hides, and skins in the country, and for retailing lint, iron, tar, and wax in the country.[222]

Sometimes purchasers from the south would venture into the sheriffdom of Aberdeen. On 13 May 1445 the alderman and council of Aberdeen forbade Thom Newman and James Elge of Dundee to buy any merchandise such as wool, hides, and skins within the freedom

[217] The woman's name is not clear in the manuscript.
[218] ACR X.82.
[219] ACR II.11.
[220] ACR V ii.828.
[221] ACR IX.63.
[222] ACR XIII.486.

(the sheriffdom) of Aberdeen under pain of escheat of such goods. If any freemen of the town were to sell any such merchandise to them or any other men of Dundee or Perth they were to be fined 40s.[223] The illegal transport of goods to the Mounth and beyond may suggest that exporters could get better prices for them if they took them to southern burghs. Peripheral regions were disadvantaged then as now. The tendency for goods to go south did not affect all exports, however, and Aberdeen's trade in salmon must have done much to attract foreign traders to the burgh.

It is also interesting to note that the authorities never, according to the surviving evidence, endeavoured to impose controls on the prices of salmon. This may have been because the production of salmon was organized rather differently from that of animal products; in particular, Aberdeen burgesses (as opposed to landmen who were the producers of animals and animal products) were often the producers and processers of salmon: thus it was ruled in the guild court of 10 October 1466 that no man in possession of water (that is, with appurtenant fishing rights) should lease it to unfreemen in future, and that no one but guild members, or their sons still living at home, should cure salmon.[224] Given that the maxima imposed on the prices of animal products were in the interests of exporting merchants it seems unlikely that merchant producers would have welcomed any curtailing of their profits. Another factor in the structure of salmon prices in the burgh, which would have made it difficult to impose maxima, is that they frequently involved a rent element. For example, on 22 October 1526 Thomas Angussoun and John Law were ordered on their own admission to deliver John Collisone the elder twelve barrels of salmon and grilse according to the terms of their obligation. They swore that they had had no further profit of his fishing than this. John for his part was to pay 40s. per barrel of salmon, and 30s. for each barrel of grilse. If, however, they failed to deliver the fish, John was to be paid at the rate of 55s. for each salmon barrel and 45s. for each barrel of grilse. Clearly, the price at which John was to be recompensed was closer to the going price of salmon than the rate at which he was to pay for it.[225] In another case, on 25 November 1533, Tom Angussoun acknowledged he owed Duncan Mar, baillie, three barrels of salmon to be paid at Lammas (1 August). Further, Duncan leased his half net's fishing of the 'Raik' to Tom for

[223] ACR V ii.702.
[224] ACR V ii.837.
[225] ACR XII i.56–7 (Salmon List 240).

that season, for which Tom was to give Duncan all the fish he caught and soused for 30s. per barrel of salmon and per barrel of grilse.[226]

There were, however, minimum prices set on certain imports, notably soap, tar, iron, and salt. These were, like the maxima for certain exports, imposed in the interest of merchants.[227] There were exceptions to these minima – for example, in an ordinance made in late November or early December 1401, which was to last until Easter, no one in town might sell a boll of salt for less than 5s.4d., or a stone of iron for less than 16d., except for sales made to neighbours of the town and lords of the country, that is, sales by the chaldron and half chaldron (of salt) or a whole rod of iron.[228] Bulk purchases were thus associated with townspeople and lords, and might be made at lower prices; and again, on 7 October 1463, it was laid down that no merchant was to 'tap' or sell salt, iron, tar, or soap for less than the given minimum prices; but while iron was to be sold retail for no less than 32d. (per stone), bulk sales were permitted more flexibility: 'and it be salde in grete as the merchande kan accorde'.[229]

The latitude permitted to merchants who traded overseas is in contrast to the strict regulations applying to burgh craftsmen. The reasons for their different treatment are complex. Apart from the fact that the merchant voice was powerful in Aberdeen, it would have been difficult in practice to calculate a fair price for the merchant's service in transporting goods from one country to another. Men understood clearly that goods were worth more in one place than in another, because they were harder to come by. The twelfth-century writer, Reginald of Durham, describing the worldly time in the life of St Godric of Finchale, shows this understanding well:

For he laboured not only as a merchant but also as a shipman . . . to Denmark and Flanders and Scotland; in all which lands he found certain rare, and therefore more precious, wares, which he carried to other parts wherein he knew them to be least familiar, and coveted by the inhabitants beyond the price of gold itself; wherefore he exchanged these wares for others coveted by men of other lands; and thus he chaffered most freely and assiduously. Hence he made great profit in all his bargains, and gathered much wealth in the sweat of his brow; for he sold dear in one place the wares which he had bought elsewhere at a small price.[230]

[226] ACR XIV.314 (Salmon List 271–2).
[227] See Salt List 30–2 and 50, and Iron List 27, 28, and 44.
[228] ACR I.197 (printed, *Extracts*, ed. Stuart, p. 380).
[229] ACR V ii.846.
[230] Quoted by G.G. Coulton, *Social Life in Britain from the Conquest to the Reformation* (Cambridge, 1919), pp. 417–18.

The relationship between prices at home and abroad was further complicated by the risks and costs in which merchants trading overseas involved themselves which were very difficult to quantify. They had to pay for their goods to be packed, stowed, and carried by ship. On the journey itself there were the vicissitudes of weather and wind and the danger of piratical raids. And when they reached their destination there were still risks and costs. Many merchants entrusted their business dealings abroad to agents. An unreliable agent could cause untold problems, by buying shoddy goods, failing to despatch them, selling goods for too low a price, or failing to settle up. The authorities in Aberdeen in fact recognized this problem and enacted legislation to ensure that no agent would engage himself to a new merchant until he had settled up with his first employer. On 18 July 1491 it was ordained for the good and common profit of merchandise that no merchant was to take another's associate from him until he and his merchant had made account, reckoning and payment, each one to the other.[231] In the guild court of 8 October 1507 it was ordained that no merchant should take another man's merchant from him until he had accounted and reckoned finally with his merchant and was freed of him.[232]

All these risks and costs constituted the service performed by merchants trading overseas; and it was these which entitled them to make some profit when they sold their goods. And conversely, it was not thought reasonable that a profit should be made without some sort of service having been performed. Thus Agnes Thomsone was amerced on 9 February 1498 for selling wine which she had bought without 'aventour' in the town.[233] 'Aventour' in this context implied the dangers and expenses associated with importing goods. It must also have been difficult to tell what price an article of merchandise might fetch or be bought for on the foreign market to which it was destined or came from. Valuations made in court of outgoing goods to recompense merchants for their loss or misdirection were frequently based on the value of other goods transported on the same voyage. It seems that the fair price for imported goods was supposed to bear some sort of relationship to the price paid for them abroad. In the case between William Baudy and John Reaucht already cited, William claimed that in August 1537 John had bought a pipe of woad from him for the same price as other neighbours (who had bought woad abroad at the price at which William had bought his) were selling their woad in Aberdeen at the time. The idea was, of course, that William's cost and profit margin should be

[231] ACR VII.261.
[232] ACR VIII.752.
[233] ACR VII.862.

the same as that of his neighbours. He claimed that James Nown's pipe of woad which was bought for £7 groot Flemish (in Flanders) was sold for £22 Scots (in Aberdeen).[234]

No consistent attempt was made by the Aberdeen authorities to impose restrictions on the prices at which overseas merchants sold their goods. There are a few exceptions to this, as when controls were occasionally imposed on the retail prices of imported wine;[235] or when individuals were charging extortionate prices far above the going rate. In March 1473 three people were amerced for breaking common ordinance in selling figs and raisins for enormous prices.[236] On 19 May 1508 Alexander Hay was given day to answer to the complaint against him by Richard Hendersone, litster, who dwelt in Old Aberdeen, about his having been overcharged for a pipe of woad. Richard claimed £5 as the difference between what he himself had paid, £11, and the price at which the rest of the woad which came at the same time was sold to Allan Litster, Duncan Wawdy, and Robert Crag.[237]

While the authorities left native merchants free for the most part to negotiate the prices of goods they imported, this is not to say that they did not influence the supply and the price of imports. Those in authority in the town were responsible for ensuring that its needs for imports were met, and legislation enacted from time to time obliged exporting merchants to bring goods back on their return journey. It is telling that such legislation was considered necessary, for it surely made sense for exporters to import and in fact it was common for native and foreign merchants to exchange goods with one another. In the guild court of 31 January 1449 it was enacted that everyone who sent goods from Aberdeen to Flanders should bring goods back in proportion. For every sack (of wool?) that went outwards two tuns of goods were to be brought back. Exporters of fish and hides were also to carry an obligation to import in accordance with the exported value. Two merchants were to be chosen by the common council on every trip to see that the statute was kept, and they were also to buy salt on the town's behalf.[238] Later, in February 1493, the merchants who had goods in the ships about to sail agreed that for every sack exported one and a half tuns of goods should be brought back to supply the town with merchandise.[239]

[234] ACR XVI.64 (below, 'Appendix of documents' no. III).
[235] E.g. ACR VI.920 and XII ii.776 (Wine List, 228, 364).
[236] ACR VI.227.
[237] ACR VIII.835–6.
[238] ACR V ii.735–6.
[239] ACR VII.406.

Part of the reason for measures of this sort was to ensure the skipper was paid for both parts of his journey. On 11 July 1496 everyone who had goods in the ships of Veere belonging to Cornelis Boll and Willekin Haunart on the most recent voyage was ordered to load them up again in accordance with the quantity of their goods; everyone who failed to comply was to pay waste freight.[240] The fact that this was to be done between then and the following Thursday shows that the ships were in Aberdeen, rather than abroad, and that the importers were here bound to export. But taken in conjunction with the fact that the Aberdeen authorities took further measures to ensure an adequate supply of imports it seems clear that much of the purpose of ensuring ships were loaded both ways was to provide for imports.

The burgh involved itelf in what may be conveniently called 'corporate purchases', in that it commissioned the purchase of goods, especially grain and salt, on behalf of the town. First, the town would commission purchases by merchants on its behalf. For example, the two merchants appointed in the guild court of 31 January 1449 to enforce the provision that exporters should import were also given the exclusive commission to buy, with the advice of the other merchants, all the salt that was to be bought for the town.[241] In August in the same year four named merchants for each of the town's quarters (sixteen men in all) commissioned David Meignes to buy a shipful of salt in Flanders and send it to Aberdeen. The commission was, at the merchants' desire, to be from the whole town, and under the secret seal, so they obliged themselves to keep the town and the commons harmless of anything David might do by virtue of it.[242]

The evidence of corporate purchases of goods which had already reached the burgh is in fact more copious. On 29 October 1444 it was ordained by the whole common council and many of the guild that Gilbert Meignes, Alexander of Kintor, John Gray, and Duncan of Clat or any two of them should have full power to buy to the common profit of the town all manner of goods that came by sea to the burgh, and to distribute them to the neighbours of the town as appropriate.[243] No one else in the burgh was to buy any such goods until the commissioned purchasers had completed their job. Similar commissions were set up in 1472 and 1475, with four men being chosen to purchase

[240] ACR VII.742.
[241] ACR V ii.735–6.
[242] ACR V ii.741.
[243] ACR V ii.686.

all imports.[244] And in 1485 a statute was enacted giving the town's right of pre-emption more permanent force. On 23 September it was ordained by the council that in future all goods that came to the burgh by sea should first be offered to the alderman or baillies and part of the council at least, in the town's name, before any man bought any part of them.[245] Similarly, on 16 March 1509, it was ruled by the provost, baillies, and council that no one was to buy any kind of merchandise that happened to come by sea – Frenchmen's or any others' – until the price was made by the provost and council or unless they were given the town's licence to sell their goods to whomever they chose.[246] In the following month – 24 April – it was judged by the whole council that Andrew Litster had greatly wronged the provost Gilbert Menzeis in intermeddling with, housing and withholding certain wheat and other stuff for which the provost had offered earnest money for the same price in the town's name, and for refusing to distribute the goods to the provost and council. So it was ordained that all the stuff that came in the said ship, 'the Hoy', should be equally distributed among the townsmen and that in future no stuff should be bought by any individual. If it were, it was to be equally distributed among the townsmen by the advice of the provost, baillies, and council. Alternatively if the town did not wish to buy the goods in question, the vendors were licensed to sell it to whomever they chose.[247]

These enactments gave the authorities the opportunity to buy up all goods, but not the obligation to do so. In fact, corporate purchases were usually of necessities. On 6 November 1444 Matheus Crukin, master of a Stralsund ship, granted that he had sold to the town all the rye in his ship for £7 10s. each Stralsund last and all his boards, at £5 10s. each hundred. The burgh council for its part agreed that the provost should be responsible for the distribution of these goods and for collecting payment for them, in return for a fee.[248] Similarly, in about September 1470 the entry of a ship was recorded with its master Andrew Lyseman and merchant ?Walter[249] Janson, and a cargo of two 'hundreds' of wheat, two 'hundreds' of salt, and a last of soap. The master and merchant had sold to the alderman – in the town's name – one hundred of wheat at 10s. the boll and one hundred of salt

[244] ACR VI.203 and 398.
[245] ACR VI.933.
[246] ACR VIII.939.
[247] ACR, VIII.950.
[248] ACR V ii.687.
[249] The man's Christian name is partly illegible in the manuscript.

for £10 groot (Flemish currency), 50s. Scots to the £ groot. The money was to be paid within fifteen days after the wheat and salt were delivered to the town.[250]

In practice there was little difference between the town setting the price at which its inhabitants were to buy goods and its buying the goods on their behalf. By the sixteenth century corporate purchases of grain were in the latter form. On 12 May 1508 it was ruled that no person was to intermeddle with the bere, meal, or wheat until it was delivered by the provost. On the same day the baillies, council, and community agreed that the provost should buy the three ships (laden) with bere, meal, and victual which were then outside the harbour for the same price at which he had bought the present ship's load (presumably that referred to in the previous entry) and that they would pay for it.[251] On 23 June 1508 Gilbert Menzies the provost enjoined the townspeople to come to the quay and collect the bere bought from the foreigners, beseeching them to come and receive as much as every man would take at the price at which it had been bought at their command; protesting if they did not receive the bere that he and his friends might have it.[252] On 9 March 1509 in the baillies' court the names of persons, including several bakers, were listed; they had bought rye, rye meal, and maslin from William Halkarstone, burgess of Edinburgh, by causing the provost Gilbert Menzies to bind himself for payment for it, and a note was made of the amount each person had bought and what he owed for it.[253]

Another arrangement was to devolve the responsibility for getting payment on to the baillies. On 22 May 1513 the provost ordered the baillies to deliver the victuals bought from the foreigners to people they would guarantee would pay for it. If the recipients failed to do so, the baillies would themselves be responsible for the payment, out of their own property.[254] On 4 May 1515 the baillies and divers members of the council and community formally agreed to receive the bere bought by the provost and town 'from the first ship' (the first ship of a convoy?) whose merchants were David Musfard and Haward Strathachin. The baillies with their officers were ordered to take two or three merchants and examine the books of those merchants who owned the bere (that is, presumably, those who had said they would buy it), and were to cause the town's 'pynors' (official carriers) to deposit quantities of bere

[250] ACR VI.120.
[251] ACR VIII.832.
[252] ACR VIII.841.
[253] ACR VIII.938.
[254] ACR IX.223.

at the door or gate of anyone who had not received any of it, in amounts according to the quality of such persons (that is, presumably, their ability to pay), until all of it had been dealt with. People of substance and others who had already received some of the bere were to take more, as judged by the baillies and the merchants they had chosen to help them. This bere was to be delivered and received before any other bere was received from the rest of the ships.[255] On 8 June Musfard and Strathachin[256] acknowledged that they had been paid for all goods – bere, meal, and merchandise – bought by the provost, baillies, and merchants of Aberdeen, and acquitted the whole town of the debt.[257] In another example from the same year, it was ruled on 7 September that all the persons whose names were written in a bill authenticated by the provost should receive the rye meal bought for the town's profit and pay for it. If anyone refused, it was to be taken to his house at his own expense and he was to pay for it.[258] On 21 August 1531 John Ratray explained in the baillies' court that he had asked the merchants and the neighbours of the town who had taken any of the Englishmen's rye several times for payment for it, and that there were some people who would not pay up. He asked that all the debtors should be obliged to pay 12s. for each boll they had received, and more, as should be ordained by the king and the Lords of Council.[259]

There was considerable incentive for people to honour their promise to pay for what they had ordered, for the corporate purchase policy was a non-profit-making one. The authorities bought goods from foreign merchants at one price negotiated in most cases by the provost, and then sold it, at that same price, to the neighbours of the town. In Edinburgh, where there was also a tradition of corporate purchase from the mid-fifteenth century, this was on the understanding that the purchasers would not resell the goods to make a profit for themselves,[260] and such may well have been the understanding in Aberdeen. In May 1541 the town's officers ordered all townspeople to come and take their share of the bere which had been bought for the whole town from foreign merchants and to pay for it so that the vendors could be paid and so that the provost and baillies who, at the whole town's command, had bought the bere for their profit would not be complained against

[255] ACR IX.440.
[256] This merchant's Christian name is now given as Albert.
[257] ACR IX.454.
[258] ACR IX.488.
[259] ACR XIII.206–7.
[260] See Nicholson, *Scotland*, p. 452. In his parliament of March 1541 James V gave burgh governments the power to buy up or set a price on imported wine, salt, or timber, so that everyone should then buy at those same prices: *APS* II.373–4.

by the foreigners or anyone else. The townspeople were warned that if they failed to come and take the bere they would forfeit the opportunity; the provost and baillies would sell it to anyone and allow them to make a profit on it, so that the foreigners could be paid. In the event, only a certain number of townspeople did turn up, so a formal record was made to make clear that the townspeople had been given ample warning. They had forfeited the opportunity and the authorities would now sell the grain to anyone who would pay for it, who would also be licensed to make a profit.[261]

The practice of corporate purchase was adopted, then, to ensure that people who wished to buy imported goods, especially grain, could do so at a price negotiated by the authorities on their behalf. The purpose was also to cut out the profit-making middleman or retailer. We may perhaps assume that it was in general the profit of foreign merchants, rather than native ones, which was affected. And of course, although the town had claimed the right to purchase all imported goods, in practice it only bought certain cargoes. There was also the fact that while the town may have imposed a lower price on foreign merchants, this may have been outweighed by the advantage of quick sales and guaranteed payments. And foreign merchants could not be squeezed too much, for they could always go elsewhere.

There is indeed some evidence to suggest that Aberdeen's price levels may have been lower than those elsewhere. We have already seen that the burgh experienced problems over ensuring that hides, wool, skins, and live animals produced within the sheriffdom made their way to the town rather than being diverted south. As far as imports are concerned, in a case brought into the baillies' court in August 1532 the freightsmen and merchants of a ship loaded at Gdansk/Danzig claimed that the agreement with the owner and skipper was that the vessel should go to Leith, Dundee, or St Andrews, whichever they preferred. They therefore claimed that the owner and skipper should be liable for any damage or cost suffered if they unloaded their goods in Aberdeen and sold them for lower prices than they might get in the ports to which they had wished to go.[262]

The control which the Aberdeen authorities exercised over prices varied according to the nature and provenance of the commodity in question. Their regulation of the prices of articles manufactured in the burgh was the most direct, and the most enduring. But the reason for the frequency of the assizes was that they were determined upon the

[261] ACR XVI.800.
[262] ACR XIII.497–8.

fluctuating prices of raw materials, over which control was not exercised in the same way. The assizes had to be fixed with a degree of flexibility to accommodate changes in the prices of raw materials, and the occasions on which widespread infringements of the assizes occurred may well indicate they were not being sufficiently sensitive to price movements. Craftsmen naturally wished their profits to be as large as possible; but acquisitiveness cannot account for all the offences we meet against the assizes of bread, ale, candle, and meat. The authorities' control over the prices of imports and exports was also limited. The prices of foreign merchants' imports could only be kept low to a certain degree, beyond which Aberdeen would cease to attract overseas traders. The prices of the burgh's exports issuing from its hinterland were, indeed, controlled directly on occasion in the fifteenth century, but again, if Aberdeen merchants were offering prices below the odds there would be an increased temptation, the burgh's monopoly on export trade notwithstanding, for landward vendors to send their goods to merchants from other burghs. Thus while the government of Aberdeen had the power to regulate the prices asked by burgh craftsmen for their wares, and those paid by townspeople for certain imports and exports, its real ability to control prices was restricted by much wider economic factors. Its efforts to increase the supply of food and other goods from the countryside and from abroad were therefore a necessary element in its influence on prices. And the fact that such efforts were made is in itself an indication that they understood that a fair price depended on the relationship between supply and demand.

Appendix of documents

I. Aberdeen Council Register, IV.143

[Aberdeen guild court, 7 October 1438]

Ordinance concerning the purchase of foodstuffs in time of dearth.

Quo die pro communi utilitate burgi, considerata magna caristia victualium iam regnante, subsequens ordinacio fuit ex consensu communis consilii facta: primo videlicet[1] quod nulla mulier emet farinam in foro sed homines tantum. Et quod farina mensurabitur tam cum dimidia ferlota quam peck' et dimid[ia] peck'. Et quod nulla regratiatrix sit in burgo nisi sponsus suus fuerit liber burgensis.

Item quod nullus qui emit farinam aut alter burgensis quicumque plus habeat de farina[2] uno die fori quam potest sibi sufficere ad rationabiles expensas domus sue[3] usque ad[4] diem fori proxime inde sequentem.

Item quod nullus burgensis emet salmones aut alios piscos[5] seu cepum martorum aut multonum a carnificibus burgi[6] vel aliis, extraneis, in una summa sed tantum de predictis quantum sibi sufficere potest ad expensas domus sue quousque deserviatur vicinis suis de predictis.

Item quod pistores panis frumenti vendant pannos[7] venales in bothis suis propriis et non regratiatrixes sub pena eschaete dictorum panium et sub pena amerciamenti octo solidorum.

II. Aberdeen Council Register, VIII.562

[Baillies' court, 28 March 1506]

Statute providing for standard measures for ale

[1] Followed by *nullus*, struck through.
[2] *de farina* interlined, with caret.
[3] Interlined.
[4] Followed by ?*primum*, struck through.
[5] *Sic*.
[6] Interlined.
[7] *Sic*.

Statut' anent the mesouris [*marginated*]

The said day it was commaundit ordanit and chargit in our soverane lordis nayme provest balzeis and offi[ciaris] of the said burghe that withtin viij dais next eftir folloing' ilkane brouster withtin this burghe sale ger mak ane poynt of tyne haldande mesour witht the richtius' jugaile and mett. Ande that ilkane of thame be signit witht the stampe and pas' to Davy Theman and ger him mett the said pontis witht the jugale and se that thai hald inlik and that the said Davy to merk thame and ilkan pont quart or chopin sale pay him[8] j d' for his labour. Ande that thai[9] aile be sauld bot witht j pont of tynn mesourit witht the richt jugale and signit witht the stamp undir the paynis of tynsale of thar haile broust' and brekin of commone ordinance. And thai chargit and commaundit be oppin proclamatioun at the mercat croce that nay manere of persone suld ask and tak ony strakis or goupnys of meile or malt undir the panis of brekin of commone ordinance.

III. Aberdeen Council Register, XVI.64–5

[Baillies' court, 18 November 1538]
Dispute over salmon and woad

Petitio Bawdy [*marginated*]

My lord prowest and balzes of this nobill burgh' of Abirdene unto zour /m/[10] humely menis and complanis I zour nychtbour and comburges William Baudy apoun' Johnne Reaucht burges of the said burgh' that quhar the said John in the moneth of Januar the zeir of God j M v^{c} xxxvij zeiris [January 1538] sauld to me withtin the burght' of Abirdene twa barrellis of salmond full reid and sweit sufficient merchand gude of the rychtous bynd of Abirdene to haf bene deliverit to me the said tyme and thareftir the samyn moneth of Januar and zeir forsaid quhen Elspet Malisone my wyf com' in my name to the said John for the said twa barrellis of salmond and desirit the same to be strekin oup and sene gif thai var sufficient or nocht the tane of thaim vas strekyn oup and[11] fundin sufficient and my said vif content tharof. And than the said John said 'Ze mistyr nocht to stryk oup the tothir; I ma nocht tary for bissenes I hef a do bot I sell ouphald it als gud and als sufficient as the tothir', and on' that conditioun my vif ressavit the same. And thareftir quhen the said twa barrellis com' to the merkat in

[8] Interlined.
[9] *Sic*; rectius *na*?
[10] *Maistershippis?*
[11] *sene. . .and* marginated with caret in text.

Franche and war strekin oup in presens of Alexander Murray my factour the said barrell the said John oupheld sufficient was all bot grilssis and bot thre or iiij laxis in the heid of it, and gaff nocht samekill as the tothir barrell salmond be four frankis. And alsua the said John in the monetht of August in the zeir of God j M v^{c} xxxvij[12] zeiris [August 1537] coft and ressavit fra me ane pipe of vade of the same price that my nychtbouris vade that was boicht of the same price that myn was bocht of was sellit in Abirdene for the tym. And that samyn tym James Nownis pipe of vade that was coft of the same price my vade was coft of, videlicet, for vij li' gryt Flemis money was sellit to Alexander Fresour litstar for xxij li' Scottis money. And the said John restis awand me as zit xl s' Scottis of my said pipe of vade of the price forsaid, and intendis to mak me na recompensatioun for the said four frankis for the skaytht of the said barrell of grilssis he oupheld to me sufficient salmond and als gud as the tothir barrell I gat fra hym nor zit to pay me the said xl s'[13] of the rest of my said pipe of vade bot wrangously and aganis the law postponis and deferris to do the same withtout he be compellit be justice tharto; beseikand heirfor zour /m/ prowest and balzes forsaid to decerne and compell be justice the said John Reaucht to oupset me the said four frankis for the skaytht of the said barrell of grilsis forsaid he oupheld sufficient salmond. And als to pay the said xl s' of the rest of my said pipe of vade [p. 65] be ressonis forsaid and conforme to justice, togidder witht my expensis maid and to be maid in the persute of the same. And gif neid beis this my petitioun to haff the strynth of ane borgh', and zour /m/ ansur heirapoun' witht justice and expe[ditioun] humely I beseik.

Note on editorial practice.

'c's and 't's, 'u's and 'v's, and 'i's and 'j's, have been standardized to accord with modern pronunciations and derivations of the words concerned; 'w's and 'v's have been left as found in the Scots texts. The medieval Scottish letter 'ȝ' has been rendered as 'z'; 'y' as th. Suspensions have been retained when the missing letters are not clear to us; probable extensions and word endings have been given in square brackets. Punctuation and capital letters have been modernized. Units of currency have been left abbreviated in the Scots texts.

[12] The final (long) minim seems to have been written over a second short minim; the intention may have been to denote viij, i.e. 1538, which would mean the second complaint was recited in correct chronological sequence.

[13] Followed by a two- or three-letter word, struck through.

3 Weights and measures

> ITEM anent mettis and mesuris it is sene speidfull that sen we haif bot a king and a lawe vniuersale throu out the Realme we sulde haif bot a met and mesur' generale to serue all the Realme.[1]

In order to be able to compare prices, we need to examine the various weights, measures, containers, and other units in which commodities were exchanged or valued. As will be seen from the Glossary, medieval Scotland knew a rich variety of weights and measures, and within each commodity series we find a number of different units. Wine, which had to be carried from abroad, and was sold in divers quantities, is the commodity for which we have met the greatest number of different vessels: tuns, pipes, puncheons, tersans, hogsheads, casks, vases, rubbours, gallons, pints, choppins, and mutchkins are all found. Yet to enable us to compare individual entries for each commodity we have, as far as possible, expressed our unit prices in terms of the unit found most commonly for that commodity. This process is by no means complete, for a number of reasons. First, it has not always been clear to us what the size or weight of a particular unit was. Secondly, although we may have found some evidence to indicate the size or weight of a unit on a particular occasion, we may not be confident that it was always of that size or weight. And finally, we believe that some units were simply not intended to represent specific quantities. The Glossary sets out the evidence on which our assumptions about the size or weight of individual units are based, and also explains which units have not been established as having a fixed size or relationship with others.

Evidence about the weights and measures used in medieval Scotland is sometimes in the form of explicit statements, but it is also, and far more copiously, implicit in the transactions themselves. Of the explicit sort of information is the medieval Scottish legislation prescribing the actual capacity or weight of particular units and stating what the relation-

[1] *APS* II.50.

ship between them ought to be. This has been an important source for our understanding of some of the medieval standards which were used widely, although the usefulness of legislation as a source is marred by inconsistencies between the statements in the texts, some of which are caused by what appear to be copyists' or transcribal errors. Even if we were dealing with authoritative texts, a more fundamental issue would remain, that is, the extent to which the government's prescriptions were in fact put into practice in the country at large. Legislation on the subject of weights and measures may have been made either because the government was itself advocating a change in existing standards which it needed to advertise, or because it was attempting to quantify and to standardize changes which had in practice taken place already, or because there were regional differences in weights and measures which it was desirable to root out. In all of these cases, the limited extent to which any medieval government, and particularly Scotland's, was able to ensure that its decrees were applied throughout its dominions makes it unlikely that any prescription for radical change will have been adopted generally and immediately.

Indeed, most explicit statements in the sources about the capacity or weight of given standards should be treated with some caution. It is on the face of it encouraging to read that, say, a barrel contained twelve stones of butter; but had every barrel been of that capacity, why was there the need to specify in the particular instance? Explicit detail about weights and measures may have been in the nature of an aide memoire, or to make a general rule better known, but it could equally record an exception to the rule rather than the rule itself. We may, however, use somewhat more confidently the statements describing the relationship between Scottish and 'foreign' or local weights and measures, because the reason for making these was probably not because that relation was inconstant, but rather because it was not well known.[2] Much of this sort of evidence comes from Aberdeen, and it is interesting to note that on one occasion the authorities tried to circumvent the problem of reconciling Scots with foreign weights and measures (or, possibly, to remove the opportunity for swindling which foreign standards might present) by ruling on 26 February 1490 that no salt was to be received overseas by anyone unless he had two witnesses with him when he

[2] See, for examples, Glossary, under boll (relation to bushel), chaldron (relation to quarter), cogall (relation to stones), ell (relation between Scots/Flemish ells), long and short hundred (relation between Scots/ Flemish hundreds; relation between hundred of 'Burvage' (Bruges) and Scots boll), last (relation between Stralsund last and Scots boll), moye (relation between moye and boll), piece (relation between piece of wax and 'leis' ' pounds), puncheon (relation between 'puntionis terceanse(?)' and boll/peck); sack (relation between small sack and Flemish wey), stone (relation between 'leis' ' pound and Scots wax stone).

bought and received it; and that importers were to bring with them the measure with which they had received salt abroad and to use that measure when they delivered it.[3] On 10 September 1499, and perhaps in accordance with this rule, John Callat, a Frenchman, who had been ordered on the previous day to deliver a quantity of salt to William Fuches, bound himself to bring the measure that the salt was measured with in Dieppe to Aberdeen.[4] The 1500 deposition cited in the Glossary about the flour contained in 'puntionis terceanse' (under puncheon) may also have been a consequence of the 1490 ruling.[5] That such matters as foreign currency and the units in which commodities were measured and sold in foreign ports could present problems to the overseas trader and on which he might welcome some guidance is further evidenced by the existence of such manuals as the late fourteenth- or early fifteenth-century 'Treaties Scots Merchandise'. This handbook explains some of the weights and measures used in the Low Countries (including those by which Scots goods were measured and which were widely used in Scotland) and presents tables calculating the prices of smaller units of articles according to the price of larger units.[6] This is a useful guide, and its didactic purpose may make it more reliable than some medieval Scottish legislation.

The bulk of the evidence about medieval Scots weights and measures is, however, implicit. When there are several units involved in a transaction we can often calculate the relationship between those units. Such calculations do not always yield precise results, especially when there are more than two units involved, or when there are fractions of units. Rounding off will have taken place, either when the transaction was negotiated, or when the accountant was calculating the unit price. Another point to bear in mind is that most medieval accountants and merchants did not grasp fractions in more than a rudimentary way. They could not, for example, see how to use a common denominator in order to combine thirds and halves or quarters[7] and it is rare to find fractions based on divisions other than these.[8] But given this kind of difficulty, often attributable to the problem of calculating in Roman rather than Arabic numerals,

[3] ACR VII.169. It was also ruled on that occasion that no wine was to be loaded with salt in future.

[4] ACR VII.982.

[5] See below, Glossary, under puncheon. Also of interest in this connection is the claim made by Thom Forman in 1447 that he had bought a Prussian last of wheat to be delivered with the measure of Scotland: ACR IV.498, and see also Chapter 2, pp. 28–9.

[6] Alison Hanham, 'A Medieval Scots Merchant's Handbook', *SHR*, 50 (1971), 107–20.

[7] For examples, see Barley List 346 (sale of 97 chaldrons, 6 bolls, 1 firlot, 2 pecks, half a peck, a third of a peck, two-thirds of a firlot) and 488 (sale of 4 bolls, half a peck and two-thirds of a peck).

[8] For rare examples, see ACR VIII.370 (debt of one fifth of a barrel of grilse) and Salmon List 261 (debt of a seventh part of a barrel of salmon).

it is remarkable how often different units and fractions are priced in exact proportion to the given unit price. The calculation of customs levies also sometimes permits us to establish the relationship between units. If we are told that custom was levied at a certain rate per stone of wool and the amount exported is given in sacks and stones we can calculate the number of stones to the sack. It sometimes happened, however, that customs officials rounded off calculations, or charged custom on smaller units at a slightly higher rate in order to boost revenues, so this source is of variable use.[9] Comparison between the charge and discharge sections of an account is sometimes a further source of implicit information about weights and measures. If, for example, an accountant charges himself with a given number of lasts of salmon, then discharges himself in terms of expenditure expressed in barrels and lasts, we can calculate the number of barrels to the last.

There is, of course, much more to understanding medieval weights and measures than comparing the results of detailed calculations such as these. Once made, judgements have to be formed about the likelihood that a particular unit had a fixed relationship to others. We have usually preferred the bland and non-committal word 'unit' so far in these pages rather than 'weights' or 'measures' because we do not believe that every unit we have met in the sources actually had the status of a fixed measure or weight. The terms we have encountered were ways of describing quantities of goods, but that is not the same thing as their having an existence as standards. Some of them, certainly, had that status, most obviously those whose size or weight was defined in legislation. There were, however, also units which apparently came into existence for the purpose of carrying or storing goods, and whose capacity might vary, especially according to the article contained in them. A barrel, for example, was a convenient way of packing and transporting many different commodities, but it was only in the fifteenth century, and only for salmon, that it came to have the status of a measure, and of a unit on which customs could be charged. The sack of wool doubtless began as a convenient way of packing and carrying that commodity, though it became standard at 24 stones and again was the unit on which wool custom was levied. The status, as a measure, of a pipe of wine is uncertain: while it may have had a known capacity, it seems, like many of the units for wine, to have been primarily a container; there is evidence, moreover, that the pipe might not always be full.[10] In contrast, there are units which did not exist physically at

[9] See Glossary, especially under the last for hides, and the sack.
[10] See Wine List 209–10.

all but were merely multiples of smaller ones, such as the chaldron of grain, or the last of hides, wool, or fish. There are also units, such as the load, which appear to us to be of uncertain size but whose meaning was perhaps established by common or customary usage. The most uncertain units are those such as the cask by which things were commonly bought or sold or transported but which did not, so far as we can tell, refer to a specific quantity.

A further point to bear in mind is that commodities are quantified differently according to the context in which they occur. For instance, wine was sold by retail in gallons or pints, but was imported or sold wholesale in tuns or pipes or other larger vessels. The retail price was high in proportion to the wholesale, and it would be wrong to convert wholesale prices into prices per gallon. Likewise, fish packed into barrels had undergone a cleaning and salting process which those counted numerically had not, so in a sense they were a slightly different commodity and it would be wrong directly to compare their prices with those for the unprocessed article.

A rather different issue from the relationship between weights and measures is that of the constancy of standards. The question of whether, over the period we have studied, particular weights and measures may have changed is of course a crucial one for price history, because any comparison of prices over a period needs to be informed by an awareness of possibly changing standards. The most obvious evidence of change is the medieval Scottish legislation on the subject of weights and measures. The earliest known Scottish legislation setting out a system of weights and measures is the 'Assisa Regis David'.[11] This, however, only survives as a part-summary, part-gloss, the chapters of which are given in both Latin and Scots. The Latin text in the *Acts of the Parliaments of Scotland* is taken from the Ayr Manuscript, which was probably written in the reign of Robert Bruce (1306–29).[12] The Scots text, which is a very loose translation of the Latin with additions and omissions of material, is a collation of the text in Adv. Libr. MS A.I. 32 (a late fifteenth-century document) with that in Balfour's *Practicks*.[13]

The 'Assisa' speaks of weights and measures laid down and in use in the time of 'King David', and we infer from this that the system it

[11] *APS* I.673–4. Also of interest is cap. xxxi of the 'Assise Regis David', a collection of laws ascribed to David I. This attempted to establish a universal standard of weights, 'quod dicitur pondus Cathanie', but it did not give any indication of the actual units on which the system was to be based: *APS* I.324.

[12] See *APS* I.179. See also Chapter 4 on currency, where it is demonstrated that the references to currency at the time of writing of the text do not necessarily date the 'Assisa'.

[13] See *APS* I.195 and 308.

sets out was based on what was known, or believed to be known, of the legislation of David I (1124–53). Of particular interest to us here is what the 'Assisa' said about the stone, the pound and the ounce, and the boll and the gallon. The stone, it said, ought to contain 15 pounds and the pound 15 ounces (though the text refers also to an 8 pound stone of which 12 made a wey).[14] The ounce in David's day contained 20 sterling pennies (though by the fourteenth century, we are told, it ought to weigh 21 because of the diminution of the money) and the sterling ought to weigh 32 grains of good and round wheat.[15] The dimensions of the boll given in the 'Assisa' suggest a vessel of 3,667.22 cubic inches.[16] The dimensions of the gallon as given in the

[14] *APS* I.673. See the Glossary for the descriptions of the stone and the pound in this document. For the writer's distinction between David's pound and that of his own day, see below, Chapter 4, pp. 114–15.

[15] *APS* I.673–4. See the Glossary for the descriptions of the ounce and the sterling in this document. The writer drew a distinction between the theoretical pennyweight and the actual weight of the penny current in his own day; the theoretical pennyweight of 32 wheat grains was the unit forming part of the weight system and would not have been affected by changes in the weight of the actual penny. For more about the currency in the 'Assisa', see Chapter 4 on currency.

[16] *APS* I.674. See the Glossary for the description of the boll in this document. There is some variation between the readings of different texts for the dimensions of the boll, and we are grateful to Dr R.D. Connor for drawing our attention to these. The Cromertie MS gives an upper diameter of 24 inches 'infra tabulas ex transverso *cum spissitudine ligni utriusque partis* [editor's italics]' (which is difficult to interpret), a lower diameter of 24½ inches 'infra tabulas ex transverso' and a lower circumference of 74 inches 'infra tabulas' (see *APS* I.308). Sir James Balfour, *Practicks: Or, a System of the More Ancient Law of Scotland* (Edinburgh, 1754), p. 88, gives the capacity as 22 gallons and the depth as 19 inches. His figures look like scribal errors, but the Cromertie readings cannot be dismissed so easily. We have, however, taken the figures given in *APS* as definitive, since most of the MSS are in agreement. If we calculate the capacity of the boll using the given dimensions, our first difficulty is with the thickness of the boards forming the vessel. This problem does not seem to affect depth or circumference. We have no examples in the legislation we have looked at of the thickness of the lower board being included in the given depth, and we have assumed it was usually not. Moreover, when the documents speak of the thickness of the boards, they usually speak of both boards. Further, as regards circumference, we believe 'in medio ligni' with reference to the upper circumference to mean in between the boards rather than at a point in the middle of the boards. The latter interpretation would be the only instance in which a measurement was taken in this way in Scottish medieval legislation. The Cromertie MS seems to indicate that the circumferences were measured within the boards although the authority of this interpretation is weakened by the apparent contradiction contained in the statement about the upper diameter in that text. However, it seems that thickness of the boards is really only a problem when we are looking at diameter.

In 1426, 1458, and 1587, the thickness of both the boards forming the firlot was specified as 1½ inches, while in 1618 the 'steps' were to be an inch at least, though it was not made clear whether this was one or both of them: *APS* II.12 and 50; III.522; and IV. 586. The Cromertie MS tells us that the thickness of both boards should be 1 inch. It seems best to regard 1 inch for both the boards as likely to be nearest the thickness of the wood of the vessels of David's day. The upper diameter

'Assisa' show a vessel of 333.39 cubic inches.[17] The text says there should be 12 gallons to the boll, so this would give a boll of 4,000.68 cubic inches, while the gallon, taken as $\frac{1}{12}$ of the dimensions of the boll, would be 305.60 cubic inches. Finally, a gallon containing 12 pounds of water (which information is given in the Scottish text only) would be 339.43 cubic inches, allowing for extra density of seawater. This would give a boll of 4,073.16 cubic inches.[18]

The above calculations are based entirely on what is explicit in the 'Assisa Regis David'. We believe that although the differences between the figures generated from the various statements are not insignificant, they are acceptable in view of all the possible causes of inaccuracy. For example, we do not know exactly how thick the boards making the vessel were; we cannot be certain that a medieval Scottish inch was the same as a modern one;[19] we do not know how much to allow for factors such as warpedness of the wood or poor standards of craftsmanship in the making of the vessels. Further, a recent study has demonstrated, with special reference to Scottish royal legislation of 1426 and 1618, that the discrepancy between the capacity of the larger grain vessels as calculated from their given dimensions, and that derived from multiplying the known capacity of smaller measures by the number of those smaller measures which the larger vessel was supposed to contain (such that the latter calculation produces a somewhat larger vessel than that

of the boll would then become 23 inches. Now, if we calculate the lower diameter from the lower circumference (which we take to have been measured between the boards) we get a lower diameter of 22.59 inches. We can take an average of the possibilities: 22.96 (i.e. average upper diameter from explicit diameter and from upper diameter as calculated from explicit upper circumference) + 22.59 (i.e. lower diameter calculated from explicit lower circumference) divided by 2 gives average diameter of 22.77; the volume from this is 3,667.22 cubic inches.

[17] *APS* I.674. See the Glossary for the description of the gallon in this document.

Dr R.D. Connor has drawn our attention to the following variations in the different MSS: Adv. MS 25.5.37 gives an upper circumference of 22 inches, and *Regiam Majestatem*, Sir John Skene (Edinburgh, 1609), gives it as 27 inches. Both these readings seem to represent errors.

Allowing 1 inch for the thickness of both the boards, the lower diameter is 7½ inches. The circumferences give no indication as to whether they were measured within or outside the boards, but the diameter can be used to help with this point. The lower circumference using the diameter with the thickness of the boards (i.e. 8½ inches) works out at 26.71 inches. So the given lower circumference of 23 inches would seem to be within the boards. Taking an average of the possibilities 8.75 (upper diameter calculated from explicit upper circumference) + 7.41 (average lower diameter from explicit lower diameter and explicit lower circumference) divided by 2 gives average diameter of 8.08. This gives a volume of 333.39 cubic inches.

[18] On the manuscripts confirming the 12 pound gallon reading, see the forthcoming work by R.D. Connor and A.D.C. Simpson, *The Weights and Measures of Scotland*, to be published by HMSO with the National Museums of Scotland.

[19] See the Glossary, under ell, for the description of the inch in the 'Assisa'.

generated from the dimensions), is caused by the use of grain rather than water as the measuring medium.[20] We feel that David's gallon and boll were compatible with each other within reasonable margins. Our confidence in David's system is further strengthened by information drawn from the legislation of James I.[21] James' 'Assisa' does, however, present its own set of problems. Although it can firmly be dated as an act of James in his parliament of 11 March 1426, there are inconsistencies in the statements about different weights and measures, caused, or at least compounded by, the absence of a single, authoritative text.[22]

James apparently made a fundamental change to the system of weights. The stone was now to weigh 16 pounds 'troyis' and the pound 'troyis' 16 ounces.[23] It would seem, on the face of it, that the pound was to gain an ounce, and the stone a pound as well as $\frac{1}{15} \times 16$. Seeing that there is no change mentioned in the weight of the ounce, and that the makers of the 1426 act were aware of David I's legislation on the subject of weights and measures,[24] in which the ounce was given as 20 sterling pennyweights, it seems most unlikely that the ounce was to be changed. This is a point to which we shall return in due course.[25]

The 'Assisa' then moved on to deal with capacity measures. The first statement it made is worth quoting in full: 'ITEM thai ordanit the boll to met with'all vitall to be devidit in foure partis videlicet four ferlotis to contene a boll Ande that ferlote nocht to be maid eftir the first mesoure na eftir the mesoure now vsit bot in a middil mesoure betuix the twa.' The dimensions of this 'new' firlot are then given, and it is here that our first real textual problem is encountered.

The 1566 edition of the *Acts of the Parliaments of Scotland*, relying on copies of the records of the parliaments of James I and James II (which were probably already lost), gave the depth of the firlot as 9

[20] A.D.C. Simpson, 'Grain Packing in Early Standard Capacity Measures: Evidence from the Scottish Dry Capacity Standards', *Annals of Science*, 49 (1992), 337–50.

[21] *APS* II.12.

[22] The statutes of James I and James II have come down to us from copies: see *APS* II.Preface.

[23] *APS* II.12, but cf. p. 10 where it is said that the stone was to weigh 15 loyal 'troyis' pounds, and was to be divided into 16 loyal Scottish pounds. See the Glossary for the descriptions of the stone in James' legislation. See also A.D.C. Simpson, 'Scots "Trone" Weight: Preliminary Observations on the Origin of Scotland's Early Market Weights', *Northern Studies*, 29 (1992), 62–81, for the observation that a pound of 15 ounces of 480 grains would be equal to a pound of 16 ounces of 450 grains. In what follows, however, we have assumed a 480 grain ounce.

[24] The 1426 act referred to the 'Statute of king Dauid' in its chapter on the ell and spoke of the 'ald boll first maid be king Dauid' in its last chapter: *APS* II.12.

[25] The 1426 act did not mention the 8 pound stone of which 12 made a wey which occurs in David's 'Assisa'. It is not clear whether this was to co-exist with the new 16 pound stone as it had done previously with the 15 pound stone.

inches.[26] The 1681 edition repeated this, and a 9 inch reading is also found in Balfour's *Practicks*.[27] But the 1874 edition, which used a number of manuscript collections in order to reduce the errors in the 1566 edition, has 6 inches.[28] This is also to be found in a contemporary copy of the 1426 act, in SRO MS PA 5/6.[29] We believe that the texts with the 6 inch reading are in themselves more authoritative. If the 9 inch texts are taken, we get a capacity of 1,810.29 cubic inches; if the 6 inch, 1,206.86 cubic inches.[30]

The dimensions of the boll are then given. We have already been told in the text that there are to be 4 'new' firlots to the 'new' boll, but the dimensions of the boll given in the text produce a vessel of 11,913.93 cubic inches,[31] far larger than 4 firlots of 1,206.86 cubic inches or even 1,810.29 cubic inches would give. Here, we believe, a mistake may have been made, and if we are right in so thinking, the whole of the act makes much better sense. Though we should prefer to impute as little as possible to scribal errors, so large a boll cannot be reconciled with many of the other statements of this act. A possible source of the error lies in the 'xix Inchys' depth. The new diameters are only slightly larger than those of David's boll: but 19 inches rather than 9 inches of the earlier boll would mark a complete change in the shape of the vessel. 'xix' instead of 'ix' would be an easy slip; and although all our texts are in agreement in giving 19 (either in words or figures) this may only serve to show that if a copyist's error was made, it was made in the original statute from which all our texts are derived. If the correct depth is 9 inches, this would produce a boll of 5,643.44 cubic inches, which, although a little larger than we might

[26] We are grateful to Dr R.D. Connor for drawing our attention to this text. See *APS* II.Preface for the 1566 edition and its sources.

[27] Sir Thomas Murray of Glendook, *The Laws and Acts of Parliament Made by King James the First, Second, Third, Fourth, Fifth, Queen Mary, King James the Sixth, King Charles the First, King Charles the Second . . . Kings and Queen of Scotland* (Edinburgh, 1681), p. 11, and Balfour, *Practicks*, p. 89.

[28] See *APS* II.Preface.

[29] We are grateful to Dr R.D. Connor for drawing our attention to this manuscript.

[30] *APS* II.12. See the Glossary for the description of the firlot in this document. It is not clear why the thickness of the boards was specified since the diameters were clearly measured within them. It may have been merely to establish the firmness of the vessel. It cannot have been because the thickness was included in the depth because both boards were mentioned.

Swinton tells us that an inspection of the records showed the depth of the firlot was 6 inches: John Swinton (Lord), *A Proposal for Uniformity of Weights and Measures in Scotland* (Edinburgh, 1779), p. 138.

[31] *APS* II.12. See the Glossary for the descriptions of the boll in this document. The first diameter given is perhaps the lower, as with the firlot in the preceding chapter. We have used an average diameter of 28.25 inches, and assumed that both diameters are within the boards.

expect, is much more compatible with 4 firlots of 1,206.86 cubic inches which would give us a boll of 4,827.44 cubic inches. The safer, though disappointing, alternative is to ignore the dimensions of the boll completely when assessing the meaning of this act. As they stand, they cannot be used.[32]

The statute then speaks of the gallon capacity of the firlot. It was to contain 2 gallons and 1 pint, each pint containing 41 ounces of the clear water of Tay, that is, 2 pounds 9 ounces 'troyis' (which clearly shows them to be the new pounds of 16 ounces) and therefore each gallon weighing 20 pounds 8 ounces. All this would give the firlot a capacity of 1,327.62 cubic inches. So, the statute said, the firlot weighed 41 pounds (which would give it a capacity of 1,249.52 cubic inches) and the boll 164 pounds (which would give it a capacity of 4,998.10 cubic inches).[33] There is an inconsistency in this last statement about the weight of the firlot, because the statute has just told us it was to contain 2 gallons and 1 pint (that is, 17 pints) whereas 41 pounds were equivalent to only 16 pints. Apart from this, the different statements about the new system of weights and measures are, within reasonable limits, self-consistent, if we accept the 6 inch depth of the firlot and the 9 inch depth of the boll. We have already drawn attention to the factors at play to create inaccuracies in medieval standards which may frustrate our modern calculations, and again, we believe the discrepancies are acceptable. So far, then, it seems clear that the new gallon was to be twice as large as the old, and the firlot and boll about one third larger than the old.

Now at this point, the statute begins to make comparisons between the old system and the new. What it says deserves close attention. First, it says that David's boll contained a sextern, that is, 12 old gallons. This is nothing more than is said in David's 'Assisa'. Then the statute states that the old gallon weighed 10 pounds 'troyis' and 4 ounces of divers waters. These are the new pounds of 16 ounces, so this would give a capacity of 312.38 cubic inches; near enough, indeed, to the capacities of the old gallon already established.[34] So, the text says, the boll weighed 123 (new) pounds, giving a capacity of 3,748.57 cubic inches – again, reasonably near to the capacities of the old boll. So, the text says, the boll weighed more than the old by 41 pounds.

[32] Swinton, *A Proposal*, p. 138, tells us that an inspection of the records showed the boll was 9 inches deep. See also Simpson, 'Grain Packing', p. 347 where the oversized boll (after correction of the depth) is explained in terms of the measure being constructed to accommodate an allowance for heaping.

[33] *APS* II.12. See the Glossary for the descriptions of the firlot and the boll in this document.

[34] See above, p. 87.

This would show a boll of 164 pounds which the statute has already given us.[35]

So the 1426 statute attempted to make three basic changes to the system of the 'Assisa Regis David'. The pound and the stone were to be increased slightly, the new gallon was to be twice as large as the old, and the new boll and firlot about one third larger than David's original, but not, we believe, one third larger than that commonly in use by the early part of the fifteenth century. We suggest that James I was trying to codify and make universal a system which was widely in use already.

There is something to be learned of the statute's intent in what it said about the firlot: the new one was not to be the same as the first measure, nor that now used, but in a middle measure between the two. Since the first measure, which we can probably assume to be David's, is smaller than the new one prescribed in the statute, we may presume the one in use to have been even larger. The increase in the size of capacity measures was something which doubtless occurred gradually over the centuries. James and his advisers were perhaps trying to standardize existing practice, conservatively.

The same cannot be said about the changes they made to the gallon. The new one was to be twice as large as David's. How much the gallon used in the market place had increased in size over the centuries can only be guessed at, but it seems unlikely that it would have grown so much. It is not clear why a change was attempted in 1426.

Nor is it clear that the innovations of the 1426 statute were put into practice, or that its attempts to standardize what was then usual practice were in fact accepted. An important difficulty in our assessment of James I's legislative measures – which covered extensive matters – is how effectively they were enforced.[36] Although Bower does not refer specifically to the weights and measures legislation, his observations on James' new laws should be taken into account:

In the following Lent [March 1426] the king held his parliament at Perth; then he prorogued it because of the approach of Easter and continued the session at Edinburgh, beginning on 12 May. There he issued various different statutes, some of which would have served the kingdom well enough for the future if

[35] *APS*, II.12. 'The ald boll first maid be king Dauid contenit a sextern' the sextern' contenit xij galon'is of the ald met Ande Ilk galon'e weyit x pundis troyis and foure vnce of diuerse wattiris swa weyit the boll vj^{xx} iij pundis Sua this new boll now maid weyis mar' than the auld boll be xlj lib' quhilk' makis twa galon'is and a half and a chopyn of the auld mete ande of the new mete now ordanit ix pyntis and thre muchekynis.'

[36] For James I's legislation, see Nicholson, *Scotland*, pp. 305–14.

they had been kept; but as it is written in the canon law: 'It is not enough to establish laws if there is no one to see to their enforcement.'[37]

One issue which will have had to be addressed if the weights and measures reforms were to be put into effect was that of ferms and other dues payable in kind. Later royal enactments on the subject of standards made it clear that the absolute quantity of such dues was not supposed to change as a consequence of the alterations in weights and measures; but such riders, whose purpose will have been in part to avoid resistance to the changes, would surely have caused administrative havoc by necessitating widespread adjustment of tenancy agreements, and it was only in the 1618 legislation that detailed procedures were laid down for making such adjustments.[38] In the absence of such arrangements in 1426 one may perhaps question the actual impact of the changes of that year.

It is nevertheless clear that a 16 ounce pound was in use in the Scottish mint, and there, indeed, we would expect the principles of royal government to appear in action.[39] It is not clear what happened in the country at large, and the prices cannot help us much. The commodity series for which the usual units were weights (wool, cheese, wax, and iron) would probably fail to reveal such a small increase in weights, even if we were sure that such an increase had occurred.[40] What seems more certain is that the gallon by which ale was sold in Aberdeen did not double in size as a result of the 1426 legislation. Though we have no data from the late 1420s, our ale prices from Aberdeen in the 1430s, though they are somewhat higher than those of the opening years of the fifteenth century, do not suggest that a dramatic change had taken place. And price increases in the first half of the fifteenth century – not only for commodities sold by the gallon but for all others as well – are explicable largely in monetary terms.[41]

If, however, there had been a dramatic change in weights as a result of the legislation of 1426, it would have had a noticeable effect upon prices. It is important when assessing the meaning of James I's legislation to take account of the theory that it introduced a heavier ounce. It has

[37] Walter Bower, *Scotichronicon*, VIII, ed. D.E.R. Watt (Aberdeen, 1987), p. 257. This is the English translation of the Latin text on p. 256.

[38] See *APS* II.50, 246, and 254; III.522; IV.587, and 588–9.

[39] See R. W. Cochran-Patrick (ed.), *Records of the Coinage of Scotland* (Edinburgh, 2 vols., 1876), I, pp. 22 and 24–7, in accounts of the king's moneyers rendered in 1438, 1441, 1442, 1443, 1447, and 1448.

[40] It is just possible that bread prices from Aberdeen, in the form of orders to bakers about the number of ounces to the penny loaf, would have helped here, but these prices do not start until the 1440s.

[41] See Chapter 4 on currency.

been thought that a system of weights heavier by one third than the Troy system was implicit in medieval Scottish legislation; and that the 'tron' system abolished in 1618 in favour of French Troy weight was none other than this heavier system.

Mr L. Burrell believed that this heavier system originated with David, and that it continued, in modified form, until 1618.[42] His belief that the tron system began with David I seems to be the result of a confusion of wheat and barley grains. David's sterling, of which 20 made an ounce, weighed 32 wheat grains. That would give an ounce of 640 wheat grains. Wheat grains are lighter by one third than barley grains on which the standard Troy system is based. Not realizing this, Mr Burrell surmised that David's ounce was heavier by one third than the Troy ounce. But 640 wheat grains were equivalent to 480 barley grains; David's was the Troy system, merely expressed in wheat rather than barley grains.

Another, related, theory is that a heavier system may have been introduced by the legislation of 1426. It is thought that this heavier system was implied by the words 'trois' and 'troyis' used to describe the new ounce and pound. The evidence of official use of a heavier ounce prior to 1618 is this: the pint or Stirling jug, of which several examples have come down to us, is thought to have been made in the fifteenth century, and not to have increased in size by 1618.[43] Now, in an act of 1587, the dimensions of the firlot which was to contain 19 pints and 2 jucats suggest a cubic capacity of 101.36 cubic inches for the pint,[44] yet the same act stated that the Stirling pint should contain 2 pounds 9 ounces 'trois' of clear water, which would give a capacity of only 78.10 cubic inches.[45] The two capacities are clearly irreconcilable.

[42] L. Burrell, 'The Standards of Scotland', *Monthly Review of the Institute of Weights and Measures Administration*, 69 (March 1961), 49–60.

[43] Burrell, 'The Standards of Scotland', esp. pp. 49 and 55–6.

[44] *APS*, III.522: 'The firlot to be augmentit and the standert tharof to be of the forme eftirspe'it and to contene nyntene pyntis and tua Jowcattis and this to be the measour of all wictuall and stuff wsit in tymes bipast to be sauld' be straik sic as quheit ry peis' bennis meill and quheit salt sauld' in mercattis or in the cuntry The wydnes / and braidnes of the qlk firlot wnder and abone ewin ovir within the burdis sall contene auchtene insches and sext part of ane insche The deipnes sevin insches and half insche / and the peck to be maid effeirand tharto And that the steppis of the said firlot be of the auld' proportione in thiknes of baytht the burdis ane insche and ane half /'. The relationship between the pint and the jucat is not clear. Burrell, 'The Standards of Scotland', p. 58, suggested the jucat was either the Scottish gill ($\frac{1}{16}$ of the pint) or another name for the mutchkin ($\frac{1}{8}$ of the pint). Taking each of these alternatives the cubic capacity works out at either 101.69 cubic inches or 101.03 cubic inches. The average of the two is 101.36 cubic inches.

[45] *APS* III.521: 'The pynt of stirling contening tua pund and nyne vnce trois wecht of cleir watter /'.

By this stage, moreover, we have independent evidence that the Stirling jug had a capacity of about 104 cubic inches, so of the two figures from 1587, 101.36 cubic inches seems more likely to be the correct one.[46]

Now, in 1618, the firlot was found to contain 21 pints and a mutchkin of the Stirling jug measure. The Stirling jug was said to contain 3 pounds 7 ounces of French Troy weight of the clear running water of Leith.[47] This would give a capacity of 104.76 cubic inches for the Stirling jug or pint. The dimensions of the firlot given in this act suggest a pint of 100.20 cubic inches.[48] These figures are compatible enough considering all the possible sources of error which have already been mentioned. It has been thought, because the pint did not apparently increase between 1426 and 1618, that the ounces which made a pint in 1426 and in 1587 were in fact heavier by one third than the ounces which made a pint in 1618, so that 41 ounces (1426 and 1587) were equivalent to 55 ounces (1618). It is suggested that these heavier ounces, and the heavier pounds and stones they generated, were the 'trone' system proscribed by the 1618 legislation.[49] It is thought that the 'trois' or 'troyis' ounce and pound referred to in the 1426 legislation were identical with that 'trone' system. This argument is severely weakened by the fact that the 1426 pint of 41 ounces can be shown, using the dimensions of the 1426 firlot, to have been smaller than the 1618 pint by one third.[50] And the admittedly less reliable boll dimensions

[46] See Burrell, 'The Standards of Scotland', pp. 49 and 55–6.

[47] *APS* IV.586: 'And the same measure and firlot being fund agreable with the said Jedge / the saids Commissioners caused praesentlie fill the same with water which being full / they fand that the same conteined Twentie ane pincts and ane mutchkin of just Sterline Jug and measure and that the foresaid jug containes within the same Thrie punds and seaven unces of frensh Troys weght / of clear running water of the water of Leith.'

[48] *APS* IV.586: 'The wydnes and Breadnes of the which Firlot vnder and above euen over within the buirds / shall contein nyneteen Inches / and sext parte inche; and the deipnes / seaven Inches / and ane thrid part of ane inche: and the Peck / halfe Peck and fourt part Peck to bee made effeirand thereto; And the steppes of the said Firlot to be in thiknes one Inche at the least:'.

[49] *APS*, IV.587: 'there shall bee onely one Just Weght through all the parts of this Kingdome /. . .to wit / The frensh Troys Stone Weght / conteining Sexteine Troys Pounds / in the Stone / and Sexteine Troys Unces in the Pound / and the lesser Weghts and Measures to be made in proportion conforme therto: (And that Weght called of old the Trone weght to bee allvtterlie abolisched and discharged / and neuer hereafter to be received nor vsed.)'. See Burrell, 'The Standards of Scotland', esp. pp. 49 and 54–6.

[50] See above, p. 89. Taking the capacity of the firlot as 1,206.86 cubic inches and dividing first by sixteen pints, we get a pint capacity of 75.43 cubic inches. Dividing by seventeen pints, we get a pint capacity of 70.99 cubic inches. (It will be remembered that there is some confusion in the 1426 act as to whether the firlot was composed of 16 or 17 pints.)

bear out a smaller 1426 pint.[51] Finally the dimensions of the firlot as laid down in 1458 also suggest a pint smaller by one third than that of 1618.[52]

Surely all this points to a one third increase in the size of the pint between 1426 and 1618, rather than a one third decrease in the weight of the ounce in 1618? This, in turn, would suggest that the surviving examples of the Stirling jug are more likely to date from the sixteenth century than the fifteenth century, and we are still left with the discrepancy in the 1587 act. Although the 1587 legislation shows the larger pint weighing 41 ounces, we are inclined to believe the discrepancy exists because the weight was taken from the 1426 text – or even from sheer force of habit – with no attempt to reconcile the weight with the increased capacity. We believe that an error of this kind is plausible; much more plausible, indeed, than the notion that a new system was introduced as relatively late as 1426, without any mention being made of it, and then dropped, equally silently, 200 years later. Both acts were explicit about the changes they did intend. It is unlikely that the most fundamental change of all would have been only tacitly understood. Both acts emphasized the 16 ounce pound and the 16 pound stone; it was these they were trying to promulgate and enforce. We admit of the existence of a tron system of weights;[53] we do not believe it to have been created by Scottish royal legislation.

We can now turn to the final piece of legislation from our period on the subject of weights and measures, that from 1458.[54] The intention of the statute was to establish one single, universal measure for the whole kingdom. It was to be based on a standard pint given by ordinance of the three estates to the burgh of Stirling during the chamberlainship of Sir John Forester (1425–48), which was to remain 'universal' throughout the realm. Here, again, is a suggestion that new legislation intended only to enforce the status quo, but the statute then

[51] See above, pp. 89–90. Taking the capacity of the 1426 boll as 5,643.44 cubic inches and dividing by 4 we get 1,410.86 cubic inches. Dividing first by 16 pints, we get a pint capacity of 88.18 cubic inches. Dividing by 17 pints, we get a pint capacity of 82.99 cubic inches.

[52] For the 1458 legislation in *APS* II.50, see below, p. 96 and n. 55. Taking the capacity of the 1458 firlot as 1,283.46 cubic inches and dividing by 18 pints we get a pint capacity of 71.30 cubic inches.

[53] Clearly there was a 'trone' system in use in Scotland in 1618, for the legislation of that year abolished it. See also Burrell, 'The Standards of Scotland', especially pp. 52–3 and 60, and more recently Simpson, 'Scots "Trone" Weight'.

[54] *APS* II.50.

went on to say that the firlot was thereafter to contain 18 pints.[55] It will be remembered that in 1426 the firlot was to contain 16 or 17 pints, so already there was to be a change in the size of the firlot.[56]

Only the diameter of the new firlot is given in the text. It has been assumed by scholars that the omission of the depth of the vessel meant it was to remain as before,[57] but, as we have already seen, the texts of the 1426 statute are not in agreement, some of them giving 6 inches and others 9 inches. Taking the former, we get a volume of 1,283.46 cubic inches, and taking the latter we get 1,925.20 cubic inches. Finally, if the firlot was to contain 18 pints each containing 41 ounces of water (as in the 1426 act) the volume of the firlot works out at 1,405.71 cubic inches. This is rather nearer to a 6 inch depth than a 9 inch depth, and the 6 inch seems more likely in any case.

What seems clear is that, in later medieval Scotland, measures of capacity, and, to a lesser degree, weights, very gradually grew. They grew over time, probably as copies of standards were made, and as the status quo was accepted and codified. The giving of generous measures, especially of grain, is an important factor here.[58] A gradual increase in the capacity of measures will have had an effect on prices, but it can by no means be said to account on its own for the price rises which demonstrably occurred. The series of currency-adjusted index prices shows that monetary factors had a much more marked effect on prices. Nevertheless, it is possible that the gradual change in the size of the boll and firlot over the centuries may have contributed to the relative buoyancy of cereal prices compared to livestock prices. Although we are unable to say that medieval Scottish weights and measures were constant over time, we can say that changes were probably extremely gradual.[59] Thus, comparison over fifty years or so is unlikely to do violence to the evidence, although longer-term comparison needs to be

[55] *APS* II.50. 'ITEM anent mettis and mesuris it is sene speidfull that sen we haif bot a king and a lawe vniuersale throu out the Realme we sulde haif bot a met and mesur' generale to serue all the Realme That is to say ane pynt quhilk was giffin be the ordinance of the thre estatis sir Jhon'e forester that tyme beande chavmerlane to the burgh of striuelling as for standart sall remane vniuersale throuout the Realme And the ferlot salbe maide thareftir That is to say ilk ferlot sall contene xviij pyntis of the sammyn mesur' rovnde and elik wyde vndir and abvne the twa burdis contenande evyne our in thiknes' ane inche and a half ande the breide our withtin the burdis xvj inchis ande a half Ande the half ferlot and pek to folowe thareftir in the sammyn kinde.'

[56] See above, p. 90.

[57] E.g. Burrell, 'The Standards of Scotland', p. 57.

[58] See below, pp. 107–9.

[59] Perhaps one third over two or three centuries, as is suggested by the new dimensions of the firlot and boll of 1426. The dating of 'David I's' assize is doubtful.

informed by an understanding of possible weights and measures distortion. Most particularly, we see no evidence for any dramatic overnight legislative changes, with the sole exception of the new gallon of 1426, which, in practice, seems to have been of very limited application.

A final problem remains. For the first century of our study, we have made close comparison of Scottish and English prices. There is evidence from the late thirteenth to the mid-fourteenth centuries, mainly from English documents relating to Scotland, that 4 English quarters were equivalent to 1 Scottish chaldron, though there were exceptions to this rule.[60] Now, if Scottish measures and English measures were growing over time, it is possible that they increased at different rates, so that there could have been a time when the rule of a 4-quarter chaldron worked more perfectly than it did at others.[61] Doubtless the equivalence was only a rough and notional one. But in order to use it to compare prices, we must know when it was operable and how accurate it was.

Trying to establish the capacity of the English bushel in absolute terms leads into difficulties because of uncertainty about the capacity of the English gallon. There is evidence of at least 3 gallons in use in England in the later middle ages, suggesting a range of *c*. 3,584 cubic inches – *c*. 4,000 cubic inches for 2 bushels (equivalent in theory to the Scottish boll).[62] These figures are surprisingly compatible with David's boll, which calculations from his 'Assisa' show to have had a capacity in the range of between 3,667.22 and 4,073.16 cubic inches. There is therefore some justification for a comparison of English and Scottish prices in the thirteenth and fourteenth centuries on the basis of a 2 bushel boll and a 4 quarter chaldron.

We have emphasized above grave doubts as to the efficacy of legislative measures apparently designed to introduce dramatic change to the system of weights and measures, but there is some evidence that certain changes did occur, for they were discernible to the contemporary eye and had to be allowed for by accountants. In his account for 1461–2, the chamberlain of royal lands of Moray and other lands beyond the Mounth was allowed 1 boll per chaldron for the difference between the smaller measure with which he had received wheat, barley, and malt from the royal farms of the earldom of Moray, and the new measure with which

[60] See the Glossary, under chaldron. Although the Coldingham evidence is in some ways a Scottish source, it can also be thought of as English, because of the Durham connection.

[61] On the progressive enlargement of English measures as a result of heaping, see esp. R.D. Connor, *The Weights and Measures of England* (London, 1987), pp. 156–8, and Simpson, 'Grain Packing'.

[62] Connor, *The Weights and Measures of England*, pp. 151–5.

the grain was sold.[63] There is also evidence of a growth of measures in the accounts of the chamberlain and subsequently the receiver of Kintore, Coull, and O'Neil in the late 1470s and in the 1480s, where a chaldron of barley due from the thanage of Kintore is described in 1477–9 accounts as 'antique mensure' and afterwards as 'parve mensure'; in the account for 1483–4 the barley is described in the charge as of small measure and in the discharge as of old measure. Clearly the old measure was the smaller.[64]

Another issue to be borne in mind is that of regional diversity of weights and measures. Where the sources contain price evidence from several parts of Scotland, or when goods were transported between regions, we sometimes meet clear evidence of regional variation. The *Exchequer Rolls* show this most clearly. Royal lands extended over many parts of Scotland, and accountants were confronted with the question of diversity of measures, either because they were accounting centrally and needed to reconcile quantities from different estates, or because it was necessary to make clear that render in kind was measured according to local standards. In the same way, the Acts of the Lords of Council and of the Lords Auditors, because they dealt with cases from all over Scotland, distinguished local measures. The relation between the regional measure to which attention was being drawn and the standard from which it differed is not always specified, but it seems clear that there was considerable diversity of measures in medieval Scotland. The west of Scotland is noteworthy for the persistence of purely local measures for cheese and meal when these were paid as render or wages, such as the caslamus and the codrus, found at Tarbert, and the castlaw (which may have been the same as the caslamus), found in Kintyre.[65] While the use of such local terms makes it difficult to assess the prices in the particular entries in which they occur, the use of purely local measures has not in fact been a major problem in our study. That is not to say that many local measures did not exist, but merely that the sources used do not usually reveal them.[66] Of greater concern is the evidence that measures bearing the same name did not mean the same thing all over Scotland. Although we do meet a large pound, for cheese, in Kintyre, nearly all the information about diversity of standards relates

[63] See *ER* VII.132–3.
[64] *ER*, VIII.528 and 612; IX.108–9, 175, 262–3, 308, 407–8, and 503. In the account for 1477–8 oats too are described as of old measure.
[65] See these terms in the Glossary. Simpson, 'Scots "Trone" Weight', is also informative about these units.
[66] Other examples of measures which are associated with particular places or accounts are the batum, the cogall, and the modius: see these terms in the Glossary.

to measures for grain.[67] First there is considerable evidence of a use of larger measures for grain in the south-west of Scotland. The Acts of the Lords of Council and the Acts of the Lords Auditors mention the met or measure of Annandale, Nithsdale, Galloway, Kirkcudbright, the sheriffdom of Wigton, and Dumfries.[68] In the *Exchequer Roll* accounts of the chamberlain of Galloway and the royal rentals for Galloway and Twynham, oatmeal from the king's granges and mills is often given 'in large measure', or by the 'great boll' of Galloway.[69]

Another geographic area where there is evidence of a local measure out of step with the recognized standard is Ross. Here, however, the local measure was a smaller one. A sale by the chamberlain of Ross in 1507–8 of 42 chaldrons, 2.5 bolls of meal and barley 'in small Ross measure' was said to be equivalent to 31 chaldrons, 10 bolls in Leith measure.[70] This suggestion that the small Ross measure was equivalent to 75% of the Leith measure is confirmed by later evidence. In the accounts of the chamberlain of Ross and the farmer (arrendatarius) of Ardmannoch for the late 1520s and for the 1530s, allowances of barley, oatmeal, and oats were made to compensate for the difference between the large and small measures of the lordship of Ross; an allowance explicitly stated to be 4 bolls per chaldron was permitted, on condition that if it were established that dues had in fact been received in large measure the allowance was to be repaid.[71] After a new assessment was made in 1539, however, this rather unsatisfactory situation was resolved and victuals were measured in the accounts of the chamberlains of Ross and Ardmannoch by the large measure of Leith, without shortfall.[72] There is also evidence of a disparity between the measures of Moray and those of Aberdeen. In the grain account of the chamberlain of the lordship of Moray for 1475–6, the Moray firlot was said to be smaller than that of Aberdeen by 1 boll per chaldron (that is, one sixteenth).[73]

In these instances local diversity is associated with more or less remote regions of Scotland; rather more worrying in terms of our confidence in the existence of any generally recognized standard is the evidence in the St Andrews rental at the very end of our period of diversity even

[67] *ER* XII.586, 703. See also *ER* I.53.

[68] *ALC* I.7, 8, 60, 283, 419. *ALA* I.65, 97.

[69] Eg. for meal, *ER* VI.348, XII.251–2, 654–6, XV.316–17, XVII.73, 75. See also *ER* X.79 where oats are specified in large measure at Spottis grange, and from Ballindune grange in small measure. In this instance the amounts had perhaps been converted from the larger local measure.

[70] *ER* XIII.47–8.

[71] *ER* XV.502–3; XVI.113–14, 202–3, 208, 278–9, 326, 406–7; XVII.35, 112–13, and 233.

[72] *ER* XVII.331–50, 437–46, 448–53, and 493–500.

[73] *ER* VIII.368.

between the measures of St Andrews and Leith. We are told, when wheat was used up in Edinburgh, or when barley was delivered to Leith, of a shortfall owing to the difference of measures; the amounts specified as compensation for this usually represent between 6.84% and 9.34% of the quantity delivered or expended, although in one instance, for a delivery of barley, it rises to 12.12%.[74]

In these instances it is possible to quantify to some degree how far a particular region's usual standards were out of step with those current elsewhere. Taken with other evidence – where our attention is drawn to regional diversity although without information to enable us to quantify it, or where it is not possible to say which part of Scotland the anomalous measure came from – it serves as a warning against too precise comparisons between prices from different regions.[75] And a further issue is the existence of water measure for goods coming by ship, which was a larger measure than that for goods coming from the land.[76] What the royal records show, however, is a clear awareness of what standards ought to be, and they demonstrate that the issue was sufficiently important to warrant attempts to reconcile them, although with uncertain success. The fact that royal lands extended over a large part of Scotland will have acted as a force working for greater uniformity of weights and measures.

The chamberlain's ayre will also have tended to encourage uniformity of standards, particularly in that there was provision for enquiry during the ayre into the weights and measures used in the burghs.[77] On a day to day basis, however, the burgh authorities were responsible for ensur-

[74] *Rentale Sancti Andree, Being the Chamberlain and Granitar Accounts of the Archbishopric in the Time of Cardinal Betoun, 1538–1546*, ed. Robert K. Hannay, SHS, 2nd ser. 4 (1913), pp. 99, 100, 113, 114, 130, and 131.

[75] For other examples of regional diversity, see *ER*, I.291–2: chamberlain, 1329–30: loss (laca) of wheat and barley through diversity of measures; 325–6: account of receiver of victuals at Clackmannan, rendered 1330: 2 bolls oats out of 2 chaldrons, 14 bolls received discounted for short measure; *ER*, XVII.97: baillie of ward of Errol, 1537–8: allowance of 3 firlots for 'lie inlaik' of wheat sent to Leith through difference of measures. In these and other examples, loss is associated with diversity of measures, and this diversity may well explain other references to 'inlac' or 'inlak' in the records. See *ER* VII.168, XII.224, XIII.146, and SHS 2, 10.100.

[76] For water measure, see ACR XV.685 (salt in Aberdeen 1538) and the Glossary, under the last for grain. Also *APS* II.10 (James I, parliament at Perth, March 1426): ordinance that the current water 'mettis' shall remain and be used through the realm in future; and that in each place and town where goods are sold and measured by the water a man shall be appointed to measure all goods saleable by the water 'mett', including coal as well as other goods; ACR VII.975 (Aberdeen, 1499): delivery ordered of 1 chaldron of wheat with the water measure or else 17 bolls with the market measure.

[77] See especially 'Fragmenta Collecta', pp. 183–4, clause xlvii, and 'Modus Procedendi', pp. 132–4 and 144, clauses i and xv.

ing just standards within the burgh.[78] In particular, the weights and measures used in the burgh had to be sealed with the burgh seal.[79] The lists of goods of heirship in the Aberdeen records show us that many burgesses indeed owned an array of weights and measures, so the job of inspecting all burgesses' weights on a regular basis must have been a daunting one if it were carried out to the letter. A particularly impressive set, including a quart, a pint, a choppin, and a mutchkin of tin, a pair of wool balances with a stone, half stone, quarter, half quarter, and pound, a pair of small balances (perhaps for weighing spices?) with appropriate weights, and a firlot and a peck, was included among the list of goods belonging to a deceased burgess, Alexander Andersone, in February 1540.[80]

The problems which the Scottish governments anticipated over practical enforcement of standards are interesting. The possibility that individuals would use one weight or measure for purchases, and another for sales, seems to have been a perennial concern.[81] It is also clear from points to be included in the chamberlain's ayre that particular types of tradespeople – alewives, taverners, and regraters – were presumed to be especially likely to offend with weights and measures.[82] The Aberdeen evidence bears out the latter concern to a certain extent. Taverners, meal sellers, alewives, and women whose trade is not specified are commonly found implicated in the use of wrongful measures.[83] The town also had to chastise individuals found using unlawful pecks, a problem rather noticeable in early 1493 and in October 1508.[84]

Further, the authorities periodically tightened up on standards, as when in October 1455 along with the assize all alewives were ordered to present the measures with which they sold ale.[85] Later on, in the

[78] 'Burgh Laws', pp. 33–4, clause lxviii, and 'Fragmenta Collecta', pp. 180–1, clause xl, tell us that the baillies were responsible for punishing the first three offences, after which the offender would be in the king's will. However, 'Fragmenta Collecta', p. 184, clause xlviii, tells us that anyone convicted concerning false weight or measure by inquisition of the baillies should be in the king's will. See also 'Articuli Inquirendi', p. 115, clause 13. It seems clear that the baillies were responsible for the examination of standards, even if not, ultimately, for the punishment of offenders.

[79] See 'Burgh Laws', p. 23, clause xlviii and 'Articuli Inquirendi', p. 121, clause 50. The Burgh Laws give the standards which burgesses were permitted to own as an unspecified measure for corn, an ell, a stone, and a pound.

[80] ACR XVI.466.

[81] See esp. *APS* I.324 (Assise Regis David, cap. xxxi) and II.376; 'Articuli Inquirendi', p. 117, clause 27; 'Modus Procedendi', pp. 142–3 and 152–3, clauses xi and xxviii.

[82] See 'Articuli Inquirendi', p. 115 and 116, clauses 12 and 15, and 'Modus Procedendi', pp. 141–2 and 146, clauses x, xviii and xix.

[83] See, for examples, *Early Records of the Burgh of Aberdeen*, ed. Dickinson, pp. 40, 41, and 115; ACR VI.734 and 736, and VIII.398.

[84] ACR VII.397, 410, and 420; VIII.882, 888, and 889.

[85] ACR V i.246.

guild court held on 8 October 1507, as part of a major series of enactments concerning the social and economic life of the burgh, it was ruled that an investigation of the 'mettis' and measures in the whole town should take place, and that wrongful ones should be destroyed and the owners punished.[86] On 12 February 1524 it was ruled that all the measures taken and examined by the baillies or their officers and found insufficient should be destroyed and burned, and that all neighbours of the burgh should be ordered, under severe penalty, to keep just 'met' and measure.[87]

These general provisions may merely indicate the authorities were doing their job; they are not in themselves indicative of a change in standards. However, the difficulties they experienced in enforcing the use of a correct pint by alewives at the turn of the sixteenth century may have been caused by a change in the standard. On 19 April 1493 the council ordered the alderman to see that all the pints of the town kept the full measure of a pint of Philip of Dunbrek's (perhaps the town's pewterer) which was presented to him.[88] In the baillies' court held on 28 March 1506 twenty-five women were convicted for holding wrongful measures – pints and quarts – and for selling ale and wine with them.[89] This entry is followed in the register by a statute concerning measures made on the same day, in which every brewster in the burgh was ordered to have a pint of tin made whose capacity was to be checked with the correct 'jugale' by Davy Theman who was then to mark them; he was to have a penny for his labour for each pint, quart, or choppin he processed.[90] In October 1507 a similar order (although the king's authority was not on this occasion explicitly brought to bear) was issued; this time the inspector was to be William Stile, pewterer.[91] On 20 December 1507 the brewsters of the burgh generally were accused of a range of infringements of the regulations concerning the purchase of victual and the selling of ale, including selling ale with pints which had not been marked and measured with the 'juggale'. The assize decided it could not acquit thirty-three women of having broken the assize of ale, and that it could not acquit the remainder of the brewsters of the points of which they had been accused.[92]

It has been suggested that the royal government was, at the end of the fifteenth century and in the opening years of the sixteenth, undertaking a

[86] ACR VIII.755.
[87] ACR XI.404.
[88] ACR VII.429.
[89] ACR VIII.561.
[90] ACR VIII.562 (above, 'Appendix of documents', no. II).
[91] ACR VIII.763.
[92] ACR VIII.784.

review of the weights and measures system, and, specifically, was attempting to enforce a pint of the larger size which we know was current by the seventeenth century.[93] For example, a statute of James IV's parliament of March 1504 ordered that all weights and measures (pint, quart, firlot, peck, ell wand, stone, and pound) should be of one quantity and measure which was to be ordained in Edinburgh by the king, chamberlain, and council. Every burgh was to come and fetch their standards from Edinburgh.[94] It is possible therefore that the Aberdeen burgh authorities' dealings with the brewsters in the early years of the sixteenth century may have had something to do with a reform of the weights and measures system advocated by the government centrally.

A similar longstanding problem concerns the barrel. First, we meet repeated attempts to ensure there was a constant size for the barrel of salmon. One special indication of the importance of the salmon trade in Aberdeen is the attention paid by the authorities, from the fifteenth century onwards, to the size and quality of the barrels in which the fish was packed, and, indeed, to the packing process itself. And the salmon barrel was also a subject for repeated royal legislation.[95] All salmon barrels made in the burgh were subject to inspection by sworn searchers who, in return for a fee, checked the barrels were the right size, of good-quality wood, and packed with good fish; those which passed inspection were sealed or branded. Each cooper was also supposed to brand the barrels he had made, so that shoddy workmanship or wrongful measure could be traced back to him.[96] The first clear evidence we have of the existence of a standard, physical measure for salmon barrels (earlier rulings speak only of sufficient measure) comes from 1472: in the Aberdeen guild court held on 9 October the four appointed searchers of the town's salmon barrels were to have two iron girths to see that each one was sufficient.[97] On 1 September 1479 it was ordained there should be a Hamburg barrel made for salmon according to the 'bande' and 'stand' ordained that year, containing 13¾ gallons of water. The barrel was to be made according to the measure of a band of iron which the provost would have made 'bath witht girth uten and e'new the barrel', and all the town's barrels were to be made according to

[93] Connor and Simpson, *The Weights and Measures of Scotland.*

[94] *APS* II.246 and 254.

[95] The royal and burghal legislation on the size of salmon barrels is summarized in the Glossary.

[96] ACR V ii.701; VI.203, 485, 558a, and 598; VII.844; VIII.755; IX.1, 427, and 441; XII i.180; and XIII.150. See, for royal legislation on these points, *APS* II.119, 179, 213, and 375.

[97] ACR VI.203.

this standard. All the coopers were to call the searchers when they had made their barrels so that they might be assayed with the same measure.[98]

Very soon afterwards we encounter suspicion about the size of barrels. On 14 August 1486 five men referred to as the town's coopers (they were probably the master coopers) swore publicly and solemnly that the barrels they were currently making were of the same size as those of three, four, and five years ago and no smaller; and they swore to keep that same measure undiminished in future.[99] The very fact that they were asked to take an oath surely suggests there may have been a decrease in the size of the barrels, discernible even over the space of a very few years, and this was a trend which continued. On 27 August 1507 the provost ordered the baillies to summon all the coopers in the burgh and to punish them for failing to make barrels of the correct measure.[100] By 1511 the authorized measure was itself reduced to 12 gallons or thereabouts. The ordinance, of 21 July,[101] was said to be made with the consent of eight named coopers and craftsmen and all other coopers who were indwellers of the burgh. (The consent of craftsmen – and not just coopers – to ordinances which affected them was very frequently recorded. It was a way of guarding against later dissent or plea of ignorance; but we should not assume that the stated consent was either explicit or the result of choice.) To ensure the standard was kept, every one of them was to have a 'bilg gyrtht' and a 'hed girtht' of iron to measure the barrel at its middle and its top. Anyone making a barrel of a capacity less or more by a pint than 12 gallons was to be excluded from the craft for a year.[102]

The standard in 1521 was still 12 gallons or thereabouts, but it was apparently not being kept by the coopers. On 18 February the searchers reported the coopers were making insufficient stuff, 'witht stawys of quhit wod, witht woud wandis and worme hollis quhilk culd nocht be kepit thecht'; they were also making barrels less than the proper measure of 12 gallons or thereabouts. Punishments were therefore laid down for those who made shoddy goods or barrels less than the proper measure, which were to be more severe in the case of notably undersized, or unmarked, barrels.[103]

[98] ACR VI.598 and see also p. 595.
[99] ACR VI.967.
[100] ACR VIII.731.
[101] The manuscript is difficult to read at this point, but the date is confirmed on p. 441, where the statute is ratified.
[102] ACR IX.1. This seems to be the meaning of the text although darkening of the manuscript makes part of the text illegible.
[103] ACR X.281–2.

The difficulty of making barrels to an exact size was evidently recognized; but the permitted margin of error will have encouraged the trend towards smaller barrels. On 14 June 1527 the provost and baillies ordered Will Chapman and Wille Make, the coopers' deacons, to inspect all the barrels made by the coopers and see they were duly marked and of the right measure, 11½, 11¾, or 12 gallons.[104]

Over a period of about fifty years, then, the authorized measure of the salmon barrel had decreased from 13¾ to (potentially) 11½ gallons, a reduction in capacity of 16.36%. This is striking in view of evidence which shows other capacity measures growing in size over time.[105] One reason for the decrease is that coopers will themselves have wished to make smaller barrels, for it presumably cut down the cost of their materials. But a decrease in the size of the units by which salmon was sold may well have had an effect on prices, and we should bear this in mind when looking at salmon prices in the later fifteenth and early sixteenth centuries. Whether the decreasing barrel size will also have had a bearing on merchants' ability to market salmon abroad is a more difficult question. Purchasers may have overcompensated for the perceived smaller size of the barrels, especially when they were buying in advance without seeing them, so that it is possible that the prices of the diminished barrels will have been lower than the actual reduction of size would warrant in itself. Worries were certainly expressed about the marketability of Aberdeen's salmon in 1529. On 25 June, in a preamble to new legislation, it was explained that because of 'ewin' packing of fish and insufficient fish and barrels, the town's fish were being 'lichtlyit' (scorned) in other parts and were not fetching the prices they used to do.[106] The underlying cause was thought to be the multitude of packers in the burgh who failed to put their mark on the barrels they packed, so that it was difficult to know who to punish for rotten or badly packed fish. (It seems, in fact, that the coopers themselves often packed fish.[107] This made sense since they were most likely to fit on the head of the barrel. Up until this piece of legislation, however, and as the preamble implies, packing was probably not the preserve of the coopers.) It was therefore decided to limit the job of packing the

[104] ACR XII i.180.
[105] See above, pp. 88–98.
[106] The royal statute of June 1478 stipulating that all salmon was to be packed in Hamburg barrels according to the old assize of Aberdeen spoke of grumbles by strangers and other salmon purchasers over the 'mynising' of the vessels and barrels that it was packed in: *APS* II.119.
[107] E.g. ACR VIII.715: on 23 July 1507 it was ordained that no cooper in the burgh was to pack or head fish, salmon or grilse, until they showed the barrel to the provost, custumar, and two or three of the council.

town's fish to three sworn packers, two of whom were Chapman and Make, the deacons of the coopers in 1527.[108] They were only to pack fish of adequate marketable quality, in tight and sufficient 'treis' (vessels; that is, barrels) of the correct and customary measure of Aberdeen. Each was to brand the barrels he had packed, and was to be accountable to the buyer in case of insufficient fish or 'treis' or 'ewin' packing. The packers were also given the task of inspecting all the barrels made in the burgh.[109] These three people will doubtless have been 'master packers' with people under them to actually carry out the work; but the point was they were responsible for whatever was done. And limiting the responsibility in this way made it much more likely that the job would be done well, for errors could much more easily be traced.

It also made sense to restrict the number of coopers. In November 1497 three coopers had to identify on oath to the alderman and council those who were worthy to exercise the craft within the burgh for the common profit.[110] Later on, in the order of 14 June 1527 already mentioned it was added that if any coopers from Old Aberdeen were found working in the town the town's coopers (that is, the authorized craftsmen) were to take their ?'tu'nns' (the vessels they had fashioned?) and present them to the provost and baillies.[111] In the same way, when in 1533 certain Frenchmen had hit on the idea of bringing their own barrels, which they assembled on the spot, for exporting salmon in, they were told firmly to set up no more barrels than they had done already in the burgh and its water, and to sell both the assembled and the unassembled ones to the neighbours of the town, or else to put them back in their ship.[112]

It was, of course, in the interests of native coopers to have the exclusive right to make barrels. But bound up with that monopoly was the obligation they bore – like all other 'free' craftsmen working in the burgh – to supply their product at a certain price and in quantities which met burgh demand. On 9 October 1472 it was ordained that no cooper should have more than 2d. for heading a barrel and making it watertight.[113] On 7 July 1506 an Englishman (whose name is not given) appeared before the baillies and explained that the coopers of the burgh had undertaken to supply everyone who had salmon with barrels; and he argued that if he happened to lack any barrels through their fault,

[108] See above, p. 105.
[109] ACR XII ii.615–16.
[110] ACR VII.844.
[111] ACR XII.i.180.
[112] ACR XIV.194–5.
[113] ACR VI.203.

he should have his money back so that he could get barrels from elsewhere to pack his master's fish.[114] In the ordinance of 21 July 1511 the coopers were told to do their best to acquire materials and to sell their barrels according to the cost of those materials.[115]

Another problem in Aberdeen in the sixteenth century was that of landmen offering, and neighbours seeking, generous measure in purchases of grain. Extra quantities were known by a variety of intriguing names: 'straiks', 'cheritys', 'goupnys', 'sampillis', 'seik sailkynnis', 'scheit saikingis'; but to offer or to seek them was doggedly forbidden by the authorities from 1487 onwards.[116] These rulings are sometimes associated with restrictions on the quantities of grain people were permitted to buy and with other stipulations about purchasing practice in the market, or with the proscription of cake baking. As a practical measure, the authorities tried to ensure authorized grain measures were readily available and that measuring occurred openly rather than secretly. In the ruling of 23 April 1487, and again on 14 November 1505, the tollman was ordered to have a firlot, peck, and half peck available for everyone's use.[117]

It is interesting to note that at the time when giving generous measures was being proscribed in Aberdeen, the giving of 'charity' was a widespread practice in sales of grain on royal estates. We also find charity in the St Andrews rental at the end of our period. Charity can be understood as a way of giving generous measure by allowing the purchaser an additional amount for which he was not charged. It was

[114] ACR VIII.591.

[115] ACR IX.1.

[116] ACR VII.12 (23 April 1487: no landman to give 'straik' of meal in future; tollman always to have ready firlot, peck, and half peck) and 34 (23 October 1487: statute that no huckster, cake baker, or market spiller should buy more meal than would serve their own needs between market days, and should take no 'straike' of meal from landmen in future); VIII.518–19 (14 November 1505: no woman to buy meal in the market unless she had agreed a price before giving earnest money, or to take any 'strakis' or 'cheriteys', or to buy more meal than would suffice herself and her household; no one to bake 'saile cakis' until it were 'divisit' by authorities; all landmen to have their sacks ready open to sell to all who wished to buy victual by the boll, half boll, firlot, peck, and half peck; tollman always to have ready a firlot, peck, and half peck to serve everyone) and 562 (28 March 1506: no one to ask for or take any 'strakis' or 'goupnys' of meal or malt; this is associated with the prescriptions regarding the pint measure for brewsters and is given in full above, 'Appendix of documents', no. II); XIII.439 (11 May 1532: in future no landward man or woman bringing victuals to the burgh to sell to give any 'semplis', 'seiksailkynnis', 'strakis', or any other 'moundmentis(?)' (emolument or benefit?) of their victuals to anyone, but [to give] the just measure of peck or firlot, and to measure openly in the market in good weather and in bad or windy weather underneath stairs or if necessary in the tolbooth); XV.219 (6 October 1536: no 'scheit saikingis' (?sheet shakings) or 'sampillis' to be taken of landward men in future).

[117] ACR VII.12 and VIII.519.

reckoned for meal, and for grains except for wheat, at 1 boll per chaldron (or $\frac{1}{16}$th, i.e. 6.25%) of the amount sold.[118] For wheat charity was with some exceptions half that amount, perhaps because wheat was a more valuable, scarcer grain, so that half a peck to the boll was considered sufficiently generous.[119] It would seem on the face of it that the Aberdeen authorities were out of step with what was going on elsewhere, unless we can view charity as a way of standardizing, and, we suggest, restricting the amount of generous measure given. The Aberdeen evidence shows that generous measures were known by a variety of terms; by implication, they were not standardized. But at the very end of our period, while proscribing the use of generous measures, the authorities explicitly sanctioned an additional allowance in purchases of malt. On 13 October 1539 it was ruled that no one in the burgh was to presume to take any 'sampillis' or 'scheit schankingis' of either meal or malt from the strangers (presumably the landmen or foreign merchants) but only the boll of malt with a peck to the boll, and only 4 'straikit' (struck) firlots of meal per boll.[120] Here, it may be suggested, the burgh was doing locally what the king's administrators had been doing for some time on his estates; that is, standardizing generous measure at an acceptable level – one sixteenth – and in so doing stamping out the practice of giving generous measures of uncertain and variable dimensions.[121] It seems, however, that the burgh was only prepared to accept an additional allowance for malt.

It is intriguing that references to generous measure should be confined in the records to the late fifteenth and the sixteenth centuries, particularly in view of the fact that this was the very time when grain prices were beginning to rise. If that price rise was a result of increased demand for grain, it is unlikely that vendors would have begun to offer generous measures in order to make their sales; and, indeed, the proscriptions of uncontrolled generous measures are frequently associated with rulings indicating concern on the part of the authorities about the supply of victual.[122]

[118] Cf. *ER* XIV.217, where for oatmeal the 'cantelis' was calculated at 1 firlot for 3 bolls, that is, $\frac{1}{12}$.

[119] For exceptions, see *ER* VIII.147, 222, 368. All three examples come from the accounts of the chamberlain of Moray. See also SHS 2,10.199.

[120] ACR XVI.359. It was also ruled that no one in town was to 'tope' (tap) or regrate any victual from their house dearer than on the preceding market day, and that no one was to take more victual than would sustain themselves and their household until the next market day.

[121] See also ACR XVI.677 for additional amounts in the Aberdeen records.

[122] See above, n. 116.

It is, surely, much more probable that generous measures existed throughout the period of our study, and that the late fifteenth and early sixteenth centuries saw this becoming standardized. In this context it is especially significant that the references to generous measures are found earliest, and most copiously, in the royal accounts. As was probably the case in 1426, the government was coming to terms with customary practice and usage, and standardizing, conservatively, the quantity of generous measure. It seems likely that generous measures were in practice a result of heaping grain in the vessel. This is suggested by the Aberdeen evidence which speaks of straiks, a term meaning the amount of grain represented by the heap, and by the emphasis on struck measures for meal in the ruling of 1539 which standardized additional quantities. The association of heaping with charity is further evidenced by the lower amount of the charity for wheat, and the explicit prescription at Aberdeen of a struck firlot for meal; both of which may foreshadow the smaller firlot for wheat, and for rye, beans, peas, meal, white salt, and other 'stuff' and victual said to have been measured formerly by struck measure, and the larger firlot for malt, bere, and oats which were said to have been customarily measured with heaps, authorized in 1618.[123] It is even possible that some of the variant regional measures considered above (such as those used in Moray), which also varied by one sixteenth, may have had their origins in locally differing practice concerning generous measure.

The above discussion draws attention to the problems we have encountered over weights and measures in our study of Scottish prices. The reader is additionally referred to the Glossary which sets out much detailed evidence about the many standards in use in medieval Scotland. In summary, we would emphasize that legislation about the weights and measures of medieval Scotland is highly problematic. It appears that weights were reasonably constant in our period, although measures of capacity certainly indicate a marked growth. But that growth was not at a speed which would have been perceptible during people's lifetime and, if not perceived, will not have influenced prices in the short term. But it is true that a sixteenth-century boll of meal would have filled more bellies than a thirteenth-century one, and on that account may be presumed to have been worth more in real terms. Thus, the growth of capacity measures, most obviously for grain, may

[123] *APS* IV.586–7; see also *APS* III.521–2 for the arrangements made in 1587 for measuring malt, bere, and oats.

well have contributed to the cereal price rise in the later middle ages.

Regional variations, particularly in capacity measures, are unquestionably a source of error. But quantification of these suggests they rarely amounted to more than the odd boll in the chaldron, reminiscent of charity, heaping, and other customary generous measures with which regional variations may be linked. It is our hope and belief that although changes over time and regional differences may blur the picture, they do not on the whole obscure it.

Metrology is not an issue to be considered separately from the history of the society and economy which produced the weights and measures under consideration. Standards came into existence because of the need to quantify the goods involved in transactions, and they changed and developed alongside changes and developments in the nature of the transactions themselves. The wool sack and the salmon barrel emerged as standards on which royal custom could be charged as wool and salmon exports grew in importance. Scottish kings became increasingly concerned with standards in order to preserve revenues from customs and from royal estates, but their assumption of responsibility for the prescription of uniform standards expressed and enhanced royal authority in the kingdom as a whole. The gradual growth of capacity measures and efforts to standardize this may well have been linked to changes in the custom and practice of market transactions. Thus, while we may wish for constant standards, and may seek to discover their absolute size or weight, the changes and uncertainties revealed contribute vitally to our understanding of developments in Scotland's medieval economy and society.

4 Currency

the mater of the mone is rycht subtile[1]

Scottish medieval prices are almost always cited in money of account, that is so much £ s. d., or marks (13s. 4d.) or half marks. However, the relationship between this money of account and the actual currency used in the transaction was not always straightforward. At the beginning of our period the only coins minted in Britain were pennies, and £1 money of account would actually have been paid over as 240 of these pence. Similarly 1s. meant 12 pence. Halfpennies and farthings were simply cut fractions of the penny. In 1280 Edward I struck round farthings and soon after halfpennies, and Alexander III followed suit at the same time. Edward I also attempted to launch a 4d. groat, but the issue was short-lived and it was not until the 1350s that this larger silver denomination was successfully issued in England and Scotland. A successful gold coinage also began in the mid-fourteenth century in the shape of a noble of 6s. 8d., with in England its half (3s. 4d.) and quarter (1s. 8d.). In Scotland at this time only the noble was struck, and that in very small quantities.

While the intrinsic content of these coins remained constant the distinction between a certain amount of money of account and the actual coins involved will not have affected prices. However, the later middle ages was a period of progressive currency depreciation everywhere in Europe. Precious metals became scarcer and their market value consequently became enhanced. The intrinsic metal content of a given unit of money of account therefore tended to fall. However, the metal content of a unit of money of account was actually fixed by government, and different European governments came to terms with the rising value of precious metals at varying speeds. In some countries, at some times, the intrinsic value of the money of account was reduced faster than the value of precious metals rose, whereas in other places it was reduced more slowly. Generally England was slow to recognize

[1] *APS* ii, 106, c. 4.

the rising value of metal on the open market, but Scotland adjusted more quickly. If government deliberately reduced the metal content of its coinage faster than the value of the metal rose, prices might be expected to rise to compensate.[2]

Thus in order to understand the movement of money of account prices it is important to be aware of the nature of the money in which transactions were actually conducted. In the thirteenth century, and for much of the fourteenth century, the currency in Scotland was dominated by English coin.[3] Alexander III twice ordered the recoinage of coin in Scotland into new Scottish types, and for a few years after these recoinages in the 1250s and 1280s, the currency will have been composed much more of Scottish coin, but until the second half of the fourteenth century transactions were for the most part accomplished in English coin. Moreover, in any case Scottish issues were designed to circulate at parity with English sterling. In the course of the fourteenth century the Scottish coinage gradually began to break away from the English. Very marginal reductions in the intrinsic content of the Scots issues may have occurred under Bruce and in the early years of David II, and these are considered below, but it was not until 1367 that Scotland clearly moved away from sterling. It took from then to the end of the century for the Scottish element in the circulation to eclipse the English.[4] This is not to suggest that English coin was then totally excluded from Scotland. Moreover, in the fifteenth and sixteenth centuries other European coins were also used in significant quantities in Scotland. Nevertheless, from the end of the fourteenth century it is reasonable to assume that it was Scottish mint issues which predominated in Scotland's currency, and when foreign coin was employed it was given a Scots valuation.[5]

[2] For a lucid discussion of the distinction between debasement and depreciation, see C.E. Challis, 'Debasement: The Scottish Experience in the Fifteenth and Sixteenth Centuries', in *Coinage in Medieval Scotland*, p. 171.

[3] Mayhew, 'Money in Scotland'.

[4] Mayhew, 'Alexander III', p. 64, citing especially W.A. Seaby and B.H.I.H. Stewart, 'A Fourteenth-Century Hoard of Scottish Groats from Balleny Townland, Co. Down', *BNJ*, 33 (1964), 94–106.

[5] The composition of the Scottish money supply may be studied through the hoards: Metcalf 'The Evidence of Scottish Coin Hoards'. This has been most usefully supplemented by J.D. Bateson, 'Roman and Medieval Coins', which also notes single finds. The evolution of the usual money of Scotland also affords useful indications: John M. Gilbert 'The Usual Money of Scotland and Exchange Rates against Foreign Coin', in *Coinage in Medieval Scotland*, pp. 131–54, and W.W. Scott, 'Sterling and the Usual Money of Scotland 1370–1415', *Scottish Economic and Social History*, 5, (1985), 4–22. Scott shows that after the debasement of 1367 the usual money of Scotland made only a gradual appearance,and that it was official Scottish policy to attempt to maintain that sterling and the Scottish currency were equal. This fiction was abandoned after the debasement of 1393 and the trickle of usual money references became a flood.

Unfortunately, the intrinsic content of Scottish coin is by no means always as easy to establish as might be imagined. In the first place the weight of surviving coins can only provide an approximate indication of the likely intended weight at the time of issue. Apart from clipping and wear during its period of use, a coin probably undergoes further weight loss in the ground when hoarded, and as a result of cleaning subsequent to its discovery. It is also important to realize that medieval coins were struck at so many to the pound, and within certain tolerances, so individual examples could legally be significantly above or below the average intended weight, even immediately after issue. It is even more difficult to attempt to gauge intended fineness (purity of metal) from surviving examples. Destructive analysis is effectively prohibited by the rarity and value of Scottish coins, but non-destructive analysis is still a young science. Relatively few Scottish coins have been analysed in this way,[6] and what has been done may not always have overcome all the technical difficulties.[7]

If the coins themselves provide only an uncertain guide, documentary evidence can be even more difficult to interpret. In the first place the written record of Scottish mint issues is very incomplete. Moreover, of what does survive, some at least appears to record unfulfilled intentions rather than concrete achievement. Thus Scottish records quite often speak of a return to sound money, when all the other indications are of a gradual but continuing reduction in intrinsic value. Conversely, English evidence for Scottish coinage tends to suggest that it was worse than it was, since English proclamations were often intended to exclude Scots coin from the English currency rather than to provide an accurate assessment of its true value. Further, even when the surviving documents do accurately record the intrinsic value of Scottish coin, they are not always easy to understand. The earliest written evidence for the weight of Scottish coin is a case in point. The assize of David I on weights and measures is known to us only from fourteenth-century manuscripts which have adjusted the original details to suit the currency of the time of copying.[8] The section relating to the weight of the pound, the ounce, and the sterling are worth quoting in full:

[6] D.M. Metcalf, 'The Quality of Scottish Sterling Silver, 1136–1280', and J.E.L. Murray, 'The Black Money of James III', both in *Coinage in Medieval Scotland*.

[7] Surface enrichment is the principal difficulty. A summary of some of the problems of analysis of silver coins by X-ray fluorescence spectrometry appears in N. J. Mayhew, *Sterling Imitations of Edwardian Type* (Oxford, 1983), pp. 142–4. New techniques have since been developed but not yet widely applied to Scottish coins.

[8] *APS* I. Preface, pp. 44, 50. The earliest text, the Ayr MS, is thought to be early fourteenth century.

De pondere libre.
Item libra debet ponderare .xxv.s.hoc erat in illo tempore assise pretacte. [Nunc autem libra ponderabit] .xxvj.s. et .iij.d. quoniam in tantum nunc minuitur nova moneta ab antiqua tunc vsitata. Item libra debet ponderare .xv. vncias.
De pondere uncie.
Item vncea continebat in se tempore Regis David .xx.d. sterlingorum.quia nova moneta nunc in tantum minuitur.
De pondere sterlingi.
Item sterlingus debet ponderare .xxxij. grana boni et rotundi frumenti.[9]

Burns assumed that the ounce mentioned here was equal to the English Tower ounce of 450 grains, giving a Tower pound of 5,400 grains (12 oz), and a Scottish pound of 6,750 grains (15 oz).[10] If this is the Tower system, a reference to it temp. David I would be the earliest known, but it has to be admitted that David's authority was often somewhat freely invoked in subsequent centuries.[11] Moreover, the weight of sterling is given as 32 wheat grains. This corresponds to the Troy pennyweight of 24 barley grains.[12] Thus, if it is the Tower ounce mentioned in one chapter of the assize, it is nevertheless definitely a Troy weight equivalent given in the next. In fact a Troy ounce of 480 grains works better throughout. David's assize could then be interpreted as an internally consistent system consisting of: a troy pennyweight of 32 wheat grains equal to 24 barley grains; a troy ounce of 20 of these pennyweights making 480 barley grains or 640 wheat grains to the ounce; a Scottish pound of 15 of these Troy ounces making 7,200 barley grains or 9,600 wheat grains to this Scottish pound. The 12 Troy ounce pound consisted of 5,760 grains, or 240 dwt each of 24 grains. The Scots pound of 15 ounces contained 300 dwt or 25 shillings. The fourteenth-century compiler was, however, aware of the distinction between the pennyweight – 24 grains – and the weight of the penny which was actually in the region of 22.5 grains.[13] Thus he speaks of a reduction

[9] *APS* I.673–4.
[10] E. Burns, *The Coinage of Scotland* (Edinburgh, 3 vols., 1887), I, pp. 228–9.
[11] It has recently been suggested that the Tower system emerged in 1158, being the weight of coin returned to the merchant by the English mint in exchange for 1 pound Troy after the deduction of mintage and seignorage. The arithmetic, however, is not exact. Pamela Nightingale, 'The Evolution of Weight Standards and the Creation of New Monetary and Commercial Links in Northern Europe from the Tenth Century to the Twelfth Century', *EcHR*, 2nd ser. 38 (1985), 205. It was Grierson who first pointed out that the Tower pound is probably later than the Troy pound, *NC*, 7th ser., 4 (1964), Presidential Address, p. xi.
[12] P. Grierson, *Dark Age Numismatics* (London, 1979), article XI, 351. Nightingale, 'The Evolution of Weight Standards', 206, notes the use of the 32 wheat grain pennyweight in the thirteenth-century English *Fleta*.
[13] It is this distinction which is recognized by the emergence of the Tower system, based on a penny of 22.5 grains, giving a Tower pound of 12 ounces, or 5,400 grains. The English penny was certainly stabilized at this 22.5 grain weight in the mid-twelfth century: D.F. Allen, *A Catalogue of English Coins in the British Museum: The Cross*

in the weight of the penny so that there were now 21 to the ounce, or 26s. 3d. to the pound.[14] Burns, working with a 450 grain ounce, believed that the weight of the penny was actually reduced in the reign of Robert Bruce to 21 to the ounce, giving an individual weight of *c.* 21.43 grains, but there is no independent evidence for this.

This illustrates clearly the sort of difficulties which typically attend the interpretation of the documentary evidence for monetary questions. Fortunately in this case the question is of little practical importance. Whether Robert Bruce made a marginal reduction in the weight of the penny or not, it will certainly not have had any effect on prices. In the first place the supposed reduction is too small. Bruce's pennies are not distinguishable by weight from those of Baliol and Alexander.[15] In the second place, even if Bruce pennies were so distinguishable, the total issue was far too small for it to have had any effect on prices. All the Scottish coins in the Aberdeen hoards accounted for less than 3% of the total, a proportion confirmed by a wide range of other Scottish hoards. The Scottish element in the currency of the early fourteenth century was too small for it to have significantly influenced the behaviour of Scottish prices.[16] For all practical purposes it is therefore safe to assume that till around the middle of the fourteenth century transactions were made in Scotland in pence of sterling weight and fineness, whether of Scottish or English origin.

After the death of Robert Bruce almost no pence were struck for some years either in Scotland or England, though halfpennies and

and Crosslets ('Tealby') Type of Henry II (London, 1951), p. xli. It is difficult to believe that Scotland ever attempted a 24 grain standard while England was operating a 22.5 grain one.

[14] 21 pence to the 480 grain Troy ounce works out at 22.8 grains.

[15] Burns' treatment of the weights of Bruce pennies in the Montrave hoard is uncharacteristically flawed, *The Coinage of Scotland*, I, p. 229. The mean weights of the Scottish coins in the two recent Aberdeen hoards was as follows: hoard 1, Alexander III 1.30, Baliol 1.31, Bruce 1.38; hoard 2, Alexander III 1.28, Baliol 1.28, Bruce 1.22; hoards 1 and 2 together, Alexander III 1.29, Baliol 1.30, Bruce 1.32. Obviously the earlier coins have lost marginally more weight, having circulated for longer before the hoards were concealed; the English coins in these two hoards confirm this point.

[16] Many of the same comments apply to Burns' suggestion that Alexander III's second coinage was struck at a slightly lower weight than his first (Burns, *The Coinage of Scotland*, I, p. 229, n. 1). The possible reduction is too small, and the part played by Scottish coins in Scotland in the thirteenth century too limited, for such reductions to have influenced prices. In any case, again, the evidence for such a reduction is by no means certain. Burns found the second coinage of lower average weight than the first, but made no allowance for the fact that the second coinage pennies will ordinarily have remained in circulation for longer than the first. Moreover, when Burns wrote of the reduced weight of the English sterling in 1279 to allow 243d. to be struck to the pound, he was unaware that Henry III had already been striking 242d. to the pound for decades.

farthings were struck on a reduced standard in modest quantities. The Scottish halfpence and farthings of this period are excessively rare. In the mid-1340s England resumed the production of pence, now of sterling fineness but reduced weight, and in 1351 the weight of this penny was stabilized at 18 grains.[17] It seems likely that these reduced-weight English pence were issued at about the weight at which much of the existing (worn) currency was already circulating. There is no evidence that the new issues inflated English prices.[18] In Scotland there was a modest issue of pennies, probably attributable to the period 1351–7, which seems to have been struck at a weight standard of *c.* 16 grains – notably below the 18 grain weight of the contemporary English counterpart.[19] These Scots pennies seem to have provoked the first official English attempt to proscribe Scots coin.[20] Significantly, the English explicitly permitted the continued circulation of old Scots money. However, although this issue does seem to have been weaker than its English counterpart, it does not seem to have been struck in sufficient quantities to have had much effect on Scottish prices. The huge Montrave hoard contained nineteen examples of this coinage, mixed among eighty-two examples of the contemporary English issue, and over 8,000 earlier English pence.

The end of the sterling standard

On David II's return to Scotland from captivity in 1357 he took steps to restore the Scottish issues to match the contemporary English standard of a penny of 18 grains. David also sought and received agreement from Edward III that English and Scots money should again be interchangeable.[21] Ten years later, however, the decision was taken to strike 352d. from the pound of 12 Troy ounces instead of 320d., resulting in a Scots penny of just over 16 grains.[22] For every pound of silver of

[17] It was at this time that groats (4d.), half groats and gold were introduced.

[18] This seems generally to have been true of all the English weight reductions of the later middle ages, and suggests that the English mint was doing no more than take account of the rising value of bullion on the open market. See N.J. Mayhew, 'From regional to central minting, 1158–1464', in C.E. Challis (ed.), *New History of the Royal Mint* (Cambridge, 1992), pp. 83–178.

[19] Burns, *The Coinage of Scotland*, I, p. 232. The average weight of the 30 coins of this type in the Ashmolean–Hunterian Sylloge was 15.8 grains. *SCBI*.

[20] Cochran-Patrick I, p. 6, 12 March 1355.

[21] *ER* II.xcvii, citing Knighton's *Chronicon*, p. 2619. (This seems to be a reference to Roger Twysden's *Historiae Anglicanae scriptores x* edition (London, 1652), pp. 2311–742.) The high standard of the 1357 issue made by Master Jacobus was recommended as a yard-stick in 1366. There is no conclusive evidence in support of Burnett's suggestion that this standard was not maintained for more than a year or two.

[22] Cochran-Patrick I, pp. 1–2, 7 October 1367. The weights of the light groats in the Balleny hoard confirm this, assuming a weight loss about the same as for the heavy

appropriate fineness the Scottish mints paid 27s. 9d., having deducted 7d. seignorage, 11d. for the master moneyer, and 1d. for the warden, from the 29s. 4d. actually made from each pound. This adjustment can be seen as an attempt to bring the intrinsic value of the Scottish coinage more closely into line with the true market price for silver. It may also be seen as a devaluation, which might be expected to discourage imports into Scotland by making them more expensive, while at the same time making Scottish exports seem better value abroad. Although a modern devaluation may be stated in these terms, in the fourteenth century it was more probably seen in bullionist terms as an attempt to restrict the outflow of silver, and to draw it into the Scottish mints – 'propter raritatem pecunie de argento ad presens in regno nostro'.[23] Thus a merchant bringing a Troy pound of silver to Britain was offered a choice between 27s. 9d. in Scottish coin, and 25s. 10d. in English coin.[24] The level of Scottish output at this time[25] suggests a number chose the Scottish option, and the English authorities were quick to respond. In December 1367 Scottish money was declared acceptable in England only as bullion,[26] and in 1373, 1374, and 1387 the English ordered an exchange rate of 3d. sterling to 4d. Scots.[27] By 1390 the English rate for Scots money had sunk to half the value of English money,[28] and in 1393 Scots money was denied currency altogether.[29] In fact the intrinsic content of Robert III's first coinage is known to us from the unusually specific Scots act of 24 October 1393, which calls for 21s. to be struck from 6 Troy ounces (2,880 grains) giving a theoretical fine silver weight of just under 11.5 grains to the penny.[30] Again it is clear that the simple 2:1 exchange rate involves an English undervaluation of the intrinsic content of the Scottish coinage.

groats. It would thus appear that the number of pence struck from the pound was increased by one tenth.

23 Cochran-Patrick, I pp. 1–2.

24 For the English mint price which was 24s. 2d. for a Tower pound of 12 Tower ounces (after payment of seignorage and mintage), see C.E. Challis (ed.), *New History of the Mint* (Cambridge, 1992), p. 705. The larger pound of 12 Troy ounces permitted a further 20d. at 18 grains to be struck.

25 Mayhew, 'Alexander III' pp. 63–4.

26 Cochran-Patrick, I p. 7.

27 Ibid., p. 10. That the terms of issue under Robert II were the same as at the end of the reign of David II appears from the Scots order of 17 June 1385, ibid., p. 8. This document also recommends a valuation of 7s. 8d. Scots for the English noble, a rate significantly more favourable to the Scots coinage. Official valuations whether English or Scottish often deliberately undervalue a competitor's currency.

28 Confirmed in 1398, ibid., p. 15.

29 Ibid., p. 14.

30 Ibid., p. 12. The same document, however, makes it clear that Scots pennies were actually to be struck with extra alloy to make the weight up to a size convenient for everyday use.

During the reign of Robert III, however, a number of complications develops. Early in the reign Robert reintroduced a Scottish gold coinage, now for the first time struck in reasonable quantities. And towards the end of the reign (and possibly during the subsequent Regency) a further, uncertain, weight reduction took place in the Scottish coinage. Robert's first issue groats were struck at approximately 46–8 grains,[31] while his earliest gold lions weighed *c.* 61 grains.[32] The light groats from late in the reign weigh about 28 grains,[33] while the light lions are particularly variable in weight, but have a possible intended weight of *c.* 38 grains.[34]

By the end of the fourteenth century the issues of the Scottish mints were accounting for a much larger proportion of the Scottish currency than had earlier been the case. At the same time the divergence of the weights of Scottish coin from the weights of English coin became more marked. For both these reasons it is reasonable to expect the reduced intrinsic content of the Scottish currency to have had a greater effect on the behaviour of Scottish prices. However, it should also be noted that the English coinage itself saw a reduction in weight in 1411, the weight of the penny falling to 15 grains, that of the noble to 108 grains. The value of bullion was obviously rising, and this makes it difficult to provide a constant measure of value against which to compare the behaviour of prices over time. The English coinage retained its intrinsic value more fully than most other European coinages, and as such provides a possible yard-stick, but it should always be borne in mind that at times England's coinage nevertheless still appears to have been distinctly undervalued. In other words the intrinsic value of English coin may have occasionally been allowed to exceed its face value. The consequences of such an undervaluation would be idle mints, clipped and worn currency, perhaps deflationary pressure on prices, and a general damping down of the economy. Many or all of these features are present in later medieval England. In short, it could be argued that

[31] Burns, *The Coinage of Scotland*, I, pp. 285–6, confirmed by the Fortrose hoard. This gives a theoretical penny sterling content of just under 11.5 grains. Burns arrived at about 46 grains which is a reasonable figure in the light of the weights of surviving examples, but his arithmetic is in fact flawed, and is based on the use of a Tower ounce of 450 grains, despite the explicit use of the Troy ounce of 480 grains used in the text of the 1393 act. Moreover, any calculations are necessarily approximate because of the uncertainty involved in the medieval concept of pure silver.

[32] Burns, *The Coinage of Scotland* I, p. 342.

[33] Ian Stewart, *The Scottish Coinage* (London, 1967), p. 39, gives 28–30 grains. The four coins in the Ashmolean–Hunterian collections average 27.25 grains, *SCBI*. These figures imply a theoretical sterling silver content for the penny of 7 – 7.5 or 6.81 grains.

[34] Stewart, *The Scottish Coinage*, p. 39.

England did not allow its currency to depreciate enough.[35] For this reason comparison with England could tend to produce an unduly unfavourable picture of currency depreciation in Scotland. Yet some reduction in the intrinsic content of the coinage – probably more than occurred in England, though perhaps not as much as occurred in Scotland – will have been a necessary response to the rising value of precious metal.

In the fifteenth century this problem is further complicated by a new variable factor. Whereas in the fourteenth century changes in the intrinsic value of the money had been achieved only by physical changes to the coinage itself, in the fifteenth century government also made alterations by leaving the coins themselves unchanged but giving them a greater nominal value. Unfortunately the documentary record of these changes is incomplete, and a number of uncertainties remains.

After the light coinage of Robert III, itself extremely rare, almost nothing appears to have been struck apart from a few pennies of Edinburgh, Inverness, and Aberdeen, till after James I's return from England in 1424.[36] The hoard record is also very sparse at this time. Thereafter the coinage was composed of gold demies and fleur-de-lis groats and pence struck from *c.* 1424 to 1451. In 1433–4 the value of the groat was raised from 5d. to 6d., at which price it was still quoted in the 1450s. It remains uncertain, however, when the groat was changed from its traditional value of 4d. to 5d.[37] The tables of intrinsic values (below, pp. 138–9) offer a plausible analysis of the Scottish coinage at this period, based on the documents, the coins, and Anglo-Scottish exchange rates, but there are other possible interpretations.[38] The overall picture which emerges is one of a continuing gradual drift downwards in the intrinsic value of Scottish money of account. The currency-adjusted prices referred to elsewhere in this work were derived by multiplying any Scots currency price by the figure in the 'deflator' column, which is merely the Scots to English coinage ratio expressed as a decimal.

[35] Nicholson, 'Scottish Monetary Problems'.

[36] Ian Stewart, 'Scottish Mints', in R.A.G. Carson (ed.), *Mints, Dies and Currency* (London, 1971), pp. 232–3.

[37] The picture is actually more complicated still, since there is evidence of an attempted lowering of face values *c.* 1430–1. On this whole period, see Mayhew, 'The Contemporary Valuation of the Fleur-de-Lis Groats of James I and II', *BNJ*, 58 (1989), 130–2.

[38] Among other complications may be noted the appearance of a 16 ounce Troy pound at the Scottish mints in 1438 and the 1440s. Cochran-Patrick I, pp. 22, 24–7. This provides interesting confirmation that the 16 ounce pound introduced in the weights and measures reform of 1426 did actually operate. *APS* ii. 12. See Chapter 3 and Connor and Simpson, *The Weights and Measures of Scotland.*

In 1451 the fleur-de-lis groats were replaced by crown groats, and an extensive document survives from this time recording the advice of the deputies of the three estates on the matter of the money.[39] This advice calls for the 6d. fleur-de-lis groats to be cried down to 4d., the new crown groats to be equal in intrinsic worth to the English groat and both to be valued at 8d. Scots. For the gold, the existing demies were to be cried down to 6s. 8d. (instead of 9s.) and the new lions, weighing half an English noble, to be worth 6s. 8d. Thus the intention was clearly to restore the Scots money to a value exactly half that of England's coinage. In fact this advice was probably never followed up; although the new crown groat was of broadly equal intrinsic value to the English, both were valued at 12d. Scots, not 8d. This is clear by August 1452 when it was ordained that the English penny was to pass at 3d. Scots.[40] John Laundale's mint account of 1453 continues to speak of 12d. crown groats,[41] as does the Perth Guildry Book.[42] In 1456 the 12d. crown groat, the 6d. fleur-de-lis groat, and the 10s. lion and demy were all confirmed.[43] These arrangements obviously aimed at a ratio of 3 to 1 between the Scottish and the English money throughout the 1450s, and in practice some such rate may have operated for some years before.

James III

The death of James II at the siege of Roxburgh in 1460 had no effect on the coinage, as the young James III's advisers continued the issue of the gold lions and silver crown groats of the previous reign. It is, however, apparent that by the time of James III, if not before, the weight of the crown groats had begun to slide. Valued at 12d. Scots, they had a theoretical weight of 60 grains being struck at 8 to the ounce.[44] These terms of issue corresponded exactly with those of the

[39] Cochran-Patrick I, pp. 19–20, October 1451.
[40] Ibid., p. 21.
[41] Ibid., p. 28.
[42] Marion L. Stavert, 'James II and his Mints: An Unknown Document', *BNJ*, 58 (1988), 132–4. I am most grateful to Mrs Stavert for an early sight of the passages of the Perth Guildry Book relating to the coinage.
[43] Cochran-Patrick I, pp. 21–2.
[44] Holmes, 'A Fifteenth-Century Coin Hoard from Leith', *BNJ*, 53 (1983), 86, gives the Scottish ounce as 471.16 grains. Given the approximate nature of our calculations I have preferred to use 480 grains. The lower figure is based on late sixteenth- and seventeenth-century investigations of English and Scots weights, but Chapter 3 shows that these tended to alter quite markedly over a long period of time, so the application of so late a figure to the fifteenth century is unlikely to be accurate either. It seems better to use the round figure and retain an awareness of its marginal inaccuracy.

English groat. In fact we know that by 1464 the Scottish mint was offering 8s. 9d. for the ounce of burnt silver, and by 1466 that figure had risen to 9s. 2d., so clearly more than eight 12d. groats were being struck from each ounce.[45] Given the weight of surviving examples of the crown groat it seems likely that the Scottish mint was actually aiming at a weight just below that of the contemporary English groat, though close enough to it to justify a tariff of 12d. Scots for both of them.

In 1464, however, the English mint reduced the weight of the groat from 60 grains (8 to the ounce) to 48 grains (10 to the ounce). The initial Scottish response was to reduce the face value of the new English groat to 10d. Scots 'and na derrare',[46] but this, like almost all attempts to stem the rising price of precious metal, failed. In 1467 new higher currency values were proclaimed: the new English groat was set at 12d., the old at 16d., while the crown groat which had already risen to 13d. was now set at 14d., and even the lighter old fleur-de-lis groat reached 8d.[47] Monetary policy, however, remained confused. Black, i.e. base, small change was also struck at this time with a predictable effect on retail prices: 'the pennyworthis ar Rysin wyth the penny and mekle derrar than thai war wont to be'.[48] Parliament complained vociferously on behalf of the rentier classes about the new higher valuations of coin, and some creditors enforced debts at the old rates.[49] An attempt was therefore made to restrain prices and to preserve the value of rents and debts by holding down the face value of coin to the rates in force before the changes of 1467. Accordingly, the new English groat was to be worth 11d. Scots, the old 13d., and the crown groat was set at 12d. and the fleur-de-lis at 6½d.[50] It is difficult to believe that these arrangements, which ignored the trend on the open market, could ever have been satisfactorily enforced, and at some time thereafter, the Scottish mint began a new issue of light groats at 12 to the ounce (40 grains) valued at 12d.[51] This was a significant reduction in the intrinsic

[45] Cochran-Patrick I, pp. 30–1.
[46] Ibid., p. 32.
[47] Ibid.
[48] Ibid., p. 34.
[49] Nicholson, *Scotland: The Later Middle Ages*, pp. 434–5.
[50] Cochran-Patrick I, pp. 34–5.
[51] The first explicit mention of this issue does not occur till 1475, ibid., pp. 37–8. It is worth noting the absence of these groats in the Leith hoard 1470–5, although Burns, *The Coinage of Scotland* II, p. 114 n. 1, records their presence in the Kilmarnock hoard of 1869 together with the thistle-head groat. Nicholson, *Scotland: The Later Middle Ages*, pp. 431–2, notes parliamentary complaints about 'the skantnes of bullioune that is in the realme' dating from 1471 and 1473. While Nicholson interprets these complaints in terms of increased demand for coin, I would see them as evidence of

value of the groat made almost inevitable by the reduction in the weight of the English groat in 1464. Perhaps issued concurrently with the light groats were the new thistle-head groats, at *c.* 77% fine and worth 8d.[52] As already noted, the way for this Scottish reduction had been prepared by the sliding fall in the intrinsic content of the crown groat and its enhanced face value. Interestingly, there is no evidence that the much more sudden English monetary adjustment affected English prices,[53] and it is unlikely that the gradual Scottish changes in the content of the silver coinage at this time affected prices north of the border either. Although Scottish coinage in baser metal did cause inflation and commercial disruption (see below), Scottish silver and gold at this time merely kept in step with changes in England made inevitable by the rising price of precious metal. Thus James III's gold coinage was a model of stability: the earlier lions and even demies were still in circulation, and their values were enhanced to correspond with the 32s. valuation then set on Edward IV's rose noble.[54] There are some indications that the prices of gold coin may have been rising in the 1470s,[55] and the Scottish gold coins struck then – crowns and new riders[56] – were probably valued accordingly, but the unicorns introduced in 1484 were set only at 20s. with the riders still valued at 24s.[57] Similarly, when in 1484 and 1485 it became necessary to effect at least a cosmetic improvement in the coinage to restore confidence after the failure of the debased currencies, the new heavier groat (10 to the ounce) also had a higher face value of 14d.;[58] the ounce of silver was therefore valued at 140d. instead of 144d. making this only a very marginal hardening of the currency compared with the light groat. Thus despite

the inadequacy of the Scots mint price for bullion until the new light groat was introduced.

52 J.E.L. Murray and M.R. Cowell, 'Some Placks and Base Groats of James III of Scotland', in D.M. Metcalf and W.A. Oddy, (eds.) *Metallurgy in Numismatics* (London, 1980), p. 182.

53 I am most grateful to David Farmer for an early sight of his appendices for the *Agrarian History of England and Wales*, II and III, in advance of publication, which allowed me to confirm this point. Thorold Rogers was so impressed by the failure of later medieval English prices to respond to changes in the English currency that he guessed (wrongly) that payments must usually have been made by weight. J.E. Thorold Rogers, *A History of Agriculture and Prices in England, 1259–1793* (Oxford, 7 vols, 1866–1902), IV, pp. 186–93.

54 Cochran-Patrick I, p. 32.

55 Ibid., pp. 37–8; see also Gilbert, 'The Usual Money of Scotland', pp. 131–51.

56 Cochran-Patrick I, p. 45, prints the mint account citing *ER*.

57 J.E.L. Murray, 'The Early Unicorns and the Heavy Groats of James III and James IV', *BNJ*, 40 (1971), 69. By 1488, however, unicorns were quoted at 18s. each, perhaps as a result of a reduction in fineness, ibid., p. 75.

58 Cochran-Patrick I, pp. 39–41.

the various issues, James III's gold and silver coinages were set at very constant values.

Billon

The billon (debased silver) coinage seems to have been more complicated. Scotland had used billon for its small change since the time of Robert III, but this device was intended solely to make inconveniently small amounts of silver into reasonably sized coins. The Leith hoard provides an invaluable glimpse of the billon currency in use in an urban environment in the 1470s. On the basis of this hoard it has been estimated that the pennies of James II may have been struck at about 45 coins to the ounce while James III's lighter issues may have numbered 65 to the ounce.[59] No thorough-going metal analysis of these issues has yet been made but documentary evidence suggests that under James III these pennies were meant to be 5d. fine.[60] If this were also true for James II and the estimates of weight were correct they would indicate that James II's billon pence were struck to a face value of 108d. from every ounce of silver bullion, while under James III the ounce of silver could have been struck into 156 billon pence. These figures fit in extremely well with the known terms of issue for the groats. Indeed, we might actually have expected the billon pence to have been slightly overvalued vis-à-vis the groats, to defray the extra costs of manufacture of the pence.

Under James III the use of billon was extended to larger denominations. In 1471 the 'new alayt groat' had its value revised downwards from 7d. to 6d.[61] This new alloyed groat was for long identified with the thistle-head groat,[62] but this identification has recently been questioned. If the thistle-head groat were the alloyed groat, it would have given an equivalence of about 130d. to the ounce of silver at the 7d. valuation, or 112d. at the 6d. rate. Since the ounce of silver when struck into light James III groats at 12d. had a value of just under 156d., there would be no grounds for resistance to the thistle-head groat valued at 7d. or 6d. Instead the alloyed groat has recently, and

[59] Holmes, 'A Fifteenth-Century Coin Hoard from Leith'.

[60] Like the placks; Cochran-Patrick I, p. 36. This seems to be confirmed by a tentative experimental investigation carried out some years ago which indicated a fineness of about 50% for both James II and III, though some James III pennies were probably significantly baser and others better. Murray, 'The Black Money of James III', p. 119.

[61] Cochran–Patrick I, p. 35.

[62] Burns, *The Coinage of Scotland*, II, pp. 112–14.

convincingly, been identified as the plack,[63] which may therefore be dated before May 1471. With a face value of either 7d. or 6d. these placks would have been heavily overvalued, which would explain the resistance they encountered. An early issue was cried down in July 1473,[64] and refused in Aberdeen on that account in August,[65] but more placks appear to have been struck later in the reign. There is conflicting parliamentary evidence in 1485–6 calling both for their withdrawal and their continued circulation, and in Aberdeen the rule was that they were not to be refused until they were actually cried down.[66] This seems to have been accomplished in the course of 1486 when all placks, including the foreign counterfeits which had evidently complicated matters, were to be accepted at the mints for 2d.[67] An original valuation of 7d. or 6d. for the placks would certainly have been very high, but the later placks and bawbees showed that such overvaluation was by no means out of the question. It has been suggested that before their withdrawal at 2d. they had been current at 4d., which was to become the traditional value of the plack, and at that rate James III's placks would not have been overvalued.[68] However, *Exchequer Roll* accounts for the year 1485–6 provide two examples of accountants receiving allowances of two-thirds against old placks accepted before their crying down, which would argue for a 6d. rate cut to 2d.[69]

It thus appears that James III's billon coinage encountered a certain amount of resistance, and that the chief problem was one of valuation. So long as the need for a petty coinage is great enough some degree of overvaluation can be sustained, but it is important that the overvaluation is not too great and that the supply of the petty coins should not be allowed to exceed demand. This problem was compounded by the appearance of counterfeits which no doubt were very base, confusing the question of the intrinsic value of the whole issue and flooding the market with excess supply. On the whole, however, the billon coinage seems to have been relatively well managed; the authorities did respond to the popular feeling that the placks were initially overvalued, and we only have evidence for their refusal either when they had been officially cried down or when they were plagued by imitations.

[63] Murray and Cowell, 'Some Placks and Base Groats of James III of Scotland', p. 182.
[64] Cochran-Patrick I, p. 36.
[65] ACR VI.263.
[66] ACR VI.921.
[67] May 1485, Cochran-Patrick I, pp. 40–1, but dated 1486? in *APS*.
[68] See Tables 4 and 5. For the 4d. valuation, see Murray and Cowell, 'Some Placks and Base Groats of James III of Scotland', p. 183.
[69] *ER* IX. 445,449.

Black Money

All these problems appear in a still more acute form with the black money. The most authoritative recent numismatic examination of the black money question identifies these coins as the regal copper farthings and the Crux Pellit coppers.[70] The documentary evidence allows us to identify two particular periods of black money in the 1460s[71] and the early 1480s. The need for copper farthings specifically for the purchase of bread and ale was articulated in parliament in 1466, and it was suggested they be legal tender for larger transactions in amounts up to 1s. in the pound. A year later parliament was already calling for the restoration of the old white small change and an end to the black issues, but although some black halfpennies were reduced to farthings the mint accounts show that black money was struck in the period to June 1468, and in the same year parliament spoke of permitting the use of farthings for business up to 3s. in the pound. In 1469 foreign black money was prohibited but base Scottish money was clearly still legal tender in 1470 when an Aberdeen baker was amerced for refusing the farthing.[72] In any base issue it is important that too many pieces should not be struck. The genuine need for small change would guarantee continued acceptance of an overvalued coin, but if the coins became too plentiful demand for them would melt away. By and large, despite predictable opposition from the hard money lobby,[73] this first period of black money does not seem to have caused excessive difficulties. If they continued to be struck and/or used in the 1470s they have left no trace of disturbance in the historical record.[74]

In 1482–3, however, black money was the subject of a rash of documentary references, making it clear that at this time it became an issue of major political and commercial importance. The entry in the Short Chronicle of 1482 which describes how the black money contributed to the attempted coup d'état of that year is worth quoting in full:

[70] Murray, 'The black money of James III'. This source has been closely followed by Norman Macdougall, *James III: A Political Study* (Edinburgh, 1982), pp. 158–62. I am also grateful to Nicholas Holmes who tells me that copper farthings are now being found in excavations as plentifully as the Crux Pellit issue.

[71] Cochran-Patrick I, pp. 32–5, 43–5.

[72] ACR VI.108.

[73] Nicholson, *Scotland: The Later Middle Ages*, p. 436.

[74] In 1478 parliament demanded an end to all minting, but there is no evidence that this was occasioned by black money problems rather than any other kind of monetary difficulty. Cochran-Patrick I, pp. 38–9. Nicholson, *Scotland: The Later Middle Ages* pp. 435–6, convincingly explains this ban on minting as an attempt to stop the reminting of existing Scots coin, there being no such objection to the coining of newly imported bullion.

Anno domini m cccc lxxxii thir was ane gret hungyr and deid in Scotland for the boll of meill was for four pundis for thir was blak cunzhe in the relame strikkin And ordinyt be king James the thred half pennys and three penny pennys Innumerabill of coppir And thai yeid twa zere and mair And als was gret were betuix Scotland and Ingland and gret distructioun throw the weris was of corne and catell And thai twa thyngs causyt baitht hungar and derth and mony pure folk deit of hunger And that sammyn zere in the moneth of Julij the king of scotland purposyt till haif passyt in Ingland with the power of scotland and passyt on gaitwart to lawdyr and thar the lordis of Scotland held thair consaill in the kirk of lauder and cryit downe the blak silver and thai slew ane part of the kingis housald and other part thai banysyt and thai tuke the king him self and thai put him in the castell of Edynburgh in firm kepyng for he wrocht mair the consaell of his housald at war bot sympill na he did of thame that was lordis And he was haldyn in the castell of Edinburgh fra the magdalyne day quhill michaelmess And than the wictall grew better chaip for the boll that was for four punds was than for xxii s. ('xxxi' erased) of quhyt silver.[75]

This suggests that this more troublesome black money may have been introduced in 1480, matters only reaching a head two years later. The Aberdeen evidence, however, suggests that the black money burst onto the scene quite suddenly in 1482. Perhaps it was only then that it was struck in excessive quantities. We read first of the refusal of the king's copper money on 26 March 1482,[76] and subsequently there is evidence of widespread commercial disruption. Bakers especially complained about the prices at which they were obliged to sell bread, and ale and meal prices were also inflated contrary to the assize. Refusing to sell was as much an offence as selling above the fixed price, while in at least one case offering to buy with white money rather than black was interpreted as forestalling. Inevitably the black money valuations of 'hard' money rose: the English groat (Henry VI) moved up to 1s. 4d. and then to 2s., while the Scots crown groat reached 22d., and James III's light groats fetched 16d. [77] Aberdeen also provides the earliest evidence for the crying down of the black money which had apparently occurred before 19 July 1482 when a disputed payment was made.[78]

[75] Macdougall, *James III*, p. 312.

[76] ACR VI.727. There were a number of further cases in July of that year. For the exceptional conditions affecting Aberdeen bakers this year, see also ACR VI.728, 747.

[77] References to the black money: ACR VI.727–8, 740–9, and for a series of less informative cases mostly to do with the repayment of debts complicated by the debasement, 774, 766, 788, 789, 792, 795, 806, 832, 866, 886, 895, 916.

[78] ACR VI.743. At a court held on 23 July 1482, David Hil claimed to have received black money in repayment of 15 English groats on 19 July. At the court Hil claimed that the black money was cried down before 19 July. The fact that he accepted the black money in the first place suggests that the news had not reached Aberdeen by Friday 19 July but had obviously done so by 23 July. James III was held in Edinburgh,

The men who had made the black money were paid off in July 1483,[79] and law suits about the payment of debts complicated by black money continued to come to court throughout 1483 and into 1484 and 1485 (when placks become an issue). Thus on the whole the Aberdeen evidence suggests that the black money incident, though extremely severe, was essentially short-lived.

The overall picture is one in which the gold and silver currency appears stable, the billon somewhat less so, and the copper subject to periodic crisis. This pattern is a familiar one elsewhere in Europe. The requirement of international trade for a strong currency was met by the gold and silver; the needs of the urban poor for an adequate supply of small change called for a series of baser issues, but mostly the good metal coinage was insulated from the petty currency by limitations placed on its validity. Such limitations seem to have been essentially de facto rather than de iure. Thus Comptroller Alexander Lesly refused a payment from the receiver of ferms of Kinclevin for the Pentecost term 1482 because it was in black money, but the auditors in 1487 granted the receiver an allowance against his losses incurred as a result.[80] Receivers of revenue, collecting a number of small payments but settling their accounts with a single larger payment, must often have been in a difficult position. Similarly, retailers who bought large quantities with good coin but sold small amounts necessarily for petty money were trapped between the upper and nether millstones of the Scottish monetary system, and it is their difficulties which loom largest in the Aberdeen records when the separate parts of the system fell out of step.[81] However, these records suggest that at the local level serious disruption was restricted to the crisis of 1482 and its aftermath. Massive issues of base coin could severely damage commercial life and undermine the precious metal currency, but the speed with which this ill-considered experiment

the deliberations at Lauder completed, by the feast of Mary Magdalen, Monday 22 July.

[79] Macdougall, *James III*, p. 159.

[80] *ER* IX.480. Comptroller Thomas Symsone similarly refused £105 in placks before their demonetisation, and the chamberlain of Moray won an allowance for them, 1486–7. *ER* IX.363. We may thus conclude that neither comptroller had any legal justification for refusing to accept large payments in black money, but it seems likely that such refusals were not uncommon.

[81] Thus on 11 July 1482 the council commanded the fleshers, brewers, and baxters to provide food at stable prices, while simultaneously confirming the currency of the black money. See H.W. Booton, 'Burgesses and Landed Men in North-East Scotland in the Later Middle Ages: A Study in Social Interaction' (Aberdeen University PhD Thesis, 1987), p. 442, citing ACR VI.742–3. One may note, however, the prosperity of at least one baxter, William Buchan, in Aberdeen. Nevertheless, the measure of his prosperity and perhaps the secret of his success lay in diversification into property, the wool trade, and flour milling.

was terminated is impressive. For the reign as a whole monetary changes are unlikely to have caused major price variations, and the Anglo-Scottish exchange rate moved only gradually above 3+:1.

James IV

At first sight the coinage of James IV appears straightforward. The gold consisted of unicorns (at 18s.) continuing from the issue of James III, and a very few crowns. Silver groats also continued as issued by James III at 10 to the ounce (48 grains) valued at 14d., though James III's portrait was quickly replaced by a more traditional facing bust in imitation of the English groat with which it was at least nominally equal. Probably around 1496 the groats were reduced in weight to *c.* 40 grains, 12 to the ounce, but their valuation was also reduced to 12d., so the intrinsic value of the groats remained unchanged.[82] A list of coin values compiled in Aberdeen in 1501 confirms these values:

the old (pre-1464) English groat 16d.
the new English groat 14d.
the old Scottish crown groat (1451 – *c.* 1467) 14d.
the new crown groat (James III and IV heavy groat 1484 – *c.* 1496) 14d.
the Spurrit groat (David II and Robert II) 16d.
the new Spurrit groat (James IV light groat, and possibly James III mullet groats?) 12d.
the fleur-de-lis groat (James I and II) 8d.

Half groats were also issued, and even a 'penny' of fine silver worth 3d. Scots. Billon Scots pennies, however, seem to have been valued at a halfpenny, at any rate by 1501.[83] As James IV's reign progressed, billon, especially in the shape of 4d. placks, began to assume growing importance. The parliament of March 1503/4 saw a number of bullionist measures to prevent the outflow of gold and silver and to encourage its 'homebringing'. The currency of worn and cracked silver was specifically

[82] The heavy groats had actually been permitted to be struck at 12s. to the ounce of sterling silver – i.e. ten 48 grain groats *and* 4d. – though without any explicit recognition of where the extra 4d. would be stolen from. In fact the groats would have been struck fractionally, and imperceptibly, light. A limit of 1 ounce in pennies to every 40 ounces of groats was set on the number of these pennies permitted to be struck.

[83] ACR VIII.3,1501. The valuations of gold coin were as follows: rose noble 35s., Harry noble 31s., angel 23s.4d., Scots rider 23s., unicorn 18s., demy 13s.4d., . . .? lyone 18s., licht lione 10s., old French crown 14s., [crown] of the sun 14s.6d., 'rall' of franche 15s.6d., lew 17s. ?6d., . . . noble 30s., Flemish rider 15s./16s., Rinsche gudling 10s.6d., postlate gudling 6s.8d., . . . crown of Bertane 13s.

confirmed.[84] Clearly, the silver coinage was in difficulties. The first documentary evidence for James IV billon placks occurs in a coinage account included in the *Treasurer's Accounts* for February 1505 – August 1506.[85] Since mint accounts for the preceding period do not survive, it is possible that placks may have been struck a little earlier, but only old (James III) placks and half placks (at 4d. and 2d.) are mentioned in the Aberdeen 1501 list. Once introduced, however, placks were to become the dominant issue during the last part of the reign of James IV, and their issue continued thereafter till 1526.

The apparent simplicity of James IV's coinage in fact conceals a reduction in the fineness of the gold and the billon issues.[86] This explains fluctuations in the valuation of the gold unicorn, which seems to have been valued first in 1485 at 20s., before falling to 18s. by 1488. The 18s. valuation held good for much of James IV's reign but rose at some time between 1508 and 1511 to 20s. again. This enhanced value reflects not a restoration of the earlier fineness, but the falling value of the Scots money of account resulting from what appears to have been quite heavy debasement of the placks. The importance of this reduction in fineness extends beyond the plack coinage. Because the fine silver coinage remained almost unchanged, holders of bullion could have received a much higher mint price for their silver if it was coined into debased placks rather than sterling silver groats.[87] As a result silver issues almost completely stopped in the later part of the reign.[88] One of the few surviving accounts illustrates the process vividly.[89] In this account the crown coined 177.5 ounces silver from its own melted plate into good silver 12d. groats; this silver yielded 172.4d. per ounce.[90] However, the crown opted to coin a much larger quantity

[84] *APS* II.242–6.

[85] Cochran-Patrick I, p. 52.

[86] Murray, 'The Early Unicorns and the Heavy Groats of James III and James IV', 92–4, for the gold; Murray, 'The Black Money of James III', p. 119, for the billon.

[87] In fact, if the crown took the lion's share of the profit with a very high seignorage rate, the mint price paid to the bullion holder need not have been so very high.

[88] I am grateful to Lord Stewartby for the observation that throughout the sixteenth century the Scottish mint had a tendency to strike either silver or billon at any one time, but not both.

[89] Cochran-Patrick I, p. 53. *Treasurer's Account* for 25 Aug. 1511–14 Aug. 1512.

[90] This exceeds the published rate for silver in fine groats which was set at 144d. per ounce sterling silver (i.e. 156d. per ounce pure silver). Either the silver in the melted amphora had been better than coinage fine, or the rare Roman lettering groats (Burns, *The Coinage of Scotland*, 698A, p. 182, 199) were of lower weight or fineness. Burns knew of two examples weighing 31.5 and 35.7 grains, against a theoretical weight of 40 grains. Mrs Murray has kindly informed me of a third example now known, weighing 35.8 grains.

These pieces were specially struck for the Maundy ceremony. See Ian Stewart, 'Some Scottish Ceremonial Coins', *PSAS*, 98 (1964–6), 254–75.

of its silver plate into placks. Just under 536 ounces were coined into placks to the value of £611, a yield of 273.6d. per ounce. In other words, one could make about 100d. per ounce more by coining bullion into placks rather than into groats.[91] Not surprisingly, this rate of return attracted a large amount of silver to the mint for conversion to billon placks: the £5,793 4s. 10½d. which the crown received in seignorage is the highest annual sum made by the mint recorded in any of the surviving accounts for the first half of the sixteenth century.[92] The fragmentary accounts also suggest that this process may have been going on since at least 1505,[93] though it was perhaps only at the very end of the reign that placks so came to dominate the currency as a whole as to affect the valuation of Scots gold, or of other foreign currencies in terms of £ s. d. Scots.

As noted above, the unicorn's face value rose from 18s. Scots to 20s. sometime between 1508 and 1511, while the Scots rate for the English angel increased somewhat more from 23s. 4d./24s. to 28s. A normal Anglo-Scots exchange rate of 1:3.5 (or 3.6) thus moved up to 1:4.2. The Scots rate against the franc (i.e. livre tournois) moved somewhat earlier: in 1501 and 1502 the franc was set at 8s. or 9s. Scots; from 1504 through to 1512 it is quoted at 10s. or once at 9s. 6d.[94]

[91] This is to ignore the mintage and seignorage charges, the levels of which are not known. For the later bawbee coinage the crown seized the lion's share of the profit on the debasement by means of very high seignorage charges. A high seignorage charge could help prolong the ignorance of the uninformed Scottish public about the true fineness of the coins. Without an assay the public's only guide to fineness was the mint price which need not rise too dramatically if the king pocketed most of the profits of debasement.

[92] Challis, 'Debasement', p. 180.

[93] Cochran-Patrick I, p. 52, and Challis, 'Debasement', p. 180. The yield then was only about 204.8d. per ounce. The difference could have arisen either because the placks were then of better quality, or because the original plate on this occasion was not as fine, or if the profit on the transaction was calculated after deduction of costs.

[94] For these rates see *TA*. See also ACR IX.170, 681, for the 10s. rate in 1513 and 1517. It is more difficult to interpret the rates for specific French coins. The 'French crown' occurs throughout the *TA* right up to 1532 at 14s. but the French crown of weight is quoted at 16s. and more usually at 18s. through to 1517. By 1538–42 it stood at 22s. It is not really satisfactory to read the crown as the écu à la couronne and the crown of weight as the écu au soleil, since a 2s. or 4s. difference would be too great. More reasonably the Aberdeen list of 1501 cites the 'old French crown' at 14s., and the crown of the sun at 14s. 6d. It may be that the écu au soleil was accorded a rising rate as the Scots currency fell on the exchange, while the écu à la couronne, which ceased to be struck after 1475, had its value frozen at 14s. because of its age and presumed wear. Thus at Aberdeen we meet French crowns at 14s. in 1512 and 1513, and at 17s. in 1511, this last presumably being the crown of weight (ACR IX.53, 85, 269). To complicate matters still further, by the 1530s a 'crown' seems to have come to mean 10s. See ACR XIII.419; XV.427.

It thus appears that although the Scottish exchange rate did fall against sterling and the franc in the first decade of the sixteenth century, it did not fall anything like as far as the debasement of the placks might have led us to expect.[95] A number of factors might help to explain this. In the first place Scottish placks and pennies were intended essentially for domestic use, international trade being carried on by the Scots either in foreign coin or in Scottish silver and gold. In this way the international market would have been at least partially insulated from Scottish domestic debasement. However, since even domestic commodity prices in this decade appear to have remained basically stable, it would seem that for the most part the government was able to enforce its valuations without either widespread refusal of the money or a general hoisting of prices.

The Aberdeen evidence, which registered the effects of serious monetary disturbance resulting from the black money of James III, is worth examining closely for similar signs at this point. They do provide one reference to the refusal of the king's money on 8 November 1504.[96] There are, of course, also the usual amercements for infringing the price statutes, but these are commonplace also in periods of sound money. What may be additionally significant are the indications that many retail traders may have been experiencing a common difficulty, as is perhaps suggested by the reminders that retailers must be prepared to sell in the smallest units as well as in larger ones, and by the repeated assertion that, bakers especially, were under obligation to serve the town and could not simply refuse to sell.[97] These are exactly the kind of developments which might be expected to arise from the difficulties of retailers who bought in bulk but sold piecemeal for base money. It must, however, be admitted that trading regulations of this kind are not restricted to periods of monetary difficulty, and there is only one reference to refusal of the money.

On balance, therefore, it appears that James IV did manage to enforce the acceptance of his placks at 4d. without causing severe disruption of trade or prices. Although the suspicion remains that some squalls did perhaps affect the domestic economy, they did not amount to

[95] The ounce of pure silver in England yielded 43d.; coined into placks it yielded 274d. Scots. This gives a ratio of over 6:1.

[96] ACR VIII.391. Donald Baxter (his profession may be significant) was amerced for refusing the king's money; in future he or any other offender was to be placed in the pillory.

[97] ACR VIII.519: victual to be sold in smallest units as well as large 1505; 784: thirty-three brewers amerced together 1507; 806: fishmongers not to refuse to sell pennyworths 1508; 1020: bakers conspiring together not to bake 1509.

anything like the monetary storm James III had caused. It seems that demand for coin was adequate to guarantee acceptance of the billon despite its overvaluation. Supply of the billon issues may also have been carefully controlled. Although there is no evidence for this under James IV, it is implicit in some of the information we have from the 1530s and 1540s that billon was not being coined continually for anyone who brought in the metal, but rather that minting in billon had to be expressly authorized and only for limited, stated, quantities of metal.[98] Thus restrictions on the quantities issued may have helped sustain demand. It is also apparent that although the valuation on the billon may have been high compared with the values set of the silver coinage, they were not as severely out of line with the values of continental billon coins.[99]

More Scottish hoards from this period would also add to our knowledge of the money in use, as opposed to the types and valuations of the recent issues. From the limited number of finds already on record, it appears that although early in the reign gold, silver, and billon were in use side by side,[100] by the end of the reign billon appears to dominate the currency.[101] Such silver or gold which was in use was likely to be foreign, or fifteenth century, or both.[102]

Failing finds, documentary evidence very occasionally provides information about the actual coins which made up a given sum. The detailed composition of a payment made by the archdeacon of Dunkeld to the bishop's chamberlain in the period March 1514 to January 1516 was as follows: '£14 13s. 4d. in plaikis, 5 French scuta of weight, 2 half-

[98] *ALCPA*, p. 399, where a projected issue of 2d. fine placks is limited to 120 stone, and pp. 508–9, where the profit of coining 1 stone was assigned to meet a debt.

[99] A thorough-going examination of the intrinsic content of the placks of James IV and V has yet to be undertaken. James III's undoubtedly finer placks were probably 5d. fine; James V's bawbees were 3d. fine; a proposed issue of placks in 1533 was to be 2d. fine. The weights of surviving placks are very variable. Much more precise information is available for the grand blanc of Francis I of France, valued at 12 denier tournois, about 2.6 to 2.8 grammes, around 4d. fine (Jean Lafaurie and Pierre Prieur, *Les Monnaies des Rois de France*, II (Paris, 1956), p. 22). In Scotland this 'greite blank of Fraunce' was accepted at 6d. Scots, *ALCPA*, pp. 186–7, Oct. 1523), corresponding to the exchange rate of 10s. Scots to the franc or livre tournois. Valued at 6d. Scots, the ounce of pure silver coined into grands blancs would have yielded a value of 207.69d. Scots. Rated at 4d. Scots, yielding 273.6d. Scots per ounce pure silver, the placks were certainly lighter and baser than the grand blanc.

[100] See the Perth 1920, and Whitburn hoards, both probably concealed fairly soon after 1496.

[101] The Creggan and Barr hoards, both concealed early in the reign of James V, were entirely billon; in the former hoard placks predominated, in the latter pennies.

[102] See the Mauchline hoard.

unicorns each of the value of 10s, in all £20 3s. 4d.'[103] The importance of placks and foreign gold, and the complete absence of Scottish silver, is confirmed by such sources. A similar account exists of a payment of some 300 marks made in 1521.[104] At this date silver coin is totally lacking, in this payment at any rate, but billon accounts for nearly £70 of the total sum. The vast majority of the gold coin which made up the balance was foreign.[105] In all there must have been just under 140 gold coins and nearly 4,000 billon (if chiefly placks rather than pennies). It seems clear that by the beginning of James V's reign Gresham's law had caused the billon to drive the silver out of the circulation.

James V

James V, or rather his mother, and subsequently the Lord Governor, struck no silver at all until 1526, but the issue of placks continued, probably as prolifically as under James IV. In 1515 the Lords of Council began to express concern,[106] and by 1517 the refusal of placks was becoming so serious a problem that the Lords of Council took action.[107] The public were trying to distinguish the quality of different placks on the basis of their colour, but the Lords asserted that all the placks of James IV and V were to be accepted irrespective of colour. They blamed current difficulties on counterfeiters, both at home and abroad, and ordered experts to sit in burgh markets across the land to distinguish true placks from false.[108] The appearance of counterfeits[109] confirms the

[103] *Rentale Dunkeldense, being Accounts of the Bishopric (AD 1505–1517),* with Myln's 'Lives of the Bishops' (AD 1483–1517), trs. and ed. Robert K. Hannay, with a note on the cathedral church by F.C. Eeles, SHS, 2nd ser., 10 (1915), p. 265.

[104] Cochran-Patrick I, p. 67.

[105] This is to regard the eagle crowns not as the Scottish pattern, none of which are known today, but as the Flemish crowns of Charles V which bear an eagle; confirmation that eagle crowns may have been foreign is to be found in *ALCPA*, p. 379 (1532).The other foreign coins present were angels, French crowns, and a couple of ducats. It must, however, be admitted that none of the three gold coins of Charles V struck for the Low Countries with an eagle exactly corresponds with the crown (H. Enno van Gelder and Marcel Hoc, *Les Monnaies des Pays-Bas Bourgnignons et Espagnols 1434–1713* (Amsterdam, 1960), nos. 183–5), while his couronne au soleil which does correspond, does not feature the eagle (no. 186). Grierson preferred to see this eagle crown as Scottish: 'The Eagle Crown: A Gold Coin of the Minority of James V of Scotland', *BNJ*, 28 (1955–7), 656–8.

[106] Cochran-Patrick I, p. 60.

[107] Ibid., p. 61.

[108] Countrymen's use of coin was explicitly recognized, though they also had to consult experts in the burghs. For more evidence of forgery, see *ALCPA*, pp. 38, 110, 270 (1515, 1518, 1527). A number of false placks may be seen in the Museum of London.

[109] One William White, who worked as a potter at the mint, was identified as a false coiner in 1515. I am grateful to Mrs Murray for these references. *TA* IV.272, V.8.

impression that the royal valuation of legitimate placks was proving more or less successful; private enterprise at home and abroad was quick to follow a scheme which permitted base placks to be valued significantly above their intrinsic content. But the success of the scheme was to prove its undoing. Either because the crown was unable to resist the temptation to coin excessive numbers of placks, or because the market was flooded with counterfeits – or perhaps for both reasons – combined with a slowly dawning awareness on the part of the general Scottish public, resistance to the placks began to grow.

From around 1524 Scottish monetary policy shifted against billon and more in favour of gold and silver. The values fixed on foreign billon were reduced, the French grand blanc falling from 6d. to 5d., while the values quoted for gold coin in Scots money of account were enhanced. In an attempt to stem the flow of gold abroad, parliament raised the rates for the rose noble to 44s., the Harry noble to 40s., the angel to 30s., and ducats, previously at 19s., to 20s.[110]

By overvaluing the placks, government had inevitably undervalued gold and silver, for if they had also overvalued gold and silver in terms of the nominal values set on the coinage, commodity prices would have had to rise sharply and the exchange rate fall, just as had occurred as a result of the debasements of the first half of the fifteenth century. Debasement of the petty currency alone, combined with vigorously enforced price control in the burghs, delayed the day of reckoning, but caused a flight of hard gold and silver money. As part of the attempt to stem this flow, a new silver coinage was ordered in 1526, and the issue of placks was halted.[111] The gold unicorns were also replaced by new Abbey crowns.

There had, of course, also been changes in England, where the angel was now enhanced to 7s. 6d. English (from 6s. 8d.), and the 4d. groat reduced in weight to *c.* 42.68 grains.[112] Thus the new Scottish groat at 11 to the ounce was struck at approximately the same weight as that in England, but at a reduced fineness of 10d. 2 grains. The traditional Scottish practice of striking coin just below the intrinsic levels prevailing in England was re-established. In Scotland, however, the resulting coin, with handsome Renaissance-style portrait, was valued at 18d. Scots, giving an Anglo-Scots exchange ratio of about 1:4.5 ignoring the better

Registrum secreti sigilli Scotorum: The Register of the Privy Seal, ed. M. Livingstone (1908–) I, nos. 2594, 2633.

110 Cochran-Patrick I, p. 54. Searchers were also set on the ports to enforce the old bullionist legislation, ibid., p. 55.

111 Ibid., pp. 62–3. The Linlithgow hoard, which contained James V silver and billon together, shows that the existing placks remained in circulation. In October 1527 it was still necessary to arrange searches for false placks. *ALCPA*, p. 270.

112 The English penny thus fell in weight from 12 to 10.66 grains.

fineness of the English piece. It may have been this high valuation for silver which encouraged Hochstetter, the mint master for the time in Scotland, to promise the crown an income of at least £3,000 a year from the mint.[113] Every ounce minted would yield a total face value of 198d. Scots,[114] constituting a significant mark-up in price compared with the groats of James IV. Thus the restoration of a reasonable silver coinage to replace the placks was only achieved by setting a high face value on the groats. Although the new coins looked like a great improvement on the placks, the face values set on the silver contained in both issues were much more closely aligned, allowing placks and silver to circulate side by side. Any other policy would have been severely deflationary. In fact the mint income accounted for by the treasurer in the late 1520s and 1530s averaged around £450 p.a. If this was the total income generated by the mint, though far below the optimistic £3,000 figure, it represented a reasonable and fairly consistent return considering the relatively sound money in production at the time.

The new Abbey crown, struck at 9 to the ounce of gold and just over 21 carats fine was worth 20s., compared with the value set on gold for the old unicorns which were originally struck at 8 to the ounce and valued at 20s. The valuation of the gold in the new crowns then corresponded with the 30s. rate for the angel, but taking no account of the superior fineness of the English coin.

Nevertheless, the attempt to restore a coinage of gold and silver soon came under fire. It was not long before the old complaints about export of money resurfaced,[115] and in 1533 the king ordered the striking of six score stone weight of alloyed money 2d. fine 'in plakkis or uthir money as thai [the treasurer and comptroller] sall think expedient'.[116]

[113] Cochran-Patrick I, p. 65, 1527.

[114] According to Hochstetter's contract mintage was charged on this sum at 20s. a pound (i.e. 15d. an ounce). In 1531 silver was bought from the mines at 168d. the ounce (*ALCPA*, pp. 360–1), which allowing 15d. mintage and 15d. seignorage works out at 198d. In 1537 twelve silver spoons from Glamis were sold to the mint at 168d. to the ounce (*ER* xvii.161.) Gold, however, was bought from the mines at £6 10s. though it was coined at £9 the ounce (see below). Either the mined gold was below coinage fineness or the rate of seignorage and/or mintage was excessively high.

[115] Cochran-Patrick I, p. 56, 1532, 1535. Also *ALCPA*, p. 398, where the king proposed a 20 carat gold crown 'becaus that the gold als wele cunzeit as uncunzeit is transportit and takin daly furth of our realm', 17 March 1533. Foreign forgeries evidently remained a problem, for a burgess of Dundee was sent to Flanders in 1527 'for serching of fals pennyis' (*TA* V.318).

[116] *ALCPA*, p. 399, 2 March 1533. Both this and the previous king's letter (see n. 115) were entered in the council book under 22 March. The call for a resumption in the issue of placks was explicitly fiscal in purpose, being justified by the 'urgent necessite and defalt of money to furnis our expens', and because 'the wele and defence of our realm and dressing of our gud materis . . . can nocht be furnist uthirways at this present tyme'.

A particular variety of James V plack has been associated with this issue,[117] but this can only have been a modest issue. However, no such reservation attaches to the new billon issue of 1538 which was substantial. Although the mint master, Acheson, declined to strike the new coins,[118] it did not prove difficult to find someone else less scrupulous. Richard Wardlaw's contract provided for the mint to buy fine silver at 17s. (204d.) an ounce. It was then debased to 3d. fine permitting the ounce of fine silver to be struck into sixty-four coins each set at 6d., giving a face value of 32s. (384d.). Mintage was charged at 5.625s. (67.5d.) and seignorage at 9.375s. (112.5d.) per ounce of fine siver.[119] Not surprisingly, the sums received by the treasurer from the mint leap into thousands of pounds, giving a similar yield to that enjoyed by James IV from his placks.[120] Once again it became profitable for the crown to send its plate to the mint.[121] Equally, counterfeiters were quick to try to issue their own versions of the new billon.[122] Wardlaw apparently quickly withdrew from mint affairs and Acheson returned, but it was the master of the mint, Alexander Orok of Sillebawby, who gave his name to the new billon issue of 'bawbees'. Predictably the Scottish exchange rate began to fall as a result of the bawbee debasement. The angel, set at 30s. to 32s. in the early to mid-1530s was quoted at 34s. in 1539 and 1540 (i.e. 1:4.5+). Also, as before, good silver coinage ceased altogether, but reasonably sound gold issues continued, helped by Scottish mined gold from Crawford Muir. The Abbey crowns were replaced by a new 'ducat' with a portrait of James V. The new coin was valued at 3 marks (40s.) and was meant to weigh about 88 grains of gold 23 carats fine. This compares with the Abbey crown set at 20s. for about 53 grains of gold 21.5 carats fine.[123]

Tables 4–7[124] permit an overview, and a number of observations may be made. Clearly the ounce of precious metal was struck into an ever

[117] Stewart, *The Scottish Coinage*, fig. 301. See also J.E.L. Murray, 'The Organisation and Work of the Scottish Mint 1358–1603', in *Coinage in Medieval Scotland*, p. 165 and n. 101.

[118] Burns, *The Coinage of Scotland*, II, pp. 264–5, with references to the Hopetoun MSS.

[119] For Wardlaw's contract, which contains an interesting list of mint equipment and appears to have escaped the notice of earlier numismatists, see *ALCPA*, pp. 472–4.

[120] Challis, 'Debasement', p. 180.

[121] Cochran-Patrick I, p. 60, 7 September 1541–16 August 1542, when the mint price had evidently fallen to 16s. 3.5d. Burns, *The Coinage of Scotland*, II, p. 264, notes it at 17s. again in 1543.

[122] One John McKesoun imported false coin *c.* 1540 (*TA* VII.244), and in 1542 a false coiner was caught in Wigtown (*TA* VIII.94).

[123] Burns, *The Coinage of Scotland*, II, p. 250, citing the Hopetoun MS. Burns' reservations about the fineness of the ducat would seem to be unfounded; see Murray 'The Early Unicorns and the Heavy Groats of James III and James IV', 92.

[124] The information contained in Tables 4–7 is derived from the text above and the notes cited there. Small discrepancies arise between the tables and the text since the tables

larger number of pence. Put another way, this means that any given unit of account – £ s. d. – had a steadily falling precious metal content. Tables 4–7 show that this process occurred both in England and in Scotland, though more markedly in the latter. It was in fact a process discernible over all of Europe at this time. Occasional attempts were made from time to time to reverse the process and strengthen the coinage, but such attempts were almost always of short duration, and sometimes amounted to no more than a proposal which was never properly implemented. The changing metal content of the money of account means that commodity prices, expressed in the money of account of the time, are difficult to interpret. In short, the yard-stick is not constant. However, because the value of the precious metal itself was not constant either, it would equally be a mistake to convert prices to pure metal content only.

In addition to largely involuntary changes in the Scottish money brought about by the rising value of precious metal, some Scottish monetary changes were deliberately made with specific policy objects in view. Sometimes the motive was fiscal, designed to raise cash for the crown. The billon coinages of the sixteenth century are the most obvious examples, although there may have been an unstated fiscal element on other occasions. At other times the intention was to draw bullion to the Scottish mints to supply a clearly felt shortage of coin within Scotland. Whatever the motive, the Scottish mint does seem to have allowed its currency to weaken beyond the point made inevitable by the rising value of precious metal.

In an attempt to neutralize the effects of Scottish debasement, while at the same time recognizing that bullion prices were rising, we have used the English mint valuation of silver as a deflator of Scottish prices. Although the English mint valuation was by no means always the 'true' price – at times it seems to have lagged behind the price of bullion on the open market – it does permit some allowance to be made for the rising value of metal, without in any sense overinflating prices.

We have preferred to use the silver deflator rather than the gold (from which at some periods it differed slightly) because Scottish silver came closer to dominating the circulation in Scotland than did Scottish gold. For international payments, where gold naturally played a larger part, foreign coins were probably always important.

If prices are to be compared with one another over time – a hazardous exercise – a new light may be thrown on the subject by multiplying each price by the appropriate deflator for the period. The resulting

calculate the values of an ounce of pure metal, while the text, based more closely on the original sources, often calculates on the basis of an ounce of metal coinage fine.

Table 4. *The value of silver in the Scottish and English medieval silver coinage*

Date	Wt Scot. penny (gr)	Wt Eng. penny (gr)	Scot.: Eng. exchange	Wt Scot. groat (gr)	d. Scot./oz pure Ag	Wt Eng. groat (gr)	d. Eng./oz pure Ag	Scot: Eng.	deflator
Bruce	21.43?	22.2	1 : 1						
1351	c. 16.0	18.0	1+: 1						
1357	c. 18.0 (72gr groat)	18 (72gr groat)	1 : 1						
1367				61	34	72	29	1.17:1	0.85
1393				46	45	72	29	1.56:1	0.64
1400s				c. 28	74	72–60	29–35	2.6/2.1:1	0.39–0.47
1420s				c. 36	58	60	35	1.67:1	0.6
					or 72	60	35	2.08:1	0.48
1430s				c. 36	86	60	35	2.50:1	0.4
1450s				60	104	60	35	3.0:1	0.33
1464				<60	>105	48	43	2.43:1	0.41
1466				<60	>110	48	43	2.54:1	0.39
1467						48 (120d. Scot)			
1467				<60	>112	48	43	2.6:1	0.38
1467				<60	>121	48	43	2.8:1	0.36
1467				60	104	48	43	2.4:1	0.42
soon after				40	156	48	43	3.6:1	0.28
soon after				32	156[a]				
1484–5				48	151	48	43	3.5:1	0.29
1496				40	156	48	43	3.6:1	0.28
1511–12				(40)	>172	48	43	3.99:1	0.25
1526				44	218	43	49	4.48:1	0.22

Note: decimal points are rounded to the nearest whole number, except for the last two columns. Small discrepancies sometimes occur because these last two columns were calculated from the full detailed data, not from the rounded figures which are given in the other columns of this table.

[a] Murray and Cowell, 'Some Placks and Base Groats of James III and James IV', based on the thistle-head groat, 77% fine, 15 to the ounce, valued at 8d.

Table 5. *The value of silver in the Scottish medieval billon coinage*

James II pence	If 5d. fine, 45 to ounce.	108d./oz pure Ag
James III pence	If 5d. fine, 65 to ounce.	156d./oz pure Ag
James III placks	If 5d. fine, 15 to ounce, at 4d.	144d./oz pure Ag
	at 6d.	216d./oz pure Ag
	at 7d.	252d./oz pure Ag
Black money	Crown groat at 22d. – at least	176d./oz pure Ag
	Light groat at 16d. – at least	192d./oz pure Ag
James IV placks		273.6d./oz pure Ag
1533	?Placks at 2d. fine	
1538 bawbees	Silver bought at	204d./oz pure Ag
	New coin valued at	384d./oz pure Ag

Table 6. *The value of the Scottish medieval gold coinage*

Scots coin	Value	Weight (gr)	Carats	d. Scot./oz pure Au	Scot:Eng
David II noble	6s. 8d.	120	24.0	320	1.00:1
Robert III lion	5s. 0d.	62	23.5	478	1.49:1
Light lion	5s. 0d.	*c.* 38	23.0	791	2.22:1
James I demy	9s. 0d.	54	23.0	1002	2.82:1
James II demy	9s. 0d.	54	22.0	1047	2.95:1
James II lion	10s. 0d.	54	21.0	1219	3.43:1
James III rider	23s. 0d.	79	22.0	1841	3.84:1
James III unicorn	18s. 0d.	59	22.0	1917	3.99:1
James IV unicorn	18s. 0d.	59	20.0	2109	4.39:1
James IV crown	13s. 4d.	52	19.5	1809	3.77:1
James V unicorn	20s. 0d.	59	20.5	2286	4.76:1
	22s. 0d.	59	20.5	2514	5.24:1
James V abbey cr.	20s. 0d.	52	21.5	2461	4.56:1
James V ducat	40s. 0d.	88	23.0	2722	5.04:1

Note: David II's noble and the English gold coinage as a whole, have been rated as pure, though actually only 23 carats 3.5 grains, i.e. 95.5/96ths

Table 7. *The value of the English medieval gold coinage*

Eng. coin	Value	d. Eng./oz pure Au
Edward III noble	6s. 8d.	320.0
Henry IV noble	6s. 8d.	355.55
Edward IV ryal	10s. 0d.	480.0
Edward IV angel	6s. 8d.	480.0
Henry VIII angel	6s. 8d.–7s. 6d.	480.0–540.0

currency-adjusted figure may then also be more directly compared with the corresponding English price. However, this method is not foolproof and should only be used with great care.

This chapter has been concerned primarily with the value of the Scottish currency. Very little has been said about its volume, chiefly because it has to be admitted that our knowledge is very thin. Perhaps surprisingly, the thirteenth-century evidence is the best. This is because Alexander III's two recoinages of 1250 and 1280 attempted with a fair degree of success to change the permitted type of the coinage and to force all coin of the old types through the mints. Estimates of mint output at this time thus provide a useful guide to the numbers of coins of the old type in circulation immediately prior to the recoinage. On this basis I have estimated elsewhere that there may have been *c.* £50,000–£60,000+ of Scottish coin in the middle of the thirteenth century and £130,000–£180,000+ around 1280.[125] Even allowing for considerable margins of error these figures suggest very remarkable monetary growth in Scotland at this time.

The currency in fourteenth-century Scotland was dominated by huge English issues, as the hoards make clear. This English dominance becomes less marked towards the end of the century, and the Scottish output in the period 1357 to 1390 has been guessed at about £100,000 but it remains unclear how much of this Scottish coin remained in Scotland, or what proportion of the total currency it comprised.[126] These difficulties become even more acute in the fifteenth century, and it is thus extremely difficult to estimate what quantity of coin was available for use in later medieval Scotland. Mint accounts, which give such good information for England, are extremely scarce north of the border. Such evidence as we have has been tabulated by Challis, [127]giving Scots mint figures for about one third of the fifteenth century. These figures suggest a very modest output, but it is impossible to know how far such partial information is representative of the whole period. Figures for certain periods of probably heavier output are known to be missing. Thus James I's fleur-de-lis groats seem to have been struck from a

[125] Mayhew, 'Money in Scotland', and 'Alexander III', pp. 61–2, and the references cited there. There are reasons for believing that both these figures may be somewhat on the low side. The 1250 estimate makes no allowance for English Long Cross coin struck since 1247 in circulation in Scotland, which would not have required recoinage. The 1280 figure may also be higher; new higher estimates of Irish mint output would permit a larger Scottish figure, on the basis of the Scots–Irish ratio suggested by the hoards.

[126] Mayhew, 'Alexander III', pp. 63–4.

[127] Challis, 'Debasement'.

large number of dies,[128] probably suggesting a large output, beginning perhaps in 1426,[129] but the mint output figures survive only from 1433. Equally we have no figures for James III's placks and black money which were certainly struck in quantity. From 1488 the *Treasurer's Accounts* give some indirect indication of mint output in the form of figures for royal profit from the mint.[130] James IV's placks and James V's bawbees made considerable profits and were struck in quantity. One and a half million bawbees seem to have been struck over four years, yielding a profit to the crown of about £14,000, or about £3,000 per annum, and adding some £37,500 to the Scottish money supply.[131] Even the regular silver issues 1526–38 achieved consistent profits of around £400 p.a., implying a reasonable output. In general it looks as if sixteenth-century output exceeded fifteenth-century levels, but given the nature of the evidence such impressions must be treated with caution.

The calculation of mint output based on die studies is also problematic. Surviving examples of the heavy groats struck 1484–96 provide evidence of twenty-eight obverse and forty-five reverse dies. This must be the minimum number of dies used, and in fact the original total was almost certainly greater, coins from some dies not having survived.[132] Contemporary groat dies of Henry VII each struck on average some 20,000 to 24,000 coins.[133] At 20,000 groats to an obverse die, the twenty-eight heavy groat dies known to have been used would have struck 560,000 groats, or £32,666 13s. 4d. Scots, each groat being worth 14d. At 10 groats to the ounce (16 ounces to the pound) this makes 3,500 pounds. This is not a huge amount for 14 years mint output,

[128] Burns, *The Coinage of Scotland*, II, p. 5: 'The groats of James I present a very great number of minor varieties, the difficulty being to find two coins in all respects precisely alike, more particularly of the Edinburgh mint.' A proper die study of the issue has yet to be carried out, but Burns' impression provides a useful initial guide.

[129] See above, p. 119.

[130] For any given profit, however, one cannot be sure whether it was derived from a low output combined with a high seignorage charge, or a low seignorage charge and a high output.

[131] R.B.K. Stevenson, 'The Bawbee Issues of James V and Mary', *BNJ* 59 (1989), 120–56. A masterly study.

[132] Statistical techniques exist which would permit us to estimate what proportion of the original number of dies used the surviving numbers represent. Such an approach, however, requires a more detailed die study than is yet available.

[133] D.M. Metcalf, *Sylloge of Coins of the British Isles XXIII: Ashmolean Museum, Oxford, Pt III: Coins of Henry VII* (London, 1976), pp. xxii–xxiv. Mint output was obviously lower in Scotland than in England, but output per die is likely to have been comparable. Scots moneyers might have underused some dies for lack of bullion, but equally legendary Scots parsimony might have led them to under-order dies, and to use what they had for longer.

and the yearly average of 250 pounds is not far from the sole surviving documentary figure we have for 1486–7 of 181 pounds. In fact, we might expect output to have been heavier at the introduction of the type *c.* 1484, and dropping below the 1486–7 figure by the end of the issue in 1496. The 250 pounds Scots Troy is equivalent to just over 355 pounds Tower. English mint silver output at this time ran at about £5,000 sterling per annum, or 2,666.66 pounds Tower. Thus Scots silver output may have been running at about 13% of English.

Before such calculations can have much value, it would be necessary to make a series of such estimates to span the whole century, and to make similar assessments of the size of the gold issues, and of the billon and copper coinages. However, it also needs to be recognized that foreign coin played a significant role in fifteenth-century Scotland. Even if much of the continental foreign coin tariffed by parliament or burgh council at the appropriate rate Scots was largely restricted to the towns, the hoards show clearly that English coin played a significant part in towns and in the country at large. Hoards from Linlithgow, Forgandenny, 'Ayrshire', Aberdeen, Glen Afton, St Andrews, Ayr, Wick, Perth, and Whitburn[134] all testify to a significant fifteenth-century English element in the Scottish currency, though the evidence is not adequate to quantify it. Equally, we await more and better hoard evidence to determine what proportion of earlier issues remained in use alongside later coinage. For the moment, however, these remarks can do little more than set the context for future work.

[134] Metcalf, 'The Evidence of Scottish Coin Hoards', nos. 172, 174, 178, 179, 183, 188, 189, 191, 193, 194.

5 The price of victual and needful merchandise

This study is based upon a detailed listing of individual Scottish prices, but the evidence thus accumulated requires some degree of organization and analysis if it is to be more readily understood. Accordingly, each commodity is considered below in turn, and the more reliable prices have been averaged in chronological periods to reveal the likely trends for each commodity more easily. By the 1460s these averages fall readily into ten-year periods, but before that date the incidence of the data varies from one commodity to another, so in the tables and graphs which follow it is important to note the time periods covered by each grouping before 1460. It is also important to realize that for the thirteenth and fourteenth centuries the numbers of individual prices behind these mean figures are often lamentably small.

Before Scots debasement begins in 1367 prices in England and Scotland can be compared directly with one another, without currency exchange complications. In the discussion which follows there is a table setting out such an Anglo-Scottish price comparison for the period before 1367 for most commodities. After 1367 Scots mean prices are calculated both in actual money terms, and after adjusting the money price to allow for Scottish debasement producing a figure more directly comparable with English money and prices.[1] In fact in the absence of information about the exact nature of the coins involved in any payment this process can never be more than a most approximate correction. Nevertheless, the value of the Anglo-Scottish comparison is such that the process seems worthwhile despite the inevitable inaccuracies it may entail.

In order to facilitate comparison between commodities and between England and Scotland, these mean money prices, adjusted as appropriate, have also been converted to index prices calculated on a fourteenth-century base. English money prices were drawn from Rogers, Beveridge, Titow, Farmer, and original manuscripts. English index prices were

[1] For the basis of this currency adjustment, see Chapter 4.

drawn from Farmer[2] whose base period was 1330/1–1346/7. Because of the scarcity of data, the Scottish base price sometimes included 1320s prices as well, a further indication of the approximate nature of these calculations. The Scottish indices need also to be used with great caution because of the problems caused by slowly evolving weights and measures, which may not always be comparable over the long term.[3]

It will not escape the notice of the reader that although these means and index prices may simplify interpretation, these calculations also involve elements of generalization and approximation, distancing the conclusions from the original evidence on which they are based. In a sense this process is common to all historical writing, but there is a danger that a column of figures may seem more impartial and objective than a page of finely turned phrases. In truth, the Scottish mean prices, especially in their currency-adjusted and indexed forms, are as much a result of the process of survival, selection, and evaluation of evidence as any other, much more readable, historical essay. This is why the listing of individual prices, the real evidence on which subsequent conjecture is founded, remains fundamental.[4]

Wheat

The overall movement of mean wheat prices is revealed in Table 8, and Figures 10 and 11. In its broadest terms the behaviour of wheat prices is common to that of most commodities. The currency-adjusted price shows that even after monetary factors have been stripped out, demand for wheat remained strong and the price high throughout our whole period. The marked fall in adjusted price in period F (1398–1414) may suggest that the weakening of the currency during the Albany period has been overestimated. The Hume Will price (period G, 1424), is slightly low, as is typical of the other will prices. Apart from the possibility of conservative valuation, it should be noted that this wheat was still growing. The indexed currency-adjusted prices in Table 8 show that inflation in wheat prices was usually as strong as, if not greater than, that of the other grains.

In the period before 1367, Table 9 shows that Scots wheat prices

[2] D.L.Farmer, in *Agrarian History of England and Wales* II, pp. 716–817, and III, pp. 431–525.

[3] See Chapter 3.

[4] The ultimate generalization is the construction of overall cereals and livestock indices, as decennial means, for comparison with similar decennial means calculated from Farmer's cereals and livestock indices as set out in Chapter 1. Readers should not forget how far these figures have travelled from the transactions at toll-booth, castle gate or market cross which are their origin.

Table 8. *Wheat summary table*

Period	Mean price	Deflated	Index
A	18.0	18.0	80.0
B–C	22.5	22.5	100.0
D	31.0	31.0	137.8
E	35.0	29.75	132.2
F	43.0	(21.5)	(95.6)
G	40.0	24.0	106.7
H	80.0	32.0	142.2
I	98.0	32.34	143.7
60s	87.0		
70s	108.0	30.24	134.4
80s	190.0		
90s	142.0	39.76	176.7
1500s	141.0	39.48	175.5
10s	144.0	36.0	160.0
20s	229.0	57.25	254.4
30s	223.0	49.06	218.1

Note: the mean price is in pence per boll; the deflated column gives the currency-adjusted sterling equivalent price. Parentheses have been used to flag up calculations which are less securely based than others – either because they are based on a smaller amount of data, or because they involve certain, possibly questionable, assumptions.

were almost invariably dearer than the English prices collected by Rogers, Titow, and Farmer, and that the Durham prices we have studied usually fall between the Scottish high and the southern English low levels. Additionally, East Anglian wheat prices used by Beveridge from Hinderclay in Suffolk suggest that English wheat prices were at their lowest here. High Scots wheat prices drew imported wheat from England and continental Europe, but the Scots price evidence also shows clearly that wheat was grown in Scotland.[5] Scots farmers anticipated wheat yields of four-fold, or at least claimed and won compensation at this rate if their cultivation was disrupted.[6] Many English medieval estates would have been pleased to average as much. Where

[5] See especially the estate records of St. Andrews and Dunkeld and the legal claims of countless smaller Scots farmers recorded in *ALA* and *ALC*.

[6] *ALC* I.15, 199. See also p. 163 below on the subject of barley yields and comparison with English yields. It is sometimes suggested that Scottish yields only equalled English, because the former were calculated in the courts without allowing for the deduction of tiends (tithes). I have seen no evidence to support this assertion. In passsing it may be noted that in the 1980s Scottish wheat and barley yields were broadly equal to those achieved in England; the important difference between the two countries was that cereal cultivation was possible far more widely in England.

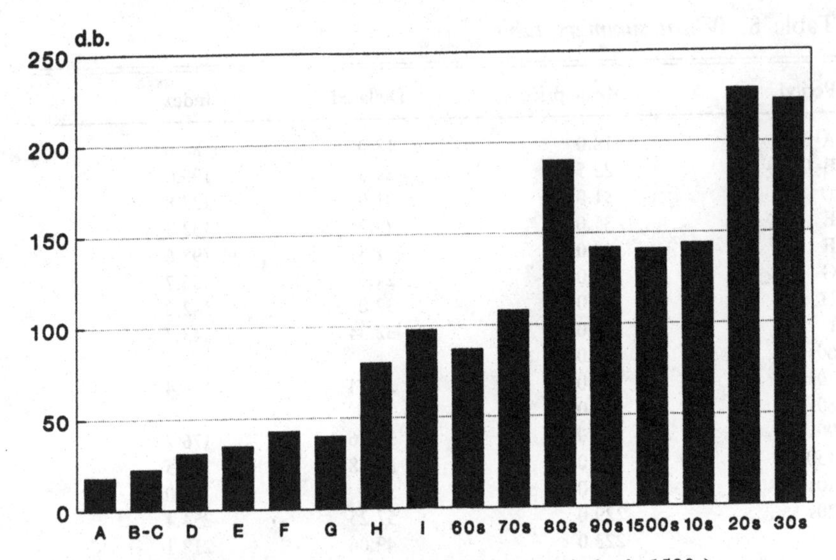

10 Wheat prices (mean prices for time periods A–1530s)
For periods A–I see, Introduction, p. 6.

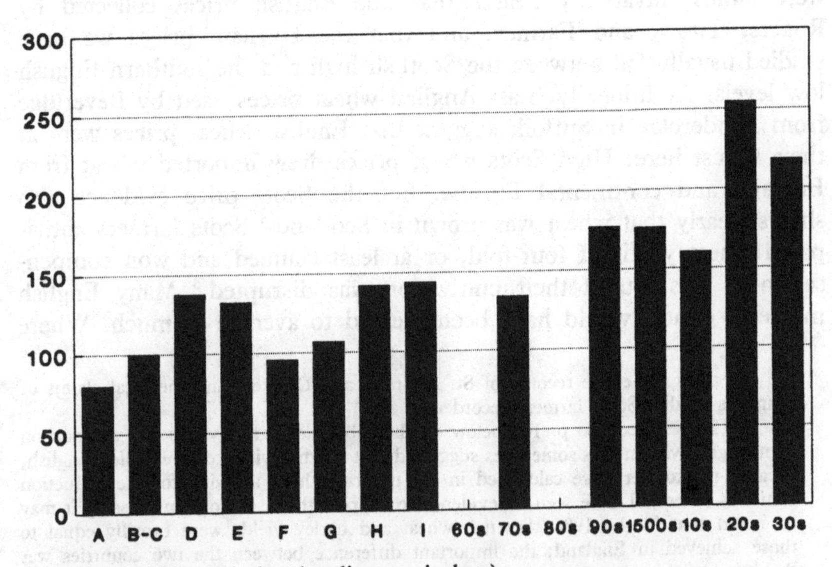

11 Wheat index (sterling equivalent)

Table 9. *Wheat prices 1263–1367: Scotland and England*

Year	Scotland	Durham	Rogers	Titow	Farmer
1263	5.0		3.95		
1264	7.63		4.33	5.29	4.19
1279	4.0		5.1		5.31
1288	3.33		3.07	3.5	2.94
	3.0				
1290	(13.33)		6.46	7.0	6.0
1291	6.67		5.6	6.06	5.54
	6.67				
1292	6.67		5.39	6.63	6.15
1295		9.93			9.23
1296	5.0		4.77	5.83	4.83
1297		8.0			6.33
1298		4.8			
1303	(8.0)		4.1	3.65	3.65
1327	9.44		3.92	5.92	
	6.67				
1328	6.67		6.46	7.25	
	8.67				
	6.67				
	6.67				
	7.0				
1329	10.0	6.98	6.55	7.67	
	9.33				
	8.0				
	8.05				
	6.67				
	6.67				
1330	8.33	9.62	7.19	9.0	
	11.09				
	10.0				
	11.92				
1331	7.81		7.94	8.08	
	10.0				
	11.25				
	10.0				
1335	8.0	4.58	5.29	5.83	
1337	5.01	4.0	3.58	4.67	
1340	6.0	5.39	3.54	4.75	
1341	6.2	3.72	3.8	5.5	
	8.2				
1342	5.6	5.93	4.14	4.75	
	7.0				
1347	7.17		6.62	7.08	
1357	6.67	8.7	6.85		
	11.52				

Table 9 (*cont.*)

Year	Scotland	Durham	Rogers	Titow	Farmer
1358	10.36	3.98	5.54		
1361	8.0	5.03	5.4		
1363	14.44	8.76/7.84		8.5	
1364	13.33	9.11	7.45		
1366	10.44	9.35	6.71		
1367	8.72	11.44	6.64		
	10.0				

Note: all prices are in shillings per quarter. Parentheses have been used to flag up calculations which are less securely based than others – either because they are based on a smaller amount of data, or because they involve certain, possibly questionable, assumptions.

the conditions permitted it, high prices will certainly have encouraged Scots farmers to grow wheat.

The Anglo-Scottish comparison also shows that the same extremely good or bad years stand out on both sides of the border. For example, 1288 was a famously good year,[7] while 1330 and 1331 were dear years both in England and Scotland. In the fifteenth century 1438 was a very bad year across Europe, but our only Scots wheat price for the year, though high, is not extremely so.[8] This is an Aberdeen assize price, and the intention to prevent wheat prices rising above this level may not in fact have been achieved, for Aberdeen certainly experienced famine in 1438. Generally, however, Aberdeen often appears to have been a relatively cheap area.[9] In contrast royal purchases, especially when made under conditions of some military stress, are often high. James II had to pay enormous sums in 1455 and Edward III may have been similarly exploited at Berwick in 1340.[10] An act of parliament in 1424 was thought necessary to protect the court from such exploitation.[11] More generally our royal purchase prices might be expected to be somewhat above sale prices to the extent that accounting officers often

[7] The sheriff of Lanark in his account for 1289 comments explicitly on the 1288 harvest, *ER* I.46.

[8] List 139.

[9] *ACR* IX.659, January 1517, where the cheapness of wheat in the region was noted by the authorities. As well as locally grown wheat, Aberdeen will have enjoyed ready access to imported grain through its port.

[10] *CDS* III.245, for Berwick merchants overcharging Edward III. List 163, 164 for high prices paid by James II.

[11] *APS* II.7.

had to buy at times of shortage and sell in times of plenty.[12] Moreover, sales are more likely on the more distant estates, and prices tend to be lower near sources of supply which are remote from centres of consumption, whatever the general state of the market. These trends, however, are by no means invariable.

The plentiful wheat evidence from Aberdeen 1398–1414 provided by the assize of bread permits us to look more closely at variation in wheat prices within a single calendar year. In an ordinary year we tend to see prices rising through spring and early summer, followed by an adjustment in late summer and autumn to reflect the success or failure of the harvest. Exceptionally the year 1400 shows prices oscillating between 40 and 48d.b. through the year revealing no seasonal pattern, but 1400 looks less irregular if viewed as part of the period 1398–1402.

If we express the difference between the maximum and minimum prices in any single year as a percentage of the minimum price at Aberdeen in this period, we find a range of variation from 0% (i.e. no variation within the year) to 100% (i.e. a doubling of price within the year). The evidence from Perth, James V's Household Book, and St Andrews in the sixteenth century, when we also have multiple entries for several years from a single source, gives a range of variation from 14% to 83% (Table 10).

Such wide variations confirm the pre-eminence of harvest fluctuations as the most important influence on wheat prices. They also indicate the desirability of using harvest years rather than calendar years for price research, although the general inadequacies of the Scottish medieval evidence precluded such an approach in this case.[13] In fact although a price variation of 100% from the same source in a single calendar year is known, variations of more than 33% are unusual.

The Aberdeen assize of bread and ale also permits us to form some impression of the usual price ratio between wheat and malt.[14] In the period 1398 to 1401 we have twenty-six comparable quotations giving ratios ranging from 1 to 1.7 and averaging 1.25. This information provides a useful guide to the likely ratio of wheat and malt prices; wheat and malt prices moving outside this range probably need to be examined with some care.

The price lists which accompany the discussions of each commodity in this chapter call for some explanation. As has already been mentioned

[12] For this reason, it is preferable to collect only directly comparable prices, but in Scotland any medieval evidence is too valuable to be discarded.

[13] See the Introduction, pp. 4–5, on dating. It should also be remembered that considerable price variation can occur within a single harvest year.

[14] Wheat price divided by malt price.

Table 10. *Wheat price variations in a single year*

Aberdeen 1398–1414		Perth 1506–14, HBJV 1526, St Andrews 1540–1
0%	1405	14% 1513, 1541
6%	1402	18% 1507
10%	1414	19% 1509
11%	1399, 1408	25% 1540
14%	1406, 1407	27% 1512
16%	1398	33% 1514, 1526
20%	1400, 1409	60% 1508
33%	1412	83% 1506
50%	1401	
60%	1413	
66%	1411	
100%	1410	

in the Introduction[15] these lists provide only a summary of the much fuller data base compiled in the course of our research and available now through the ESRC data archive at the University of Essex. A 'hard copy' of the full data base may also be consulted at the Ashmolean Museum, Oxford. The essential information for the most usable prices is, however, published here. To draw attention to the often disparate nature of many of the prices, the 'Source' column in the following tables often ends with a letter-code to give some idea of the type of price involved:

Key to the letter-code

Aw. = Judgement or damages awarded in court.
C. = Claim made in court.
Ch. = Entry in Chronicle.
O. = Obligation recognized by debtor.
P. = Purchase.
R. = Price repeated on separate occasions for same year in one source.
V. = Valuation.
W. = Will.
Wi. = Witness' statement.

Inevitably this simple code creates as many difficulties as it solves. Even the most straightforward purchase prices would, of course, have been sales if the evidence for them had come down to us through the seller's accounts. Such sales account for the vast majority of those prices

[15] See above, pp. 5–7.

Table 11. *Wheat price list*

No.	Year	Place	Unit price	Source
1	1263	Edinburgh	15d.b.	*ER* I.25
2	1264	Ayr	22.88d.b.	*ER* I.5 P
3	1279	Berwick	12d.b.	James Raine, *The History and Antiquities of North Durham* (London, 1852), Appendix, p.16
4	1288	Edinburgh	9d.b.	*ER* I.41
5	1288	Jedburgh	10d.b.	*ER* I.44 P.
6	1290	Hinernairn	40d.b.	*DHS* I.184 P.
7	1291	Bothkennar	20d.b.	*CDS* II.132–3
8	1291	Bothkennar	20d.b.	*CDS* II.129
9	1292	Bothkennar	20d.b.	*DHS* I.275–6
10	1296	Coldstream	5s.qr(=15d.b.)	*DHS* II.32
11	1303	Stirling	24d.b. wheatmeal	PRO E101/366/1. P.
12	1327	Berwick	28.33d.b.	*ER* I.81
13	1327	Berwick	20d.b.	*ER* I.63–4
14	1328	Berwick	20d.b.	*ER* I.217
15	1328		26d.b.	*ER* I.184
16	1328	Cardross	20d.b.	*ER* I.124 P.
17	1328		23s.4d.1pipe 3bar. wheatmeal	*ER* I.117 P.
18	1328	Edinburgh	20d.b.	*ER* I.115
19	1328		21d.b.	*ER* I.219 P.
20	1329	Moray?	30d.b.	*ER* I.289 P.
21	1329	Earlston	28d.b. baked wheat	DPS Exp.'29a P.
22	1329		24d.b.	*ER* I.283
23	1329		24.16d.b.	*ER* I.289 P.
24	1329	Galloway	20d.b.	*ER* I.152 P.
25	1329		20d.b.	*ER* I.240
26	1330	Liberton	25d.b.	*ER* I.340
27	1330	Berwick	30d.b.? with malt	*ER* I.341
28	1330		33.27d.b.	*ER* I.341 P.
29	1330	Liberton	30d.b.	*ER* I.340
30	1330		35.75d.b.	*ER* I.337
31	1331		23.44d.b.	*ER* I.396
32	1331	Liberton	30d.b.	*ER* I.402
33	1331		33.75d.b.	*ER* I.400 P.
34	1331		30d.b.	*ER* I.396
35	1335	Roxburgh	24d.b.	*CDS* III.322
36	1335	Cramond, etc.	15d.b.	*CDS* III.327ff pre-war V.
37	1336	Cramond, etc.	15d.b.	*CDS* III.377ff pre-war V.
38	1337	Berwick	15.04d.b.	*CDS* III.373
39	1340	Berwick	6s.qr(=18d.b.)	*CDS* III.245
40	1341	Aberdeen	18.58d.b.	*ER* I.530 P.
41	1341		24.61d.b.	*ER* I.505 P.
42	1342	Coldingham	16d.b.	CP 1342–3 P.

Table 11 (*cont.*)

No.	Year	Place	Unit price	Source
43	1342	Edinburgh	21d.b.	*ER* I.536
44	1347	Coldingham?	21.51d.b.	CP 1347–8 P.
45	1357	Crail	20d.b.	*ER* I.565
46	1357	Edinburgh	34.5d.b.	*ER* I.609
47	1357	Stirling	21.8d.b.? with oatmeal	*ER* I.577
48	1358	Edinburgh	31.05d.b.	*ER* I.617
49	1361	Morphy	24d.b.	*ER* II.111
50	1363		43.31d.b.	*ER* II.252 P.
51	1364	Berwick, etc.	40d.b.	SS 12.xlvii P.
52	1366		31.27d.b.	*ER* II.252 P.
53	1367		26.18d.b.	*ER* II.294 P.
54	1367	Bothkennar	30d.b.	*ER* II.304
55	1368	Dune	30d.b.	*ER* II.304
56	1369	Moray	34.33d.b.	*ER* II.352
57	1372		29.72d.b.	*ER* II.367–8 P.
58	1372		33.76d.b.	*ER* II.369 P.
59	1373		35.39d.b.	*ER* II.450–1 P.
60	1373		39.98d.b.	*ER* II.454 P.
61	1374	Dundee	36d.b.	*ER* II.449
62	1375	Edinburgh	204.67d.b.?	*ER* II.475 clerk's error?
63	1380		38.42d.b.	*ER* III.39 P.
64	1380	Edinburgh	45d.b.	*ER* III.653 P.
65	1384		28.75d.b.	*ER* III.106 P.
66	1398	Aberdeen	48d.b.	SHS 3,49.27 assize V.
67	1398	Aberdeen	40d.b.	SHS 3,49.34 assize V.
68	1399	Aberdeen	40d.b.	SHS 3,49.39 assize V.
69	1399	Aberdeen	40d.b.	SHS 3,49.41 assize V.
70	1399	Aberdeen	40d.b.	SHS 3,49.46 assize V.
71	1399	Aberdeen	40d.b.	SHS 3,49.53–4 assize V.
72	1399	Aberdeen	36d.b.	SHS 3,49.63 assize V.
73	1399	Aberdeen	36d.b.	SHS 3,49.75 assize V.
74	1399	Aberdeen	36d.b.	SHS 3,49.113 assize V.
75	1400	Aberdeen	48d.b.	SHS 3,49.121 assize V.
76	1400	Aberdeen	40d.b.	SHS 3,49.126 assize V.
77	1400	Aberdeen	40d.b.	SHS 3,49.129 assize V.
78	1400	Aberdeen	42d.b.	SHS 3,49.134 assize V.
79	1400	Aberdeen	40d.b.	SHS 3,49.137 assize V.
80	1400	Aberdeen	42d.b.	SHS 3,49.138 assize V.
81	1400	Aberdeen	48d.b.	SHS 3,49.148 assize V.
82	1400	Aberdeen	42d.b.	SHS 3,49.155 assize V.
83	1400	Aberdeen	48d.b.	SHS 3,49.159 assize V.
84	1400	Aberdeen	40d.b.	SHS 3,49.162 assize V.
85	1400	Aberdeen	42d.b.	ACR I.168 assize V.
86	1400	Aberdeen	48d.b.	ACR I.172 assize V.
87	1401	Aberdeen	48d.b.	ACR I.177 assize V.

Table 11 (*cont.*)

No.	Year	Place	Unit price	Source
88	1401	Aberdeen	54d.b.	ACR I.179 assize V.
89	1401	Aberdeen	54d.b.	ACR I.181 assize V.
90	1401	Aberdeen	40d.b.	ACR I.213 assize V.
91	1401	Aberdeen	60d.b.	ACR I.217 assize V.
92	1402	Aberdeen	60d.b.	ACR I.222 assize V.
93	1402	Aberdeen	64d.b.	ACR I.229 assize V.
94	1405	Aberdeen	32d.b.	ACR I.249 assize V.
95	1405	Aberdeen	32d.b.	ACR I.263 assize V.
96	1405	Aberdeen	32d.b.	ACR I.265 assize V.
97	1405	Aberdeen	32d.b.	ACR I.267 assize V.
98	1406	Aberdeen	32d.b.	ACR I.276 assize V.
99	1406	Aberdeen	28d.b.	ACR I.278 assize V.
100	1406	Aberdeen	28d.b.	ACR I.247 assize V.
101	1407	Aberdeen	28d.b.	ACR I.317 assize V.
102	1407	Aberdeen	32d.b.	ACR I.321 assize V.
103	1407	Aberdeen	30d.b.	ACR I.324 assize V.
104	1408	Aberdeen	36d.b.	ACR II.22 assize V.
105	1408	Aberdeen	40d.b.	ACR II.23 assize V.
106	1409	Aberdeen	40d.b.	ACR II.33 assize V.
107	1409	Aberdeen	48d.b.	ACR II.34 assize V.
108	1409	Aberdeen	48d.b.	ACR II.42 assize V.
109	1410	Aberdeen	44d.b.	ACR II.58 assize V.
110	1410	Aberdeen	54d.b.	ACR II.61 assize V.
111	1410	Aberdeen	54d.b.	ACR II.63 assize V.
112	1410	Aberdeen	60d.b.	ACR II.65 assize V.
113	1410	Aberdeen	72d.b.	ACR II.66 assize V.
114	1410	Aberdeen	40d.b.	ACR II.66 assize V.
115	1410	Aberdeen	36d.b.	ACR II.102 assize V.
116	1410	Aberdeen	40d.b.	ACR II.103 assize V.
117	1411	Aberdeen	40d.b.	ACR II.69 assize V.
118	1411	Aberdeen	48d.b.	ACR II.105 assize V.
119	1411	Aberdeen	48d.b.	ACR II.106 assize V.
120	1411	Aberdeen	48d.b.	ACR II.106 assize V.
121	1411	Aberdeen	30d.b.	ACR II.114 assize V.
122	1412	Aberdeen	36d.b.	ACR II.120 assize V.
123	1412	Aberdeen	48d.b.	ACR II.129 assize V.
124	1413	Aberdeen	48d.b.	ACR II.132 assize V.
125	1413	Aberdeen	54d.b.	ACR II.135 assize V.
126	1413	Aberdeen	60d.b.	ACR II.137 assize V.
127	1413	Aberdeen	64d.b.	ACR II.141 assize V.
128	1413	Aberdeen	36d.b.	ACR II.193 assize V.
129	1413	Aberdeen	40d.b.	ACR II.197 assize V.
130	1414	Aberdeen	40d.b.	ACR II.209 assize V.
131	1414	Aberdeen	44d.b.	ACR II.206 assize V.
132	1424	Dunglas	40d.b.	HMS 12,8.87 W.

Table 11 (*cont.*)

No.	Year	Place	Unit price	Source
133	1433	Aberdeen	84d.b.	William Kennedy, *Annals of Aberdeen from the Reign of King William the Lion* (London, 2 vols., 1818), p.1 assize V.?
134	1434	Edinburgh	72d.b.	*ER* IV.622 P.
135	1434	Aberdeen	84d.b.	ACR IV.53 assize V.
136	1435	Aberdeen	72d.b.	ACR IV.51 assize V.
137	1436	Aberdeen	84d.b.	ACR IV.60 assize V.
138	1437	Edinburgh	108d.b.	*ER* V.36 P.
139	1438	Aberdeen	108d.b.	ACR IV.142 assize V.
140	1441	Aberdeen	60d.b.	ACR IV.257 assize V.
141	1442	Aberdeen	60d.b.	ACR IV.281 assize V.
142	1443	Aberdeen	84d.b.	ACR IV.297 assize V.
143	1443	Aberdeen	72d.b.	ACR IV.323 assize V.
144	1443	Aberdeen	72d.b.	ACR IV.327 assize V.
145	1444	Irvine	144d.b	*ER* V.260 V.
146	1444	Aberdeen	96d.b.	ACR IV.334 assize V.
147	1445	Inverk'g	120d.b.	*ER* V.223 P.
148	1446	Irvine	144d.b.	*ER* V.280–1 V.
149	1446	Ayr	144d.b.	*ER* V.261 P.
150	1447	Aberdeen	72d.b.	ACR IV.494 assize V.
151	1447	Aberdeen	48d.b./54d.b.	ACR IV.498 C/Wi.
152	1448	Dunbar	96d.b.	*ER* V.341 P.
153	1448	Edinburgh	75.18d.b./84d.b.	*ER* V.347 P.av./max. price
154	1448	Inverness	108d.b.	*ER* V.405 P.
155	1448	Edinburgh	96d.b.	*ER* V.347 P.
156	1450	Aberdeen	72d.b.	ACR V i.69 assize V.
157	1450	Aberdeen	80d.b.	ACR V i.101 assize V.
158	1450	Falkland?	96d.b.	*ER* V.471–2 P.
159	1451	Linlithgow	80d.b.	*ER* V.505 P.
160	1452	Aberdeen	72d.b.	ACR V i.147 assize V.
161	1453	Aberdeen	108d.b.	ACR V i.180 assize V.
162	1455	Perth	114d.b.	*ER* VI.244 V.
163	1455	Galloway	336d.b.	*ER* VI.209
164	1455	Galloway	252d.b.	*ER* VI.203–4 P.
165	1456	Ferny	160d.b.	*ER* VI.418
166	1461	Moray	108d.b.	*ER* VII.122
167	1461	Aberdeen	120d.b.	*ER* VII.143 P.
168	1462	Aberdeen	72d.b.	ACR V i.449 Wi.
169	1462	Aberdeen	72d.b.	ACR V i.461 assize V.
170	1462	Brechin	60d.b.	*ER* VII.167
171	1464	Moray	80d.b.	*ER* VII.351
172	1464	N. Berwick	96d.b.	*ER* VII.366
173	1465	North of Tay	80d.b.	*ER* VII.409–1

Table 11 (*cont.*)

No.	Year	Place	Unit price	Source
174	1465	N. Berwick	96d.b.	*ER* VII.425–6
175	1466	Edinburgh	100d.b.	*ER* VII.502 P.
176	1468	Aberdeen	3.5 Scots crowns p.moye	ACR VI.61–2 Wi.
177	1468	Moray	74.08d.b.	*ER* VII.641
178	1469	Aberdeen	96d.b.	ACR VI.88 Wi.
179	1469	Moray	80d.b.	*ER* VIII.85
180	1470	Aberdeen	120d.b.	ACR VI.120 P.
181	1472	Moray	60d.b.	*ER* VIII.147–8
182	1472	Dunbar	96d.b.	*ER* VIII.188 V.
183	1472	St Andrews	108d.b.	*ER* VIII.196 P.
184	1473	Moray	60d.b.	*ER* VIII.222
185	1474	Stirlingsh.	100d.b.	*ER* VIII.282
186	1474	Moray	60d.b.	*ER* VIII.303
187	1475	Stirlingsh.	111d.b.	*ER* VIII.329
188	1475	Stirlingsh.	111d.b.	*ER* VIII.329
189	1475	Stirlingsh.	111d.b.	*ER* VIII.330
190	1475	Moray	82.5d.b.	*ER* VIII.368
191	1475	Aberdeen	84d.b.	ACR VI.404 assize V.
192	1476	Moray	80d.b.	*ER* VIII.409
193	1476	Stirlingsh.	96d.b.	*ER* VIII.430
194	1476	Fife	108d.b.	*ER* VIII.447
195	1476	Stirlingsh.	120d.b.	*ER* VIII.505
196	1477	Fife	120d.b.	*ER* VIII.447
197	1477	Berwick	120d.b.	*ER* VIII.539
198	1477	Berwick	90d.b.	*ER* VIII.539
199	1477	Leith	102d.b.	*ER* VIII.546
200	1477	Dumbarton	204d.b.	*ER* VIII.549
201	1478	Schanbody	240d.b.	ALA I.75 C.
202	1478	Schanbody	144d.b.	ALA I.87 Aw.
203	1478	Stirlingsh.	144d.b.	*ER* VIII.564
204	1478	Moray	84d.b.	*ER* VIII.579
205	1479		108d.b.	*ER* IX.4
206	1479	Linlithgowsh.	108d.b.	*ER* IX.16
207	1479	Moray	84d.b.	*ER* IX.49
208	1479	Moray	70d.b.	*ER* IX.49
209	1479	Carrick	120d.b.	*ER* IX.123
210	deleted			
211	1480	Stirlingsh.	192d.b.	*ER* IX.95
212	1480	Fife	168d.b.	*ER* IX.100
213	1480	Abircorne	162.96d.b.	*ER* IX.104
214	1480	Ballincrefe	168d.b.	*ER* IX.127
215	1480	Moray	96d.b.	*ER* IX.142
216	1482	Dunmure	160d.b.	ALC I.199 C.
217	1482	Wauchtoun'	216d.b.	ALC I.429 Aw.
218	1483	Wauchtoun'	240d.b.	ALC I.166 Aw.
219	1483	Wauchtoun'	240d.b.	ALC I.166 Aw.

Table 11 (*cont.*)

No.	Year	Place	Unit price	Source
220	1483	Perthshire	288d.b.	ALA I.*116 Aw.
221	deleted			
222	1483	Carrick	160d.b.	*ER* IX.274
223	1484	Quhittingam	160d.b.	ALC I.*90 Aw.
224	1484	Broxmouth'	168d.b.	ALA I.*134 Aw.
225	1484	Broxmouth'	168d.b.	ALA I.*134 Aw.
226	1484	Moray	90d.b.	*ER* IX.314
227	1485		120d.b.	ALC I.*102 C.
228	1486	Fethirkern	168d.b.	*ER* IX.481
229	deleted			
230	1488	Dun/Dummure	240d.b.	ALC I.86 Aw.
231	1488	Abirnethy	192d.b.	ALC I.90 Aw.
232	1488	Arth'	240d.b.	ALC I.98 Aw.
233	1488	Prestoun'	240d.b.	ALC I.12 Aw.
234	1488	Abirnethy etc.	360d.b.	ALA I.114 C.
235	1488	Carrick etc.	120d.b.	*ER* X.126
236	1489	Kynfaunis etc.	180d.b	ALC I.102 C.
237	1489	Aberdeen	216d.b.	ACR VII.101 assize V.
238	1489	Fife	168d.b.	*ER* X.205
239	1490	Lundy etc.	160d.b.	ALC I.140 Aw.
240	1490	Ballinbrech	160d.b./120d.b.	ALC I.15 C/Aw. + bear
241	1490	Lesle	160d.b./120d.b.	ALC I.15 C/Aw. + bear
242	1490	Hollis of Ar	180d.b.	ALA I.137 C.
243	1490	Essilmont	120d.b.	ALA I.183 Aw. + bear
244	1490	Dundee?	180d.b.	*ER* X.301
245	1491	the Raith?	120d.b.	ALC I.172
246	1491	Ballincrefe	120d.b.	*ER* X.337
247	1492	Edinburgh	120d.b.	ALC I.220 C.
248	1492	Edinburgh	288d.b.	ALC I.220 C.
249	1492		120d.b.	ALC I.221 C.
250	1492	Inchecometh	120d.b.	ALA I.161 Aw.
251	1492	Edinburgh	168d.b.	*ER* X.387
252	1494	Crancho	96d.b.	ALC I.33 Aw.
253	1494	Perth	240d.b.	ALC I.359 C.
254	1494	Kilmarone	60d.b.	ALC I.403 Aw.
255	1494	Coutty	96d.b.	ALA I.190 Aw.
256	1494	Kirkton'	160d.b.	ALA I.203 C.
257	1494	Glasgow	100d.b.	*ER* X.472
258	1495	Setoun'	84d.b.	ALC I.399 Aw. + bear
259	1495	Ballegarno	96d.b.	ALC I.422 Aw.
260	1495	Hallis of Ar	216d.b.	ALC I.430 C.
261	1497	Falkland	150d.b.	*ER* XI.75
262	1497	Dunbar	160d.b.	*ER* XI.75
263	1497	Falkland	160d.b.	*ER* XI.75
264	1498	Edinburgh	120d.b.	*ER* XI.233
265	1499	Aberdeen	216d.b.	ACR VII.950 C.

Table 11 (*cont.*)

No.	Year	Place	Unit price	Source
266	1499	Aberdeen	1 French crown/bar.	ACR VII.957
267	1499	Fife	151.94d.b.	*ER* XI.243
268	1500	Aberdeen	85.71d.b.	*ER* XI.375
269	1501	Threave castle	192d.b.	*ER* XII.16
270	1502	Aberdeen	1 French crown b.	ACR VIII.175 Wi.
271	deleted			
272	1504	Kinlos	112.5d.b.	*ER* XII.224
273	1504	Fife	120d.b.	*ER* XII.310
274	1504	Ballincreif	33.33d.b.	*ER* XII.313 V.
275	1504	Edinburgh	109.7d.b.	*ER* XII.372
276	1505	Clony	144d.b.	SHS 2,10.18
277	1505	Moray	133.9d.b.	*ER* XII.439
278	1505	Murthocarny	80d.b.	*ER* XII.444–5 V.
279	1505	C'brandspeth	150d.b.	*ER* XII.519
280	1505	C'brandspeth	132d.b.	*ER* XII.519
281	1505	Moray	74.42d.b.	*ER* XII.396
282	1506	Perth	119.22d.b.	SHS 2,10.197 P.
283	1506	Perth	138d.b.	SHS 2,10.197 P.
284	1506	Perth	140d.b.	SHS 2,10.199 P.
285	1506	Perth	150d.b.	SHS 2,10.199 P.
286	1506	Perth	138d.b.	SHS 2,10.199 P.
287	1506	Perth	160,198,220d.b.	SHS 2,10.204 P.
288	1506	Moray	118.86d.b.	*ER* XII.492
289	1506	Fife	144d.b.	*ER* XII.525
290	1506	Fife	137.8d.b.	*ER* XII.525
291	1506	Stirling	150d.b.	*ER* XII.541
292	1506	Stirling	150d.b.	*ER* XII.541
293	1506	Dunbar	109.5d.b.	*ER* XII.559
294	1507	Perth	204,210d.b.	SHS 2,10.206 P.
295	1507	Perth	192,216,228d.b.	SHS 2,10.206 P.
296	deleted			
297	1507	Fife	212.57d.b.	*ER* XII.6
298	1507	Pittenweem	144d.b.	*ER* XIII.89
299	1508	Perth	100,106,160d.b.	SHS 2,10.211 P.
300	1508	Lothian	240d.b.	SHS 2,10.248
301	1508	Lothian	120d.b.	SHS 2,10.250
302	1508	Moray	96d.b.	*ER* XIII.204
303	1508	Moray	96d.b.	*ER* XIII.209
304	1508	Moray	96d.b.	*ER* XIII.209
305	1509	Perth	84d.b.	SHS 2,10.214 P.
306	1509	Perth	84,100d.b.	SHS 2,10.214 P.
307	1509	Perth	100.83d.b.	SHS 2,10.217 P.
308	1509	Abbirlathy	84d.b.	SHS 2,10.259
309	1509	Abbirlathy	84,100d.b.	SHS 2,10.259
310	1510	Aberdeen	120d.b.	ACR VIII.108 Aw.
311	1510	Dunkeld	100d.b.	SHS 2,10.112

Table 11 (*cont.*)

No.	Year	Place	Unit price	Source
312	1510	Perth	135.93d.b.	SHS 2,10.222 P.
313	1510	Abbirlathy	100d.b.	SHS 2,10.259
314	1510	Abbirlathy	100d.b.	SHS 2,10.259
315	1511	Dunkeld	160d.b.	SHS 2,10.120
316	1511	Lothian	84d.b.	SHS 2,10.254
317	1511	Lothian	82.50d.b.	SHS 2,10.257
318	1511	Lothian	100d.b.	SHS 2,10.257
319	1511	Moray	80d.b.	*ER* XIII.460
320	1512	Perth	160,168,192,204d.b.	SHS 2,10.227 P.
321	1512	Moray	120d.b.	*ER* XIII.522
322	1513	Perth	188.91d.b.	SHS 2,10.228 P.
323	1513	Perth	192d.b.	SHS 2,10.231 P.
324	1513	Perth	180d.b.	SHS 2,10.231 P.
325	1513	Perth	168d.b.	SHS 2,10.231 P.
326	1513	Lothian	160d.b.	SHS 2,10.262
327	1514	Perth	159.55d.b.	SHS 2,10.232 P.
328	1514	Perth	155.95d.b.	SHS 2,10.236
329	1514	Perth	120d.b.	SHS 2,10.240
330	1515	Inchegarvy	168d.b.	TA V.20 P.
331	1515	Moray	100d.b.	*ER* XIV.118
332	1515	Moray	100d.b.	*ER* XIV.133
333	deleted			
334	1515	Fife	120d.b.	*ER* XIV.177
335	1515	Perth	144d.b.	*ER* XIV.196 P.
336	1516	Moray	100d.b.	*ER* XIV.134
337	1516	Moray	100d.b.	*ER* XIV.283
338	1516	Fife	149.90d.b.	*ER* XIV.291
339	1517	Aberdeen	144d.b.	ACR IX.659 assize V.
340	1517	Aberdeen	160d.b.	ACR IX.663 Aw.
341	1517		228d.b.	*ER* XIV.352 P.
342	1518		240d.b.	TA V.163 P.
343	1518	Fife	144d.b.	*ER* XIV.412
344	deleted			
345	1520	Aberdeen	240d.b.	ACR X.212 Aw.
346	1521	Aberdeen	240d.b.	ACR X.390 Aw.
347	1523		268.8d.b.	*ER* XV.89 P.
348	1524	Fife	150d.b. poor wheat	*ER* XV.208–9
349	1525	Edinburgh	276d.b./288d.b.	HBJV, p. 5 P.
350	1525	Edinburgh	264d.b.	HBJV, p. 5 P.
351	1525	Edinburgh?	288d.b.	HBJV, p. 10 P.
352	1525		288d.b.	HBJV, App., p. 4 P.
353	1525		160d.b.	*ER* XV.293
354	1526	Edinburgh?	162d.b.	HBJV, p. 39 P.
355	1526	Edinburgh?	180d.b.	HBJV, p. 46 P.
356	1526	Edinburgh?	216d.b.	HBJV, p. 51 P.
357	1526	Stirling	216d.b.	HBJV, p. 55 P.

Table 11 (*cont.*)

No.	Year	Place	Unit price	Source
358	1526	Stirling?	192d.b.	HBJV, p. 61 P.
359	1526	Edinburgh	222d.b.	HBJV, App., p. 7 P.
360	1526	Leith	204d.b.	HBJV, App., p. 8 P.
361	1526	Ruthillut	120d.b.	*ER* XV.231
362	1526	Fife	160d.b.	*ER* XV.353–4
363	1526		168d.b.	*ER* XV.388
364	1527	Fife	216d.b.	*ER* XV.397–8
365	1527	Fife	216d.b.	*ER* XV.398
366	1527	Ruthillut	192d.b.	*ER* XV.398
367	1527		216d.b.	*ER* XV.466
368	1528	Edinburgh	300d.b.	HBJV, p. 130 P.
369	1528		252d.b.	HBJV, App., p. 13 P.
370	1528	Fife	216d.b.	*ER* XV.475
371	1528	Fife	192d.b.	*ER* XV.479
372	1528		192d.b.	*ER* XV.551
373	1529	Edinburgh	276d.b.	HBJV, p. 144 P.
374	1529	Falkland	288d.b.	HBJV, p. 213 P.
375	1529	Edinburgh?	276d.b.	HBJV, App., p. 18 P.
376	1529	Leith	277.09d.b.	HBJV, App., p. 24 P.
377	1529	Edinburgh?	216d.b.	HBJV, App., p. 26 P.
378	1529		336d.b.	HBJV, App., p. 26 P.
379	1529	Aberdeen	300d.b.	ACR XII ii.6 Aw.
380	1529	Fife	150d.b.	*ER* XVI.15
381	1530	Edinburgh	252d.b.	HBJV, p. 227 P.
382	1530	Ayr?	409.92d.b. adipis	HBJV, App., p. 28 P.
383	1530	Fife	160d.b.	*ER* XVI.93
384	1530	Fife	200d.b.	*ER* XVI.93
385	1530		180d.b.	*ER* XVI.139
386	1532	Aberdeen	288d.b.	ACR XIII.437 assize V.
387	1532	Aberdeen	18s barrel	ACR XIV.66 Aw.
388	1534	Fife	192d.b.	*ER* XVI.430
389	1535	Fife	301.71d.b.	*ER* XVI.467
390	1535		240d.b.	*ER* XVI.481
391	1537	Errol	174d.b.	*ER* XVII.97
392	1537	Glamis etc.	170d.b.	*ER* XVII.146
393	1537	Glamis etc.	168d.b.	*ER* XVII.147
394	1537	Glamis etc.	160d.b.	*ER* XVII.147
395	1537		168d.b.	*ER* XVII.174
396	1538	St Andrews	192d.b.	SHS 2,4.79
397	1538	Kyrklistoun	180d.b.	SHS 2,4.79
398	1538	Eistfeild	180d.b.	SHS 2,4.80
399	1538	Errol	216d.b.	*ER* XVII.216
400	1538	Errol	216d.b.	*ER* XVII.216
401	1538	Glamis etc.	192d.b.	*ER* XVII.250
402	1539	Aberdeen	264d.b.	ACR XVI.385 C.
403	1539	St Andrews	221.81d.b.	SHS 2,4.99

Table 11 (*cont.*)

No.	Year	Place	Unit price	Source
404	1539		168d.b.	*ER* XVII.293
405	1539	Errol	240d.b.	*ER* XVII.362
406	1540	St Andrews	192,216,240d.b.	SHS 2,4.113
407	1540	Glamis	288,240d.b.	*ER* XVII.418
408	1541	St Andrews	252,264,276,288d.b.	SHS 2,4.130
409	1541	Glamis	240d.b.	*ER* XVII.478
410	1541	Linlithgowsh.	264d.b.	*ER* XVII.564
411	1541	Linlithgowsh.	264d.b.	*ER* XVII.567
412	1541	Stirlingsh.	240d.b.	*ER* XVII.598
413	1542	St Andrews	264d.b.	SHS 2,4.148

which appear in the list without any letter-code. However, the ambiguity of many medieval sales has prevented the use of a simple S to distinguish this group: such sales were often more properly accounting devices to set a money-figure on an accounting officer's answerability, or even commutations of obligations in kind. Thus 'sales' can often merge imperceptibly with valuations. This category can include allowances to accounting officers for goods disbursed, as well as more careful assessments of value; sometimes they can be the result of a careful inquest, but they can equally be notional sums fixed decades before. Assize valuations, set in burgh courts after careful examination of the state of the market in the region, have been specially noted. Perhaps enough has been said to provide a warning of the limited nature of the information conveyed by the letter-code. Its real purpose is to convey some impression of the highly variegated character of the evidence.

Barley[16]

Thirteenth- and fourteenth-century barley prices are scarce, and not particularly reliable. Deteriorated barley which had been kept in store too long cannot well be compared with other prices although its formal valuation by the men of Roxburgh is a point of interest.[17] Equally, barley meal is not met often enough for the price given at List 3 to have much value. On a number of other occasions our accountants

[16] The Scots bere (or bear) has been recorded where it was met but the distinction between bere and barley chiefly reflects the use of the vernacular or Latin (ordeum) in the original source, rather than a more careful choice of terminology.

[17] List 2. Another, later hint about the process of valuation occurs in List 177 where a value had to be proved before the Lords in Council.

make no distinction in price between barley and malt.[18] Since Rogers, and our own barley and malt averages suggest malt was generally dearer, the failure to distinguish the prices of these commodities is a handicap, especially early in the series when other evidence is scarce.[19] Before the fifteenth century the only grouping of barley prices which encourages any degree of confidence is the clutch of seven prices between 1328 and 1331.[20] Even here the range of price is wide, the highest prices more than doubling the lowest, and purchase prices usually significantly exceeding sales. After the Black Death the evidence is particularly weak, three of our five surviving prices coming from Agnes de Batella's annual allowance from the farms of Rait.[21] List 20, although of special interest, excusing barley below 10d.b. from the $\frac{1}{20}$th tax assessment of 1373, is scarcely a reliable guide to price.

Consequently the Table 12 and Figure 12 summarizing average prices for barley throughout the period have to be regarded with due scepticism, especially as regards the periods A to F. Having regard to the weakness of the barley evidence, and the comparative information provided by the other cereals, the barley average price in the second half of the fourteenth century looks especially suspect.

Comparison with English barley prices (Table 13) also casts doubt on the Scots evidence at this point, since it is only for these post-Plague barley figures that the rule of Scots cereals exceeding English in price is seriously questioned.

In the fifteenth and sixteenth centuries the evidence is much more plentiful, and the message of Table 12 and Figure 12 can be taken more seriously for this period. The Hume Will price of period G is characteristically on the low side; the barley in question had yet to be sown.[22] Thereafter prices rise sharply, and the currency-adjusted price and its index (Table 12, Figure 13) show that although currency alterations were the chief cause, barley prices rose strongly even after monetary factors have been stripped out. These generous prices offered

[18] List 4–6, 8–10, 56, 74, 87, 90, 92, 94, 111, and 400.

[19] Barley is also joined in price occasionally with wheat (List 151–2, 155, 187, 325, 327), with oats (List 224, 226, 277), once with rye (List 156) and most often with oatmeal, to which it was usually nearest in price (List 73, 145, 153, 182, 236, 238, 249, 253–4, 261–3, 265–6, 286, 293, 367, 382–4, 398, 405–8, 412, 419–20, 430, 436, 455, 508). Occasionally, the price was too low to be an economic price in any case (List 286, 367), but usually these prices look reasonably realistic, and barley and oatmeal were teamed together so often that in Scotland the unspecified term 'victual' very often meant a mixture of these two cereals.

[20] These are vital for the base period used in the indexation of barley prices. See Table 12.

[21] List 16–18.

[22] List 21.

Table 12. *Barley summary table*

Period	Mean price	Deflated	Index
A	10	10.0	55.5
B–C	18	18.0	100.0
D	11	11.0	61.1
E	(10)	(9.35)	(51.9)
F			
G	24	14.4	80.0
H	51	20.4	113.3
I	55	18.15	100.8
60s	55		
70s	80	22.4	124.4
80s	136		
90s	107	29.96	166.4
1500s	105	29.4	163.3
10s	114	28.5	158.3
20s	119	29.75	165.3
30s	142	31.24	173.6

Note: the mean price is in pence per boll; the deflated column gives the currency-adjusted sterling equivalent price. Parentheses have been used to flag up calculations which are less securely based than others – either because they are based on a smaller amount of data, or because they involve certain, possibly questionable, assumptions.

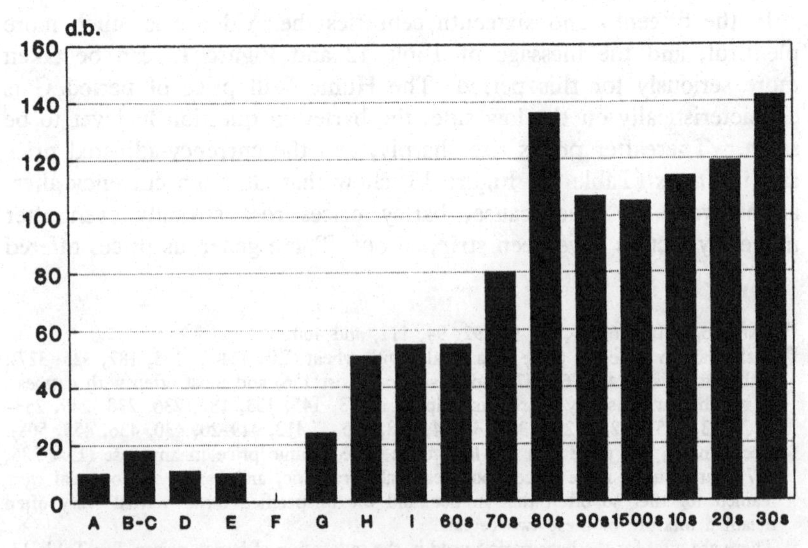

12 Barley prices (mean prices for time periods A–1530s)
For periods A–I, see Introduction, p. 6.

Table 13. *Barley prices 1263–1367: Scotland and England*

Year	Scotland	Durham	Rogers	Farmer
1263	3.33		3.56	
1264	(2.0)		4.0	3.48
1290	(2.5)		4.45	4.29
1296	5.0		3.76	3.83
1327		5.0		
1328	5.0		4.48	
	5.52			
	5.76			
	6.0			
	5.52			
	4.0			
1329	6.0	6.21	4.51	
	7.4			
1330		7.13		
1331	5.0		6.32	
	6.67			
	9.67			
1359	3.33	4.94/4.26	4.35	
1360	4.0	4.9/4.53	4.54	
1361	4.0	5.58	4.6	
1367	3.71	6.26	4.14	

Note: all prices are in shillings per quarter. Parentheses have been used to flag up calculations which are less securely based than others – either because they are based on a smaller amount of data, or because they involve certain, possibly questionable, assumptions.

in Scotland for barley will comfortably have exceeded English prices[23] even in terms of hard sterling, a fact which satisfactorily explains the continued English export of barley to Scotland, even though this grain was so plentifully grown north of the border. Thus a number of our prices provide evidence for barley imported to Scotland.[24]

Strong import demand, however, does not obscure the fact that barley was a major home-grown Scottish product. Anticipated yields of Scots barley were very much in line with those expected in England,[25] and compensation claims were also entered in the courts if manuring[26] or

[23] Farmer's index shows that prices in England often failed to equal their fourteenth-century base period price.

[24] *ER* VIII.320. List 90, 91–2, 101–3, 178, 209, 217, 244, 258, 269, 291.

[25] List 117, 151–2, 163 speak of four-fold yields. List 167, 169 of three-fold. See also the comments made about wheat yields, above, p. 145.

[26] List 154.

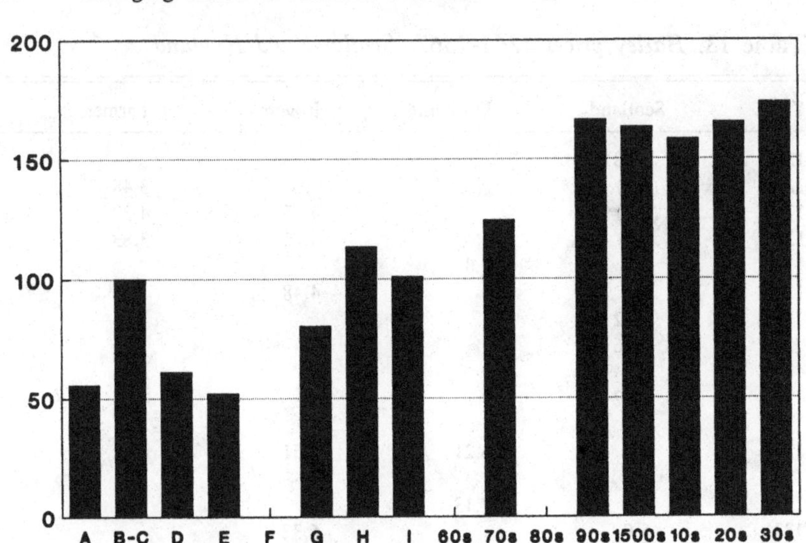

13 Barley index (sterling equivalent)

provision of oxen[27] were interfered with, as well as for the more normal appropriation of land. Although some barley was consumed in its basic state, huge quantities were malted and then brewed into ale and beer.[28] Wages were sometimes paid, at least in part, in barley, given a money value set against the value of the work,[29] and even more exalted feudal fees were sometimes partially settled in kind.[30]

However, the clearest evidence for the almost universal cultivation of barley, from the lowlands to Orkney, or from the east coast to the Western Isles, derives from the incidence of rents, grassums,[31] or other renders paid in kind, upon which various different kinds of monetary value were set. The value of these various 'sales', allowances, valuations, or commutations for the study of prices is highly variable. In the first place the actual terminology used is often but a poor guide to the nature of the payment involved. Thus we sometimes meet a transaction

[27] List 166, 181.

[28] See List 196, the building of a malt house and malt kiln; List 369–70, 375, 378–9, and 402–3, 411, for the expected yield of usually *c.* 10 gallons of ale from 1 boll (but List 402 gives almost 20 gallons from a boll), and List 84 for mention of the malt makers in Leith, evidently a national centre of malting, but see also the malt prices series and commentary pp. 177–88.

[29] List 293 paid to men working on the bridge at Dunkeld, 304.

[30] List 68, for 20 marks paid in kind to John Stewart, Lord Darnley.

[31] A kind of entry fine.

described as 'Vendicionem seu commutationem',[32] a clear enough description in this case, but one which throws doubt on other 'sales'. Moreover, even explicit commutations may or may not be of importance for the study of prices, depending on when the original commutation was arranged, and whether the payment was fixed, or variable.[33] Sometimes these payments were made by the landowner to his husbandmen for renders in kind. In other words the term of the tack or lease involved the provision of goods to the landowner at what may even have begun as a low price, but which soon lost all connection with the going rate. On other occasions rents in kind were commuted to money payments, or even 'sold' to the accounting officer.[34]

Thus Adam Smith warned 'the writers who have collected the price of corn in ancient times seem frequently to have mistaken what is called in Scotland the conversion price for the actual market price'.[35] However, such valuations and conversions have not been totally excluded from our study. In some cases, if they are up-to-date, they may even provide a better guide to general year on year price levels than true market prices which can be distorted by unusual conditions of one particular time or place. More often, of course, they are more or less out of date, but it is only when they become markedly so that they can be identified with confidence as frozen or fossilized. Moreover, in remote regions far from the market centres, these valuations, even when out of date, will have contributed to the local sense of price. Grain surrendered by farmers at one price will often have been sold on at a much greater one by landlords, but some awareness of these parallel pricing systems is an essential part of our understanding of the nature of price in the middle ages, and of the way in which it differed from what one would now call a market price. Although these various valuations have been retained in the full data base and even to some extent in the price lists, they have been excluded from the mean price calculations when they can be clearly seen to be out of date by comparison with other prices.[36] This is obviously a matter of judgement, and we have probably erred on the side of caution, continuing to calculate from prices which may have begun to grow out of date. Where this is the case our calculated

[32] *ER* X.328.

[33] Even variable payments may be expected to show a certain stickiness, and lag behind open market prices.

[34] See especially Murray, 'Exchequer and Crown Revenue', pp. 83–6 on these valuations.

[35] Smith, *The Wealth of Nations*, p. 166.

[36] The circularity of the argument that anomalous prices are excluded when they look anomalous compared to the others does not escape us. Students with a more rigorously philosophical approach may recalculate means themselves from the full data base. See also in this connection the discussion of marts prices, below, pp. 232–3.

Table 14. *Barley price list*

No.	Year	Place	Unit price	Source
1	1263	Maccuswell	10d.b.	*ER* I.17
2	1264	Roxburgh	6d.b. deteriorated	*ER* I.29
3	1290	Kincardine	7.5d.b. barley meal	*ER* I.49
4	1296	Coldstream	5s.qr (=15d.b.) with malt	*DHS* II.33 V.
5	1328	Cardross	15d.b. with malt	*ER* I.124–5 P.
6	1328	Cardross	16.5d.b. with malt	*ER* I.124–5 P.
7	1328	Berwick?	12d.b.	*ER* I.206
8	1328	Cardross	18d.b. with malt	*ER* I.124–5 P.
9	1328	Cardross	17.25d.b. with malt	*ER* I.124–5 P.
10	1328	Cardross	16.5d.b. with malt	*ER* I.124–5 P.
11	1329		18d.b.	*ER* I.241 V.
12	1329		22.18d.b. with malt	*ER* I.289 P.
13	1331		29d.b.	*ER* I.400 P.
14	1331		20d.b.	*ER* I.396
15	1331		15d.b.	*ER* I.396
16	1359	(Rait)	10d.b.	*ER* II.52. V.
17	1360	Rait	12d.b.	*ER* II.81 V.
18	1361	(Rait)	12d.b.	*ER* II.117 V.
19	1367		11.12d.b.	*ER* II.294. P.
20	1373	Lanark	10d.b.	*ER* II.418 not a price
21	1424	Dunglas,etc.	24d.b.	HMS 12,8.87 W.
22	1433	Leith	80d.b.	*ER* IV.579
23	1434	Edinburgh?	7s.barrel	*ER* IV.627 P.
24	1437	Feichley,Mar	60d.b.	*ER* V.55
25	1442	Bute & Arran	40d.b.	*ER* V.167
26	1442	Bute & Arran	40d.b.	*ER* V.167
27	1442	Bute & Arran	40d.b.	*ER* V.166–7
28	1444	Bute & Arran	40d.b.	*ER* V.213
29	1445	Bute	72.63d.b.	*ER* V.253 grassum
30	1446	Bute	60d.b.	*ER* V.290 grassum
31	1447	Bute & Arran	60d.b.	*ER* V.334
32	1447	Bute & Arran	60d.b.	*ER* V.354
33	1447	Bute & Arran	60d.b.	*ER* V.333
34	1448	Bute & Arran	60d.b.	*ER* V.365
35	1448	Bute & Arran	60d.b.	*ER* V.365
36	1449	Bute & Arran	48d.b.	*ER* V.412
37	1449	Bute & Arran	45d.b.	*ER* V.411
38	1450	Bute & Arran	60d.b.	*ER* V.454
39	1450	Bute & Arran	45d.b.	*ER* V.453
40	1455	Bute & Arran	54d.b.	*ER* VI.232
41	1456	Bute & Arran	69d.b. or 70d.b.	*ER* VI.330–1
42	1456	Bute & Arran	70.15d.b.	*ER* VI.331
43	1457	Bute & Arran	40d.b.	*ER* VI.422
44	1457	Bute & Arran	40d.b.	*ER* VI.422
45	1457	Strath'ney	36d.b.	*ER* VI.423
46	1458	Strath'ney	36d.b.	*ER* VI.575

Table 14 (*cont.*)

No.	Year	Place	Unit price	Source
47	1459	Bute & Arran	48d.b.	*ER* VI.630–1
48	1459	Strathearn	80d.b.	*ER* VI.635
49	1459	Bute & Arran	48d.b.	*ER* VI.630
50	1459	Bute & Arran	48d.b.	*ER* VI.630
51	1460	Bute & Arran	40d.b.	*ER* VII.14
52	1461	Bute & Arran	60d.b.	*ER* VII.110
53	1461	Fife	24d.b.	*ER* VII.80
54	1461	Bute & Arran	60d.b.	*ER* VII.110
55	1461	Bute & Arran	60d.b.	*ER* VII.110–11
56	1461	Moray	96d.b. with malt	*ER* VII.122
57	1461	Bute & Arran	60d.b.	*ER* VII.110
58	1461	Garioch	80d.b.	*ER* VII.89–90
59	1461	Bute & Arran	60d.b.	*ER* VII.110
60	1462	Bute & Arran	72d.b.	*ER* VII.276
61	1462	Bute & Arran	50d.b.	*ER* VII.276
62	1462	Bute	60d.b.	*ER* VII.275–6 grassum
63	1462	Garioch	40d.b.	*ER* VII.162
64	1462	le Halch	60d.b.	*ER* VII.167
65	1464	Bute	50d.b.	*ER* VII.339
66	1464	Moray	80d.b. with malt	*ER* VII.351
67	1465	Bute & Arran	50d.b.	*ER* VII.406
68	1467	Bute	60d.b.	*ER* VII.491
69	1468	Moray	45.61d.b.	*ER* VII.642
70	1468	Fife	60d.b.	*ER* VIII.97
71	1472	Moray	40d.b.	*ER* VIII.148
72	1472	Moray	40d.b.	*ER* VIII.148
73	1472	Ardmannoch	12d.b. with oatmeal	*ER* VIII.184 V.
74	1472	Ardmannoch	40d.b. with malt	*ER* VIII.376
75	1473	Moray	40.01d.b.	*ER* VIII.222
76	1473		60d.b.	*ALA* I.24 C.
77	1473	Orkney & Shetl.	80d.b.	*ER* VIII.225
78	1474	Orkney & Shetl.	80d.b.	*ER* VIII.276
79	1474	Orkney & Shetl.	80d.b.	*ER* VIII.276 V.
80	1474	Orkney & Shetl.	80d.b.	*ER* VIII.276 V.
81	1474	Moray	50d.b.	*ER* VIII.303
82	1474	Orkney	80d.b.	*ER* VIII.275 V.
83	1474	Orkney & Shetl.	83d.b.	*ER* VIII.276 V.
84	1475	Orkney & Shetl.	80d.b.	*ER* VIII.364 V.
85	1475	Moray	65.46d.b.	*ER* VIII.369
86	1476	Ross	8d.b.	*ER* VIII.597 V.
87	1476	Fife	90d.b. with malt	*ER* VIII.448
88	1476	Stirlingsh.	80d.b.	*ER* VIII.431
89	1476	Moray	80d.b.	*ER* VIII.410
90	1476	N. Berwick	120d.b.English with malt	*ER* VIII.469
91	1477	N. Berwick	160d.b.English	*ER* VIII.624
92	1477	Dysart	160d.b.English with malt	*ER* VIII.549

Table 14 (*cont.*)

No.	Year	Place	Unit price	Source
93	1477	Moray	96d.b.	*ER* VIII.526
94	1477	Fife	46d.b. with malt	*ER* VIII.448
95	1478	Aberdeen	86d.b.	ACR VI.528 C.
96	1478		80d.b.	*ALC* I.8 Aw.
97	1478	Stirlingsh.	120d.b. with malt	*ER* VIII.565
98	1479	Linlithgowsh.	96d.b.	*ER* IX.16–17
99	1479	Moray	50d.b.	*ER* IX.49
100	1479	Ross	36d.b.	*ER* IX.60
101	1479	Dysart & P't'w	120d.b. English	*ER* IX.71
102	1479	N. Berwick	108d.b. English	*ER* IX.68
103	1479	Kinghorn	108d.b. English	*ER* IX.73
104	1479	Newmekill etc.	8d.b.	*ER* IX.59 V.
105	1480		80d.b.	*ALC* I.54 Aw.
106	1480	Aberdeen	50d.b.	ACR VI.671
107	1480	Abircorne	115.2d.b.	*ER* IX.104
108	1480	Menteith	60d.b.	*ER* IX.115
109	1480	Moray	84d.b.	*ER* IX.142
110	1480	Stirlingsh.	120d.b.	*ER* IX.95–6
111	1480	Fife	120d.b. with malt	*ER* IX.100
112	1481	Orkney & Shetl.	50d.b.	*ER* IX.184
113	1481	Raith	288d.b.	*ALA* I.*112 Aw.
114	1481	Burnhus & hall	288d.b.	*ALA* I.*112 Aw.
115	1482	Raith	216d.b.	*ALA* I.*112 Aw.
116	1482	Burnhus & hall	216d.b.	*ALA* I.*112 Aw.
117	1482	Dunmure	120d.b.	*ALC* I.199 C.
118	1482	Wauchtoun'	192d.b.	*ALC* I.429 Aw.
119	1483	Wauchtoun'	192d.b.	*ALC* I.166 Aw.
120	1483	Ltl.Preston	160d.b.	*ALA* I.*118
121	1483	Perthshire	240d.b.	*ALA* I.*116 Aw.
122	1483	Stirlingsh.	115.55d.b.	*ER* IX.252
123	1484	Quhittingam	108d.b.	*ALC* I.*90 Aw.
124	1484	Aberdeen	120d.b.,160d.b.	ACR VI.859 Aw.
125	1484	Broxmouth	120d.b.	*ALA* I.*134 Aw.
126	1484	Broxmouth	120d.b.	*ALA* I.*134 Aw.
127	1484	Mukkersy	100d.b.	*ALA* I.*134 Aw.
128	1485	Davidstoun	216d.b.	*ALA* I.115–16 Aw.
129	1485	Ryflat etc	120d.b.	*ALC* I.*107 Aw.
130	1485		80d.b.	*ALC* I.*102 Aw.
131	1485	Forteviot	120d.b.	*ALC* I.*94 Aw.
132	1486	Orkney	84d.b.	*ER* IX.490–1
133	1486	Orkney & Shetl.	84d.b.	*ER* IX.490
134	1486	Bute	60d.b.	*ER* IX.489
135	1486	Bute	50d.b.	*ER* IX.489
136	1486	Bute	60d.b.	*ER* IX.489 V.
137	1487	Colpmalindy	240d.b.	*ALA* I.142–3 C.
138	1487	Innes	144d.b.	*ALA* I.118 Aw.

Table 14 (*cont.*)

No.	Year	Place	Unit price	Source
139	1487	the Hirne	96d.b.	*ALC* I.107 Aw.
140	1488	Abernethy	192d.b.	*ALC* I.90 Aw.
141	1488	Aberdeen	144d.b.	ACR VII.95 O.
142	1488	Orkney & Shetl.	50d.b.	*ER* X.40
143	1488	Abirnethy	216d.b.	*ALA* I.114 C.
144	1488	Dun/Dummure	160d.b.	*ALC* I.86 Aw.
145	1489		192d.b. with meal	*ALC* I.119 C.
146	1489	Ardendracht	100d.b.	*ALC* I.243,256 Aw.
147	1489	Kyrkinnyr'	84d.b.	*ALC* I.117 C.
148	1489	Balcarhous	144d.b.	*ALC* I.113 Aw.
149	1489	Davidstone	228d.b.	*ALC* I.102 C.
150	1489	Kynfawnis	150d.b.	*ALC* I.102 C.
151	1490	Ballinbrech	120d.b. with wheat	*ALC* I.156 Aw.
152	1490	Leslie	120d.b. with wheat	*ALC* I.156 Aw.
153	1490	Innoch & Crai.	120d.b. with meal	*ALC* I.181 C.
154	1490	Delgatie castle	96d.b.	*ALC* I.289 Aw.
155	1490	Essilmont	120d.b. with wheat	*ALA* I.183 Aw.
156	1490	Foulefurd	192d.b. with rye	*ALC* I.152 Aw.
157	1490	W. Glasfurd	96d.b	*ALC* I.316 Aw.
158	1490	Glentoun'	60d.b.	*ALC* I.270 Aw.
159	1490	Edinburgh?	180d.b.	*ALC* I.16 Aw.
160	1490	Foulefurd	192d.b.	*ALC* I.152 Aw.
161	1490	Glasfurd'	96d.b.	*ALC* I.316 Aw.
162	1491	Ros'neth'?	240d.b.	*ALC* I.181 Wi.
163	1491	Torwechquhy	96d.b. with fodder	*ALC* I.181 C.
164	1491	Arth'	240d.b.	*ALC* I.195 Aw.
165	1491	Inverquhoth	60d.b.	*ALC* I.202 Aw.
166	1491		96d.b.	*ALC* I.335 Aw.
167	1491	Quhitnacloi	60d.b.	*ALC* I.363 Aw.
168	1491	?Edinburgh	180d.b.	*ALC* I.171 O.
169	1491	Quhitnacloi	60d.b.	*ALC* I.363 Aw.
170	1491	Raith/Bawber	77d.b.	*ALC* I.172 Aw.
171	1491	the Raith	72d.b.	*ALC* I.172 Aw.
172	1492	Trewin & Lochl	96d.b.	*ALC* I.211 C.
173	1492	Earlsferry	10s.barrel	*ALC* I.245 Aw.
174	1492		123d.b. with fodder	*ALC* I.248 Aw.
175	1492	Quhite Crag	96d.b. av. price	*ALC* I.316 Aw.
176	1492		96d.b.	*ALC* I.221 C.
177	1492		96d.b. with fodder	*ALC* I.219 Aw.
178	1493	Edinburgh	120d.b. English	*ER* X.460
179	1493	Fife	72d.b.	*ER* X.452
180	1493		120d.b.	*ALC* I.286 C.
181	1494	Coutty	80d.b.	*ALA* I.190 Aw.
182	1494	Kirkton	120d.b. with meal	*ALA* I.203 C.
183	1494	Kilmarone	54d.b.	*ALC* I.403 Aw.
184	1494	Perth	192d.b.	*ALC* I.359 C.

Table 14 (*cont.*)

No.	Year	Place	Unit price	Source
185	1494	Crancho	72d.b.	*ALC* I.333 Aw.
186	1495		132d.b.	*ALC* I.425 Aw.
187	1495	Setoun'	84d.b. with wheat	*ALC* I.399 Aw.
188	1495	WesterGarts.	60d.b.	*ALC* I.403 Aw.
189	1495	Ballegarno	72d.b.	*ALC* I.422 Aw.
190	1496	Orkney & Shetl.	50d.b.	*ER* XI.19
191	1496	Orkney & Shetl.	84d.b.	*ER* XI.19
192	1496	Bute	79.06d.b.	*ER* XI.5
193	1497	Ballincreif	112.94d.b.	*ER* XI.93
194	1497	Fife	175.8d.b.	*ER* XI.76
195	1497	Dunbar	120d.b.	*ER* XI.75–6 V.
196	1498	Fife	60d.b.	*ER* XI.154 V.
197	1498	Orkney	100d.b.	*ER* XI.165 P.
198	1498	Falkland	115.67d.b.	*ER* XI.77
199	1498	Falkland	118d.b.	*ER* XI.77
200	1498	Falkland	120d.b.	*ER* XI.77
201	1498	Fife	120d.b.	SHS 3,50.77
202	1498	Ballincreif	160d.b.	*ER* XI.211
203	1499	Fife	115.64d.b.	*ER* XI.243
204	1500	Aberdeen	62.8d. b.	ACR VII.1034 Aw.
205	1500	Peebles	60d.b.	*ER* XI.309*
206	1500	Bute	80d.b.	*ER* XI.326
207	1500	Bute & Arran	80d.b.	*ER* XI.325
208	1501	Bute	80d.b.	*ER* XII.67
209	1502	Edinburgh	159.55d.b. English	*ER* XII.162
210	1502		60d.b.?	*TA* II.294 P.
211	1502	Bute	93.76d.b.	*ER* XII.248
212	1503	Cameron	120d.b.	*ER* XII.195
213	1503	Stirling	168d.b.	*TA* II.394 P.
214	1503	Ballincreif	100d.b.	*ER* XII.179
215	1503	Ross	10d.b.	*ER* XII.239 V.
216	1503	Ardmannoch	120d.b.	*ER* XII.245
217	1503	Edinburgh	180d.b. imported	*ER* XII.262
218	1503	Fife	148.41d.b.	*ER* XII.195–6
219	1503	Fife	120d.b.	*ER* XII.195
220	1503	Fife	120d.b.	*ER* XII.195
221	1503	Kinlos	101.2d.b.	*ER* XII.225
222	1504	Fife	108d.b.	*ER* XII.310
223	1504	Fife	228.28d.b.	*ER* XII.283–4
224	1504	Bute	53.01d.b. with oats	*ER* XII.319
225	1504	Fife	108d.b.	*ER* XII.310
226	1505	Bute	48d.b. with oats	*ER* XII.430
227	1505	Montblairy	60d.b.	*ER* XII.438
228	1505	Colbrandspet	100d.b.	*ER* XII.519
229	1505	S.Kintyre	40d.b.	*ER* XII.586
230	1505	Murthocarny	30d.b.	*ER* XII.446 V.

Table 14 (*cont.*)

No.	Year	Place	Unit price	Source
231	1505	Moray	108d.b.	*ER* XII.446
232	1505	Moray	85.98d.b.	*ER* XII.439
233	1506	Stirling	100d.b.	*ER* XII.543
234	1506	Perth	96d.b.	SHS 2,10.195
235	1506	Ferische etc.	10d.b.	*ER* XII.550 V.
236	1506	Auchterhouse	60d.b. with meal	*ER* XII.486
237	1506	Ardmannoch	72d.b.	*ER* XII.557
238	1506	Strathdon	60d.b. with meal	*ER* XII.508
239	1506	Ross & Ardman.	60d.b.	*ER* XII.515 V.
240	1506	Perth	108d.b.	SHS 2,10.201
241	1506	Moray	53.33d.b.	*ER* XII.493
242	1506	Bute	72d.b.	*ER* XII.512
243	1506	Dunbar	75.01d.b.	*ER* XII.559
244	1506	Edinburgh	101.49d.b. English	*ER* XII.593
245	1506	Kyrkhill	80d.b.	SHS 2,10.93
246	1506	Dunkeld	108d.b.	SHS 2,10.90
247	1506	Dunkeld	96d.b.	SHS 2,10.81
248	1506	Dunkeld	80d.b.	SHS 2,10.90
249	1507	Montblairy	50d.b. with meal	*ER* XIII.51–2
250	1507	Ferische etc.	10d.b.	*ER* XIII.45 V.
251	1507	Ross	127.40d.b.	*ER* XIII.47–8
252	1507	Ardmannoch	144d.b.	*ER* XIII.49
253	1507	Auchterhouse	150.43d.b. with meal	*ER* XIII.30
254	1507	Strathdon	120d.b. with meal	*ER* XIII.73
255	1507	Perth	216d.b.	SHS 2,10.208
256	1507	Perth	160d.b.	SHS 2,10.208
257	1507	Clony	216d.b.	SHS 2,10.168
258	1507	Edinburgh	194.25d.b. English	*ER* XIII.95
259	1508	Aberdeen	192d.b.	ACR VIII.838 Wi.
260	1508	Lothian	120d.b.	SHS 2,10.251
261	1508	Kynnacrag	10d.b. with meal	*ER* XIII.145 V.
262	1508	Auchterhouse	76.52d.b. with meal	*ER* XIII.153
263	1508	Montblairy	59.37d.b. with meal	*ER* XIII.176
264	1508	Orkney	72d.b.	*ER* XIII.181 P.
265	1508	Mekill Strat	60d.b. with meal	*ER* XIII.195
266	1508	Kildrummy	50d.b. with meal	*ER* XIII.198
267	1508	Moray	72d.b.	*ER* XIII.204
268	1508	Moray	71.64d.b.	*ER* XIII.209
269	1508	Edinburgh	132d.b. English	*ER* XIII.229
270	1508	Bute	72d.b.	*ER* XIII.139
271	1508	Perth	108d.b.	SHS 2,10.211
272	1508	Lothian	178.56d.b.	SHS 2,10.248
273	1509	Moray	48d.b.	*ER* XIII.294
274	1509	Aberdeen	214.4d.b.	ACR VIII.965 Wi.
275	1509	Kincarny	120d.b.	SHS 2,10.172
276	1509	Bute	72d.b.	*ER* XIII.313

Table 14 (*cont.*)

No.	Year	Place	Unit price	Source
277	1509	Auchterhouse	50d.b. with oats	*ER* XIII.343
278	1509	Dunkeld	61.25d.b.	SHS 2,10.109
279	1509	Dunkeld	72d.b.	SHS 2,10.110 V.
280	1509	Dunkeld	120d.b.	SHS 2,10.111 V.
281	1509	Ramorganye	90d.b.	*ER* XIII.289 V.
282	1509	Fife	66d.b.	*ER* XIII.289
283	1509	Abbirlathy	84d.b.	SHS 2,10.259
284	1509	Perth	72d.b.	SHS 2,10.216
285	1509	Dunmakerf	72d.b.	SHS 2,10.111 V.
286	1510	Petdinne	30d.b. with meal	*ER* XIII.454 V.
287	1510	Dunkeld	80d.b.	SHS 2,10.112
288	1510	Dunkeld	80d.b.	SHS 2,10.113
289	1510	Perth	80d.b.	SHS 2,10.220
290	1510	Lothian	84d.b.	SHS 2,10.254
291	1510	Edinburgh	109.86 English	*ER* XIII.390
292	1510	Abbirlathy	84d.b.	SHS 2,10.259
293	1511	Dunkeld	80d.b. with meal	SHS 2,10.285 V.
294	1511	Moray	60d.b.	*ER* XIII.459
295	1511	Sutherland	100.12d.b.	*ER* XIII.449
296	1511	Lothian	84d.b.	SHS 2,10.257
297	1511	Lothian	150d.b.	SHS 2,10.261
298	1511	Lothian	160d.b.	SHS 2,10.261
299	1511	Dunkeld	144d.b.	SHS 2,10.126 V.
300	1511	Lothian	72d.b.	SHS 2,10.257
301	1511	Perth	144d.b.	SHS 2,10.224
302	1511	Dunkeld	144d.b.	SHS 2,10.121
303	1511	Dunkeld	120d.b.	SHS 2,10.121
304	1511	Dunkeld	80d.b.	SHS 2,10.120 V.
305	1512	Moray	120d.b.	*ER* XIII.523
306	1512	Methven	144d.b.	*ER* XIII.550
307	1513	Lothian	156.21d.b.	SHS 2,10.262
308	1513	Linlithgow	121.78d.b.	*ER* XIV.3
309	1513	Bute	80d.b.	*ER* XIV.21
310	1513	Stirling	120d.b.	*ER* XIV.42
311	1513	Ferisch etc.	9.75d.b.	*ER* XIV.85 V.
312	1513	Dunkeld	144d.b.	SHS 2,20.129
313	1513	Dunkeld	120d.b.	SHS 2,10.129
314	1513	Dunkeld	108d.b.	SHS 2,10.129
315	1513	Perth	160d.b.	SHS 2,10.230
316	1514	Perth	96d.b.	SHS 2,10.240
317	1514	Perth	120d.b.	SHS 2,10.240
318	1514	Clony	120d.b.	SHS 2,10.152 V.
319	1514	Tullemule	120d.b.	SHS 2,10.152 V.
320	1514	Dunkeld	120d.b.	SHS 2,10.152 V.
321	1514	Perth	144d.b.	SHS 2,10.234
322	1514	Perth	120d.b.	SHS 2,10.242 P.

Table 14 (*cont.*)

No.	Year	Place	Unit price	Source
323	1514	Perth	96d.b.	SHS 2,10.240
324	1514	Perth	120d.b.	SHS 2,10.240
325	1515	Fife	90d.b. with wheat	*ER* XIV. 177
326	1515	Fife	100d.b.	*ER* XIV.179
327	1515	Moray	100d.b. with wheat	*ER* XIV.118
328	1515		68.55d.b.	*ER* XIV.224
329	1515	Dunkeld	120d.b.	SHS 2,10.146
330	1515	Moray	100d.b.	*ER* XIV.133–4
331	1516	Cultiscroft	120d.b.	SHS 2,10.151
332	1516	Arleweicht	64d.b.	SHS 2,10.151 V.
333	1516	Lennox	60d.b.	*ER* XIV.232
334	1516	Ross	72d.b.	*ER* XIV.283
335	1516	Ross	92d.b.	*ER* XIV.283
336	1516	Fife	90.31d.b.	*ER* XIV.291
337	1516	Dunkeld	160d.b.	SHS 2,10.151
338	1516	Moray	72d.b.	*ER* XIV.283
339	1516	Strauthhurd	120d.b.	SHS 2,10.151
340	1516	Stobhale	120d.b.	SHS 2,10.151
341	1517	Ross	81.85d.b.	*ER* XIV.305
342	1517	Fife	144d.b.	*ER* XIV.347
343	1517	Cupar,Fife	80d.b.victual $\frac{1}{3}$ meal	*SCBF*, p. 79 Aw.
344	1517	Aberdeen	6.67s.barrel	ACR IX.746 Aw.
345	1517	Fife	144d.b.	*ER* XIV.321
346	1518		144d.b.	*ER* XIV.471–2
347	1518	Fife	100d.b.	*ER* XIV.414
348	1518	Balbrechy	96d.b.	*ER* XIV. 409
349	1518	Largo	192d.b.	*ER* XIV. 407
350	1518	Cupar,Fife	240d.b.	*SCBF*, p. 208 C.
351	1521	Ross	90d.b.	*ER* XV.24
352	1521	Aberdeen	192d.b. with fodder	ACR XI.119 C.
353	1521	Ferisch etc.	10d.b.	*ER* XV.23 V.
354	1522	Lennox	60d.b.	*ER* XV.8
355	1522	Aberdeen	160d.b.	ACR XI.31–5 C.
356	1522	Aberdeen	144d.b.	ACR XI,36–7 C.
357	1522	Aberdeen	144d.b.	ACR XI.52 Aw.
358	1523	Ross	168d.b.	*ER* XV.100–1
359	1523	Aberdeen	120d.b.	ACR XI.298 O.
360	1523	Aberdeen	216d.b.	ACR XI.372 Aw.
361	1524	Ross	100d.b.	*ER* XV.171–2
362	1524	Ardmannoch	100d.b.	*ER* XV.175–6
363	1524		160d.b.	*ER* XV.209
364	1524	Fife	144d.b.	*ER* XV.132–3
365	1524	Balbreky	96d.b.	*ER* XV.121–2
366	1524	Murthocarny	66.66d.b.	*ER* XV.119–20 V.
367	1524	Kincrag,etc.	10d.b. with meal	*ER* XV.170 V.
368	1525		108d.b	*ER* XV.294

Table 14 (*cont.*)

No.	Year	Place	Unit price	Source
369	1526	Edinburgh	150d.b.	HBJV. App., pp. 8,9 P.
370	1526	Edinburgh	144d.b.	HBJV. p. 57 P.
371	1526	Edinburgh	132d.b.	HBJV. App., p. 10 P.
372	1526	Ross	108d.b.	*ER* XV.330
373	1526	Ardmannoch	100d.b.	*ER* XV.341
374	1526	Ruthillutt	120d.b.	*ER* XV.353
375	1526	Edinburgh	150d.b.	HBJV, p. 41 P.
376	1526	Fife	120d.b.	*ER* XV.354
377	1526		120d.b.	*ER* XV.388
378	1526	Edinburgh	144d.b.	HBJV, p. 58 P.
379	1526	Edinburgh	150d.b.	HBJV, p. 47 P.
380	1526	Fife	100d.b.	*ER* XV.353
381	1526	Fife	100d.b.	*ER* XV.354
382	1527	Ross	100d.b.? with meal	*ER* XV.407
383	1527	Ardmannoch	100d.b. with meal	*ER* XV.412–13
384	1527	Ardmannoch	100d.b. with meal	*ER* XV.413
385	1527	Fife	120d.b.	*ER* XV.400
386	1527		168d.b.	*ER* XV.466
387	1527	Fife	100d.b.	*ER* XV.399
388	1527	Fife	180d.b.	*ER* XV.399
389	1527	Aberdeen	240d.b.	ACR XII i.18 Aw.
390	1527	Ruthillut	160d.b.	*ER* XV.399
391	1527	Bute	100d.b.	*ER* XV.425
392	1528	Aberdeen	20s barrel	ACR XII i.42
393	1528	Fife	132d.b.	*ER* XV.475
394	1528	Bute	80d.b.	*ER* XV.497
395	1528		120d.b.	*ER* XV.552
396	1528	Fife	100d.b.	*ER* XV.475
397	1528	Fife	120d.b.	*ER* XV.480
398	1528	Ardmannoch	90d.b. with meal	*ER* XV.506
399	1529	Fife	100d.b.	*ER* XVI.15
400	1529	Fife	100d.b. with malt	*ER* XVI.16
401	1529	Bute	80d.b.	*ER* XVI.24
402	1529	Edinburgh	180d.b.	HBJV, p. 144 P.
403	1529	Edinburgh	175.29d.b.	HBJV, p. 151 P.
404	1529	Aberdeen	192d.b.	ACR XIV 612 C.
405	1529	Estwemis	100d.b. with meal	*ER* XVI.112–13
406	1529	Ross	100d.b. with meal	*ER* XVI.113
407	1529	Ross	100d.b. with meal	*ER* XVI.113
408	1529	Ross	90d.b. with meal	*ER* XVI.113
409	1529	Ardmannoch	100d.b.	*ER* XVI.118–9
410	1529	Hiltoun etc.	20d.b.	*ER* XVI.119 V.
411	1529	Edinburgh	180d.b.	HBJV, App., p. 18 P.
412	1529	Kincrag	10d.b. with meal	*ER* XVI.111.V.
413	1529	Bute	80d.b.	*ER* XVI.24
414	1529	Fyschrie etc.	10d.b.	*ER* XVI.110 V.

Table 14 (*cont.*)

No.	Year	Place	Unit price	Source
415	1529	Ardmannoch	12.75d.b. victual	*ER* XVI.116 V.
416	1530	Fife	100d.b.	*ER* XVI.94
417	1530		144d.b.	*ER* XVI.144
418	1530	Fife	100d.b.	*ER* XVI.95
419	1531	Ross	160d.b. with meal	*ER* XVI.203
420	1531	Ross	160d.b. with meal	*ER* XVI.203
421	1531	Fife	100d.b.	*ER* XVI.195
422	1531	Ardmannoch	160d.b.	*ER* XVI.207
423	1531	Aberdeen	76.36d.b.	ACR XIII.197 Aw.
424	1531	Mekle Suthy	160d.b.	*ER* XVI.207
425	1531	Ardmannoch	160d.b.	*ER* XVI.207
426	1531	Hiltoun etc	160d.b.	*ER* XVI.207
427	1532	Ross	72d.b.	*ER* XVI.279
428	1532	Aberdeen	96d.b.	ACR XIII.352 C.
429	1533	Aberdeen	14s.barrel	ACR XIV.185 Aw.
430	1533	Ardmannoch	75d.b. with meal	*ER* XVI.327
431	1533	Leith	72d.b.	*ER* XVI.322–3
432	1533	Aberdeen	240d.b.	ACR XIV.94 O.
433	1534	Leith	120d.b.	*ER* XVI.406
434	1534	Ross	100d.b.	*ER* XVI.407
435	1534	Ardmannoch	100d.b.	*ER* XVI.410
436	1534	Ardmannoch	100d.b. with meal	*ER* XVI.410
437	1534	Fife	132d.b.	*ER* XVI.431
438	1535	Bute	80d.b.	*ER* XVII.29
439	1535	Fife	207.36d.b.	*ER* XVI.468
440	1535	Aberdeen	168d.b.	ACR XVI.837 C.
441	1535		259.78d.b.	*ER* XVI.481
442	1536	Ross	120d.b.	*ER* XVII.35
443	1536	Fischerie etc.	10d.b.	*ER* XVII.33 V.
444	1536	Murthocarny	66.67d.b.	*ER* XVII.8 V.
445	1536	Aberdeen	168d.b.	ACR XVI.735 C.
446	1536	Kincrag	10d.b.	*ER* XVII.33 V.
447	1537	Glamis etc	100d.b.	*ER* XVII.148
448	1537	Glamis etc.	108d.b.	*ER* XVII.148
449	1537	Glamis etc.	30d.b.	*ER* XVII.149
450	1537	Glamis etc.	108d.b. aride multure	*ER* XVII.149
451	1537		120d.b.	*ER* XVII.175
452	1537		120d.b.	*ER* XVII.175
453	1537	Tantallon	100d.b.	*ER* XVII.133 V.
454	1537	Ardmannoch	90d.b.	*ER* XVII.117
455	1537	Ross	90d.b. with meal	*ER* XVII.114
456	1537	Glamis etc.	108d.b.	*ER* XVII.149
457	1538	Glamis	144d.b.	*ER* XVII.255
458	1538	Kyrklistoun	120d.b.	SHS 2,4.80
459	1538	Bute	100d.b.	*ER* XVII.199
460	1538	Errol	168d.b.	*ER* XVII.217

Table 14 (*cont.*)

No.	Year	Place	Unit price	Source
461	1538	Ardmannoch	144d.b.	*ER* XVII.240
462	1538	Glamis etc.	144d.b.	*ER* XVII.251
463	1538	Glamis etc.	132d.b.	*ER* XVII.251
464	1538	Glamis etc.	120d.b. aride multure	*ER* XVII.251
465	1538	Glamis	144d.b.	*ER* XVII.255
466	1538	Tiree	72d.b.	*ER* XVII.92
467	1538	Aberdeen	160d.b.	ACR XV.516–17 C.
468	1538	Aberdeen	144d.b. seed	ACR XVI.81–2 C.
469	1538	Glamis	72d.b. lycht beir	*ER* XVII.255
470	1538	Estfeild	120d.b.	SHS 2,4.80
471	1539	Errol	180d.b.	*ER* XVII.362
472	1539	West Migvy	80d.b.	*ER* XVII.370
473	1539	Glamis & Brig.	200d.b.	*ER* XVII.424
474	1539	St Andrews	160d.b.	SHS 2,4.100
475	1539		181.38d.b.	*ER* XVII.294
476	1539	St Andrews	180d.b.	SHS 2,4.100
477	1539	St Andrews	168d.b.	SHS 2,4.83
478	1539	Glamis & Brig.	150d.b.	*ER* XVII.423
479	1539	St Andrews	192d.b.	SHS 2,4.100
480	1540	Fife	200d.b.	*ER* XVII.407
481	1540	West Migvy	150d.b.	*ER* XVII.413
482	1540	Glamis etc.	160d.b. + aride multure	*ER* XVII.419
483	1540	Fife	204d.b.	*ER* XVII.407
484	1540	Fife	192d.b.	*ER* XVII.407
485	1540	Errol	200d.b.	*ER* XVII.435
486	1540	Draffane etc.	160d.b.	*ER* XVII.582
487	1540	Glamis etc.	216d.b.	*ER* XVII.420
488	1540	St Andrews	141.41d.b.	SHS 2,4.160
489	1540	St Andrews	180d.b.	SHS 2,4.114
490	1540	Aberdeen	144d.b.	ACR XVI.677 Aw.
491	1540	Aberdeen	18s.barrel	ACR XVI.505 Aw.
492	1540	Glamis etc.	200d.b. + aride multure	*ER* XVII.419
493	1540	St Andrews	204d.b.	SHS 2,4.114
494	1541	Linlithgowsh	192d.b.	*ER* XVII.567
495	1541	Avandale	200d.b.	*ER* XVII.588
496	1541	Kilmarnock	200d.b.	*ER* XVII.594
497	1541	Stirlingsh.	192d.b.	*ER* XVII.600
498	1541	St Andrews	192d.b.	SHS 2,4.131
499	1541	Halis,Trapyr	192d.b.	SHS 2,4.131
500	1541	St Andrews	200d.b.	SHS 2,4.131
501	1541	Linlithgowsh	192d.b.	*ER* XVII.564
502	1541	Mull,Tiree	100d.b.	*ER* XVII.535
503	1541	Tiree	100d.b.	*ER* XVII.535
504	1541	Fife	200d.b.	*ER* XVII.513
505	1541	Ross	192d.b. aride multure	*ER* XVII.496
506	1541	Tiree	92d.b.	*ER* XVII.486

Table 14 (*cont.*)

No.	Year	Place	Unit price	Source
507	1541	Glamis	150d.b.	*ER* XVII.480
508	1542	Lempitlaw	120d.b. with meal	*ALCPA*, p. 519 Wi.
509	1542	St Andrews	204d.b.	SHS 2,4.149

means will then be too low, but this seems preferable to discarding evidence too readily. The Sutherland Will price, which is actually a genuine sale price, of 6s. 8d. per boll (1456) was discovered too late for inclusion in our lists and calculations, but it confirms the suspicion that our calculated mean price for this date may be too low.[37]

Malt

Malt was usually made from barley[38] but other grains, notably oats, could also be malted.[39] Very rarely we can compare the price of barley malt and oat malt,[40] the latter being notably cheaper than the former, confirming Rogers' finding and the Durham evidence.[41] Unfortunately, however, in most cases the exact nature of the malt is unstated, and though the means calculated for Table 15 and Figure 14 exclude oat malt when it is explicit, unspecified malt may well include oat malt, and therefore perhaps depress the calculated prices. We also occasionally meet details of the nature or quality of the malt priced. Malt was sold ground or unground.[42] Best malt at Aberdeen cost 6d. more than good malt in 1442.[43] Malt spoilt by seawater[44] or otherwise 'quasi putrefacti'[45] will clearly have been cheaper as a result. More often, however, the type or quality of the malt goes unremarked, and our prices are correspondingly approximate.

English imported malt is frequently encountered[46] but locally pro-

[37] *Bannatyne Miscellany*, III, ed. David Laing (Edinburgh, 1855), p. 95. I am grateful to Dr Barbara Crawford for the reference.

[38] List 7, 13–14, 17–18, 21, 209, 211, 213 are explicitly for barley malt, but all malt has been presumed to be barley malt in the absence of evidence to the contrary.

[39] Oat malt is explicit in List 11–13, 210, 212, 214.

[40] List 209–14, barley malt 40d.b., oat malt 16d.b.

[41] Table 16.

[42] List 187, 238, 270.

[43] List 114–15.

[44] List 144, 193.

[45] List 254.

[46] The duty regularly paid on imported malt suggests it may have been England's main export to Scotland in the later middle ages. I am grateful to Dr A. Stevenson for this observation. For prices see List 121, 123, 141–3, 145, 147, 149, 151, 155–7, 159–60, 164–6, 169, 171, 173–4, 205, 207–8.

Table 15. *Malt summary table*

Period	Mean price	Deflated	Index
A	10	10.0	50.0
B–C	20	20.0	100.0
D	28	28.0	140.0
E	32	27.2	136.0
F	33	(16.5)	82.5?
G			
H	51	20.4	102.0
I	81	26.73	133.7
60s	102		
70s	106	29.68	148.4
80s	157		
90s	129	36.12	180.6
1500s	123	33.44	167.2
10s	154	38.5	192.5
20s	197	49.25	246.3
30s	158	34.76	173.8

Note: the mean price is in pence per boll; the deflated column gives the currently-adjusted sterling equivalent price. Parentheses have been used to flag up calculations which are less securely based than others – either because they are based on a smaller amount of data, or because they involve certain, possibly questionable, assumptions.

duced malt is equally evident in valuations and renders in kind from Cramond, Kintyre, Ardmannoch, and Aberdeen.[47] Royal purchase prices were likely to be higher than sale prices, because of the usual tendency to sell surplus and buy in need. For example, on one occasion we meet malt sold because it could not be transported.[48] On the other hand, Edward III's officials were clear that they were having to pay inflated prices[49] while the locals could buy more cheaply. The prior of Coldingham certainly managed to buy malt at this lower price.[50]

The evidence from the Aberdeen assize of ale (1398–1414) and from Dunkeld (1506–7) is plentiful enough to provide information on price variation within the year. Aberdeen assize prices can usually be dated to the month, if not the day, and they generally reveal a predictable seasonal pattern, tending to rise through the summer, falling after the

[47] List 17–18, 209–14, 269, 131–2, 134, 136–7, 139, 259, 261. For an idea of the difficulties involved in using these valuations, see pp. 164–5 on barley valuations.
[48] List 31, sold 'pro defectu cariagii'.
[49] *CDS* III.245, a petition of the warden of Berwick.
[50] List 23.

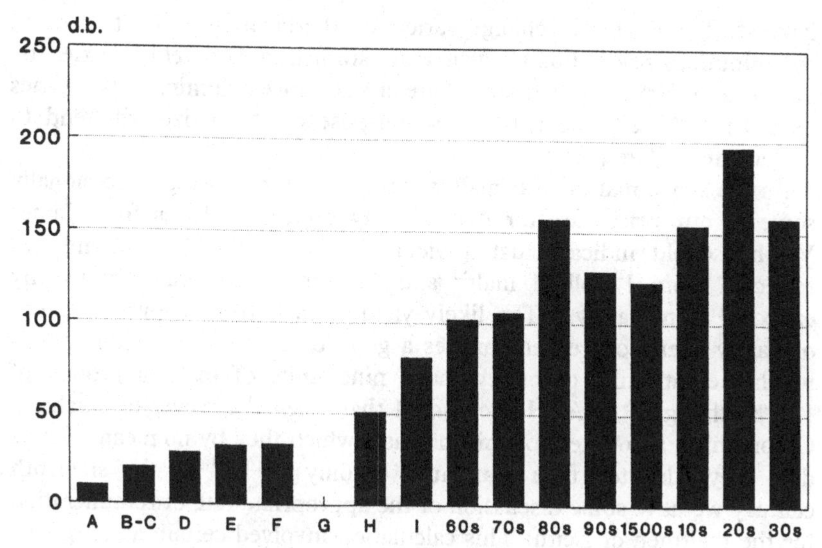

14 Malt prices (mean prices for time periods A–1530s)
For periods A–I, see Introduction, p. 6.

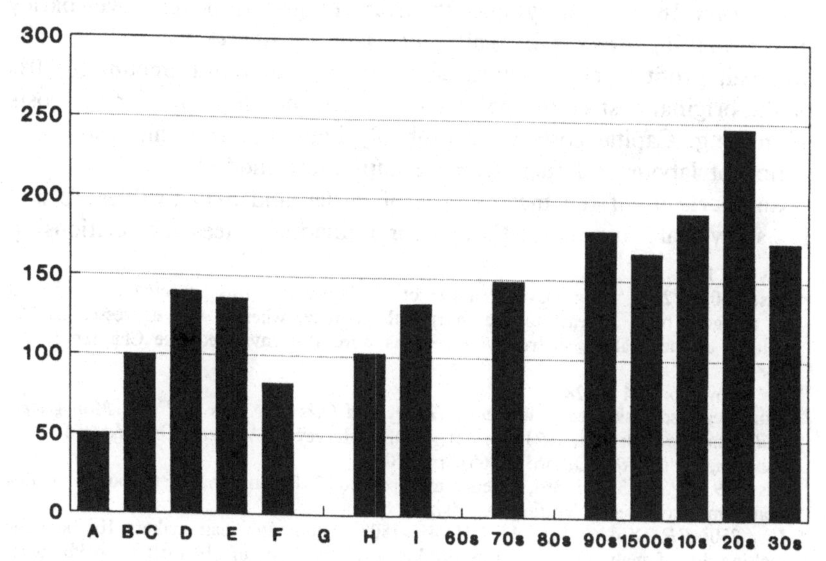

15 Malt index (sterling equivalent)

harvest. The degree of change varied at Aberdeen from 0% to 60% of the minimum price. For the two years studied at Dunkeld it varied by 28.6% and 50%. In periods where assize prices dominate the series (e.g. List 36–129) the nature and purpose of the assize will tend to understate higher prices.

As the assize makes clear malt was required for brewing. Occasionally some of our prices are for malt already brewed.[51] Prices from James V's household indicate that a yield of about 10 gallons of ale was expected from 1 boll of malt[52] and the same yield was also usually expected from barley.[53] The likely yield of malt from a given quantity of barley exercised contemporaries a good deal. Walter of Henley tells us that eight units of barley made nine units of malt, a growth of 12.5%, though P.D.A. Harvey noted that when the reeves of Cuxham, Oxfordshire, accounted for this increase, which they by no means always did, they admitted to a maximum of only 7.5%.[54] In the sixteenth century we have some discussion of the appropriate rate of remuneration for the maltmen of Leith. This calculation involved certain assumptions about the yield of malt from barley, the costs of malting, and the appropriate pricing of the grain. The simplest formula suggested malt should cost 2s.b. more than bere,[55] but an alternative system suggested that 15b. of malt be sold for the price of 1 celdra of barley (16b.).[56] Under the latter system, if barley sold at 100d.b., malt would cost 106.66d.b., but the maltster might be expected to make 3b. of malt from every 16b. of barley, and 2b. from the growth of malt over barley in the malting process if Walter of Henley's figures were right. The 3b. malt profit of every celdra of barley malted would amount to 20% of the original cost of the barley, but makes no allowance for the costs of malting. Capital costs were probably high, but running costs, consisting of labour and fuel, were perhaps more modest.

Comparisons of the mean prices of barley and malt (Tables 12 and 15) show malt cost more, though for individual prices the relationship

[51] List 5, 195.

[52] List 240–1, 243. 'King David's' assize of ale shows that this expected ratio of malt to ale goes back at least to the fourteenth century, when it was expressed as 160 gallons to the chalder; alternative strengths were also envisaged: see Chapter 2, pp. 148–9.

[53] See above, p. 164 n. 28.

[54] Dorothea Oschinsky (ed.), *Walter of Henley and Other Treatises on Estate Management and Accounting* (Oxford, 1971), p. 421. P.D.A. Harvey, *A Medieval Oxfordshire Village: Cuxham, 1240–1400* (Oxford, 1965), pp. 70–1.

[55] List 239. *APS* II.351 (1536), orders a malt price of 2s.b. more than bere, but complains that some have been charging 4s., 5s., or 6s. more.

[56] List 250. *ER* IX.436, 485. *APS* II.245 (1503), allows the malt makers 1b. bere for making 1c. of malt. Oat malt was produced on the basis of 8b. malt from 9b. oats; *ER* I.132.

Table 16. *Malt prices 1263–1367: Scotland and England*

Year	Scotland	Durham	Rogers (i) *capitalis*	Rogers (ii) *cursalis*
1263	3.36			
	2.5			
	3.39			
	2.5			
	2.5			
1264	2.5			
1287	3.33[a]		3.35	2.17
1288	2.5		2.6	
	2.5			
1290	2.5		6.23	3.0
1302		3.61[a] 2.07[b]		
1303	2.5[b]		4.3	2.33
1328	3.16[b]		4.59	3.65
1329	4.69[a&b]	6.12[a]	6.4	3.13
	3.33[a]			
	4.0[a]			
1330	8.4	6.84[a] 4.0[b]	8.09	4.37
1331	9.16		6.22	5.94
1340	5.0	4.0[a]	3.44	3.33
1341	8.0	4.12[a]	3.62	3.12
	8.24			
1342	5.08	4.5[a] 2.0[b]	3.57	3.67
	5.0			
	(6.57)[a]			
1364	10.8		6.0	3.67
1366	9.0	7.5[a]	5.39	4.0
1367	8.28	6.84[a]	6.0	

Note: all prices are in shillings per quarter. Parentheses have been used to flag up calculations which are less securely based than others – either because they are based on a smaller amount of data, or because they involve certain, possibly questionable, assumptions. [a] Barley malt [b] Oat malt.

is less clear, and we have some instances of barley and malt sold together undifferentiated in price.[57] On one occasion we meet wheat and malt similarly undistinguished,[58] and malt and oatmeal were customarily linked in the Ardmannoch payments, though in this case both were so heavily undervalued that the difference in value between the two was much less significant than the difference between the valuation and the market price.

[57] List 140, 148, 158–9, 163, 166, 170, 172.
[58] List 188.

Table 17. *Malt price list*

No.	Year	Place	Unit price	Source
1	1263	Perth	7.5d.b.	*ER* I.2
2	1263	Kinross	10.16d.b.	*ER* I.16 P.
3	1263	Edinburgh	7.5d.b.	*ER* I.25
4	1263	Linlithgow	7.5d.b.	*ER* I.25
5	1263	Dumfries	10.07d.b. braciatas	*ER* I.16
6	1264	Forres	7.5d.b.	*ER* I.15
7	1287	Maldisley	10d.b. barley	*ER* I.40
8	1288	Edinburgh	7.5d.b.	*ER* I.48
9	1288	Edinburgh	7.5d.b.	*ER* I.42
10	1290	Kincardine	7.5d.b.	*ER* I.49
11	1303	Annandale	2s.6d.qr (= 7.5d.b.) oat	*CDS* II.427
12	1328	Cardross	9.48d.b. oat	*ER* I.125 P.
13	1329		14.06d.b. barley + oat	*ER* I.250 V.
14	1329	Galloway	10d.b., 12d.b. barley	*ER* I.152
15	1330		25.21d.b.	*ER* I.341 P.
16	1331	Inverk'g	28.40d.b.	*ER* I.370 P.
17	1335	Cramond etc.	10d.b. barley	*CDS* III.327 pre-war V.
18	1336	Cramond etc.	10d.b. barley	*CDS* III.377 pre-war V.
19	1340	Berwick	5s.qr (= 15d.b.)	*CDS* III. 245 Wi.
20	1341	Aberdeen	24d.b.	*ER* I.480 P.
21	1341		24.68d.b. barley	*ER* I.505 P.
22	1342	Dundee	15.25d.b.	*ER* I.527 O.
23	1342	Coldingham	15d.b.	CP 1342–3. P.
24	1364		32.34d.b.	*ER* II.228 P.
25	1366		27.04d.b.	*ER* II.253 P.
26	1367		24.79d.b.	*ER* II.294 P.
27	1372		29.03d./b.24.66d.b.	*ER* II.368 P.
28	1372		29d.b.	*ER* II.369 P.
29	1373		30.56d.b.	*ER* II.451 P.
30	1374	Scone	32d.b.	*ER* II.449
31	1374		32d.b.	*ER* II.453
32	1380	Edinburgh	40d.b.	*ER* III.653 P.
33	1380		33.87d.b./28.80d.b.	*ER* III.40 P.
34	1382	Edinburgh	40d.b.	*ER* III.87–8 P.
35	1384		26.76d.b.	*ER* III.107 P.
36	1398	Aberdeen	32d.b.	SHS 3,49.34 assize V.
37	1398	Aberdeen	40d.b.	SHS 3,49.27 assize V.
38	1399	Aberdeen	36d.b.	SHS 3,49.39 assize V.
39	1399	Aberdeen	36d.b.	SHS 3,49.46 assize V.
40	1399	Aberdeen	30d.b.	SHS 3,49.53 assize V.
41	1399	Aberdeen	32d.b.	SHS 3,49.63 assize V.
42	1399	Aberdeen	36d.b.	SHS 3,49.41 assize V.
43	1399	Aberdeen	32d.b.	SHS 3,49.113 assize V.
44	1399	Aberdeen	36d.b.	SHS 3,49.75 assize V.
45	1400	Aberdeen	32d.b.	SHS 3,49.121 assize V.
46	1400	Aberdeen	36d.b.	SHS 3,49.126 assize V.

Table 17 (*cont.*)

No.	Year	Place	Unit price	Source
47	1400	Aberdeen	36d.b. town made	SHS 3,49.129 assize V.
48	1400	Aberdeen	36d.b. country made	SHS 3,49.129 assize V.
49	1400	Aberdeen	36d.b.	SHS 3,49.134 assize V.
50	1400	Aberdeen	36d.b.	SHS 3,49.137 assize V.
51	1400	Aberdeen	36d.b. good	SHS 3,49.121 assize V.
52	1400	Aberdeen	48d.b.	SHS 3,49.148 assize V.
53	1400	Aberdeen	42d.b.	SHS 3,49.155 assize V.
54	1400	Aberdeen	40d.b.	SHS 3,49.159 assize V.
55	1400	Aberdeen	32d.b.	SHS 3,49.162 assize V.
56	1400	Aberdeen	32d.b.	ACR I.169 assize V.
57	1400	Aberdeen	30d.b.	ACR I.172 assize V.
58	1400	Aberdeen	36d.b.	SHS 3,49.138 assize V.
59	1401	Aberdeen	32d.b.	ACR I.177 assize V.
60	1401	Aberdeen	(32d.b.)	ACR I.181 assize V.
61	1401	Aberdeen	36d.b.	ACR I.184 assize V.
62	1401	Aberdeen	28d.b.	ACR I.213 assize V.
63	1401	Aberdeen	32d.b.	ACR I.179 assize V.
64	1402	Aberdeen	36d.b.	ACR I.222 assize V.
65	1402	Aberdeen	54d.b.	ACR I.236 C.
66	1405	Aberdeen	24d.b.	ACR I.249 assize V.
67	1405	Aberdeen	24d.b.	ACR I.265 assize V.
68	1405	Aberdeen	24d.b.	ACR I.267 assize V.
69	1405	Aberdeen	24d.b.	ACR I.263 assize V.
70	1406	Aberdeen	20d.b.	ACR I.278 assize V.
71	1406	Aberdeen	20d.b.	ACR I.247 assize V.
72	1406	Aberdeen	24d.b.	ACR I.276 assize V.
73	1407	Aberdeen	24d.b.	ACR I.317 assize V.
74	1407	Aberdeen	24d.b.	ACR I.321 assize V.
75	1407	Aberdeen	24d.b.	ACR I.324 assize V.
76	1408	Aberdeen	30d.b.	ACR II.22 assize V.
77	1408	Aberdeen	32d.b.	ACR II.23 assize V.
78	1409	Aberdeen	32d.b.	ACR II.33 assize V.
79	1409	Aberdeen	40d.b.	ACR II.42 assize V.
80	1409	Aberdeen	40d.b.	ACR II.34 assize V.
81	1410	Aberdeen	36d.b.	ACR II.61 assize V.
82	1410	Aberdeen	40d.b.	ACR II.63 assize V.
83	1410	Aberdeen	40d.b.	ACR II.65 assize V.
84	1410	Aberdeen	42d.b.	ACR II.66 assize V.
85	1410	Aberdeen	36d.b.	ACR II.66 assize V.
86	1410	Aberdeen	36d.b.	ACR II.58 assize V.
87	1410	Aberdeen	30d.b.	ACR II.103 assize V.
88	1410	Aberdeen	28d.b.	ACR II.102 assize V.
89	1411	Aberdeen	28d.b.	ACR II.105 assize V.
90	1411	Aberdeen	30d.b.	ACR II.106 assize V.
91	1411	Aberdeen	24d.b.	ACR II.106 assize V.
92	1411	Aberdeen	24d.b.	ACR II.114 assize V.

Table 17 (*cont.*)

No.	Year	Place	Unit price	Source
93	1411	Aberdeen	28d.b.	ACR II.69 assize V.
94	1412	Aberdeen	24d.b.	ACR II.120 assize V.
95	1412	Aberdeen	32d.b.	ACR II.129 assize V.
96	1413	Aberdeen	36d.b.	ACR II.132 assize V.
97	1413	Aberdeen	42d.b.	ACR II.137 assize V.
98	1413	Aberdeen	48d.b.	ACR II.141 assize V.
99	1413	Aberdeen	40d.b.	ACR II.193 assize V.
100	1413	Aberdeen	32d.b.	ACR II.196 assize V.
101	1413	Aberdeen	32d.b.	ACR II.197 assize V.
102	1413	Aberdeen	48d.b.	ACR II.135 assize V.
103	1414	Aberdeen	36d.b.	ACR II.202 assize V.
104	1414	Aberdeen	32d.b.	ACR II.209 assize V.
105	1426		54d.b.	*ER* IV.413 P.
106	1428	Dundee	60d.b.	*ER* IV.470 P.
107	1429	Aberdeen	60d.b.	*ER* IV.510
108	1433	Aberdeen	48d.b.	Kennedy, *Annals of Aberdeen*, p.1 ?assize V.
109	1435	Aberdeen	54d.b.	ACR IV.51 assize V.
110	1435	Aberdeen	48d.b.	ACR IV.53 assize V.
111	1436	Aberdeen	48d.b.	ACR IV.60 assize V.
112	1441	Aberdeen	36d.b.	ACR IV.257 assize V.
113	1442	Strathearn	60d.b.	*ER* V.174–5 P.
114	1442	Aberdeen	48d.b. best	ACR IV.281 assize V.
115	1442	Aberdeen	42d.b. good	ACR IV.281 assize V.
116	1443	Aberdeen	72d.b.	ACR IV.323 assize V.
117	1443	Aberdeen	84d.b.	ACR IV.327 assize V.
118	1443	Aberdeen	84d.b.	ACR IV.297 assize V.
119	1444	Aberdeen	80d.b.	ACR IV.334 assize V.
120	1446	Linlithgow	120d.b.	*ER* V.267
121	1447	Leith	122.8d.b. English	*ER* V.317 P.
122	1447	Aberdeen	60d.b.	ACR IV.494 assize V.
123	1447	Leith	120d.b. English	*ER* V.317 P.
124	1449	Strathurd	66d.b.	*ER* V.395
125	1450	Aberdeen	60d.b.	ACR V i.101 assize V.
126	1450	Aberdeen	42d.b.	ACR V i.69 assize V.
127	1452	Aberdeen	60d.b.	ACR V i.147 assize V.
128	1452	Droune	80d.	*ER* V.605–6 P.
129	1453	Aberdeen	60d.b.	ACR V i.180 assize V.
130	1455	Dundee	160d.b.	*ER* VI.127 P.
131	1456	Ardmannoch	12d.b. with meal	*ER* VI.520 V.
132	1457	Ardmannoch	12d.b. with meal	*ER* VI.520 V.
133	1457	Elgin	72d.b.	*ER* VI.468–9 P.
134	1458	Ardmannoch	12d.b. with meal	*ER* VI.520 V.
135	1459	Aberdeen	40d.b.	*ER* VI.658 P.
136	1459	Ardmannoch	12d.b. with meal	*ER* VI.659 V.
137	1459	Ardmannoch	12d.b. with meal	*ER* VI.654–5 V.

Table 17 (*cont.*)

No.	Year	Place	Unit price	Source
138	1461	Fife	108d.b., 120d.b.	*ER* VII.83
139	1464	Ardmannoch	80d.b.	*ER* VII.351
140	1464	Moray	80d.b. with barley	*ER* VII.351
141	1465	N.Berwick	120d.b. English	*ER* VII.426
142	1466	N.Berwick	114d.b. English	*ER* VII.506
143	1467	N.Berwick	96d.b. English	*ER* VII.581
144	1467	Berwick	40.76d.b. damaged	*ER* VII.579 V.
145	1468	N.Berwick	96d.b. English	*ER* VII.656
146	1469	Moray	79.68d.b.	*ER* VIII.85
147	1470	Berwick	115.83d.b. English	*ER* VIII.118
148	1472	Ardmannoch	40d.b. with barley	*ER* VIII.376
149	1473		96d.b. English	*ER* VIII.255
150	1474	Stirlingsh.	80d.b.	*ER* VIII.283
151	1474		100d.b. English	*ER* VIII.313
152	1475	Stirlingsh.	99d.b.	*ER* VIII.330
153	1475	Stirlingsh.	96d.b.	*ER* VIII.330
154	1475	Stirlingsh.	90d.b.	*ER* VIII.331
155	1475	N.Berwick	108d.b. English	*ER* VIII.382
156	1475	Disart	96d.b. English	*ER* VIII.385 V.
157	1476	Berwick	96d.b. English	*ER* VIII.389
158	1476	Fife	90d.b. with barley	*ER* VIII.448
159	1476	N.Berwick	120d.b. English with barley	*ER* VIII.469
160	1476	Berwick	109.6d.b. English	*ER* VIII.455
161	1476	Stirlingsh.	96d.b.	*ER* VIII.506
162	1476	Stirlingsh.	96d.b.	*ER* VIII.431
163	1477	Fife	46d.b. with barley	*ER* VIII.448
164	1477	Berwick	108d.b. English	*ER* VIII.539
165	1477	N.Berwick	160d.b. English	*ER* VIII.542
166	1477	Dysart	160d.b. English with barley	*ER* VIII.549
167	1478	Stirlingsh.	120d.b.	*ER* VIII.565
168	1478	Fife	80d.b.	*ER* VIII.574
169	1478	Berwick	144d.b. English	*ER* VIII.620
170	1478	Stirlingsh.	120d.b. with barley	*ER* VIII.565
171	1479	N.Berwick	120d.b. English	*ER* IX.67–8
172	1480	Fife	120d.b. with barley	*ER* IX.100
173	1480	Berwick	132d.b. English	*ER* IX.145
174	1480	Leith	144d.b. English	*ER* IX.155
175	1480	Stirlingsh.	120d.b.	*ER* IX.95
176	1482	Aberdeen	282d.b.	ACR VI.745 C.
177	1482	Aberdeen	360d. black money b.	ACR VI.748 C.
178	1482	Aberdeen	144d.b.	ACR VI.762 Aw.
179	1482	Aberdeen	300d.b.	ACR VI.745 C.
180	1484	Quhittingam	120d.b.	*ALC* I.*90 Aw.
181	1485	Fettercairn	80d.b.	*ER* IX.397 V.

Table 17 (*cont.*)

No.	Year	Place	Unit price	Source
182	1486	Aberdeen	23s.6d. meil	ACR VI.945 Aw.
183	1486	Aberdeen	84.8d.b.	ACR VI.957 Aw.
184	1486	Aberdeen	23s.6d.meil	ACR VI.239 C.
185	1486	Orkney	84d.b.	*ER* IX.490
186	1486	Orkney & Shetl.	120d.b.	*ER* IX.490
187	1488	Arth'	240d.b. unground	*ALC* I.98 Aw.
188	1488	Prestoun'	240d.b. with wheat	*ALC* I.127 Aw.
189	1488	Arth'	240d.b.	*ALC* I. 98 Aw.
190	1489	Morinche	144d.b.	ALA I.156 Aw.
191	1489	Kilmarnock	80d.b.	*ER* X.160–1
192	1489	Leith	132d.b.	*ER* X.231
193	1489	Leith	84d.b. part water-spoilt	*ER* X.231
194	1489	Kilmarnock	100d.b.	*ER* X.159
195	1491	Arth'	160d.b. in ale	*ALC* I.195 Aw.
196	1491	Fife	120d.b.	*ER* X. 374
197	1492	Trewin & Lochl	96d.b., 120d.b.	*ALC* I.211 C.
198	1493		240d.b.	*ALC* I.287 Aw.
199	1493	Overtoun'	80d.b.	*ALC* I.415 C.
200	1493	Aberdeen	120d.b./barrel	ACR VII.480 C.
201	1499	Kilmarnock	84d.b.	*ER* XI.361 V.
202	1499	Edinburgh	144d.b.	*ER* XI.274
203	1501	Kilmarnock	84d.b.	*ER* XII.22 V.
204	1503	Aberdeen	80d.b.	ACR VIII.290 Aw.
205	1503	Pittenweem	204d.b. English	*ER* XII.260
206	1503	Fife	120d.b.	*ER* XII.195
207	1504	Edinburgh	180d.b. English	*ER* XII.375
208	1504	Edinburgh	120d.b. English	*ER* XII.372
209	1505	S.Kintyre	40d.b. barley	*ER* XII.586
210	1505	S.Kintyre	16d.b. oat	*ER* XII.586
211	1505	N.Kintyre	40d.b. barley	*ER* XII.586
212	1505	N.Kintyre	16d.b. oat	*ER* XII.586
213	1505	N.Kintyre	40d.b. barley	*ER* XII.703
214	1505	N.Kintyre	24d.b. oat	*ER* XII.703
215	1506	Dunkeld	84d.b.	SHS 2,10.90
216	1506	Dunkeld	96d.b.	SHS 2,10.90
217	1506	Dunkeld	96d.b.	SHS 2,10.93 V.
218	1506	Dunkeld	96d.b.?	SHS 2,10.93 V.
219	1506	Stirling	108d.b.	*ER* XII.543
220	1506	Stirling	84d.b.	*ER* XII.543
221	1506	Dunkeld	108d.b.	SHS 2,10.90
222	1507	Dunkeld	168d.b.	SHS 2,10.98
223	1507	Dunkeld	204d.b.	SHS 2,10.98
224	1507	Dunkeld	144d.b.	SHS 2,10.98
225	1507	Tulicultre	126.87d.b.	*ER* XIII.27
226	1507	Dunkeld	216d.b.	SHS 2,10.98
227	1508	Tulicultre	84d.b.	*ER* XIII.164

Table 17 (*cont.*)

No.	Year	Place	Unit price	Source
228	1509	Tulicultre	84d.b.	*ER* XIII.273
229	1511	Dunkeld	144d.b.	SHS 2,10.121
230	1511	Clony	132d.b.	SHS 2,10.179
231	1513	Dunkeld	144d.b.	SHS 2,10.129
232	1515	Inchegarvy	172d.b.	TA V.20 P.
233	1515	Dunbar	138.95d.b.	*ER* XIV.219 P.
234	1516	Cupar, Fife	96d.b.	*SCBF* p. 51 Aw.
235	1517		192d.b.	*ER* XIV.352 P.
236	1518		216d.b.	TA V.163 P.
237	1522	Aberdeen	288d.b.	ACR XI.114 C.
238	1523	Edinburgh	45s./laid of 9f., ground	*ALCPA* p. 184
239	1524	Leith	2s.b. more than bere	*ALCPA* p. 201–2 V.
240	1525	Edinburgh	240d.b.	HBJV p. 6 P.
241	1525	Edinburgh	240d.b.	HBJV p. 12 P.
242	1525	Aberdeen	240d.b.	ACR XI.526 Aw.
243	1526	Stirling	168d.b.	HBJV p. 56 P.
244	1527	Aberdeen	192d.b.	ACR XII i.15 C.
245	1528	Fife	132d.b.	*ER* XV.476
246	1528	Fife	120d.b.	*ER* XV.480
247	1529	Edinburgh	204d.b.	HBJV, p. 144 P.
248	1529	Fife	100d.b.	*ER* XVI.16
249	1530	Fife	100d.b.	*ER* XVI. 95
250	1531	Leith	15b malt for 16b bere	*ALCPA*, pp. 366–7 V.
251	1531	Aberdeen	184.8d.b.	ACR XIII.310 Aw.
252	1531	Aberdeen	180d.b.	ACR XIII.311 Aw.
253	1533	Aberdeen	160d.b.	ACR XV.547 C.
254	1537	Dunbar	84d.b. quasi putrefacti	*ER* XVII.159
255	1537		120d.b.	*ER* XVII.176
256	1538	Aberdeen	160d.b.	ACR XV.561 C.
257	1538	Aberdeen	144d.b.	ACR XV.595 C.
258	1538	Aberdeen	156d.b.	ACR XVI.81–2 C.
259	1538	Aberdeen	160d.b.	ACR XVI.425 C.
260	1538	Aberdeen	120d.b.	ACR XV.619 Aw.
261	1539	Aberdeen	132d.b.	ACR XVI.88 C.
262	1539	Aberdeen	120d.b.	ACR XVI.88 C.
263	1540	Aberdeen	180d.b.	ACR XVI.67 Aw.
264	1540	Aberdeen	168d.b.	ACR XVI.75 C.
265	1540	Fife	216d.b.	*ER* XVII.408
266	1540	Aberdeen	156d.b.	ACR XVI.495 Aw.
267	1540	Draffane etc.	160d.b.	*ER* XVII.582
268	1540	Aberdeen	160d.b.	ACR XVI.88 C.
269	1541	Kintyre	60d.b.	*ER* XVII.625 V.
270	1541	Kilmarnock	200d.b. ground	*ER* XVII.594
271	1541	Desschier	120d.b.	*ER* XVII.484

Overall the malt price evidence looks reasonably reliable, though the thirteenth-century prices look low compared with the normally reliable Cramond valuation of pre-war prices, and it is the higher price which has been used on the summary Table 15. After the Plague the rise in malt prices confirms doubts about the possibly aberrant barley prices of this time. Comparison with English malt prices and with the Durham series is complicated by the incidence of oat malt, but so far as comparison is possible, malt confirms the impression of high Scots grain prices compared with England (Table 16).

Oats

Oats were much grown in Scotland where climate and relief made the cultivation of more valuable, but less hardy, crops difficult. We have only one price for imported oats[59] but evidence of its Scottish cultivation is widespread. Three-fold yields were anticipated[60] in the courts, which would be a reasonable agricultural performance for the time. Perhaps because of its general availability in Scotland, oat prices there were closer to English norms than was usually the case for cereals.[61] However, it should be noted that the whole Scottish oat price series is characterized by a rather wide spread of prices, presenting a somewhat blurred picture which makes such comparison difficult. As with other cereals, harvest fluctuations affected prices dramatically, and in certain extreme years this phenomenon provoked comment.[62]

The wide range of prices may also be attributed in part to the basic sale/purchase price contrast noted in less extreme form for other commodities. Additionally, for oats the widespread cultivation and ready availability of this crop make its use for grassums,[63] and other rents and renders in kind common, and these customary payments often became frozen and, in an age of inflation, uneconomic.[64] Ross, Mar, and Bute provide the best examples. However, certain sales from the same farms and estates producing totally uneconomical valuations of renders show that some other prices in these remote regions were also significantly below the usual town rates.[65] Of course, one cannot always

[59] List 189.
[60] List 120–1, 140, 143–4.
[61] See Table 19 for Anglo-Scots comparison.
[62] Oatmeal List 7 was a high price 'propter temporis caristiam', while Oatmeal List 9 was much cheaper 'propter bonum forum bladi'.
[63] E.g. List 74.
[64] E.g. List 37–8, 44, 49, 59–61, 74, 85, 177, 180, 187, 190, 201, 233, 258, 261, 271, 334, 342, etc.

Table 18. *Oat summary table*

Period	Mean price	Deflated	Index
A	6	6.0	66.7
B–C	9	9.0	100.0
D	10	10.0	111.1
E	10	8.79	97.7
F			
G	15	9.0	100.0
H	26	10.4	115.6
I	43	14.19	157.7
60s	50		
70s	46	12.88	143.1
80s	84		
90s	59	16.52	183.6
1500s	46	12.88	143.1
10s	48	12.0	133.3
20s	83	20.75	230.6
30s	62	18.26	202.9

Note: the mean price is in pence per boll; the deflated column gives the currency-adjusted sterling equivalent price.

be clear that some of these sales should not more truly be described as commutations,[66] but some sales do seem less fixed than the frozen valuations and allowances. Moreover, regal revaluations of renders due from remote estates made in the sixteenth century remain well below the current average price levels.[67] Thus even when obviously frozen allowances and valuations are excluded from the average prices, the range of prices contributing to the calculated average remains wide. Purchase prices paid by the army or the royal household[68] will regularly be far in excess of the sale prices common on remote estates. Thus particular care should be taken with the interpretation of the average prices in Table 18 and Figure 16, when a particular source is dominant. Compare, for example the high numbers of crown purchases inflating the average in the 1520s, and the newly assessed allowances and valuations from remote regions which depress the average for the 1530s.

Such difficulties are by no means restricted to the sixteenth century. The high prices paid for oats by John de Rystone as he accompanied

[65] E.g. List 39, 181, 217, 234, 240, 244–5, 259, 263, 267, 295, etc.
[66] E.g. List 63, 86–7.
[67] List 373–4, 376, 383.
[68] List 24, 264, 304, and all the HBJV prices.

Table 19. *Oat prices 1296–1367: Scotland and England*

Year	Scotland	Durham	Rogers	Farmer
1296	2.0		2.27	2.33
1303	2.0		2.16	1.67
	2.0			
1304	4.33		2.4	2.25
	4.33			
	4.33			
	4.33			
1306		1.46		
1307		2.8		
1328	2.5		3.08	
	1.67			
	2.0			
	2.0			
	3.27			
1329	3.33		2.48	
	2.0			
	3.51			
	3.33			
	3.33			
1330	5.4	4.17	2.93	
1335	2.0	2.75	2.2	
	3.52			
1340	3.0	2.09	1.92	
1344	2.0	1.37	1.79	
1363	5.0	2.92	2.89	
1365	3.0	2.64	2.48	
1367	2.5	3.47	3.13	

Note: all prices are in shillings per quarter

Edward I's horses south in 1304 are a case in point.[69] At the beginning of our period when the evidence is also much scarcer the distorting effect of such factors is likely to be correspondingly greater. Thus in Table 18 an adjusted estimate has been used instead of a simple mean. After the Plague oat prices hold their own but do not rise significantly till the fifteenth century. The Hume Will prices[70] are for oats 'sown and to be sown', so they may understate the rise in household oat prices. Monetary factors account for the bulk of the later price rise, but the currency-adjusted series shows strong demand for home-grown cereal to the end of our period (Table 18 and Figure 17).

[69] List 5–8. Royal officials in a hurry and with money in their purse often paid more. See Bain, *CDS* II, no. 1581, p. 410.

[70] List 31–2.

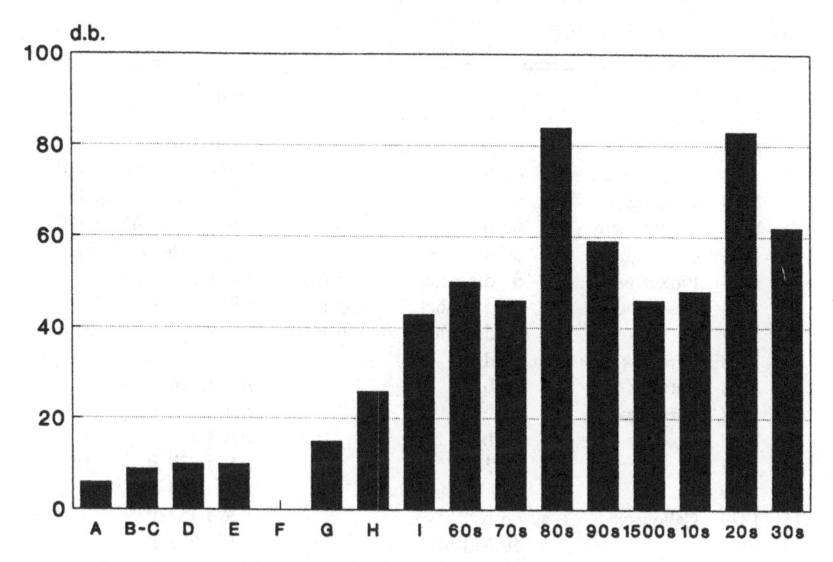

16 Oat prices (mean prices for time periods A–1530s)
For periods A–I, see Introduction, p. 6.

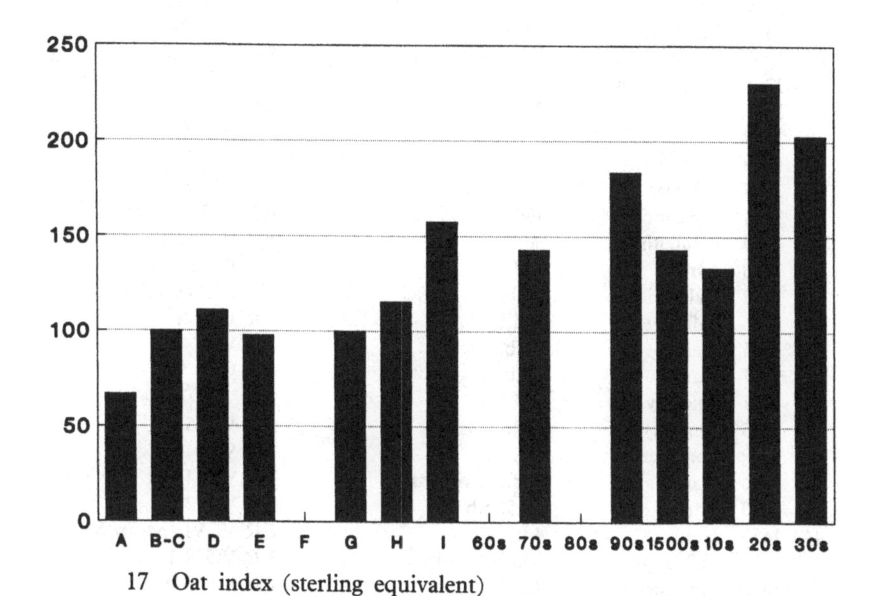

17 Oat index (sterling equivalent)

Table 20. *Oat price list*

No.	Year	Place	Unit price	Source
1	1296	Coldstream	2s.qr (= 6d.b.)	DHS II.33 V.
2	1303	Linlithgow	6d.b.	PRO E101/365/9m4 P.
3	1303	Linlithgow	6d.b.	PRO E101/365/9m4 P.
4	1303	Coldingham	6d.b.	PRO E101/365/9m4 P.
5	1304	Coldingham	6.5d.bushel (= 13d.b.)	PRO E101/98/33 P.
6	1304	Pinkerton	6.5d.bushel (= 13d.b.)	PRO E101/98/33
7	1304	Musselburgh	6.5d.bushel (= 13d.b.)	PRO E101/98/33 P.
8	1304		6.5d.bushel (= 13d.b.)	PRO E101/98/33 P.
9	1328	Cardross	7.5d.b.	*ER* I.125. P.
10	1328	Berwick?	5d.b.	*ER* I.206
11	1328	Cardross	6d.b.	*ER* I.125 P.
12	1328		6d.b.	*ER* I.117 P.
13	1328		9.82d.b.	*ER* I.219 P.
14	1329		10d.b. large oats	*ER* I.240 P.
15	1329	Galloway	6d.b.	*ER* I.152 P.
16	1329		10.54d.b.	*ER* I.289 P.
17	1329	Earlston	10d.b.	DPS Exp.'29a V.
18	1329	Earlston	10d.b.	DPS Exp.'29a V.
19	1330		16.20d.b.	*ER* I.341 P.
20	1335	Cramond etc.	4d.b.	*CDS* III.327f pre-war V.
21	1335	Edinburgh	6d.b.	*CDS* III.p342
22	1335	Roxburgh	10.57d.b.	*CDS* III.p322
23	1336	Cramond etc.	3.75d.b.	*CDS* III.377f pre-war V.
24	1340	Berwick	3s.qr (= 9d.b.)	*CDS* III.245 Wi.
25	1344	Coldingham	6d.b.	C.S.1344–5ii P.
26	1363	Coldingham	15d.b.	SS 12.xliv–xlv P.
27	1365	Coldingham	9d.b.	SS 12.1 P.
28	1367		7.5d.b.	*ER* II.304 P.
29	1369	Moray	8.19d.b.	*ER* II.352
30	1379	Strathearn	12d.b.	*ER* III.38. P.
31	1424	Dunglas	15d.b.	HMS 12,8.87 W.
32	1424	Aldcambus	15d.b.	HMS 12,8.87 W.
33	1430	Menteith	30d.b.	*ER* IV.530 P.
34	1433	Ayr	24d.b.	*ER* IV.595
35	1433	Dalpatrik	6d.b.	*ER* IV.595 V.
36	1436	Ballincrefe	10d.b.	*ER* V.64 V.
37	1436	Mar	4d.b.	*ER* V.58 V.
38	1437	Mar	4d.b	*ER* V.60 V.
39	1437	Feichley	24d.b.	*ER* V.54
40	1445	Linlithgow	60d.b.	*ER* V.225 P.
41	1449	Corntoun	30d.b.	*ER* V.394–5
42	1450	Mar	36d.b. with hay	*ER* V.464 P.
43	1450	Fife	56.56d.b.	*ER* V.472 P.
44	1450	Mar	4d.b.	*ER* V, VI. *passim* V.
45	1451	Falkland?	30d.b./24d.b.	*ER* V.538 P.
46	1453	Strathurd	30d.b.	*ER* V.603 P.

Table 20 (*cont.*)

No.	Year	Place	Unit price	Source
47	1453	Strathearn	31.58d.b.	*ER* V.662 P.
48	1453	Balkerow	10d.b.	*ER* V.677 V.
49	1453	Bute etc.	12d.b.	*ER* V. VI *passim* V.
50	1454	Falkland?	60d.b./72d.b.	*ER* VI.79–80 P.
51	1455	Methven?	50d.b.	*ER* VI.253 P.
52	1455	Falkland?	60d.b.	*ER* VI.254 P.
53	1456	Down	40d.b.	*ER* VI.284 V.
54	1456	Pety	30d.b. with straw	*ER* VI.483 V.
55	1456	N.of Spey	36d.b. with straw	*ER* VI.483 P.
56	1457	Strathearn	24d.b.	*ER* VI.426 V.
57	1459	Falkland?	60d.b.	*ER* VI.615 V.
58	1459	Methven	40d.b./50d.b.	*ER* VI.637 P.
59	1460	Bute & L.Cumbr.	12d.b.	*ER* VII *passim* V.
60	1460	Mar	4d.b.	*ER* VII *passim* V.
61	1461	Bute etc.	12d.b.	*ER* VII.108 V.
62	1461	Stirling	60d.b.	*ER* VII.139 V.
63	1462	Mar	12d.b.	*ER* VII.162
64	1464	Falkland	36d.b.	*ER* VII.269 P.
65	1464	Fife	60d.b.	*ER* VII.334 P.
66	1466	Kindeleith	40d.b.	*ER* VII.452 V.
67	1466	Fife	45d.b.	*ER* VII.456 V.
68	1466	Fife	45d.b.	*ER* VII.457 V.
69	1467	Falkland	50d.b.	*ER* VII.570 V.
70	1468	Falkland?	48d.b.	*ER* VII.655 V.
71	1469	Falkland?	48d.b.	*ER* VII.655 P.
72	1473		30d.b.	*ALA* I.24 C.
73	1476	Fife	47.2d.b.	*ER* VIII.449
74	1476	Ross	4d.b.	*ER* VIII.597 V. grassum
75	1477	Fife	49.41d.b.	*ER* VIII.449
76	1478	Dunberny	80d.b.	*ALA* I.61 Aw.
77	1478		40d.b.	*ALC* I.8 Aw.
78	1478	Schanbody	120d.b.	*ALA* I.75 C.
79	1479		30d.b.	*ALA* I.68 Aw.
80	1479	Corswod	24d.b.	*ALA* I.81–2 Aw.
81	1479	Corswod	24d.b.	*ALA* I.81–2 Aw.
82	1479		48d.b.	*ALC* I.28 Aw.
83	1479	Schanbody	80d.b.	*ALA* I.87 Aw.
84	1479	Linlithgow	48d.b.	*ER* IX.17
85	1479	Newmekill	4d.b.	*ER* IX *passim* V.
86	1479	Ross	8d.b.	*ER* IX.60
87	1479	Ross	12d.b.	*ER* IX.61
88	1480		60d.b.	*ALC* I.54 Aw.
89	1480		60d.b.	*ALC* I.71 Aw.
90	1480	Stirlingsh.	48d.b.	*ER* IX.96
91	1480	Fife	48d.b.	*ER* IX.101

Table 20 (*cont.*)

No.	Year	Place	Unit price	Source
92	1480	Fife	60d.b.	*ER* IX.101
93	1480	Fife	60d.b.	*ER* IX.101
94	1480	Abircorne	56.46d.b.	*ER* IX.104
95	1480	Menteith	48d.b.	*ER* IX.115
96	1482	Dunmure	80d.b.	*ALC* I.199 C.
97	1482	Wauchtoun	120d.b.	*ALC* I.429 Aw.
98	1483	Wauchtoun	120d.b.	*ALC* I.166 Aw.
99	1483	Pentland'	132d.b.	*ALA* I.*112–13 Aw.
100	1483	Perthshire	120d.b.	*ALA* I.*116 C.
101	1483	Torcrake	80d.b	*ALA* I.*118 Aw.
102	1484	Broxmouth	72d.b.	*ALA* I.*134 Aw.
103	1484	Broxmouth	72d.b.	*ALA* I.*134 Aw.
104	1484	Mukkersy	80d.b.	*ALA* I.*134 Aw.
105	1484	Culquhalye	40d.b.	*ALA* I.*134 O.
106	1484	Westergagy	72d.b.	*ALC* I.*85 Aw.
107	1484	Quhittingam	80d.b.	*ALC* I.*90 Aw.
108	1485		40d.b.	*ALC* I.*102 C.
109	1485	Ryflat	60d.b.	*ALC* I.*107 C.
110	1485	Davidstoun	120d.b.	*ALA* I.115–16 C.
111	1486	Dumbarton	96d.b.	*ALC* I.124 C.
112	1487	the Hirne	48d.b.	*ALC* I.107 C.
113	1487	Aberdeen	120d.b.	ACR VII.37 C.
114	1488	Dun/Dummure	100d.b. with fodder	*ALC* I.86 C.
115	1488	Abirnethy	160d.b.	*ALA* I.114 C.
116	1488	Abernethy	100d.b.	*ALC* I.90 Aw.
117	1488	Straithall.	144d.b.	*ALC* I.92 Aw.
118	1489	Flawcrag	120d.b.	*ALC* I.108 C.
119	1489	Ardendracht	60d.b.	*ALC* I.243 Aw.
120	1489	Ballinbrech	100d.b./80d.b.	*ALC* I.156 C./Aw.
121	1489	Lesle	100d.b./80d.b.	*ALC* I.156 C./Aw.
122	1490		100d.b.	*ALC* I.162 Aw.
123	1490	Glentoun'	30d.b.	*ALC* I.270 Aw.
124	1490	Drummond	60d.b.	*ALA* I.139–40 Aw.
125	1490	Essilmont	60d.b.	*ALA* I.183 Aw.
126	1490	Dunkeld	96d.b.	*ALC* I.128 Aw.
127	1490	Essilmont	80d.b.	*ALA* I.183 Aw.
128	1490		72d.b.	*ALC* I.145 Aw.
129	1490	Pettindrech	120d.b.	*ALC* I.152 Aw.
130	1490	Foulefurd	120d.b.	*ALC* I.152 Aw.
131	1490	Dumbarton	96d.b. with fodder	*ALC* I.157 Aw.
132	1490	Dumbarton	96d.b. with fodder	*ALC* I.157 Aw.
133	1490	Hollis of A.	80d.b.	*ALA* I.137 C.
134	1490	Dumbarton	96d.b. with fodder	*ALC* I.124 C.
135	1490		90d.b.	*TA* I.131 P.
136	1490	Newby	120d.b.	*ALC* I.149 Aw.
137	1491	the Raith'	48d.b.	*ALC* I.172 Aw.

Table 20 (*cont.*)

No.	Year	Place	Unit price	Source
138	1491	the Raith'	48d.b.	*ALC* I.172 Aw.
139	1491	Brigland	28d. thrave	*ALC* I.177 C.
140	1491	Torwechquhy	50d.b. with fodder	*ALC* I.184 C.
141	1491	Inverquhoth	30d.b.	*ALC* I.202 Aw.
142	1491		40d.b.	*ALC* I.335 Aw.
143	1491	Quhitnacloi	40d.b. with fodder	*ALC* I.363 Aw.
144	1491	Quhitnacloi	40d.b.	*ALC* I.363 Aw.
145	1491	Tellin & Polg.	30d.b.	*ER* X.321
146	1491	Stirlingsh.	48d.b.	*ER* X.375
147	1492	Inchecometh	48d.b.	*ALA* I.161 Aw.
148	1492		48d.b. with fodder	*ALC* I.219 Aw.
149	1492		40d.b.	*ALC* I.221 C.
150	1493	Crawfurdlan	40d.b.	*ALC* I.300 Aw.
151	1493	Dumbarton	36d.b. with fodder	*ALA* I.185 Aw.
152	1493	Dingwall	40d.b.	*ER* X.438 P.
153	1494	Crancho	40d.b.	*ALC* I.333 Aw.
154	1494	Coutty	36d.b.	*ALA* I.190 Aw.
155	1494	Kilmarone	30d.b.	*ALC* I.403 Aw.
156	1494	Telyne & Polg.	24d.b.	*ER* X.479
157	1494	Strathearn	36d.b.	*ER* X.488
158	1495	Setoun'	72d.b.	*ALC* I.399 Aw.
159	1495	Arran	20d.b.	*ER* X.551
160	1495	Methven	24d.b.	*ER* X.559
161	1495	Ballegarno	40d.b.	*ALC* I.422 Aw.
162	1495	Hallis of A.	80d.b.	*ALC* I.430 C.
163	1495	Arran	13.55d.b.	*ER* X.551
164	1495	W. Gartscho	20d.b.	*ALC* I.403 Aw.
165	1495	Forstare Hill	80d.b.	*ALC* I.424 C.
166	1495	Tellyn & Polg.	24.9d.b.	*ER* XI.103 P.
167	1496	Largo	36d.b.	*ER* X.591 P.
168	1496	Bute	24d.b.	*ER* XI.6
169	1496	Moray/Kinl.	24d.b.	*ER* XI.13 P.
170	1496	Fife/Falkl.	72d.b.	*ER* XI.40 P.
171	1496	Falkland	72d.b.	*ER* XI.41 P.
172	1497	Falkland	100d.b.	*ER* XI.74 P.
173	1497	Lanark	24d.b.	*ER* XI.353–4
174	1498	Davidstone	120d.b.	*ALC* I.102 C.
175	1498	Stirling?	50d.b.	*TA* I.384 P.
176	1499	Fife	81.8d.b. with wheat	*ER* XI.300 V.
177	1500	Bute & Arran	12d.b.	*ER* XI.325 V.
178	1500	Peebles	30d.b.	*ER* XI.309*
179	1501		30d.b.	*TA* II.44 P.
180	1501	Bute	12d.b.	*ER* XII *passim* V.
181	1501	Bute	24d.b.	*ER* XII.67
182	1502	Bute	33.73d.b.	*ER* XII.248
183	1502	Kettyll	48d.b.	*ER* XII.617–8 V.

Table 20 (*cont.*)

No.	Year	Place	Unit price	Source
184	1502	Newtown Falk.	40d.b.	*ER* XII.618 V.
185	1502	Auchtermuch.	48d.b.	*ER* XII.619 V.
186	1503	Falkland	50d.b.	T.A. II.272 P.
187	1503	Ross	2.5d.b.	*ER* XII *passim* V.
188	1503	Ross	112.2d.b.	*ER* XII.240
189	1503	Pittenweem	60d.b. imported	*ER* XII.260
190	1503	Strathdon	4d.b.	*ER* XII.327 V.
191	1504	Bute	6d.b.	*ER* XII.319 P.
192	1505	Clony	40d.b.	SHS 2,10.18 P.
193	1505	Cameron	50d.b.	*ER* XII.448
194	1506	Bute	35.97d.b.	*ER* XII.512
195	1506	Ross & Ardman.	24d.b.	*ER* XII.515
196	1506	Ferische etc.	40d.b.	*ER* XII.550 V.
197	1507	Clony	44d.b.	SHS 2,10.20 V.
198	1507	Dunkeld	72d.b.	SHS 2,10.157
199	1507	Ballinbla	15d.b.	*ER* XIII *passim* V.
200	1507	Ferische etc.	40d.b.	*ER* XIII.45 V.
201	1507	Bute	12d.b.	*ER* XIII.80 V.
202	1508	Dunkeld	48d.b.	SHS 2,10.157
203	1508	Lothian	96d.b.	SHS 2,10.247
204	1508	Lothian	144d.b.	SHS 2,10.247
205	1508	Strathdon	24d.b.	*ER* XIII.199
206	1508	Moray	23.19d.b.	*ER* XIII.205
207	1508	Lothian	60d.b.	SHS 2,10.251
208	1508	Kynnacrag	64d.b.	*ER* XIII.145 V.
209	1508	Ross	17.39d.b.	*ER* XIII.147
210	1508	Lothian	117.67d.b.	SHS 2,10.284
211	1508	Bute	36d.b.	*ER* XIII.139
212	1509	Dunkeld	30d.b.	SHS 2,10.158
213	1509	Abbirlathy	50d.b.	SHS 2,10.259 V.
214	1509	Moray	13.91d.b.	*ER* XIII.295
215	1509	Bute	36d.b.	*ER* XIII.313
216	1509	Auchterhouse	50d.b.	*ER* XIII.343
217	1509	Ross	13.04d.b.	*ER* XIII.349
218	1510	Clony	40d.b.	SHS 2,10.175 P.
219	1510	Lothian	50d.b.	SHS 2,10.254
220	1510	Abbirlathy	60d.b.	SHS 2,10.259 V.
221	1511	Dunkeld	48d.b. with fodder	SHS 2,10.161 V.
222	1511	Lothian	50d.b.	SHS 2,10.257
223	1511	Lothian	60d.b.	SHS 2,10.257
224	1511	Lothian	60d.b.	SHS 2,10.261
225	1511	Lothian	80d.b.	SHS 2,10.262
226	1511	Lothian	80d.b.	SHS 2,10.262
227	1511	Dunkeld	30d.b.	SHS 2,10.280 P.
228	1511	Dunkeld	60d.b.	SHS 2,10.280 P.
229	1513		64d.b.	T.A. IV.529 P.

Table 20 (*cont.*)

No.	Year	Place	Unit price	Source
230	1513	Lothian	73.25d.b.	SHS 2,10.262
231	1513	Dunkeld	60d.b.	SHS 2,10.289 P.
232	1513	Fife	48d.b.	*ER* XIV.16
233	1513	Bute	12d.b.	*ER* XIV *passim* V.
234	1513	Bute	36d.b.	*ER* XIV.21
235	1514	Dunkeld	58.58d.b.	SHS 2,10.291 P.
236	1514	Dunmure	48d.b.	*ER* XIV.168
237	1514	Ballinbla	15d.b.	*ER* XIV *passim* V.
238	1515	Auld Lindori	40d.b.	*ER* XIV.181
239	1515	Fife	40d.b.	*ER* XIV.182
240	1515	Ross	30d.b.	*ER* XIV.217
241	1516	Cupar,Fife	48d.b.	*SCBF*, p. 51 Aw.
242	1516	Dunkeld	37.89d.b.	SHS 2,10.297 P.
243	1516	Fife	38.88d.b.	*ER* XIV.291
244	1516	Ross	30d.b.	*ER* XIV.306
245	1516	Lennox	24d.b.	*ER* XIV *passim* V.
246	1517	Fife	60d.b.	*ER* XIV.323
247	1517	Fife	60d.b.	*ER* XIV.323
248	1517		60d.b.	*ER* XIV.347
249	1518	Largo	16d.b.	*ER* XIV.410
250	1518	Fife	48d.b.	*ER* XIV.411
251	1518	Fife	48d.b.	*ER* XIV.411
252	1518	Fife	40d.b.	*ER* XIV.411
253	1518	Balbrechy	48d.b.	*ER* XIV.411
254	1518	Fife/Largo	30d.b.	*ER* XIV.411
255	1518	Fife	40d.b.	*ER* XIV.412
256	1518		40d.b.	*ER* XIV.472
257	1519	Aberdeen	4d. peck = 64d.b.	ACR X.151 assize V.
258	1521	Ferisch etc.	2.5d.b.	*ER* XV *passim* V.
259	1521	Ross	24d.b.	*ER* XV.24
260	1522	Bogfarlay	80d.b. with fodder	ACR XI.34–5 C.
261	1522	Bute	12d.b.	*ER* XV *passim* V.
262	1522	Ballinba	15d.b.	*ER* XV *passim* V.
263	1522	Lennox	24d.b.	*ER* XV *passim* V.
264	1523	Edinburgh	7d./8d.peck = 112d.b./ 128d.b.	*ALCPA*, p. 183 P.
265	1523	Ross	57.76d.b.	*ER* XV.101
266	1523		60d.b.	*ER* XV.101
267	1524	Ross	24d.b.	*ER* XV.171–2
268	1524	Balbreky	46.5d.b.	*ER* XV.123
269	1524	Fife	60d.b.	*ER* XV.123–4
270	1524	Balbreky	36d.b.	*ER* XV.135
271	1524	Kincrag	4d.b.	*ER* XV *passim* V.
272	1524	Largo	60d.b.	*ER* XV.123
273	1525	Strathdee	36d.b.	*ER* XV.213–14
274	1526	Edinburgh	84d.b.	HBJV, p. 103 P.

Table 20 (*cont.*)

No.	Year	Place	Unit price	Source
275	1526	Stirling	72d.b.	HBJV, p. 104 P.
276	1526	Edinburgh	60d.b.	HBJV, p. 110 P.
277	1526	Fife	50d.b.	*ER* XV.234
278	1526	Fife	40d.b.	*ER* XV.394–5
279	1526	Fife	60d.b.	*ER* XV.355
280	1526	Auchtermuch.	48d.b.	*ER* XV.355
281	1527	Aberdeen	120d.b.	ACR XII i.227 C.
282	1527	Fife	80d.b.	*ER* XV.401
283	1527	Fife	80d.b.	*ER* XV.401
284	1527	Estircasche	60d.b.	*ER* XV.402
285	1527	Balbreky	48d.b.	*ER* XV.402
286	1527	Bute	52d.b.	*ER* XV.425
287	1528	Edinburgh	100d.b.	HBJV, p. 196 P.
288	1528	Edinburgh	156d.b.	HBJV, p. 196 P.
289	1528	Edinburgh	156d.b.	HBJV, p. 196 P.
290	1528		100d.b.	HBJV, p. 197 P.
291	1528		128d.b.	HBJV, p. 197 P.
292	1528	Fife	50d.b.	*ER* XV.477
293	1528	Fife	72d.b.	*ER* XV.477
294	1528	Edinburgh	8d.peck = 128d.b.	HBJV, p. 198 P.
295	1528	Bute	40d.b.	*ER* XV.497
296	1528	Edinburgh	8d.peck = 128d.b.	HBJV, p. 199 P.
297	1528	Edinburgh	108d.b.	HBJV, p. 200 P.
298	1528	Stirling	84d.b.	HBJV, p. 200 P.
299	1528	Stirling	90d.b.	HBJV, p. 201 P.
300	1528	Stirling	96d.b.	HBJV, p. 201–2 P.
301	1528	Edinburgh	128d.b.	HBJV, p. 202 P.
302	1528	Fife	50d.b.	*ER* XV.477
303	1528	Stirling	105.33d.b.	HBJV, p. 198 P.
304	1528	East Lothian	8d.peck = 128d.b.	*ALCPA*, p. 290 P.
305	1528	Stirling	84d.b.	HBJV, p. 199 P.
306	1529	Stirling	96d.b.	HBJV, p. 203 P.
307	1529	Edinburgh	109.53d.b.	HBJV, p. 203–4 P.
308	1529	Stirling	96d.b.	HBJV, p. 204 P.
309	1529	Edinburgh	144d.b.	HBJV, p. 205 P.
310	1529	Edinburgh	128d.b.	HBJV, p. 206, P.
311	1529	Stirling	96d.b.	HBJV, p. 206–7 P.
312	1529	Edinburgh	128d.b.	HBJV, p. 207
313	1529	Edinburgh	128d.b.	HBJV, p. 207 P.
314	1529	Stirling	113.28d.b.	HBJV, p. 208 P.
315	1529	Edinburgh	128d.b.	HBJV, p. 208 P.
316	1529		124d.b.	HBJV, p. 208 P.
317	1529	Kincrag	64d.b.	*ER* XVI *passim* V.
318	1529	Fife	50d.b.	*ER* XVI.17–18
319	1529		128d.b.	HBJV, p. 209 P.
320	1529		60d.b.	*ER* XV.538

Table 20 (*cont.*)

No.	Year	Place	Unit price	Source
321	1529	Ballinbla	15d.b.	*ER* XVI *passim* V.
322	1529	Fife	50d.b.	*ER* XVI.17
323	1529		128d.b.	HBJV, p. 210 P.
324	1529	Fife	50d.b.	*ER* XVI.18
325	1529	Bute	12d.b.	*ER* XVI *passim* V.
326	1529	Bute	40d.b.	*ER* XVI *passim*
327	1529	Fyschrie	40d.b.	*ER* XVI *passim* V.
328	1529		138.78d.b.	HBJV, p. 209 P.
329	1530	Fife	60d.b.	*ER* XVI.96–7
330	1532	Fife	66.66d.b.	*ER* XVI.271
331	1532	Fife	47.41d.b.	*ER* XVI.271
332	1533	Fife	72d.b.	*ER* XVI.316
333	1533	Bute	44d.b.	*ER* XVI.333
334	1535	Bute	12d.b.	*ER* XVII *passim* V.
335	1535	Bute	44d.b.	*ER* XVII.29
336	1536	Aberdeen	80d.b.	ACR XVI.735 C.
337	1536	Ballinbla	15d.b.	*ER* XVII *passim* V.
338	1536	Fife	80d.b.	*ER* XVII.11
339	1536	Fife	80d.b.	*ER* XVII.11
340	1536	Strathdee	60d.b.	*ER* XVII *passim*
341	1536	Fischerie	40d.b.	*ER* XVII *passim* V.
342	1536	Kincrag etc.	4d.b.	*ER* XVII *passim* V.
343	1536	Ross	36d.b.	*ER* XVII.35
344	1536	Keig & Monym.	36d.b.	SHS 2,4. 81
345	1537	Errol	40d.b.	*ER* XVII.97
346	1537	Largo	84d.b.	*ER* XVII.106
347	1537	Drumtennand	48d.b.	*ER* XVII.107
348	1537	Ross	36d.b.	*ER* XVII.114
349	1537	Glamis etc	116d.b.	*ER* XVII.144 P.
350	1537	Glamis etc.	80d.b.	*ER* XVII.144 P.
351	1537	Glamis	54d.b.	*ER* XVII.152
352	1537	Glamis	54d.b.	*ER* XVII.152
353	1537	Glamis	54d.b.	*ER* XVII.153
354	1537	Glamis	48d.b.	*ER* XVII.153
355	1537	Glamis	60d.b.	*ER* XVII.153
356	1538	Kyrklistoun	80d.b.	SHS 2,4.81
357	1538	Kyldeleith	50d.b.	SHS 2,4.81
358	1538	Eistfeild	80d.b.	SHS 2,4.81
359	1538	Byrehillis	100d.b.	SHS 2,4.81
360	1538	Fife	48d.b. + 72d.b.	*ER* XVII.107
361	1538	Bute	48d.b.	*ER* XVII.199
362	1538	Fife	100d.b.	*ER* XVII.212
363	1538	Errol	60d.b.	*ER* XVII.218
364	1538	Ross	48d.b.	*ER* XVII.235
365	1538	Ardmanach	72d.b.	*ER* XVII.240
366	1538	Glamis	72d.b.	*ER* XVII.256

Table 20 (*cont.*)

No.	Year	Place	Unit price	Source
367	1538	Glamis	120d.b.	*ER* XVII.256
368	1539	St Andrews	112d.b.	SHS 2,4.101
369	1539	Keig & Monym.	48d.b.	SHS 2,4.101
370	1539	Estir Culles	80d.b.	*ER* XVII.329
371	1539	Fife	100d.b.	*ER* XVII.330
372	1539	Ross	40d.b.	*ER* XVII.342
373	1539	Strathdee	40d.b.	*ER* XVII *passim* V.
374	1539	West Migvy	40d.b.	*ER* XVII.370
375	1539	St Andrews	80d.b.	SHS 2,4.101
376	1539	Strathdee	40d.b.	*ER* XVII *passim* V.
377	1539	St Andrews	104d.b.	SHS 2,4.101
378	1539	St Andrews	50d.b.	SHS 2,4.101
379	1539	St Andrews	100d.b.	SHS 2,4.101
380	1540	St Andrews	100d.b.	SHS 2,4.115
381	1540	Kildeletht	80d.b.	SHS 2,4.115
382	1540	St Andrews	92.8d.b.	SHS 2,4.161
383	1540	West Migvy	40d.b.	*ER* XVII.413
384	1540	St Andrews	120d.b.	SHS 2,4.115
385	1541	Ross	40d.b.	*ER* XVII.497
386	1541	Glamis	40d.b.	*ER* XVII.480
387	1541	Keig & Monym.	36d.b.	SHS 2,4.163
388	1541	Kyldeleith	50d.b.	SHS 2,4.132
389	1541	St Andrews	120d.b.	SHS 2,4.132
390	1542	St Andrews	144d.b.	SHS 2,4.151

Oatmeal

Comparison of oats prices with those of other grains and with oatmeal prompts a number of comments. An English manual of husbandry tells us that it required rather more than 2 quarters of oats to make 1 quarter of oatmeal, and that a quarter of meal would be worth about the same as 1 quarter of wheat.[71] This relationship is confirmed in the account of the Scottish chamberlain for 1328, in which he charged himself with 8½ chaldrons of oatmeal issuing from 17 chaldrons of oats.[72] However, much could depend on the extent to which the oatmeal was ground. We know of coarse meal (farina grossa), ordinary meal (farina communa) and fine or white meal (farina alba).[73] Very roughly

[71] Oschinsky (ed.), *Walter of Henley and Other Treatises*, p. 471.
[72] *ER* I.120.
[73] *ER* I.133. 'Item computat iij celdras et vj bollas avene, factas in j celdram farine albe, et in xiij bollas farine communis, et in ix bollas farine grosse et j firlotam'. Thus in

then one might expect oats to be worth half as much as oatmeal or wheat.[74] Of course, one should never forget the very approximate nature of such relationships, but they do provide a rough yard-stick to check the prices emerging from the data. It would suggest, for example, that in the 1520s the mean price of oats is too high and/or that for meal too low (Tables 18, 21).

The explanation for this disparity is most likely to be found in an examination of the sources providing price data. For oats there are several high prices paid by the royal household and the army who both needed oats chiefly to feed horses and spent freely to meet their needs. Oatmeal, on the other hand, was a staple for the mass of the population, but was not much bought by the army or the household who preferred wheat bread and could afford to buy it. Within the oatmeal series a similar contrast may be drawn between prices in the 1490s, which were much influenced by the legal claims which dominate our records in this decade, and in the 1500s when estate prices from Perth and Dunkeld are common. Plaintiffs never understated the value of goods in dispute, but grain prices at the point of production were sometimes relatively low. This was especially true around harvest time. Robert Egew wrote to Lord Sinclair from Newburgh in Buchan, 7 August 1511, 'gif I will sell the said meile to dais I can nocht get of hand siluer for the boll iiij schillingis and will I sell it to Martymes I will gett for the boll v schillingis vi peneyis'. Even the later November price looks well below our other oatmeal prices of this period; perhaps Egew exaggerated somewhat in order to explain to Sinclair the difficulty of finding ready money in the country. He went on, 'And sa gif ever your Lordschipe thinkis to gett reddy monee or ony price for wittall in thir partis ye man sett it to a man wnder ane soume that he may sell it to ane day and mak monee of it for the siluer is nocht wer to gett in Orknay and Scheitland thane it is in Buchane.'[75]

The overall movement of meal prices is revealed in Table 21 and Figure 18, and the general trends are familiar. A marked rise occurred

this instance 38¼ bolls of meal were produced from 54 bolls of oats. See also *ER* IX.436, 15c.7b.1f. oats yielding 10c.8b.2f. meal. Note also that in a Scottish context farina = oatmeal, rather than wheat flour. White meal was a superior product costing more than coarse meal (List 244–6, 249–51) but white and black meal were not always distinguished in price (List 485–6).

[74] While this theoretical relationship holds reasonably true for oats and oatmeal, it significantly understates the value of wheat. Farmer's English prices confirm that oats sometimes stand at more like ⅓ rather than ½ wheat prices.

[75] *Illustrations of the Topography and Antiquities of the Shires of Aberdeen and Banff*, Spalding Club, 9 (Aberdeen, 1843), p. 106. These 4s.b. and 5s.6d.b. prices were discovered too late for inclusion in the price list or the calculated means.

Table 21. *Oatmeal summary table*

Period	Mean price	Deflated	Index
A	10.5	10.5	50.0
B	21.0	21.0	100.0
C			
D–E	20.0		
D	20.0	(20.0)	(95.2)
E	20.0	(17.0)	(80.9)
F	37.0	18.5	88.1
G			
H–I	69.0	22.4	106.9
60s	80.0		
70s	(90.0)	25.2	120.0
80s	124.0		
90s	109.0	30.5	145.3
1500s	90.0	25.2	120.0
10s	98.0	24.5	116.7
20s	101.0	25.25	120.2
30s	129.0	28.4	135.1

Note: the mean price is in pence per boll; the deflated column gives the currency-adjusted sterling equivalent price. Parentheses have been used to flag up calculations which are less securely based than others – either because they are based on a smaller amount of data, or because they involve certain, possibly questionable, assumptions.

in the early fourteenth century over thirteenth-century levels; prices held up well after the Plague. Fifteenth-century prices are strongly inflated by debasement, but the index of currency-adjusted prices (Table 21, Figure 19) shows prices were rising above early fourteenth-century levels even after the effect of currency changes have been stripped out. It is nevertheless clear that this deflated meal price level does not rise as much as that of all other grains. It has been observed above that the contrasting behaviour of oats and meal in the 1520s may be partly explained in terms of the different sources providing data, but the consistent tendency of meal prices to rise less than the price of other cereals may also reflect both the care taken by burgh authorities to regulate and protect the supply of this essential foodstuff and the poverty of most of the buyers.[76] Oatmeal was the staple food of the mass of the population.

[76] Oatmeal was not sold wholesale, purchasers being enjoined to provide only for their own household's immediate needs. Oatcakes, cheaper than bread and with a higher calorific content, were not to be sold, reserving meal supplies to those providing only for their private needs. See Chapter 2, pp. 40–2.

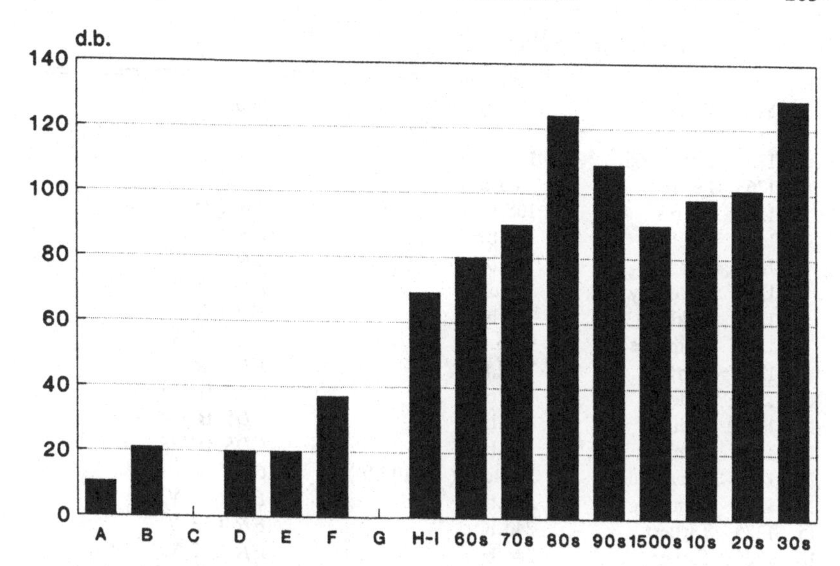

18 Oatmeal prices (mean prices for time periods A–1530s)
For periods A–I, see Introduction, p. 6.

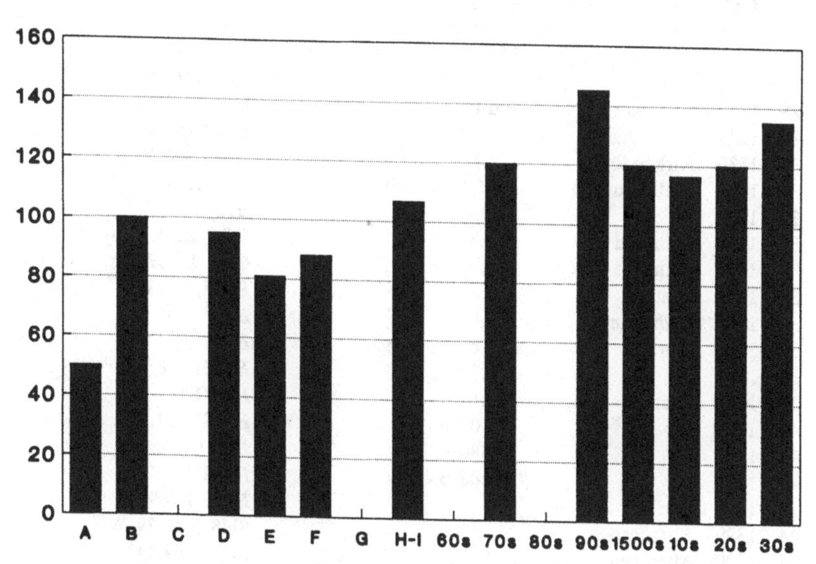

19 Oatmeal index (sterling equivalent)

Table 22. *Oatmeal price list*

No.	Year	Place	Unit price	Source
1	1263	Edinburgh	10d.b.	*ER* I.25
2	1263	Perth	9.8d.b.	*ER* I.2
3	1264	Forres	10d.b.	*ER* I.15
4	1264	Crail	10d.b.	*ER* I.4 V.
5	1264	Ayr	15d.b.	*ER* I.5
6	1287	Maldisley	10.5d.b.	*ER* I.39–40
7	1287	Selkirk	15d.b.	*ER* I.46 V.
8	1288	Dumfries	9d.b.	*ER* I.36 V.
9	1290	Cartland	7.5d.b.	*ER* I.46 V.
10	1302	Cader	10d.b.	*CDS* II.424
11	1302	Cadihou	10d.b.	*CDS* II.424
12	1302	Camb'naythan	10d.b.	*CDS* II.423
13	1303	Annandale	3s. 4d.qr(= 10d.b.)	*CDS* II.427
14	1325	Man	24d.b.	*ER* I.53 V.
15	1325	Tarbert	24d.b.	*ER* I.53 V.
16	1325	Tarbert	24d.b.	*ER* I.53 V.
17	1325	Tarbert	7d.pond. with cheese	*ER* I.58 V.
18	1325	Tarbert	24d.b. with barley	*ER* I.53 P.
19	1325	Tarbert	24d.b.	*ER* I.54 P.
20	1325	Ile	7d.pond. with cheese	*ER* I.52–3 V.
21	1325	Tarbert	24d.b.	*ER* I.55 V.
22	1325	Tarbert	20d.b.	*ER* I.53 V.
23	1325	Tarbert	7d.caslamus with cheese	*ER* I.55 V.
24	1325	Tarbert	24d.b.	*ER* I.57 V.
25	1325	Tarbert	24.86d.b.	*ER* I.57 V.
26	1328	Cardross	15d.b.	*ER* I.124 P.
27	1328		15.23d.b.	*ER* I.219 P.
28	1329	Galloway	10d.b.	*ER* I.152 P.
29	1329		15.23d.b.	*ER* I.289 P.
30	1330	Kirkcudb.	20d.b.	*ER* I.356 V.
31	1330	Linlithgow	*c.* 26.6d.b. with malt	*ER* I.301 P.
32	1330		24.07d.b.	*ER* I.341 P.
33	1335	Cramond	10d.b.	*CDS* III.327 pre-war V.
34	1336	Cramond	10d.b.	*CDS* III.377 pre-war V.
35	1355	Kinross	15d.b.	*ER* I.581 V.
36	1367	Bothkennar	24d.b.	*ER* II.304
37	1369	Moray	25d.b. with malt	*ER* II.352
38	1372		20.38d.b.	*ER* II.368 P.
39	1372	Kinross	20d.b.	*ER* II.419 V.
40	1374		71.10d.b. (*sic*)	*ER* II.454 P.
41	1380		25.58d.b.	*ER* III.40 P.
42	1384		20.20d.b.	*ER* III.106 P.
43	1391	Forfar	15d.b.	*ER* III.269 V.
44	1399	Aberdeen	24d.b.	SHS 3,49.79 Wi.
45	1400	Aberdeen	36d.b.	SHS 3,49.143 C.
46	1402	Edinburgh	£5 last	*ER* III.566 V.

Table 22 (*cont.*)

No.	Year	Place	Unit price	Source
47	1413	Aberdeen	48d.b.	ACR II.194 Aw.
48	1413	Inverness	40d.b.	*ER* IV.227–8 P.
49	1429	Aberdeen	54d.b.	*ER* IV.510 V.
50	1433	Aberdeen	44d.b.	Kennedy, *Annals of Aberdeen*, p.1 assize V.
51	1435	Aberdeen	44d.b.	ACR IV.53 assize V.
52	1435	Jed Forest	216d.b. *recte* 1438?	Bower, *Scotichronicon*, p.298 Ch.
53	1436	Lit.Cumbray	24d.b.	*ER* V.84 V.
54	1442	Lit.Cumbray	24d.b.	*ER* V.163 V.
55	1443	Aberdeen	120d.b.	ACR IV.323 C.
56	1444	Aberdeen	68d.b.	ACR IV.349 C.
57	1444	Lit.Cumbray	24d.b.	*ER* V.209 V.
58	1445	Lit.Cumbray	24d.b.	*ER* V.250 V.
59	1446	Lit.Cumbray	24d.b.	*ER* V.288 V.
60	1447	Lit.Cumbray	24d.b.	*ER* V.332 V.
61	1448	Lit.Cumbray	24d.b.	*ER* V.363 V.
62	1449	Cessintuly	59.79d.b.	*ER* V.394
63	1449	Cessintuly	48d.b.	*ER* V.394
64	1449	Bothkennar	48d.b.	*ER* V.395
65	1449	Lit.Cumbray	24d.b.	*ER* V.410 V.
66	1450	Bothkennar	50d.b.	*ER* V.476
67	1450	Lit.Cumbray	24d.b.	*ER* V.452
68	1454	Edinburgh	72s.last	*ER* VI.3 P.
69	1454	Dowcrufe	34.29d.b.	*ER* VI.51–2 P.
70	1454	Forfar	15d.b.	*ER* VI.181–2 V. temp. Rob I
71	1455	Kirkcud't?	60d.b.	*ER* VI.205
72	1455	Ettrick	120d.b.	*ER* VI.227 V.
73	1455	Strathearn	60d.b.	*ER* VI.285–6
74	1456	Strathearn	60d.b.	*ER* VI.208
75	1456	Ormyshuche	37.5d.b.	*ER* VI.341 V.
76	1456	Galloway	96d.b.	*ER* VI.348
77	1456	Melrose?	120d.b.	*ER* VI.372 V.
78	1457	Galloway	54d.b.	*ER* VI.458–9
79	1458	Mar & Moray	48d.b.	*ER* VI.522
80	1458	Doune	30d.b.	*ER* VI.575
81	1459	Galloway	72d.b.	*ER* VI.644
82	1459	Galloway	60d.b.	*ER* VI.647
83	1460	Galloway	120d.b.	*ER* VII.9,10
84	1460	Galloway	120d.b.	*ER* VII.10
85	1460	Galloway	80d.b.	*ER* VII.10–11
86	1460	Galloway	69.38d.b.	*ER* VII.11
87	1460	Galloway	96d.b.	*ER* VII.11
88	1460		80d.b.	*ER* VII.11 P.
89	1461	Stirlingsh.	60d.b.	*ER* VII.70

Table 22 (*cont.*)

No.	Year	Place	Unit price	Source
90	1461	Galloway	120d.b.	*ER* VII.116
91	1461	Bothkennar	60d.b.	*ER* VII.120
92	1462	le Halch	48d.b.	*ER* VII.167
93	1462	Bothkennar	54d.b.	*ER* VII.201
94	1463	Bothkennar	48d.b.	*ER* VII.246
95	1463	le Halch	48d.b.	*ER* VII.351
96	1463	Galloway	96d.b.	*ER* VII.611
97	1464	le Halch	54d.b.	*ER* VII.351
98	1465	Spottis	80d.b.	*ER* VII.611
99	1465	Spottis	80d.b.	*ER* VII.611–12
100	1466	Galloway	80d.b.	*ER* VII.612
101	1466	Galloway	80d.b.	*ER* VII.612
102	1467	Falkland	96d.b.	*ER* VII.570 V.
103	1468	Balndone	80d.b.	*ER* VII.612
104	1468	Spottis	80d.b.	*ER* VII.612
105	1468	Spottis	80d.b.	*ER* VII.612
106	1468	Galloway	80d.b.	*ER* VII.612
107	1468	Spottis?	80d.b.	*ER* VII.612
108	1468	Balndone	100d.b.	*ER* VII.612
109	1468	Galloway	80d.b.	*ER* VII.612–13
110	1471	Spottis	80d.b.	*ER* VIII.90
111	1471	Galloway	80d.b.	*ER* VIII.90
112	1471	Galloway	80d.b.	*ER* VIII.91
113	1473	Galloway	60d.b.	*ER* VIII.217
114	1473	Galloway	60d.b.	*ER* VIII.217
115	1474	Aberdeen	14s.barrel	ACR VI.295 Aw.
116	1474	Galloway	80d.b.	*ER* VIII.288
117	1475	Galloway	90d.b.	*ER* VIII.344
118	1476	Fife	75.14d.b.	*ER* VIII.373 V.
119	1476	Galloway	102d.b.	*ER* VIII.421
120	1476	Ross	40d.b.	*ER* VIII.594 V.
121	1476	Ross	12d.b.	*ER* VIII.597 V. grassum
122	1477	Galloway	144d.b.	*ER* VIII.491
123	1477	Galloway	120d.b.	*ER* VIII.491
124	1477	Galloway	144d.b.	*ER* VIII.490 V.
125	1478	Kyrkmichill	160d.b.	*ALC* I.8 Aw.
126	1478	Fife	80d.b.	*ER* VIII.571 V.
127	1478	Galloway	96d.b.	*ER* VIII.607
128	1479	Aberdeen	12s.barrel	ACR VI.580 O.
129	1479	Langschaw	120d.b.	*ALA* I.78 C.
130	1479	Skraisburgh	120d.b.	*ALC* I.40 Aw.
131	1479	Baldune	50d.b.	*ER* IX.21
132	1479	Galloway	60d.b.	*ER* IX.21
133	1479	Newmekill	12d.b.	*ER* IX.59 V.
134	1479	Ross	36d.b.	*ER* IX.60
135	1479	Ross	36d.b.	*ER* IX.61

Table 22 (*cont.*)

No.	Year	Place	Unit price	Source
136	1480	Twa Penek	120d.b. with malt	*ALC* I.58 Aw.
137	1480	Stirlingsh.	80d.b.	*ER* IX.96
138	1480	Menteith	60d.b.	*ER* IX.115
139	1480	Menteith	40d.b.	*ER* IX.115
140	1480	Menteith	41.14d.b.	*ER* IX.115
141	1480	Galloway	60d.b.	*ER* IX.126
142	1480	Galloway	80d.b.	*ER* IX.126
143	1481	Raith'	240d.b.	*ALA* I.*112 Aw.
144	1481	Burnhus & Hall	240d.b.	*ALA* I.*112 Aw.
145	1481	Baldone	192d.b.	*ER* IX.193
146	1481	Sannack & Cul.	240d.b.	*ER* IX.193
147	1481	Spottis	240d.b.	*ER* IX.193
148	1482	Raith'	168d.b.	*ALA* I.*112 Aw.
149	1482	Burnhus & Hall	168d.b.	*ALA* I.*112 Aw.
150	1483	Litil Prest.	144d.b.	*ALA* I.*118 Aw.
151	1483	Baldune	100d.b.	*ER* IX.247
152	1483	Bothkennar	80d.b.	*ER* IX.252
153	1484	Kiddisdale	14.28d.b.	*ER* IX.301
154	1484	Ballindune	194.06d.b.	*ER* IX.301–2
155	1484	Bothkennare	60d.b.	*ER* IX.328
156	1485	Ballindune	80d.b.	*ER* IX.382
157	1485	Spottis	80d.b.	*ER* IX.382
158	1485	Culven mill	80d.b.	*ER* IX.382
159	1486	Baldone etc.	100d.b.	*ER* IX.463
160	1486	Galloway	80d.b.	*ER* IX.463
161	1486	Spottis	100d.b.	*ER* IX.464
162	1486	Bothkennare	49.65d.b.	*ER* IX.486
163	1487	Innes	144d.b.	*ALA* I.118 Aw.
164	1487	Colpmalindy	160d.b.	*ALA* I.142–3 C.
165	1488		120d.b.	*ALC* I.94 Aw.
166	1488	Arth'	192d.b.	*ALC* I.98 Aw.
167	1488	Prestoun'	120d.b.	*ALC* I.127 Aw.
168	1488	Bothkennare	97.67d.b.	*ER* X.1
169	1488	Stirlingsh.	99.62d.b.	*ER* X.5
170	1488	Spottis	53.05d.b.	*ER* X.79
171	1488	Ballindune	144d.b.	*ER* X.79
172	1488	Sannak	144d.b.	*ER* X.79
173	1489	Kynfawnis	80d.b.	*ALC* I.102 C.
174	1489	Lekraw	192d.b.	*ALC* I.106 Aw.
175	1489		216d.b.	*ALC* I.110 Aw.
176	1489	the Trabeau	192d.b.	*ALC* I.110 C.
177	1489	Kyrkinnyr'	66d.b.	*ALC* I.117 C.
178	1489	Kyrkinnyr'	66d.b.	*ALC* I.117 C.
179	1489		192d.b. with bear	*ALC* I.119 C.
180	1489	Aberdeen	9.25s.barrel	ACR VII. 144 Wi.
181	1489	Inglistoun	120d.b.	*ALC* I.426 C.

Table 22 (*cont.*)

No.	Year	Place	Unit price	Source
182	1489	Galloway	100d.b.	*ER* X.222
183	1489	Kilmarnock	84d.b.	*ER* X.158–9
184	1490	Colpmalindy	180d.b. cut to 168d.b.	*ALA* I.144 Aw.
185	1490	Dunkeld?	160d.b.	*ALC* I.128 Aw.
186	1490	Dunkeld?	160d.b.	*ALC* I.128 Aw.
187	1490	Dunkeld	160d.b.	*ALC* I.128 Aw.
188	1490	Sauchquhy	120d.b.	*ALC* I.147 C.
189	1490	Innoch & Craic	120d.b. with bear	*ALC* I.181 C.
190	1490	Delgatie castle	120d.b.	*ALC* I.289 Aw.
191	1490	Glasfurd	96d.b. with bear	*ALC* I. 31 Aw.
192	1490	W.Glasfurd	96d.b. with bear	*ALC* I.316 Aw.
193	1491	Edinburgh?	144d.b.	*ALC* I.171 C.
194	1491	Ros'neth'?	168d.b.	*ALC* I.181 Aw.
195	1491		120d.b.	*ALC* I.189 Aw.
196	1491	Arth'	120d.b. in bread	*ALC* I.195 Aw.
197	1491	Cammis	120d.b.	*ALA* I.147 Aw.
198	1491	Culwen	83.75d.b.	*ER* X.372
199	1491	Culwen mill	80d.b.	*ER* X.342
200	1491	Sannak mill	80d.b.	*ER* X.342
201	1491	Bothkennar	60d.b.	*ER* X.374
202	1492	Crewach	192d.b.	*ALC* I.226 Aw.
203	1492	Quhite Crag	96d.b.with bear	*ALC* I.316 Aw.
204	1492	Kilmadok	144d.b.	*ALC* I.429 Aw.
205	1493		80d.b.	*ALC* I.283 Aw.
206	1493		160d.b.	*ALC* I.297 C.
207	1494	Perth	160d.b.	*ALC* I.359 C.
208	1494	Kirkton'	120d.b.	*ALA* I.203 C.
209	1494		4s.b.	*TA* I.244 P.
210	1494	Lany	108d.b.	*ALC* I.429 Aw.
211	1495	Bute	40d.b.	*ER* X.549,576
212	1495	Kittisdale	22.86d.b.	*ER* X.573 V.
213	1495	Spottis & Sann	80d.b.	*ER* X.574
214	1495	Galloway	72.73d.b.	SHS 3,50.63
215	1496	Rothesay	40d.b.	*ER* XI.6
216	1496	Kittisdale	22.86d.b.	*ER* XI.110 V.
217	1497	Ayr	11s.b.	*TA* I.343 P.
218	1497		100d.b.	*TA* I.314
219	1497	Aberdeen	96d.b.	ACR VII.841 Wi.
220	1497	Bothkennar	97.67d.b.	*ER* XI.134
221	1497	Baldoune	72.72d.b.	*ER* XI.112
222	1498	(Ayr)	120d.b.	*TA* I.382 P.
223	1498	Bothkennar	120d.b.	SHS 3,50.77
224	1498	Ballindune	72.72d.b.	*ER* XII.64
225	1499	Kilmarnock	64d.b.	*ER* XI.361
226	1499	Torwood	132d.b.	*ER* XI.315 V.
227	1499	Torwood	80d.b.	*ER* XI.314–15 V.

Table 22 (*cont.*)

No.	Year	Place	Unit price	Source
228	1501	Kilmarnock	64d.b.	*ER* XII.22 V.
229	1502	Baldone	66.66d.b.	*ER* XII.656
230	1503	Ross	128d.b.	*ER* XII.239 V.
231	1503	Ross	112.2d.b. with oats	*ER* XII.240
232	1503	Sannak	86d.b.	*ER* XII.251
233	1503	Spottis	100d.b.	*ER* XII.251
234	1503	Culven	80d.b.	*ER* XII.251
235	1503	Baldoune	66.67d.b.	*ER* XII.252
236	1504	Dumbarton?	100d.b.	*TA* II.428 P.
237	1504	Dunkeld	80d.b.	SHS 2,10.82 V.
238	1504	Ardmannoch	12d.b. victual	*ER* XII.307 V.
239	1504	Stirling	64d.b.	*ER* XII.342
240	1505	Linlithgow	84d.b.	*ER* XII.389 V.
241	1505	Stirling	60d.b.	*ER* XII.406
242	1505	Auchterhouse	75.18d.b. victual	*ER* XII.427
243	1505	Montblairy	50d.b.	*ER* XII.438
244	1505	S.Kintyre	6.12d. cast. white meal	*ER* XII.586
245	1505	S.Kintyre	3.63d. cast. coarse meal	*ER* XII.586
246	1505	N.Kintyre	8.84d./8d. cast. white meal	*ER* XII.586
247	1505	Kettil	48d.b.	*ER* XII.689 V.
248	1505	Newtown Falk.	40d.b.	*ER* XII.689 V.
249	1505	N.Kintyre	8d. cast. white meal	*ER* XII.703
250	1505	N.Kintyre	4d. cast. coarse meal	*ER* XII.703
251	1505	N.Kintyre	4.73d.cas./4d.cas. coarse	*ER* XII.586
252	1506	Dunkeld	72d.b.	SHS 2,10.80
253	1506	Dunkeld	80d.b.	SHS 2,10.80
254	1506	Dunkeld	88d.b.	SHS 2,10.80
255	1506	Dunkeld	72d.b.	SHS 2,10.89
256	1506	Kyrkhill	80d.b.	SHS 2,10.93
257	1506	Dunkeld	88d.b.	SHS 2,10.93
258	1506	Clony	84d.b.	SHS 2,10.166
259	1506	Perth	64d.b.	SHS 2,10.196
260	1506	Perth	72d.b.	SHS 2,10.197
261	1506	Perth	80d.b.	SHS 2,10.197
262	1506	Perth	84d.b.	SHS 2,10.197
263	1506	Perth	84d.b.	SHS 2,10.199 V.
264	1506	Perth	68d.b.	SHS 2,10.202
265	1506	Perth	72d.b.	SHS 2,10.202
266	1506	Perth	72d.b.	SHS 2,10.202
267	1506	Perth	80d.b.	SHS 2,10.202
268	1506	Perth	84d.b.	SHS 2,10.202
269	1506	Perth	88d.b.	SHS 2,10.202
270	1506	Perth	92d.b.	SHS 2,10.202
271	1506	Perth	96d.b.	SHS 2,10.202
272	1506	Perth	100d.b.	SHS 2,10.202
273	1506	Auchterhouse	60d.b. with barley	*ER* XII.486

Table 22 (*cont.*)

No.	Year	Place	Unit price	Source
274	1506	Strathdon	60d.b.	*ER* XII.508
275	1506	Ross & Ardman.	50d.b.	*ER* XII.515
276	1506	Ross & Ardman.	60d.b.	*ER* XII.515 V.
277	1506	Stirling	60d.b.	*ER* XII.543
278	1506	Ferische	8d.b.	*ER* XII.550 V.
279	1506	Leith	66.27d.b.	*ER* XII.552
280	1507	Dunkeld	100d.b.	SHS 2,10.89
281	1507	Lt.Dunkeld	100d.b.	SHS 2,10.97
282	1507	Dunkeld	120d.b.	SHS 2,10.97
283	1507	Dunkeld	144d.b.	SHS 2,10.97
284	1507	Dunkeld	192d.b.	SHS 2,10.97
285	1507	Dunkeld	192d.b.	SHS 2,10.97
286	1507	Megilhauch	168d.b.	SHS 2,10.100 V.
287	1507	Dunkeld	168d.b.	SHS 2,10.100 V.
288	1507	Clony	100d.b.	SHS 2,10.169
289	1507	Clony	192d.b.	SHS 2,10.169
290	1507	Perth	100d.b.	SHS 2,10.206 V.
291	1507	Spottis	100d.b.	*ER* XII.654–5
292	1507	Culven	80d.b.	*ER* XII.655
293	1507	Auchterhouse	150.43d.b. with barley	*ER* XIII.30
294	1507	Ferische	8d.b.	*ER* XIII.45 V.
295	1507	Ross	95.6d.b./127.4d.b.	*ER* XIII.47–8 Ross/Leith b.
296	1507	Ardmannoch	12d.b.	*ER* XIII.49 V.
297	1507	Strathdon	120d.b. with barley	*ER* XIII.73
298	1508	Lothian	192d.b.	SHS 2,10.249 P.
299	1508	Bute	80d.b.	*ER* XIII.138
300	1508	Kynnacrag	10d.b.	*ER* XIII.145 V.
301	1508	Ross	70.45d.b.	*ER* XIII.146
302	1508	Montblairy	59.37d.b. with barley	*ER* XIII.176
303	1508	Mekill Strat	60d.b. with barley	*ER* XIII.195
304	1508	Kildrummy	50d.b. with barley	*ER* XIII.198
305	1508	Dunkeld	96d.b.	SHS 2,10.104
306	1508	Dunkeld	84d.b.	SHS 2,10.104
307	1508	Dunkeld	80d.b.	SHS 2,10.104
308	1508	Perth	80.76d.b.	SHS 2,10.211
309	1509	Fordowy	192d.b.	SHS 2,10.172 V.
310	1509	Bute	80d.b.	*ER* XIII.313
311	1509	Perth	56d.b.	SHS 2,10.217
312	1509	Perth	60d.b.	SHS 2,10.217
313	1509	Dunkeld	52d.b.	SHS 2,10.109
314	1509	Dunkeld	64d.b.	SHS 2,10.109
315	1510	Dunkeld	64d.b.	SHS 2,10.116
316	1510	Dunkeld	80d.b.	SHS 2,10.116
317	1510	Dunkeld	80d.b.	SHS 2,10.117 V.
318	1510	Perth	64d.b.	SHS 2,10.221

Table 22 (*cont.*)

No.	Year	Place	Unit price	Source
319	1510	Perth	68d.b.	SHS 2,10.221
320	1510	Perth	72d.b.	SHS 2,10.221
321	1510	Perth	80d.b.	SHS 2,10.221
322	1510	Dunkeld	132d.b.	SHS 2,10.288 V.
323	1510	Leperseit	16d.b. victuals	*ER* XIII.454 V.
324	1510	Petdinne	30d.b. with barley	*ER* XIII.454
325	1511	Dunkeld	80d.b.	SHS 2,10.123 V.
326	1511	Dunkeld	80d.b.	SHS 2,10.123
327	1511	Dunkeld	132d.b.	SHS 2,10.123
328	1511	Clony	108d.b.	SHS 2,10.177 V.
329	1511	Clony	80d.b.	SHS 2,10.178 V.
330	1511	Perth	100d.b.	SHS 2,10.225
331	1511	Stirling	144d.b.	*ER* XIII.404 P.
332	1511	Linlithgow	80d.b.	*ER* XIII.409 V.
333	1511	Ardmannoch	12.75d.b. victuals	*ER* XIII.446 V.
334	1512	Dunkeld	132d.b.	SHS 2,10.126 V.
335	1512	Perth	108d.b.	SHS 2,10.225
336	1512	Perth	120d.b.	SHS 2,10.225
337	1512	Perth	132d.b.	SHS 2,10.225
338	1512	Stirlingsh.	120d.b.	*ER* XIII.567 P.
339	1513	Perth	132d.b.	SHS 2,10.228 V.
340	1513	Perth	132d.b.	SHS 2,10.229 V.
341	1513	Dunkeld	108d.b.	SHS 2,10.132
342	1513	Dunkeld	100d.b.	SHS 2,10.141
343	1513	Dunkeld	120d.b.	SHS 2,10.141
344	1513	Bute	80d.b.	*ER* XIV.21
345	1513	Stirling	100d.b.	*ER* XIV.39 P.
346	1513	Stirling	80d.b.	*ER* XIV.42 P.
347	1513	Ardmannoch	12.75d.b.	*ER* XIV.89 V.
348	1514	Perth	100d.b.	SHS 2,10.235
349	1514	Perth	96d.b.	SHS 2,10.235
350	1514	Perth	112d.b.	SHS 2,10.235
351	1514	Perth	112d.b.	SHS 2,10.237 V.
352	1514	Perth	112d.b.	SHS 2,10.238 V.
353	1514	Perth	96d.b.	SHS 2,10.240
354	1514	Perth	100d.b.	SHS 2,10.240
355	1514	Perth	100d.b.	SHS 2,10.240 V.
356	1514	Perth	100d.b.	SHS 2,10.242
357	1514	Perth	100d.b.	SHS 2,10.242
358	1514	Dunkeld	80d.b.	SHS 2,10.294 V.
359	1514	Brechin	80d.b. victuals	*ER* XIV.81 V.
360	1515	Inchegarvy	144d.b.	*TA* V.20 P.
361	1515	Dunkeld	80d.b.	SHS 2,10.146 V.
362	1515	Dunkeld	100d.b.	SHS 2,10.148
363	1515	Ross	72d.b.	*ER* XIV.217
364	1515	Arbroath	66d.b.	*ER* XIV.217

Table 22 (*cont.*)

No.	Year	Place	Unit price	Source
365	1515	Perth	100d.b.	SHS 2,10.243 V.
366	1516	Dunkeld	100d.b.	SHS 2,10.151
367	1516	Banf	80d.b.	SHS 2,10.151
368	1516	Alytht	100d.b.	SHS 2,10.151 V.
369	1516	Tullemurdo	100d.b.	SHS 2,10.151 V.
370	1516	Cultiscroft	100d.b.	SHS 2,10.151 V.
371	1516	Stobhale	100d.b.	SHS 2,10.151 V.
372	1516	Strauthhurd	100d.b.	SHS 2,10.151 V.
373	1516	Estircapeth	100d.b.	SHS 2,10.151 V.
374	1516	Fordye	100d.b.	SHS 2,10.152 V.
375	1516	Tullemule	100d.b.	SHS 2,10.152 V.
376	1516	Dunkeld	100d.b.	SHS 2,10.152 V.
377	1516	Dunkeld	80d.b.	SHS 2,10.299 P.
378	1516	Lennox	80d.b.	*ER* XIV.232–3
379	1516	Ross	76.81d.b.	*ER* XIV.283
380	1517	Ross	72.30d.b.	*ER* XIV.306
381	1517		144d.b.	*ER* XIV.347
382	1518		120d.b.	*ER* XIV.472
383	1519	Aberdeen	120/96d.b.	ACR X.150 Wi.
384	1521	Aberdeen	18s barrel	ACR X.303 Aw.
385	1521	Ferisch	8d.b.	*ER* XV *passim* V.
386	1521	Ross	90d.b.	*ER* XV.24
387	1521	Ardmannoch	12.75d.b. victuals	*ER* XV.27 V.
388	1522	Aberdeen	80d.b.	ACR XI.47 O.
389	1522	Lennox	80d.b.	*ER* XV.8
390	1523	Stirling	288d.b.	*ER* XV.91 P.
391	1523		277.96d.b. victuals	*ER* XV.89 P.
392	1524	Kincrag	10d.b. with barley	*ER* XV *passim* V.
393	1524	Ross	100d.b.	*ER* XV.171–2
394	1524	Ardmannoch	100d.b.	*ER* XV.175–6
395	1524		160d.b.	*ER* XV.209
396	1525	Ross	80d.b.	*ER* XV.258
397	1525	Ardmannoch	12d.b.	*ER* XV *passim* V.
398	1526	Fife	80d.b.	*ER* XV.234
399	1526	Sannak	96d.b.	*ER* XV.316
400	1526	Spottis	100d.b.	*ER* XV.316
401	1526	Culven	80d.b.	*ER* XV.316
402	1526	Ballindone	66.67d.b.	*ER* XV.317
403	1526	Drumnachtane	65d.b.	*ER* XV.329
404	1526	Drumnachtane	80d.b.	*ER* XV.329
405	1527	Aberdeen	384d.b.	ACR XII i.190 C.
406	1527	Aberdeen	32s.tun	ACR XII i.227 C.
407	1527	Ross	100d.b. with barley	*ER* XV.407
408	1527	Ardmannoch	100d.b. with barley	*ER* XV.412–13
409	1527	Ardmannoch	100d.b. with barley	*ER* XV.413
410	1527	Bute	80d.b.	*ER* XV.425

Table 22 (*cont.*)

No.	Year	Place	Unit price	Source
411	1528	Bute	80d.b.	*ER* XV.497
412	1528	Ardmannoch	90d.b.	*ER* XV.506
413	1528	Stirling	120d.b.	*ER* XV.549–50 V.
414	1529	Aberdeen	192d.b.	ACR XII ii.553 assize V.
415	1529	Stirling	120d.b.	*ER* XV.538 V.
416	1529	Fife	100d.b.	*ER* XVI.18
417	1529	Bute	80d.b.	*ER* XVI.24
418	1529	Fyschrie	8d.b.	*ER* XVI *passim* V.
419	1529	Estwemis	100d.b. with barley	*ER* XVI.112–3
420	1529	Ross	100d.b. with barley	*ER* XVI.113
421	1529	Ross	100d.b. with barley	*ER* XVI.113
422	1529	Ross	90d.b. with barley	*ER* XVI.113
423	1529	Ardmannoch	12.75d.b. victuals	*ER* XVI *passim* V.
424	1530	Stirling	120d.b.	*ER* XVI *passim* V.
425	1530		120d.b.	*ER* XVI.144
426	1531	Aberdeen	160d.b.	ACR XIII.174 O.
427	1531		150d.b.	*TA* V.459 P.
428	1531	Ross	160d.b. with barley	*ER* XVI.203
429	1531	Ross	160d.b. with barley	*ER* XVI.203
430	1532	Aberdeen	288d.b./240d.b.	ACR XIII.478 Wi.
431	1532	Aberdeen	192d.b.	ACR XIV.66 Aw.
432	1532	Fife	120d.b.	*ER* XVI.271
433	1532	Ross	72d.b.	*ER* XVI.279
434	1533	Glasgow	96d.b.	*TA* VI.164 P.
435	1533	Fife	80d.b.	*ER* XVI.317
436	1533	Ardmannoch	75d.b. with barley	*ER* XVI.327
437	1534	Aberdeen	132d.b.	ACR XIV.338 Aw.
438	1534	Ross	148d.b.	*ER* XVI.406
439	1534	Ross	100d.b.	*ER* XVI.407
440	1534	Ardmannoch	100d.b.	*ER* XVI.410
441	1535	Aberdeen	72d.b.	ACR XIV.594 Aw.
442	1535	Fife	160d.b.	*ER* XVI.471
443	1535		156.11d.b.	*ER* XVI.481
444	1535	Bute	80d.b.	*ER* XVII.29
445	1535	Ardmannoch	12.75d.b. victuals	*ER* XVII *passim* V.
446	1536	Aberdeen	144d.b./160d.b.	ACR XV.139 Wi.
447	1536	Fife	120d.b.	*ER* XVII.11
448	1536	Fischerie	128d.b.	*ER* XVII *passim* V.
449	1536	Kincrag	160d.b.	*ER* XVII *passim* V.
450	1537	Sannak	96d.b.	*ER* XVII.73
451	1537	Spottis	100d.b. large measure	*ER* XVII.73
452	1537	Culven	80d.b. large measure	*ER* XVII.73
453	1537	Ballindone	66.66d.b. large measure	*ER* XVII.75
454	1537	Errol	112d.b.	*ER* XVII.96
455	1537	Largo	96d.b.	*ER* XVII.106
456	1537	Ross	90d.b. with barley	*ER* XVII.114

Table 22 (*cont.*)

No.	Year	Place	Unit price	Source
457	1537	Douglas	210d.b.	*ER* XVII.124
458	1537	Craufurdjohn	100d.b.	*ER* XVII.128 P.
459	1537	Kingorne	96d.b.	*ER* XVII.150
460	1537	Glamis	100d.b.	*ER* XVII.150
461	1537	Stirling	120d.b.	*ER* XVII.163 V.
462	1538	Aberdeen	120d.b.	ACR XVI.429 C.
463	1538	Bonkle	100d.b.	*ER* XVII.121 V.
464	1538	Bute	100d.b.	*ER* XVII.199
465	1538	Fife	100d.b.	*ER* XVII.212
466	1538	Errol	168d.b.	*ER* XVII.217
467	1538	Douglas	120d.b.	*ER* XVII.272
468	1538	Ross	144d.b.	*ER* XVII.235
469	1538	Ardmannoch	144d.b.	*ER* XVII.240
470	1538	Glamis etc.	132d.b. + 144d.b.	*ER* XVII.252
471	1539	St Andrews	144d.b.	SHS 2,4.102
472	1539		160d.b.	*ER* XVII.290 V.
473	1539	Edinburgh	120d.b.	*ER* XVII.291 V.
474	1539	Linlithgow	120d.b.	*ER* XVII.291 V.
475	1539		140d.b.	*ER* XVII.294
476	1539	West Migvy	80d.b.	*ER* XVII.370
477	1539	Glamis & Brig.	150d.b. + 144d.b.	*ER* XVII.423
478	1540	West Migvy	96d.b.	*ER* XVII.413
479	1540	Glamis	132d.b. + 120d.b.	*ER* XVII.421
480	1540	Glamis	150d.b.	*ER* XVII.421
481	1540		87.03d.b.	*TA* VII.384
482	1540	St Andrews	144d.b.	SHS 2,4.116
483	1541	Aberdeen	96d.b.	ACR XVI.738 C.
484	1541	St Andrews	144d.b.	SHS 2,4.133
485	1541	Desschier & T.	120d.b. white meal	*ER* XVII.484
486	1541	Desschier & T.	120d.b. black meal	*ER* XVII.484
487	1541	Ross	192d.b.	*ER* XVII.496
488	1541	Ross	192d.b. aride multure	*ER* XVII.496
489	1541	Ross	160d.b.	*ER* XVII.496
490	1541	Fife	80d.b.	*ER* XVII.515
491	1541	Mull,Tiree	16d. stone	*ER* XVII.529 V.
492	1541	Douglas	160d.b.	*ER* XVII.560
493	1541	Linlithgowsh	168d.b.	*ER* XVII.568
494	1541	Bonkle & Pres.	192d.b.	*ER* XVII.573
495	1541	Kilbride	200d.b.	*ER* XVII.580
496	1541	Draffane	160d.b.	*ER* XVII.582
497	1541	Avandale	150d.b.	*ER* XVII.588
498	1541	Kilmarnock	150d.b.	*ER* XVII.595
499	1541	Kintyre	16d. stone	*ER* XVII.625 V.
500	1542	St Andrews	192d.b.	SHS 2,4.153

The central importance of oatmeal in the diet of the mass of the Scottish people is demonstrated by the use of meal in wages in kind.[77] Although the cash valuations set on these payments in kind may sometimes have exhibited a certain stickiness, they give a much more reliable indication of price than the various commutations, valuations, and allowances associated with landholding.[78] Equally, the care with which the Aberdeen authorities policed the market in meal[79] testifies to its importance in the diet of the majority of townsfolk.

At the same time as the Aberdeen authorities took care to ensure a reasonable supply of meal for the town and a just distribution of it once it had arrived, those buying oatmeal were people least able to afford inflated prices. This does not mean that meal prices did not rise sharply in time of crisis: the 1480s show that they did, but then, and throughout the later middle ages, meal prices rose less than other cereals. Oatmeal prices were probably relatively low because there was no export demand, the crop was widely grown in Scotland, and there was also a genuine ceiling on the price the Scottish poor could afford to pay.

Wine

A large number of Scottish prices for wine have been collected and are printed in the list of prices, but it should be admitted at the outset that they are only of limited value. The difficulties involved in using this material are such that the cumulative figures give us little more than a crude indication of long-term inflation, while the individual entries can only provide anecdotal evidence.

David I's assize of wine[80] is a rather terse attempt to regulate the relationship between wholesale tun (doleum) prices and retail gallon (lagena) prices. As with David's other assizes, the actual figures given are appropriate only to the very beginning of our prices series, but the principles intended to govern this relationship are of more general interest. It was there stated that every 10s. on the tun price should raise the gallon price by 1d., so a 30s. tun should lead to a 3d. gallon,

[77] List 226–7, 316, 328, 382, 358, 361, 415, 424, 473–4, and SHS 2, 10,281.

[78] As with barley and oats, the lowest valuations were set on customary payments made to husbandmen for renders in kind associated with their tenancies; List 278, 294, 385 from Ferische; 300, 392, 449 from Kincrag; 238, 296, 347, 387, 397, 423, 445 from Ardmannoch, 121 from Ross. Other low 'sales' commutations, allowances, and valuations are also met; List 133, 153, 212, 216, 323.

[79] See Chapter 2.

[80] *APS* I.676. As with bread and ale, the attribution to David I may be regarded with some scepticism.

a 60s. tun to a 6d. gallon. It was then implicit that 120 gallons of wine should be sold retail for the cost of a wholesale tun.

However, another document from around the beginning of the fourteenth century records different figures. The Corpus Christi College, Cambridge MS no. 37[81] records a jury's verdict that a tun of wine should contain 100 (5 score) gallons retail. They went on to state that with the tun bought at £4 the gallon should be sold at 12d., a tun at 53s. 4d. gives a gallon of 8d., and a tun of 40s. gives a gallon at 6d. On this system 80 gallons sold retail would cover the wholesale cost of one of these 100 gallon tuns. Thus the assize and the Corpus Christi College MS suggest slightly different pricing structures and tun sizes. Even more disturbingly, they speak of tun sizes which appear to be in the region of half the size of the English tun.

Thorold Rogers, and more recently Connor, found that the English tun contained 252 gallons.[82] Since wine had to be imported both to England and Scotland one might have hoped that tuns in Scotland would not have been significantly different but this does not always seem to have been the case.[83] This uncertainty seriously complicates the interpretation of the tun series, and also makes comparison of tun and gallon prices difficult. This in turn obscures our understanding of retail profit margins.

Scottish burgh custom generally disapproved of retail profits. It was usually held that goods should not be sold on at a profit unless some value were added in the process, but the special problems of wine retailers do seem to have been recognized. One such problem was that unsold wine quickly turned sour. It seems clear that medieval wine did not age well. New wine was consistently prized more highly than old,[84] and despite annual harvest fluctuations no attempt seems to have been made to store the more plentiful vintages for sale in scarcer years. The current price was always dramatically affected by the latest shipments. Under these circumstances, retail wastage was probably high.

It may also be that the assize was less protective towards consumers

[81] SHS 44, Miscellany, p. 26.

[82] J.E. Thorold Rogers, *Six Centuries of Work and Wages: The History of English Labour* (Oxford, 1890) p. 135. See also Connor, *The Weights and Measures of England*, pp. 170–1.

[83] Gallons, like so many of our measures, will also have varied over time, and sometimes differed from the English measure. See Chapter 3, and the Glossary.

[84] List 13–15. Margery K. James, 'The Fluctuations of the Anglo-Gascon Wine Trade during the Fourteenth Century', in E.M. Carus Wilson (ed.), *Essays in Economic History*, II (London, 1962), p. 128, notes that the demand for the newest wine was such that prices could fall by as much as 13s. 4d. a tun within eight days of the first sales of the harvest.

because wine was never regarded as essential. While Scottish burghs went to considerable lengths to safeguard supplies of bread and ale, luxury products like wine did not justify such concern. More especially, we may also note that retailers and wholesalers of wine were often one and the same, and belonged very definitely to the community of international merchants dominating the upper echelons of Scottish burgh life.[85] We need not be surprised if the regulations they imposed to control their own profits weighed less heavily than those they imposed on others. In Aberdeen wine price regulation is extremely rare, compared with the regular legislation on bread and ale, and when it does occur it is much less onerous.[86]

Comparison of wholesale and retail wine prices is also complicated by the question of carriage. Tun prices in Scotland usually include the cost of freight from the wine growers (for exceptions see List 174 and 224) but may or may not include additional carriage costs within Scotland.[87] The gallon price of course has to cover all additional costs incurred right up to the point of consumption. The Scottish evidence for carriage is not sufficient to permit us to calculate a carriage rate per mile/tun or gallon, but English legislation shows that these costs were considerable. The usual fourteenth-century inland rates were in the order of $\frac{1}{2}$d. a gallon for carriage of twenty-five to thirty miles.[88] Wine in Oxford consistently cost at least 1d. a gallon more than in London.[89] Rogers estimated wine carriage at about 3$\frac{1}{2}$d. per tun per mile,[90] so a range from 3d. to 5d. per tun/mile looks about right. Sea-freight was usually cheaper, but could become dramatically more expensive in time of war.[91]

Ultimately, however, the marked discrepancy between retail and wholesale wine prices and uncertainty about the size of the tun makes it very difficult to compare prices in gallons with those in tuns.[92] We

[85] Burgesses are met constantly as suppliers of luxuries to the royal and noble households. Occasionally we find wine issued in taverns as borough hospitality (List 127–34, 136).

[86] List 364 expressly permitted totally free wholesale pricing and sales by one wine merchant, and set a high price for pint retail sales.

[87] Carriage costs were explicitly included for some prices (List 11, 113, 120, 227, 255, *TA* VII.60) and excluded for others (List 69, 284–5, 372). Sometimes carriage costs are given separately (List 107, 198, 273), or special coastal carriage discussed (List 293, 378).

[88] James, 'Fluctuations of the Anglo-Gascon Wine Trade', pp. 133, 138. An attempt to fix a rate of $\frac{1}{2}$d. a gallon for fifty miles, introduced in 1381 was repealed in 1383 (ibid., p. 144).

[89] Ibid., p. 132.

[90] Rogers, *Six Centuries of Work and Wages* p. 135.

[91] James, 'Fluctuations of the Anglo-Gascon Wine Trade', p. 135.

[92] The David I formula was not in force in the fourteenth century in England either. E.g. ibid., p. 144.

Table 23. *Wine summary table (gallons)*

Period	Mean price	Deflated	Index
A			
B–C	10	10.0	100.0
D	26	26.0	260.0
E	33	27.65	276.5
F	40	20.18	201.8
G			
H	83	33.39	333.9
I	74	24.36	243.6
60s			
70s	84	23.4	234.0
80s	107		
90s	76	21.28	212.8
1500s	92	24.91	249.1
10s	125	34.94	394.4
20s	85	21.19	211.9
30s			

Note: the mean price is in pence per gallon; the deflated column gives the currency-adjusted sterling equivalent price.

are effectively left with two separate wine series. Gallon prices are consistently very much dearer than tun prices. English gallon prices are also dearer vis-à-vis the tun price but generally Scottish prices – tun and gallon – are dearer than English. This disparity – already clear in the mid-fourteenth century – becomes more marked later. For example, while English gallon prices stood around 6d. for much of the first half of the fifteenth century, Scots prices (Table 23) exceeded English by far more than the factor of debasement.[93] England's rule in Gascony probably enabled her to buy wine more cheaply, and Scotland will certainly have suffered from its additional distance from the wine growers and from the danger of English privateers. Moreover, despite the high prices paid in Scotland, it was sometimes the poorest quality wine which was sent north.[94]

All these very considerable difficulties and uncertainties seriously complicate any understanding of the central problem of wine prices, that is, the great variety of wines of variable quality. Margery James

[93] There is no table of comparison between Scots and English prices before 1367 because Rogers' prices are given in gallons while most Scots prices of this date are in tuns.
[94] *CDS* IV, no. 122, p. 27, for 'thin wine' sent to Scotland.

found that even within a single year, and restricting her consideration only to Gascon wines, wine prices could often fluctuate by as much as 50%. The wines bought in Scotland and noted here make an even less homogeneous group, and this wide price variation from different types and qualities of wine means that the mean prices can be heavily affected by the accident of which particular types and qualities happen to fall in any given group of averaged prices. The value of these aggregated and averaged wine prices is thus limited in the extreme. (See Table 23 and Figures 20 and 21 for mean gallon prices, and the currency-adjusted gallon price index; Table 24 and Figures 22 and 23 for mean tun prices and the currency-adjusted tun price index.)

On the other hand, the variety of wines available in Scotland is not without its own interest. Apart from otherwise undistinguished red and white wine, the wines of Gascony and the Rhine are those most commonly encountered. About the end of the fifteenth century references to Gascon wine become less common, while 'claret' is increasingly mentioned. Clearly the change is merely one of terminology, though it may be noted that at that time the term 'claret' was not restricted solely to the wines of south-west France.[95] The wine of Beaune was specially prized[96] while Anjou and Poitou wine was also distinguished by name.[97] Malmsey, muscadet, and grenache were much appreciated[98] while Spanish, Portuguese, Greek, and Roman wine are also met.[99]

Although the place of origin can give some guide to price, it is impossible to establish any objective guide to quality. Royal purchases were often of superior wine, but poorer varieties of wine were also bought in quantity by the king for the less exalted members of his household or for military garrisons. Extremely expensive wines can readily be spotted and excluded from our calculations, but even so the range of more normal prices was wide, making it difficult to identify shifts in price attributable to economic factors. Thus Tables 23 and 24, for the mean prices of wine in gallons and tuns, and their adjusted indexes, can only provide the most general information. Buying by the gallon was much more expensive than buying by the tun. Wine in Scotland was dearer than in England. Prices clearly rose markedly over the period as a whole, but the absence of a long run of comparable prices makes further analysis of wine price changes over time hazardous.

[95] List 288: 'claret de Burgunye et le Beaune'.
[96] List 153, 201, 288–9.
[97] List 209, 237, 337, 339, 351.
[98] List 54, 89, 146–7, 191, 213, 215, 219, 223, 231, 238, 265, 271, 278, 282–4, 331, 350, 360.
[99] List 124–5, 165, 242, 252, 368, 373.

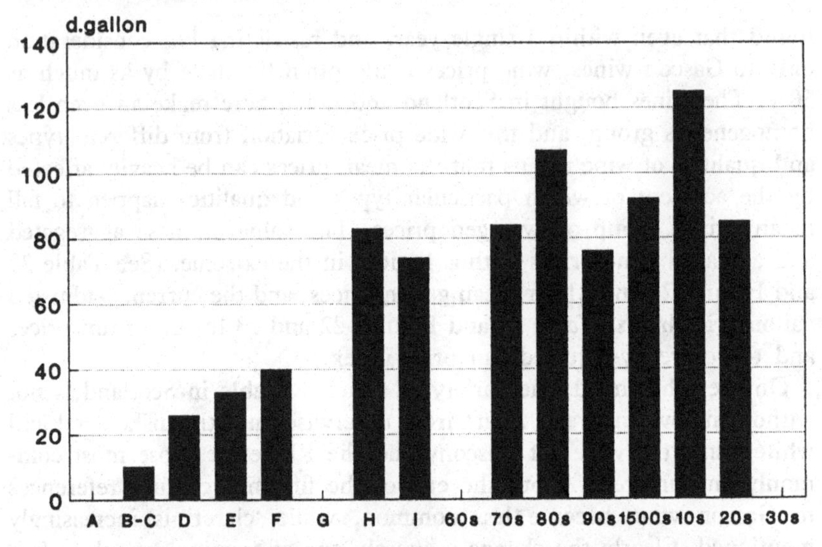

20 Wine gallon prices (mean prices for time periods A–1530s)
For periods A–I, see Introduction, p. 6.

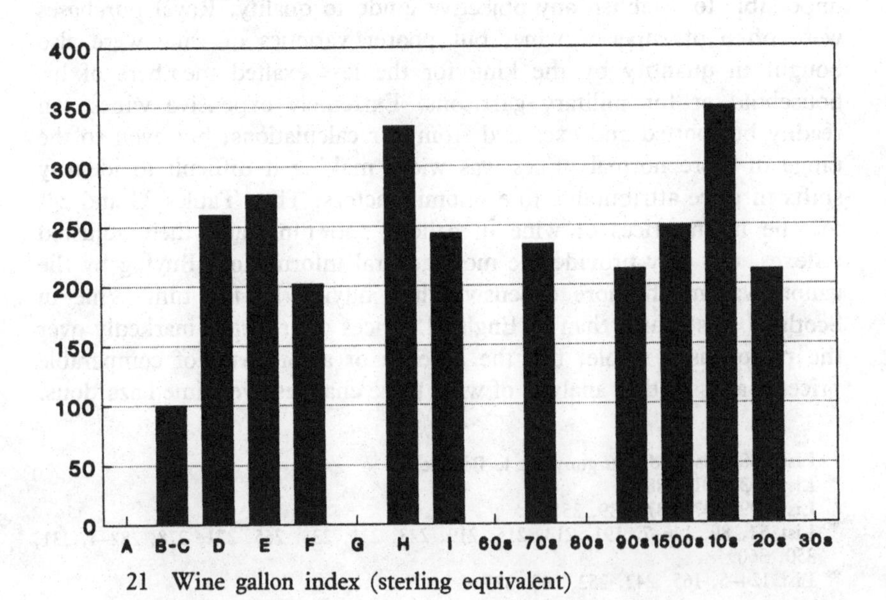

21 Wine gallon index (sterling equivalent)

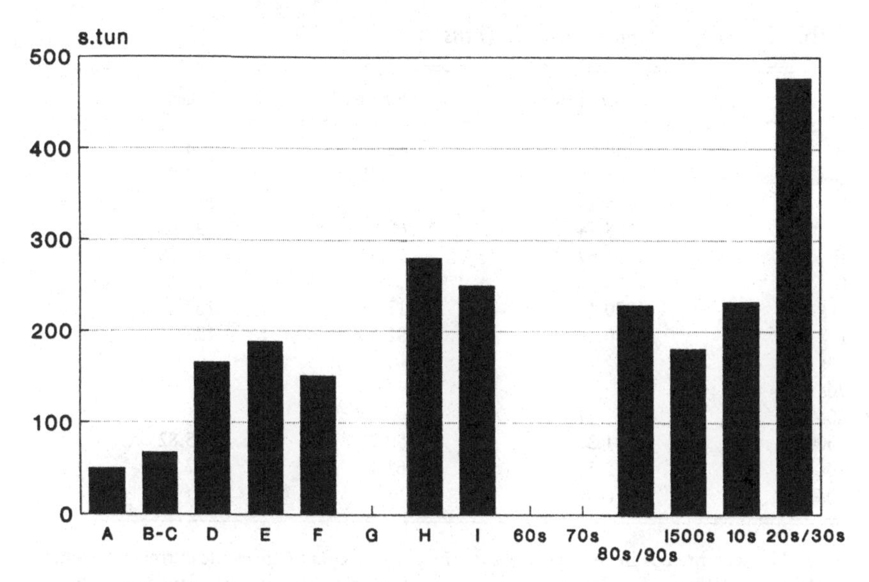

22 Wine tun prices (mean prices for time periods A–1530s)
For periods A–I, see Introduction, p. 6.

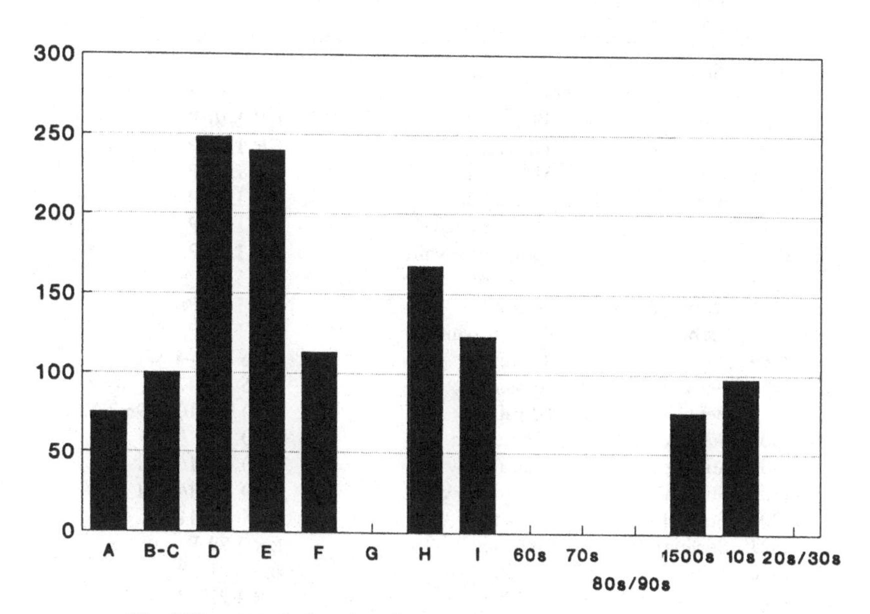

23 Wine tun index (sterling equivalent)

Table 24. *Wine summary table (tuns)*

Period	Mean price	Deflated	Index
A	50.06	50.06	74.77
B–C	66.95	66.95	100.0
D	166.14	166.14	248.16
E	188.74	160.43	239.63
F	151.67	75.84	113.28
G			
H	280.1	112.04	167.35
I	250.06	82.52	123.26
60s			
70s			
80s–90s	(229.17)		
1500s	181.3	50.76	75.82
10s	232.5	65.1	97.24
20s–30s	(476.89)		

Note: the mean price is in shillings per tun; the deflated column gives the currency-adjusted sterling equivalent price. Parentheses have been used to flag up calculations which are less securely based than others – either because they are based on a smaller amount of data, or because they involve certain, possibly questionable, assumptions.

Table 25. *Wine price list*

No.	Year	Place	Unit price	Source
1	1263		49.4s.tun	*ER* I.10 P.
2	1264		110.77s.tun	*ER* I.10 P.
3	1264	Forres	51.79s.tun	*ER* I.15 P.
4	1265	Ayr	36.67s.tun red	*ER* I.28 P.
5	1265	Ayr	30.5s.tun red	*ER* I.28 P.
6	1265	Ayr	36.67s.tun white	*ER* I.28 P.
7	1265	Ayr	40.33s.tun white	*ER* I.288 P.
8	1288	Jedburgh	40s.tun	*ER* I.44 P.
9	1288	Jedburgh	45s.tun white	*ER* I.44 P.
10	1289		44s.tun	*DHS* I.71–8 Wi.
11	1294	Berwick	65.5s.tun	*DHS* II.247 P.
12	1303	Berwick	6d.gal.	PRO E101/365/9m2 V.
13	1303	Stirling	60s.tun old	PRO E101/366/1 P.
14	1303	Stirling	80s.tun new	PRO E101/366/1 P.
15	1303	Stirling	80s.tun new	PRO E101/366/1 P.
16	1304	Berwick	66.5s.tun	*CDS* II.444 V.
17	1327	Stirling?	100s.tun	*ER* I.79 P.
18	1328		80s.tun	*ER* I.211 P.
19	1328		64.33s.tun	*ER* I.219 P.
20	1328		40s.tun	*ER* I.185 P.

Table 25 (*cont.*)

No.	Year	Place	Unit price	Source
21	1328	Berwick	75s.tun	*ER* I.119 P.
22	1328		12d.gal.	*ER* I.219 P.
23	1328		12d.gal.	*ER* I.219 P.
24	1328		93.33s.tun	*ER* I.216 P.
25	1329		80s.tun	*ER* I.245 P.
26	1329		66.67s.tun	*ER* I.237
27	1329	Ayr	86.67s.tun	*ER* I.285 P.
28	1329	Perth	66.67s.tun	*ER* I.288 P.
29	1329		70s.tun	*ER* I.289 P.
30	1330		54.04s.tun	*ER* I.341 P.
31	1331		53.33s.tun	*ER* I.403 P.
32	1331		79.44s.tun	*ER* I.400 P.
33	1331	Inverk'g	106.67s.tun	*ER* I.369 P.
34	1331		40.22s.tun	*ER* I.397
35	1331		80s.tun new	*ER* I.397
36	1331	Inverk'g	100s. tun	*ER* I.370
37	1341	Aberdeen	80s.tun	*ER* I.530 P.
38	1341		56.67s.tun	*ER* I.505
39	1341	Aberdeen	56.67s.tun	*ER* I.531 P.
40	1341		48s.tun	*ER* I.505 P.
41	1341		60s.tun	*ER* I.505 P.
42	1341	Aberdeen	53.33s.tun	*ER* I.532 P.
43	1341	Ayr	60s.tun red	*ER* I.495 P.
44	1341		73s.4d.tun	*ER* I.505 P.
45	1342	Edinburgh	66.67s.tun	*ER* I.522
46	1342	Edinburgh	53.33s.tun	*ER* I.535 V.
47	1342	Inverness	12d.and 8d.gal.	*ER* I.479
48	1342	Aberdeen	53.33s.tun	*ER* I.481 P.
49	1342	Aberdeen	11.43d.gal. white	*ER* I.482 P.
50	1342	Edinburgh	12d.gal.	*ER* I.522
51	1344	Berwick?	6.5d.gal.	HI 1344–5,b P.
52	1357	Perth	160s.tun	*ER* I.597 P.
53	1357		160s.tun	*ER* II.3 P.
54	1357	Edinburgh	32d.gal. grenache	*ER* I.609 V.
55	1357	Linlithgow	160s.tun	*ER* I.599 P.
56	1357	Linlithgow	160s.tun	*ER* I.599 P.
57	1357	Perth	24d.gal.	*ER* II.3–4 P.
58	1357	Edinburgh	24d.gal. Rhine	*ER* I.609 V.
59	1357	Linlithgow	160s.tun	*ER* I.599 P.
60	1357	Perth	160s.tun	*ER* I.597 P.
61	1358	Dundee	200s.tun Rhine	*ER* II.6 P.
62	1358	Edinburgh	24d.gal.	*ER* I.617 V.
63	1359	Aberdeen	133.33s.tun	*ER* II.32 P.
64	1359	Linlithgow	160s.tun	*ER* II.12 P.
65	1360	Linlithgow	200s.tun	*ER* II.79 P.
66	1360		186.67s.tun	*ER* II.83 P.

Table 25 (*cont.*)

No.	Year	Place	Unit price	Source
67	1360		200s.tun	*ER* II.82 P.
68	1360		293.34s.tun Rhine	*ER* II.78 V.
69	1360		160s.tun	*ER* II.52 P.
70	1360	Edinburgh?	120s.tun	*ER* II.65 P.
71	1360	Perth?	160s.tun	*ER* II.82 P.
72	1360	Linlithgow	146.75s.tun	*ER* II.67 P.
73	1361	Stirling	193.33s.tun	*ER* II.115 P.
74	1361		126.67s.tun	*ER* II.113 P.
75	1361		160s.tun	*ER* II.117 P.
76	1362	Edinburgh	133.34s.tun	*ER* II.128 P.
77	1362	Edinburgh	290s.roda Rhine	*ER* II.128 V.
78	1362	Linlithgow	146.66s.tun	*ER* II.125 V.
79	1362		133.33s.tun	*ER* II.166 P.
80	1362	Linlithgow	160s.tun	*ER* II.124 P.
81	1362	Glasgow	200s.tun	*ER* II.126 P.
82	1362	Dundee	173.33s.tun	*ER* II.140 V.
83	1362	Linlithgow	186.67s.tun	*ER* II.124 V.
84	1363	Edinburgh	146.67s.tun	*ER* II.177 P.
85	1363	Coldingham	226.67s.tun	SS 12.xliii P.
86	1364		155.56s.tun	*ER* II.227 P.
87	1364		146.67s.tun	*ER* II.222 V.
88	1364	Linlithgow?	133.34s.tun	*ER* II.221.P.
89	1364		83.33s.butt grenache	*ER* II.228 P.
90	1364	Edinburgh	133.33s.tun	*ER* II.200 P.
91	1365	Perth	220s.tun Rhine & red Gascon	*ER* II.222 P.
92	1366		138.73s.tun	*ER* II.252 P.
93	1368	Stirling	146.67s.tun	*ER* II.306 P.
94	1371	Scone?	32.5d.gal.	*ER* II.365 P.
95	1372		222.69s.tun	*ER* II.369 P.
96	1373	Edinburgh	163.20s.tun	*ER* II.368 V.
97	1373		200s.tun	*ER* II.452 P.
98	1373		218.97s.tun	*ER* II.451 P.
99	1373		34.03d/30.51d.gal.venalis	*ER* II.451 P.
100	1374	Stirling	93.33s.tun	*ER* II.462
101	1374	Dundee	71.16s.tun Gascon	*ER* II.449 V.
102	1374	Edinburgh	200s.tun	*ER* II.463 P.
103	1374	Melrose	232.5s.tun	*ER* II.463 P.
104	1375	Edinburgh	281.17s.vasa Rhine	*ER* II.475 P.
105	1375	Edinburgh	160s.tun	*ER* II.521 P.
106	1376	Montrose	32d.gal. Rhine	*ER* II.531 P.
107	1376	Edinburgh	180s.tun	*ER* II.520 V.
108	1377	Edinburgh	125.84s.tun	*ER* II.553 V.
109	1377	Edinburgh	180s.tun	*ER* II.554 P.
110	1378	Edinburgh	160s.tun	*ER* II.608 P.
111	1378	Edinburgh	133.33s.tun	*ER* II.608 P.

Table 25 (*cont.*)

No.	Year	Place	Unit price	Source
112	1378	Linlithgow	156.67s.tun	*ER* II.605 P.
113	1379	Edinburgh	126.67s.tun	*ER* III.2 P.
114	1379	Edinburgh	253.33s.tun	*ER* III.3 P.
115	1379	Edinburgh	240s.tun	*ER* III.3 P.
116	1379	Edinburgh	240s.tun	*ER* III.3 P.
117	1379	Edinburgh	160s.tun	*ER* III.3 P.
118	1380	Edinburgh	225s.tun	*ER* III.53 P.
119	1380	W. Scotland	333.33s.tun Rhine	*ER* III.40 V.
120	1380	Montrose	174.08s.tun	*ER* III.654 P.
121	1380		133.33s.tun	*ER* III.652 P.
122	1380		40.48d.gal./35.12d.gal.	*ER* III.40 P.
123	1381	Bute	186.67s.tun	*ER* III.82 P.
124	1381	Edinburgh	266.67s.tun de Respyne	*ER* III.81 P.
125	1381	Edinburgh	240s.tun Spanish	*ER* III.81 P.
126	1384	Bute	160s.tun	*ER* III.107 V.
127	1399	Aberdeen	5.40d.pint	SHS 3,49.81 P.
128	1399	Aberdeen	6d.pint	SHS 3,49.81 P.
129	1399	Aberdeen	4d.pint	SHS 3,49.81 P.
130	1399	Aberdeen	64d.gal.	SHS 3,49.81 P.
131	1399	Aberdeen	4d.pint	SHS 3,49.81 P.
132	1399	Aberdeen	32d.gal.	SHS 3,49.81 P.
133	1399	Aberdeen	6.4d.pint	SHS 3,49.81 P.
134	1399	Aberdeen	4d.pint	SHS 3,49.81 P.
135	1399	Perth	180s.tun	*ER* III.495 P.
136	1399	Aberdeen	4d.pint	SHS 3,49.81 P.
137	1402	Linlithgow	133.33s.tun	*ER* III.569 V.
138	1407		133.33s.tun red	*ER* IV.66 V.
139	1409		160s.tun	*ER* IV.130 P.
140	1425	Perth	220s.butt de Osaye	*ER* IV.406 V.
141	1425	Edinburgh	140s.tun	*ER* IV.411 P.
142	1427	Edinburgh	240s.vasa Rhine	*ER* IV.436 P.
143	1427	Linlithgow	190s.butt Rhine	*ER* IV.450 P.
144	1428	Leith	360s.tun Rhine	*ER* IV.471 P.
145	1429	Aberdeen	160s.tun	*ER* IV.511 P.
146	1429	Coupar	320s.tun grenache	*ER* IV.499 P.
147	1433	Perth	260s.butt muscadet	*ER* IV.563–4 P.
148	1433	Perth	83.48d.gal. Rhine	*ER* IV.564 P.
149	1433	Aberdeen	373.33s.tun Gascon	*ER* IV.568 P.
150	1433	Edinburgh	180s.tun	*ER* IV.578 V.
151	1433	Perth	168s.cade Rhine	*ER* IV.563 P.
152	1433	Edinburgh	180s.tun	*ER* IV.574 P.
153	1434	Edinburgh	640s.tun Beaune	*ER* IV.622 P.
154	1434	Edinburgh	320s.tun Gascon	*ER* IV.622 P.
155	1434	Edinburgh	320s.tun Gascon	*ER* IV.620 P.
156	1434	Edinburgh	324s.tun	*ER* IV.620–1 P.
157	1434	Aberdeen?	360s.tun Gascon	*ER* IV.628 P.

Table 25 (*cont.*)

No.	Year	Place	Unit price	Source
158	1434	Perth	240s.tun	*ER* IV.607 P.
159	1434	Edinburgh	373.33s.tun Gascon	*ER* IV.623 P.
160	1434	Edinburgh	320s.tun Gascon	*ER* IV.621 P.
161	1434	Edinburgh?	320s.tun Gascon	*ER* IV.626 P.
162	1437	Perth	394.67s.tun	*ER* V.19 P.
163	1437	Aberdeen	111.67s.pipe	ACR IV.94 Aw.
164	1437	Edinburgh	200s.tun red	*ER* V.36 V.
165	1437	Edinburgh	£10 per butt Greek	*ER* V.36 V.
166	1438	Perth	266.67s.tun	*ER* V.73 P.
167	1439	Aberdeen	226.78s.tun bastard	ACR IV.172 Aw.
168	1440	Perth	288s.tun	*ER* V.99 P.
169	1440	Dunbar	560s.tun Gascon	*ER* V.100 P.
170	1440	Ayr	186.67s.tun	*ER* V.129–30 P.
171	1441	Perth	288s.tun	*ER* V.114 P.
172	1442	Perth	266.67s.tun	*ER* V.128 P.
173	1443	Perth	266.67s.tun	*ER* V.156 P.
174	1444	Edinburgh	171s.tun	*ER* V.150 P.
175	1444	Perth	285s.tun	*ER* V.185 P.
176	1444	Perth	200s.tun	*ER* VI.493 P.
177	1445	Aberdeen	320s.tun Gascon	*ER* V.235 P.
178	1445	Dumbarton	144s.tun	*ER* V.224 P.
179	1445	Perth	253.33s.tun	*ER* V.231 P.
180	1446	Edinburgh	234s.tun	*ER* V.276 P.
181	1447	Perth	200s.tun	*ER* V.302 P.
182	1448	Perth	200s.tun	*ER* V. 354 V.
183	1448	Edinburgh	184s.tun white	*ER* V.346 P.
184	1449	Perth	88.88s.tun	*ER* V.378 V.
185	1449	Edinburgh	400s.tun	*ER* V.387 P.
186	1449	Perth	200s.tun	*ER* V.402 V.
187	1450	Perth	200s.tun	*ER* V.425 V.
188	1451	Perth	200s.tun	*ER* V.496 V.
189	1451	Aberdeen	280s.tun	*ER* V.509 P.
190	1452	Aberdeen	80d.gal.	ADG fol. 2r P.
191	1452	Aberdeen	80d.gal. Malmsey & red	ADG fol. 2r P.
192	1452	Aberdeen	64d.gal. red	ADG fol. 2r P.
193	1452	Aberdeen	64d.gal. red	ADG fol. 2r P.
194	1452	Aberdeen	64d.gal. red	ADG fol. 2r P.
195	1452	Aberdeen	64d.gal. red	ADG fol. 2r P.
196	1454	Edinburgh	400s.tun Gascon	*ER* VI.4 P.
197	1455	Aberdeen	200s.tun	ACR V i.249 Aw.
198	1455	Dumbarton	10.29d.pint	*ER* VI.295 P.
199	1455	Galloway	180s.tun	*ER* VI.202 P.
200	1456	Stirling	8s.gal.	*ER* VI.326 P.
201	1457	Edinburgh	1000s.tun Beaune	*ER* VI.384 P.
202	1457		218.5s.pipe Rhine	*ER* VI.308 V.
203	1458	Aberdeen	8s.gal. Rhine	*ER* VI.501–2 P.

Table 25 (*cont.*)

No.	Year	Place	Unit price	Source
204	1458	Galloway	200s.tun	*ER* VI.572 V.
205	1459	Edinburgh	320s.tun	*ER* VI.582 V.
206	1459	Inverness?	200s.pipe Gascon	*ER* VI.658 P.
207	1459	Inverness?	4s.gal. red	*ER* VI.658 P.
208	1459	Inverness?	100s pipe red	*ER* VI.658 P.
209	1461	Galloway	180s.tun white of Poitou	*ER* VII.8 P.
210	1461	Galloway	6d.pint white	*ER* VII.8 P.
211	1462		210s.tun	*ER* VII.228 P.
212	1462	Mar & Garioch	53.88s. 'rubbour' Rhine	*ER* VII.163 V.
213	1470	Aberdeen	128d.gal. Malmsey	ADG Ac1000 P.
214	1470	Aberdeen	64d.gal. red	ADG Ac1000 P.
215	1470	Aberdeen	?128d.gal. Malmsey	ADG Ac1000 P.
216	1470	Aberdeen	56d.gal. red & white	ADG Ac1000 P.
217	1470	Aberdeen	64d.gal.	ADG Ac1000 P.
218	1470	Aberdeen	64d.gal.	ADG Ac1000 P.
219	1470	Aberdeen	128d.gal. Malmsey	ADG Ac1000 P.
220	1470	Aberdeen	56d.gal. red & white	ADG Ac1000 P.
221	1471	Aberdeen	64d.gal. red	ADG Ac1000 P.
222	1477	Aberdeen	£50 roda Rhine	ACR VI.481 Wi.
223	1482	Aberdeen	£18 butt Malmsey	ACR VI.723–4 C.
224	1483	Wigtown	27 crowns tun = 270s.	*ALA* I. *122 Aw.
225	1484		£11 tun Gascon	*ER* IX.448 P.
226	1485	Edinburgh?	£5 puncheon Gascon	*ER* IX.451 V.
227	1485	Methven	219s. 4d. pipe Gascon	*ER* IX.358 P.
228	1485	Aberdeen	6d. pint	ACR VI.920 V.
229	1488	Edinburgh?	£34 'qw' Rhine	*ALC* I.97 Aw.
230	1488	Edinburgh?	8s.gal.	*ALC* I.97 Aw.
231	1488	Edinburgh?	13s.4d.gal. Malmsey	*ALC* I.97 Aw.
232	1488	Edinburgh?	8s.gal. Gascon	*ALC* I.97 Aw.
233	1488	Edinburgh?	280s.tun Gascon	*ALC* I.97 Aw.
234	1488	Edinburgh?	16s.gal. Rhine	*ALC* I.97 Aw.
235	1490	Perth	£7 puncheon	*TA* I.134 P.
236	1494	Stirling	£6 13s. 4d.pipe	*ER* X.510 V.
237	1496	Aberdeen	180s.tun ?Poitou	ACR VII.722 V.
238	1496	Aberdeen	14d pint Malmsey	ACR VII.723 V.
239	1496		2s. quart	*TA* I.302 P.
240	1497	Aberdeen	4s.gal. claret	ACR VII.839 P.
241	1497	Aberdeen	200s.tun	ACR VII.839 P.
242	1497	Falkland	£13 tun? some Spanish	*ER* XI.72 V.
243	1497	Orkney & Shetl.	£6 tun	*ER* XI.82 P.
244	1497	Ayr	£3 puncheon	*ER* XI.121 V.
245	1497		160s.tun	*TA* I.352 P.
246	1497	Ayr	160s.tun	*TA* I.343 P.
247	1497	Aberdeen	4s.gal. claret	ACR VII.839 P.
248	1498		£12 tun	*TA* I.391 P.
249	1498	Edinburgh	210s.tun spiced claret	*ER* XI.233–4 V.

Table 25 (*cont.*)

No.	Year	Place	Unit price	Source
250	1498	Aberdeen	32s.stik(cask)	ACR VII.920 C.
251	1498	Dumbarton?	£12 tun	*TA* I.392 P.
252	1498	Dumbarton	260s.tun Spanish	SHS 2,10.80 P.
253	1499	Aberdeen	100s./10crowns pipe claret	ACR VII.985 P.
254	1499	Stirling	222s. vase Rhine	*ER* XI.265 V.
255	1501	Aberdeen	1.31s.pint Rhine	*TA* II.44 P.
256	1504	Perth	£10 tun	*ER* XII.376 P.
257	1504	Dumbarton	£7 tun	*TA* II.428 P.
258	1504	Dumbarton	£7 tun	*TA* II.434 P.
259	1505	Moray	£2 puncheon claret	*ER* XII.394 P.
260	1505	Perth	£10 tun	*ER* XII.470 P.
261	1505	Falkland	140s. vase Rhine	*ER* XII.470–1 P.
262	1506	Moray	40s.puncheon	*ER* XII.491 P.
263	1506	Aberdeen	£9 6s.8d. tun Rhine	*ER* XII.600 P.
264	1507	Menteith	£10 tun	*ER* XIII.60 P.
265	1507	Perth	132d.gal. Malmsey	SHS 2,10.206 P.
266	1507		£6 puncheon	*TA* IV.79 P.
267	1508	Lothian	70s.punch. claret & Gascon	SHS 2,10.248 P.
268	1508	Lothian	64d.gal. claret	SHS 2,10.248 P.
269	1508	Darnaway	£10 tun	*ER* XIII.203 P.
270	1508	Dundee	16d.pint Rhine	*ER* XIII.235 P.
271	1508	Lothian	16d.pint Malmsey	SHS 2,10.248 P.
272	1508	Dumbarton	£10 tun	*ER* XIII.226 P.
273	1509	Aberdeen	85s.puncheon	ACR VIII.93 P.
274	1509	Aberdeen	64d.gal. claret	ACR VIII.937 P.
275	1509	Aberdeen	48d.gal. white	ACR VIII.93 P.
276	1509	Dunkeld	165s.tun claret & Gascon	SHS 2,10.7 P.
277	1509	Perth	64d.gal. claret	SHS 2,10.214 P.
278	1509	Aberdeen	112d.gal. Malmsey	ACR VIII.93 P.
279	1511	Dunkeld	64d.gal.	SHS 2,10.124 P.
280	1512	Ayr	£10 tun	*ER* XIII.570 P.
281	1512	Wigtown etc.	£13 5s.tun	*ER* XIII.577 P.
282	1513	Forth	16s.gal. muscadet	*TA* IV.474 P.
283	1513	Forth	16s.gal. Malmsey	*TA* IV.474 P.
284	1513	Forth	2s.gal. Malmsey	*TA* IV.470 P.
285	1513	Forth	£4 puncheon	*TA* IV.474 P.
286	1514	Perth	99d. 1gal.1mutchkin claret	SHS 2,10.233 P.
287	1515	Edinburgh	10d.pint claret	*ER* XIV.205 P.
288	1515	Edinburgh	£20 tun claret & Beaune	*ER* XIV.200 P.
289	1515	Edinburgh	£20 tun Beaune	*ER* XIV.201 P.
290	1517	Aberdeen	40s.puncheon	ACR IX.720 Aw.
291	1517	Paisley	£4 10s.punch. claret	*ER* XIV.352–3 P.
292	1518	Weddirburn	£4 punch. claret	*ER* XIV.463 P.
293	1523	Aberdeen	£5 puncheon claret	ACR XI.434 C.
294	1525	Aberdeen	70s.puncheon claret	ACR XV.665 C.

Table 25 (*cont.*)

No.	Year	Place	Unit price	Source
295	1525	Aberdeen	£30 great styk Rhine	ACR XI.592 C.
296	1525	Edinburgh?	£6 claret & white	HBJV, p. 85 P.
297	1525	Edinburgh?	£6 15s.punch. claret	HBJV, p. 85 P.
298	1525	Edinburgh	12d. pint conflated	HBJV, pp. 86–7 P.
299	1525	Edinburgh?	£7 punch. claret	HBJV, p. 86 P.
300	1525	Edinburgh	£7 10s.punch. white	HBJV, p. 86 P.
301	1525	Edinburgh?	£7 punch. claret	HBJV, p. 85 P.
302	1525	Edinburgh?	£6 punch. claret	HBJV, p. 85 P.
303	1526	Edinburgh?	£21 tun claret & white	HBJV, p. 88 P.
304	1526	Edinburgh?	106s. 8d.ters. claret & white	HBJV, p. 88 P.
305	1526	Edinburgh?	£4 5s.punch. claret & white	HBJV, p. 88 P.
306	1526	Edinburgh?	14d.pint Rhine	HBJV, p. 88 P.
307	1526	Stirling	12d.pint conflated	HBJV, pp. 91–2 P.
308	1526	Edinburgh?	8d.pint claret	HBJV, p. 92 P.
309	1526	Edinburgh	£8 tersan claret	HBJV, p. 87 P.
310	1526	Edinburgh?	70s.punch. claret & white	HBJV, p. 93 P.
311	1526	Leith	12d.pint. claret	HBJV, p. 93 P.
312	1526	Edinburgh	10d.pint conflated	HBJV, pp. 87–94 P.
313	1526	Edinburgh	14d. pint conflated	HBJV, p. 87 P.
314	1526	Edinburgh	£7 punch. claret	HBJV, p. 87 P.
315	1526	Edinburgh?	12d.pint white	HBJV, p. 93 P.
316	1528	Edinburgh?	24d.pint Rhine	HBJV, p. 189 P.
317	1528	Edinburgh?	£6 10s.punch. claret	HBJV, p. 189 P.
318	1528	Stirling?	£6 10s.punch. new claret	HBJV, p. 186 P.
319	1528	Edinburgh?	£4 10s.punch. claret	HBJV, p. 185 P.
320	1528	Edinburgh	£7 punch. white	HBJV, p. 188 P.
321	1528	Edinburgh?	£24 tun new claret	HBJV, p. 190 P.
322	1528	Edinburgh?	8.64d.pint claret	HBJV, p. 189 P.
323	1528	Edinburgh?	£3 17s. 6d.punch. claret	HBJV, p. 185 P.
324	1528	Edinburgh?	£5 15s.punch. claret	HBJV, p. 187 P.
325	1528	Edinburgh	2s.pint Rhine	HBJV, p. 189 P.
326	1528	Edinburgh?	18d.pint Rhine	HBJV, p. 189 P.
327	1528		12d.pint conflated	HBJV, pp. 185–6 P.
328	1528	Edinburgh	8d.pint conflated	HBJV, pp. 186–8 P.
329	1528	Edinburgh	10d.pint conflated	HBJV, pp. 187–9 P.
330	1528	Edinburgh?	£5 5s.punch. claret	HBJV, p. 185 P.
331	1528	Perth	18.86d. pint Malmsey	HBJV, p. 185 P.
332	1528	Edinburgh?	£6 punch. new white	HBJV, p. 190 P.
333	1529	Edinburgh?	£12 pipe white	HBJV, p. 193 P.
334	1529		£8 13s. 4d. tersing claret	HBJV, p. 193 P.
335	1529	Leith	£6 punch. claret	HBJV, p. 190 P.
336	1529	Edinburgh	£5 10s.punch. claret	HBJV, p. 194 P.
337	1529	Edinburgh?	14d.pint white Anjou	HBJV, p. 191 P.
338	1529	Edinburgh?	£12 pipe white	HBJV, p. 194 P.
339	1529		7d.pint white Anjou	HBJV, p. 192 P.

Table 25 (*cont.*)

No.	Year	Place	Unit price	Source
340	1529	Leith	£5 10s.punch. claret	HBJV, p. 194 P.
341	1529	Edinburgh?	£12 pipe white	HBJV, p. 192 P.
342	1529		9.45d.pint claret	HBJV, p. 194 P.
343	1529	Edinburgh	£6 punch. white	HBJV, p. 193 P.
344	1529	Edinburgh?	£5 punch. claret	HBJV, p. 194 P.
345	1529	Edinburgh?	£6 punch. white	HBJV, p. 193 P.
346	1529	Edinburgh?	£5 10s.punch. claret	HBJV, p. 194 P.
347	1529	Edinburgh?	£8 13s. 4d.tersing claret	HBJV, p. 193 P.
348	1529	Edinburgh?	£12 pipe white	HBJV, p. 194 P.
349	1529	Stirling?	£5 10s.punch. claret	HBJV, p. 191 P.
350	1529		2s.pint Malmsey	HBJV, p. 195 P.
351	1529		14d.pint white Anjou	HBJV, p. 192 P.
352	1529		£5 punch. claret	HBJV, p. 195 P.
353	1529	Edinburgh?	£6 10s.punch. claret	HBJV, p. 193 P.
354	1529	Edinburgh?	£5 5s.punch. claret	HBJV, p. 191 P.
355	1529		10.77d.pint	HBJV, p. 192 P.
356	1529	Edinburgh?	£6 punch. white	HBJV, p. 192 P.
357	1529	Edinburgh?	£6 10s.punch. claret	HBJV, p. 193 P.
358	1529		12d.pint conflated	HBJV, pp. 190–5 P.
359	1529		10d.pint conflated	HBJV, pp. 190–5 P.
360	1529		2s.pint muscadet	HBJV, p. App., p. 33 P.
361	1529		9.85d.pint	HBJV, p. 190 P.
362	1529	Linlithgow	12d.pint	HBJV, p. 134 P.
363	1529	Edinburgh?	£5 10s.punch. claret	HBJV, p. 191 P.
364	1530	Aberdeen	10d.pint	ACR XII.11 V.
365	1531		£24 tun claret	*TA* V.459 P.
366	1532		£26 tun	*TA* VI.40 P.
367	1533	Aberdeen	£4 puncheon	ACR XIV.195 Aw.
368	1533	Aberdeen	236s.pipe Roman	ACR XIV.125 Aw.
369	1534	Aberdeen	£3 10s.puncheon	ACR XIV.360 Aw.
370	1534	Aberdeen	£4 16s.puncheon claret	ACR XIV.532 Aw.
371	1536	Rouen	40 francs tun white	*TA* VII.40 P.
372	1536	Rouen	37.5 francs tun claret	*TA* VII.40 P.
373	1536	Rouen	3 francs 15s.barrel allacant	*TA* VII.40 P.
374	1537	Dumbarton		*ER* XVII.161
375	1538		£6 puncheon	*TA* VI.390 P.
376	1539	Kelso	£4 punch.	*ER* XVII.274
377	1541	Edinburgh	£21 puncheon	SHS 2,4.12 P.
378	1542	Edinburgh	26.66s.punch. white & cla.	SHS 2,4.14 P.

Marts

Marts were beef cattle intended for eating, the name being derived from the customary slaughter of selected animals around St Martin's day, 11 November. Occasionally, however, oxen were also eaten, so such instances have been listed here with the marts series. Otherwise oxen are presumed to be labouring beasts; they cost significantly more than marts, and have therefore been listed and analysed separately.

Beef cattle specially fattened for eating are listed here but their price was always higher than for ordinary marts and they have been excluded from our calculations.[100] Similarly, veal prices have not been counted in the mart price figures.[101] In other aspects, however, the mart evidence is surprisingly homogeneous. Fresh beef and salted appear similarly priced, and marts on the hoof and with their hides are not distinguishable by price from ready slaughtered animals. Treated hides, of course, were a valuable commodity in their own right (see below pp. 277–83) but the value of raw hides does not appear to have raised the price of live marts significantly above that of ready butchered ones. Similarly the 2s. value put on the offal of a mart in 1508[102] was only a small proportion of the total price. It seems that the by-products of the industry were more or less off-set by the costs of slaughter and butchery, travelling and salting. Live animals, of course, were easier to move on land, and a certain amount of evidence survives for the cost of driving cattle to market or the larder.[103] Though sometimes a flat rate was charged for driving a group of beasts, often the charge *c.* 1500 seems to have been 1s. per mart whether driven from Galloway or from Kildrummy in the north to centres such as Edinburgh or Stirling. Occasionally, animals are described as being on the hoof[104] but usually no such detail is given. One can sometimes judge from the context when animals were already slaughtered. Shipments from Orkney, for example, were often said to be salted, and beef is sometimes met as a 'side' or 'quarter'. Insights into the butchery trade are rare. We read, for instance, of a meat appraiser quarrelling with the baillie who had to write down the prices of meat set.[105] But more usually the mart series is dominated by agricultural price evidence, rather than by town prices.

The Scottish countryside appears to have been teeming with marts, from Lewis and Bute to Orkney and Ettrick. They appear so plentifully in our records because the particular suitability of so much of rural Scotland for rough grazing gave the mart a specially important role in

[100] List 75, 121, 228, 363, 367, 416, 418, 420, 422, 465, 467, 511, 532–3, 561.
[101] List 198, 364, 402–8, 426–34, 450–5, 480–95, 513–14, 537.
[102] List 301. List 1 and 36 are also associated with further information about hides and offal.
[103] List 55, 57–62, 214, 263–4.
[104] List 354, 536.
[105] List 203. See also Chapter 2, p. 29.

agricultural rental agreements. On one occasion we even find amercements being paid in marts.[106] Whether as rent in kind, entry fines, or under a customary obligation to sell produce to the landlord at a fixed price, marts loom large in the royal estate accounts which provide the bulk of our evidence. Unfortunately for our purposes, however, when marts occur in tenancy agreements their valuation almost always became frozen at a price which even at the initiation of the rental was often conservative. With the passage of years in a period of inflation such prices rapidly become laughably anachronistic. Sometimes we can see the same animals priced first on the customary basis, but subsequently marketed on a commercial one: thus the same Galloway marts could be priced at 5s. and sold at 20s.[107]

We have not excluded all these commuted or customary valuations. In the first place, they can provide a useful guide to the general prices of the time when they were first introduced. Moreover, although the nature of these payments is sometimes explicit in the record, this was not always the case, so any attempt to discard all such prices would in fact let some slip by unnoticed. Accordingly, we have continued to include such prices in our calculations until they become obviously anachronistic. Thus 5s. marts have been excluded from 1400, 6s.8d. marts from 1450, 10s. and 12s. marts from 1470, and 13s. and 15s. marts from 1500. Marts below 20s. were excluded from 1530. It should be stressed that those customary, frozen prices are excluded only from the calculated means and index prices. All available material, including the anachronistic prices, have been retained in the data base, and almost all of it appears in the list of prices where the atypical nature of the frozen prices can be seen at a glance.

Because of our reluctance to exclude frozen prices before they had become entirely divorced from genuine prices, we may have included them in our calculation of mean and indexed prices for too long. This may be a contributory factor partly explaining the low mean, currency-adjusted and indexed prices of the fifteenth century in this series. Cows, by contrast, were not commonly used in landholding agreements and cow prices appear significantly less depressed than mart prices.[108] Obviously, the balance between excluding customary prices too early or too late is a difficult one to strike. Interestingly, the administrators of the royal estates encountered similar difficulties. When

[106] List 87.

[107] List 173–5. See also List 106 for marts in an account for Mar, Moray, and Ross priced at 5s. and 15s.

[108] This may, however, reflect the productive capacity of cows. See below pp. 249–56.

Table 26. *Mart summary table*

Period	Mean price	Deflated	Index
A	7.0	7.0	96.3
B–C	7.27	7.27	100.0
D	6.27	6.27	86.2
E	6.09	5.18	71.3
F	(7.37)	(3.69)	(50.8)
G			
H	11.98	4.79	65.9
I	16.41	5.42	74.6
60s	15.8		
70s	16.76	4.69	64.5
80s	18.41		
90s	18.5	5.18	71.3
1500s	18.45	5.17	71.1
10s	19.6	4.9	67.4
20s	27.31	6.08	83.6
30s	27.43	6.03	82.9

Note: the mean price is in shillings each; the deflated column gives the currency-adjusted sterling equivalent price.

in the sixteenth century they imposed new and more realistic valuations on livestock,[109] tenants and accounting officers produced feu-farm charters successfully to defend and reinstate the old, uneconomic rates.[110] Renewed efforts were being made to impose realistic rates in 1539 and 1541.[111]

The existence of large numbers of such uneconomically priced marts complicates the whole concept of 'price'. Their total exclusion from the calculation of an open market price, though an attractively simple solution, would do violence to the truth that no medieval price was ever a truly open market price. The weighting which the customary sector should be given, and the way in which it actually influenced the level of more genuinely economic prices, must remain for the moment open questions.

All these reservations should be held in mind when considering the overall pattern revealed by Table 26, and Figure 24 of mean, and Figure 25 of currency-adjusted index prices. Even allowing for the

[109] E.g. *ER* XV.423 and List 507, 515.

[110] List 519: 'Compotans ostendat cartam feodifirme solventem quindecim solidos pro qualibet marta.' Also List 528–9, and *ER* XVII. 16, 23, 84, 201, 226, 317, 341, 348, 375, 430, 437, 492, 493.

[111] List 574, 577–8, 580–2, 584.

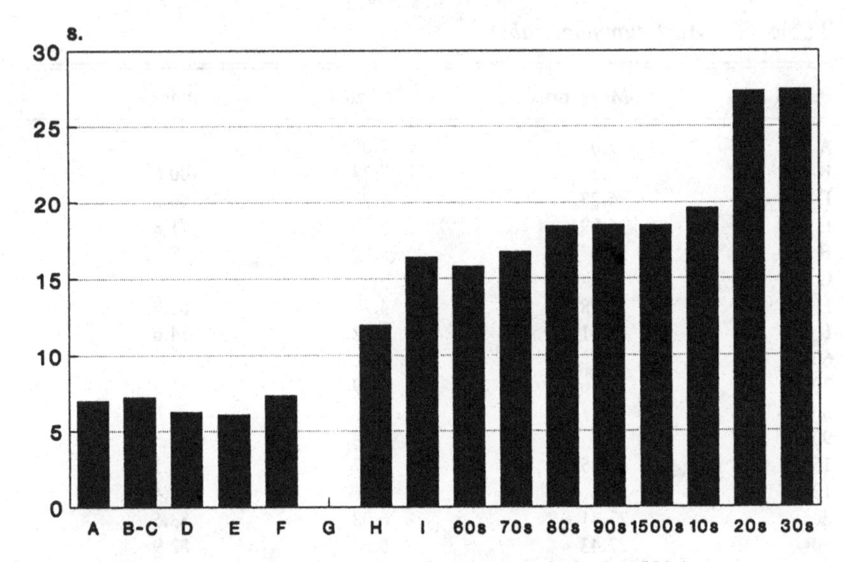

24 Mart prices (mean prices for time periods A–1530s)
For periods A–I, see Introduction, p. 6.

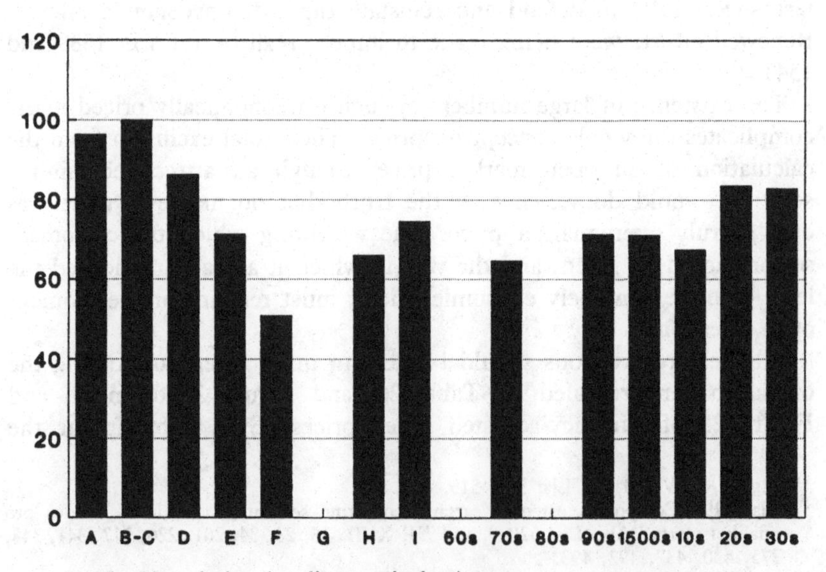

25 Mart index (sterling equivalent)

Table 27. *Mart prices 1298–1367: Scotland and England*

Year	Scotland	Durham	Farmer (Sales)
1298	7.0		12.31
1327	8.0	8.93	
1328	5.0	9.73	
	8.31		
	8.0		
	(4.0)		
	6.67		
	7.82		
	(2.5)		
	9.09		
	9.05/8.06		
	(6.67)		
1329	10.0	12.04	
	7.0		
	(6.82)		
1330	8.6/7.45	13.13	
1331	13.33		
	6.99		
1342	5.0	6.74	
1355	5.0	9.12	
1363	(8.0)	8.0	
1367	(6.67)	14.75	
	(24.88)		

Note: all prices are in shillings each. Parentheses have been used to flag up calculations which are less securely based than others – either because they are based on a smaller amount of data, or because they involve certain, possibly questionable, assumptions.

possible effect of included customary prices, mart prices were clearly severely depressed from the late fourteenth century to the sixteenth century when the first signs of recovery become evident. Thus it is not until the very end of our period that the deflated price levels return to anything like the early fourteenth-century peak. As will be seen below, sheep and oxen present a picture broadly similar to that of marts.

There can also be little doubt that beef cattle were cheaper in Scotland than in England. Table 27 compares English (chiefly Durham) prices with those of Scotland before 1367, but even after the divergence of the two currency systems Scots livestock generally remained cheaper than English.[112] Overall total demand for meat no doubt fell with

[112] See Figures 2 and 4, Tables 1 and 2, above in Chapter 1, pp. 20–4.

Table 28. *Mart price list*

No.	Year	Place	Unit price	Source
1	1298	Roxburgh	7s.	*DHS* II.326 P.
2	1327	Dunbarton	8s.	*ER* I.258. V.
3	1328	Cardross	5s.	*ER* I.125 P.
4	1328	Cardross	8.31s.	*ER* I.125 P.
5	1328	Cardross	8s.	*ER* I.125 P.
6	1328		4s. carcase	*ER* I.197
7	1328	Glenkill	6.67s.	*ER* I.185 P.
8	1328	Berwick?	6.67s. carcase	*ER* I.206
9	1328	Dumfries	7.82s.	*ER* I.74 P.
10	1328	Dumfries	2.5s. dead	*ER* I.74
11	1328	Perth	9.09s.	*ER* I.118 P.
12	1328		9.05s./8.06s.	*ER* I.219 P.
13	1329		10s.	*ER* I.289 P.
14	1329		7s.	*ER* I.241
15	1329		6.82s. carcase	*ER* I.289 P.
16	1330		8.60s/7.45s.	*ER* I.341 P.
17	1331	Dundee	13.33s.	*ER* I.368 V.
18	1331	Scone	6.99s.	*ER* I.375 P.
19	1342	Peebles	5s.	*ER* I.517 V.
20	1355	Kinross	5s.	*ER* I.580–1 P.
21	1363	Coldingham	8s. carcase	SS 12.xliv P.
22	1367	Clackmannan	6.67s.	*ER* II.294 P.
23	1368	Edinburgh	8s./6.67s.	*ER* II.306 P.
24	1368	Aberdeen	5s.	*ER* II.309 P.
25	1372		11.03s. carcase	*ER* II.368 P.
26	1372		5s.	*ER* II.369 P.
27	1372		7.87s. carcase	*ER* II.369 P.
28	1373		5s.	*ER* II.451 P.
29	1373		7.12s. carcase	*ER* II.451 P.
30	1374	Perth	5s. carcase	*ER* II.449 V.
31	1379	Foulis	5s.	*ER* III.35 V.
32	1380	Fife etc.	5.42s./4.64s.	*ER* III.40–1 P.
33	1380		5.43s. carcase	*ER* III.41 P.
34	1380	Methven	10s.	*ER* III.40–1 V.
35	1380	Edinburgh	6.67s.	*ER* III.653 P.
36	1384		6.61s./5.97s.	*ER* III.107 P.
37	1384		7.46s./6.23s. carcase	*ER* III.107 P.
38	1399	Aberdeen	16d.qr beef	SHS 3,49.76 Aw.
39	1413	Inverness	7.37s.	*ER* IV.228 P.
40	1433	Menteith	13.88s./12s.	*ER* IV.590 P.
41	1433	Stra'gartney	14.40s./12s.	*ER* IV.590 P.
42	1433	Lennox	14.21s./12s.	*ER* IV.590 P.
43	1433	Carrick	10s.(*recte* 12s.)	*ER* IV.596 V.
44	1433	Carrick	12s.	*ER* IV.596 V.
45	1435	Edinburgh	11.86s.	*ER* V.26 P.
46	1436	Fermartyn	5s.	*ER* V.10 V.

Table 28 (*cont.*)

No.	Year	Place	Unit price	Source
47	1436	Mar	5s.	*ER* V.58 V.
48	1436	Bute & Aran	5s.	*ER* V.81 V.
49	1437	Kildrummy	12s.	*ER* V.60 P.
50	1437	Mar	5s.	*ER* V.60 V.
51	1437	Mar	5s.	*ER* V.60 V.
52	1439	Bute & Arran	5s. 'mail'	*ER* V.85 V.
53	1439	Bute & Arran	5s.	*ER* V.85 V.
54	1442	Bute	5s.	*ER* V.166 V.
55	1442	Arran	5s.	*ER* V.164 V.
56	1442	Strathearn	5s.	*ER* V.172 V.
57	1443	Bute	5s. 'mail'	*ER* V.164 V.
58	1444	Bute	5s. 'mail'	*ER* V.210 V.
59	1445	Bute	5s. 'mail'	*ER* V.210 V.
60	1446	Bute	5s. 'mail'	*ER* V.251 V.
61	1447	Bute	5s. 'mail'	*ER* V.288 V.
62	1448	Bute & Arran	5s. 'mail'	*ER* V.332 V.
63	1449	Bute & Arran	5s. 'mail'	*ER* V.363–4 V.
64	1450		16s.	*ER* V.395 V.
65	1450	Bute & Arran	5s. 'mail'	*ER* V.410 V.
66	1450	Methven	18s.	*ER* V.485 V.
67	1450	Bute etc.	5s.	*ER* V.452 V.
68	1451	Mar	16s.	*ER* V.519 V.
69	1451	Arran	13.33s.	*ER* V.575 V.
70	1451	Menteith	17s.	*ER* V.594 V.
71	1451	Menteith	20s.	*ER* V.598 V.
72	1451	Bute etc.	5s.	*ER* V.519 V.
73	1452	Strathearn	24.43s.	*ER* V.585 P.
74	1452	Menteith	15.82s.	*ER* V.593 V.
75	1452		43.75s. fattened	*ER* V.605 V.
76	1452	Methven	17.21s.	*ER* V.605 V.
77	1452	Brechin	18s.	*ER* V.605 V.
78	1453	Menteith	15.87s.	*ER* V.594–5 P.
79	1453	Menteith	20s.	*ER* V.598 V.
80	1453	Menteith	15.83s.	*ER* V.677 V.
81	1453	Strath'ney	13.33s.	*ER* V.677 V.
82	1453	Strabrok	21s.	*ER* VI.91 V.
83	1453	Bute etc.	5s.	*ER* V.657 V.
84	1454	Cluny forest	13.33s.	*ER* VI.53 V.
85	1454	Bute etc.	5s.	*ER* VI.45 V.
86	1454	Strathearn	6.67s.	*ER* VI.287 V.
87	1455	Wigtown	18s.	*ER* VI.190 V.
88	1455	Bute etc.	5s.	*ER* VI.154 V.
89	1455	Strathearn	6.67s.	*ER* VI.283 V.
90	1456	Galloway	18.34s./16.54s.	*ER* VI.349 P.
91	1456	Aberdeen?	17.56s.	*ER* VI.363 P.
92	1456	Aberdeen?	11.66s. carcase	*ER* VI.363 P.

Table 28 (*cont.*)

No.	Year	Place	Unit price	Source
93	1456	Kirkcud't	18s.	*ER* VI.449 V.
94	1456	Kirkcud't	18s.	*ER* VI.449 V.
95	1456	Ardmannoch	14.76s.	*ER* VI.484 P.
96	1456	Elgin	13.33s.	*ER* VI.485–6 V.
97	1456	Bute etc.	5s.	*ER* VI.329 V.
98	1456	Menteith	6.67s.	*ER* VI.244 V.
99	1457	Strathearn	15s.	*ER* VI.423
100	1457	Bute etc.	5s.	*ER* VI.420 V.
101	1458	Balvany	15s.	*ER* VI.529 V.
102	1458	Galloway	13s.	*ER* VI.570
103	1458	Fettercairn	13.33s.	*ER* VI.622 V.
104	1458	Bute etc.	5s.	*ER* VI.515–16 V.
105	1459	Kirkcud't	18s.	*ER* VI.594 V.
106	1459	Mar etc.	15s.	*ER* VI.663–4 V.
107	1459	Bute etc.	5s.	*ER* VI.622 V.
108	1460	Spottis	6s. 8d.	*ER* VII.7 V.
109	1460	Elgin?	14.42s	*ER* VII.20–1 P.
110	1460	Discher etc.	6s. 8d.	*ER* VII.2–3 V.
111	1460		5s.	*ER* VII.7 V.
112	1461	Brechin	15s.	*ER* VII.89,92
113	1461		5s.	*ER* VII.58 V.
114	1462	Brechin	15s. 4d.	*ER* VII.168 P.
115	1462	Moray	15s.	*ER* VII.209 V.
116	1462		5s.	*ER* VII.164 V.
117	1462	Wigtown	14s.	*ER* VIII.40 V.
118	1463	Stirling?	18s.	*ER* VII.252 P.
119	1463	Strathearn	19.81s	*ER* VII.257 V.
120	1463	Methven	20.33s	*ER* VII.481 P.
121	1464	Fife	30s. fattened	*ER* VII.335 P.
122	1464	North of Tay	21.95s./18.84s.	*ER* VII.358–9 V.
123	1464	Bute & Arran	15s.	*ER* VII.338 V.
124	1464		5s.	*ER* VII.327 V.
125	1465		5s.	*ER* VII.398 V.
126	1466	Yarow	12s.	*ER* VII.496–7
127	1466		5s	*ER* VII.448 V.
128	1467	Ettrick	12s.	*ER* VII.528–9
129	1467	Elgin & Inv.?	19s.	*ER* VII.544 P.
130	1467		5s.	*ER* VII.541 V.
131	1468	Yarow	12s.	*ER* VII.622
132	1468	Moray	20s.	*ER* VII.638 P.
133	1468		5s.	*ER* VII.614 V.
134	1468	Glenderowane	12.12s.	*ER* VIII.508 V.
135	1470	Galloway	16.67s.	*ER* VIII.90 V.
136	1470	Yarow	12s.	*ER* VIII.100
137	1470		5s.	*ER* VIII.8 V.
138	1471	Strathearn	22s.	*ER* VIII.58 V.

Table 28 (*cont.*)

No.	Year	Place	Unit price	Source
139	1471	Galloway	17.39s.	*ER* VIII.89–90
140	1471	Discher	6s. 8d.	*ER* VIII.59 V.
141	1471	Ettrick	12s.	*ER* VIII.101 V.
142	1472	Tweed	12s.	*ER* VIII.140
143	1472	Tweed	10s.	*ER* VIII.149
144	1472	Galloway	20s.	*ER* VIII.165 V.
145	1472		5s.	*ER* VIII.145 V.
146	1472	Ettrick	12s.	*ER* VIII.141 V.
147	1473	Galloway	20s.	*ER* VIII.217
148	1473	Orkney & Shet.	13s. 4d.	*ER* VIII.225 V.
149	1473		5s.	*ER* VIII.215 V.
150	1474	Orkney & Shet.	13s. 4d.	*ER* VIII.276 V.
151	1474	Orkney & Shet.	13s. 4d. salted	*ER* VIII.276 V.
152	1474	Galloway	20s.	*ER* VIII.289
153	1474		5s.	*ER* VIII.287 V.
154	1474	Ettrick	12s.	*ER* VIII.209 V.
155	1475	Galloway	20s.	*ER* VIII.345
156	1475	Orkney & Shet.	13s. 4d.	*ER* VIII.364 V.
157	1475	Orkney & Shet.	13s. 4d.	*ER* VIII.364 V.
158	1475	Moray	17s.	*ER* VIII.369
159	1475		5s.	*ER* VIII.342 V.
160	1475	Ettrick	12s.	*ER* VIII.268 V.
161	1476	Ovirardmach.	12s.	*ALA* I.50 C.
162	1476	Moray	15s.	*ER* VIII.410
163	1476		5s.	*ER* VIII.407 V.
164	1476	Ettrick	12s.	*ER* VIII.357 V.
165	1476	Ross	4s.	*ER* VIII.597 V.
166	1477	Fettercairn	10s.	*ER* VIII.516
167	1477		5s.	*ER* VIII.489 V.
168	1477	Ettrick	12s.	*ER* VIII.433 V.
169	1478	Kincardine	10s.	*ER* VIII.591
170	1478		5s.	*ER* VIII.577 V.
171	1478	Ettrick	12s.	*ER* VIII.478 V.
172	1479	Discher	6s. 8d.	*ER* IX.11 V.
173	1479	Galloway	5s.	*ER* IX.20 V.
174	1479	Galloway	20s.	*ER* IX.22
175	1479	Galloway	20s.	*ER* IX.22
176	1479	Cowale	12s. 3d.	*ER* IX.25 V.
177	1479	Tweed	12s.	*ER* IX.30
178	1479	Ettrik	12s.	*ER* IX.33 V.
179	1479	Petty,Brach.	5s.	*ER* IX.35–6 V.
180	1479	Strathearn	5s.	*ER* IX.42 V.
181	1479	Strathearn	21s.	*ER* IX.42–3
182	1479	Elgin & Forres	5s.	*ER* IX.47 V.
183	1479	Newmekill	4s.	*ER* IX.59 V.
184	1479	Ross	10s.	*ER* IX.60

Table 28 (*cont.*)

No.	Year	Place	Unit price	Source
185	1479	Ross	14s.	*ER* IX.61
186	1479	Ross	13s. 4d.	*ER* VIII.598 V.
187	1479	Ettrick	12s.	*ER* VIII.586 V.
188	1480	Discher	20s.	*ER* IX.112
189	1480	Strathearn	20s.	*ER* IX.119
190	1480	Galloway	15s.	*ER* IX.126
191	1480	Fettercairn	10s.	*ER* IX.132
192	1480	Tweed	12s.	*ER* IX.135
193	1480	Yarow	11.83s.	*ER* IX.137
194	1480	Ettrick	12s.	*ER* IX.139
195	1481	Fettercairn	10s.	*ER* IX.176
196	1481	Orkney & Shet.	13s. 4d. salt	*ER* IX.184
197	1483	Glennessil	5s.quarter salt beef	*ALC* I.*83–4 Aw.
198	1483	Areschene	13s. 4d. fed veal	*ALA* I.*121 Aw.
199	1483	Wauchtoun'	20s.	*ALC* I.166 Aw.
200	1483	Wauchtoun'	20s. salt	*ALC* I.166 Aw.
201	1483	Fettercairn	5s.	*ER* IX.275 V.
202	1483	Garioch	5s.	*ER* IX.280 V.
203	1484	Aberdeen	18s./17s./16s. carcase	ACR VI.884 Wi.
204	1484	Galloway	5s.	*ER* IX.300 V.
205	1484	Strathdon	5s.	*ER* IX.333 V.
206	1485	Bute	5s.	*ER* IX.352 V.
207	1485	Ross	23.53s.	*ER* IX.405 V.
208	1485	Yarow	9s.	*ER* IX.420 V.
209	1486	Methven	25s.	*ER* IX.358 V.
210	1486	Moray	23s.	*ER* IX.499
211	1486	Orkney & Shet.	20s. barrel salted	*ER* IX.490
212	1487	Tweed	22s.	*ER* X.13
213	1487	Tweed	12s.	*ER* X.13
214	1487	Galloway	5s.	*ER* X.30 V.
215	1487	Elgin & Forres	5s.	*ER* X.37 V.
216	1487	Kinkellis	5s.	*ER* X.42 V.
217	1487	Yarrow	12s.	*ER* X.97 V.
218	1487	Fettercairn	15s.	*ER* X.112
219	1488	Orkney & Shet.	13s. 4d. salted	*ER* X.40
220	1488	Uchtirtyr etc.	5s.	*ER* X.75 V.
221	1488	Galloway	20s.	*ER* X.80
222	1488	Fettercairn	5s.	*ER* X.111–12 V.
223	1490	Forres? Moray	20.69s. salted	*ER* X.278 P.
224	1491	Arth'	24s. salted	*ALC* I.195 Aw.
225	1492	Orkney & Shet.	12s.	*ER* XI.450 V.
226	1494	Bute	5s.	*ER* X.478 V.
227	1494	Discher	6s. 8d.	*ER* X.521 V.
228	1495	Stirlingsh.	£5 fattened	*ER* X.554 P.
229	1495	Ettrick	12s.	*ER* XI.8–9 V.
230	1496	Bute	5s.	*ER* XI.6 V.

Table 28 (*cont.*)

No.	Year	Place	Unit price	Source
231	1496	Elgin & Forres	5s.	*ER* XI.14 V.
232	1496	Orkney & Shet.	13s. 4d. salted	*ER* XI.19 V.
233	1496	Drumquharran	20s.	*ER* XI.22,24 V.
234	1496	Cree	5s.	*ER* XI.109 V.
235	1496	Strathearn	5s.	*ER* XI.182 V.
236	1497	Ayr	17s.	*TA* I.343 P.
237	1497	Strathearn	20s.	*ER* XI.91
238	1498	Strathearn	20s.	*ER* XI.182
239	1498	Coule	15s.	*ER* XI.310
240	1498	Oneile	15s.	*ER* XI.310
241	1498	Newark	12s.	*ER* XI.207–8
242	1499	Galloway	5s.	*ER* XI.336 V.
243	1499	Strathearn	20s.	*ER* XI.345
244	1501	Fettercairn	15s.	*ER* XII.2
245	1501	Orkney & Shet.	12s. salted	*ER* XII.30 P.
246	1501	Orkney & Shet.	12s. salted	*ER* XII.30 P.
247	1501	Yarrow	12s.	*ER* XII.35 V.
248	1501	Strathearn	20.11s.	*ER* XII.51
249	1501	Elgin & Forres	5s.	*ER* XII.53 V.
250	1501	Urquhart	13s. 4d.	*ER* XII.61–2 V.
251	1501	Bute	5s.	*ER* XII.66 V.
252	1501	Coiss	15s.	*ER* XII.291–2
253	1501	Coule	15s.	*ER* XII.292
254	1501	Menibrig	20s.	*ER* XII.312 P.
255	1502	Carrick?	20s.	*ER* XII.178
256	1502	Glen Artney	22.33s.	*ER* XII.186 V.
257	1502	Glen Artney	23.76s.	*ER* XII.186
258	1502	Strathnavern	13s. 4d.	*ER* XII.186 P.
259	1502	Strathdee	20s.	*ER* XII.297
260	1502	Kintyre	18s.	*ER* XII.365 P.
261	1502	Buchquhopill	24s.	*ER* XII.631 V.
262	1503	Strathearn	20s.	*ER* XII.212
263	1503	Cree	5s.	*ER* XII.254 V.
264	1503	Strathdon	5s.	*ER* XII.326–7 V.
265	1503	Strathdon	20s.	*ER* XII.327
266	1504	Ardmannoch	5s.	*ER* XII.307 V.
267	1505	Menteith	20s.	*ER* XII.414
268	1505	Petty & Brauc.	5s.	*ER* XII.416–17 V.
269	1505	Bute	20s.	*ER* XII.428
270	1505	Strathearn	20s.	*ER* XII.456
271	1505	South Kintyre	21.05s.	*ER* XII.586
272	1506	Perth	14.86s. carcase	SHS 2,10.198 P.
273	1506	Discher	6s. 8d.	*ER* XII.489 V.
274	1506	Strathearn	20s.	*ER* XII.500
275	1506	Coule	15s.	*ER* XII.501
276	1506	Corse	15s.	*ER* XII.502

Table 28 (*cont.*)

No.	Year	Place	Unit price	Source
277	1506	Ross & Ardman.	16s.	*ER* XII.515
278	1506	Stirling	32s.	*ER* XII.540 P.
279	1506	Ferische	4s.	*ER* XII.550 V.
280	1506	Ross	18s.	*ER* XII.553
281	1506	Ardmannoch	18s.	*ER* XII.557
282	1507	Elgin & Forres	5s.	*ER* XIII.12 V.
283	1507	Ferische	4s.	*ER* XIII.45 V.
284	1507	Ardmannoch	5s.	*ER* XIII.49 V.
285	1507	Kinclaven	20s.	*ER* XIII.57
286	1507	Menteith	20s.	*ER* XIII.60
287	1507	Fettercairn	15s.	*ER* XIII.67
288	1507	Strathdon	5s.	*ER* XIII.69 V.
289	1507	Bute	5s.	*ER* XIII.80
290	1507	Bute	20s.	*ER* XIII.80
291	1508	Buchquhopill	24s.	*ER* XIII.629 V.
292	1508	Buchquhidder	24s.	*ER* XIII.633 V.
293	1508	Tullelum	14.61s. carcase	SHS 2,10.66 P.
294	1508	Dunkeld	13.33s. carcase	SHS 2,10.66 P.
295	1508	Bute	20s.	*ER* XIII.140
296	1508	Coule	15s.	*ER* XIII.142
297	1508	Strathearn	20s.	*ER* XIII.183
298	1508	Strathdon	15s.	*ER* XIII.199
299	1508	Garioch	15s.	*ER* XIII.200
300	1508	Elgin & Forres	5s.	*ER* XIII.202 V.
301	1508	Lewis	13.85s./12s.	*ER* XIII.253 V.
302	1509	Monydi	24s.	SHS 2,10.67 P.
303	1509	Monydi	24.33s.	SHS 2,10.67 P.
304	1509	Perth	26s. 8d.	SHS 2,10.213 P.
305	1509	Moray	14s.	*ER* XIII.292 V.
306	1509	Moray	16s.	*ER* XIII.293 P.
307	1509	Darnaway	16s.	*ER* XIII.293 P.
308	1509	Strathearn	20s.	*ER* XIII.316
309	1509	Kintyre	20s.	*ER* XIII.321
310	1509	Garioch	5s.	*ER* XIII.338 V.
311	1509	Kynnacrag	4s.	*ER* XIII.347 V.
312	1511	Clony	13. 21s. carcase	SHS 2,10.179 P.
313	1511	Fettercairn	18s.4d.	*ER* XIII.402
314	1511	Orkney & Shet.	12s. salted	*ER* XIII.419 V.
315	1511	Ardmannoch	15.77s.	*ER* XIII.446
316	1511	Sutherland	16s.	*ER* XIII.444
317	1511	Cree	5s.	*ER* XIII.471 V.
318	1511	Carnyburg	20s.	*ER* XIV.419 V.
319	1512	Forth	16s.	*TA* IV.459 P.
320	1512	Perth	15s. carcase	SHS 2,10.225 P.
321	1512	Orkney & Shet.	12s. salted	*ER* XIII.419 V.
322	1512	Orkney & Shet.	12s. salted	*ER* XIII.515 P.

Table 28 (*cont.*)

No.	Year	Place	Unit price	Source
323	1512	Cree	20s.	*ER* XIII.535
324	1513	Forth	32s. fresh	*TA* IV.467 P.
325	1513	Forth	10s. side	*TA* IV.464 P.
326	1513	Forth	10s. side	*TA* IV.467 P.
327	1513	Forth	10s. side	*TA* IV.464 P.
328	1513	Forth	12s. side	*TA* IV.463 P.
329	1513	Forth	6s. 8d. side	*TA* IV.468 P.
330	1513	Forth	9s. side	*TA* IV.464 P.
331	1513	Forth	12s.	*TA* IV.491 P.
332	1513	Forth	20s. conflated	*TA* IV.469 P.
333	1513	Forth	10s. half	*TA* IV.485 P.
334	1513	Forth	21s.	*TA* IV.485 P.
335	1513	Forth	22s.	*TA* IV.485 P.
336	1513	Forth	23s.	*TA* IV.485 P.
337	1513	Forth	24s.	*TA* IV.485 P.
338	1513	Dunkeld	26s.	SHS 2,10.141 P.
339	1513	Dunkeld	26s.	SHS 2,10.141 P.
340	1513	Dunkeld	26.55s.	SHS 2,10.141 P.
341	1513	Dunkeld	24s.	SHS 2,10.141 P.
342	1513	Bute	5s.	*ER* XIV.20 V.
343	1513	Bute	23s.	*ER* XIV.20–1 P.
344	1513	Bute	20s.	*ER* XIV.21
345	1513	Bute	16.07s.	*ER* XIV.22 P.
346	1513	Strathearn	20s.	*ER* XIV.24 P.
347	1513	Fettercairn	15s.	*ER* XIV.26
348	1513	Orkney & Shet.	12s. salted	*ER* XIV.32 P.
349	1513	Cree	5s.	*ER* XIV.35 V.
350	1513	Garioch	5s.	*ER* XIV.77 V.
351	1513	Ferisch	4s.	*ER* XIV.85 V.
352	1513	Ardmannoch	5s.	*ER* XIV.89 V.
353	1513	Kinclaven	23.68s.	*ER* XIV.157 V.
354	1514	Dunkeld?	26s. on hoof	SHS 2,10.266 P.
355	1514	Dunkeld?	25.88s.	SHS 2,10.266 P.
356	1514	Dunkeld	26.55s.	SHS 2,10.266 P.
357	1514	Dunkeld	24s.	SHS 2,10.74 P.
358	1514	Perth	24s. carcase	SHS 2,10.236 P.
359	1514	Perth	26s.	SHS 2,10.237 P.
360	1514	Coule	15s.	*ER* XIV.77–8
361	1515	Dumbarton	20s.	*TA* V.16 P.
362	1515	Inchegarvy	17s. 8d.	*TA* V.20 P.
363	1515	Inchegarvy	56s. fattened	*TA* V.20 P.
364	1515	Inchegarvy	9s. 8d. veal	*TA* V.21 P.
365	1515	Fordoun	15s.	*ER* XIV.126 V.
366	1515	Glentarkane	4s.	*ER* XIV.126 V.
367	1515	Arbroath	£4 6s. 8d. fattened	*ER* XIV.217 P.
368	1516	Cupar, Fife	18s.	*SCBF*, p. 51 Aw.

Table 28 (*cont.*)

No.	Year	Place	Unit price	Source
369	1516	Discher	6s. 8d.	*ER* XIV.228 V.
370	1516	Galloway	20s.	*ER* XIV.237
371	1516	Lennox	13s. 4d.	*ER* XIV.223 V.
372	1518	Ross	20s.	*ER* XIV.384 P.
373	1518	Strathearn	19s. 11. 24d.	*ER* XIV.393
374	1518	Strathearn	20s.	*ER* XIV.393
375	1518	Coule	15s.	*ER* XIV.431
376	1518		20s.	*ER* XIV.472
377	1521	Ferisch	4s.	*ER* XV.23 V.
378	1521	Ardmannoch	5s.	*ER* XV.27 V.
379	1522	Galwalmoir	15s.	*ER* XV.2 V.
380	1522	Glentarkane	4s.	*ER* XV.2 V.
381	1522	Orkney & Shet.	12s. salted	*ER* XV.6
382	1522	Bute	5s.	*ER* XV.8 V.
383	1522	Bute	13s. 4d.	*ER* XV.8–9
384	1522	Discher	6s. 8d.	*ER* XV.9 V.
385	1522	Over Bertoun	20s.	*ER* XV.12
386	1522	Upper Cree	5s.	*ER* XV.16 V.
387	1522	Galloway	20s.	*ER* XV.19
388	1522	Coule	15s.	*ER* XV.30
389	1522	Fettercairn	15s.	*ER* XV.146
390	1522	Kintyre	20s.	*ER* XV.165
391	1522	Kintyre	20s.	*ER* XV.167
392	1523		20s.	*ER* XV.101
393	1524	Kincrag	4s.	*ER* XV.170 V.
394	1524	Ross	20s.	*ER* XV.171–2
395	1524	Ardmannoch	20s.	*ER* XV.175–6
396	1525		32s. conflated	HBJV, pp. 3,5,9 P.
397	1525		30s. conflated	HBJV, p. 6 P.
398	1525	Stirling	28s.	HBJV, p. 16 P.
399	1525	Glasgow	36.41s.	HBJV, App., p. 5 P.
400	1525	Edinburgh	36s.	HBJV, p. 20 P.
401	1525	Edinburgh	38s.	HBJV, p. 20 P.
402	1525		14s. veal conflated	HBJV, pp. 5–6 P.
403	1525	Peebles	18s. veal	HBJV, p. 3 P.
404	1525		12s. veal	HBJV, p. 5 P.
405	1525	Edinburgh	28s. veal	HBJV, p. 10 P.
406	1525	Edinburgh	12s. veal	HBJV, p. 12 P.
407	1525	Stirling	12s. veal	HBJV, p. 15 P.
408	1525	Edinburgh	20s. veal	HBJV, p. 18 P.
409	1525	Strathdee	24s.	*ER* XV.213
410	1525	Strathearn	13s. 4d.	*ER* XV.244
411	1525	Oneile	15s.	*ER* XV.245–6
412	1525	Galloway	23.30s.	*ER* XV. 249
413	1525	Kintyre	£1 6s. 8d.	*ER* XV.434
414	1526	Edinburgh?	42s.	HBJV, p. 22 P.

Table 28 (*cont.*)

No.	Year	Place	Unit price	Source
415	1526	Edinburgh	56s.	HBJV, p. 25 P.
416	1526	Stirling	90s. fattened	HBJV, p. 57 P.
417	1526	Stirling	30s.	HBJV, p. 57 P.
418	1526	Edinburgh	96s. fattened	HBJV, p. 58 P.
419	1526	Edinburgh	30s.	HBJV, p. 58 P.
420	1526	Edinburgh	100s. fattened	HBJV, p. 59 P.
421	1526	Edinburgh	80s. ox with hide	HBJV, p. 59 P.
422	1526	Edinburgh	128s. fattened	HBJV, p. 60 P.
423	1526	Stirling?	36s.	HBJV, p. 61 P.
424	1526	Edinburgh	48s.	HBJV, p. 63 P.
425	1526	Edinburgh	36s.	HBJV, p. 64 P.
426	1526	Edinburgh	26s. veal	HBJV, p. 25 P.
427	1526	Stirling	13s. veal	HBJV, p. 57 P.
428	1526	Stirling	3s. 2d. small veal	HBJV, p. 57 P.
429	1526	Edinburgh	22s. veal	HBJV, p. 58 P.
430	1526	Edinburgh	18s. veal	HBJV, p. 60 P.
431	1526	Stirling	17s. veal	HBJV, p. 61 P.
432	1526	Sterling	3s. 4d. small veal	HBJV, p. 61 P.
433	1526	Edinburgh?	15s. veal	HBJV, p. 63 P.
434	1526	Linlithgow	32s. veal	HBJV, App., p. 7 P.
435	1526	Strathearn	15s.	*ER* XV.310
436	1527	Strathearn	15s.	*ER* XV.423
437	1527	Bute	20s.	*ER* XV.425
438	1528		32s. conflated	HBJV, p. 119 P.
439	1528	Camesmor	40s. 9d.	HBJV, p. 114 P.
440	1528	Falkland	28s.	HBJV, p. 115 P.
441	1528	Falkland?	29s.	HBJV, p. 116 P.
442	1528	Perth	30s.	HBJV, p. 117 P.
443	1528	Edinburgh	32.4s.	HBJV, p. 119 P.
444	1528	Edinburgh	30.3s.	HBJV, p. 123 P.
445	1528	Stirling	28.8s.	HBJV, p. 124 P.
446	1528	Linlithgow	29.6s.	HBJV, p. 125 P.
447	1528	Edinburgh?	34.58s.	HBJV, App., p. 16 P.
448	1528	Stirling	35.53s.	HBJV, App., p. 16 P.
449	1528	Edinburgh	41s. 4d.	HBJV, p. 132 P.
450	1528	Camesmor	20s. veal	HBJV, p. 114 P.
451	1528	Perth	12s. veal	HBJV, p. 117 P.
452	1528	Edinburgh	14s. veal	HBJV, p. 119 P.
453	1528	Edinburgh	14s. veal	HBJV, p. 121 P.
454	1528	Stirling	12s. veal	HBJV, p. 124 P.
455	1528	Edinburgh	22s. veal	HBJV, p. 132 P.
456	1528	Bute	20s.	*ER* XV.497
457	1528	Orkney & Shet.	12s.	*ER* XV.553 V.
458	1529		36s. conflated	HBJV, p. 135 P.
459	1529		40s. conflated	HBJV, p. 137 P.
460	1529	Linlithgow	32s.	HBJV, p. 134 P.

Table 28 (*cont.*)

No.	Year	Place	Unit price	Source
461	1529	Stirling	33s.	HBJV, p. 134 P.
462	1529	Linlithgow	34.29s.	HBJV, p. 135 P.
463	1529	Edinburgh	40s.	HBJV, p. 135 P.
464	1529	Linlithgow	26s. 8d.	HBJV, p. 136 P.
465	1529	Edinburgh	96s. fattened	HBJV, p. 137 P.
466	1529	Edinburgh	43s.	HBJV, p. 145 P.
467	1529	Stirling	88s. fattened	HBJV, p. 152 P.
468	1529	Jedburgh	50s.	HBJV, p. 155 P.
469	1529	Peebles	41.05s.	HBJV, p. 156 P.
470	1529	Stirling	35s.	HBJV, p. 158 P.
471	1529	Linlithgow	29s.4d.	HBJV, p. 160 P.
472	1529	Stirling	34s.	HBJV, p. 162 P.
473	1529	Falkland	33s.	HBJV, p. 213 P.
474	1529	Linlithgow	32s.	HBJV, p. 216 P.
475	1529	Stirling	38s.	HBJV, App., p. 24 P.
476	1529	Linlithgow	24s.	HBJV, p. 219 P.
477	1529	Edinburgh	28s.	HBJV, App., p. 25 P.
478	1529	Edinburgh	39s.	HBJV, p. 220 P.
479	1529	Edinburgh	29s.	HBJV, p. 220 P.
480	1529		20s. veal conflated	HBJV, p. 136 P.
481	1529	Linlithgow	12s. veal	HBJV, p. 134 P.
482	1529	Linlithgow	15s. veal	HBJV, p. 135 P.
483	1529	Edinburgh	22s. veal	HBJV, p. 135 P.
484	1529	Edinburgh	24s. veal	HBJV, p. 137 P.
485	1529	Edinburgh	27.27s. veal	HBJV, p. 145 P.
486	1529	Edinburgh	3s. 8d. small veal	HBJV, p. 145 P.
487	1529	Edinburgh	21s. veal	HBJV, p. 148 P.
488	1529	Edinburgh	22s. veal	HBJV, p. 150 P.
489	1529	Stirling	18s. veal	HBJV, p. 152 P.
490	1529	Stirling	3s. small veal	HBJV, p. 152 P.
491	1529	Stirling	18s. 8d. veal	HBJV, p. 153 P.
492	1529	Stirling	9s. veal	HBJV, p. 158 P.
493	1529	Linlithgow	16s. veal	HBJV, p. 162 P.
494	1529	Linlithgow	14s. veal	HBJV, p. 216 P.
495	1529		14s. veal	HBJV, App., p. 23 P.
496	1529	Discher	6s. 8d.	*ER* XVI.3 V.
497	1529	O'Neile	15s.	*ER* XVI.5 V.
498	1529	Fettercairn	15s.	*ER* XVI.7 V.
499	1529	Galwelbeg	15s.	*ER* XVI.19 V.
500	1529	Strathearn	15s.	*ER* XVI.20–1
501	1529	Bute	5s.	*ER* XVI.23 V.
502	1529	Bute	20s.	*ER* XVI.24
503	1529	Cree	5s.	*ER* XVI.26 V.
504	1529	Galloway	28.24s.	*ER* XVI.28
505	1529	Orkney & Shet.	12s.	*ER* XVI.30
506	1529	Coule	15s.	*ER* XVI.33

Table 28 (*cont.*)

No.	Year	Place	Unit price	Source
507	1529	Hiltoun	20s./30s.	*ER* XVI.119
508	1529	Ardmannoch	5s.	*ER* XVI.116 V.
509	1530		36s.	HBJV, App., p. 28 P.
510	1530	Glasgow	30s.	HBJV, p. 224 P.
511	1530	Stirling	£4 6s. 8d. fattened	HBJV, p. 225 P.
512	1530	Peebles	46s.	HBJV, p. 226 P.
513	1530	Glasgow	20s. veal	HBJV, p. 224 P.
514	1530	Stirling	18s. veal	HBJV, p. 225 P.
515	1530	Galwegbeg	15s. changed to 30s.	*ER* XVI.106 V.
516	1530	Strathearn	30s.	*ER* XVI.107
517	1530	Fyschrie	4s.	*ER* XVI.110 V.
518	1530	Kincrag	4s.	*ER* XVI.111 V.
519	1530	Fettercairn	30s.	*ER* XVI.121
520	1530	Strathdee	29.63s.	*ER* XVI.124
521	1530		30s.	*ER* XVI.140
522	1530	Orkney & Shet.	12s.	*ER* XVI.140 P.
523	1530	Orkney & Shet.	18s.	*ER* XVI.141
524	1531	Edinburgh	12s.	*ER* XVI.178 V.
525	1531		30s.	*ER* XVI.180
526	1531	Hiltoun	20s.	*ER* XVI.207
527	1531	Galloway	30s.	*ER* XVI.211
528	1531	Coule	30s.	*ER* XVI.216–17
529	1531	Strathearn	20s.	*ER* XVI.221
530	1532	Dundee	28s.	HBJV, p. 230 P.
531	1532	Edinburgh	36s.	HBJV, p. 231 P.
532	1533	Edinburgh	£5 13s. 4d. fattened	HBJV, p. 233 P.
533	1533	Edinburgh	£5 fattened	HBJV, p. 235 P.
534	1533	Edinburgh	40s.	HBJV, p. 235 P.
535	1533	Glasgow	24s. carcases	*TA* VI.164 P.
536	1533	Glasgow	29s. 9d. on the feit	*TA* VI.164 P.
537	1533	Edinburgh	24s. veal	HBJV, p. 234 P.
538	1533	Kinclaven	30s.	*ER* XVI.306
539	1533	Strathdee	30s.	*ER* XVI.412
540	1534	Bute	30s.	*ER* XVI.446
541	1535	Bute	5s.	*ER* XVII.29 V.
542	1535	Bute	24s.	*ER* XVII.29
543	1535	Bute	30s.	*ER* XVII.30
544	1535	Ardmannoch	5s.	*ER* XVII.37 V.
545	1535	Ardmannoch	24s.	*ER* XVII.39
546	1536	Strathearn	20s.	*ER* XVII.14
547	1536	Fettercairn	15s.	*ER* XVII.16 V.
548	1536	Cree	5s.	*ER* XVII.20–1 V.
549	1536	Galloway	30s.	*ER* XVII.22
550	1536	Coule	15s.	*ER* XVII.23
551	1536	Discher	6s. 8d.	*ER* XVII.24 V.
552	1536	Kinclaven	30s.	*ER* XVII.25

Table 28 (*cont.*)

No.	Year	Place	Unit price	Source
553	1536	Strathdee	30s.	*ER* XVII.27
554	1536	O'Neile	15s.	*ER* XVII.30 V.
555	1536	Fischerie	4s.	*ER* XVII.33 V.
556	1536	Kincrag	4s.	*ER* XVII.33 V.
557	1536	Ross	24s.	*ER* XVII.35–6
558	1537	Ross	24s.	*ER* XVII.114
559	1537	Shetland	12s.	*ER* XVII.168 V.
560	1537	Cowell	26s. 8d.	*ER* XVII.205
561	1537	Baiky	47s. fattened ox	*ER* XVII.144 P.
562	1538		33s.	*TA* VI.391 P.
563	1538	Bute	24s.	*ER* XVII.199
564	1538	Cullarde	30s.	*ER* XVII.223
565	1538	Cullarde	22.86s.	*ER* XVII.224 V.
566	1538	Ross	26s. 8d.	*ER* XVII.235
567	1538	Ardmannoch	26s. 8d.	*ER* XVII.240
568	1539	Monymusk	24s.	SHS 2,4.105
569	1539	Cullarde	30s.	*ER* XVII.432
570	1539		26s.	*ER* XVII.275
571	1539	Ross	30s.	*ER* XVII.335 V.
572	1539	Fischerie	4s.	*ER* XVII.341 V.
573	1539	Ross	30s.	*ER* XVII.343
574	1539	Ardmannoch	30s.	*ER* XVII.344 V.
575	1539	Ardmannoch	30s.	*ER* XVII.349
576	1539	Cowell	30s.	*ER* XVII.356
577	1539	Strathdee	30s.	*ER* XVII.364 V.
578	1539	Strathdee	30s.	*ER* XVII.657 V.
579	1541	Monymusk	24s.	SHS 2,4.118
580	1541	Mull,Tiree	26s. 8d.	*ER* XVII.529 V.
581	1541	Jura	26s. 8d.	*ER* XVII.535 V.
582	1541	Islay	26s. 8d.	*ER* XVII.545 V.
583	1541	Cowell	30s.	*ER* XVII.569
584	1541	Kintyre	26s. 8d.	*ER* XVII.625 V.

population levels on both sides of the border[113] but livestock prices seem to have held up better in England. The supply of livestock in Scotland probably failed to adjust adequately to reduced demand after the Plague, chiefly because so much Scots agricultural land was good for little other than rough grazing.

[113] Though individuals seem to have consumed more meat. Dyer, *Standards of living*, p. 159. Also Alexander Gibson and Christopher Smout, 'Scottish Food and Scottish History, 1500–1800' in R.A. Houston and I.D. Whyte (eds.), *Scottish Society 1500–1800* (Cambridge, 1989).

Table 29. *Cow summary table*

Period	Mean price	Deflated	Index
A	4.57	4.57	66.1
B–C	6.91	6.91	100.0
D–E			
F	(12.0)		
G	13.33	8.0	115.8
H			
I	16.07	5.3	76.7
60s	21.67		
70s	20.5	5.74	83.1
80s	25.74		
90s	24.71	6.92	100.1
1500s	26.33	7.37	106.7
10s			
20s	31.67	7.92	114.6
30s	30.14	6.63	95.9

Note: the mean price is in shillings each; the deflated column gives the currency-adjusted sterling equivalent price. Parentheses have been used to flag up calculations which are less securely based than others – either because they are based on a smaller amount of data, or because they involve certain, possibly questionable, assumptions.

Cows

Cows were much less commonly traded than marts, probably being seen more as a capital asset than as a market product. Thus the acquisition of a cow was regarded as a prudent investment for a man in receipt of an unexpected windfall.[114] The income generated by a cow in terms of milk and calves was estimated in one case at 13s.4d. a year[115] and a live cow was also worth considerably more than its meat and hide value.[116] The prudent farmer was thus generally reluctant to sell cows, and will normally have attempted to bring them up through his own herd from birth rather than buy them.[117]

The scarcity of cow sales not only makes the whole series relatively short, but also makes legal valuation of cows in court cases one of the chief sources of evidence. Records of forfeited goods also provide a

[114] List 159, a reward for finding treasure trove.

[115] List 39. Much earlier in 1337 the chamberlain estimated the yield of a cow at 5 stones of cheese and 1 stirk per year (*ER* I.437). Cf. Oschinsky (ed.), *Walter of Henley and Other Treatises*, pp. 334–5, 425–7.

[116] *ALC* I.300.

[117] List 129–30, 133, for the rising value of calves over three years.

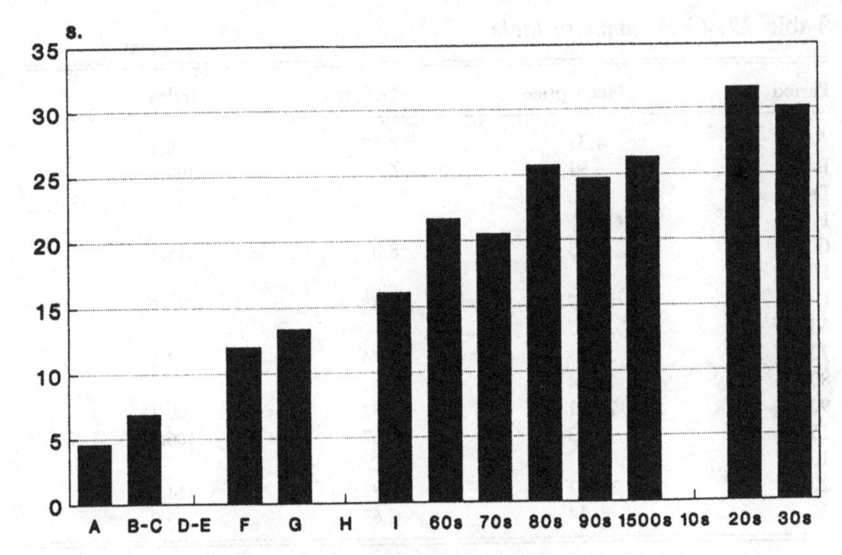

26 Cow prices (mean prices for time periods A–1530s)
For periods A–I, see Introduction, p. 6.

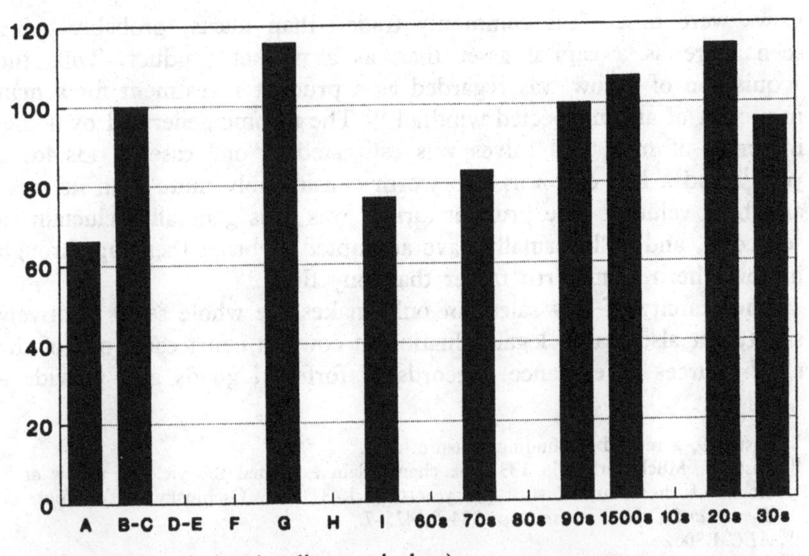

27 Cow index (sterling equivalent)

Table 30. *Cow prices 1263–1364: Scotland and England*

Year	Scotland	Durham	Rogers	Farmer
1263	5.0			
	5.0			
	5.0			
	4.5/3.75			
	5.0			
	4.5			
1264	5.0		8.0	6.06
	5.0			
	3.0			
	4.0			
1290	5.0		7.5	8.75
1302	5.0		6.15	8.25
1304	6.67		6.96	6.63
1310		11.0		
1311	5.0		12.69	12.5
1328	10.0		10.1	
1333	9.0	7.41	11.19	
1335	6.67	10.13	10.33	
	8.81			
1336	7.0	7.5	9.9	
	6.67			
	6.67			
1337	5.5	10.82	6.73	
	5.5			
1344	7.33	7.5	9.29	
1364	(9.0)	9.52	15.92	

Note: all prices are in shillings each. Parentheses have been used to flag up calculations which are less securely based than others – either because they are based on a smaller amount of data, or because they involve certain, possibly questionable, assumptions.

number of prices which are more truly valuations.[118] Rents seem only rarely to be paid in the form of cows, the royal receipts from Ettrick being a notable exception.[119] The cow prices given here have not therefore been depressed by many outdated valuations of rents in kind.[120]

There were thus good and sufficient reasons for real cow prices consistently exceeding the price of marts. Yet exceptionally in the thirteenth and early fourteenth centuries cow prices do look low relative

[118] List 8, 12, 17–24, 30, 31.

[119] Though even this may arise from too literal a reading of 'bowky' which were often actually marts. See *ER* VII.623, 'marts called bowky'.

[120] Cf. Marts above, p. 232.

Table 31. *Cow price list*

No.	Year	Place	Unit price	Source
1	1263	Forfar	4.5s.	*ER* I.8 V.
2	1263	Inverness	5s.	*ER* I.20 V.
3	1263	Inverkoych	5s.	*ER* I.4
4	1263	Banff	4.5s./3.75s.	*ER* I.15 V.
5	1263	Kinross	5s.	*ER* I.16
6	1263	Inverness	5s.	*ER* I.19 V.
7	1264	Forfar	5s.	*ER* I.26 V.
8	1264	Fife	5s.	*ER* I.31 V.
9	1264	Kintyre	3s.	*ER* I.11 V.
10	1264	Brewevill	4s.	*ER* I.5 V.
11	1290	Kincardine	5s.	*ER* I.49
12	1302	Peebles	5s.	*CDS* II.425
13	1304	Stirling	6s. 8d.	*CDS* IV.465 P.
14	1311	Stirling	5s.	*CDS* III.402 V.
15	1328	Cardross	10s.	*ER* I.125 V.
16	1333	Scotland?	9s.	DB 1333–4 P.
17	1335	Roxburgh	6.67s.	*CDS* III.322
18	1335	Berwick	8.81s.	*CDS* III.326
19	1336	Berwick	7s.	*CDS* III.371
20	1336	Roxburgh	6.67s.	*CDS* III.375
21	1336	Roxburgh	6.67s.	*CDS* III.375
22	1337	Berwick	5.5s.	*CDS* III.373
23	1337	Berwick	5.5s.	*CDS* III.373
24	1344	Coldingham	7.33s.	CS 1344–5ii
25	1364	Coldingham	9s. carcase	SS 12.xlvii P.
26	1398	Aberdeen	12s.	SHS 3,49.31 Aw.
27	1424	Dunglas	13.33s.	HMS 12,8.87 W.
28	1444	Aberdeen	18s.	ACR IV.350 Aw.
29	1448	Aberdeen	24s.	ACR V.i 5 C.
30	1454	Peebles	15s.	*ER* VI.86
31	1457	Annandale	13.33s.	*ER* VI.446
32	1458	Galloway	10s.	*ER* VI.570
33	1466	Yarow	22s.	*ER* VII.497
34	1467	Daldres	20s.	*ALA* I.8 Aw.
35	1467	Ettrick	22s.	*ER* VII.528–9
36	1467	Yarow	22s.	*ER* VII.530
37	1468	Yarow	22s.	*ER* VII.622
38	1468	Tweda	22s.	*ER* VII.623 P.
39	1470		40s.	*ALA* I.56–7 Aw.?C.
40	1471	Ettrick	22s.	*ER* VIII.101 V.
41	1474		20s. and 18s.	*ALA* I.34 Aw.
42	1474	Galloway	20s.	*ER* VIII.287 P.
43	1478	Noligrey	24s. with oxen	*ALC* I.6 Aw.
44	1479	Corswod	20s.	*ALA* I.81–2 Aw.
45	1479		25s. with oxen	*ALC* I.28 Aw.
46	1479	Corswod	20s.	*ALA* I.81–2 Aw.

Table 31 (*cont.*)

No.	Year	Place	Unit price	Source
47	1479		20s.	*ALA* I.82 C.
48	1479		20s.	*ALC* I.35 Aw.
49	1479		20s.	*ALC* I.35 Aw.
50	1479	Corswod	20s.	*ALA* I.81–2 Aw.
51	1479	Fettercairn	10s.	*ER* IX.12
52	1479	Tweed	22s.	*ER* IX.30
53	1479	Ettrick	22s.	*ER* IX.33 V.
54	1479	Falkland	24s.	*ER* IX.54 P.
55	1480		24s./20s. with oxen	*ALC* I.54 C./Aw.
56	1480		20s.	*ALC* I.68 Aw.
57	1480	Yarow	22.65s.	*ER* IX.137
58	1482	Stew-toun	36s.	*ALA* I.107 Aw.
59	1483	Glennessil	13s. 4d. yeld (barren)	*ALC* I.*83 Aw.
60	1483	Glennessil	28s. with calf	*ALC* I.*83 Aw.
61	1483	Glennessil	25s. without calf	*ALC* I.*83 Aw.
62	1483	Litil Prest.	30s. with oxen	*ALA* I.*118 Aw.
63	1483	Areschene	24s. grete	*ALA* I.*121 Aw.
64	1483	Areschene	13s. 4d. 2yr old	*ALA* I.*121 Aw.
65	1483	Lile	21s. 4d.	*ALA* I.*123 Aw.
66	1483	Wauchtoun'	26s. 8d. old	*ALC* I.166 Aw.
67	1483	Wauchtoun'	26s. 8d. young cow & calf	*ALC* I.166 Aw.
68	1484	Inglistoun	26s. 8d. with oxen	*ALA* I.*131 Aw.
69	1484	Kirkhop	30s.	*ALA* I.*136 Aw.
70	1484	Haltre	26s. 8d. with oxen	*ALA* I.*137 Aw.
71	1484	Tynyngam	30s.	*ALA* I.*137 Aw.
72	1484	Kilgrossan	26s. 8d. with oxen	*ALA* I.*141 Aw.
73	1484	Perte?	24s. with oxen	*ALC* I.389 Aw.
74	1485	Tracquar	24s. and 20s.	*ALC* I.*95 Aw.
75	1485		30s. with oxen	*ALC* I.*98 Aw.
76	1485	Ryflat	30s.	*ALC* I.*107 Aw.
77	1485	Ester Rossy	30s.	*ALC* I.*110 Aw.
78	1487	Yarrow	22s.	*ER* X.97 V.
79	1488	Balgoner	26s. 8d.	*ALA* I.115 Aw.
80	1488	Ardwell	18s.	*ALA* I.118 Aw.
81	1488	Ballincref	24s.	*ALC* I.90 Aw.
82	1488	Estir Beltj	26.67s.	*ALC* I.90 Aw.
83	1488	Straithallo.	40s.	*ALC* I.92 Aw.
84	1489	Ballaly	26s. 8d./30s. with oxen	*ALA* I.122 Aw./C.
85	1489	Lekraw	40s.	*ALC* I.106 Aw.
86	1489	Craghall	35s.	*ALC* I.108 Aw.
87	1489		30s.	*ALC* I.108 Aw.
88	1489	Brigland'	30s. new calfit	*ALC* I.114 Aw.
89	1489	Brigland'	20s.	*ALC* I.114 Aw.
90	1489	Brigland'	26s. 8d.	*ALC* I.115 Aw.
91	1489	Kyngarth	26s. 8d.	*ALC* I.115 C.
92	1489	Kyrkinnyr'	40s.	*ALC* I.117 C.

Table 31 (*cont.*)

No.	Year	Place	Unit price	Source
93	1489	Kirkcudbrig.	24s. per cow	*ALA* I.131 C.
94	1490	Foulartoun'	24s.	*ALC* I.165 Aw.
95	1490	the Birs'	26s. 8d.	*ALA* I.141 C.
96	1490	Delgatie castle	24s.	*ALC* I.289 Aw.
97	1490		24s.	*ALC* I.132 C.
98	1490	Essilmont	20s. with oxen	*ALA* I.183 Aw.
99	1490	Thornetoun	36s.	*ALC* I.146 C.
100	1490	Newby?	26s. 8d. with oxen	*ALC* I.149 Aw.
101	1490	Glengelt	26s. 8d. with oxen	*ALC* I.156 Aw.
102	1490	Est Fortoun	26s. 8d.	*ALC* I.157 Aw.
103	1490		40s. with oxen	*ALC* I.158 Aw.
104	1490	the Birs'	26s. 8d.	*ALA* I.141 C.
105	1490	Kirkcudbrig.?	30s.	*ALC* I.137 Aw.
106	1490	Thornetoun	36s.	*ALC* I.146 C.
107	1491	Raith/Bawb.	26s. 8d.	*ALC* I.172 Aw.
108	1491	Lanraky	40s. with oxen	*ALC* I.177 C.
109	1491	Strathalloun	40s. with oxen	*ALC* I.177 C.
110	1491	Brigland	40s. with oxen	*ALC* I.177 C.
111	1491	Balconie,Fife	26s. 8d.	*ALC* I.178 C.
112	1491	Gowgask	26s. 8d. with oxen	*ALC* I.196 C.
113	1491	Kowgask	35s. and 18s. with oxen	*ALA* I.156 Aw.
114	1491	Aberdeen	20s.	ACR VII.275 Aw.
115	1491	Cromarty	13s. 4d.	*ALC* I.273 Aw.
116	1492	Trewin	32s. with oxen	*ALC* I.211 C.
117	1492		40s. with oxen	*ALC* I.228 Aw.
118	1492	Petlour/Dem.	30s.	*ALC* I.212 C.
119	1492		20s. young, with oxen	*ALC* I.219 Aw.
120	1492		20s.	*ALC* I.219 Aw.
121	1492		20s.	*ALC* I.221 C.
122	1492	Balbegy	26s. 8d.	*ALC* I.231 Wi.
123	1492	Balbegy	13s. 4d.	*ALC* I.231 Wi.
124	1492	Kirkcudbrig.	30s.	*ALC* I.232 Aw.
125	1493	Kirkcudbrig.?	25s.	*ALC* I.278 Aw.
126	1493	Balgethray	40s.	*ALC* I.281 Wi.
127	1493	Ouer Cullane	20s. with oxen	*ALC* I.282 Aw.
128	1493	Petlour	26s. young	*ALC* I.296 Aw.
129	1493	Delgatie castle	13s. 4d. 3yr old	*ALC* I.289 Aw.
130	1493	Delgatie castle	5s. 1 yr old	*ALC* I.289 Aw.
131	1493	Petlour	24s. milk cow	*ALC* I.296 Aw.
132	1493	Condy	26s. 8d.	*ALC* I.282 C.
133	1493	Delgatie castle	8s. 2 yr old	*ALC* I.289 Aw.
134	1493	Glencarn'	20s. nolts, with oxen	*ALA* I.179 Aw.
135	1493	Abircorn	26s. 8d.	*ALA* I.183 Aw.
136	1493	Crawfurdland	20s.	*ALC* I.300 Aw.
137	1493	Crawfurdland	30s.	*ALC* I.300 Aw.
138	1493	Cullory	30s.	*ALC* I.301 C.

Table 31 (*cont.*)

No.	Year	Place	Unit price	Source
139	1493		26s. 8d. with oxen	*ALC* I.305 Aw.
140	1494	Aberdeen	24s.	ACR VII.528 Aw.
141	1494		20s. cow with calf	*ALC* I.323 Aw.
142	1494	Kynlyn	20s.	*ALC* I.327 Aw.
143	1494	Kynlyn	20s.	*ALC* I.327 Aw.
144	1494		26s.8d. with oxen	*ALC* I.337 Aw.
145	1494	Dysart	13s.4d.	*ALC* I.364 Wi.
146	1494	Dysart	20s.	*ALC* I.364 Wi.
147	1494	Orkky	32s. with oxen	*ALC* I.370 C.
148	1494	Murdoston'	26s.8d.	*ALA* I.187 C.
149	1494	Lochinnall.	26s.8d. with calf	*ALA* I.193–4 Aw.
150	1494	the Ard'	20s.	*ALA* I.206 Aw.
151	1495	Water of Urr	30s. with oxen	*ALC* I.394 Aw.
152	1495		24s.	*ALC* I.394 Aw.
153	1495	Inverness	20s.	*ALC* I.398 Aw.
154	1495	Cowsland'	30s. with oxen	*ALC* I.405 C.
155	1495	Smetoun'	26s.8d.	*ALC* I.411 C.
156	1495	Monquhanny	26s. 8d./26s.	*ALC* I.413 C./Aw.
157	1495	Ballaly	26s. 8d. with oxen	*ALC* I.413 Aw.
158	1495	Ettrick	22s.	*ER* XI.8 V.
159	1496		24s.	*TA* I.277 V.
160	1500	Aberdeen	22s. cow and calf	ACR VII.1035 C.
161	1501	Lupno & Loss.	24s.	*ER* XII.74 V.
162	1503	Stirling	30s. with calf	*TA* II.394 P.
163	1507	Aberdeen	18s.	ACR VIII.657 C.
164	1508	Sclaty,Abdn	23s.	ACR VIII.909 Aw.
165	1509	Aberdeen	12s.	ACR VIII.1027 Aw.
166	1509	Moray	24s.	*ER* XIII.292 P.
167	1514	Dunkeld	30s.	SHS 2,10. 73 V.
168	1516	Cupar,Fife	2 at 53s. 4d. 1 at 24s.	*SCBF*, p. 51 Aw.
169	1522	Cupar,Fife	40s. with calf	*SCBF*, p. 262 Aw.
170	1522	Cupar,Fife	13s. 4d. young	*SCBF*, p. 262 Aw.
171	1522	Cupar,Fife	40s. old, 26s. 8d. young	*SCBF*, p. 267 Aw.
172	1522	Aberdeen	50s.	ACR XVI.860 C.
173	1526	Aberdeen	32s.	ACR XI.681 Aw.
174	1526	Aberdeen	28s.	ACR XI.681 Aw.
175	1531	Aberdeen	14s. young	ACR XIII.173 Wi.
176	1531	Aberdeen	24s. with calf	ACR XIII.173 Wi.
177	1535	Aberdeen	33s.	ACR XIV.538 Aw.
178	1536	Aberdeen	16s./17s.	ACR XV.507 Wi.
179	1536	Aberdeen	28s./30s.	ACR XV.507 Wi.
180	1539		40s./50s.	*TA* VII.169 P.
181	1539	Galloway	30s.	*ER* XVII.289 P.

to other livestock, and this observation raises doubts about the validity of the cow price used as a base of the adjusted index. If this doubt is well founded, it could provide an explanation of the relatively high currency-adjusted index price scored by cows in the fifteenth and sixteenth centuries (Table 29 and Figure 27).

We may thus tentatively conclude that cows are generally closer in price to oxen than to marts, but that despite the high calculated currency-adjusted index price, in reality cows probably did no better than other livestock over the whole period. The general trend of cow prices, and Scottish prices relative to English ones,[121] conform to the established patterns.

Oxen

Oxen, like cows, were not commonly sold, and several of the court cases which consequently provide the lion's share of our prices make specific reference to compensation for the loss of profits caused by the removal of oxen. We read of compensation for land unploughed, or for the need to hire oxen. On one occasion the profit of an ox was estimated in grain at 6 firlots of meal per ox per year.[122] Such was the productive value of an ox that, like cows, a live ox was judged to exceed the value of a dead animal by 10s.[123]

In addition to ploughing, oxen were regularly used as draught animals. We meet them shifting timber at Falkland[124] and drawing guns south to Flodden.[125] Bulls are occasionally mentioned in this series,[126] as well as the younger animals, nolts and stirks.

The predominance of legal valuations in the ox series carries with it the possibility that our prices may be somewhat high. Claimants are unlikely to underestimate the value of their stock, while there are several instances of valuations being reduced by the courts.[127] Nevertheless, the very possibility of claims being cut back by the courts, and the care which was obviously taken to establish realistic values[128] suggest that any upward trend in court valuations was kept within reasonable limits.

Oxen were not commonly demanded as rents in kind, though they

[121] Table 30.
[122] List 155, 169, 201.
[123] *ALC* I.300.
[124] List 42.
[125] List 220–2.
[126] List 70, 114.
[127] List 98, 107, 111, 212, 214.
[128] See List 119 for a valuation under oath.

Table 32. *Ox summary table*

Period	Mean price	Deflated	Index
A			
B–C	9.6	9.6	100.0
D			
E	8.24	7.0	72.9
F	12.11	6.06	63.1
G	13.33	8.0	83.3
H	(10.5)	(4.2)	
I	20.5	6.77	70.5
60s	17.72		
70s	23.8	6.66	69.4
80s	30.26		
90s	28.93	8.1	84.4
1500s	22.19	6.21	64.7
10s	30.62	7.66	79.8
20s	31.33	7.83	81.6

Note: the mean price is in shillings each; the deflated column gives the currency-adjusted sterling price. Parentheses have been used to flag up calculations which are less securely based than others – either because they are based on a smaller amount of data, or because they involve certain, possibly questionable, assumptions.

do occur for the more occasional feudal fines of seisin (entry) and heriot (death duty). The seisin ox, however, seems to have been early commuted to a fixed money sum,[129] and therefore from 1400 onwards prices of 6s.8d. and below have been judged to be frozen, and excluded from the calculated mean prices (Table 32 and Figures 28 and 29). The origins of this 6s.8d. price may be traced at least as far back as the beginning of the fourteenth century,[130] and this seems to have been used on occasion as a standard price throughout the century.

The overall movement of ox prices is broadly in line with that of livestock prices in general, and the marked tendency of Scottish livestock to undercut English before 1367 continues (Table 33). Indeed, so well established was this last feature, that Durham monks regularly stocked their manor with Scots livestock,[131] and we may presume they were not alone in doing so.

[129] List 17, 28, 29, 38; heriot 30.

[130] Corpus Christi College, Cambridge, MS no. 37. SHS 44, Miscellany, pp. 25–6. Three-year-old animals were priced at 6s.8d., 'colpundagh' of two years at 40d., and stirks of one year at 20d. The difficulty of dating this document prevents its inclusion in the full listing of prices. It must refer to a time after 1286 and before 1309.

[131] E.g. List 8–10.

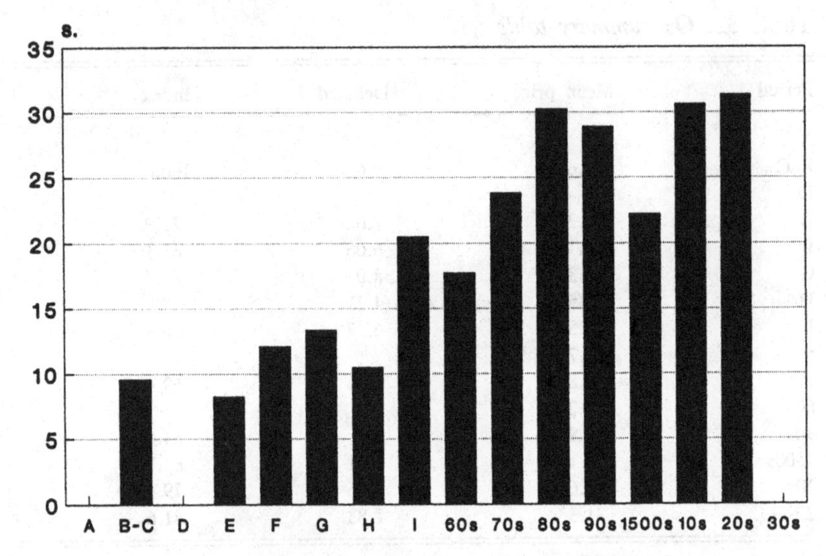

28 Ox prices (mean prices for time periods A–1530s)
For periods A–I, see Introduction, p. 6.

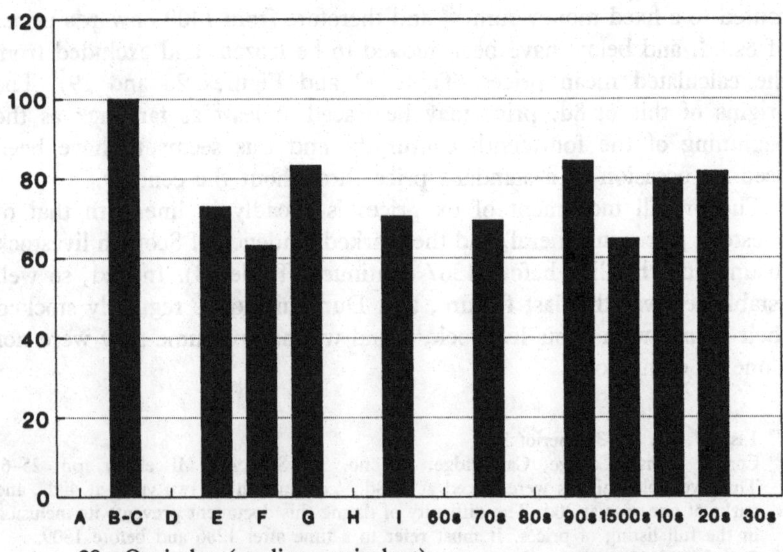

29 Ox index (sterling equivalent)

Table 33. *Ox prices 1296–1349: Scotland and England*

Year	Scotland	Durham	Rogers	Farmer (purchases)
1296	(3.0)		9.58	11.31
1297		10.08		
1302	7.0	11.87	9.33	10.79
1304	8.0		9.02	10.21
	20.0			
1306	10.0	13.29	11.19	14.83
1328	14.0	13.33	13.58	
1329	10.67	17.38	12.58	
1330	9.0	14.33	15.71	
	8.26			
1335	8.0	14.54	13.75	
	13.33			
1336	(7.5)	13.65	13.54	
	6.67			
1349	10.6	8.84	6.73	

Note: This table includes oxen which are undistinguished in the records, as well as those which were labouring animals. For oxen which were to be eaten, see marts. All prices are in shillings each. Parentheses have been used to flag up calculations which are less securely based than others – either because they are based on a smaller amount of data, or because they involve certain, possibly questionable, assumptions.

Table 34. *Ox price list*

No.	Year	Place	Unit price	Source
1	1296	Coldstream	3s. and cows	*DHS* II.33 V.
2	1302	Lochmaban	7s.	*CDS* II.342–3
3	1304	Scotland	8s.	*CDS* II.418 P.
4	1304	Dumfries	8s.	*CDS* II.396–7 P.
5	1304	Dumfries	20s.	*CDS* II.397 V.
6	1306	Scotland	10s.	DB 1306–7a+b P.
7	1328	Forfar?	14s.	*ER* I.215 V.
8	1329	Durham	10.67s.	DB 1329–30b P.
9	1330	Roxburgh	9s.	DB 1330–1a P.
10	1330	Roxburgh	8.26s.	DB 1330–1a P.
11	1335	Roxburgh	8s.	*CDS* III.322
12	1335	Edinburgh	13s. 4d.	PRO E101/19/21 P.
13	1336	Berwick	7.5s. and cows	*CDS* III.372
14	1336	Roxburgh	6.67s.	*CDS* III.375
15	1349	Roxburgh?	10s. 6d.	DB 1349–50a+b P.
16	1368	Perth	6.67s.	*ER* II.298 V.
17	1368	Lethendy	6.67s.	*ER* II.297 V.

Table 34 (*cont.*)

No.	Year	Place	Unit price	Source
18	1379	Foulis	11.39s.	*ER* III.35 P.
19	1400	Aberdeen	13.33s.	SHS 3,49.199 V.
20	1400	Aberdeen	8s.	SHS 3,49.145 C.
21	1412	Coldingham	15s.	SS 12.lxxxii V.
22	1424	Dunglas	13.33s.	HMS 12,8.87 W.
23	1436	Feichley	10s.	*ER* V.55
24	1440	Aberdeen	11s.	ACR IV.218 C.
25	1445	Aberdeen	20s.	ACR IV.419 Aw.
26	1447	Coldingham	6s.	SS 12.lxxxiv V.
27	1447	Aberdeen	20s.	ACR IV.482 Aw.
28	1450	Menteith	6.67s.	*ER* V.479 V.
29	1451	Brechin	6.67s.	*ER* V.525 V.
30	1451	Petlandy	20s.	*ER* V.543 V.
31	1453	Methven?	20s.	*ER* V.604 P.
32	1454	Methven?	22s., 20s., 18s.	*ER* VI.283 P.
33	1455	Galloway	19.19s.	*ER* VI.203 P.
34	1455	Balmaclellan	17s. 2d. and cows	*ER* VI.203 P.
35	1456	Ballyndone	20s.	*ER* VI.348 P.
36	1456	Methven	22s.	*ER* VI.357 P.
37	1457	Methven	24.36s.	*ER* VI.425 P.
38	1458	Mar	6.67s.	*ER* VI.516 V.
39	1461	Galloway	15s. young	*ER* VII.116
40	1462	Stirlingsh.	21.61s.	*ER* VII.190 P.
41	1463	Kirkcudbrig.	18s.	*ER* VII.313
42	1464	Fife	20s.	*ER* VII.335 V.
43	1466	Aberdeen	14s.	ACR V i.578 C.
44	1470	Balnabreich	22s. 6d.	*ER* VIII.76 V.
45	1472	Kittydy?	26s. 8d.	*ALA* I.20 C.
46	1473		40s.	*ALA* I.24 C.
47	1474	Galloway	26s.8d.	*ER* VIII.287 P.
48	1474	Galloway	20s.	*ER* VIII.289
49	1476	Lettupane	20s. and cows	*ALA* I.55 C.
50	1478	Craufurd	27.03s.	*ALC* I.18 Aw.
51	1478	Hume	20s.	*ALC* I.19 Aw.
52	1479		16s.	*ALA* I.68 Aw.
53	1479		10s.	*ALA* I.77 Aw.
54	1479		20s.	*ALA* I.80 Aw.
55	1479		26s.	*ALC* I.28 Aw.
56	1479		6s. 8d. young nolt	*ALC* I.35 Aw.
57	1479		24s.	*ALC* I.39 Aw.
58	1479	Rossy	26s.8d.	*ALC* I.45 Aw.
59	1480		24s.	*ALC* I.68 Aw.
60	1480		13s. 4d. young nolt	*ALC* I.68 Aw.
61	1480	Fife?	20s.	*ALC* I.68 Aw.
62	1482	Aberdeen	23.5s.	ACR VI.764 Aw.
63	1482	Wauchtoun'	30s.	*ALC* I.429 Aw.

Table 34 (*cont.*)

No.	Year	Place	Unit price	Source
64	1483	Wauchtoun'	26s. 8d.	*ALC* I.166 Aw.
65	1483	Wauchtoun'	26s. 8d.	*ALC* I.166 Aw.
66	1483	Litil Prest.	30s. and cows	*ALA* I.*118 Aw.
67	1483	Torcrake	30s.	*ALA* I.*118 Aw.
68	1483	Pitgorno	30s.	*ALA* I.*118 Aw.
69	1483		30s.	*ALA* I.*120 C.
70	1483	Areschene	30s. and bulls	*ALA* I.*121 Aw.
71	1483	Lasinstoun	35s.	*ALA* I.*125–6 Aw.
72	1484	Murhous	35s.	*ALA* I.*130 Aw.
73	1484	Inglistoun	26s. 8d. and cows	*ALA* I.*131 Aw.
74	1484	Haltre	26s. 8d. and cows	*ALA* I.*137 Aw.
75	1484	Tynyngam	40s. old	*ALA* I.*137 Aw.
76	1484	Tynyngam	26s.8d. young	*ALA* I.*137 Aw.
77	1484	Tynyngam	20s. young	*ALA* I.*137 Aw.
78	1484	Tynyngam	10s. young nolt	*ALA* I.*137 Aw.
79	1484	Kilgrossan	26s. 8d. and cows	*ALA* I.*141 Aw.
80	1484	Aberdeen	20s.	ACR VI.853–4 C.
81	1484	Perte?	24s. and cows	*ALC* I.389 Aw.
82	1484	Westergagy	30s.	*ALC* I.*85 Aw.
83	1484	Erdhous	40s.	*ALC* I.*86 C.
84	1484	Erdhous	40s.	*ALC* I.*86 C.
85	1484	Erdhous	40s.	*ALC* I.*86 C.
86	1484	Quhittingam	20s.	*ALC* I.*90 Aw.
87	1485	Tracquar	5s. stirks	*ALC* I.*95 Aw.
88	1485	Tracquar	13.33s. young nolts	*ALC* I.*98 Aw.
89	1485		40s.	*ALC* I.*102 C.
90	1485		6s. 8d. young nolt	*ALC* I.*102 C.
91	1485	Gargu'no	40s.	*ALC* I.*104 Aw.
92	1485	Ryflat	40s.	*ALC* I.*107 C.
93	1485	Ryflat	10s. young nolt	*ALC* I.*107 C.
94	1485	Symontoun'	40s.	*ALC* I.*107 C.
95	1485	Ester Rossy	10s. young nolt	*ALC* I.*110 Aw.
96	1485	Bannolly	17s. 6d. and cows	*ALC* I.*112 C.
97	1485	Davidstoun	26s. 8d.	*ALA* I.115–16 Aw.
98	1488	Dunmure	40s./24s.	*ALC* I.86 C./Aw.
99	1488		24s./30s.	*ALC* I.204 Aw.
100	1488	Balgoner	30s.	*ALA* I.115 Aw.
101	1488	Balgoner	6s. 8d. young nolt	*ALA* I.115 Aw.
102	1488	Balgoner	13s. 4d. young	*ALA* I.115 Aw.
103	1488	Balgoner	6s. 8d.young 2 yr old nolt	*ALA* I.115 Aw.
104	1488	Ardwell	24s.	*ALA* I.118 Aw.
105	1488	Ballincref	32s. and cows	*ALC* I.90 Aw.
106	1488	Straithallo.	28s.,32s.	*ALC* I.92 Aw.
107	1489	Ballaly	30s./26s. 8d. and cows	*ALA* I.122 C./Aw.
108	1489	Davidstone	26.67s.	*ALC* I.102 C.
109	1489	Lekraw	40s.	*ALC* I.106 Aw.

Table 34 (*cont.*)

No.	Year	Place	Unit price	Source
110	1489	Lekraw	13s. 4d. young nolt	*ALC* I.106 Aw.
111	1489	Craghall	40s./30s.	*ALC* I.108 C./Aw.
112	1489	Logy Murtho	33s. 4d.	*ALC* I.110 Aw.
113	1489	Balcarhous	26s. 8d.	*ALC* I.113 Aw.
114	1489	Brigland	20s. bull	*ALC* I.114 Aw.
115	1489	Brigland	13s. 4d. stots	*ALC* I.114 Aw.
116	1489	Kirkcudbrig.	32s.	*ALA* I.131 C.
117	1490	Turny dik'	28s.	*ALC* I.130 Aw.
118	1490		32s.	*ALC* I.132 C.
119	1490	the Birs	30s.	*ALA* I.141 C.
120	1490	the Birs	30s.	*ALA* I.141 C.
121	1490		30s.	*ALA* I.144 Aw.
122	1490		30s.	*ALC* I.137 Aw.
123	1490		20s. 3yr old nolt	*ALC* I.137 Aw.
124	1490		13s. 4d. 2yr old nolt	*ALC* I.137 Aw
125	1490		6s. 8d. stirk	*ALC* I.137 Aw.
126	1490	Thornetoun	40s.	*ALC* I.146 C.
127	1490	Thornetoun	40s.	*ALC* I.146 C.
128	1490	Newby?	26s. 8d. and cows	*ALC* I.149 Aw.
129	1490	Glengelt	26s. 8d. and cows	*ALC* I.155 Aw.
130	1490	Peebles	30s. cattle	*ALC* I.155 Aw.
131	1490	Est Foftoun'	30s.	*ALC* I.157 Aw.
132	1490	Est Fortoun'	40s. and cows	*ALC* I.158 Aw.
133	1490	Delgatie castle	24s.	*ALC* I.289 Aw.
134	1490	Essilmont	20s. and cows	*ALA* I.183 Aw.
135	1491	the Raith'	26s. 8d.	*ALC* I.172 Aw.
136	1491	Bawbertane	26s. 8d.	*ALC* I.172 Aw.
137	1491	Raith/Bawb.	6s. 8d. stirk	*ALC* I.172 Aw.
138	1491	Raith/Bawb.	10s. young nolt	*ALC* I.172 Aw.
139	1491	W.Essuntuly	30s.	*ALC* I.177 C.
140	1491	Lanraky	40s. and cows	*ALC* I.177 C.
141	1491	Strathalloun	40s. and cows	*ALC* I.177 C.
142	1491	Brigland	40s. and cows	*ALC* I.177 C.
143	1491	Brigland	14s. 4d. young cattle	*ALC* I.177 C.
144	1491	Balcomie	30s.	*ALC* I.178 C.
145	1491	Torwechquhy	30s.	*ALC* I.184 Aw.
146	1491	Arth'	15s. nolt	*ALC* I.195 Aw.
147	1491	Gowgask	26s. 8d. and cows	*ALC* I.196 C.
148	1491	Glennegas?	24s. nolt	*ALA* I.148 Aw.
149	1491	Seitoun'	40s.	*ALA* I.152 C.
150	1491	Kowgask	35s.,18s. and cows	*ALA* I.156 Aw.
151	1491	Stantoun'	30s.	*ALC* I.202 Aw.
152	1491	Dulbaty	26s. 8d.	*ALC* I.202 Aw.
153	1491	Dulbaty	30s.	*ALC* I.202 Aw.
154	1491	Inverquhoth.	20s. nolts	*ALC* I.202 Aw.
155	1491		24s.	*ALC* I.335 Aw.

Table 34 (*cont.*)

No.	Year	Place	Unit price	Source
156	1492	Inchecometh	26s. 8d.	*ALA* I.161 Aw.
157	1492	Trewin & Loch.	32s./20s. and cows	*ALC* I.211 C./C.
158	1492	Petlour	40s.	*ALC* I.212 C.
159	1492	Petlour	20s. young	*ALC* I.212 C.
160	1492	Tolcors	20s. stirks and cows	*ALC* I.215 Aw.
161	1492		30s.	*ALC* I.219 Aw.
162	1492		26s. 8s.	*ALC* I.219 Aw.
163	1492		20s. young	*ALC* I.219 Aw.
164	1492		26s. 8d./20s.	*ALC* I.221 Aw.
165	1492		10s. 2yr old nolt	*ALC* I.221 Aw.
166	1492		5s. 1yr old nolt	*ALC* I.221 Aw.
167	1492		40s. and cows	*ALC* I.228 Aw.
168	1492	Balbegy	20s.	*ALC* I.231 Wi.
169	1492	Kynnard	22s.	*ALC* I.401 Aw.
170	1493	Mekle Crage	16s. and cows	*ALC* I.274 Aw.
171	1493	Mekle Crage	12s.	*ALC* I.274 Aw.
172	1493	Mekle Crage	10s. 2/3yr old stirks	*ALC* I.274 Aw.
173	1493		13s. 4d. young nolt	*ALC* I.278 Aw.
174	1493	Kirkcudbri.?	30s.	*ALC* I.278 Aw.
175	1493	Petscotty	27s.	*ALC* I.280 Aw.
176	1493	Ouer Cullan	20s. and cows	*ALC* I.282 Aw.
177	1493	Ouer Cullan	12s. young nolt	*ALC* I.282 Aw.
178	1493	Condy	30s.	*ALC* I.282 C.
179	1493		30s.	*ALC* I.287 Aw.
180	1493	Slanis	24s.	*ALC* I.287 Aw.
181	1493		26s. 8d.	*ALC* I.288 Wi.
182	1493	Petlour	26s. 8d.	*ALC* I.296 Aw.
183	1493	West.Quhitb.	26s. 8d.	*ALA* I.172 C.
184	1493	West.Quhitb.	26s. 8d.	*ALA* I.172 C.
185	1493	West.Quhitb.	26s. 8d.	*ALA* I.172 C.
186	1493	Glencarn	20s. nolts and cows	*ALA* I.179 Aw.
187	1493	Abircorn'	35s.	*ALA* I.183 Aw.
188	1493	Abircorn'	6s. 8d. stirks	*ALA* I.183 Aw.
189	1493	Crawfurdland	40s.	*ALC* I.300 Aw.
190	1493		26s. 8d. and cows	*ALC* I.305 Aw.
191	1494	Estertoun	40s.	*ALC* I.325 C.
192	1494		26s. 8d. and cows	*ALC* I.337 Aw.
193	1494	Burnetoun	35s.	*ALC* I.338 C.
194	1494	Perthshire	24s.	*ALC* I.348 Aw.
195	1494	Dysart	24s.	*ALC* I.364 Wi.
196	1494	Dysart	6s. young nolt	*ALC* I.364 Wi.
197	1494	Dysart	20s.	*ALC* I.364 Wi.
198	1494	Dysart	16s. stots	*ALC* I.364 Wi.
199	1494	Orkky	32s. and cows	*ALC* I.370 C.
200	1494	Ard'	20s. nolt	*ALC* I.333 Aw.
201	1494	Coutty	30s.	*ALA* I.190 Aw.

Table 34 (*cont.*)

No.	Year	Place	Unit price	Source
202	1494	Lochinnall	30s.	*ALA* I.193–4 Aw.
203	1495	Akynbar	32s.	*ALC* I.388 C.
204	1495	Water of Urr	30s. and cows	*ALC* I.394 Aw.
205	1495	Water of Urr	20s. 3yr old	*ALC* I.394 Aw.
206	1495	Water of Urr	10s. younger	*ALC* I.394 Aw.
207	1495		30s.	*ALC* I.394 Aw.
208	1495	Inverness	20s.	*ALC* I.398 Aw.
209	1495	Cowsland	30s. and cows	*ALC* I.405 Aw.
210	1495	Peebles	40s. and cows	*ALC* I.410 Aw.
211	1495	Smetoun	40s.	*ALC* I.411 C.
212	1495	Monquhanny	30s./26s.	*ALC* I.413 C./Aw.
213	1495	Ballaly	26s. 8d. and cows	*ALC* I.413 Aw.
214	1495	Sadsiff	35s./22.9s.	*ALC* I.430 C./Aw.
215	1501		22s.	*TA* II.44 P.
216	1501	Lupno & Loss.	5s. stirks	*ER* XII.74 V.
217	1506	Crawmound	30.56s. ploughing	SHS 2,10.246 P.
218	1509	Aberdeen	14s.	ACR VIII.1041 Aw.
219	1512	Clony	26s. 8d.	SHS 2,10.71 P.
220	1513	Dunblane	29.09s	*TA* IV.515 P.
221	1513	Dalkeith	32s.	*TA* IV.519 P.
222	1513	Dunmure	£1 13s. 4d.	*ER* XIV.319 V.
223	1515	Cupar,Fife	32s.	*SCBF*, pp. 6–7 Aw.
224	1520	Cupar,Fife	40s.	*SCBF*, pp. 196,201 Aw.
225	1522	Cupar,Fife	14s. young	*SCBF*, p. 262 Aw.
226	1522	Cupar,Fife	40s.	*SCBF*, p. 267 Aw.
227	1531	Aberdeen	24s. young	ACR XIII.173 O.
228	1540	Nathane	80s.	*TA* VII.384

Sheep

The principal difficulty in interpreting the series of sheep prices concerns the wide variety of animals which were all called sheep. We meet the adult animals, rams or tups, wethers and ewes, as well as younger sheep ranging from the lambs up to the hogs, gimmers, and dinmonts.[132] Lambs, of course, were markedly cheaper than adult animals[133] but hogs, gimmers, and dinmonts were also regularly about half to two-thirds the price of sheep. Despite this consistent price differentiation, on

132 A gimmer was an ewe and a dinmont a wether, between their first and second shearing. List 272–7, 279, for the relative values of a full range of these animals: rams, ewes with lambs, wethers, hogs, dinmonts, and gimmers, as priced by the court at Cupar.

133 List 83–4, 125–6, 189–90, 280, 282, 286–7, 344–5, 349–50, 380–1.

occasion our records make no distinction but include a variety of types of sheep under a single price.[134] Unfortunately, in most cases we can only guess at the precise nature of the animals described simply as sheep.

A further consideration which unquestionably affected sheep prices involved the by-products – wool, fleece, offal, milk, and cheese – of animals bought chiefly for their meat. In some cases these items receive detailed consideration,[135] but in most it is difficult to be sure if animals were dead or alive, shorn or unshorn, skinned or disembowelled.[136] Sheep carcases were usually cheaper than live animals, but since in many cases we cannot know the state of the sheep sold it has not been possible to distinguish separate series of prices to reflect these variations.

Like marts, sheep were often involved in various types of customary payments, grassums, and rents in kind. These dues were often commuted to cash, or valued in cash terms in the accounts, and the values applied quickly became frozen. From 1400 we have excluded valuations of 16d. and below from our calculated means, because these were clearly outdated as prices, but other commutations have been included although they may have been slightly low compared to an open market price.[137]

In the late fifteenth century court cases provide a growing number of the prices. One might suspect that these legal claims were likely to exaggerate the value of lost or damaged livestock, but the courts did not accept these valuations totally uncritically.[138] Similarly in the 1520s royal purchases recorded in the Household Book of James V, in quantity and at high prices, dominate the series, while in the 1530s the imposition of new rentals contributed a number of rather modest prices to the series. Equally butchers' prices for the mutton bouk are generally on the low side, especially those held down by Aberdeen's assize of flesh.[139]

It is thus clear that the prices in the sheep series are nothing like a homogeneous group. Yet although our information is sufficient to make this clear, it is not good enough over the whole period to allow us to

[134] SHS 2, 10.179–80, *TA* VII.383.

[135] See *ER* III.41, 107, V.605, VI.363, 438; *ALA* I.115, 179; *ALC* I.113. *SCBF*, p. 267; ACR XV.561–2.

[136] For explicit mention of carcases, see List 15, 22–3, 26, 28, 30, 33, 35, 119. Bouks are discussed below.

[137] E.g. Dunkeld commutations, List 224, 227, 237–8, 240, 242, 244, 246, 248, 251, 258–9. In the 1530s the crown set new rates, which still look on the low side (List 356, 359, 362–3, 365–7, 372–3, 379, 382–4) but the old rates were surprisingly persistent (List 374). For a fuller discussion of the problems interpreting these valuations, see above pp. 164–5 and 232–3.

[138] List 87 for a claim reduced. More often the numbers of sheep claimed were reduced rather than the valuation, see *ALA* I, p. 115; *ALC* I.231.

[139] See Chapter 2, p. 44. Bouks are identified in the list of prices.

Table 35. *Sheep summary table*

Period	Mean price	Deflated	Index
A	9	9.09	55.9
B–C	16	16.27	100.0
D–E	14	14.38	88.4
F		(12.22)	(75.1)
G	13	12.9	79.3
H	31	12.58	77.3
I	46	15.28	93.3
60s	(60)		
70s	38	10.56	64.9
80s	59		
90s	49	13.65	83.9
1500s	39	10.98	67.5
10s	40	10.07	61.9
20s	67	16.69	102.6
30s	53	11.74	72.2

Note: the mean price is in pence rounded to the nearest penny; the deflated column gives the currency-adjusted sterling equivalent price. Parentheses have been used to flag up calculations which are less securely based than others – either because they are based on a smaller amount of data, or because they involve certain, possibly questionable, assumptions.

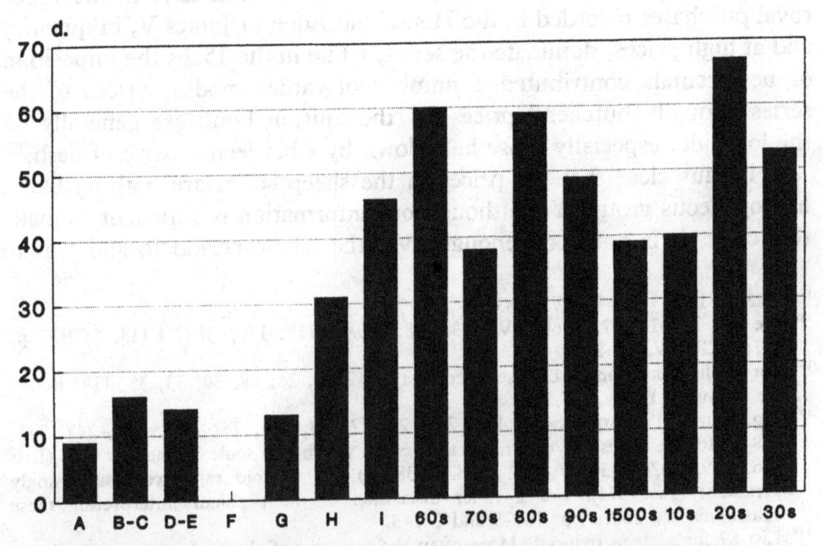

30 Sheep prices (mean prices for time periods A–1530s)
For periods A–I, see Introduction, p. 6.

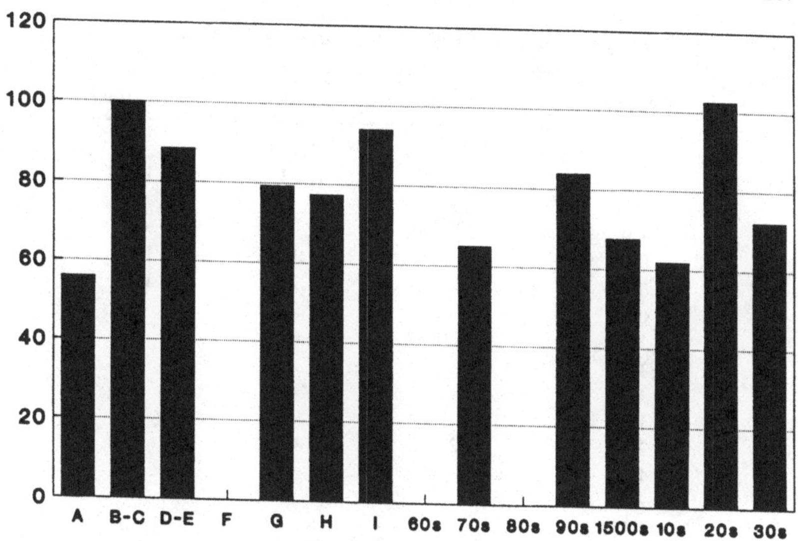

31 Sheep index (sterling equivalent)

separate the different types of sheep into separate series.[140] In these circumstances the picture of sheep prices is inevitably blurred. Moreover, there is a danger that any individual decade may not be properly comparable with other decades because of the incidence of a clutch of younger or older animals which could lead to a particularly distorted price.

These difficulties mean that sheep prices need to be approached with particular circumspection. The general level of sheep prices seems similar to that of livestock in general, but the rather erratic movement of prices from decade to decade in the fifteenth century can probably be explained in terms of the bunching of prices of one particular type from one particular source (Table 35 and Figures 30 and 31). At the beginning of our period sheep price movements follow the usual pattern, rising in the early fourteenth century, but the Anglo-Scottish comparison shows English and Scottish prices fairly closely aligned (Table 36). It might have been expected that Scots sheep would have followed the usual pattern for livestock and been cheaper than in England. Perhaps the very extensive practice of sheep farming all over most of England kept English prices down.

[140] In the calculation of means and index prices, only lambs have been excluded.

Table 36. *Sheep prices 1263–1364: Scotland and England*

Year	Scotland	Durham	Rogers	Farmer
1263	0.83		1.11	
1264	0.8		1.23	1.15
	0.83			
	1.0			
1296	0.67[a&b]		1.1[a]	1.25[a]
	0.67		1.27	1.29
	0.5[c]		1.25[c]	
1328	1.5	1.92/1.67	1.0	
	1.0			
	1.44			
	1.5			
1329	2.0	1.52	1.6	
	1.25			
	2.0			
	(1.17)			
1330	2.11/1.77	0.67	2.08	
1331	1.89/1.5		1.25	
1335	1.0	1.41	1.42	
1336	0.67/0.56	0.83/0.7[d]	1.42	
1341	1.2/1.0	0.67	0.85	
1345	1.29	0.71	1.19	
1363	0.67		1.92	
1364	(0.75)	1.45	1.85	

Note: all prices are in shillings each. Parentheses have been used to flag up calculations which are less securely based than others – either because they are based on a smaller amount of data, or because they involve certain, possibly questionable, assumptions. Where the type of sheep is distinguished in the Scottish sources comparison has been made with the appropriate type of sheep from Rogers' and Farmer's tables. Otherwise we have compared *multones*, *oves*, and *bidentes* of the record with muttons.

[a]Ewe.
[b]Lamb.
[c]Hoggasters.
[d]Figure includes hoggasters.

Table 37. *Sheep price list*

No.	Year	Place	Unit price	Source
1	1263	Strathylif	10d.	*ER* I.9 V.
2	1264	Lanark	9.6d.	*ER* I.30 P.
3	1264	Barry	10d.	*ER* I.9 V.
4	1264	Edinburgh	12d.	*ER* I.33 P.
5	1296	Coldstream	8d. 1 ewe + lamb	*DHS* II.33 V.

Table 37 (*cont.*)

No.	Year	Place	Unit price	Source
6	1296	Coldstream	8d.	*DHS* II.33 V.
7	1296	Coldstream	6d. hog	*DHS* II.33 V.
8	1328	Cardross	18d.	*ER* I.125 P.
9	1328	Cardross	12d.	*ER* I.125 P.
10	1328	Berwick?	17.32d.	*ER* I.206
11	1328	Berwick	18d.	*ER* I.206
12	1329	Earlston	24d.	DPS Exp.'29a V.
13	1329		15d	*ER* I.240.
14	1329		24d.	*ER* I.289
15	1329		14d. carcase	*ER* I.289 P.
16	1330		25.28d./21.24d.	*ER* I.341 P.
17	1331		21.6d./18d.	*ER* I.400 P.
18	1335	Berwick	12d.	*CDS* III.326
19	1336	Berwick	8d./6.67d.	*CDS* III.371
20	1341		14.4d./12d	*ER* I.504
21	1345	Coldingham	15.48d.	CP 1345–6
22	1363	Coldingham	8d. carcase?	SS 12.xliv P.
23	1364	Coldingham	9d. carcase	SS 12.xlvii P.
24	1368	Edinburgh	1.20s./1s.	*ER* II.306 P.
25	1372		1.19s./0.99s.	*ER* II.368 P.
26	1372		1.19s. carcase	*ER* II.368 P.
27	1372		1.96s.	*ER* II.369 P.
28	1372		1.21s./1.07s. carcase	*ER* II.369 P.
29	1373		1s.	*ER* II.451 P.
30	1373		2.31s./2.04s. carcase	*ER* II.451 P.
31	1374	Coldingham	2.07s./1.73s.	SS 12.lxxiv
32	1380		1.20s./1s.	*ER* III.41 P.
33	1380		1.26s./1.13s. carcase	*ER* III.41 P.
34	1380	Edinburgh	1.6s./1.33s.	*ER* III.653 P.
35	1384		1.13s./1.02s. carcase	*ER* III.108 P.
36	1384		1.31s./1.10s.	*ER* III.107 P.
37	1424	Dunglas	3s. or 2s. ewes	HMS 12,8.87 W.
38	1424	Dunglas	2s.	HMS 12,8.87 W.
39	1424	Dunglas	2s. tups	HMS 12,8.87 W.
40	1424	Dunglas	14d. hog	HMS 12,8.87 W.
41	1427	Aberdeen	2.41s./2.17s.	*ER* IV.443 P.
42	1427	Aberdeen	2.59s./2.17s.	*ER* IV.443 P.
43	1427	Aberdeen	2.59s./2.18s.	*ER* IV.443 P.
44	1433	Aberdeen	2.67s. bouk	Kennedy, *Annals of Aberdeen*, p.10 assize V.?
45	1436	Kintyre etc.	2.36./2s.	*ER* V.9 V.
46	1443	Aberdeen	4.5s.	*ER* V.155–6 P.
47	1444	Aberdeen	2s. 8d. bouk	Spalding Club 12.11 assize V.
48	1450	Mar	3.5s.	*ER* V.464 V.
49	1455	Mar	4s.	*ER* VI.438 V.

Table 37 (*cont.*)

No.	Year	Place	Unit price	Source
50	1456	Strathearn	3.6s.	*ER* VI.358 P.
51	1456	Mar	4.33s.	*ER* VI.363 P.
52	1456	Elgin etc.	12d. wether	*ER* VI.482 V.
53	1457	Elgin etc.	12d. wether	*ER* VI.469–70 V.
54	1458	Elgin etc.	12d.	*ER* VI.516 V.
55	1459	Elgin etc.	12d.	*ER* VI.651 V.
56	1460	Elgin etc.	12d.	*ER* VII.18 V.
57	1461	Elgin etc.	12d.	*ER* VII.125 V.
58	1462	Elgin etc.	12d.	*ER* VII.237 V.
59	1464	Elgin etc.	12d.	*ER* VII.356 V.
60	1465	Elgin etc.	12d.	*ER* VII.413 V.
61	1466	Mar & Garioch	5.83s./5s.	*ER* VII.463 V.
62	1466	Elgin etc.	12d.	*ER* VII.448 V.
63	1467	Elgin etc.	12d.	*ER* VII.541 V.
64	1467	Ettrick	12d. lamb	*ER* VII.528–9
65	1468	Aberdeen	1.6s.	ACR V i.626 Aw.
66	1468	Ettrick	12d. lamb	*ER* VII.623 V.
67	1468	Elgin etc.	12d.	*ER* VII.636 V.
68	1470	Elgin etc.	12d.	*ER* VIII.82–4 V.
69	1471	Ettrick	12d. lamb	*ER* VIII.101 V.
70	1474		4s. ewe	*ALA* I.34 Aw.
71	1476	Aberdeen	2.9s. ewe	ACR VI.428 Aw.
72	1476	Glenscherop	3.51s.	*ALA* I.46 C.
73	1476	Ross	8d.	*ER* VIII.597 V.
74	1478	Rachich	3s.	*ALC* I.18 Aw.
75	1479	Newmekill	8d.	*ER* IX.59 V.
76	1479	Ross	16d.	*ER* IX.60
77	1479	Ross	2s.	*ER* IX.61
78	1479	Corswod	4s. ewe	*ALA* I.81–2 Aw.
79	1479		3.33s.	*ALC* I.35 Aw.
80	1479		2s. hog	*ALC* I.35 Aw.
81	1479		3s. 4d. ewe	*ALC* I.35 Aw.
82	1479	Hallishawis	4s. milk ewe	*ALC* I.37 Aw.
83	1479	Berwickshire	30d. gimmer/dinmont	*ALC* I.46 Aw.
84	1479	Berwickshire	12d. lamb	*ALC* I.46 Aw.
85	1479	Ettrick	12d.	*ER* IX.30–1
86	1480	Menteith	2s.	*ER* IX.115–16
87	1480		4s. 6d./3s. 6d. old	*ALC* I.54 C./Aw.
88	1480	Twa Penek	2s. 6d. wether	*ALC* I.58 Aw.
89	1482	Conred	5s.	*ALA* I.99 C.
90	1483	Wauchtoun'	6s. 8d. ewe/wether	*ALC* I.166 Aw.
91	1483	Glennessil	5s. ewe	*ALC* I.*83 Aw.
92	1483	Keth'	6s. 8d. wether/ewe	*ALA* I.*117 Aw.
93	1483	Keth'	3s. 4d. hog	*ALA* I.*117 Aw.
94	1483	Litil Prest.	6s. 8d. ewe	*ALA* I.*118 Aw.
95	1483	Nether Keth	3s. 4d. hog	*ALA* I.*118 Aw.

Table 37 (*cont.*)

No.	Year	Place	Unit price	Source
96	1483	Litil Prest.	4s. hog	*ALA* I.*118 Aw.
97	1483	Torcrake	40d. hog	*ALA* I.*118 Aw.
98	1483	Nether Keth	6s. 8d. ewe	*ALA* I.*118 Aw.
99	1483	Nether Keth	6s. 8d. wether	*ALA* I.*118 Aw.
100	1483	Torcrake	6s. 8d. wheter/ewe	*ALA* I.*118 Aw.
101	1483	Lile	4s. wether	*ALA* I.*123 Aw.
102	1483	Lile	33d. gimmer/dinmont	*ALA* I.*123 Aw.
103	1483	Lile	4s. ewe	*ALA* I.*123 Aw.
104	1484	Aberdeen	10d.qr/40d.the bouke	ACR VI.824 assize V.
105	1484	Moray	1s.	*ER* IX.316 V.
106	1484	Inglistoun	4s.	*ALA* I.*131 Aw.
107	1484	Haltre & Brok.	3s. 4d. hog	*ALA* I.*137 Aw.
108	1484		7s. ewe/wether	*ALA* I.*136 Aw.
109	1484	Haltre & Brok.	6s. 8d. ewe/wether	*ALA* I.*137 Aw.
110	1484	Haltre & Brok.	3s. 4d. hog	*ALA* I.*137 Aw.
111	1484	Haltre & Brok.	6s. 8d. ewe/wether	*ALA* I.*137 Aw.
112	1484	Haltre & Brok.	6s. 8d. ewe	*ALA* I.*137 Aw.
113	1484	Haltre & Brok.	6s. 8d. ewe/wether	*ALA* I.*137 Aw.
114	1484	Haltre & Brok.	3s. 4d. hog	*ALA* I.*137 Aw.
115	1484	Tynyngam & Dun	7s. ewe + lamb	*ALA* I.*137 Aw.
116	1484	Tynyngam & Dun	7s. wether, old	*ALA* I.*137 Aw.
117	1484	Westergagy	5s.	*ALC* I.*85 Aw.
118	1484	Quhittingam	5s. old	*ALC* I.*90 Aw.
119	1484	Quhittingam	16d. lamb, carcase?	*ALC* I.*90 Aw.
120	1487	Elgin etc.	12d.	*ER* X.37 V.
121	1487	Ettrick	1.16s. lamb	*ER* X.13
122	1487	Ettrick	12d. lamb	*ER* X.97 V.
123	1488	Balgoner	6s. 8d. sheep + lamb	*ALA* I.115 Aw.
124	1488	Balgoner	5s.	*ALA* I.115 Aw.
125	1488	Estir Beltj	4s. wether	*ALC* I.90 Aw.
126	1488	Estir Beltj	2s. lamb	*ALC* I.90 Aw.
127	1488		6s. 8d. wether	*ALA* I.153 Aw.
128	1488	Glencarn	3s. ewe/gimmer/dinmot	*ALA* I.179 Aw.
129	1489	Ballaly	5s.	*ALA* I.122 C.
130	1489	Crivy	6s. 8d. wether	*ALC* I.106 Aw.
131	1489	Brigland'	20d. lamb	*ALC* I.114 Aw.
132	1489	Kirkpatrik	21. 6d./18d. lamb	*ALA* I.130–1 C.
133	1489	Crivy	2s. hog	*ALC* I.106 Aw.
134	1489	Balcarhous	5s. old, with wool	*ALC* I.113 Aw.
135	1489	Brigland'	4s.	*ALC* I.114 Aw.
136	1489	Crivy	5s. ewe	*ALC* I.106 Aw.
137	1489	Lekraw	6s. 8d.	*ALC* I.106 Aw.
138	1489	Morinche	40d. wether	*ALA* I.156 Aw.
139	1490	Lekraw	6s. 8d.	*ALC* I.132 Aw.

Table 37 (*cont.*)

No.	Year	Place	Unit price	Source
140	1490		4s.	*ALC* I.145 Aw.
141	1490	Glengelt	5s. ewe	*ALC* I.155 Aw.
142	1490	Glengelt	5s. wether	*ALC* I.155 Aw.
143	1490	Glengelt	3s. hog	*ALC* I.155 Aw.
144	1490	Delgatie castle	4s. ewe	*ALC* I.289 Aw.
145	1490	Delgatie castle	4s. wether	*ALC* I.289 Aw.
146	1490	Essilmont	3s. ewe	*ALA* I.183 Aw.
147	1491	Raith/Bawb't	5s. ewe	*ALC* I.172 Aw.
148	1491	Raith/Bawb't	4s. old	*ALC* I.172 Aw.
149	1491	Raith/Bawb't	2s. 6d. hog	*ALC* I.172 Aw.
150	1491	Brigland	3s.	*ALC* I.177 C.
151	1491	Peeblesshire	5.26s. ewe + lamb/hog	*ALA* I.148 C.
152	1491	Glennegas?	6s.	*ALA* I.148 Aw.
153	1491	Edinburgh	6s. 8d. wether/ewe	*ALA* I.157 C.
154	1491	Cromarty	2s.	*ALC* I.273 Aw.
155	1492	Clydesdale	6s. 8d. wether	*ALC* I.207 C.
156	1492	Balbegy	16d. lamb	*ALC* I.231 Wi.
157	1492	Kirkcudbrigh.	6s. wether/ewe	*ALC* I.232 Aw.
158	1492	Petlour etc.	2s. hog	*ALC* I.212 C.
159	1492		2s. 6d. gimmer/dinmont	*ALC* I.221 Aw.
160	1492	Balbegy	40d. ewe	*ALC* I.231 Wi.
161	1492	Petlour etc.	5s.	*ALC* I.212 C.
162	1492		4s. 6d. wether/ewe	*ALC* I.221 Aw.
163	1492	Kynnard	4s. ewe	*ALC* I.401 Aw.
164	1492	Kynnard	2s. hog	*ALC* I.401 Aw.
165	1493	Kirkcudbrig.?	6s. 8d. wether	*ALC* I.278 Aw.
166	1493	Petscotty	5s. ewe	*ALC* I.280 Aw.
167	1493	Petscotty	5s. wether	*ALC* I.280 Aw.
168	1493	Petscotty	30d. hog	*ALC* I.280 Aw.
169	1493		5s. ewe	*ALC* I.288 Wi.
170	1493	Petlour	4s.	*ALC* I.296 Aw.
171	1493	Petscotty	4s. 6d. wether	*ALC* I.280 Aw.
172	1493	Petlour	30d. hog	*ALC* I.296 Aw.
173	1493	Petscotty	4s. 2d. ewe	*ALC* I.280 Aw.
174	1493	Abircorn'	4s. old	*ALA* I.183 Aw.
175	1493	Petscotty	30d. hog	*ALC* I.280 Aw.
176	1493	Abircorn'	30d. hog	*ALA* I.183 Aw.
177	1493	Petscotty	4s. 6d. wether	*ALC* I.280 Aw.
178	1493	Delgatie castle	40d. lambs now 3 years	*ALC* I.289 Aw.
179	1493	Petscotty	30d. hog	*ALC* I.280 Aw.
180	1493	Delgatie castle	3s. lambs now 2 years	*ALC* I.289 Aw.
181	1493	Petscotty	4s. 2d. ewe	*ALC* I.280 Aw.
182	1493	Delgatie castle	18d. hog	*ALC* I.289 Aw.
183	1493	Petscotty	4s. 6d. wether	*ALC* I.280 Aw.
184	1493	Petscotty	4s. 2d. ewe	*ALC* I.280 Aw.
185	1493	Ouer Cullane	4s.	*ALC* I.282 Aw.

Table 37 (*cont.*)

No.	Year	Place	Unit price	Source
186	1493	Petscotty	30d. hog	*ALC* I.280 Aw.
187	1493	Petscotty	4s. 2d. ewe	*ALC* I.280 Aw.
188	1494	Kynlyn	2s. sheep and goats	*ALC* I.327 Aw.
189	1494	Ard'	40d. old	*ALC* I.333 Aw.
190	1494	Ard'	18d. lamb	*ALC* I.333 Aw.
191	1494	Peebles	5s. ewe/wether	*ALC* I.357 Aw.
192	1494	Peebles	5s. ewe/wether	*ALC* I.357 Aw.
193	1494	Dumfries	5s. 6d. ewe/wether	*ALC* I.358 C.
194	1494	Dumfries	4s. 6d. gimmer/dinmont	*ALC* I.358 C.
195	1494		4s. 6d.	*ALC* I.372 Aw.
196	1494	Lochinnall	4s.	*ALA* I.193–4 Aw.
197	1494	Renfrewshire	4d. lamb	*ALA* I.192 ancient V.
198	1494	EsterFernway	2s. sheep/goat	*ALA* I.206 Aw.
199	1495		5s. ewe/wether	*ALC* I.403 Aw.
200	1495		3s. hog	*ALC* I.403 Aw.
201	1495	Brakynsid	4s. ewe/wether	*ALC* I.412 Aw.
202	1495	Ettrick	12d. lamb	*ER* XI.9 V.
203	1496	Elgin & Forres	12d.	*ER* XI.14 V.
204	1497	Ayr	2s. 10d.	*TA* I.344 P.
205	1497	Elgin & Forres	12d.	*ER* XI.84 V.
206	1497	Ettrick	4.81s.	*ER* XI.99 V.
207	1498	Moray	4s.	*ER* XI.84 V.
208	1498	Tynnes	5.42s.	*ER* XI.206 P.
209	1499	Kilmarnock	3s.	*ER* XI.361 V.
210	1499	Dunbar	34.29d./30d.ewe with lamb	*ER* XI.299 P.
211	1500	Balnagask	5s. wether	ACR VII.1046 Wi.
212	1501	Kilmarnock	3s.	*ER* XII.22 V.
213	1501	Elgin & Forres	12d.	*ER* XII.53 V.
214	1501	Garlacleuch	5s. 6d. unshorn	*ER* XII.34 P.
215	1501	Lupno	3s. wether	*ER* XII.73 V.
216	1501	Lupno	2s. 2d. gimmer/dinmont	*ER* XII.74 V.
217	1503	Ross	8d.	*ER* XII.239 V.
218	1503	Ettrick	4s. 6d.	*ER* XII.204 P.
219	1504	Ardmannoch	12d.	*ER* XII.307 V.
220	1505	Petty & Brauch	12d.	*ER* XII.416–17 V.
221	1505	Ardmannoch	2s.	*ER* XII.453 V.
222	1505	S.Kintyre	2s.	*ER* XII.586
223	1505	N.Kintyre	2s.	*ER* XII.586
224	1505	Dunkeld	40d. wether	SHS 2,10.60
225	1505	Lupno	4s. 6d. ewe with lamb	*ER* XII.74 V.
226	1506	Ferische	8d.	*ER* XII.550 V.
227	1506	Dunkeld	40d. wether	SHS 2,10.62
228	1506	Stirling	1s. 2d. lamb	*ER* XII.540 P.
229	1506	Ferische	8d.	*ER* XII.550 V.
230	1507	Aberdeen	32d. bouk	ACR VIII.708 assize V.
231	1507	Elgin & Forres	12d.	*ER* XIII.12 V.

Table 37 (*cont.*)

No.	Year	Place	Unit price	Source
232	1507	Ferische	8d.	*ER* XIII.45 V.
233	1507	Ardmannoch	12d.	*ER* XIII.49 V.
234	1507	Elgin	3s.	*ER* XIII.12 V.
235	1508	Mekill Strath	3s.	*ER* XIII.195
236	1508	Stirling	2s. lamb	*ER* XIII.248 P.
237	1508	Dunkeld & Clon	40d. wether	SHS 2,10.65
238	1508	Dunkeld & Clon	40d.	SHS 2,10.65
239	1508	Aberdeen	32d. best bouk	ACR VIII.854 assize V.
240	1509	Dunkeld	40d. wether	SHS 2,10.34 V.
241	1509	Auchtertool	40d. wether	SHS 2,10.268
242	1509	Dunkeld	40d. wether	SHS 2,10.66
243	1509	Kynnacrag	8d.	*ER* XIII.347 V.
244	1510	Dunkeld	3.33s. wether	SHS 2,10.69
245	1510	St Serf	46.48d. wether	SHS 2,10.175 P.
246	1510	Dunkeld	2.37s./2.05s. gimmer/dinmont	SHS 2,10.68 P.
247	1510	Clony	32.48d. gimmer/dinmont	SHS 2,10.175 P.
248	1511	Dunkeld	3.33s. wether	SHS 2,10.70
249	1511	Clony	27.13d. various	SHS 2,10.179 P.
250	1511	Moray	3s.	*ER* XIII.459 V.
251	1512	Dunkeld	3.33s. wether	SHS 2,10.71
252	1512	Clony	30d. various	SHS 2,10.180 P.
253	1513	Forth	2s. 10d.	*TA* IV.464 P.
254	1513	Forth	3s. R.	*TA* IV.464,etc. P.
255	1513	Forth	3s.4d. R.	*TA* IV.464,469 P.
256	1513	Dunkeld	2.24s.	SHS 2,10.142–3 P.
257	1513	Ardmannoch	12d.	*ER* XIV.89 V.
258	1513	Dunkeld	40d. wether	SHS 2,10.43
259	1513	Dunkeld	3.33s. wether	SHS 2,10.141
260	1513	Forth	4s. conflated	*TA* IV.486,501 P.
261	1515	Inchegarvy	2s. lamb	*TA* V.21 P.
262	1515	Ferisch	8d.	*ER* XIV.143 V.
263	1515		4s. bouk	*TA* V.21 P.
264	1516	Cupar,Fife	4s.	*SCBF*, p. 51 Aw.
265	1516	Aberdeen	40d. bouk	ACR IX.574 assize V.
266	1517	Cupar,Fife	10s. ewe	*SCBF*, p. 69 Aw.
267	1517	Cupar,Fife	20d. hog	*SCBF*, p. 69 Aw.
268	1518		9s.	*TA* V.163 P.
269	1521	Ferisch	8d.	*ER* XV.23 V.
270	1521	Ross	2s.	*ER* XV.24
271	1521	Ardmannoch	12d.	*ER* XV.27 V.
272	1522	Cupar,Fife	6s. 8d. ram	*SCBF*, p. 262 Aw.
273	1522	Cupar,Fife	8s. ewe with lamb	*SCBF*, p. 262 Aw.
274	1522	Cupar,Fife	3s. hog	*SCBF*, p. 262 Aw.
275	1522	Cupar,Fife	6s. wether with wool	*SCBF*, p. 267 Aw.
276	1522	Cupar,Fife	4s. dinmont with wool	*SCBF*, p. 267 Aw.

Table 37 (*cont.*)

No.	Year	Place	Unit price	Source
277	1522	Cupar,Fife	4s. gimmer with wool	*SCBF*, p. 267 Aw.
278	1522	Aberdeen	3.33s.	ACR XI.137 C.
279	1522	Cupar,Fife	6s.8d. wether	*SCBF*, p. 262 Aw.
280	1523	Aberdeen	36d. best bouk	ACR XI.300 assize V.
281	1523	Edinburgh	5s.	*ALCPA*, p. 184 P.
282	1523	Aberdeen	20d. lamb best bouk	ACR XI.300 assize V.
283	1524	Aberdeen	40d. bouk	ACR XI.458 assize V.
284	1524	Kincrag	8d.	*ER* XV.170 V.
285	1524	Ross	2s.	*ER* XV.171–2.
286	1525	Aberdeen	32d. and 28d. lamb	ACR XI.589–90 Wi.
287	1525	Aberdeen	2s. best lamb bouk	ACR XI.590 assize V.
288	1525	Peebles	62d. conflated	HBJV, pp. 3,5 P.
289	1525		56d. conflated	HBJV, pp. 6–7,11–14 P.
290	1525	Edinburgh	58d.	HBJV, p. 6 P.
291	1525	Stirling	42d.	HBJV, p. 16 P.
292	1525	Edinburgh	57.1d.	HBJV, p. 10 P.
293	1525		3s. lamb conflated	HBJV, pp. 5,9, App., p. 3 P.
294	1525	Stirling	43.2d.	HBJV, p. 15 P.
295	1525		60d.	HBJV, p. 9 P.
296	1525	Edinburgh	52d.	HBJV, p. 17 P.
297	1525	Aberdeen	40d. best bouk	ACR XI.645 assize V.
298	1525		60d.	HBJV, App., p. 5 P.
299	1525	Edinburgh	64d.	HBJV, p. 18 P.
300	1525	Edinburgh	64d.	HBJV, p. 20 P.
301	1525	Aberdeen	4s. best bouk	ACR XI.590 assize V.
302	1526	Edinburgh	72d.	HBJV, p. 64 P.
303	1526		3s. lamb conflated	HBJV, pp. 57–61, 63–4 P.
304	1526		68d.	HBJV, App., p. 8 P.
305	1526	Edinburgh?	64d.	HBJV, p. 22 P.
306	1526	Aberdeen	4s. wether	ACR XI.689 Aw.
307	1526	Edinburgh?	96d. conflated	HBJV, pp. 58–60 P.
308	1526	Stirling?	90d.	HBJV, p. 61 P.
309	1526	Edinburgh?	84d.	HBJV, p. 63 P.
310	1526	Linlithgow	84d.	HBJV, App., p. 7 P.
311	1526	Edinburgh	79.2d.	HBJV, p. 25 P.
312	1526	Stirling	67.2d.	HBJV, p. 57 P.
313	1528		56d. conflated	HBJV, pp. 116 etc. P.
314	1528	Edinburgh	64d. conflated	HBJV, pp. 119,127–8 P.
315	1528	Edinburgh	69d.	HBJV, p. 123 P.
316	1528	Linlithgow	68.2d.	HBJV, p. 129 P.
317	1528	Edinburgh	68d.	HBJV, p. 130 P.
318	1528	Edinburgh	81.6d./67.2d.	HBJV, p. 132 P.
319	1528	Falkland?	3s.	HBJV, App., p. 14 P.
320	1528		60d. conflated	HBJV, pp. 115, etc. P.
321	1529	Edinburgh	68.5d.	HBJV, p. 133 P.

Table 37 (*cont.*)

No.	Year	Place	Unit price	Source
322	1529	Stirling	66d.	HBJV, p. 134 P.
323	1529	Linlithgow	66d.	HBJV, p. 134 P.
324	1529	Edinburgh	102d.	HBJV, p. 148 P.
325	1529	Stirling	90d.	HBJV, p. 153 P.
326	1529	Edinburgh	72d.	HBJV, p. 136 P.
327	1529	Peebles	91.32d.	HBJV, p. 156 P.
328	1529	Edinburgh	84d.	HBJV, p. 137 P.
329	1529		3s. 6d. lamb conflated	HBJV, pp. 148 etc, P.
330	1529	Aberdeen	8s. wether	ACR XII ii.5 C.
331	1529		96d. conflated	HBJV, pp. 149–53,155 P.
332	1529	Edinburgh	4s. 6d. lamb	HBJV, p. 145 P.
333	1529	Linlithgow	80d.	HBJV, p. 136 P.
334	1529	Edinburgh	79.2d.	HBJV, p. 138 P.
335	1529	Edinburgh	117d.	HBJV, p. 145 P.
336	1529	Edinburgh	84d.	HBJV, p. 135 P.
337	1529		64d. conflated	HBJV, pp. 160 etc, P.
338	1529	Edinburgh	6s.8d.	*ALCPA*, p. 476 C.
339	1529	Fyschrie	8d.	*ER* XVI.110 V.
340	1529	Kincrag	8d.	*ER* XVI.111 V.
341	1529	Ardmannoch	12d.	*ER* XVI.116 V.
342	1529	Linlithgow	73.59d.	HBJV, p. 135 P.
343	1530	Linlithgow	72.28d.	HBJV, App., p. 28 P.
344	1530	Stirling	96d.	HBJV, p. 225 P.
345	1530	Stirling	3s. 4d. lamb	HBJV, p. 225 P.
346	1530	Glasgow	80d.	HBJV, p. 224 P.
347	1531	Aberdeen	3s. 6d.	ACR XIII.173 Wi.
348	1532	Edinburgh	61.4d.	HBJV, p. 231 P.
349	1533	Edinburgh	81.84d.	HBJV, p. 234 P.
350	1533	Edinburgh	3.45s. lamb	HBJV, p. 234 P.
351	1533	Edinburgh	3s. 3d. lamb	HBJV, p. 235 P.
352	1533	Edinburgh?	84d.	HBJV, p. 235 P.
353	1533	Fyschrie	4d.	*ER* XVI.321 V.
354	1535	Ardmannoch	12d.	*ER* XVII.37 V.
355	1536	Kincrag	8d.	*ER* XVII.33 V.
356	1536	Ross	3s.	*ER* XVII.36
357	1536	Fischerie	8d.	*ER* XVII.33 V.
358	1537	Fischerie	4d.	*ER* XVII.112 V.
359	1537	Ross	3s.	*ER* XVII.114
360	1537	Quhitecleuch	4s. young ewe	*ER* XVII.129
361	1537	Balgray	30d. lamb	*ER* XVII.129
362	1538	Ross	3s.	*ER* XVII.235
363	1538	Ardmannoch	3s.	*ER* XVII.240–1
364	1538	Aberdeen	9.33s. ewe/wether	ACR XV.561–2 C.
365	1539	Ross	3s.	*ER* XVII.335–9
366	1539	Ross	3s.	*ER* XVII.343
367	1539	Ardmannoch	3s.	*ER* XVII.344–7

Table 37 (*cont.*)

No.	Year	Place	Unit price	Source
368	1539	Monymusk	4s. wether	SHS 2,4.105
369	1539	Craufurdmur	3.53s./3.01s.	*ER* XVII.274
370	1539		2s. lamb	*ER* XVII.287 P.
371	1539		2s. lamb	*ER* XVII.288 P.
372	1539	Strathdee	12d. lamb	*ER* XVII.364 V.
373	1539	Strathdee	1s. lamb	*ER* XVII.657 V.
374	1539	Fischerie	4d.	*ER* XVII.341 V.
375	1540	Aberdeen	4s. bouk	ACR XVI.506 C.
376	1540		5.92s./5.13s. ewe	*TA* VII.383
377	1541	Aberdeen	16d. flanks	ACR XVI.735 C.
378	1541	Monymusk	4s. wether	SHS 2,4.118
379	1541	Kintyre	2s. wether	*ER* XVII.625 V.
380	1541	Craufurdjohn	4s. young ewe	*ER* XVII.571
381	1541	Craufurdjohn	3d. lamb	*ER* XVII.571
382	1541	Avandale	5s. wether	*ER* XVII.584 V.
383	1541	Avandale	5s. wether	*ER* XVII.587 V.
384	1541	Jura	2s. wether	*ER* XVII.536 V.

Hides

The hide prices collected were almost entirely for cattle hides, so the occasional horse hide encountered has been listed[141] but excluded from calculations. Ox hides, being larger, were generally dearer than cow hides[142] but mart hides are most commonly met. In the absence of evidence to the contrary mart hides may be assumed. Very dear hides, such as that bought for the king's jacket[143] or specially coloured hides[144] have been excluded from the averages, as have the larger hides bought for currocks.[145] Hides specially described as 'barkit' or tanned have also been excluded from calculations.[146] Of course, the possibility remains that hides of these excluded categories may have slipped through unrecognized where the original source gives no description.

[141] List 8, 69.
[142] List 28–9.
[143] List 49.
[144] List 41, 47.
[145] I.e. leather covered boats, with a light wooden frame, coated in tar. List 63, 68, 70, 73, 75. List 33, however, is included as our sole price between 1456 and 1478.
[146] A tanned hide seems to have been its finished state. Cleaned and salted hides were often shipped prior to final finishing. List 37, 66.

Table 38. *Hide summary table*

Period	Mean price	Deflated	Index
A	1.79	1.79	93.75
B–C	1.6	1.6	100.0
D	0.88	0.88	55.0
E	1.34	1.14	71.25
F	(1.5)		
G			
H			
I	3.13	1.03	64.4
60s	(4.5)		
70s	(4.0)		
80s	(3.98)		
90s	4.41	1.23	76.9
1500s	5.92	1.66	103.75
10s	5.36	1.34	83.75
20s	5.0	1.25	78.1
30s	5.78	1.27	79.3

Note: the mean price is in shillings each; the deflated column gives the currency-adjusted sterling price. Parentheses have been used to flag up calculations which are less securely based than others – either because they are based on a smaller amount of data, or because they involve certain, possibly questionable, assumptions.

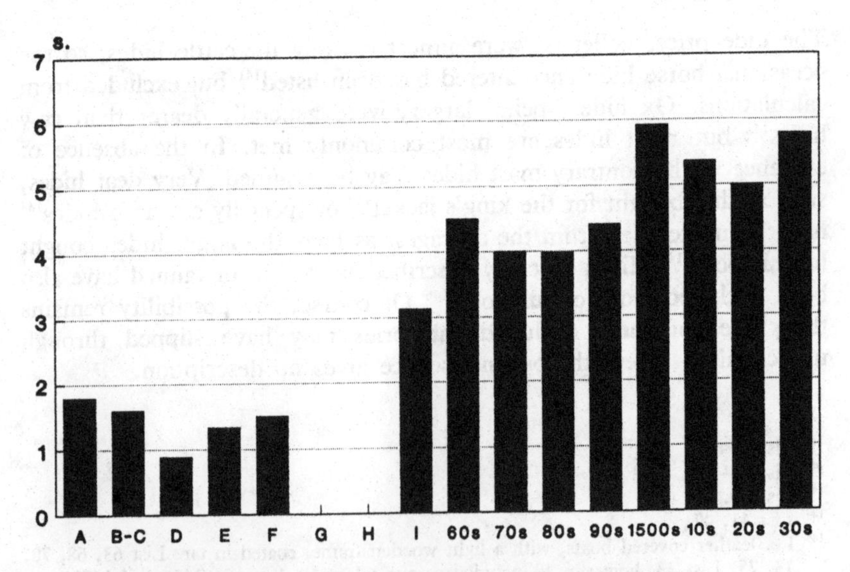

32 Hide prices (mean prices for time periods A–1530s)
For periods A–I, see Introduction, p. 6.

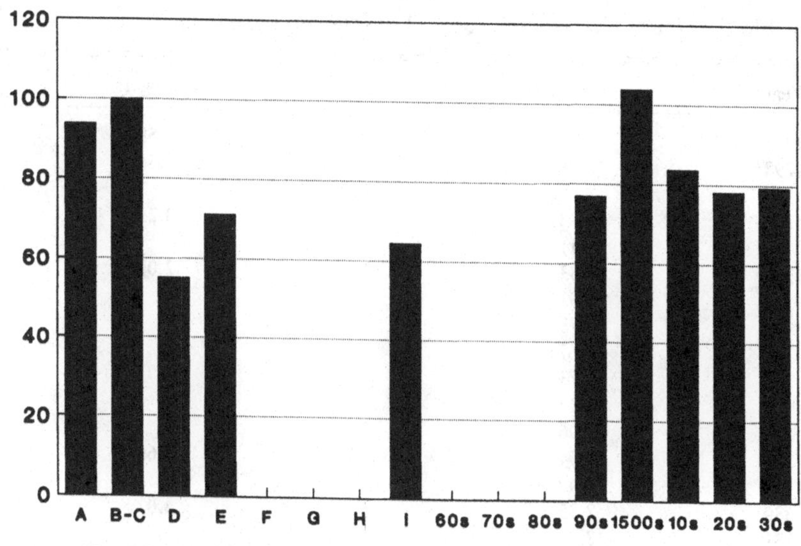

33 Hide index (sterling equivalent)

Despite such uncertainties, the hide price series presents a picture broadly in line with that of livestock generally in Scotland (see Table 38 and Figure 32). Early fourteenth-century prices show a rise over thirteenth-century levels, but after the Plague prices fell. Until 1367 we can see that Scots hides were cheaper than hides in England (Table 39), but after Scottish debasements begin the Scots price naturally rises. However, if an allowance is made for this debasement, the currency-adjusted index (Table 38 and Figure 33) shows that prices did not recover the early fourteenth-century peak till the sixteenth century. The lower prices apparent from Table 38, 1510–40, may at least in part be an effect of the widespread use of an artificially low 5s. fixed price.

Burgh regulation of hide prices was known[147] but rare, so it seems unlikely that prices were held down artificially. Indeed, any such regulation would have been especially difficult for a commodity so much sought after for exports.[148] Exported hides will also complicate the price series because of the effect of customs duty.[149] Local demand for hides

[147] List 28–9.

[148] *ER passim*. Also List 3–4, 21, 37, 42, 84, and 92.

[149] The custom on hides was first levied at a rate of 13s.4d. per last (temp. Robert I, *ER* I.xcix). Like the custom on wool and woolfells it was doubled in 1358, tripled in 1359, and finally quadrupled to 53s.4d. a last in 1368 (*ER* II.xli, lxxii). Since the last contained 200 or 240 hides, at its height the customs duty would have added 2d. or 3d. to the price of an exported hide.

Table 39. *Hide prices 1263–1367: Scotland and England*

Year	Scotland	Durham	Rogers
1263	1.5		1.58
1298	(2.08)	3.23	2.36
1302		4.25	
1304	(1.33)		3.23
	(1.1)		
1328	1.33		2.08
	2.0		
	1.73		
	(0.67)		
	1.73		
	1.24		
	2.06		
1329	1.54	2.5	2.66
	2.4		
1330	2.35		4.0
1331	2.3		
	1.64		
1335	1.25		3.17
1341	1.0		3.0
1362	1.0	1.47	2.46
1367	0.76	1.72	2.0

Note: all prices are in shillings each. Parentheses have been used to flag up calculations which are less securely based than others – either because they are based on a smaller amount of data, or because they involve certain, possibly questionable, assumptions.

is also very evident in our price series. Shoes, bellows, currocks, harness, and clothing all generated Scots demand for leather.[150]

The number of cases involving money owing for hides, whether at local or at an international level, shows that credit was an essential lubricant at all levels of the trade in hides.[151] Occasional law suits also involve questions of damage to hides[152] but the vast majority of court cases arise from the breakdown of credit arrangements which seem to have stretched from the farmer or butcher to the international merchant or local consumer and back again, in a way very much reminiscent of the English wool trade.

150 Shoes: List 71, 91, 97. Bellows: List 69.
151 List 25–6, 35–7, 39, 42–3, 71, 76, 81–4, 89–91. Cordwainers were also a particularly prominent group in the London money market: *Calendar of Letter-Books of the City of London: Letter-Book A c.1275–1298*, ed. Reginald R. Sharpe (London, 1899) passim.
152 List 31, 97.

Table 40. *Hide price list*

No.	Year	Place	Unit price	Source
1	1263	Elgin	1.5s.	*ER* I.33
2	1298	Berwick	2.08s. + offal	*DHS* II.326 P.
3	1304	Berwick	1.33s.	*CDS* II.440 V.
4	1304	Berwick	1.1s.	*CDS* II.436 V.
5	1328		1.33s.	*ER* I.201
6	1328	Stirling	2s.	*ER* I.113
7	1328	Cardross	1.73s.	*ER* I.124
8	1328	Cardross	8d. horse hide	*ER* I.124
9	1328	Berwick	1.73s.	*ER* I.184
10	1328	Berwick?	1.24s.	*ER* I.206
11	1328	Berwick?	2.06s.	*ER* I.206–7
12	1329		1.54s.	*ER* I.195
13	1329		2.40s.	*ER* I.249
14	1330		2.35s.	*ER* I.336
15	1331		2.30s.	*ER* I.396
16	1331		1.64s.	*ER* I.380
17	1335	Edinburgh	1.25s.	*CDS* III.343
18	1341		1s.	*ER* I.503
19	1362		1s.	*ER* II.183
20	1367		0.76s.	*ER* II.294
21	1368	Edinburgh	1.5s.	*ER* II.304
22	1374		1.50s.	*ER* II.453
23	1390		1.03s.	*ER* III.242
24	1392	N.of Forth	1.33s.	*ER* III.318
25	1401	Aberdeen	1.5s.	ACR I.211 Wi.
26	1446	Aberdeen	3.6s.	ACR IV.427 Aw.
27	1449		2s.	*ER* V.395
28	1450	Aberdeen	3s. ox hide	ACR V ii.757 assize V.
29	1450	Aberdeen	2s. cow hide	ACR V ii.757 assize V.
30	deleted			
31	1453	Aberdeen	3s.	ACR V i.188 Aw.
32	1456	Aberdeen	1.62s.	*ER* VI.360
33	1468	Linlithgow	4.5s.	*ER* VII.630
34	1478		4s.	*ALC* I.18 Aw.
35	1482	Aberdeen	3s.	ACR VI.745 Aw.
36	1484	Quhittingam	4s. nolt hide	*ALC* I.*90 Aw.
37	1485		5s. 7d. salted hides	*ALC* I.*104 Aw.
38	1487	Aberdeen	3.33s.	ACR VII.27 Aw.
39	1490	Aberdeensh.?	6s. 8d.	*ALA* I.132–3 Aw.
40	1491		3.33s.	*ER* X.375
41	1492		6s. red hides	*ALC* I.228 Aw.
42	1492	Aberdeen	5s.g.'licht money'	ACR VII.358 C.
43	1493	Aberdeen	4s. 6d.	ACR VII.386 Aw.
44	1495		4.65s.	SHS 3,50.65
45	1496		9.1s. barkit	*TA* I.283 P.
46	1496		6s. barkit	*TA* I.290 P.

Table 40 (*cont.*)

No.	Year	Place	Unit price	Source
47	1496		16s. white	*TA* I.293 P.
48	1496		4s.	SHS 3,50.71
49	1497		40s. for king's jacket	*TA* I.310 P.
50	1497	Orkney & Shetl.	4.5s.	*ER* XI.80 P.
51	1498		4s.	*ER* XI.254
52	1499	Fife	4s.	*ER* XI.245
53	1499		4s.	*ER* XI.254
54	1502		5s.	*ER* XII.180
55	1504		6s.	*TA* II.286 P.
56	1506		6s.	*TA* III.89 P.
57	1506		£5 great barkit hides	*TA* III.264 P.
58	1506	Dunkeld	6s. ox hides	SHS 2,10.62
59	1507	Montrose	6s.	*ER* XIII.107
60	1507		7s.	*ER* XIII.125
61	1508	Dunkeld	5s.	SHS 2,10.65 P.
62	1508	Dunkeld & Clo.	5s.	SHS 2,10.65
63	1508	Dunkeld	8s.	SHS 2,10.66 V.
64	1508		7s.	*ER* XIII.118
65	1508		7s.	*ER* XIII.253–4
66	1509	Dunkeld	6s. salted	SHS 2,10.3–4
67	1509	Dunkeld	5s.	SHS 2,10.6
68	1509	Dunkeld	10s. 4d.	SHS 2,10.110 P.
69	1510	Dunkeld	5s. horse hide	SHS 2,10.117 P.
70	1510	Dunkeld	8s. ox hide	SHS 2,10.117 P.
71	1513	Aberdeen	6s.	ACR IX.213 O.
72	1513		6s.	*TA* IV.529 P.
73	1513	Dunkeld	10s. ox hide	SHS 2,10.133 P.
74	1513	Dunkeld	4.5s. ox hide	SHS 2,10.72
75	1513	Dunkeld	10s. ox hide	SHS 2,10.142 P.
76	1515	Aberdeen	6.4s.	ACR IX.473 O.
77	1515		5s.	*ER* XIV.118 V.
78	1515	Ross	5s.	*ER* XIV.217
79	1516		5s.	*ER* XIV.284
80	1517		5s.	*ER* XIV.347
81	1521	Aberdeen	? 5s.	ACR X.271 O.
82	1522	Aberdeen	5s.	ACR XI.24–5 Wi.
83	1522	Aberdeen	5s.	ACR XI.216 Aw.
84	1523	Aberdeen	6 crowns per dicker	ACR XI.258
85	1523		5s.	*ER* XV.87
86	1524		5s.	*ER* XV.197
87	1526		5s.	*ER* XV.377–8
88	1530		5s.	*ER* XVI.131
89	1532	Aberdeen	1 crown (= 10s.) hide	ACR XIII.419 Aw.
90	1532	Aberdeen	8s.	ACR XIII.419 Aw.
91	1532	Aberdeen	6s.	ACR XIII.419 Aw.
92	1533	Aberdeen	7s. 4d.	ACR XIV.154 Aw.

Table 40 (*cont.*)

No.	Year	Place	Unit price	Source
93	1535		5s.	*ER* XVI.480 K P.
94	1535		5s.	*ER* XVI.480 K V.
95	1537	Coule	5s.	*ER* XVII.161
96	1537		5s.	*ER* XVII.170 P.
97	1538	Aberdeen	7s.	ACR XV.624 Aw.
98	1539	Cowell	5s.	*ER* XVII.275

Wool

The wool price series is extremely disappointing for such an important commodity. We have no thirteenth-century data, though the Dunwich valuations of Scottish wool in 1242 should be noted.[153] The evidence for the first half of the fourteenth century is reasonable, but thereafter the fixed price for wool collected in connection with David II's ransom obscures the picture.[154] Again, in the fifteenth century the evidence from 1450 to 1489 is extremely scarce and probably somewhat unreliable, since the Aberdeen fixed price of 5s. a stone at this time looks low, while the 1482 black money price is obviously atypical. A further problem affecting interpretation of the series as a whole arises from the incidence of prices per sack which predominate at the beginning of the period, and prices per stone which take over from the beginning of the fifteenth century. Sack prices may reflect a greater export orientation of the trade; stone prices may indicate more domestic trading. In Table 41 mean prices are quoted per stone, converted on the basis of 24 stones to the sack,[155] but sack and stone prices may not be properly comparable if bulk purchase attracted a discount or if sack prices included customs duty paid.[156]

Wool, of course, was a commodity of variable quality, the product

[153] 40s. per sack, *CDS* I, no. 1594, p. 291.

[154] The Scone council of November 1357 empowered the king to requisition wool at cost price, and use the profit on its sale to pay the ransom. He usually seized wool at 66s.8d. a sack, though council had suggested 53s.4d. *ER* II.xxxviii–xxxix, and Nicholson, *Scotland: The Later Middle Ages*, pp. 164–5.

[155] See the Glossary under sack.

[156] As noted above, wine retail and wholesale prices were clearly not comparable, but for most other commodities burgh authorities tried to discourage a retail mark-up in an attempt to protect the interest of the small consumer. Customs duties may also have affected some hide and salmon prices.

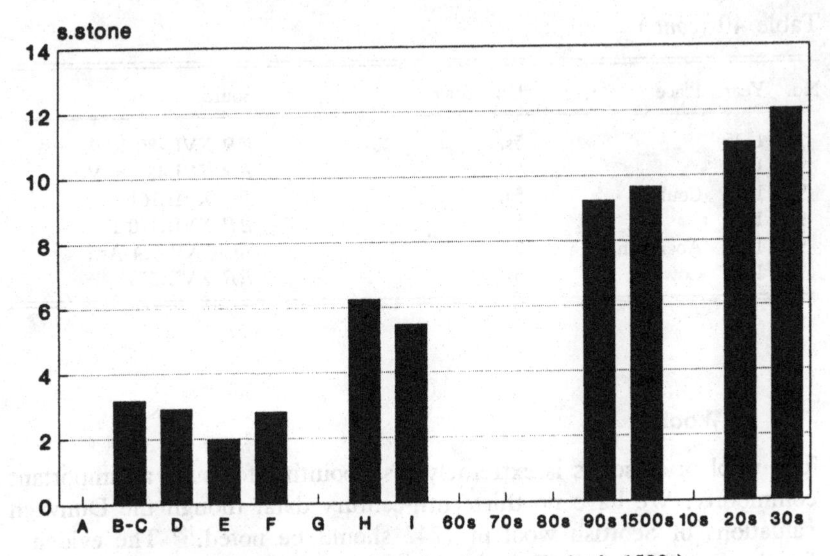

34 Wool prices (mean prices for time periods A–1530s)
For periods A–I, see Introduction, p. 6.

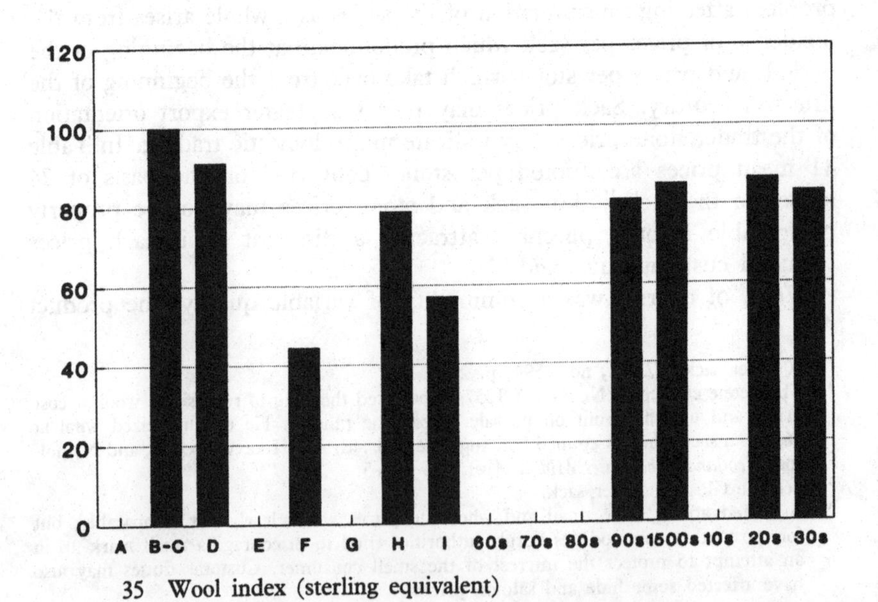

35 Wool index (sterling equivalent)

Table 41. *Wool summary table*

Period	Mean price	Deflated	Index
A			
B–C	3.18	3.18	100.0
D	2.9	2.9	91.2
E	(1.98)		
F	2.81	1.41	44.3
G			
H	6.25	2.5	78.6
I	5.47	1.81	56.9
90s	9.24	2.59	81.4
1500s	9.66	2.71	85.2
20s	11.0	2.75	86.5
30s	12.03	2.65	83.3

Note: the mean price is in shillings per stone; the deflated column gives the currency-adjusted sterling equivalent price. Parentheses have been used to flag up calculations which are less securely based than others – either because they are based on a smaller amount of data, or because they involve certain, possibly questionable, assumptions.

of certain regions being much more highly prized than that of others.[157] This consideration largely vitiates the Anglo-Scottish comparison (Table 42) which shows Scots wool was generally cheaper than English, since the Scots product was usually found to be of poorer quality.[158] In addition to the variable quality of the wool of different regions, the Aberdeen authorities seem also to have taken account of the status of the wool growers, permitting a higher price for the wool of lords and free tenants.[159] It seems doubtful whether this policy was in reality operable.

[157] For differential pricing of wools of Mar, Buchan, and Garioch, see List 36–9, 41–2, 50–3. Thus Robert Egew, chaplain to Lord Sinclair, observed in 1511, 'It will gif ilk stane vij. schillingis and that is ane gud price for Buchane woll considering the ter that is in it' (*Illustrations of the Topography and Antiquities of the Shires of Aberdeen and Banff*, p. 107). This price was discovered too late for inclusion in the list and table of calculated mean prices.

[158] Duncan, *Scotland: The Making of the Kingdom*, p. 430, tabulates Pegolotti's prices of wool of different qualities sold from Scottish religious houses into Flanders. These can be usefully compared with the prices for English wool, tabulated by T.H. Lloyd, *The Movement of Wool Prices in Medieval England (EcHR* Supplement, no. 6, 1973), pp. 52–61. See also James Campbell, 'England, Scotland and the Hundred Years' War in the Fourteenth Century', in J.R. Hale, J.R.L. Highfield, and B. Smalley (eds.), *Europe in the Late Middle Ages* (London and Evanston, 1965), pp. 184–216, especially at pp. 204–5 for English wool exported to and through Scotland. Such considerations suggest that the origin of wool is not always evident.

[159] List 36, 38.

Table 42. *Wool prices 1304–67: Scotland and England*

Year	Scotland	Durham	Rogers	Lloyd
1304	80.0		123.24	106.34
	(60.0)			
1327	(80.0)		138.84	136.24
1328	93.33	85.59	133.88	125.84
1329	(80.0)	80.0	95.16	115.7
	(80.0)			
1342	72.0	79.95	84.76	96.46
1344	73.33	83.41	99.84	100.62
	80.0			
1345	80.0		102.96	94.38
1346	70.0		89.96	102.7
1347	66.0	61.93	98.28	94.12
1357	(66.67)	71.23	95.16	83.46
	(66.67)			
1358	(69.04)	65.91	89.96	85.8
	(66.65)			
	(66.67)			
	(71.67)			
	(66.67)			
	(66.67)			
1359	(66.67)	83.06	96.2	67.86
	(66.67)			
	(56.56)			
	(66.67)			
1362	(66.67)	65.73	94.12	88.66
	(66.67)			
1363	64.0	82.5	88.92	77.74
1364	65.0		117.0	80.34
1365	63.33	66.74	120.12	104.78
1366	72.0	80.74	130.0	105.04
1367	84.0	79.23	151.84	120.38

Note: all prices are in shillings per sack. We have converted Rogers' prices which are given in shillings per clove of 7 pounds to sacks assuming 2 cloves per *petra* and 26 *petre* to the English sack. Lloyd's figures, which are given in shillings per petra, have been similarly converted. Most of the Durham prices are for sacks and have not required conversion, but where conversion had proved necessary we have again assumed that there were 26 *petre* to the sack. Parentheses have been used to flag up calculations which are less securely based than others – either because they are based on a smaller amount of data, or because they involve certain, possibly questionable, assumptions.

Despite the inadequacies of the wool price evidence it does throw some light on other questions. Royal finances were obviously intimately involved with the wool trade. This was most true for David II, but wool was also involved in the arrangements for James I's 'Financia', and was also used to settle at least one royal debt in 1495.[160] This royal involvement in the wool trade arose largely because wool's role as an export product made it more easily convertible into ready money than most domestic products.[161] Indeed the crown's attempt to tap this source of ready money was merely typical of mercantile life in Scotland generally. Wool was inextricably involved with debts and their settlement throughout Scots society. Wool was often handed over in settlement of a debt of money or other goods.[162] On other occasions wool was owed but not supplied. Since many deals were initially agreed without goods or cash changing hands, wool was sometimes withheld because payment had not been forthcoming. In such circumstances it is often unclear whether cash or other goods had been advanced against wool or vice versa. The picture can be further complicated by intermediaries, carriers, factors, or sureties, who may have exploited their position or failed to meet their responsibilities. However, whatever the complexities of the picture, the importance of the role of wool in international trade and royal and merchant debt is clear.[163]

Towards the end of our period the survival of Halyburton's Ledger provides much interesting information on Scottish wool exports which went chiefly to Middleburg (especially from Edinburgh) and Veere (especially from Aberdeen). The best wool was then sold on to Bruges merchants, but there was also a ready demand for poorer wools and fells, particularly at times when the heavy draperies were experiencing difficulties. In the early sixteenth century Scots wool exports were thus quite buoyant, though competition from Baltic wools posed a growing threat, particularly when currency devaluation in the Baltic improved the competitiveness of Ostland wool.[164]

Nevertheless, the domestic trade remained subject to the conventional rules of burgh price setting and the punishment of traders forestalling, or breaking price.[165] These sort of controls may have influenced the domestic price. Equally, domestic and the international price will have

[160] List 13–26, 43, 80.
[161] For wool as an export see List 1–3, 5–6, 47–8, 57, 63, 73, 94–6.
[162] List 49, 54, 95, 96, 107.
[163] List 33, 46–7, 49, 54, 56, 58, 60–3, 65, 67–8, 70, 72, 78–9, 93, 95–6, 98–101, 107.
[164] See Ian Blanchard, 'Northern Wools and the Netherlands Markets at the Close of the Middle Ages', *Studies in Economic and Social History*, Discussion Paper 3 (Edinburgh, 1992).
[165] List 34–9, 41–2, 50–3.

Table 43. *Wool price list*

No.	Year	Place	Unit price	Source
1	1304	Berwick	80s.sack	*CDS* II.440
2	1304	Berwick	60s.sack	*CDS* II.436 V.
3	1327	Inverkeith'g	80s.sack	*ER* I.78 V.
4	1328	Edinburgh	93.33s.sack	*ER* I.175 P.
5	1329	Edinburgh?	80s.sack	*ER* I.211 P.
6	1329	Edinburgh?	80s.sack	*ER* I.245 P.
7	1342	Coldingham	72s.sack	CP 1342–3.
8	1344	Coldingham	73.33s.sack	CS 1344–5ii
9	1344	Coldingham	80s.sack	CP 1344–5
10	1345	Coldingham	80s.sack	CP 1345–6
11	1346	Coldingham	70s.sack	CP 1346–7
12	1347	Coldingham?	66s.sack	DB 1347–8a+b V.
13	1357	Aberdeen	66.67s.sack	*ER* I.587 P.
14	1357	Edinburgh	66.67s.sack	*ER* I.606–7 P.
15	1358	Inverness	69.04s.sack	*ER* I.611 V.
16	1358	Forfar	66.67s.sack	*ER* I.615 P.
17	1358	Montrose	66.67s.sack	*ER* I.612 P.
18	1358	Aberdeen	71.67s.sack	*ER* I.553 P.
19	1358	Dundee	66.67s.sack	*ER* I.615 P.
20	1358	Aberdeen	66.67s.sack	*ER* I.549 V.
21	1359	Aberdeen	66.67s.sack	*ER* II.32 P.
22	1359	Edinburgh	66.67s.sack	*ER* II.8 P.
23	1359		56.56s.sack	*ER* II.49 P.
24	1359	Kinneff	66.67s.sack	*ER* II.51 P.
25	1362	Linlithgow	66.67s.sack	*ER* II.125 P.
26	1362	Lindores	66.67s.sack	*ER* II.139–40 P.
27	1363	Coldingham	64s.sack	SS 12.xliv
28	1364	Coldingham	65s.sack	SS 12.xlvii
29	1365	Coldingham	63s. 4d.sack	SS 12.l
30	1366	Coldingham	72s.sack	SS 12.lii
31	1367	Coldingham	84s.sack	SS 12.lvii
32	1390	Edinburgh	48s.sack	*ER* III.219 V.
33	1401	Aberdeen	3.33s.stone	ACR I.184 C.
34	1406	Aberdeen	4s. 6d.stone	ACR I.289 Wi.
35	1406	Aberdeen	4s.stone	ACR I.225 Wi.
36	1409	Aberdeen	30d.stone Buchan wool	ACR II.52 assize V.
37	1409	Aberdeen	30d.stone Mar wool	ACR II.52 assize V.
38	1409	Aberdeen	2s.stone Buchan wool	ACR II.52 assize V.
39	1409	Aberdeen	30d.stone Garioch wool	ACR II.52 assize V.
40	1412	Coldingham	53.33s.sack	SS 12.lxxxii
41	1417	Aberdeen	2s.stone Buchan wool	Kennedy, *Annals of Aberdeen*, p.1 assize V?
42	1417	Aberdeen	2.5s.stone Mar & Garioch	Kennedy, *Annals of Aberdeen*, p.1 assize V?
43	1430		200s.sack	*ER* IV.684
44	1433	Linlithgow	120s.sack	*ER* IV.555

Table 43 (*cont.*)

No.	Year	Place	Unit price	Source
45	1435	Edinburgh	160s.sack	*ER* V.27 P.
46	1437	Aberdeen	5s.stone	ACR IV.100 Wi.
47	1438	Aberdeen	65.17s.g. small sack	ACR IV.129 Wi.
48	1439	Aberdeen	26.5 marks g./21 marks g. sarpler	ACR IV.161 Wi.
49	1442	Aberdeen	6.67s.stone	ACR IV.265 O.
50	1442	Aberdeen	6s. 8d.stone	ACR V ii.654 assize V.
51	1444	Aberdeen	5s.stone	ACR V ii.679 assize V.
52	1445	Aberdeen	4s.stone	ACR V ii.702 assize V.
53	1445	Aberdeen	5s.stone Mar wool	ACR V ii.702 assize V.
54	1449	Aberdeen	16s.stone died blue	ACR V i.49 Wi.
55	1458	Aberdeen	5s.stone	*ER* VI.510
56	1471	Aberdeen	11s.6g. sarpler lambswool	ACR VI.135
57	1472	Aberdeen	£9 10s. 7d.g. sack	ACR VI.11 O.
58	1478	Aberdeen	5s.stone lambswool	ACR VI.533 Aw.
59	1479	(Bruges)	£9 10s.g.sarpler	*ALC* I.28
60	1482		14s.stone	ALA I.103 C.
61	1483	Aberdeen	£24 sarpler	ACR VII.67 C.
62	1484	Aberdeen	5.33s.stone	ACR VI.826 Aw.
63	1487	Aberdeen	£14 g.? sarpler	ACR VII.38 C.
64	1489	Lekraw	4s.qu	*ALC* I.106 Aw.
65	1489	Aberdeen	10s.stone	ACR VII.124 Aw.
66	1489	Kirkpatrick	10s.stone	ALA I.130–1 C.
67	1489	Aberdeen	7s.stone	ACR VII.155 Aw.
68	1490	Edinburgh?	266s.8d. sack	*ALC* I.13 Aw.
69	1490	Delgatie castle	8s.stone	*ALC* I.289 Aw.
70	1491	Aberdeen	10s.stone	ACR VII.235 O.
71	deleted			
72	1492	Aberdeen	7.5s.stone	ACR VII.312 Aw.
73	1492	Veere	£6 8s. 7g. pok	ACR VII.520
74	1493		8s.stone	*ALC* I.287 Aw.
75	1493	Delgatie castle	8s.stone lambswool	*ALC* I.289 Aw.
76	1493	Delgatie castle	8s.stone lambswool	*ALC* I.289 Aw.
77	1493	Delgatie castle	8s.stone lambswool	*ALC* I.289 Aw.
78	1495	Aberdeen	7s.stone	ACR VII.617 O.
79	1495		266s.8d.sack	*ALC* I.424 Aw.
80	1495		280s.sack unpacked	TA I.220 V.
81	1495		800s. sarpler packed	TA I.220 V.
82	1495		280s.sack	TA I.220 P.
83	1498	Yarrow	£13 sack	*ER* XI.203–4
84	1499		13.74d. fells	*ER* XI.245
85	1499		6d. pelt	*ER* XI.245
86	1499		1.19s./1.01s. fells	*ER* XI.254–5
87	1499		8d. pelt	*ER* XI.255
88	1502		5d. pelt	*ER* XII.180
89	1507		7.5g. per pound	TA III.275 P.

Table 43 (*cont.*)

No.	Year	Place	Unit price	Source
90	1507	Montrose	10s.stone	*ER* XIII.107
91	1508		1.64s./1.38s. fells	*ER* XIII.254
92	1510	Birnane	13.16s. stone	SHS 2,10.175
93	1511	Aberdeen	9.32s. stone	ACR IX 46 O.
94	1522	Aberdeen	0.9francs stone	ACR XI.145 C.
95	1524	Aberdeen	8s.stone	ACR XI.462 V.
96	1524	Aberdeen	8s.stone	ACR XI.462 V.
97	1524		9.55d. fells	*ER* XV.197
98	1526	Aberdeen	3s.9g. stone	ACR XII i.18 Aw.
99	1529	Aberdeen	18s.stone	ACR XII ii.572 C.
100	1529	Aberdeen	10s.stone	ACR XII ii.629 V.
101	1532	Aberdeen	£12 6s.7g. sarpler	ACR XIII.427
102	1538	Aberdeen	12s.stone	ACR XV.595 C.
103	1538	Aberdeen	20s.stone	ACR XVI.102 C.
104	1539	Aberdeen	8.89s.stone	ACR XVI.263 Aw.
105	1539		10s.stone	*ER* XVII.287 P.
106	1539		10s.stone	*ER* XVII.288 P.
107	1540	Aberdeen	10s.stone	ACR XVI.573 Wi.
108	1542	Lempitlaw	13s. 4d.stone	*ALCPA*, p. 519 V.

differed because of customs charges paid on the latter, which could be considerable.[166] The great custom on wool reached its highest point in 1368 at 26s. 8d. per sack. In the late fourteenth century, when wool prices began to fall but before debasement had begun to erode the customs rate, the custom on wool must have weighed heavily. Most of the prices listed here will clearly not have included the customs charge, and as the fifteenth century progressed the proportional effect of customs on price will have dwindled markedly. Nevertheless, uncertainty over the customs payment unquestionably contributes to our doubts over the value of this series.

Cheese

As one would expect in a society so much devoted to animal husbandry, cheese was widely produced in medieval Scotland. A cow might be expected to yield a stone of cheese a year, and a ewe 0.2 of a stone, presumably in addition to raising their own young.[167] As one of the

[166] List 32.
[167] List 41–2; see also List 57 for a different estimate of the cheese yield of a ewe, though the time period involved in this case is not explicit.

commonest of livestock products, cheese was widely used for the payment of wages and rents in kind, though in practice many of these renders were 'sold', that is to say commuted to cash.[168] Given the importance of cheese, both in the diet and in the social economy of Scotland, it is all the more disappointing that the price series offered here is so especially weak. Not only are cheese prices quite scarce, but they are also unevenly distributed across our period leaving large gaps, most notably 1330–1400, when we have no evidence at all.

Table 44 displays mean prices in groupings into which the evidence most conveniently falls but this material can only be used with care, for the prices in any one grouping tend to be dominated by a single source or type of price which is often scarcely comparable with the others. Thus the *ER* prices which are important in the period 1456–64 may be somewhat depressed by conventional valuations of rents in kind, while the legal valuations important during 1478–89 may be slightly high. Royal purchases recorded in the Household Book of James V are consistently high. Cheese prices were also much affected by considerations of quality, mature cheese being worth more.[169] This question of variable quality must have complicated attempts at price regulation. However, Aberdeen did attempt to control cheese prices, especially as part of the policing of hucksters' trade.[170] Finally, it should be noted that the usual problems with weights and measures become particularly acute in the cheese series. Locally varied techniques of manufacture produced a range of local weights. The codrus[171] may be equated with the cudthrom, or Gaelic stone, while the cogall[172] was a unit of 6 stones, and the castlaw[173] is probably the same as the caslamus.[174] But even more familiar units are not without their pitfalls: we meet local and 'large' pounds,[175] and even the number of pounds to the stone is a matter of uncertainty. Given these flaws in the Scottish evidence for cheese, the comparison with English prices (Table 45) must be especially doubtful. It appears that Scottish cheese was cheaper than English, which would accord with the dominance of livestock in Scottish agriculture, but evidence of this quality can only give the most general of indications.

[168] List 6, 11; 1, 2–3, 18–20, 29, 30, 50–5, 69–76.
[169] List 6–7; household purchases under James V range in price from 3s. to 6s. a stone.
[170] List 22.
[171] List 5–9, 11–13, 16–17.
[172] *ER* I.6–7, 21, 49.
[173] List 51, 53–4.
[174] See Chapter 3 and the Glossary.
[175] List 4, 55.

Table 44. *Mean cheese prices 1263–1530*

Years	Mean price	Number of entries
1263–90	6	3
1325	7	13
1328–30	12	3
1325–30	8	16
1433	30	1
1456–64	25	11
1478–89	39	9
1490–1501	28	10
1515	38	2
1525–9	56	13
1525–30	55	14

Note: the mean price is in pence per stone.

Table 45. *Cheese prices 1263–1330: England and Scotland*

Year	Scotland	Durham	Rogers
1263	6.0		8.75
	6.05		
1290	6.0		7.0
1325	7.0	6.63	12.0
	7.0		
	12.0		
	7.0		
	6.5		
	6.0		
	8.0		
	7.0		
	7.0		
	6.0		
	7.2/6.0		
	7.0		
	7.0		
1328	14.4/12.0	6.43	8.57
1329	14.4/12.0	8.36	
1330	12.0/10.0	9.00	10.86

Note: all prices are in pence per stone.

Table 46. *Cheese price list*

No.	Year	Place	Unit price	Source
1	1263	Kincardine	6d.stone	*ER* I.21
2	1263	Forfar etc.	6.05d.stone	*ER* I.6–7
3	1290	Kincardine	6d.stone	*ER* I.49
4	1325	Kintyre	12d. local weight	*ER* I.53 V.
5	1325	Tarbert	7d.codrus	*ER* I.55 V.
6	1325	Tarbert	7d.codrus	*ER* I.55 V.
7	1325	Tarbert	12d.codrus	*ER* I.55–6 V.
8	1325	Tarbert	7d.codrus	*ER* I.56 V.
9	1325	Tarbert	6.5d.codrus	*ER* I.56 V.
10	1325	Tarbert	6d.stone	*ER* I.56 V.
11	1325	Tarbert	8d.codrus	*ER* I.57 V.
12	1325	Tarbert	7d.codrus	*ER* I.57 V.
13	1325	Tarbert	7d.codrus	*ER* I.57 V.
14	1325	Tarbert	6d.stone	*ER* I.58 V.
15	1325	Tarbert	7.2d./6d.stone	*ER* I.58 V.
16	1325	Tarbert	7d.codrus	*ER* I.58 V.
17	1325	Tarbert	7d.codrus	*ER* I.57 V.
18	1328	Touchs	14.4d./12d.stone	*ER* I.178 V.
19	1329	Touchs	14.4d./12d.stone	*ER* I.178 V.
20	1330	Touchs	12d./10d.stone	*ER* I.296 V.
21	1433		30d.stone	*ER* IV.591 P.
22	1448	Aberdeen	1.5d.pound	ACR V i.8 assize V.
23	1456	Galloway	30d.stone	*ER* VI.348
24	1457	Galloway	24d.stone	*ER* VI.454
25	1458	Galloway	24d.stone	*ER* VI.570
26	1459	Methven	30d.stone	*ER* VI.635
27	1459	Galloway	24d.stone	*ER* VI.644
28	1461	Galloway	24d.stone	*ER* VII.116
29	1462	Le Halch	24d.stone	*ER* VII.167
30	1464	Le Halch	24d.stone	*ER* VII.351
31	1478	Noligrey	36d.stone	*ALC* I.6 Aw.
32	1483	Glennessil	4s.stone	*ALC* I.*83 Aw.
33	1483	Wauchtoun'	48d.stone	*ALC* I.166 Aw.
34	1483	Wauchtoun'	48d.stone	*ALC* I.166 Aw.
35	1483	Lile	3s.stone	ALA I.*123 Aw.
36	1484	Quhittingam	4s.stone, old	*ALC* I.*90 Aw.
37	1484	Quhittingam	30d.stone, new	*ALC* I.*90 Aw.
38	1489	Brigland'	30d.per stone	*ALC* I.114 Aw.
39	1489	Kilmarnock	2s.stone	*ER* X.159
40	1490	Cladanis	24d.stone	*ALC* I.147 Aw.
41	1490	Delgatie castle	2s.stone cows' cheese	*ALC* I.289 Aw.
42	1490	Delgatie castle	2s.stone ewes' cheese	*ALC* I.289 Aw.
43	1493		36d.stone	*ALC* I.287 Aw.
44	1493	Cladanis	24d.stone	*ALC* I.428 Aw.
45	1497	Ayr	26.67d.stone	TA I.344 P.
46	1499	Catburnbiri	14.4d.stone	*ER* XI.358 V.

Table 46 (*cont.*)

No.	Year	Place	Unit price	Source
47	1499	Kilmarnock	2s.stone	*ER* XI.361 V.
48	1501	Kilmarnock	2s.stone	*ER* XII.22 V.
49	1501	Cullery	4.74s.stone	*ER* XII.23 V.
50	1505	S.Kintyre	12d.pound	*ER* XII.586
51	1505	S.Kintyre	8d.castlaw	*ER* XII.586
52	1505	N.Kintyre	1s.pound	*ER* XII.586
53	1505	N.Kintyre	8d.castlaw	*ER* XII.586
54	1505	N.Kintyre	8d.castlaw	*ER* XII.703
55	1505	N.Kintyre	12d.large pound	*ER* XII.703
56	1515	Inchegarvy	3s.stone	TA V.21 P.
57	1515	Cupar, Fife	40d.stone	*SCBF*, pp. 6–7 Aw.
58	1525	Edinburgh	42. 11d.stone	HBJV, App., p. 4 P.
59	1525	Edinburgh	3s. 4d.stone	HBJV, p. 17 P.
60	1525	Dalkeith	4s.stone	HBJV, p. 19 P.
61	1526		5s.stone	HBJV, App., p. 7 P.
62	1526	Edinburgh	5s. 4d.stone conflated	HBJV, p. 27 etc. P.
63	1526	Stirling	3s.stone	HBJV, p. 61 P.
64	1528	Stirling	5s. 4d.stone	HBJV, p. 122 P.
65	1528	Edinburgh?	6s.stone	HBJV, App., p. 16 P.
66	1529	Falkland	3.21s.stone	HBJV, p. 159 P.
67	1529	Edinburgh?	5s. 4d.stone	HBJV, p. 221 P.
68	1530	Aberdeen	42d.stone	ACR XII ii.750 Aw.
69	1537	Balgray	3s.stone	*ER* XVII.129
70	1541	Clochrane	3s.stone	*ER* XVII.482 V.
71	1541	Mull,Tiree	2s.stone	*ER* XVII.529 V.
72	1541	Jura etc.	2s.stone	*ER* XVII.535 V.
73	1541	Islay	16d.stone	*ER* XVII.545 V.
74	1541	Craufurdjohn	3s.stone	*ER* XVII.571
75	1541	Drumclog	3s.stone	*ER* XVII.587
76	1541	Kintyre	2s.stone	*ER* XVII.625 V.

Butter

Although we have butter prices only after 1478 (Table 47), it is nevertheless apparent that butter was much more expensive than cheese. The inflated level of prices paid by the household emerges very clearly from the butter series. Minimum household purchase prices for butter seem to begin at the maximum price paid elsewhere.

Table 47. *Mean butter prices 1478–1533*

Years	Mean price	Number of entries
1478–93	64	6
1513–16	67	14
1525–33	96	41

Note: the mean price is in pence per stone.

Table 48. *Butter price list*

No.	Year	Place	Unit price	Source
1	1478	Noligrey	60d.stone	*ALC* I.6 Aw.
2	1483	Glennessil	5s.stone	*ALC* I.*83 Aw.
3	1483	Wauchtoun'	6s. 8d.stone	*ALC* I.166 Aw.
4	1483	Wauchtoun'	6s. 8d.stone	*ALC* I.166 Aw.
5	1493		45d.stone	*ALC* I.282 Aw.
6	1493		60d.stone	*ALC* I.287 Aw.
7	1513	Forth	24s. barrel	*TA* IV.470 P.
8	1513	Forth	5s.stone	*TA* IV.489 P.
9	1513	Forth	5s. 4d.stone	*TA* IV.492 P.
10	1513	Forth	5s. 4d.stone conflated	*TA* IV.496ff. P.
11	1513		6s.stone Orkney butter	*TA* IV.511 P.
12	1513		6s.stone Orkney butter	*TA* IV.515 P.
13	1515	Inchegarvy	6s. 8d.stone	*TA* V.21 P.
14	1515	Cupar,Fife	6s.stone.	*SCBF*, pp. 6–7 Aw.
15	1516	Cupar,Fife	5s. 4d.stone	*SCBF* p. 51 Aw.
16	1525	Edinburgh	6s. 8d.stone	HBJV, p. 6 P.
17	1525	Edinburgh	6s. 8d.stone	HBJV, p. 13 P.
18	1525	Edinburgh	7s.stone	HBJV, p. 17 P.
19	1525		8s.stone	HBJV, App., p. 5 P.
20	1525	Dalkeith	8s.stone	HBJV, p. 19 P.
21	1526	Edinburgh	8s.stone conflated	HBJV, pp. 27 etc. P.
22	1526	Edinburgh?	9.6s.stone	HBJV, p. 54 P.
23	1526	Edinburgh	6s. 8d.stone	HBJV, p. 58 P.
24	1526	Stirling	7s. 1.33d.stone	HBJV, p. 61 P.
25	1528		7s. 6d.stone conflated	HBJV, pp. 113–14 P.
26	1528	Perth	11s. 3d.stone	HBJV, p. 117 P.
27	1528	Edinburgh	8s. 6d.stone	HBJV, p. 118 P.
28	1528	Stirling	9s. 4d.stone	HBJV, p. 122 P.
29	1528	Edinburgh	8s.stone	HBJV, p. 123 P.
30	1528	Edinburgh	9s.stone	HBJV, p. 127 P.
31	1528	Edinburgh?	9s.stone	HBJV, App., p. 16 P.
32	1529	Edinburgh	9s.stone conflated	HBJV, pp. 135,137 P.
33	1529		8s.stone conflated	HBJV, pp. 154–5 etc P.
34	1529	Stirling	7.93s.stone	HBJV, p. 142 P.
35	1529	Stirling	6s. 8d.stone	HBJV, p. 158 P.

Table 48. (*cont.*)

No.	Year	Place	Unit price	Source
36	1529	Falkland	8.8s.stone	HBJV, p. 159 P.
37	1529	Stirling	7.15s.stone	HBJV, p. 159 P.
38	1529	Stirling	6s. 8d.stone	HBJV, p. 163 P.
39	1529	Falkland	9s. 4d.stone	HBJV, p. 213 P.
40	1529	Linlithgow?	7s.stone	HBJV, p. 215 P.
41	1529	Edinburgh?	7s.stone	HBJV, p. 215 P.
42	1529	Stirling?	13.65s.stone	HBJV, p. 217 P.
43	1532	Perth	9s.stone	HBJV, p. 229 P.
44	1532	Dundee	10.29s.stone	HBJV, p. 230 P.
45	1533	Glasgow	58.66d.stone	*TA* VI.164 P.

Candle

Our prices for candle begin only in 1482, and are dominated by Aberdeen data. The occasional prices which we have been able to record from elsewhere are of little comparative use since they are often priced by number while the Aberdeen price regulations were consistently fixed by weight. There is also some uncertainty, as usual, over the number of pounds in the stone, though a 16 pound stone looks to be a possibility.[176] Nevertheless, despite the short duration and the dominance of Aberdeen the series is not without interest.

The burgh's insistence that candlemakers must have candle ready to sell, available to all, has a familiar ring to it, perhaps suggesting that prices were kept so low as to deny any adequate profit, but convictions of candlemakers seldom provide price details.[177] The appropriate price for candle was determined chiefly by the price of tallow.[178] The quality of candle made was also a consideration, it being important that they were clean, dry, and small wicked.[179] Candles were also to be available in a variety of sizes.[180] We know that on one occasion at least the trade was restricted to a group of six women, a provision which again may suggest a refusal by some to accept the assize, but at other times business seems to have been more open. Fleshers' wives, however, were specifically excluded.[181] This may have been to spread the available

[176] *TA* IV.509 provides the information (List 27) that 5 lb cost 20d., and a stone 5s.4d.
[177] List 18 for a rare example.
[178] See ACR X.9; XI.645; XIII.234; XIV.8.
[179] List 36. The wicks for 1 stone of candle were to weigh only 0.5 lb.
[180] List 16–17, 21–2, 24, provide for anything between one and four candles to the penny.
[181] ACR VIII.614.

Table 49. *Candle price list*

No.	Year	Place	Unit price	Source
1	1482	Aberdeen	3d.pound	ACR VI.758 assize V.
2	1483	Wauchtoun'	40d. per 100/120	*ALC* I.166 Aw.
3	1484	Aberdeen	3d.pound	ACR VI.883 assize V.
4	1485	Aberdeen	3d.pound	ACR VI.935 assize V.
5	1490	Aberdeen	6 oz per 1d.	ACR VII.207 assize V.
6	1491	Aberdeen	3d.pound	ACR VII.273 assize V.
7	1492	Aberdeen	3d.pound	ACR VII.354 assize V.
8	1495	Aberdeen	3d.pound	ACR VII.671 assize V.
9	1496	Aberdeen	3d.pound	ACR VII.762 assize V.
10	1497	Ayr	5s. per 100/120	*TA* I.344 P.
11	1497	Aberdeen	3d.pound	ACR VII.841 assize V.
12	1498	Aberdeen	3d.pound	ACR VII.908 assize V.
13	1499	Aberdeen	2.5d.pound	ACR VII.989 assize V.
14	1502	Aberdeen	3d.pound	ACR VIII.163 assize V.
15	1504	Aberdeen	3d.pound	ACR VIII.384 assize V.
16	1505	Aberdeen	3d.pound	ACR VIII.507 assize V.
17	1506	Aberdeen	3d.pound	ACR VIII.614 assize V.
18	1506	Aberdeen	0.75pound for 3d.?	ACR VIII.625 Wi.
19	1507	Aberdeen	3d.pound	ACR VIII.753 assize V.
20	1509	Aberdeen	3d.pound	ACR VIII.1033 assize V.
21	1509	Perth	1d. and ½d. each	SHS 2,10.217 P.
22	1510	Aberdeen	3d.pound	ACR VIII.1127 assize V.
23	1510	Clony	1d. each on SH	SHS 2,10.68 P.
24	1511	Aberdeen	3d.pound	ACR IX.36 assize V.
25	1512	Forth	5.44s.stone	*TA* IV.459 P.
26	1513	Forth	5s. 4d.stone conflated	*TA* IV.464–501 P.
27	1513		5s. 4d.stone	*TA* IV.509 P.
28	1515	Aberdeen	3d.pound	ACR IX.509 assize V.
29	1516	Cupar,Fife	3s. 6d.stone	*SCBF*, p. 51 Aw.
30	1518	Aberdeen	4d./3d.pound	ACR X.9 assize V.
31	1525	Aberdeen	5d.pound	ACR XI.645 assize V.
32	1531		10s.stone	*TA* V.459 P.
33	1531	Aberdeen	6d.pound	ACR XIII.234 assize V.
34	1532	Aberdeen	6d.pound	ACR XIV.8 assize V.
35	1533	Glasgow	8s.stone	*TA* VI.164 P.
36	1533	Aberdeen	4d./5d.pound	ACR XIV.286 assize V.
37	1539	Leith/Edinb.	8s.stone conflated	*TA* VII.343,345 P.
38	1540	Leith/Edinb.	8s.stone conflated	*TA* VII.346 etc. P.
39	1541	Leith/Edinb.	8s.stone conflated	*TA* VII.490,VIII.120 P.

employment more widely, or to prevent them from exploiting a favourable supply of tallow.

The actual price fixed by the Aberdeen assize seems to have been remarkably constant. The 1482 price of 3d. per pound (fixed after the

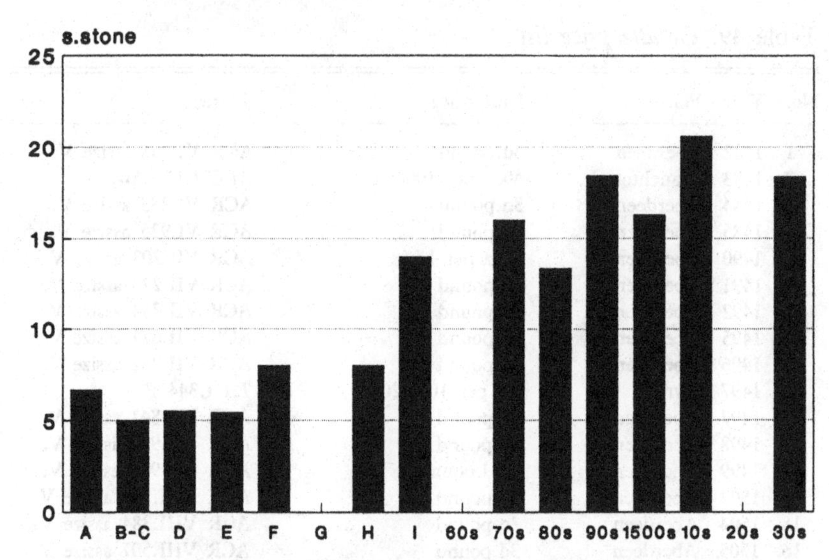

36 Wax prices (mean prices for time periods A–1530s)
For periods A–I, see Introduction, p. 6.

withdrawal of the black money) was held with little alteration[182] till 1518. Even then, the rise in price was only conceded on an exceptional basis[183] but the subsequent movement of prices in later years shows that the rise was in fact permanent and irreversible.[184] Despite the difficulty of comparing the Aberdeen prices with data from elsewhere,[185] and despite the inevitably somewhat artificial nature of the assize, the picture of prices holding broadly steady from 1482 to 1518, followed by a marked jump, finds some confirmation in some other series, notably marts and sheep, the chief sources of tallow. For all the weaknesses of our candle prices, the simple message of stable prices at the turn of the century, followed by a marked rise in the 1520s, sounds convincing.

Wax

Wax was generally used for sealing documents or for making the finest quality candles.[186] We also meet it once when wax was used to treat

[182] List 5, 13 for rare reductions in price.
[183] List 30. This price was intended to last for less than a month with a reduction envisaged thereafter. [184] List 31, 33, 34.
[185] List 25–7 for apparently dearer *Treasurer's Accounts* prices, List 29 for a cheaper price from Fife.
[186] List 3, 4, 19, 42, 53, 56, 75, 81–2, 84–5 for candles; List 8, 12, 14, 23, 27, 31–2, 34, for seals.

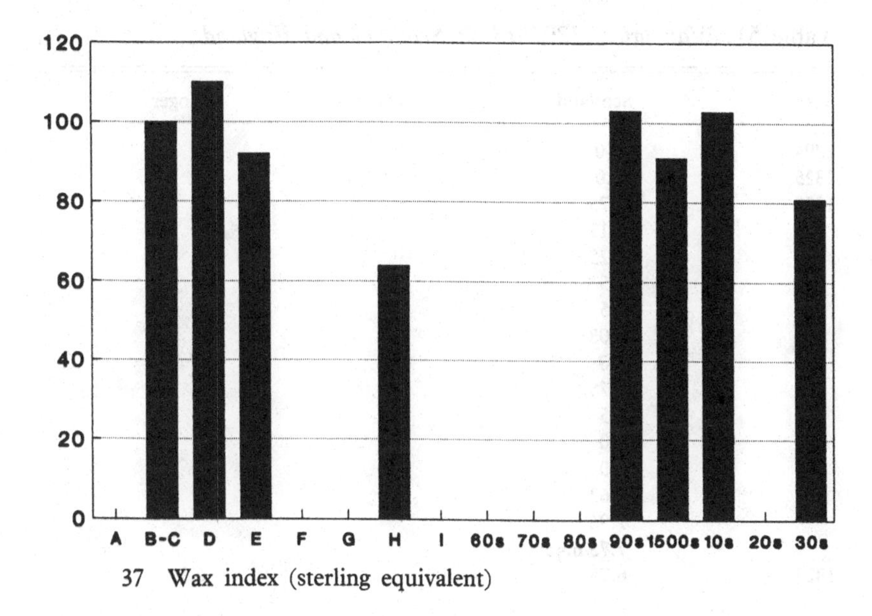

37 Wax index (sterling equivalent)

Table 50. *Wax summary table*

Period	Mean price	Deflated	Index
A	(6.67)		
B–C	5.01	5.01	100.0
D	5.51	5.51	110.0
E	5.42	4.61	92.0
F	(8.0)		
G			
H	7.99	3.2	63.9
I	(14.0)		
60s			
70s	(16.0)		
80s	(13.33)		
90s	18.44	5.16	103.0
1500s	16.29	4.56	91.0
10s	20.61	5.15	102.8
20s			
30s	18.39	4.05	80.8

Note: the mean price is in shillings per stone; the deflated column gives the currency-adjusted sterling equivalent price. Parentheses have been used to flag up calculations which are less securely based than others – either because they are based on a smaller amount of data, or because they involve certain, possibly questionable, assumptions.

Table 51. *Wax prices 1294–1366: Scotland and England*

Year	Scotland	Durham	Rogers
1294	10.0		
1325	10.0	6.63	
1328	9.75	6.43	
	8.13		
	7.25		
	7.5		
	7.5		
	8.08		
	6.0		
	4.75		
	7.5		
	9.0		
	9.0		
	7.62		
	7.96		
	7.75/6.46		
1329	6.75		6.5
	7.25		
	6.0		
	7.08		
	7.5		
	8.13		
	9.0		
1330	7.5	9.0	6.0
	9.0		
	8.13		
	8.86/7.58		
1331	7.5		7.5
	6.76		
	7.5		
	7.5		
1334	7.5		6.0
1341	6.75	6.0	
	7.19		
1343	6.0	4.89	
1344	5.5	5.47	5.0
	5.25		
1353	7.75	7.1/6.23	6.25
1358	9.07	8.07	
1361	9.0	8.11	
1364	8.25	9.0	6.75
1365	5.2	7.51	7.25
1366	7.5	6.77	6.0

Note: all prices are in pence per pound.

Table 52. *Wax price list*

No.	Year	Place	Unit price	Source
1	1281	Berwick	£4 20d.pisa	*DHS* II.245 V.
2	1294	Berwick?	6.67s.stone	*DHS* II.247 V.
3	1325	Tarbert	6.67s.stone	*ER* I.56 P.
4	1328	Berwick	6.5s.stone	*ER* I.118 P.
5	1328	Dundee	5.5s.stone	*ER* I.171 P.
6	1328		4s.10d.stone	*ER* I.220 P.
7	1328		5s.stone	*ER* I.220 P.
8	1328		5s.stone	*ER* I.221 P.
9	1328		5.39s.stone	*ER* I.220 P.
10	1328		4s.stone	*ER* I.220 P.
11	1328		4.67s.stone	*ER* I.220 P.
12	1328	Perth	5s.stone	*ER* I.88 V.
13	1328	Perth	6s.stone	*ER* I.88 V.
14	1328	Perth	6s.stone	*ER* I.176 V.
15	1328	Dundee	5.08s.stone	*ER* I.171 V.
16	1328		5.31s.stone	*ER* I.140 P.
17	1328	Berwick	5.17s/4.31s.stone	*ER* I.119 P.
18	1329		4.5s.stone	*ER* I.290 P.
19	1329	Berwick	4.84s.stone	*ER* I.288 V.
20	1329		4s.stone	*ER* I.243–4
21	1329		4.72s.stone	*ER* I.250 P.
22	1329	Perth	5s.stone	*ER* I.264 V.
23	1329	Dundee	5.5s.stone	*ER* I.276 V.
24	1329	Perth	6s.stone	*ER* I.168 V.
25	1330	Perth	5s.stone	*ER* I.264 V.
26	1330	Perth	6s.stone	*ER* I.307 V.
27	1330	Dundee	5.5s.stone	*ER* I.317 V.
28	1330		5.91s./5.05s.stone	*ER* I.343 P.
29	1331	Perth	5s.stone	*ER* I.364 V.
30	1331		4.69s./4.51s.stone	*ER* I.401 P.
31	1331	Perth	5s.stone	*ER* I.365 V.
32	1331	Berwick	5s.stone	*ER* I.362 V.
33	1334		5s.stone	*ER* I.453 P.
34	1341		4.5s.stone	*ER* I.511 V.
35	1341	Ayr	4.79s.stone	*ER* I.487–8 P.
36	1343	Perth	4s.stone	*ER* I.539 V.
37	1344	Coldingham	3.67s.stone	CS 1344–5i P.
38	1344	Coldingham	3.5s.stone	CS 1344–5ii P.
39	1353	Coldingham	5.17s.stone	SS 12.xxviii P.
40	1358	Coldingham	6.05s.stone	SS 12.xxxv P.
41	1361	Linlithgow	6s.stone	*ER* II.102 V.
42	1364	Coldingham	8.25d.pound(= 6.5s.stone)	SS 12.xlvii P.
43	1365	Coldingham	4s.4d.stone	SS 12.l P.
44	1366	Coldingham	5s.stone	SS 12.liii P.
45	1373		5.41s/4.70s.stone	*ER* II.440 P.

Table 52 (*cont.*)

No.	Year	Place	Unit price	Source
46	1373		4.04s.stone	*ER* II.443 P.
47	1374		6.24s/5.57s.stone	*ER* II.466 P.
48	1375		6.44s.stone	*ER* II.507 P.
49	1377		6.63s.stone	*ER* II.547 P.
50	1385	Broxfeld	5.33s.stone	*ER* III.163 V.
51	1387	Broxfeld	5.33s.stone	*ER* III.161 V.
52	1387	Fife	5.33s.stone	*ER* III.165
53	1397	Edinburgh	8s.stone	*ER* III.438 P.
54	1424	Linlithgow	6.67s.stone white	*ER* IV.390–1 P.
55	1430	Edinburgh	8s.stone white	*ER* IV.543 P.
56	1436	Edinburgh	9.29s.stone white	*ER* V.26–7 P.
57	1458	Edinburgh	168d.stone	*ER* VI.495 P.
58	1479	Aberdeen	2s. per pound	ACR VI.585–6 Aw.
59	1479	Aberdeen	2s.pound	ACR VI.595 Aw.
60	1487	Aberdeen	13s.4d.stone	ACR VII.21–4 Aw.
61	1491	Arth'	30d.pound	*ALC* I.195 Aw.
62	1493		33d.lb.	*ALC* I.282 Aw.
63	1496	Aberdeen	20s.stone	ACR VII.722 V.
64	1497	Aberdeen	18s.stone	ACR VII.787 V.
65	1497	Aberdeen	18s.stone	ACR VII.787 V.
66	1497	Aberdeen	18s.stone	ACR VII.839 P.
67	1497	Falkland	12s.stone	*ER* XI.73 P.
68	1497	Lanark	20s.stone	*ER* XI.351*
69	1499	Aberdeen	1 unicorn, i.e. 18s.stone	ACR VII.985 P.
70	1500	Kelle	2s.pound	*ER* XI.363*
71	1501	Aberdeen?	18s.stone	*TA* II.75 P.
72	1508		2s.pound	*TA* IV.116 P.
73	1508		26d.pound	*TA* IV.136 P.
74	1508	Aberdeen	15d.pound	ACR VIII.881 C.
75	1509	Aberdeen	18s.stone	ACR VIII.937 P.
76	1509	Perth	28d.pound	SHS 2,10.214 P.
77	1514	Perth	33.67d.pound	SHS 2,10.236 P.
78	1514	Perth	20s.stone	SHS 2,10.237 P.
79	1514	Perth	20s.stone	SHS 2,10.238 P.
80	1516	Perth	20s.stone	SHS 2,10.243 P.
81	1539	St Andrews	183.43d.stone	SHS 2,4.103 P.
82	1541	St Andrews	248d.stone	SHS 2,4.124 P.
83	1541	Edinburgh	30d.pound	*TA* VIII.125 P.
84	1542	St Andrews	216d.stone	SHS 2,4.155 P.
85	1542	St Andrews	216d.stone	SHS 2,4.141 P.

canvas for drying gunpowder.[187] Although white wax is occasionally specified[188] we have no real information about quality. Our calculations have assumed the use of a long hundred[189] and an 8 pound stone.[190]

The high thirteenth-century wax price should probably be treated with some caution. It is difficult to believe that wax was cheaper in the fourteenth century than in the thirteenth, and since the fourteenth-century evidence is relatively plentiful it seems likely that it is the isolated early price which is misleading. The fifteenth-century prices, when deflated to correct for debasement, are below the fourteenth-century levels, only recovering to the index base level in the 1490s. (Table 50, and Figures 36, 37). Wax in Scotland seems to have usually been dearer than in England (Table 51).

Salmon

Salmon were important in the medieval Scottish economy, both as a constituent of the diet and as an export item. That importance is reflected in the extent of our series of salmon prices. Some problems are, however, inherent in the nature of this commodity, tending to obscure the price trends. It is also noticeable that the early prices are usually fixed in terms of so much per fish, but from the fifteenth century barrel prices are the norm, making comparison over the whole period impossible.

The price per fish series particularly reveals not only enormous fluctuations from year to year but also huge variations within years. The determining factor seems to have been chiefly the time of year in which the fish were caught, for it was the season which dictated both availability and size. During the summer months there was a great number of salmon in the rivers but they were of varying stages of maturity. In the winter the fish were more scarce. Thus, salmon bought in the summer tended to be cheaper, although large fish fetched high prices even then.[191] A memorandum in the account of the provosts of Perth for Pentecost term 1343 enables us to pin down the time of year at which prices changed more clearly. All salmon issued to the king before Easter were to be caught and delivered at 12d. each, while those caught after that time were to be delivered at 4d. each.[192] The fact that

[187] List 57.
[188] List 54–6.
[189] *ER* I.220, 290.
[190] *ER* I.56; ACR VII.21–4.
[191] List 7–8, 11, 15, 19, 26, 28–30 give an indication of the time of year.
[192] List 28–30.

salmon were consumed in greater quantities during Lent so that Easter would herald a period of lower demand, together with the gradual increase in the availability of the fish, made Easter an obvious point at which to fix a change in the price.

That salmon were cheaper after Easter is borne out by evidence from the accounts of the cellarer at Durham. His purchases of meat, fish, and dairy produce were broken down into months and weeks, so that we can see at what times of the year salmon were consumed at Durham and at what prices they were purchased. The evidence is unequivocal. In 1328–9 the cellarer was buying salmon between February and April at prices which never fell below 17½d. apiece, and rose as far as 25.33d. apiece. In May prices declined sharply, and, except for one aberrant purchase price of 3s. for a single salmon, the prices ranged generally between 7d. and 12d. from May to June, and between 5¾d. and 9½d. apiece in July and early August when the last purchase of the year was made.[193] The account of 1329–30 shows that no salmon were bought between September and March. After Easter prices dropped dramatically, though we cannot trace further seasonal price fluctuations since the weekly accounts break off at the end of April.[194] On the strength of this evidence, and on that from Scotland, it seems that there were basically two separate price levels for salmon priced by the piece depending on the time of year, though there were, of course, exceptions to the rule of cheap summer and expensive winter salmon. Scottish salmon were generally cheaper than those found at Durham (Table 53).

Another factor affecting the price of salmon was the quantity in which they were purchased. When salmon were bought by the hundred or more, they were always relatively cheap,[195] though not all cheap salmon were bought in large quantities.[196] Variable quality, of course, affected prices, but it does not seem to be too much of a problem for the salmon series, mainly because enough prices survive to compensate for those lost through such uncertainty. Moreover, because of the value of this commodity explanations are normally offered for lower priced stock.[197] Similarly, younger fish are readily identified as grilse and lax.[198] In general terms the best-quality fish were usually described as 'full

[193] Durham Dean and Chapter Archives, Cellarer's Account, 1328–29.
[194] Durham Dean and Chapter Archives, Cellarer's Account, 1329–30.
[195] List 2–3, 9, 14, 16–20, 22–4, 26–7.
[196] List 5, 8, 30.
[197] E.g. List 219, grilse 'non erant sufficientes mercantie'.
[198] E.g. List 240, 245 for different pricing of grilse and salmon on the same occasion.

Table 53. *Salmon prices 1311–43: Scotland and England*

Year	Scotland	Durham
1311	12.0	16.62
1327	6.06	
1328	(4.68)	15.38
	18.53	
	6.0	
	24.0	
1329	12.0	24.22
	8.0	
	7.53/6.37	
	7.2	
	30.75	
	4.19	
	12.0	
1330	4.3	
	72.0	
	5.24/4.39	
1331	4.39	
	7.2/6.0	
	7.2/6.0	
1333	7.2/6.0	
1341	9.0	
	3.2	
	3.02	
	6.28	
	6.0	
1342	9.6/8.0	
	2.33/2.0	
1343	12.0	
	12.0	
	4.0	

Note: all prices are in pence each. Parentheses have been used to flag up calculations which are less securely based than others – either because they are based on a smaller amount of data, or because they involve certain, possibly questionable, assumptions.

red, sweet, sufficient merchant goods'.[199] The cost of heading,[200] scaling, gutting, salting, and barrelling[201] must have been considerable given the labour involved, and the cost of the salt[202] and the barrels, but we have little detailed information on the subject, since from the fifteenth century

[199] *ER* XI.172–3, and List 258. Sweet may perhaps refer to fresh, unsalted fish?
[200] List 238.
[201] List 226.
[202] E.g. *ER* I.66.

salmon is usually sold by the barrel with such costs included in the overall price.[203] Yet despite these costs, and the highly commercial nature of the trade in export centres such as Aberdeen, we still occasionally meet outdated valuations in rural backwaters surviving alongside more commercial sales.[204] In the countryside salmon, like marts or barley, was the subject of customary valuations co-existing with genuine market sales.

Our earliest price for barrelled salmon comes in 1380[205] and from 1425 the barrel becomes the almost invariable unit of sale.[206] Salmon were normally stored, shipped, and sold in the large Hamburg barrel, as distinct from the smaller Herring barrel, and considerable attention was devoted to establishing and maintaining a standard barrel size.[207] There were usually 12 barrels (large or small) to the last.[208] Although fresh fish continue to be sold occasionally by the piece,[209] the way in which barrelled salmon dominate the trade from the fifteenth century onwards suggests that the preservation and marketing of cleaned and salted salmon in barrels constituted something of a technical innovation, possibly introduced from Hamburg which gave its name to the standard barrel size.[210] If this were so, it could explain the absence of significant evidence for the bulk export of salmon before the fifteenth century, and the crown's failure to raise custom on it prior to James I.[211]

From the 1420s salmon assumes an importance in the record of the commercial life of Aberdeen which it would be difficult to overestimate. Unfailing demand for this fish in the markets of northern Europe made salmon as acceptable as ready money in trading and financial circles in the north-east. Although often sent to England,[212] it was export to

[203] List 277 suggests such costs may have run at about 10%.

[204] See the Ardmannoch valuations and sales contrasted in List 226, 227.

[205] List 35.

[206] In England also, Thorold Rogers found salmon first barrelled in the late fourteenth century, this becoming the norm in the fifteenth. Rogers, *A History of Agriculture and Prices in England*, I, p. 613; IV, p. 52.

[207] 14 gallons to the Hamburg barrel, *ER* IX.lxxii–lxxiii; see also Aberdeen measure, List 140. See Chapter 2, pp. 68–9 and Chapter 3, pp. 103–7.

[208] List 40, 41.

[209] E.g. List 249, 250; or even for part of a fish, List 194.

[210] cf. herrings. The necessary techniques for barrelling salted herring were introduced by a Dutchman at this very time, see below, p. 318.

[211] Customs were levied at 2s.6d. in the £ from 1426. The duty was 3s. per barrel in 1466, and was raised to 4s. per barrel in 1480. *ER* IX.lxx, lxxii–lxxiii. List 48, Ayr; List 193, Perth. Aberdeen burghers enjoyed privileged exemption till the reign of James III. Despite this, receipts from the custom on salmon were consistently highest at Aberdeen.

[212] List 39, 42, 44, 52–4, 57, 153, 154, 155. The Customs Accounts, and the Aberdeen Cocket Book of 1499 suggest that salmon was Scotland's principal export to England; I am grateful to Alexander Stevenson for this point. On one occasion, however, in 1475 salmon seems to have been imported to Berwick from England, List 121.

continental Europe which accounted for the lion's share of the trade. Flanders, particularly Bruges and Veere, figures largely,[213] though Amsterdam,[214] Zeeland,[215] Hamburg,[216] Copenhagen,[217] and Gdansk[218] also figure in the easterly trade. France, particularly Dieppe, becomes an important customer for salmon a little later, and equalled or probably surpassed Flanders in the sixteenth century.[219]

In short, salmon became a major export item to all the established centres of Scotland's continental trade. One can also perhaps discern a changing role for Edinburgh in the salmon trade. Initially, the capital appears as a customer for salmon, chiefly through the purchases of the royal household.[220] Apart from evidence of royal consumption of salmon, which occurs plentifully throughout the series, the crown also bought salmon to supply the navy.[221] Royal officials in the north-east sometimes settled their accounts with the crown in salmon,[222] though more often salmon owing was 'sold', that is usually to say commuted.[223] However, although the capital's predominance may have been founded on its role as a royal home and administrative centre, by the end of our period Edinburgh's stranglehold seems to have been gaining a more clearly commercial character. The salmon owed by Aberdeen litsters to Edinburgh merchants for woad[224] seem symptomatic; Edinburgh extending credit to Aberdeen, protected by recognition of the debt in the Aberdeen court. The importance of Edinburgh in such vital sectors as dye-stuffs and credit helped her to carve herself a role even in those sectors, like salmon, where the local advantages of the north-east might otherwise have made it difficult for the capital to compete.

The almost limitless demand for salmon on the export market gave

[213] List 61, 71, 96, 98, 112–13, 117, 133, 135, 141, 146, 153, 164, 175, 202, 207, 210, 213, 220, 231, 235, 242, 244, 258, 261, 264, 273, 276.

[214] List 235.

[215] List 241.

[216] List 238.

[217] List 273.

[218] List 142, 287.

[219] List 108, 168, 206, 232, 253, 258, 268, 274, 286, 296. A.Stevenson confirms this impression from his study of the Edinburgh Cocket Books of 1510–11 and 1512–13. See also Athol Murray's comments on the surviving Edinburgh custom book of 1537–8, and the destination of ships putting out of Leith. 'Foreign Trade and Scottish Ports 1471 and 1542', in McNeill and Nicholson (eds.), *An Historical Atlas of Scotland*, p. 75. The Scots enjoyed special customs concessions in Normandy in the early sixteenth century. Jenny Wormald, *Court, Kirk, and Community: Scotland 1470–1625* (London, 1981), p. 47.

[220] E.g. List 56. In 1434 it cost 46s. to ship 5 lasts from Aberdeen to Leith.

[221] List 205, 208–9, 211, 260.

[222] List 79, 89, 100.

[223] List 109, 114–15, 127–31, 136, 149–50, 178, 182, 189–91, 195–7, 199–200, 203–4, 216, 226–7, 233, 254, 277.

[224] List 279, 283, 285.

this commodity a key role in the winning of credit. Historians of the medieval wool and cloth trades have shown clearly that the trade would have been impossible but for the long line of credit running from grower to the European markets via numerous local fairs, and finishing processes, and back again. Such trust was only possible among a network of regular contacts, kept happy by the trickle of coin provided ultimately by strong demand for the finished product. In just the same way, demand for salmon was such that ready sales on profitable terms could confidently be predicted. So long as this was so, salmon became so creditworthy as to be as good as money itself. Our price series contains plentiful records of money owing for salmon, and salmon owing for money, while in the settlement of debts it seems to be almost a matter of indifference whether final payment be made in coin or fish or both.

William Voket was owed money by a number of people whom he pursued in the Aberdeen court by means of a royal writ, but he was willing to accept salmon or money as repayment.[225] The scale of Voket's operations may indicate he was a money lender. Similar obligations were incurred at almost every level of the trade in salmon. Fishermen made deals to sell their catch at attractive rates[226] to the holders of the fishings who in turn could settle their obligations to the burgh in salmon.[227] On other occasions the commitment to supply an entire catch to one dealer is not explicitly part of a rental arrangement, and may have arisen either as a means of debt repayment or as a more open marketing deal.[228] Disputes arising from the export of salmon were legion, and fishermen, fleshers, merchants, sailors, porters, factors, partners, and sureties had repeated recourse to the courts to resolve problems. Given the number of different parties likely to be involved in the export of a single barrel it is surprising things did not go wrong more often. A merchant sailor might fail to deliver salmon to Flanders,[229] or fail to return the proceeds of sales.[230] We even meet an agent sued by both vendor and buyer.[231] The value of salmon in Flanders could also be a subject of dispute.[232]

Not surprisingly, special procedures were set up to protect those obliged to trust others. Sureties were often introduced as a third party

[225] List 67.
[226] List 263, 269, 271–2.
[227] List 160, 198.
[228] List 292, 295; the deal was evidently broken, for 34 barrels were sold elsewhere in defiance of the agreement.
[229] List 112.
[230] List 90, 244, 280.
[231] List 232.
[232] List 98, 133.

to a deal, to guarantee the performance of obligations by one of the principals. In the event of a default, the surety himself was liable[233] and might even have to take action himself against the debtor.[234] Whether cash or salmon were originally advanced lenders might often secure their loans demanding pledges of land, rents, or fishing tackle as a guarantee of repayment.[235] Such agreements could be recorded in the court book when the loan was agreed to facilitate prosecution if repayment failed.[236] In addition to such agreements inscribed in the court record, merchants were clearly increasingly likely in the sixteenth century to give and receive written receipts, acknowledgements, or acquittances for payments made, goods handed over, or for debts or sales agreed.[237]

The importance of credit based on salmon, and the impression of more or less chronic liquidity problems, are reinforced by the use of salmon in barter agreements. The example of the exchange of woad for salmon has already been noted, but we also meet salmon exchanged for a horse, for wheat, for cloth, and for a doublet.[238] The salmon was nevertheless priced in money terms, and as we have already observed for most Scots merchants, whether in Aberdeen, Leith or Bruges, salmon so nearly was money as to make very little difference.

Barrel prices can be compared from the 1420s to the 1580s (Table 54 and Figure 38). A more or less steady rise is evident across this period with the exception of the 1450s which show a marked, though unexplained, fall. This may be the result of the chance coincidence of some low Aberdeen court, and *Exchequer Roll* valuations. This fairly steady rise in the price of salmon disappears when the price is adjusted to allow for currency debasement.[239] For European merchants, buying with hard currency, the price of Scottish salmon will have fallen sharply to the middle of the century, rising again thereafter only slowly and hesitantly. It should be noted that the high base price of period G (1425–30) depends on a somewhat uncertain deflator, but it nevertheless remains clear that as a result of Scottish devaluation, Scottish salmon will have represented especially good value for money in continental Europe and in England.

[233] List 92–3, 111, 116, 151, 156, 165, 177, 231, 253, 281, 290.
[234] List 147.
[235] List 104, 125, 156.
[236] List 104, 290. In the latter case a complex agreement was annulled when payment was actually made.
[237] List 224, 235, 238, 262, 270, 274, 298.
[238] List 110, 108, 281, 230.
[239] Table 54 also includes currency-adjusted prices.

Table 54. *Mean salmon prices 1380–1541*

Year	Mean price	Number of entries (mean of)	Deflated price
1380	(22)	1	(18.7)
1425–30	38.06	12	(22.84)
1433–40	38.35	9	15.34
1441–9	37.95	11	15.18
1450–9	30.76	21	10.15
1463–9	42.79	7	
1470–9	43.58	19	12.2
1480–9	49.3s	19	
1490–9	47.54	21	13.31
1501–9	43.64	15	12.22
1510–18	49.52	14	12.38
1520–9	54.3	27	13.58
1530–41	62.7	36	13.79

Note: the mean price is in shillings per barrel[a]; the deflated column gives the currently-adjusted equivalent price. Parentheses have been used to flag up calculations which are less securely based than others – either because they are based on a smaller amount of data, or because they involve certain, possibly questionable, assumptions.

[a] Including barrels, large barrels, Hamburg barrels, and Aberdeen barrels. Excluding small barrels and herring barrels.

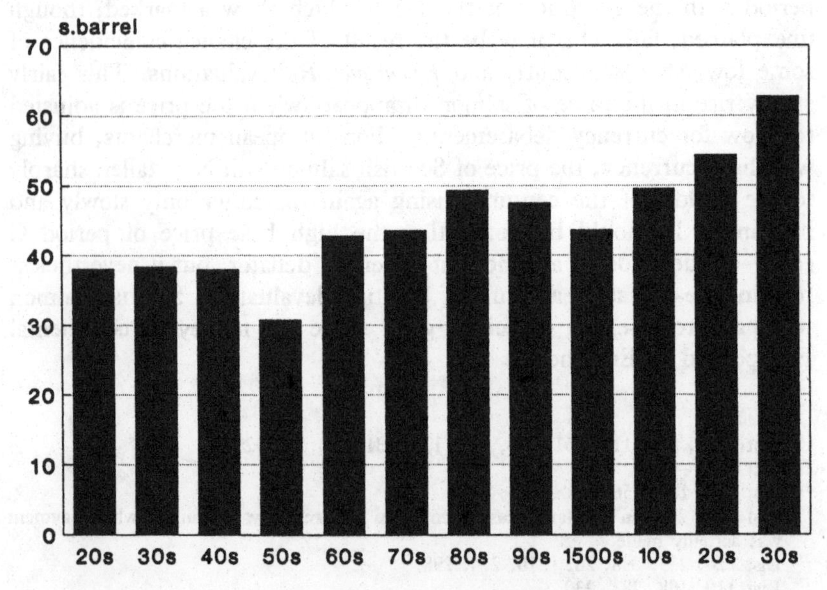

38 Salmon prices (mean prices for 1425–1541)

Table 55. *Salmon price list*

No.	Year	Place	Unit price	Source
1	1311	Stirling	12d.	*CDS* III.405 V.
2	1327	Scone	7.15d.	*ER* I.66 P.
3	1328	Perth	4.68d.	*ER* I.168 P.
4	1328	Stirling	18.53d. cleaned	*ER* I.160 V.
5	1328	Cardross	6d. salted	*ER* I.125 P.
6	1328	Perth	24d.	*ER* I.88 P.
7	1329	Ednam	12d.	DPS Exp.'29b P.
8	1329	Earlston	8d.	DPS Exp.'29a P.
9	1329	Berwick	7.53d./6.37d.	*ER* I.289 P.
10	1329	Perth	7.20d.(salted)	*ER* I.264 P.
11	1329	Perth	30.75d.	*ER* I.176 P.
12	1329	Dumbarton	4.19d.	*ER* I.269 V.
13	1329		12d.	*ER* I.241
14	1330		4.39d.	*ER* I.342 P.
15	1330	Perth	72d.?	*ER* I.306
16	1330		5.24d./4.39d.	*ER* I.337 V.
17	1331	Berwick	4.39d.?	*ER* I.362 P.
18	1331		7.2d./6d.	*ER* I.396
19	1331	Perth	7.2d./6d.	*ER* I.365 V.
20	1338	Aberdeen	7.2d./6d.	*ER* I.456 P.
21	1341	Aberdeen	9d.	*ER* I.479 V.
22	1341	Perth	3.2d.	*ER* I.485
23	1341	Perth	3.02d.	*ER* I.486
24	1341	Perth	6.28d.	*ER* I.485 P.
25	1341	Aberdeen	6d.	*ER* I.479 V.
26	1342	Inverness	9.6d./8d. winter salmon	*ER* I.479 V.
27	1342	Aberdeen	2.33d./2d.	*ER* I.482 P.
28	1343	Dundee	12d.	*ER* I.524 V.
29	1343	Perth	12d.	*ER* I.523 V.
30	1343	Perth	4d.	*ER* I.523 V.
31	1368	Aberdeen	12d.	*ER* II.308 P.
32	1374	Banff	12d.	*ER* II.492 V.
33	1378	Banff	6d.	*ER* II.599 V.
34	1378	Inverness	9d.	*ER* II.599 V.
35	1380	Edinburgh	22s.barrel	*ER* III.653 P.
36	1380		18.91d./15.80d.	*ER* III.42 P.
37	1384		20.76d./17.36d.	*ER* III.109 P.
38	1385		47d.	*ER* III.109 V.
39	1425	Montrose	30s.barrel	*ER* IV.407 P.
40	1427	Aberdeen	46s.8d.HaB	*ER* IV.443–4 P.
41	1427	Aberdeen	23s.4d.SmB	*ER* IV.444 P.
42	1427	Aberdeen	33.33s.barrel	*ER* IV.444
43	1428	Montrose	30s.barrel	*ER* IV.448–9 P.
44	1428	Aberdeen	36.67s.barrel	*ER* IV.478
45	1428	Aberdeen	45s.LgeB,25s.SmB	*ER* IV.479 P.
46	1428	Montrose	30s.HaB	*ER* IV.505 V.

Table 55 (*cont.*)

No.	Year	Place	Unit price	Source
47	1429	Montrose	30s.HaB	*ER* IV.476 P.
48	1429	Ayr	7d./6d.	*ER* IV.498
49	1429	Montrose	45s.barrel	*ER* IV.505 V.
50	1429	Aberdeen	45s.LgeB,25s.barrel	*ER* IV.510–11 P.
51	1429	Banff	40s.HaB	*ER* IV.522 P.
52	1430	Aberdeen	45s.barrel	*ER* IV.536 P.
53	1433	Aberdeen	47.14s.HaB	*ER* IV.567 P.
54	1433	Aberdeen	40s.HaB salted	*ER* IV.569 P.
55	1433	Banff	40s.barrel salted	*ER* IV.647 V.
56	1434	Aberdeen	38s.barrel salted	*ER* IV.616 P.
57	1434	Aberdeen	42s.HaB	*ER* IV.616
58	1437	Schiveses	36s.HaB salted	*ER* V.52 V.
59	1437	Aberdeen	40s.HaB salted	ACR IV.112 Aw.
60	1439	Aberdeen	16d.	ACR IV.160 Wi.
61	1440	Aberdeen	20s.barrel salted	ACR IV.192 Aw.
62	1440	Aberdeen	40s.barrel large fish	*ER* V.93 P.
63	1440	Monymusk	40s.HaB	*ER* V.94 P.
64	1441	Aberdeen	40s.barrel salted	*ER* V.117 P.
65	1442	Aberdeen	38.10s.barrel salted	*ER* V.134 P.
66	1443	Aberdeen	40s.barrel	*ER* V.155 P.
67	1444	Aberdeen	40s.HaB	ACR IV.368 O.
68	1444	Aberdeen	40s.barrel salted	*ER* V.187 P.
69	1444	Aberdeen	40s.barrel salted	*ER* V.191–2 P.
70	1444	Aberdeensh.	40s.HaB salted	*ER* V.207–8 P.
71	1445	Aberdeen	13.33s.g.barrel salted	ACR IV.391 C.
72	1445	Aberdeen	40s.barrel salted	*ER* V.234–5 P.
73	1446	Aberdeen	7d.	ACR IV.434 C.
74	1446	Aberdeen	12d.	ACR IV.435 C.
75	1446	Aberdeen	40s.barrel salted	*ER* V.270 P.
76	1449	Aberdeen	5d.	ACR V i.50 C.
77	1449	Aberdeen	26s.HaB	ACR V i.71 O.
78	1450	Aberdeen	30s.barrel salted	*ER* V.389 P.
79	1450	Aberdeen	28.89s.barrel salted	*ER* V.404 P.
80	1450	Aberdeen	33.33s.HaB salted	*ER* V.432
81	1450	Aberdeen	33.33s.HaB salted	*ER* V.432 P.
82	1450	Mar?	33.33s.barrel	*ER* V.465 P.
83	1451	Aberdeen	30s.barrel	ACR V i.118 Aw.
84	1451	Aberdeen	33.33s.barrel salted	*ER* V.508–9 V.
85	1451	Aberdeen	33.33s.barrel salted	*ER* V.509 P.
86	1451	Aberdeen	33.33s.barrel salted	*ER* V.509 V.
87	1452	Aberdeen	33.33s.barrel	*ER* V.561 P.
88	1453	Aberdeen	33.47s.barrel salted	*ER* V.629–30 P.
89	1454	Banff	33.33s.barrel salted	*ER* VII.303–4 V.
90	1455	Aberdeen	5s.g.HaB? salted	ACR V i.231 C.
91	1455	Aberdeen	5.33d.	ACR V i.234 Aw.
92	1455	Aberdeen	15s.HaB	ACR V i.241 Aw.

Table 55 (*cont.*)

No.	Year	Place	Unit price	Source
93	1455	Aberdeen	20s.barrel	ACR V i.248 Aw.
94	1455	Aberdeen	40s.barrel	*ER* V.128 V.
95	1455	Banff	36.19s.HaB salted	*ER* VI.319 V.
96	1456	Aberdeen	20s.HaB salted	ACR V i.267 Wi.
97	1456	Aberdeen	33.33s.HaB salted	*ER* VI.304 V.
98	1457	Aberdeen	20s.g.HaB salted	ACR V i.306 O.
99	1457	Aberdeen	33.33s.barrel	*ER* VI.397 V.
100	1457	Aberdeen	32.5s.barrel salted	*ER* VI.404 V.
101	1458	Moray?	26.67s.barrel	*ER* VI.521 P.
102	1459	Aberdeen	20s.HaB	ACR V i.369 O.
103	1463	Aberdeen	40s.HaB	ACR V i.493 C.
104	1465	Aberdeen	45s.HaB	ACR V i.561 O.
105	1467	Moray	36s.barrel salted	*ER* VII.544 P.
106	1468	Aberdeen	40s.barrel	ACR V i.628 C.
107	1468	Aberdeen	40s.barrel	ACR VI.77 O.
108	1469	Aberdeen	4 Fr.crowns barrel	ACR VI.88 V.
109	1469	Spey	48.5s.barrel	*ER* VIII.86
110	1470	Aberdeen	40s.barrel	ACR VI.17 O.
111	1471	Aberdeen	46s.barrel	ACR VI.132 Aw.
112	1471	Aberdeen	21s.g.3g.barrel	ACR VI.139 C.
113	1473		50s.barrel	*TA* I.67 P.
114	1473	Spey	40s.barrel	*ER* VIII.223
115	1473	Spey	40s.barrel	*ER* VIII.223
116	1474	Aberdeen	40s.barrel	ACR VI.287 O.
117	1474	Aberdeen	14s.g.barrel	ACR VI.312 Aw.
118	1474	Aberdeen	60d.	ACR VI.321 Wi.
119	1474	Aberdeen	20d.	ACR VI.321 Wi.
120	1475	Spey	40s.barrel	*ER* VIII.370 V.
121	1475	Berwick	45.56s.barrel salted	*ER* VIII.455
122	1476	Aberdeen	18d. lax	ACR VI.418 Aw.
123	1476	Aberdeen	40s.barrel	ACR VI.418 Aw.
124	1477	Aberdeen	33.33s.barrel salted	ACR VI.490 O.
125	1477	Aberdeen	66s.8d.barrel	ACR VI.491–2 O.
126	1477	Aberdeen	33.33s.barrel	ACR VI.503 O.
127	1477	Berwick	50s.barrel	*ER* VIII.456
128	1478	Berwick	50s.barrel	*ER* VIII.634
129	1478	Berwick	43s.4d.barrel	*ER* VIII.634
130	1478	Berwick	50s.barrel	*ER* VIII.634
131	1479	Berwick	31s.8d.barrel	*ER* IX.82
132	1480	Aberdeen	14d. lax	ACR VI.622 Aw.
133	1480	Aberdeen	24s.g.barrel	ACR VI.640 Aw.
134	1480	Aberdeen	28.89s.barrel	ACR VI.640 O.
135	1480	Aberdeen	29s.g.barrel	ACR VI.666 Aw.
136	1480	Moray	35s.barrel	*ER* IX.143
137	1480	Berwick	45s.barrel	*ER* IX.145 P.
138	1481	Aberdeen	12d.	ACR VI.678 Aw.

Table 55 (*cont.*)

No.	Year	Place	Unit price	Source
139	1481	Aberdeen	20s.barrel	ACR VI.700 Aw.
140	1481	Aberdeen	25s.barrel	ACR VI.706 O.
141	1482	Aberdeen	16.66s.g.barrel custom free	ACR VI.717 Aw.
142	1482	Aberdeen	50s.barrel	ACR VI.750 O.
143	1482	Aberdeen	50s.barrel	ACR VI.764–5 C.
144	1483	Aberdeen	16d. lax	ACR VI.780 V.
145	1485	Aberdour?	43.33s.barrel	A.L.C I.*108 Aw.
146	1486	Aberdeen	60s.barrel	ACR VI.244 Aw.
147	1486	Aberdeen	26s.8d.barrel	ACR VI.246 C.
148	1486	Aberdeen	53s.4d.barrel	ACR VI.976 Aw.
149	1486	Pisc.de Spey	45s.barrel	*ER* IX.502
150	1487	Kinclaven	12s.	*ER* X.10 V.
151	1488	Aberdeen	60s.barrel	ACR VII.52 O.
152	1488	Aberdeen	60s.barrel	ACR VII.87
153	1489	Kinghorn	87s.6d.barrel	*ALC* I.123 Aw.
154	1489	Aberdeen	50s.barrel	ACR VII.148 Aw.
155	1490	Aberdeen or Edinburgh?	75s.barrel	*ALC* I.136 Aw.
156	1490	Aberdeen	66s.8d.barrel	ACR VII.185 O.
157	1491	Aberdeen	66s.8d.barrel	ACR VII.272 Aw.
158	1491	Aberdeen	51s.8d.barrel	*ER* X.363 V.
159	1493	Aberdeen	18s.?barrel	ACR VII.391 O.
160	1494	Aberdeen	50s.barrel	ACR VII.548 O.
161	1494		60s.barrel	ALA I.201 Aw.
162	1495	Findhorn,Mo.	32s.barrel	*ALC* I.396 Aw.
163	1495	Findhorn,Mo.	26s.8d.barrel grilse	*ALC* I.396 Aw.
164	1496	Aberdeen	10s.g.barrel grilse	ACR VII.715 Aw.
165	1496	Aberdeen	43s.barrel	ACR VII.760 Aw.
166	1496	Leith	40s.barrel	SHS 3,50.80 P.
167	1497	Melrose	36d.	*TA* I.320 P.
168	1497	Aberdeen	37s.4d.barrel salm. & grilse	ACR VII.790 O.
169	1497	Aberdeen	40s.barrel salm. & grilse	ACR VII.824 Aw.
170	1497	Moray	40s.barrel	*ER* XI.84
171	1498	Aberdeen	50s.barrel	ACR VII.606
172	1498	Moray	26s.8d.barrel	*ER* XI.84–5
173	deleted			
174	1498	Moray	50s.barrel	*ER* XI.180 P.
175	1499	Aberdeen	42s.barrel	ACR VII.950 Aw.
176	1499	Aberdeen	60s.barrel	ACR VII.976 O.
177	1499	Aberdeen	50s.barrel	ACR VII.979 O.
178	1499		50s.barrel	*ER* XI.250
179	1500	Aberdeen	20s.barrel grilse	ACR VII.1044 O.
180	1501	Aberdeen	20s.barrel grilse	ACR VIII.1 V.
181	1501	Aberdeen	40s.barrel	ACR VIII.29
182	1502	Moray	40s.barrel	*ER* XII.179

Table 55 (*cont.*)

No.	Year	Place	Unit price	Source
183	1503	Aberdeen	56s.barrel	ACR VIII.258 O.
184	1503	Stirling	50s.barrel	*ER* XII.217 P.
185	1504	Aberdeen	40s.barrel	ACR VIII.312 C.
186	1504	Stirling	1s.8d.	*ER* XII.336
187	1504	Stirling	50s.barrel salted	*ER* XII.336 P.
188	1505	Aberdeen	45s.barrel	ACR VIII.467 V.
189	1505	Spey	40s.barrel	*ER* XII.398
190	1506	Stirling	1s.8d.	*ER* XII.540
191	1507	Conain	36.67s.barrel	*ER* XIII.50
192	1508	Aberdeen	18s.g.barrel	ACR VIII.800 O.
193	1508	Perth	50s.barrel	SHS 2,10.211 P.
194	1508	Perth	3s. salmon	SHS 2,10.65 P.
195	1508	Moray	40s.barrel	*ER* XIII.208 V.
196	1508	Moray	42.86s.barrel	*ER* XIII.209
197	1508	Moray	28.07s.barrel	*ER* XIII.210
198	1509	Aberdeen	42s.barrel	ACR VIII.104 Aw.
199	1509	Conain	16.67s.barrel	*ER* XIII.350 V.
200	1510	Moray	50s.barrel	*ER* XIII.296
201	1510	Aberdeen	50s.barrel	*ER* XIII.389 V.
202	1511	Aberdeen	2s. lax	ACR IX.18 O.
203	1511	Stirling	13.6d.	*ER* XIII.404
204	1511	Conain	8.33s.barrel	*ER* XIII.447 V.
205	1512	Forth	55s.barrel	*TA* IV.459 P.
206	1512	Aberdeen	14s.barrel grilse	ACR IX.159 Aw.
207	1512	Aberdeen	50s.barrel	*ER* XIII.573 P.
208	1513	Forth	45s.barrel	*TA* IV.470 P.
209	1513	Forth	45s.barrel	*TA* IV.469 P.
210	1513	Aberdeen	60s.barrel	ACR IX.212 O.
211	1513	Forth	50s.barrel conflated	*TA* IV.492 P.
212	1513	Aberdeen	32s.barrel	ACR IX.292 O.
213	1513	Aberdeen	50s.barrel salted	*ER* XIV.98 P.
214	1514	Perth	43s.barrel	SHS 2,10.237 V.
215	1515	Inchegarvy	28d. salted	*TA* V.21 P.
216	1516	Ardmannoch	10s.barrel	*ER* XIV.308 V.
217	1517	Kinclaven	2s.	*ER* XIV.295 P.
218	1517	Dingwall	43.33s.barrel	*ER* XIV.347
219	1517	Dingwall	33.33s.barrel poor grilse	*ER* XIV.347
220	1518	Aberdeen	60s.barrel	*ER* XIV.438 V.
221	1518		60s.barrel	*ER* XIV.463 P.
222	1520	Aberdeen	58s.barrel	ACR X.282 C.
223	1520	Aberdeen	16d. lax	ACR X.228 Aw.
224	1521	Aberdeen	55s.barrel	ACR X.334 P.
225	1521	Ardmannoch	38.33s.barrel	*ER* XIV.455–6
226	1521	Conane	10s.barrel	*ER* XV.28 V.
227	1521	Conane	33.33s.barrel	*ER* XV.28–9
228	1522	Aberdeen	50s.barrel	ACR XI.195 Aw.

Table 55 (*cont.*)

No.	Year	Place	Unit price	Source
229	1522	Aberdeen	60s.barrel	*ER* XV.67 V.
230	1522	Aberdeen	45s.barrel grilse	ACR XI.105 C.
231	1523	Aberdeen	72s.barrel grilse	ACR XI.244 Aw.
232	1524	Aberdeen	9 francs barrel	ACR XI.431 C.
233	1524	Ardmannoch	33.33s.barrel	*ER* XV.175–6
234	1525	Aberdeen	70s.barrel	ACR XI.574 Aw.
235	1525	Aberdeen	23s.4g.barrel	ACR XI.621
236	1525		69.5d. grilse	HBJV,App., p. 5 P.
237	1525		34.5d. salted	HBJV,App., p. 5 P.
238	1525	Aberdeen	80s.barrel	ACR XI.620 Wi.
239	1526	Stirling	44d. fresh	HBJV, p. 61 P.
240	1526	Aberdeen	40s.barrel (or 55s.)	ACR XII i.56 Aw.
241	1526	Aberdeen	74s.barrel grilse	ACR XII i.60 Aw.
242	1526	Aberdeen?	10s.–12s.g.barrel	ACR XII i.89 Wi.
243	1526	Ardmannoch	40s.barrel	*ER* XV.342
244	1526	Aberdeen	60s.barrel Grilse	ACR XI.717 C.
245	1526	Aberdeen	30s.barrel (or 45s.) grilse	ACR XII i.56 Aw.
246	1527	Ardmannoch	40s.barrel	*ER* XV.413
247	1528	Aberdeen	60s.barrel	ACR XII i.408 O.
248	1528	Edinburgh	70s.barrel salted	HBJV, p. 126
249	1528	Aberdeen	16s.dozen? fresh	ACR XII ii.454 C.
250	1528	Edinburgh	8s.4d. fresh	HBJV, p. 131 P.
251	1529	Edinburgh	65s.barrel salted	HBJV, App., p. 26 P.
252	1529	Edinburgh	65s.barrel salted	HBJV, p. 144 P.
253	1529	Aberdeen	85s.barrel	ACR XIII.98 Aw.
254	1529	Ardmannoch	40s.barrel	*ER* XVI.117–9
255	1529	Falkland	16d. grilse	HBJV, p. 159 P.
256	1529	Edinburgh	70s.barrel salted	HBJV, p. 221 P.
257	1530	Aberdeen	66.67s.barrel	ACR XII ii.783 C.
258	1530	Aberdeen	60s.barrel	ACR XIII.35 O.
259	1531	Aberdeen	28s.g.barrel with grilse	ACR XIII.216 C.
260	1531		62s.barrel	*TA* V.459 P.
261	1532	Aberdeen	60.38s.barrel	ACR XIV.606 Aw.
262	1532	Aberdeen	66s.barrel	ACR XIII.490 O.
263	1532	Aberdeen	30s.barrel	ACR XIII.498 C.
264	1532	Aberdeen	60s.barrel	ACR XIII.414 Wi.
265	1532	Perth	51d. fresh	HBJV, p. 229 P.
266	1532	Perth	3s.4d. salted	HBJV, p. 229 P.
267	1532	Perth	1s.2d. grilse	HBJV, p. 229 P.
268	1532	Aberdeen	100s.barrel	ACR XIII.390 Wi.
269	1532	Aberdeen	20s.barrel grilse	ACR XIII.498 C.
270	1533	Aberdeen	88.87s.barrel	ACR XIV.251 O.
271	1533	Aberdeen	30s.barrel	ACR XIV.314 O.
272	1533	Aberdeen	30s.barrel grilse	ACR XIV.314 O.
273	1533	Aberdeen	75s.barrel	ACR XIV.242 Aw.
274	1533	Aberdeen	60s.barrel	ACR XIV.173 Aw.

Table 55 (*cont.*)

No.	Year	Place	Unit price	Source
275	1535	Aberdeen	80s.barrel	ACR XIV.505 Wi.
276	1535	Aberdeen	84s.barrel	ACR XIV.559 Aw.
277	1535	Conane	50s.barrel	*ER* XVII.38–9
278	1535		60s.barrel	*ER* XVI.480 V.
279	1537	Aberdeen	65s.barrel	ACR XV.629 C.
280	1537	Aberdeen	88s.barrel	ACR XV.578 C.
281	1537	Aberdeen	55s.6d.barrel	ACR XV.404 Aw.
282	1537		60s.barrel	*ER* XVII.170 V.
283	1539	Aberdeen	45.83sbarrel	ACR XVI.246 O.
284	1539	Aberdeen	70s.barrel	ACR XVI.342 O.
285	1539	Aberdeen	50s.barrel	ACR XVI.245 O.
286	1539	Aberdeen	48s.barrel	ACR XVI.674 C.
287	1539	Aberdeen	50s.barrel	ACR XVI.759 C.
288	1539	Conane, Ross	60s.barrel	*ER* XVII.274
289	1539		66s.barrel	*ER* XVII.289 V.
290	1539	Aberdeen	60s.barrel	ACR XVI.145 O.
291	1539	Aberdeen	16d/13.71d. lax	ACR XVI.378 C.
292	1540	Aberdeen	52s.barrel grilse	ACR XVI.739 C.
293	1540	Aberdeen	60s.barrel	ACR XVI.638 Aw.
294	1540	Aberdeen	7 crowns Scots barrel	ACR XVI.676 C.
295	1540	Aberdeen	58s.barrel	ACR XVI.739 C.
296	1540	Aberdeen	7 crowns barrel	ACR XVI.577 C.
297	1540	Aberdeen	43s.barrel	ACR XVI.578 C.
298	1540	Aberdeen	50s.barrel	ACR XVI.452 P.
299	1541	Aberdeen	55s.barrel	ACR XVI.817 O.
300	1541	Aberdeen	4d. grilse	ACR XVI.870 Aw.
301	1541	Stirlingsh.	8.8d. salmon	*ER* XVII.601

Herring[240]

Herring did not vary in size as much as salmon, but there is nonetheless a good deal of variety in the herring prices we have. Though usually salted,[241] we do still meet fresh herring, and cured 'red' herrings.[242] All such preserved fish had first to be cleaned[243] though this was only rarely mentioned. Drying was also occasionally used to improve the keeping

[240] This note on herring has benefited considerably from the comments of Dr A. Stevenson. The failings which remain may be attributed perhaps to my failure to take all his advice.
[241] Explicitly so, List 2, 17, 40, 42, 45, 47, 48, 55, 56.
[242] List 32, 42, 56, 59, 90–1.
[243] List 3.

qualities of the fish.[244] We meet barrelled herring first only in the 1360s,[245] but as with salmon, from the fifteenth century this is the usual method of storing and marketing salted and cleaned fish. The discovery that if herring are cleaned, salted, and tightly barrelled within twenty-four hours of the catch, their 'shelf' life is prolonged is usually attributed to a late fourteenth-century Dutchman, William Beukels(zoon).[246] The implications of this development for the herring and salmon trades may be comparable with the impact of canning in the nineteenth and freezing in the twentieth centuries, yet the subject has received little attention.

We have no prices at all between 1436 and 1483, which is curious since before and after those dates there is no shortage of information. Stevenson's 1425–31 'Table of Customs'[247] shows herring was then only customed at Ayr. It is possible that some migration moved the shoals away from the eastern Scottish fishing grounds at this time, only to bring them back towards the end of the century.[248] Thereafter, they seem to resume their earlier importance, and an assize of herring was instituted.[249] The west coast of Scotland then gains an importance it had not previously enjoyed. While Crail, Pittenweem, and Dysart traditionally dominated the market, in the later period western herring are consistently more prized than eastern.[250] Quantitatively, however, the east coast recovered its pre-eminence, at least as far as the custom on exports is concerned.[251]

Interpretation of surviving Scottish price evidence is complicated by the sale of herring in various different units – by the last, the cade or

[244] List 40, 55, 56.

[245] List 35; Thorold Rogers noted the handling of white herring only from the late fourteenth century, Rogers, *A History of Agriculture and Prices in England*, I, p. 610. The packed herring noted by A. Saul, 'The Herring Industry at Gt Yarmouth', *Norfolk Archaeology*, 38 (1981) p. 40, in 1324 are red herring.

[246] F. Braudel, *The Structures of Everyday Life* (London, 1981), p. 215; Peter Heath, 'North Sea Fishing in the Fifteenth Century: the Scarborough Fleet', *Northern History*, 3, (1968), 61–2.

[247] *Scottish Historical Atlas*, II, forthcoming.

[248] Nicholson, *Scotland: The Later Middle Ages* p. 439. Cf. the much cited migration of herring from the Baltic to the North Sea which seems to be a myth; Heath, 'North Sea Fishing'. However, herring shoals do move. M. Bailey, 'Coastal Fishing off S.E. Suffolk in the Century after the Black Death', *Proceedings of the Suffolk Institute of Archaeology and History* 37 (1990), p. 111, regards depletion of the shoals after *c.* 1370 as unlikely, but he and Saul ('The Herring Industry') note a decline in herring fishing at this time and seem at a loss to explain it. Suggestions include wartime disruption of exports to Gascony, and increased competition from Low Countries and Hanseatic fishermen, who paid more attention to salting and packing standards.

[249] List 75, 77, 79–82, 92.

[250] See List 79, 89, 92–5, 97–8.

[251] Stevenson, in *Scottish Historical Atlas,* II.

mease, the barrel, and by number, usually following the long hundred.[252] It appears that there were 10 or 12 barrels to the last, 2 cades to a barrel, and about 600 fish to a cade, but such rules of thumb are not invariable. Very roughly there seem to have been about 12,000 loose fish or 14,400 barrelled fish to a last. However, prices for one unit cannot always be converted for another. Bulk purchases were probably cheaper, and barrelled fish would necessarily have to be cleaned and preserved. One might therefore anticipate that barrelled fish would be dearer than the corresponding number of loose fish, and this does appear to have been the case. Moreover, there seems to have been a wide variation in medieval herring prices even from the same time and place and measured in the same units. Thus the prices paid by the Durham cellarer in 1328–9 varied between about 5s. and 9s. per thousand, while in 1329–30 they varied from 4s. 7½d. to 8s. 4d.[253] When such a wide price range for a single year seems to be normal, it makes the interpretation of fragmentary evidence particularly difficult. Equally, comparison between English (i.e. Rogers' prices from Norfolk and Suffolk) and Scottish herring prices seem to show Scots herring to be generally cheaper, but this conclusion needs to be treated with caution.

Thirteenth-century Scots herring seem to have been cheap and plentiful. The early prosperity of Crail was probably founded on the fish, and Scottish herring were known and appreciated in London alongside those of Great Yarmouth.[254] In the fourteenth century prices were clearly rising, but the problem of comparing early loose last prices with later fourteenth- and fifteenth-century barrelled prices precludes any very satisfactory longer-term comparison. Barrelled herring are notably dearer than loose fish, but it is not clear how much of the rise in price can be attributed to the cost of cleaning, salting, and barrelling as opposed to a shift in the availability of herring.[255] Both factors may have been involved, for there can be little doubt that herring became scarcer in the fifteenth century. Prices are few and far between, and it is only in the 1470s that the customs accounts indicate some recovery. Restricting any price comparison solely to barrelled herring, such late fourteenth-century prices as we have suggest herring prices moved astonishingly

[252] A.Hunter, *Treatise of Weights, Mets and Measures of Scotland* (Edinburgh, 1624), states that herring were counted in long hundreds. I am grateful to A. Stevenson for this reference.

[253] Durham Dean and Chapter Archives, Cellarer's Account 1328–9, b; 1329–30.

[254] *Munimenta Gildhallae Londoniensis, Liber Albus*, ed. H.T. Riley, Rolls Series (London, 1861), p. 376. I am grateful to A. Stevenson for this reference.

[255] Saul, 'The Herring Industry', p. 41, found Yarmouth herring dearer *c.* 1400 than *c.* 1300, but turn over was substantially down.

Table 56. *Herring prices 1263–1362: Scotland and England*

Year	Scotland	Durham	Rogers
1263	1.33		5.96
1264	1.59		5.67
1298	6.67	4.15[a]	5.71
1327	4.0	6.88[a]	
	4.0		
	4.0		
1328	6.67	8.32[a] 6.5[b]	
	15.55		
	4.0		
	2.03		
	8.0		
	6.76		
1329	10.1	5.25[a] 5.23[b]	7.19
	6.9	6.84	
	8.33		
	3.45		
	6.67		
	9.33		
	8.0		
1330	2.09		
	2.12		
	7.27		
1331	8.0		7.52
	4.0		
	2.09		
	5.0		
	2.09		
1341	2.08		
	2.08		
1342	1.67		9.17
	2.08		
1359	2.09	12.75[b]	11.77
1362	6.67		11.5[b]

Note: all prices are in shillings per 1,000/1,200.
[a]White.
[b]Red.

little over 150 years into the sixteenth century. If allowance is also made for Scottish currency alterations, it is clear that the silver price of barrelled herring had fallen dramatically by the sixteenth century, perhaps as a result of the return of the herring shoals from around the 1470s.

Table 57. *Herring price list*

No.	Year	Place	Unit price	Source
1	1263	Inverness	13.33s. last	*ER* I.19 P.
2	1264	Fife	15.92s. last	*ER* I.4 P.
3	1298	Berwick	6s.8d.1,000/1,200	*DHS* II.326 P.
4	1327	Ayr	40s. last	*ER* I.69 V.
5	1327	Rutherglen	40s. last	*ER* I.70-1 P.
6	1327	Ayr	40s. last	*ER* I.69 V.
7	1328	Dumbarton	66.67s. last	*ER* I.161 V.
8	1328		155.56s. last	*ER* I.117-18 P.
9	1328	Ayr	40s. last	*ER* I.89 V.
10	1328	Crail	20.3s. last	*ER* I.159 P.
11	1328	Ayr	4s. mease (= 80s. last)	*ER* I.162 P.
12	1328		67.59s. last	*ER* I.219 P.
13	1329	Ayr	101s. last	*ER* I.268 P.
14	1329		69s. last	*ER* I.289 P.
15	1329		68.37s. last	*ER* I.289 P.
16	1329	Earlston	83.33s. last	DPS Exp.'29a V.
17	1329	Crail	34s.6d. last	*ER* I.265 V.
18	1329	Perth	66.67s. last	*ER* I.265 P.
19	1329	Linlithgow	93.33s. last	*ER* I.273 P.
20	1329		80s. last	*ER* I.283
21	1330	Dysart	20.87s. last	*ER* I.266 P.
22	1330	Crail	21.19s. last	*ER* I.305 V.
23	1330		72.73s. last	*ER* I.341-2 P.
24	1331	Dundee	80s. last	*ER* I.350 V.
25	1331	Rutherglen	40s. last	*ER* I.357 V.
26	1331	Crail	20.93s. last	*ER* I.363 V.
27	1331		50s. last	*ER* I.396
28	1331	Crail	20.88s. last	*ER* I.363 V.
29	1341	Crail	20.83s. last	*ER* I.494 P.
30	1341	Crail	20.83s. last	*ER* I.494 P.
31	1342	Inverness	16.67s. last	*ER* I.516 P.
32	1342	Crail	20.83s. last red	*ER* I.521 P.
33	1359	Crail	20.85s. last	*ER* II.31 P.
34	1362	Crail	66.67s. last	*ER* II.156 V.
35	1364		10.89s. barrel	*ER* II.228
36	1367		13.33s. barrel	*ER* II.294 P.
37	1373		9.44s. barrel	*ER* II.432 V.
38	1374		113.33s. last	*ER* II.449 V.
39	1375	Crail	33s. last	*ER* II.495 P.
40	1376	Crail	27s. last	*ER* II.540 P.
41	1377	Crail	166.75s. last autumn	*ER* II.575 V.
42	1377	Crail	16.67s. last red	*ER* II.575 V.
43	1378	Crail	44.59s. last	*ER* II.596 P.
44	1379	Crail	25.83s. last	*ER* III.24 V.
45	1380	Crail	31.94s. last	*ER* III.57 V.
46	1380		15.78s. barrel	*ER* III.42 V.

Table 57 (*cont.*)

No.	Year	Place	Unit price	Source
47	1381	Crail	39.10s. last	*ER* III.73 P.
48	1382	Crail	37.06s. last	*ER* III.102-3 P.
49	1385		20s. barrel	*ER* III.108 V.
50	1391	Crail	71.70s. last	*ER* III.308 P.
51	1396	Crail	37.43s. last	*ER* III.423 V.
52	1397	Crail	41.29s. last	*ER* III.450 V.
53	1398	Crail	53.68s. last	*ER* III.479 V.
54	1401	Crail	73.33s. last	*ER* III.557 P.
55	1402	Crail	37.50s. last	*ER* III.580 P.
56	1404	Crail	36.67s. last red	*ER* III.638 P.
57	1404	Crail	130s. last	*ER* III.638-9 P.
58	1427	Edinburgh	42s./32s. barrel	*ER* IV.438 P.
59	1428	Edinburgh	*c.* 275s. last white & red	*ER* IV.473 V.
60	1428	Aberdeen	20s. barrel	*ER* IV.479 P.
61	1433		198.04s. last	*ER* IV.591 P.
62	1436	Scone	27s. barrel salted	*ER* V.32 P.
63	1483	Wauchtoun'	2s. per 100/120	*ALC* I.166 Aw.
64	1492	Dumbarton	240s. last	*ALC* I.226 Aw.
65	1496	Leith?	18s. barrel	SHS 3,50.80 V.
66	1497	Ayr	32s. hogshead	*TA* I.344 P.
67	1498	Ayr	10s. mease	*TA* I.382 P.
68	1510	Ayr	16s.4d. barrel	*ER* XIII.382 P.
69	1513	Forth	1.6s. per 100/120	*TA* IV.463 P.
70	1513	Forth	£8 last	*TA* IV.489 P.
71	1513	Forth	2s. per 100/120 conflated	*TA* IV.464 P.
72	1513	Forth	20s. barrel conflated	*TA* IV.465 P.
73	1515	Inchegarvy	5s.3d. per 100/120	*TA* V.21 P.
74	1515	Ross	£10 last western coast	*ER* XIV.217
75	1516	Pittenweem	216s. last	*ER* XIV.267
76	1517	Western seas	14s. barrel salted	*ER* XV.60
77	1518	Pittenweem	14s. barrel	*ER* XIV.370
78	1520	Pittenweem	11s. per thousand	*ER* XIV.436 P.
79	1522	Western seas	18s. barrel salted	*ER* XV.57
80	1522	Pittenweem	13s.4d. barrel	*ER* XV.59
81	1524	Pittenweem	13s.4d. barrel	*ER* XV.178
82	1525	Leith	14s. barrel	*ER* XV.294
83	1525	Western seas	20s. barrel	*ER* XV.294
84	1526		20s. West. 14s. eastern coast barrel	*ER* XV.389
85	1527	Western seas	20s. barrel	*ER* XV.467
86	1527	Eastern seas	14s. barrel	*ER* XV.467
87	1528	Edinburgh	34s. 860/1,020	HBJV, p. 131 P.
88	1528	Western seas	20s. barrel	*ER* XV.552
89	1528	Eastern seas	14s. barrel	*ER* XV.552
90	1529	Edinburgh	35s. 1,000/1,200 salted	HBJV, p. 221 P.
91	1529	Edinburgh	16s. 400/480 fresh	HBJV, p. 221 P.

Table 57 (*cont.*)

No.	Year	Place	Unit price	Source
92	1530	Pittenweem	14s. barrel	*ER* XVI.62 V.
93	1530	Western seas	20s. barrel	*ER* XVI.140
94	1530	Eastern seas	14s. barrel	*ER* XVI.141 P.
95	1531	Eastern seas	14s. barrel	*ER* XVI.178
96	1532	Perth	6s. 2d. 160/180	HBJV, p. 229 P.
97	1537		20s. barrel western coast	*ER* XVII.176
98	1537		14s. barrel eastern coast	*ER* XVII.176
99	1541	Kilmarnock	20s. 1,000/1,200	*ER* XVII.595

Salt

There was a very considerable demand for salt in later medieval northern Europe.[256] In Scotland we find it used for treating hides,[257] and preserving meat,[258] but most especially for preserving fish.[259] An improvement in the technique of barrelling salted fish dating from the late fourteenth century may have enormously increased demand for salt,[260] and the traditional sources of salt – chiefly Lüneburg and the Low Countries – were overtaken by the huge output of the French salt pans centred around the Bay of Bourgneuf.[261]

The salt industries of different regions gave rise to different types of salt. Lüneburg salt was derived from brine springs, and English deposits in Cheshire and Worcestershire were similarly a result of the local geology, but most other medieval salt was derived from the treatment of seawater.[262] Seawater contains a much lower concentration of salt than brine, but both require heating to evaporate the water and crystallize the salts. A fast boiling creates small crystals and fine salt, while natural evaporation by the sun gives rise to large crystals and coarser salt. Thus French salt was likely to be coarse or great salt, while salts made further north by boiling were fine or small. French bay salt coming from Brittany and all the way round the Bay as far as Poitou was

[256] Medieval salt consumption has been estimated at 20g. per person per day, about twice the present figure (Braudel, *The Structures of Everyday Life*, p. 209–10).
[257] List 61.
[258] List 4, 11, 14, 59, 108.
[259] List 5, 10, 17, 35, 39, 54–5; 24, 38, 73; 43–4, 71.
[260] See herring and salmon above, pp. 306 and 318.
[261] A.R. Bridbury, *England and the Salt Trade in the Later Middle Ages* (Oxford, 1955).
[262] In the Low Countries salts deposited by seawater in peat were used as a source.

apparently grey, that from Normandy was black, while the northern boiled salt was typically white.[263]

Bridbury was clear that English fine white salt was superior to coarse grey or black salt from France and that it cost more.[264] However, the real picture may be more complicated. Thorold Rogers believed white salt was generally dearer than undesignated salt, but that great salt was generally dearer than small.[265] Unless Bridbury's identification of white fine small salt and darker coarse great salt is at fault, Rogers' perceptions have clearly become confused. Bridbury devoted a special appendix to Rogers' conclusions on price, and argued that Rogers' undesignated salt may often in fact have been Bay salt. However, while Rogers' extensive work on salt prices does seem confused, Bridbury's treatment of salt *prices* is only cursory.

Evidence for salt prices in Scotland is equally complicated by the combination of a variety of description and no description at all. Our list of prices contains 119 entries. Of these 24 were described as great or coarse salt, 3 were black, 1 came from Poitou, 1 from Burwage (?Brouage, Charent-Inf.), and 3 were clearly of French origin though the salt itself was not explicitly so designated. On the other hand we have 20 entries for white salt, 2 for fine salt, and 3 for small salt. Just over half our salt prices therefore are for salt with no further indication of type or origin. If we concentrate first on salt with information about type, and divide the prices following Bridbury's identification of fine, white, small boiled salt as opposed to coarse, great, black/grey French salt, as arranged chronologically in Table 58, we see clearly that white salt and its associated types in Scotland are consistently cheaper than French salt in Scotland. The same point emerges from consideration of the few cases where we have comparable prices for both varieties from the same time.[266] Thus in Scotland it seems clear that great salt was consistently significantly dearer than fine.

The conflict with at least one interpretation of the English evidence is not easy to resolve. It is possible that carriage costs may have

[263] Bridbury attributes the colour of French salt to surviving impurities, *Salt Trade*, p. 52 and n. 4. See P. Boissonnade, 'Le mouvement commercial entre la France et les Iles Britanniques au XVIIe siècle', *Revue historique*, 134 (1920) 228, for the black salt of Normandy.

[264] Bridbury, *Salt Trade* pp. 94–5.

[265] Rogers, *A History of Agriculture and Prices in England*, I, p. 456, IV, p. 390.

[266] List 31–2, 57, 109–10, 115–16. See also the prices of salt in Gdansk in 1485: Bay salt 40 marks a last, Lüneburg salt 38 marks a last; and Scottish salt 22 marks a last. S.G.E. Lythe, 'Economic Life', in *Scottish Society in the Fifteenth Century*, Jennifer M. Brown (ed.) (London, 1977), p. 78.

Table 58. *Salt prices 1298–1535*

White, fine, small		French, great, black, coarse	
		1298	12.5d.b.
1327	12.83d.b.	1327	12.83d.b.
1329	18d.b.	1329	15.57d.b.,18d.b.
1341	9d.b.	1341	20d.b.
1367	28.67d.b.	1367	28.67d.b.
1409	32d.b.		
		1429	40d.b.
1433	13.76d.b.		
1434	32d.b.		
1436	10.5d.b.,13.5d.b.,16d.b.	1436	80d.b.
		1446	27d.b.
1450	24d.b.	1450	96d.b.
1456	25.71d.b.,48d.b.		
1460	60d.b.	1460	120d.b.,108d.b.
1461	40d.b.		
		1467	96d.b.
		1476	96d.b.
		1477	113.6d.b.
		1480	96d.b.
		1492	(320d.b.)
		1503	96d.b.
1513	25d.b.		
1525	120d.b.	1525	120d.b.
1528	60d.b.	1528	192d.b.
1532	44d.b.		
1533	76.27d.b.	1533	192d.b.
		1535	102d.b.

Note: parentheses have been used to flag up calculations which are less securely based than others – either because they are based on a smaller amount of data, or because they involve certain, possibly questionable, assumptions.

significantly affected some prices,[267] or considerations of quality about which we are ill- or un-informed may have a role to play. It must also be remembered that some price variation was to be expected, even for one grade of salt.[268] Given the scarcity of the Scottish evidence it seems likely that it will be further work on English prices which will finally resolve this problem.

[267] E.g. List 35–6, 98–9 give information on this point, but other prices may be similarly affected without our knowing.

[268] List 84, 86, 95, 100 for price variation at Perth.

Table 59. *Salt prices 1265–1367: Scotland and England*

Year	Scotland	Durham	Rogers
1265	3.88		3.63
1288	2.25		2.63
1298	6.25[a]		3.88
	6.0		
1327	6.42[b]		4.5
1328	8.34		4.63
	5.45		
1329	10.0	4.59	4.88
	11.0	3.75[b]	
	7.79[b]		
	9.0[b]		
1330	9.0[b&c]	8.34	6.88
	6.0		
1331	6.0		4.25
	5.79		
	6.0		
1341	4.5[c]		4.5
	10.0[b]		
1357	12.0		8.63
1361	10.0		9.38
1362	12.0	10.01	9.38
1364	20.0		8.88
1367	14.34[b&c]	7.19	12.07

Note: all prices are in pence per bushel.
[a]Poitou salt.
[b]Coarse salt.
[c]Fine salt.

For the moment difficulties afflicting this particular series are such that any table of mean prices seems inappropriate. It appears that at least two distinct price levels seem to be involved but our evidence is often inadequate to attribute particular prices to one series rather than the other except on grounds of price. Such a procedure could only tell us that dear salt was more expensive than cheap salt! The full listing of prices, however, does suggest a marked rise in prices in the second half of the fourteenth century, perhaps to be associated with demand arising from new techniques in salting barrelled fish as well as any effects of the Black Death or the Hundred Years War on supply. Comparison between English and Scottish salt prices before 1367 shows that salt of whatever type was generally dearer in Scotland than in England (Table 59). Fifteenth-century prices look somewhat stagnant, especially considering Scottish currency changes, but there are signs of an upturn in salt prices towards the end of our period. These rather general comments on the movement of salt prices apply to both the dearer and the cheaper range of salt. In passing, it should perhaps be noted that the chronicle price dated to 1435 may properly belong to the famine year of 1438.[269]

Scotland both imported and exported salt. The home-produced salt came most notably from Prestonpans, with fuel for boiling derived from the Tranent coal mine.[270] The record shows quite clearly that this was white salt (as one would expect from boiling), and that it belonged in the cheaper price series. Similarly, we may note the juxtaposition of coal and saltpans at Culross, while Arbroath Abbey owned a saltworks at Stirling, and Kelso owned saltpans on the coast.[271] Nevertheless, salt was unquestionably also imported.[272] Aberdeen, no doubt because of its commitment to salmon, marts, and hides, had a particularly great demand for salt, and the burgh itself was prepared to take measures in order to secure a sufficient supply to meet the town's requirements. Exporting merchants were sometimes obliged to invest part of their profits in salt for importing to Aberdeen.[273] Also the burgh bought on its own account for redistribution within the town.[274] Further, the burgh also took the unusual step of setting a *minimum* price for salt.[275] Burgh price regulations more typically set maximum prices, to protect the consumer, but these minimum price fixings applied to wholesale transactions outside the burgh, and the price was deliberately set unreasonably high, in an attempt to prevent salt leaving the burgh. Aberdeen's merchants, of course, also bought salt individually. List 80 shows salt bought in an unhelpful French quantity which prevents our understanding of the price, but nevertheless the case is full of interest. Aberdeen burgesses arranged for delivery of the salt by French shipowners with payment due eight days after delivery. Payment seems to have been made at Leith in April, and formally acknowledged in the Aberdeen court record in September. The French contact and the involvement

[269] List 40.
[270] List 41–3, 45. See also Stevenson, *Scottish Historical Atlas* II for evidence of export.
[271] Margaret Sanderson, *Cardinal of Scotland: David Beaton c. 1494–1546* (Edinburgh, 1986), pp. 6, 21. Norman F. Shead, 'The Abbey of Kelso in the Twelfth and Thirteenth Centuries' and 'Nunneries in the Twelfth and Thirteenth Centuries', in McNeil and Nicholson (eds.), *Scottish Historical Atlas*, I, pp. 44, 46.
[272] List 66, 68–9 for duty paid on imports. See also of course the evidence for French salt.
[273] Chapter 2, pp. 71–3.
[274] List 64, though the price itself looks unreliable. For such corporate purchasing, see also p. 71.
[275] List 30–2, 50.

Table 60. *Salt price list*

No.	Year	Place	Unit price	Source
1	1265	Berwick	7.75d.b.	*ER* I.27 P.
2	1288	Jedburgh	4.5d.b.	*ER* I.44 P.
3	1298	Berwick	12.5d.b. Poitou	*DHS* II.326 P.
4	1298	Berwick	4s.qr (= 12d.b.)	*DHS* II.326 P.
5	1327	Scone	12.83d.b. coarse & white	*ER* I.66 P.
6	1328	Cardross	16.67d.b.	*ER* I.125 P.
7	1328		10.9d.b.	*ER* I.219 P.
8	1329	Galloway	20d.b.	*ER* I.152 P.
9	1329	Galloway	22d.b.	*ER* I.152 P.
10	1329	Berwick	15.57d.b. coarse	*ER* I.313 P.
11	1329	Selkirk	18d.b. coarse	*ER* I.313 P.
12	1330		18d.b. coarse & fine	*ER* I.342 P.
13	1330	Perth	12d.b.	*ER* I.306 V.
14	1331	Berwick	12d.b.	*ER* I.362 P.
15	1331	Perth	11.57d.b.	*ER* I.365 P.
16	1331	Berwick	12d.b.	*ER* I.362 P.
17	1341	Perth	9d.b. fine	*ER* I.485-6 P.
18	1341		20d.b. coarse	*ER* I.505 P.
19	1357	Edinburgh	24d.b.	*ER* I.609 P.
20	1361	Edinburgh	20d.b.	*ER* II.112 P.
21	1362	Kildrummy	24d.b.	*ER* II.166 P.
22	1364	Coldingham	40d.b.	SS 12.xlvii P.
23	1367		28.67d.b. coarse & white	*ER* II.294 P.
24	1377	Crail	20d.b.	*ER* II.575 V.
25	1380		45.28d.b.	*ER* III.42 P.
26	1381	Edinburgh	30d.b.	*ER* III.81 V.
27	1381		48d.b.	*ER* III.42 V.
28	1385	Stirling	15d.b.	*ER* III.683 P.
29	1400	Aberdeen	19.5d.b.	SHS 3,49.148 C.
30	1401	Aberdeen	64d.b.	ACR I.197 assize V.
31	1409	Aberdeen	64d.b.	ACR II.52 assize V.
32	1409	Aberdeen	32d.b. white	ACR II.52 assize V.
33	1413	Inverness	30d.b.	*ER* IV.228 V.
34	1428	Inverness	48d.b.	*ER* IV.498 V.
35	1429	Aberdeen	40d.b. coarse	*ER* IV.509-10 V.
36	1429	Aberdeen	40d.b. coarse	*ER* IV.509 V.
37	1433	S.of Forth	13.76d.b. white	*ER* IV.600 P.
38	1434	Crail	32d.b. white	*ER* IV.637 P.
39	1434	Aberdeen	80d.b.	*ER* IV.617 V.
40	1435	Jed Forest	216d.b.	Bower, *Scotichronicon*, p. 298 Ch.
41	1436	Tranent	10.5d.b white	*ER* V.53 V.
42	1436	Tranent	16d.b white	*ER* V.53 V.
43	1436	Tranent	16d.b. white	*ER* V.53 V.
44	1436	Bute + Arran	80d.b. coarse	*ER* V.85 V.
45	1436	Tranent	13.5d.b. white	*ER* V.53 V.

Table 60 (*cont.*)

No.	Year	Place	Unit price	Source
46	1437	Aberdeen	10s. large barrel white	ACR IV.88 O.
47	1439	Aberdeen	52s. petit qr coarse	ACR IV.170 C.
48	1446	Ayr	27d.b. coarse	*ER* V.261-2 V.
49	1450	Stirling	24d.b. white	*ER* V.479 P.
50	1450	Aberdeen	96d.b. coarse	ACR V ii.757 assize V.
51	1456	Inverness?	25.71d.b. white	*ER* VI.483 P.
52	1456	Elgin	48d.b. white	*ER* VI.484 P.
53	1456	Elgin	48d.b. white	*ER* VI.484 P.
54	1457	Dumbarton	50d.b. coarse & white	*ER* VI.504 P.
55	1457	Dumbarton	36d.b.	*ER* VI.591 P.
56	1460	Galloway	120d.b. coarse	*ER* VII.8 P.
57	1460	Inverness?	60d.b. white, 108d.b. coarse	*ER* VII.19 P.
58	1461	Inverness?	40d.b. white	*ER* VII.127 P.
59	1461	Moray	60d.b	*ER* VII.127 P.
60	1462	Stirlingsh.	33.5d.b.	*ER* VII.190 P.
61	1463	Stirling	32d.b.	*ER* VII.289 V.
62	1467	Elgin & Inver?	96d.b. coarse	*ER* VII.544 P.
63	1468	Moray	96d.b. coarse	*ER* VII.638 P.
64	1470	Aberdeen	375d.b.?	ACR VI.120 P.
65	1474		24d.b.	ALA I.35 Aw.
66	1476	Berwick	96d.b. coarse imported	*ER* VIII.389
67	1477	Aberdeen	72d.b.	ACR VI.486 Aw.
68	1477	Berwick	113.6d.b. great imported	*ER* VIII.539
69	1480	Berwick	96d.b. great imported	*ER* IX.145
70	1484	Quhittingam	6s. 8d. laid	*ALC* I.*90 Aw.
71	1492	Aberdeen	320d.b. great	ACR VII.321 Aw.
72	1498	Dysart	42d.b.	*ER* XI.222 V.
73	1498	Dunbar	24d.b.	*ER* XI.223 V.
74	1498	Edinburgh	25.75d.b.	*ER* XI.234 V.
75	1499	Aberdeen	80d.b.	ACR VII.1010 Wi.
76	1499	Dysart	20.45d.b.	*ER* XI.268 V.
77	1502	Linlithgow	26.25d.b.	*ER* XII.156 P.
78	1503	Ross	40d.b.	*ER* XII.239 P.
79	1503	Ross	96d.b. coarse	*ER* XII.239 P.
80	1505	Aberdeen	80s. moury great	ACR VIII.495 Wi.
81	1506	Perth	31.52d.b.	SHS 2,10.198 P.
82	1506	Perth	32d.b./36d.b./40d.b.	SHS 2,10.203 P.
83	1506	Perth	32d.b.	SHS 2,10.205 P.
84	1507		19.5d.b.	*TA* III.386 P.
85	1507	Perth	48d.b.	SHS 2,10.206 P.
86	1508	Perth	28d.b./30d.b./40d.b.	SHS 2,10.211 P.
87	1509	Perth	32.67d.b.	SHS 2,10.217 P.
88	1509	Perth	30.95d.b.	SHS 2,10.217 P.
89	1510	Perth	32.62d.b.	SHS 2,10.222 P.
90	1511	Aberdeen	15s.g. petty quarter	ACR VIII.119 Aw.

Table 60 (*cont.*)

No.	Year	Place	Unit price	Source
91	1512	Dysart	22.5d.b. met salt	*TA* IV.307 P.
92	1512	Forth	36d.b.	*TA* IV.459 P.
93	1512	Perth	30.75d.b.	SHS 2,10.227 P.
94	1513	Aberdeen	£4 petty quarter	ACR IX.224-5 C.
95	1513	Perth	32d.b./48d.b.	SHS 2,10.231 P.
96	1513	Forth	24.75d.b. conflated salt & small salt	*TA* IV.489etc P.
97	1513	Forth	25d.b. conflated salt & small salt	*TA* IV.497 P.
98	1513	Stirling	24d.b.	*ER* XIV.32 P.
99	1513	Leith	24d.b.	*ER* XIV.32-3 P.
100	1514	Perth	36d.b./48d.b.	SHS 2,10.236 P.
101	1514	Perth	36d.b.	SHS 2,10.236 P.
102	1514	Perth	36d.b.	SHS 2,10.236 P.
103	1514	Aberdeen	192d.b.	ACR IX.358-9 C.
104	1525	Edinburgh	10.07s.b. white & black	HBJV, App., p. 6 P.
105	1526	Aberdeen	25s.qr	ACR XII.i 37 Aw.
106	1527	Aberdeen	17s.pette quarter	ACR XII.i 27 Aw.
107	1528	Stirling	192d.b. black	HBJV, App., p. 16 P.
108	1528	Stirling	63.64d.b.	HBJV, App., p. 16 P.
109	1528	Edinburgh	192d.b. black	HBJV, App., p. 16 P.
110	1528	Edinburgh	60d.b. white	HBJV, App., p. 16 P.
111	1529	Aberdeen	144d.b.	ACR XII ii.4 Aw.
112	1531		45d.b.	*TA* V.460 P.
113	1532	Perth	80d.b.	HBJV, p. 229 P.
114	1532	Edinburgh	44d.b. white	HBJV, p. 232 P.
115	1533	Glasgow	76.27d.b. small	*TA* VI.164 P.
116	1533	Glasgow	192d.b. great	*TA* VI.164 P.
117	1535	Aberdeen	102d.b.	ACR XIV.546-7 Aw.
118	1538	Aberdeen	240d.b.	ACR XV.685 O.
119	1540	Aberdeen	128d.b.	ACR XVI.779 C.

of Leith in an Aberdeen deal are typical sixteenth-century developments. Equally, the deferred payment, and the need for a legal record of payment, are by then increasingly normal procedures. The record is full of cases of money or salt owing but withheld,[276] or wrongfully taken away.[277] In short, despite our uncertainty about the price structure of medieval salt, there can be no doubt about its importance.

[276] List 29, 45–6, 104–5, 110, 116, 118.
[277] List 102.

Canvas

Canvas, that is hemp measured by the ell,[278] was extensively used as a sacking material to make bags to contain items as various as lime or spices, gold or wool, documents or feathers.[279] But in addition to its role as an all purpose packing material, it was also used for tents, for example, for those camped outside Threave castle during the siege,[280] and to make sails for ships.[281] We also meet it as a sheet for drying gunpowder[282] or in straps for horse girths.[283]

Not surprisingly for a material with so many different applications, the exact type and quality of canvas under discussion will also have varied. Unfortunately, additional information about the particular type of canvas priced is only provided towards the end of our period and even then such particulars are seldom as precise as one would like. From 1495 canvas is often spoken of as Bertane or Bartane (?Breton) canvas. Subsequently, we meet also small Bertane canvas, and 'blechit' (i.e. bleached) canvas, both of which seem to be fairly consistently dearer than other types. We also meet canvas described as Vitrisch,[284] Flemish,[285] French,[286] Barres,[287] fine,[288] and great.[289] Although there is some evidence that different types of canvas were differently priced, this was by no means always the case.[290] Moreover, even when we are reasonably sure that a particular variety was liable to be specially priced, as is the case for small and bleached Bertane canvas, we cannot be certain that such types were always explicitly recognized in the text.[291] The ambiguity of the unqualified term canvas is also revealed by the way in which the term seems to merge imperceptibly with linen.[292] While linen is made of flax and canvas of hemp, the 'small' fine canvas may have contained a mixture of flax and hemp.

[278] Hemp measured by the stone could be made into rope rather than canvas. List 15, 16, 64.
[279] List 17, 92; 2, 12; 4, 31; 25; 31, 38, 122; 97. See also *ER* IV.132.
[280] List 36, and *ER* VI.119.
[281] List 29, 32, 74.
[282] List 37.
[283] List 34.
[284] List 56.
[285] List 65. The Flemish ell was one third as big again as the Scots ell.
[286] List 99–100.
[287] List 122.
[288] List 110.
[289] List 111–12, 129–30.
[290] List 135 for canvas, Bertane canvas, and great canvas all equally priced.
[291] List 124 gives three examples at the same dear price, but only the last is described as bleached. In other cases the price may look dear, but no explanation is given, e.g. List 83, 87, 104, 115.
[292] List 147 concerns 'canvas' used as sheets for the prince. G. Whittington and K.J. Edwards, 'The Cultivation and Utilisation of Hemp in Scotland', *Scottish Geographical Magazine*, 106 (1990), 167–73, were also aware of the rather blurred distinction between canvas and linen, citing *ER* I.65, XVIII.147, XIX.174.

Table 61. *Canvas summary table*

Period	Mean price	Deflated	Index
A			
B–C	3	3.08	100.0
D	6	(5.87)	(190.6)
E	6	(4.99)	(162.0)
F			
G			
H	13	5.15	167.2
I	11	3.68	119.5
60s			
70s	14	3.99	129.5
80s	(16)		
90s	12	3.42	111.0
1500s	14	4.05	131.5
10s+20s	13	3.35	108.8
30s	18	3.97	128.9

Note: the mean price is in pence per ell; the deflated column gives the currency-adjusted sterling equivalent price. Parentheses have been used to flag up calculations which are less securely based than others – either because they are based on a smaller amount of data, or because they involve certain, possibly questionable, assumptions.

As a result of this uncertainty, the single price trend suggested for canvas (Table 61) conceals, and may be distorted by, a good deal of variety, though figures have been calculated excluding the dearer canvas types when these are explicitly recorded. However, despite these considerable difficulties some observation on the movement of canvas prices may be generally valid. The prices of canvas in England and Scotland seem to be broadly comparable (Table 62). It is apparent that prices rose sharply after the Black Death, and even in the depths of the fifteenth-century depression, prices remained above their early fourteenth-century index base (Table 61 and Figure 40) even after correcting for monetary changes.

We have no direct evidence for the domestic production of canvas, and considerable evidence of its foreign origin at least in the sixteenth century. However, the raw material, hemp, was unquestionably cultivated in medieval Scotland, as pollen analyses from Fife have shown, suggesting that the local production of rope and canvas may have been likely.[293]

[293] Whittington and Edwards, 'Hemp in Scotland' and 'Palynological Evidence for the Growing of Cannabis Sativa L. (Hemp) in Medieval and Historical Scotland', *Transactions of the Institute of British Geographers* (1990), 60–9.

Table 62. *Canvas prices 1302–66: Scotland and England*

Year	Scotland	Durham	Rogers
1302		4.03/3.61	
1304	3.0		3.0
1325	3.07		3.07
1327	4.32/3.6		1.88
1328	3.0	3.25	3.5
	3.6/3.0		
	3.62/3.03		
1329	2.0	4.19/3.62	2.5
	3.0		
1330	3.55/3.0	4.0	2.83
	3.75/3.17		
1331	3.53		2.33
1335	4.0	3.0	3.0
1338	3.5		3.75
1341	2.0	2.81/2.5	1.79
1344	3.24		2.35
1363	6.5	4.77	
1364	6.5	5.19	6.33
1366	5.0	4.52	5.5

Note: all prices are in shillings per dozen ells.

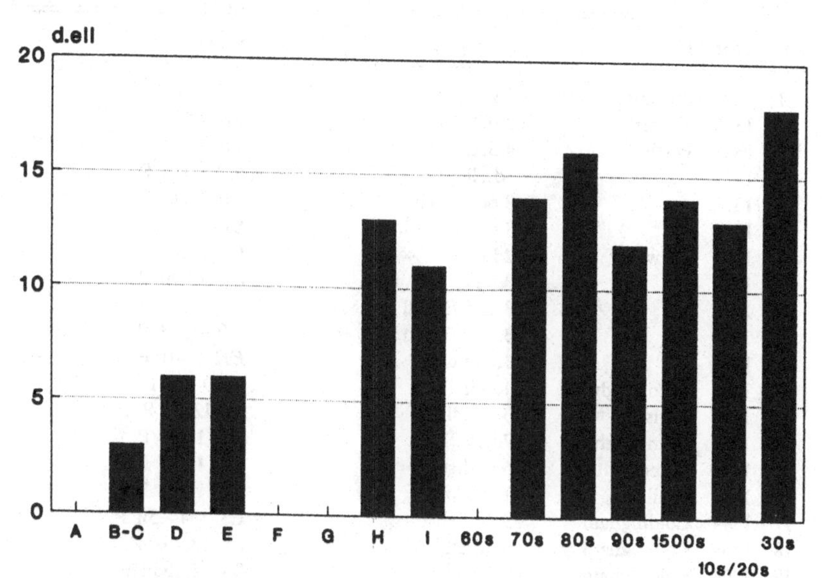

39 Canvas prices (mean prices for time periods A–1530s)
For periods A–I, see Introduction, p. 6.

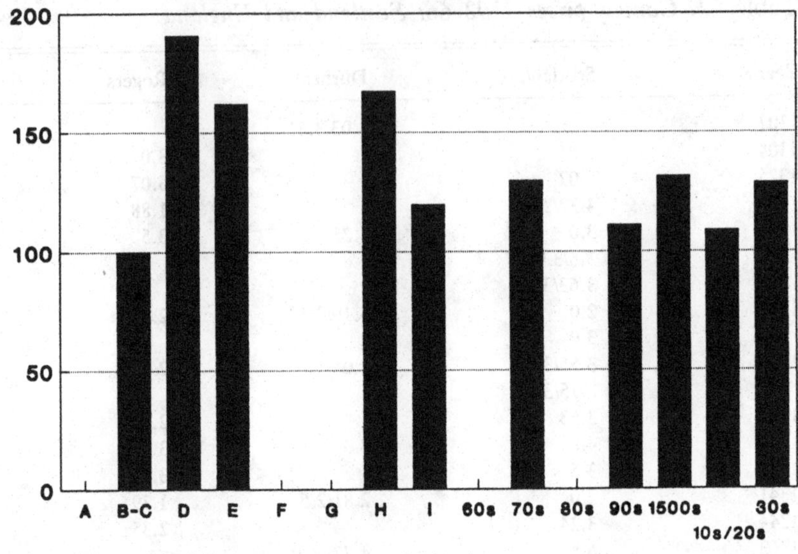

40 Canvas index (sterling equivalent)

Table 63. *Canvas price list*

No.	Year	Place	Unit price	Source
1	1304	Stirling?	3d.ell	*CDS* IV.465 P.
2	1325	Tarbert	3.07d.ell	*ER* I.57 P.
3	1327	Perth	4.32d./3.6d.ell	*ER* I.78 V.
4	1328		3d.ell	*ER* I.117 P.
5	1328		3.6d./3d.ell	*ER* I.117 P.
6	1328		3.62d./3.03d.ell	*ER* I.220 P.
7	1329	Berwick?	2d.ell	*ER* I.243
8	1329		3d.ell	*ER* I.290 P.
9	1330		3.55d./3d.ell	*ER* I.343 P.
10	1330		3.75d./3.17d.ell	*ER* I.343 P.
11	1331		3.53d.ell	*ER* I.401 P.
12	1335	Edinburgh	4d.ell	PRO E101/19/21 P.
13	1338	Earlston	3.5d.ell	SS 12.xii P
14	1341	Edinburgh	2d.ell	*ER* I.490 P.
15	1341	Inverkeith'g	6.53d.stone	*ER* I.487 P.
16	1341	Crail	1.04s.stone	*ER* I.494 P.
17	1344	Coldingham	3.24d.ell	CS 1344–5ii P.
18	1363	Coldingham	6.5d.ell	SS 12.xliv P.
19	1364	Coldingham	6.5d.ell	SS 12.xlviii P.
20	1366	Edinburgh	5d.ell	*ER* II.246 V.
21	1373		7.07d./5.97d.ell	*ER* II.440 P.

Table 63 (*cont.*)

No.	Year	Place	Unit price	Source
22	1373		6.48d./5.58d.ell	*ER* II.443 P.
23	1374		5.89d.ell	*ER* II.466 P.
24	1375		5.37d.ell	*ER* II.507 P.
25	1376	Perth	6d.ell	*ER* II.541 P.
26	1377		7.03d./5.93d.ell	*ER* II.548 P.
27	1379	Stirling	15.42d.ell	*ER* III.6 V.
28	1380		6d.ell	*ER* III.43 P.
29	1427	Dundee	12.53d.ell	*ER* IV.433 P.
30	1427	Edinburgh	10d.ell	*ER* IV.438 V.
31	1428	Stirling	12d.ell	*ER* IV.467 P.
32	1437	Dundee	16d.ell	*ER* V.15 P.
33	1444	Perth	14d.ell	*ER* V.186–7 P.
34	1453	Edinburgh	14d.ell	*ER* V.615–16 P.
35	1455	Aberdeen	6d.ell	ACR V i.225 Aw.
36	1457		10.28d./8.57d.ell	*ER* VI.310 P.
37	1458	Edinburgh	18d.ell	*ER* VI.497 P.
38	1460	Methven?	8d.ell	*ER* VII.3 P.
39	1463	Perth	12d.ell	*ER* VII.232 P.
40	1473		16d.ell	*TA* I.16 P.
41	1473		12d.ell conflated	*TA* I.32,55 P.
42	1473		14d.ell conflated	*TA* I.56,58 P.
43	1474		16d.ell conflated	*TA* I.21,24, P.
44	1474		14.4d.ell	*TA* I.60 P.
45	1474		12d.ell conflated	*TA* I.35,60 P.
46	1474		12.26d.ell	*TA* I.61 P.
47	1485	Aberdeen	16d.ell	ACR VI.903 Aw.
48	1493		10d.ell	*ALC* I.282 Aw.
49	1493		7.2d.ell	*ALC* I.282 Aw.
50	1495		18d.ell Bartane	*TA* I.257 P.
51	1496		3s.ell small Bartane	*TA* I.260 P.
52	1496		11.6d.ell	*TA* I.282 P.
53	1496		13.2d.ell	*TA* I.285 P.
54	1496		12d.ell	*TA* I.299 P.
55	1497		12d.ell	*TA* I.319 P.
56	1497		12d.ell Vitrisch	*TA* I.345 P.
57	1497		14d.ell	*TA* I.349 P.
58	1501		12d.ell Bertane	*TA* II.24 P.
59	1501		12d.ell conflated	*TA* II.26 P.
60	1502		12d.ell conflated	*TA* II.37 P.
61	1503		12d.ell conflated	*TA* II.214 P.
62	1503		18d.ell conflated	*TA* II.215 P.
63	1503		19.2d.ell	*TA* II.203 P.
64	1503	Ross	2s.stone	*ER* XII.239 P.
65	1504		12d.Scots ell Flemish	*TA* II.228 P.
66	1504		12d.ell	*TA* II.446 P.
67	1505		14d.ell conflated	*TA* III.34 P.

Table 63 (*cont.*)

No.	Year	Place	Unit price	Source
68	1505		12d.ell conflated	*TA* III.35 P.
69	1506		13d.ell	*TA* III.48 P.
70	1506		12d.ell conflated	*TA* III.50 P.
71	1506		10d.ell Bertane	*TA* III.80 P.
72	1506		10d.ell	*TA* III.295 P.
73	1506		2s.ell small	*TA* III.249 P.
74	1506		14d.ell sail	*TA* III.347 P.
75	1506		14d.ell	*TA* III.355 P.
76	1506		16d.ell	*TA* III.332 P.
77	1506		18d.ell small	*TA* III.313 P.
78	1506		18d.ell	*TA* III.313 P.
79	1507		2s.ell conflated	*TA* III.250 P.
80	1507		2s.ell small conflated	*TA* III.257 P.
81	1507		16d.ell conflated	*TA* III.254 P.
82	1507		14d.ell conflated	*TA* III.255 P.
83	1507		2s.4d.ell	*TA* III.257 P.
84	1507		11d.ell	*TA* III.259 P.
85	1507		12d.ell conflated	*TA* III.275 P.
86	1507		20d.ell small	*TA* III.317 P.
87	1507		20d.ell conflated	*TA* IV.14 P.
88	1507		12d.ell	*TA* IV.82 P.
89	1508		12d.ell conflated	*TA* IV.61 P.
90	1508		14d.ell	*TA* IV.65 P.
91	1510	Dunkeld	14.5d.ell Bertane	SHS 2,10.4 P.
92	1510	Dunkeld	6.43d.ell	SHS 2,10.117 P.
93	1511		12d.ell conflated	*TA* IV.209 P.
94	1511		14d.ell conflated	*TA* IV.317 P.
95	1512		14d.ell	*TA* IV.321 P.
96	1512		10d.ell conflated	*TA* IV.297 P.
97	1513	Lothian	14d.ell Bartane	SHS 2,10.263 P.
98	1516	Aberdeen	12d.ell French	ACR IX.640 C.
99	1517		18d.ell French veten	*TA* V.120 P.
100	1517		16d.ell French	*TA* V.145 P.
101	1526		18d.ell	*TA* V.311 P.
102	1526	Holyrood	16d.ell	*TA* V.325 P.
103	1530		3s.ell small	*TA* V.367 P.
104	1531		2s.ell	*TA* V.411 P.
105	1531		16d.ell conflated	*TA* V.423 P.
106	1531		32d.ell small	*TA* VI.19 P.
107	1532		16d.ell conflated	*TA* VI.24 P.
108	1532		40d.ell	*TA* VI.22 P.
109	1532		34.29d.ell	*TA* VI.29 P.
110	1532		18d.ell fine	*TA* VI.74 P.
111	1533		12d.ell great	*TA* VI.79 P.
112	1533		16d.ell great	*TA* VI.81 P.
113	1533		15.75d.ell	*TA* VI.86 P.

Table 63 (*cont.*)

No.	Year	Place	Unit price	Source
114	1533	Glasgow	16.25d.ell	*TA* VI.165 P.
115	1534	Stirling	42d.ell	*TA* VI.189 P.
116	1534		17d.ell Bartane	*TA* VI.192 P.
117	1534		16d.ell	*TA* VI.192 P.
118	1534		10.91d.ell	*TA* VI.194 P.
119	1534		40d.ell Bertane	*TA* VI.200 P.
120	1535		16d.ell	*TA* VI.247 P.
121	1535		18d.ell	*TA* VI.251 P.
122	1535		18d.ell Barres	*TA* VI.261 P.
123	1536		18d.ell conflated	*TA* VI.256 P.
124	1536		48d.ell Bertane conflated	*TA* VI.256 P.
125	1536		28d.ell	*TA* VI.275 P.
126	1536	France	5s.tournois	*TA* VII.43 P.
127	1536	France	5s.tournois	*TA* VII.44 P.
128	1537		42d.ell Bartane	*TA* VI.299 P.
129	1537		16d.ell great	*TA* VI.329 P.
130	1537		18d.ell great	*TA* VI.332 P.
131	1537		16d.ell conflated	*TA* VI.333 P.
132	1537		18d.ell	*TA* VI.338 P.
133	1537		20d.ell	*TA* VI.341 P.
134	1537	Aberdeen	36d.,40d.ell small	ACR XV.511 Aw.
135	1538		16d.ell conflated	*TA* VI.386 P.
136	1538		24d.ell Bertane	*TA* VI.418 P.
137	1538		32d.ell small Bertane	*TA* VI.388 P.
138	1538		36d.ell small Bertane	*TA* VI.388 P.
139	1538		16d.ell conflated	*TA* VII.89 P.
140	1539		16d.ell conflated	*TA* VII.136 P.
141	1539		20d.ell	*TA* VII.179 P.
142	1539		18d.ell	*TA* VII.252 P.
143	1540		16d.ell conflated	*TA* VII.286 P.
144	1540		18d.ell conflated	*TA* VII.299 P.
145	1540		18.66d.ell	*TA* VII.413 P.
146	1540		20d.ell conflated	*TA* VII.311 P.
147	1540		4s.ell small Bertane	*TA* VII.409 P.
148	1541		16d.ell conflated	*TA* VII.419 P.
149	1541		18d.ell Bertane	*TA* VII.426 P.
150	1541		20d.ell Bertane	*TA* VII.434 P.
151	1541		44d.ell	*TA* VII.446 P.
152	1541		£4 bolt	*TA* VII.444 P.
153	1541		16d.ell conflated	*TA* VIII.23
154	1541		17d.ell	*TA* VIII.28 P.
155	1541		32d.ell	*TA* VIII.38 P.
156	1542		16d.ell conflated	*TA* VIII.64 P.
157	1542		20d.ell	*TA* VIII.53 P.
158	1542		26d.ell	*TA* VIII.57 P.

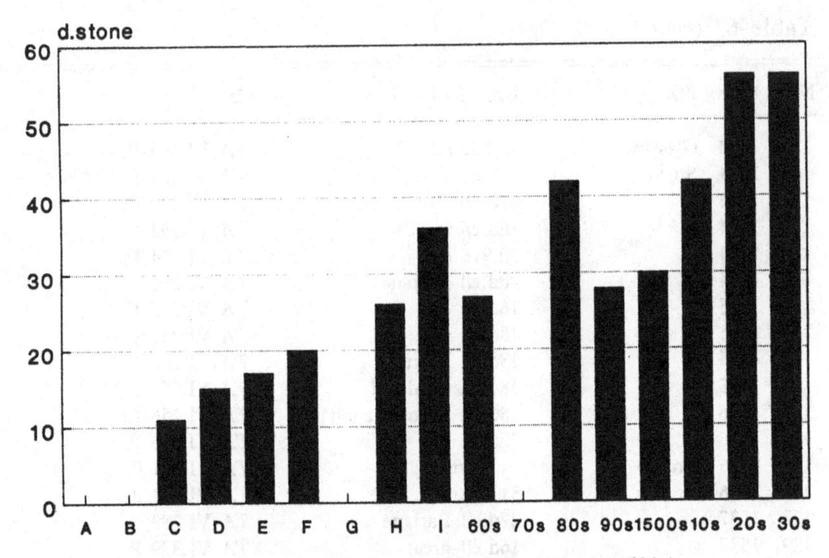

41 Iron prices (mean prices for time periods A–1530s)
For periods A–I, see Introduction, p. 6.

Iron

Iron was widely used for a variety of purposes. The fixtures and fittings for doors, gates, and windows were of iron, especially in castles where extra security was required.[294] It was used occasionally for shoeing the horses of the rich, and for shoeing wheels,[295] and we meet an iron plough(share), an iron chimney, and some unspecified iron tools.[296] Aberdeen's attempt to guarantee its own supplies by setting a high minimum price for iron sold outside the burgh[297] suggests that demand for iron was considerable, but it has to be admitted that such demand is not apparent from the numbers of surviving iron prices.[298]

One major growth area in iron use was its application in the field of artillery. From the middle of the fifteenth century the crown began to interest itself in armaments of this kind.[299] Strangely, we have no prices for iron employed in more traditional weapons manufacture; the best weapons were probably imported ready made.

[294] List 2–5, 7–9, 11, 16–17, 19, 40.
[295] List 43, 49; 68. *ER* V.686.
[296] List 107; 93; 9, 12, 13.
[297] List 27, 28, 44. Froissart commented on the difficulty of getting hold of iron in Scotland, quoted by Lythe, 'Economic Life', p. 73.
[298] Coal purchases for blacksmiths, however, do suggest a more lively iron trade, see p. 345.
[299] List 45, 51–2, 58, 60, 63, 69, 71, 73, 75–7, 79, 81, 83, 122(Aberdeen), 133.

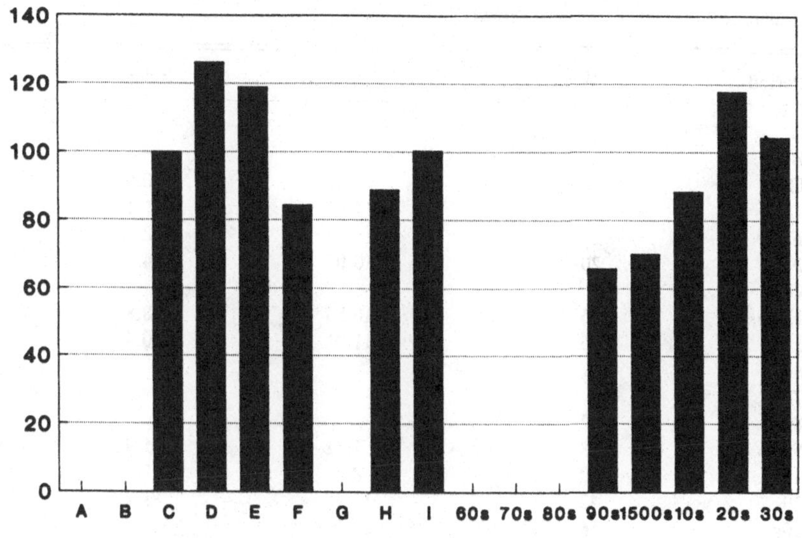

42 Iron index (sterling equivalent)

From the beginning of our period Spanish iron is established as the best available, and this is a position which it continues to hold to the end, despite the growing importance of French iron in the sixteenth century.[300] The occasional juxtaposition of French and Spanish iron prices confirms the general impression that Spanish was dearer, French only once exceeding the contemporary Spanish price.[301] We also meet a 'Prussian' iron seller, and iron brought from Hamburg in exchange for wool,[302] but local Scots iron was also available, notably from Ross and Sutherland.[303]

Table 64 and Figure 41 of mean prices present a reasonably clear-cut picture. This table has been calculated on prices per stone, walls or weighs of iron being converted at the rate of 12 stone.[304] It is clear

[300] French braid pan iron seems to have enjoyed a premium. List 158, 163, 164.

[301] List 69–70, 71–2, 138–44, 149–50, 156–7; for the dearer French price 161–2.

[302] List 29, 135.

[303] 'Testament of Alexander Suthyrland of Dunbeath', *Bannatyne Miscellany* III, p. 95, priced at 2s. a wedy, and p. 97 at 8s. a wedy. See also *ER* XIII.263–9, where large numbers of wethyis of iron occur in the Sutherland rental 1509–12. I am most grateful to Dr Barbara Crawford for these references, and also through her to Prof. Robin Adam.

[304] List 29, 58, 64, 82, 83, 93, 128. Wethys have been excluded from the calculations, as have any prices which are known to include the cost of working in the price (e.g. List 54). List 31, 61, 73, 80, 82, 115, 122, 133–4 cost working separately at rates varying from 14s. or 16s. per stone extra down to 16d. per stone extra, according to the difficulty of the work.

Table 64. *Iron summary table*

Period	Mean price	Deflated	Index
A			
B			
C	11	11.86	100.0
D	15	14.95	126.1
E	17	14.09	118.8
F	20	10.0	84.3
G			
H	26	10.53	88.8
I	36	11.91	100.4
60s	27		
70s			
80s	42		
90s	28	7.81	65.9
1500s	30	8.32	70.2
10s	42	10.48	88.4
20s	56	13.96	117.7
30s	56	12.37	104.3

Note: the mean price is in pence per stone; the deflated column gives the currency-adjusted sterling equivalent price.

Table 65. *Iron price list*

No.	Year	Place	Unit price	Source
1	1301	Glasgow	2d.pecia	PRO E101/9/12 P.
2	1335	Edinburgh	14d.stone	PRO E101/19/21 P.
3	1335	Stirling	14d.stone Spanish	*CDS* III.349 P.
4	1335	Stirling	12d.stone Spanish	*CDS* III.349 P.
5	1335	Stirling	14d.stone Spanish	*CDS* III.350 P.
6	1335	Edinburgh	14d.stone	PRO E101/19/21 P.
7	1335	Stirling	12d.stone Spanish	*CDS* III.350 P.
8	1336	Stirling	12d.stone Spanish	*CDS* III.351 P.
9	1336	Stirling	12d.stone	*CDS* III.353 P.
10	1336	Stirling	14d.stone	*CDS* III.356 P.
11	1336	Stirling	14d.stone Spanish	*CDS* III.351 P.
12	1336	Stirling	5d.stone Spanish	*CDS* III.367 P.
13	1336	Edinburgh	12d.stone	*CDS* III.358 P.
14	1338	Perth	9d.stone	*CDS* III.238 P.
15	1344	Berwick	8d.stone	*CDS* III.261 V.
16	1352	Coldingham	21.43d.stone	SS 12.xxvi P.
17	1362	Berwick	12d.stone	PRO E101/482/28 P.
18	1364	Coldingham	15.5d.stone	SS 12.xlvii P.

Table 65 (*cont.*)

No.	Year	Place	Unit price	Source
19	1364	Coldingham	15.5d.stone	SS 12.xlviii P.
20	1365	Coldingham	17d.stone	SS 12.lj P.
21	1366	Kinghorn	15d.stone	*ER* II.259 P.
22	1367		16.86d./14.69d.stone	*ER* II.294 P.
23	1374	Stirling	21.60d./18d.stone	*ER* II.462 V.
24	1374	Edinburgh	17.78d.stone	*ER* II.462 V.
25	1382	See notes	18.48d./15.40d.stone	*ER* III.660 P.
26	1384	Edinburgh	18.19d./15.15d.stone	*ER* III.118 P.
27	1401	Aberdeen	16d.stone	ACR I.197 assize V.
28	1409	Aberdeen	2s.stone	ACR II.52 assize V.
29	1427	Edinburgh	14d.stone	*ER* IV.437 P.
30	1427	Aberdeen	32s.wey = 32d.stone	*ER* IV.443 P.
31	1428	Ayr	16d.'clof'	SHR 31.144. P.
32	1428	Ayr	12d.'clowf'	SHR 31.144 P.
33	1429	Edinburgh	30d.stone	*ER* IV.508 P.
34	1433	Kirkc'bright	28s.wey = 28d.stone	*ER* IV.558 P.
35	1434	Kirkc'bright	20.40s./18s.wey = 18d.stone	*ER* IV.606 P.
36	1434		23.25d.stone	*ER* IV.627 P.
37	1434	Kirkc'bright	18s.wey = 18d.stone Spanish	*ER* IV.607 P.
38	1436	Edinburgh	30s.wey = 30d.stone Spanish	*ER* V.34 P.
39	1436	Aberdeen	42d.stone	*ER* V.58 P.
40	1437	Edinburgh	28d.stone Spanish	*ER* V.36 V.
41	1445	Cupar	36d.stone	*ER* V.227 P.
42	1445	Cupar	35.91d.stone	*ER* V.227 P.
43	1446	Cupar	35.97d.stone	*ER* V.261 V.
44	1450	Aberdeen	3s.stone	ACR V ii.757 assize V.
45	1451	Edinburgh	41.14d.stone	*ER* V.502 P.
46	1452	Aberdeen	3s.stone	ADG fol. 2v. V.
47	1452	Aberdeen	32d.'wethy'	ADG fol. 2v. V.
48	1453	Linlithgow	32d.stone	*ER* V.623 P.
49	1454	Fife	36d.stone	*ER* VI.71 P.
50	1457		123d. 100/120 pounds	*ER* VI.308 P.
51	1457	Galloway	40d.stone	*ER* VI.456 P.
52	1458	Edinburgh	1.8d./1.5d.stone	*ER* VI.496 P.
53	1459	Edinburgh	32s.dozen = 32d.stone	*ER* VI.581 P.
54	1461	Falkland	52d.stone	*ER* VII.79 P.
55	1465	Edinburgh	26d.stone	*ER* VII.422 P.
56	1465	Cupar	28d.stone	*ER* VII.429 P.
57	1473	Aberdeen	23d.per wethy	ACR VI.222 Aw.
58	1482	Edinburgh	39.67d./33.47d.stone	*ER* IX.218–19 P.
59	1484	Quhittingam	45.18d.stone	*ALC* I.*90 Aw.
60	1494		3s.stone	*TA* I.255 P.
61	1496		25s.weigh	*TA* I.281 P.

Table 65 (*cont.*)

No.	Year	Place	Unit price	Source
62	1496		28s.weigh Spanish	*TA* I.282 P.
63	1496		25s.weigh	*TA* I.283 P.
64	1496	Stirling?	32s.weigh Spanish	*TA* I.284 P.
65	1496		31s.weigh Spanish	*TA* I.285 P.
66	1496		25s.weigh French	*TA* I.287 P.
67	1496		25.01s.weigh	*TA* I.290 P.
68	1496	Leith?	25s.weigh	*TA* I.290 P.
69	1496		25s.weigh French	*TA* I.291 P.
70	1496		32s.weigh Spanish	*TA* I.291 P.
71	1496		32s.weigh Spanish	*TA* I.292 P.
72	1496		25s.weigh French	*TA* I.292 P.
73	1496		25s.weigh	*TA* I.293 P.
74	1496		33s.weigh	*TA* I.296 P.
75	1496		25s.weigh French	*TA* I.299 P.
76	1497	Edinburgh	24.92s.	*TA* I.319 P.
77	1497		28s.weigh	*TA* I.321 P.
78	1497	Stirling	28s.weigh	*TA* I.322 P.
79	1497		28s.weigh	*TA* I.334 P.
80	1497	Dunbar?	28s.weigh	*TA* I.335 P.
81	1497		28d.stone	*TA* I.349 P.
82	1497		28s.weigh	*TA* I.349 P.
83	1498	Dundee	28s.weigh	*TA* I.384 P.
84	1498	Edinburgh	27s.6d.weigh	*TA* I.391 P.
85	1498		27s.6d.weigh	*TA* I.391 P.
86	1501		25s.weigh	*TA* II.82 P.
87	1502	Dundee	27s.weigh	*TA* II.89 P.
88	1502		30d.wyddy	*TA* II.48 P.
89	1502		32s.weigh	*TA* II.270 P.
90	1502		32s.weigh Spanish	*TA* II.270 P.
91	1502		*c.* 8d.stone French	*TA* II.270 P.
92	1503		31s.weigh Spanish	*TA* II.271 P.
93	1503		33.86d.stone	*TA* II.406 P.
94	1505		28s.weigh	*TA* III.82 P.
95	1505		28s.weigh	*TA* III.136 P.
96	1506		£7 each thousand	*TA* III.296 P.
97	1506	Perth	84d. 42d. 49d. widdy	SHS 2,10.203 P.
98	1507		30s.weigh	*TA* III.299 P.
99	1507		29s.weigh	*TA* III.299 P.
100	1507		31s.weigh conflated	*TA* IV.45 P.
101	1507		30s.weigh	*TA* IV.45 P.
102	1507	Dunkeld	36.80d.widde	SHS 2,10.100 P.
103	1508		30s.weigh conflated	*TA* IV.45–7 P.
104	1508		31s.weigh	*TA* IV.113 P.
105	1508		25s.weigh Spanish	*TA* IV.48 P.
106	1508	Lothian	32d.stone	SHS 2,10.248 P.
107	1508	Lothian	32d.stone	SHS 2,10.252 P.

Table 65 (*cont.*)

No.	Year	Place	Unit price	Source
108	1510	Dunkeld	45.04d.widde	SHS 2,10.117 P.
109	1510	Dunkeld	42.03d./36.64d.widde	SHS 2,10.283 P.
110	1510	Dundee	37.42d.stone	SHS 2,10.283 P.
111	1510	Stirling	40s. + 36s.weigh	*ER* XIII.387 P.
112	1511		42s.weigh	*TA* IV.278 P.
113	1511		40s.weigh conflated	*TA* IV.286 P.
114	1511	Dunkeld	42.41d.widde	SHS 2,10.124 P.
115	1511	Dunkeld	32d.wydde	SHS 2,10.124 P.
116	1512		40s.weigh conflated	*TA* IV.291 P.
117	1512		4s.wedy	*TA* IV.462 P.
118	1513		46s.weigh conflated	*TA* IV.509 P.
119	1513		50s.weigh conflated	*TA* IV.510 P.
120	1513		48s.weigh	*TA* IV.512 P.
121	1513		23.08s.weigh	*TA* IV.481 P.
122	1513	Aberdeen	48d.stone	ACR IX.293 P.
123	1513	Dunkeld	44.12d.widde	SHS 2,10.142 P.
124	1515	Inchegarvy	3s.6d.stone	*TA* V.24 P.
125	1515		42s.weigh	*TA* V.34 P.
126	1515		42s.weigh	*TA* V.38 P.
127	1515		3s. 10d.stone	*TA* V.39 P.
128	1515		48s.weigh	*TA* V.55 P.
129	1516		42s.weigh	*TA* V.68 P.
130	1516	Edinburgh	3s. 8d.stone	*TA* V.68 P.
131	1522	Edinburgh	42s.weigh	*TA* V.200 P.
132	1522	Aberdeen	12d.quarter	ACR XI.280 P.
133	1523		5s.stone	*TA* V.222 P.
134	1523		5s.stone	*TA* V.223 P.
135	1524	Aberdeen	31.11s.barrel Osmond iron	ACR XI.462 P.
136	1526		5s.stone	*TA* V.267 P.
137	1527		5s.stone Spanish	*TA* V.322 P.
138	1527		5s.stone Spanish	*TA* V.322 P.
139	1527		4s.stone French	*TA* V.322 P.
140	1527		5s.stone Spanish	*TA* V.322 P.
141	1527		5s.stone Spanish	*TA* V.326 P.
142	1527		4s.stone French	*TA* V.327 P.
143	1527		4s.stone French	*TA* V.327 P.
144	1525		60s.weigh	*TA* V.257 P.
145	1529		60d.stone Spanish	*TA* V.372 P.
146	1531	Aberdeen	32d./36d. widde	ACR XIII.288 V.
147	1532	Aberdeen	50s.barrel	ACR XIII.338 Aw.
148	1532		4s.stone	*TA* VI.157 P.
149	1536		4s.stone French	*TA* VI.303 P.
150	1537		5s.stone Spanish	*TA* VI.349 P.
151	1537		5s.stone Spanish	*TA* VI.349 P.
152	1537		5s.stone Spanish	*TA* VI.349 P.
153	1537		4s. 4d.stone	*TA* VI.349 P.

Table 65 (*cont.*)

No.	Year	Place	Unit price	Source
154	1537		4s. 8d.stone	*TA* VI.349 P.
155	1537		4s. 4d.stone	*TA* VI.349 P.
156	1539	Leith/Edinb.	4s. 6d.stone conflated Spanish	*TA* VII.211–2 P.
157	1539	Leith/Edinb.	4s.stone French conflated	*TA* VII.210 P.
158	1539	Leith/Edinb.	4s. 4d.stone French pan iron	*TA* VII.212 P.
159	1540	Leith/Edinb.	4s. 6d.stone Spanish	*TA* VII.346 P.
160	1540	Leith/Edinb.	4s. 8d.stone Spanish conflated	*TA* VII.349 P.
161	1540	Leith/Edinb.	5s.stone Spanish conflated	*TA* VII.351 P.
162	1540	Leith/Edinb.	5s. 4d.stone French	*TA* VII.351 P.
163	1540	Leith/Edinb.	4s. 10d.stone French conflated	*TA* VII.353 P.
164	1540	Leith/Edinb.	4s. 8d.stone French	*TA* VII.360 P.
165	1540	Edinburgh	4s. 9d.stone Spanish	*TA* VII.487 P.
166	1540	Leith/Edinb.	4s. 8d.stone braid pan iron	*TA* VII.489 P.
167	1541	Leith/Edinb.	4s. 4d.stone French	*TA* VII.491 P.
168	1541	Leith/Edinb.	5s.stone Spanish conflated	*TA* VII.492–3 P.
169	1541	Leith/Edinb.	5s. 4d.stone Spanish conflated	*TA* VII,VIII P.
170	1541	Aberdeen	60d.stone	ACR XVI.764 P.
171	1541	Aberdeen	?61.71d.stone Spanish	ACR XVI.768 C.
172	1541	Aberdeen	?40d.stone	ACR XVI.779 C.
173	1541	Leith/Edinb.	5s.stone French	*TA* VII.496 P.
174	1541		4s. 8d.stone French	*TA* VII.496 P.
175	1541	Leith/Edinb.	4s. 6d.stone French	*TA* VII.500 P.
176	1541	Leith/Edinb.	4s. 6d.stone Vernour iron	*TA* VII.501–2 P.
177	1541	Leith/Edinb.	4s. 6d.stone French	*TA* VIII.120–1 P.
178	1542	Leith/Edinb.	5s. 4d.stone Spanish conflated	*TA* VIII.122 P.
179	1542	Leith/Edinb.	5s.stone French	*TA* VIII.128 P.
180	1542	Leith/Edinb.	5s.stone Spanish	*TA* VIII.128 P.

that prices rose sharply in the second half of the fourteenth century, and never again achieved such heights in our period, if allowance is made for debasement (Table 64 and Figure 42). Unusually, the lowest currency-adjusted prices fall in the 1490s–1500s, when our series is dominated by Treasurer's purchases, by no means a normal source for low prices. By the 1520s and 1530s, however, the iron prices adjusted index had surpassed the base period price level.

Table 66. *Mean coal prices 1265–1542*

Year	Mean price	Number of entries (mean of)
1265–95	2d.b.	2
1325–46	4d.b.	8
1364–84	5d.b.	8
1401–2	8d.b.	2
1434–6	5d.b.	2
1459	9d.b.	3
1479	3d.b.	1
1492–9	8d.b.	2
1506	28d.b.	1
1507	11d.b.	1
1509–10	24d.b.	3
1512–13	13d.b.	5
1514–16	32d.b.	3
1531–42	24d.b.	7

Coal

The coal price series is perhaps of more use for the light it throws on the use of iron in Scotland,[305] than as a priced commodity in its own right. This is chiefly because of the frequent use of difficult measures, such as seams, or especially 'loads', which are effectively unquantifiable. Additionally, carriage is likely to have been a significant factor distorting prices, since coal was quite cheap to buy but difficult to transport. For example List 118 suggests that the 6s. 8d. it cost to carry a celdra of coal from Leith to Edinburgh castle was almost a quarter of the price of a celdra of coal on the quayside. Variable quality may have been another distorting factor, for we sometimes read of 'smithy' coal which was clearly superior to other grades.

We meet seacoal collected from the beaches[306] and charcoal,[307] but it is clear that some mines were operating. The mine at Tranent[308] owned by the Setons returned its own accounts, while in ward to the crown, which also owned pits at Largo and Markinch. The coal owed as a

[305] See the repeated issues to blacksmiths, and, towards the end of the series, the identification of a distinct and superior quality 'smyddy' coal.

[306] List 1, 2, 16, 101. See also the early thirteenth-century charter granting coals to Newbattle Abbey 'et in accessu maris et in recessu', R.W.Cochran-Patrick, *Early Records relating to Mining in Scotland* (Edinburgh, 1878), p. 1.

[307] List 52, 62, 63.

[308] List 53, 55–6. The thirteenth-century de Quincy charter granting a mine to Newbattle was witnessed by a Seton.

Table 67. *Coal prices 1265–1366: Scotland and England*

Year	Scotland	Durham	Rogers
1265	0.75		
1295	0.48		1.25
1298		0.24/0.21	
1325	0.33	0.31	
1327	2.92		1.06
1328	0.73	0.28	
1329		0.3	
1331	(0.33)		1.0
1335	2.0	0.32	1.0
	1.44		
	1.11		
	1.33		
1336	4.0	0.32	1.0
	4.0		
	4.0		
	4.0		
	4.0		
	4.0		
	4.0		
	4.0		
	4.0		
	4.0		
1346	1.07		
1364	2.0	0.17	
1366	1.19	0.18	2.0

Note: all prices are in shillings per quarter. Parentheses have been used to flag up calculations which are less securely based than others – either because they are based on a smaller amount of data, or because they involve certain, possibly questionable, assumptions.

render in kind from Newtown, Fife,[309] suggests a mine in the district, and coal heuchs are noted by Sanderson around Pittenweem, Culross, and Dunfermline.[310] Additionally, Dunlop notes the monastic mining interests of Newbattle, Holyrood, and St Andrews.[311]

The exclusion of non-boll prices and the complications arising from

[309] List 64.

[310] Sanderson, *Cardinal of Scotland*, p. 6.

[311] A.I. Dunlop, *The Life and Times of James Kennedy, Bishop of St Andrews* (Edinburgh, 1950), pp. 375–7. Cochran-Patrick, *Mining in Scotland*, pp. xliii–xlv, and 1–4, usefully collects and prints a number of references to coal mining by Newbattle, Dunfermline, and Paisley Abbeys.

Table 68. *Coal price list*

No.	Year	Place	Unit price	Source
1	1265	Berwick	2.25d.b. sea	*ER* I.27 P.
2	1295	Berwick	1.63d.b. sea	*DHS* II.16.
3	1301	Linlithgow?	4d.seam	PRO E101/9/12 P.
4	1301	Linlithgow?	4d.seam	PRO E101/9/12 P.
5	1325	Tarbert	1d.b.	*ER* I.56–7 P.
6	1327	Berwick	8.75d.b.	*ER* I.64 V.
7	1328		2.18d.b.	*ER* I.219 P.
8	1331		1d.b.	*ER* I.403 V.
9	1335	Stirling	3d.pound	*CDS* III.349 P.
10	1335	Stirling	3d.pound	*CDS* III.350 P.
11	1335	Roxburgh	6d.b.	PRO E101/19/27 P.
12	1335	Roxburgh	4.31d.b.	PRO E101/19/27 P.
13	1335	Roxburgh	3.33d.bushel	PRO E101/19/27 P.
14	1335	Berwick	4d.bushel	PRO E101/19/27 P.
15	1336	Stirling	3d.pound	*CDS* III.351 P.
16	1336	Roxburgh	12d.bata sea	PRO E101/19/27 P.
17	1336	Roxburgh	12d.b.	PRO E101/19/27 P.
18	1336	Stirling	3d.pound	*CDS* III.353 P.
19	1336	Roxburgh	12d.b.	PRO E101/19/27 P.
20	1336	Stirling	3d.pound	*CDS* III.353 P.
21	1336	Roxburgh	12d.b.	PRO E101/19/27 P.
22	1336	Stirling	3d.pound	*CDS* III.354 P.
23	1336	Roxburgh	12d.b.	PRO E101/19/27 P.
24	1336	Stirling	3d.pound	*CDS* III.355 P.
25	1336	Roxburgh	12d.b.	PRO E101/19/27 P.
26	1336	Stirling	3d.pound	*CDS* III.355 P.
27	1336	Roxburgh	12d.b.	PRO E101/19/27 P.
28	1336	Stirling	3d.pound	*CDS* III.356 P.
29	1336	Roxburgh	12d.b.	PRO E101/19/27 P.
30	1336	Stirling	3d.pound	*CDS* III.356 P.
31	1336	Roxburgh	12d.b.	PRO E101/19/27 P.
32	1336	Stirling	3d.pound	*CDS* III.357 P.
33	1336	Roxburgh	12d.b.	PRO E101/19/27 P.
34	1336	Roxburgh	12d.b.	PRO E101/19/27 P.
35	1336	Edinburgh	3.5d.pound	*CDS* III.358 P.
36	1337	Edinburgh	4d.pound	*CDS* III.359 P.
37	1337	Edinburgh	3d.pound	*CDS* III.359 P.
38	1337	Edinburgh	4d.pound	*CDS* III.359 P.
39	1337	Edinburgh	4d.pound	*CDS* III.359 P.
40	1346	Crail	3.21d.b.	*ER* I.565 P.
41	1364	Coldingham	6d.b.	SS 12.xlvii P.
42	1366		3.56d.b.	*ER* II.253 P.
43	1367		29s.barrel	*ER* II.294 P.
44	1368	Stirling	4.64d.b.	*ER* II.306 P.
45	1374	Dundee	7.5d.b.	*ER* II.449 V.
46	1380	Stirling	5.20d.b.	*ER* III.654–5 V.

Table 68 (*cont.*)

No.	Year	Place	Unit price	Source
47	1380	Edinburgh	4.13d.b.	*ER* III.653 P.
48	1381	Edinburgh?	6d.b.	*ER* III.81 P.
49	1384		6d.b.	*ER* III.109 V.
50	1401	Perth	9.24d.b.	*ER* III.562 P.
51	1402	Kinghorn	6d.b.	*ER* III.574 V.
52	1425	Forfar	4.5d.b. charcoal	*ER* IV.423 V.
53	1433	Tranent	17.84s.onus	*ER* IV.600 P.
54	1434	Dundee	6.88d.b.	*ER* IV.615 P.
55	1436	Tranent	3.27d.b.	*ER* V.53 V.
56	1436	Tranent	3.6/3d.per onus	*ER* V.53 V.
57	1459	Aberdeen?	9d.b.	*ER* VI.658 P.
58	1459	Inverness?	7.5d.b.,10.5d.b.	*ER* VI.659 P.
59	1461	Stirling	5.4d.per onus	*ER* VII.60 P.
60	1461	Stirling	6d.onus	*ER* VII.66 P.
61	1462	Stirling	6d.per onus	*ER* VII.188 P.
62	1473	Menteith etc.	9d.b. charcoal	*ER* VIII.234 V.
63	1474	Menteith etc.	8.25d.b. charcoal	*ER* VIII.275 V.
64	1479	Newtoun	3.125d.b.	*ER* IX.51–2 V.
65	1492	Earlsferry	9d.b.	*ALC* I.245 Aw.
66	1497	Melrose	3s.laid	*TA* I.328 P.
67	1498	(Ayr)	5d.laid	*TA* I.382 P.
68	1499	Dysart	7.27d.b.	*ER* XI.268 P.
69	1506	Perth	10d.	SHS 2,10.198 P.
70	1506	Perth	45s.boat load	SHS 2,10.198 P.
71	1506	Perth	70s.boat load	SHS 2,10.203 P.
72	1506	Perth	10d./11d.load	SHS 2,10.203 P.
73	1506	Perth	28d.b. smithy	SHS 2,10.203 P.
74	1506	Edinburgh	8d.load	SHS 2,10.247 P.
75	1507		12d.b. conflated	*TA* IV.72 P.
76	1507	Dysart	11.62d.b.	*TA* IV.72 P.
77	1507		6d.laid	*TA* IV.78 P.
78	1507		9d.b.	*TA* IV.82 P.
79	1507		6d.laid	*TA* IV. 84 P.
80	1507	Stirling	6s.load	*ER* XIII.24 P.
81	1508		5d.laid	*TA* IV.99 P.
82	1508	Perth	10d.load	SHS 2,10.211 P.
83	1509	Perth	11d.load	SHS 2,10.217 P.
84	1509	Perth	24d.b. smithy	SHS 2,10.218 P.
85	1509	Perth	24d.b. smithy	SHS 2,10.218 P.
86	1510	Perth	10d.load	SHS 2,10.222 P.
87	1510	Dunkeld	24.84d.b. smithy	SHS 2,10.283 P.
88	1512	Forth	14d.laid	*TA* IV.459 P.
89	1512	Forth	12d.b.	*TA* IV.462 P.
90	1512	Perth	10d.load	SHS 2,10.227 P.
91	1513	Forth	12d.laid conflated	*TA* IV.466 P.
92	1513	Forth	14d.laid conflated	*TA* IV.466 P.

Table 68 (*cont.*)

No.	Year	Place	Unit price	Source
93	1513	Forth	16d.laid	*TA* IV.466 P.
94	1513		6d.laid	*TA* IV.523 P.
95	1513		11.33d.laid	*TA* IV.508 P.
96	1513		12d.laid	*TA* IV.509 P.
97	1513		14d.laid	*TA* IV.509 P.
98	1513		14d.b.	*TA* IV.510 P.
99	1513		13.5d.b.	*TA* IV.510 P.
100	1513		10d.laid	*TA* IV.511 P.
101	1513		15d.laid sea	*TA* IV.511 P.
102	1513		10d.laid	*TA* IV.511 P.
103	1513		12d.b.	*TA* IV.513 P.
104	1513		12d.b.	*TA* IV.514 P.
105	1513	Forth	9.2d.laid	*TA* IV.500 P.
106	1513	Forth	11.5d.laid	*TA* IV.501 P.
107	1513	Perth	10d.load	SHS 2,10.231 P.
108	1514	Perth	11d.load	SHS 2,10.236 P.
109	1514	Perth	32d.b. smithy	SHS 2,10.238 P.
110	1515		32d.b. smithy	*TA* V.39 P.
111	1515	Dunbar	5.2d.load	*ER* XIV.130 V.
112	1516	Dunkeld	32d.b. smithy	SHS 2,10.298 P.
113	1522	Dunbar	3.7d.load	*ER* XV.6–7 P.
114	1531	Aberdeen	25.5d.b.	ACR XIII.288 Aw.
115	1532	Temptalloune	12d.laid	*TA* VI.156 P.
116	1535	Aberdeen	26.25d.b.	ACR XIV.594 O.
117	1537	Aberdeen	64d.b. smithy	ACR XV.629 C.
118	1539	Leith/Edinb.	21d.b. conflated	*TA* VII.215 P.
119	1539	Leith/Edinb.	16d.laid	*TA* VII.226 P.
120	1540	Leith/Edinb.	21d.b. conflated	*TA* VII.346 P.
121	1541	Leith/Edinb.	21d.b. conflated	*TA* VII.490 P
122	1541	Leith/Edinb.	25d.b. conflated	*TA* VII.492 P.
123	1541	Leith/Edinb.	18d. laid	*TA* VIII.125 P.
124	1542	Leith/Edinb.	25d.b. conflated	*TA* VIII.122 P.
125	1542	Leith/Edinb.	16s. dozen laid	*TA* VIII.126 P.
126	1542	Leith/Edinb.	12d. laid	*TA* VIII.130 P.
127	1542	St Andrews	£11 boat load	SHS 2,4.139 P.
128	1542	St Andrews	£9 10s. boat load	SHS 2,4.155 P.

different varieties of coal and differing costs of carriage all significantly diminish the value of this series. Table 66 collects such evidence as remains, and the picture it gives of a rising money price for coal seems broadly acceptable, but the series is too weak to permit currency adjustment and indexation. Table 67 suggests that coal was sometimes dearer in England than in Scotland, though the Durham series is notably low in price as one would expect. A simple Anglo-Scottish comparison cannot adequately reflect the decisive effect of the location of coal fields and the costs of transport on the behaviour of prices.

Cloth

Cloth in medieval Scotland is a large and very important topic, to which these brief observations can scarcely do justice. The subject is worth a full-length study in its own right. The earliest burgh legislation makes it clear that already by the twelfth century coarse undyed cloth was manufactured in the countryside, while finer, shorn, and dyed stuff was meant to be reserved to the towns.[312] The archaeological evidence, however, suggests that only some 30% of cloth in use in medieval Perth was dyed. Moreover, finds of weaving and spinning artifacts in Aberdeen and Perth argue for the continued use of simpler technology in these burghs as late as the fourteenth century.[313] Lacking any real technological edge, the burghs may have been hard put to sustain the superiority of their product, and if the English experience provides a valid analogy, it seems probable that rural competition posed a growing threat to the urban industry.[314] Thus in thirteenth-century Scotland the urban industry found the quality end of the market dominated by Flemish imports, while rural manufactures may have claimed an increasing share of the domestic trade. Duncan has concluded that the urban trade in cloth in the thirteenth century without actually contracting, failed to sustain its earlier rate of growth, or keep pace with other sectors of a buoyant economy.[315] This at least is one interpretation of the very limited showing of the cloth and textile trades in the thirteenth-century evidence. It should, however, be remembered that the weavers and waulkers, being of only lowly status, would not perhaps be expected to figure largely in the record,[316] while dyers – the aristocracy of the industry, handling significant quantities of capital, and actively engaged in inter-

312 Duncan, *Scotland: The Making of the Kingdom*, pp. 470–1, 491. H.L. Macqueen and William J. Windram, 'Laws and Courts in the Burghs', in *SMT*, pp. 208–9.

313 Traces of the spinning wheel and the horizontal loom – familiar in Flanders and England at this date – have yet to be found for Scotland, where spindle whorls and traces of vertical weaving are found. R.M. Spearman, 'Workshops, Materials and Debris – Evidence of Early Industries', in *SMT*, pp. 137–8. Penelope Walton, 'Textiles', in John Blair and Nigel Ramsey (eds.), *English Medieval Industries* (London, 1991), pp. 325–8.

314 E.Miller, 'The Fortunes of the English Textile Industry in the Thirteenth Century', *EcHR*, 2nd ser. 18 (1965), 64–82.

315 Duncan, *Scotland: The Making of the Kingdom*, p. 510.

316 Though Duncan, *Scotland: The Making of the Kingdom*, p. 500, notes a weaver in Berwick in 1250.

national trade for the import of dye-stuffs, especially woad – not only do appear in the gild merchant, but are often found actively suppressing the aspirations of lower cloth and textile workers.[317]

The tension existing between craftsman and merchant is one of the most frequently discussed themes in later medieval Scottish social and economic history. To the earlier observation that merchant oligarchies seem to have used their power and influence in burgh courts and parliament to suppress the crafts and buttress their own position, Michael Lynch has recently brought a more complex and sensitive analysis which questions any such *general* tendency and sees in its place a much more locally and chronologically varied picture. Some burgh councils dominated by relatively wealthy merchants may have imposed price and trading regulations on local manufacturers, and especially in times of inflation the crafts may well have needed to fight their corner, whether by seeking better representation on the council, or by more direct action involving withdrawal of labour or street protests. Yet on other occasions the burgh may have been more successful in identifying a community of interest embracing both merchant and craftsmen. In truth, it was often difficult to distinguish between the two: the dyers, capitalist craftsmen engaged in international trade, are a case in point. Equally, baxters seem to have often been active in milling and corntrading as well as baking. Moreover, often craft co-operation with, and agreement to, burgh legislation was actively sought, and the crises arising from the failure of agreement should not blind us to the decades of successful negotiation. Equally, craftsmen themselves were eager to invoke burgh rules which protected their interests against other crafts, strangers, outdwellers, foreigners, and even against unfree townsfolk.

The frontiers between these conditions and sorts of men, together with the rules governing their employment, were liable to change from time to time and place to place. The very different circumstances pertaining in smaller burghs, and between the various larger burghs themselves,[318] mean that local rules cannot be assumed to have had a national validity, and even parliamentary legislation was often only a response to a particular local crisis. As the crisis eased, or other counsels prevailed, even the most comprehensive and unyielding legislation could be quickly set aside.

[317] Ibid., p. 491.

[318] Elizabeth P. D. Torrie, 'The Guild in Fifteenth-Century Dunfermline', in *SMT*, pp. 245–60, shows how different and inclusive the guild was in the small burgh of Dunfermline, while Lynch draws attention to differences between the larger burghs, Edinburgh, Perth, Dundee, and Aberdeen, 'Social and Economic Structure', pp. 270–81.

As well as illustrating the craft–merchant question, the cloth trade must figure importantly in any discussion of the relationship between internal and international trade. The export of Scots wool in the thirteenth and fourteenth centuries generated a significant inflow of silver, in turn permitting Scotland to import larger quantities of manufactured goods.[319] Conversely, after the down-turn in wool exports at the end of the fourteenth century, Scotland may have been obliged to develop her own manufactures more fully, rather than go on importing foreign goods which she could no longer so well afford.[320] This interpretation seems much more convincing than the idea of a large and sustained negative trade balance, which simply could not have been financed for long. The decline in Scotland's international trade could thus have stimulated domestic cloth making.

Of course, the domestic cloth trade (with some exports) had continued throughout the thirteenth and fourteenth centuries, and must have absorbed considerable quantities of Scots wool. Grant has drawn attention to the way in which Scots wool exports in 1372 could be dramatically increased almost overnight to take advantage of a temporary unavailability of English wool in Flanders, pointing out that the extra Scots wool then exported must normally have been absorbed by Scots cloth manufacture.[321] In the fifteenth century, this Scots cloth industry may have been well placed to take advantage of a marked price advantage (see below), together with much easier availability, to supply a growing share of the domestic market. Scots cloth even began to be exported, chiefly through Edinburgh, but also as a Dundee speciality aimed especially at the Baltic. The presence of an active Scots cloth trade is confirmed by the Aberdeen sources. The prices of cloth and woad 1400–1540 do not make a usable series, because of the variety of types and measures, but they leave no doubt about the existence of the trade, even in Aberdeen which never made much of a speciality of cloth compared with Edinburgh, Dundee, or Kirkcudbright.[322]

[319] Froissart was particularly struck by Scotland's dependence on imported manufactures in the fourteenth century. Alexander Stevenson, 'Trade with the South, 1070–1513' in *SMT*, p. 189.

[320] Ibid., p. 202. Lynch, 'Social and Economic Structure', p. 235.

[321] Grant, *Independence and Nationhood*, p. 75.

[322] David Ditchburn, 'Trade with Northern Europe, 1297–1540', in *SMT*, pp. 163–4, draws attention to the importance of Dundee, suggested by the Sound Toll Registers 1497–1540, and, p. 167, also notes significant quantities of Scots cloth in Gdansk, not all of it having been duly customed and cocketted in Scotland. Stevenson, 'Trade with the South', p. 192, notes the 'considerable value to the Scottish economy' of cheap cloth exported to Flanders, and, p. 198, estimates the value of Scottish cloth exports at some £3,000 p. a. in the 1430s, falling to about £1,000 p. a. in the 1450s' recession before climbing again into the sixteenth century. Stevenson's tables, *Scottish*

One of the problems which makes the study of cloth prices so difficult is the enormous range of types and qualities of cloth. In the face of this bewildering variety we have limited our analysis to two of the more commonly encountered types, the luxury material, velvet, and the cheaper 'black'. Nevertheless, the *Treasurer's Accounts* still yielded so many price quotations for velvet and 'black' that we have departed from our regular practice of listing each entry, and moved directly to the calculation of mean prices for the years available.

Velvet, a silk cloth of almost exclusively Italian manufacture, was a luxury item of importance to only the very rich.[323] The velvet prices collected were those for velvet of unspecified type, purple velvet, for example, being notably more expensive.[324] Velvet prices over the period 1473–1542 were surprisingly stable. After a break in the *Treasurer's Accounts*, velvet prices look high from 1488 to 1496, perhaps reflecting severe political and currency instability in the Burgundian Netherlands 1485–96, which may have disrupted the distribution of Italian velvet into northern Europe.[325] Velvet prices remained low from 1497 till 1513, rising thereafter, but only then holding steady till the end of our period at about the same level as that indicated in the 1470s.

'Black' cloth was chosen for the opportunities it provides to compare Scots and continental products.[326] In the earliest *Treasurer's Accounts* 'black' was not usually distinguished in type. Only one French black (42s. per ell) and two Scots black cloths (5s. per ell) are explicitly recorded. However, at least two distinct price groups emerge: up to 20s., and above 30s. per ell. The dearer range is probably all French, while the cheaper range certainly included Scots, though this cheaper range makes a tighter price group in 1474 than in 1473.[327] The later *Treasurer's Account* prices are usually more specific about exact types of cloth, and this permits us to confirm the distinction between cheaper, often Scots' cloth, and dearer, usually French, cloth.

In addition to the quality of the material, the method of dying

Historical Atlas, II, illustrate the rise of Dundee and in the west, on a much smaller scale, of Kirkcudbright.

323 A. Geijer, *A History of Textile Art* (London, 1982), pp. 61–2, 148–51. I am most grateful to Dr Frédérique Lachaud for this reference and that in n. 326, and for her advice on medieval cloth.

324 After 1515 the entries become much less numerous because velvet is more often of specified type, though it then becomes clear that black velvet was usually the same price as unspecified velvet.

325 For the coinage in the Netherlands, see Enno Van Gelder and Hoc, *Les Monnaies des Pays-Bas Bourgnignons*, esp. at p. 31.

326 On the fashion for black cloth in the fifteenth century, see F. Piponnier, *Costume et Vie Sociale à la Cour d'Anjou (XIVe–XVe Siècles)* (Paris and the Hague, 1970).

327 A 4s. price in 1473 was for 'narrow' cloth.

employed also affected costs. Dark blues and blacks were traditionally achieved by repeated dying with woad and then 'saddening' the colour with madder or weld. This was a skilled and costly process, but cheaper blacks were also made with tannin-bearing dyes like oak galls and sumach.[328] Yet by the sixteenth century 'March' or 'Mars' black, made with Martial vitriol, i.e. sulphate of iron and gall, as a black dye was among the most costly of blacks.[329]

French black exhibits the same decline in price as velvet from 1497, though it recovers somewhat later, *c.* 1522. Until *c.* 1506 French and Rissillis (Lille, from its Dutch name, Rijssell) black were close in price; indeed, French probably often was Rissillis. From *c.* 1506 we may note the emergence of a much more expensive Paris black, though Rissillis was still commonly met till the 1530s. Thereafter (1530 plus or minus two years), Rissillis began to drift downward in price as Paris black began to dominate the luxury end of the market. By the later 1530s Rissillis emerges as clearly cheaper than French black which is usually slightly cheaper than Paris. However, both Paris and Rissillis were then cheaper than in the 1520s. Paris and French black seem to recover in price 1540–2, but this is not true of Rissillis.

Changes in terminology thus obscure the price pattern somewhat, but it is clear that velvet and most types of French black showed no sign of the steadily rising price exhibited by Scottish black over this whole period. It is not known whether Scottish weavers and dyers achieved any improvement in quality, but Scottish black prices rise consistently over this period, while the more expensive cloths rarely do better than hold their own. Scots black remained, however, significantly cheaper than any of the alternatives.

[328] Walton, 'Textiles', p. 335.
[329] *TA* 1503.

Table 69. *Mean velvet prices*[a]

Date	Price, s. per ell	Number of entries
1473	54.0	20
1474	48.86	21
1488	65.0	12
1489	65.41	22
1490	70.0	6
1491	68.33	6
1494	58.57	7
1494–5	60.0	3[b]
1495	60.71	14
1496	55.15	13
1497	42.6	5
1498	40.0	1
1500	40.0	4
1501	37.55	31
1502	38.09	23
1503	41.62	42
1504	44.25	34
1505	43.53	47
1506	44.57	51
1507	43.84	32
1508	44.97	37[c]
1511	44.17	54
1512	46.97	34
1513	58.0	9
1514	55.0	1[d]
1515	55.0	1
1516	50.0	2
1518	46.0	1
1522	50.0	1
1523	60.0	1
1524	60.0	2
1525	60.0	1
1526	59.63	8
1527	55.0	1
1530	57.5	2
1531	56.13	8
1532	54.0	8
1533	52.18	11
1534	52.19	16
1535	53.2	5
1536	53.5	2
1537	50.0	1
1541	55.33	3
1542	57.5	2

[a]All *TA* prices except where noted. [b]So dated by *TA* editor.
[c]See *SHS* 2,10.249, velvet at 45s. per ell, not included in this calculation. Bought for Bishop of Dunkeld by granitar in Lothian. [d]*ER* XIV.107.

Table 70. *French black prices*

Date	Price, s. per ell	Number of entries	Price range, s.
Black cloth, probably usually French			
1473	36.5	12	32s.–42
1474	35.18	17	30s.–40
1480	36.0[a]	1	
French black			
1488	45.0	1	
1489	43.44	9	40s.–45
1490	45.63	8	45s.–50
1491	42.86	7	35s.–60
1492	38.5	2	32s.–45
1494	36.14	7	35s.–40
1495	40.0[b]	1	
1496	32.0	1	
1497	28.66[c]	3	28s.–30
1498	28.0	1	
1501	27.44	6	26s.–28
1502	26.88	3	26s.–28
1503	27.33[d]	2	26s.–28
1504	27.14[e]	7	26s.–30
1505	23.86[f]	10	20s.–28
1506	26.66[g]	1	
1537	29.42	12	26s.–33
1538	32.0	3	32s.
1539	32.86	7	32s.–36
1540	32.0	5	30s.–34
1541	33.15	24	30s.–40
1542	33.2	5	30s.–38

[a] *ER* IX.154. Black woollen cloth of Flanders.
[b] Unspecified black, deemed French.
[c] One unspecified black, deemed French.
[d] One unspecified black at 26.66 deemed French.
[e] Two unspecified black at 26.66 and 30.0, deemed French.
[f] Four unspecified black at 20.0 and 26.66, deemed French.
[g] Unspecified black, deemed French.

Table 71. *Rissillis black prices*

Date	Price, s. per ell	Number of entries	Price range
1515	28.0	1	
1518	28.0	1	
1522	32.0	2	28s.–36s.
1525	31.66	3	30s.–33s.
1526	31.64	7	28s.–36s.
1527	32.28	6	25s.–36s.
1529	28.0	1	
1530	30.0[a]	2	30s.
1531	28.49	4	28s.–30s.
1532	26.66	5	26.66s.
1533	28.93	3	28s.–30s.
1535	26.66	2	26.66s.
1536	27.16	8	26s.–28s.
1538	25.33	3	24s.–28s.
1539	25.55	6	24s.–26s.
1540	26.0	1	
1541	26.0[b]	1	

[a]One unspecified black at 30s. deemed Rissillis.
[b]Unspecified black, deemed Rissillis.

Table 72. *Paris black prices*

Date	Price, s. per ell	Number of entries	Price range
1507	50.0	1	
1508	52.5	4	50s.–60s.
1511	45.0	4	40s.–50s.
1512	60.0	1	
1513	70.0	1	
1524	60.0	1	
1526	38.75	4	35s.–40s.
1527	46.0	2	42s.–50s.
1529	48.33	3	45s.–50s.
1530	36.0	1	
1531	60.0	2	60s.
1533	47.7	5	36s.–55s.
1534	70.0[a]	1	
1535	32.0	1	
1536	60.0[a]	1	
1537	58.0[a]	5	50s.–60s.
1537	42.66	6	32s.–50s.
1538	34.53	15	32s.–42s.
1539	36.63	8	32s.–45s.
1540	42.0	3	36s.–50s.
1541	48.82	17	36s.–60s.
1542	43.33	3	35s.–50s.

[a]'Fyne' Paris black.

Table 73. *Mean Scots black prices*

Date	Price, s. per ell	Number of entries	Price range
1494	10.66	1	
1495	8.0	1	
1497	12.0	1	
1498	12.0	1	
1501	8.0	10	8s.–14s.
1502	10.0	6	9s.–12s.
1503	13.0	4	10s.–14s.
1504	13.24	14	10s.–15s.
1505	12.66	9	10s.–13s.
1506	12.27	13	10s.–15s.
1507	13.16	16	12s.–13s.
1508	11.11	3	8s.–13s.
1511	12.0	1	
1512	11.67	2	10s.–13s.
1513	14.0	1	
1523	17.0	1	
1526	17.5	4	14s.–20s.
1527	16.66	3	16s.–18s.
1533	18.0	1	
1536	18.0	1	
1537	17.09	11	15s.–18s.
1538	18.0	1	
1539	16.0	2	16s.
1541	18.22	9	16s.–22s.
1542	17.0	2	14s.–20s.

Note: all *TA* prices.

Table 74. *Mean Scots and unspecified black prices*

Date	Price, s. per ell	Number of entries	Price range
1460	4.8[a]	1	
1473	9.73	21	4s.–20s.
1474	8.81	16	6s.–12s.
1488	15.0	1	
1494	15.33	2	10s.–20s.
1495	10.7	2	8s.–13s.
1496	10.0	2	10s.
1497	12.0	1	
1498	12.0	1	
1501	8.0	10	8s.–14s.
1502	10.0	6	9s.–12s.
1503	13.0	4	10s.–14s.
1504	13.18	18	10s.–15s.
1505	12.4	15	10s.–13s.
1506	12.52	17	10s.–15s.
1507	13.17	17	12s.–13s.
1508	11.11	3	8s.–13s.
1511	12.0	1	
1512	11.67	2	10s.–13s.
1513	14.0	2	14s.
1517	16.0	1	
1523	17.0	1	
1526	16.6	7	14s.–20s.
1527	16.66	3	16s.–18s.
1529	30.0	1	
1533	18.0	1	
1536	18.0	1	
1537	17.09	11	15s.–18s.
1538	18.0	1	
1539	16.0	2	16s.
1541	18.22	9	16s.–22s.
1542	17.0	2	14s.–20s.

[a] *ACR* Vi.408. Unspecified black in Aberdeen dispute. Other prices all *TA*.

6 Prices and the Scottish economy, 1260–1540

> a change in prices and wages as measured by money is capable of transferring wealth from one class to another, and redistributing fortune in a way which baffles anticipation and upsets design.
>
> John Maynard Keynes, 1920

It is hoped that the information collected in this volume will advance our knowledge and understanding of medieval Scotland. Prices provide significant clues about the performance of the economy, and price movements can reflect or even bring about important social changes. The interpretation of this interplay of cause and effect is necessarily a much more subjective matter than the collection of data (and it has already been observed that even the collection of data is a good deal less objective than it might at first sight appear), but in this final chapter it seems appropriate to sketch out one such interpretation. Though other scholars will need to draw their own conclusions, this final chapter may serve as an example of the sort of contribution prices can make to history, as well as a record of how the medieval Scottish economy looked to us.

It is probably not pointed out often enough that prices presuppose markets, and the more efficiently flexible prices reflect the relationship between supply and demand the more successfully the market economy was working. Conversely, unmoving prices suggest a market which is limited in some way. Some limitation of this kind is very common in the middle ages. Custom, and the isolation of remote settlements, were the most important obstacles to the free market in medieval Scotland, and they have left their mark on Scottish price history in the form of the customary prices often put on renders in kind. Such prices have been retained in this study as an important reminder of one stage in the development of 'economic man'. The obligations of a feudal and/ or Gaelic society must frequently have set limits to the free rein of economic self-interest in a way which modern man perhaps dimly recalls when he hesitates to do business with friends or relatives. It would, however, be a mistake to allow a sentimental and erroneous picture of gift-exchange and barter in a cash-free world to obscure our understanding of the role of coin and freely negotiated prices in medieval Scotland. One should instead recall that the other great limitation on the free market was the official regulation of markets and prices, made necessary by the fear of church, crown, and burgh that the destructive power of naked economic self-interest might otherwise run riot. Given the care taken to control 'economic man', there can be no doubt of his existence in medieval Scotland. He also left his mark on the more fully commercial prices which are the principal subject of this study.

The earliest group of Scottish prices dates from the 1260s, but there are some indications of marked European economic growth, with rising prices, from the end of the twelfth century, and it seems likely that Scotland shared this experience.[1] Where we do have comparable English and Scottish prices before the Black Death, the trends indicated for each country are very similar.[2] This observation holds so consistently true that we have argued that prices may also have behaved in a similar manner during the long periods when Scottish price data do not survive. If Scottish price trends did follow the much more firmly established English pattern, they will also have been in step with what is known of European price movements generally. Rising European prices from the late twelfth century to the beginning of the fourteenth were probably coincident with rising money supply levels, rising population, and growing levels of trade.[3]

The Scottish evidence leaves no doubt that Scots money supply grew dramatically in the course of the thirteenth century.[4] Direct evidence of Scottish demographic growth is more difficult to find, but rising land values and the extension of arable cultivation on to marginal uplands have rightly been interpreted as evidence of rising population.[5]

[1] For the European monetary and commercial boom, see Spufford, *Money and its Use*, and for Scottish thirteenth-century prosperity, see Mayhew, 'Money in Scotland', and 'Alexander III'.

[2] See above, pp. 14–15. An important distinction needs to be borne in mind, between similar English and Scottish price *trends*, and disparate price *levels*. Thus while trends up and down were broadly similar north and south of the border, Scottish cereals were generally dearer than English, while her livestock was cheaper.

[3] There is no need to debate the primacy of monetary or demographic factors, for in this period both were pulling strongly in the same direction.

[4] Mayhew, 'Money in Scotland', and Chapter 4 above, p. 140. For the find evidence, transformed by recent discoveries, see Bateson, 'Roman and Medieval Coins'.

[5] Duncan, *Scotland: The Making of the Kingdom*, pp. 366, 516. M.L. Parry, 'Secular Climatic Change and Marginal Agriculture', *Transactions of the Institute of British Geographers* 64 (1975), 1–13. For a general upward review of rents, see A. McKerral, 'Ancient Denominations of Agricultural Land in Scotland', *PSAS*, 78 (1944), 68.

Table 75. *The* Antiqua Taxatio *and Bishop Halton's assessment by diocese*

Diocese	*Antiqua Taxatio* (£)	Bishop Halton (£)
St Andrews	8,018	13,723
Glasgow	4,080	11,143
Aberdeen	1,610	3,439
Moray	1,418	2,496
Dunkeld	1,206	2,525
Dunblane	606	1,376
Caithness	386	464
Whithorn	358	1,322
Ross	351	681
Brechin	341	1,008
Argyll	281	661
Sodor and Man	—	536

Source: Thompson and Tout (eds.), *Register of John de Halton.*

Again, in this respect Scotland seems to have shared a common European development. This economic growth in Scotland is perhaps most clearly displayed in a series of contemporary assessments of church wealth. These assessments have not been as fully used as might have been expected because of confusion surrounding their dating, so a renewed consideration of this source is called for.[6]

Comparison of the diocesan figures for the *Antiqua Taxatio* and Bishop Halton's assessment can only provide a rather generalized indication of thirteenth-century Scottish economic growth (Table 75). If the comparability of these two assessments is accepted, it suggests a doubling in the value of the Scottish dioceses over the thirteenth century. There was considerable variation from diocese to diocese, arising no doubt in part from the variable reliability of the surveys, but also perhaps depending on the level of early development already apparent by 1200. This latter factor may explain the comparatively modest growth in the richest diocese, St Andrews. A slightly more focused picture of part of this diocese emerges if we compare available data church by church. Such detailed parish figures for the Halton assessment are only available for the archdeaconry of Lothian in the diocese of St Andrews.[7] Table

[6] What follows is based on the premise that the *Antiqua Taxatio* dates from the early thirteenth century.

[7] They survive in James Raine (ed.), *Correspondence, Inventories, Account Rolls and Law Proceedings of the Priory of Coldingham*, SS 12 (1841). Tout identified this roll as part of Halton's assessment. The monks of Coldingham were responsible for the preparation of the Lothian returns for Halton.

76 sets out figures permitting comparison of individual Lothian parishes on the basis of the *Antiqua Taxatio*, Baiamund's roll from the 1270s, and the Halton assessment. The figures in the old assessment are for whole churches - ecclesiae - while the last assessment distinguishes between rectories and vicarages. Since the income of both rector and vicar were both drawn from the original endowment, where vicarages have been established, their value needs to be added to that of the rectory, for comparison with the old assessment ecclesia figure. Where the surviving data permits such calculations they indicate a rise in Scottish church wealth in Lothian over the thirteenth century of something over 50%. In fact, of course, rising prices alone might explain such a rise, if Scottish thirteenth-century inflation was anything like the English. In reality, increased output produced by a growing population probably also contributed, suggesting that some assessments underestimated growth and that the true average value of these parishes probably rose by more than 50%.

Whatever the approximations involved in these assessments and in the calculations based on them, they do provide a useful, very roughly quantifiable, indication of Scots economic growth in the thirteenth century. As such they confirm a development long recognized by many. Whatever reservations one may harbour about the data, the picture of thirteenth-century growth which they reveal is hardly controversial.

Comparison of the *Antiqua Taxatio* and Bishop Halton's assessment with the *Verus Valor* of 1366 is much less straight-forward, though once more an understanding of the prices background is essential. Detailed parish figures for the *Verus Valor* do not, so far as I am aware, survive,[8] but the diocesan figures indicate a fall in values in 1366 not only from the late thirteenth-century peak but even to well below the early thirteenth-century figures. Indeed, the drop in values revealed by the *Verus Valor* of 1366 is so huge that historians would probably have been unwilling to regard this valuation as comparable with earlier assessments if such comparison had not been made from the beginning. The deliberate contemporary juxtaposition of the *Antiqua Taxatio* and the new *Verus Valor* in 1366 leaves no room for doubt that the new valuation was intended for comparison with, and as a correction to, the old assessment.

An explanation for the fall in values reflected in the *Verus Valor* has

[8] An apparently mid-fourteenth-century roll of Moray churches is not firmly dated, so the values it suggests - on average about half those suggested by Baiamund - are difficult to use. The crucial question is whether this roll dates from before or after the Black Death. *Registrum Episcopatus Moraviensis*, ed. C. Innes, Bannatyne Club, (Edinburgh, 1837), pp. xvii and 362. The crude diocesan figures for Moray are as follows: *Antiqua Taxatio* £1,419, Baiamund *c.* £2,200 (assuming the assessment to be ten times the actual yield), Halton £2,496, undated Moray roll £928, *Verus Valor* £559.

Table 76. *Thirteenth-century taxation assessments for the parishes of the archdeaconry of Lothian*

Parish	*Antiqua Taxatio*	Baiamund's roll – first year of assessment	Baiamund's roll – second year of assessment (a)	Baiamund's roll – second year of assessment (b)	Bishop Halton
Stirling	40 0 0		15 0 0 V	15 0 0	26 13 4 V 45 14 0 E
Penicuik	13 6 8				13 6 8 E
Pentland	8 0 0	4 0 0 E	5 6 8 E		17 1 1 E?
Lasswade	60 0 0	13 6 8 V	6 13 4 V	6 13 4 V	
Melville	13 6 8		13 6 8 E	13 6 8 E	11 1 2 E
Wymeth	13 6 8				6 4 6 V
Duddingston	16 13 4	6 13 4	6 13 4 V		10 13 4 V
Restalrig	16 13 4	20 0 0 E	20 0 0 E		19 4 2 E
St Giles	17 6 8	3 6 8 V	5 0 0V		6 13 4 E? 10 0 0 V
St Cuthbert	106 13 4		3 6 8 V	3 6 8 V	11 0 0 V 162 9 3 E
Gogar	8 0 0	6 13 4 procurator	4 0 0 E	4 0 0 E	10 19 9 E
Hailes	40 0 0	13 6 8 E?	6 13 4 E?	6 13 4 E?	16 0 0 V
Ratho	46 13 4	40 0 0 E	40 0 0 E		50 3 4 E +
Kinleith	33 6 8	33 6 8 E	33 6 8 E	33 6 8 E	118 9 10 E+
Newton	10 0 0	10 0 0 E	10 0 0 E		16 5 10 E
Calder Clere	20 0 0		2 0 0 V	2 0 0 V	5 7 6 V 26 13 4 E
Calder Comitis	26 13 4				46 5 10 E
Binny	6 13 4				
Strathbrock	26 13 4	17 6 8 E	16 5 0 E	5 8 4 E	36 16 7 E
Ec'machin	16 0 0		6 13 4 E	6 13 4 E	18 6 2
Livingston	16 13 4	6 13 4 V	3 6 8 V	3 6 8 V	12 0 0 V 28 13 4 E
Bathgate	20 0 0	1 6 8 V	4 0 0 V	4 0 0 V	6 13 4 V 31 6 8 E
Dalmeny	33 6 8		3 6 8 V 21 0 0 E	3 6 8 V	13 6 8 V 46 13 4 E
Liston	46 13 4	44 0 0 E +	40 0 0 E	40 0 0 E	60 0 0E
Carriden	16 13 4	3 6 8 V			8 19 10 V 32 13 4 E
Kinnell	16 13 4				11 7 10 V 18 13 4 E
Linlithgow	73 6 8	10 13 4 V		10 13 4 V	18 11 2 V 108 6 8½ E
Falkirk	80 0 0	16 13 4 V	6 13 4 V	10 0 0 V	13 6 8 V 137 13 4 E
Slamannan	2 13 4	1 16 8 E	2 11 8 E	2 10 0 E	6 13 4 E

Table 76 (*cont.*)

Parish	*Antiqua Taxatio*	Baiamund's roll – first year of assessment	Baiamund's roll – second year of assessment (a)	Baiamund's roll – second year of assessment (b)	Bishop Halton
Dunipace	20 0 0				31 13 4
Larbert	2 13 4				8 0 0
Kirkton	40 0 0		23 6 8 V	10 0 0 V	26 13 4 V
					83 6 8 E
Airth	43 6 8			2 13 4	7 7 10 V
					35 13 4 E
Bothkenner	13 6 8				
Auldcathie	2 13 4				5 12 4 E
Oldh'stocks	40 0 0	68 17 3 E	20 0 0 E		53 6 8 E
Innerwick	20 0 0	13 6 8 V			18 0 0 V
		33 6 8 E			71 0 0 E
Dunbar	120 0 0	146 13 4 E	76 13 4 E	76 13 4 E	240 0 0 E
Tyninghame	26 13 4	60 0 0 E	30 0 0 E	30 0 0 E	53 6 8 E
Hamer	6 13 4				23 7 3 E
Auldhame	4 0 0	2 0 0 E	3 0 0 E	2 16 8 E	9 4 2 E
Linton	66 13 4	80 0 0 E	40 0 0 E	40 0 0 E	93 6 8 E
N. Berwick	66 13 4	11 13 4 V	6 13 4 V	6 13 4 V	13 6 8 V
					31 4 2 E
Haddington	80 0 0	10 0 0 V	6 13 4 V	6 13 4 V	11 13 6 V
					106 7 4 E
St Martins	3 6 8				2 0 0
Athelst'ford	6 13 4				6 17 4
Garvald	10 0 0				16 16 7 E
Bara	16 13 4				18 13 4 E
Morham	13 6 8	16 0 0 E	8 0 0 E	8 0 0 E	11 12 10 E
Bothans	20 0 0	20 0 0 E	20 0 0 E	20 0 0 E	46 13 4 E
Bolton	13 6 8	6 13 4 V	3 6 8 V	3 6 8 V	8 6 8 V
					16 18 4 E
Saltoun	20 0 0				39 7 10 E
Pencaitland	26 13 4	4 0 0 E	5 6 8 E	5 6 8 E	33 6 8 E
Gullane	53 6 8	16 13 4 V	9 0 0V		48 0 0 E
Seton	12 0 0	13 6 8 E	6 13 4 E	6 13 4 E	20 0 0 E
Tranent	43 6 8		7 0 0 V	5 0 0 V	15 19 2 V
					59 6 0 E
Musselburgh	46 13 4		3 6 8 V	3 6 8 V	9 6 8 V
Cranston	40 0 0	6 13 4 V	6 13 4 V		6 0 0 V
					9 6 8 E
Crichton	20 0 0	20 0 0 E	10 0 0 E	10 0 0 E	24 0 0 E
Keith Humble	20 0 0	6 13 4 V	3 6 8 V	3 6 8 V	7 14 6 V
					20 0 0 E
Keith Marischall	8 0 0	13 6 8 E	6 13 4 E	6 13 4 E	13 6 8 E
Fala	4 0 0				

Table 76 (*cont.*)

Parish	*Antiqua Taxatio*	Baiamund's roll – first year of assessment	Baiamund's roll – second year of assessment (a)	Baiamund's roll – second year of assessment (b)	Bishop Halton
Loquhariot	26 13 4	10 0 0 V	3 6 8 V	3 6 8 V	40 6 8 E
Carrington	12 0 0				10 0 0 V
					19 6 8 E
Cockpen	13 6 8	24 13 4 E	13 6 8 E	13 6 8 E	22 0 0
Clerkington	5 6 8		3 5 0 E	3 6 8 E	13 6 8 E
Masterton	2 13 4				
Heriot	20 0 0	25 6 8 E	12 13 4 E		23 13 4 E
Mt Lothian	8 0 0				13 0 0 E
Ormiston	8 0 0			10 0 0 E	10 0 0 E
Old Cambus	10 0 0	10 0 0 E	4 0 0 V	2 0 0 V	10 10 0 V
					10 13 4 E
Coldingham	80 0 0				102 19 6 E
Lamberton	10 0 0				6 1 2 V
					13 6 8 E
Berwick	73 6 8	26 13 4 V	13 6 8 V	13 6 8 V	29 6 8 V
					66 10 8 E
Mordington	16 0 0	26 13 4 E	13 6 8 E	13 6 8 E	20 0 0
Foulden	16 0 0	44 0 0 E	13 6 8 E	13 6 8 E	31 1 2
Chirnside	33 6 8	(80 0 0 E)		44 0 0 E	40 1 2
Edrom	66 13 4	20 0 0V	3 6 8 V	3 6 8 V	13 6 8 V
					66 0 0 E
Duns	73 6 8				80 0 0
Ellem	17 6 8	26 13 4 E	13 6 8 E	13 6 8 E	19 13 4
Cranshaws	8 0 0				20 0 0
St Bathans	0 13 4				
Langton	20 0 0	13 6 8 V	5 0 0 V	5 0 0 V	18 0 0 V
					13 6 8 E
Fishwick	20 0 0		3 6 8 V	3 6 8 V	6 13 4 V
					1 0 0 E?
Horndean	5 0 0				5 0 0
Hutton	16 0 0			20 0 0 E	25 0 10
Upset'ton	13 6 8	15 0 0 E			21 18 2
Hilton	12 0 0	15 0 0 E	7 10 0 E	7 10 0 E	20 12 10
Whitsome	30 0 0	(80 0 0 E)		36 13 4	30 1 2
Simprim	10 0 0				12 0 0 E
Swinton	23 6 8	6 13 4 V	3 6 8 V	3 6 8 V	7 0 10 V
					22 0 0 E
Lennel	20 0 0				49 9 7 E
Fogo	26 13 4	10 0 0 V	5 0 0 V	5 0 0 V	7 9 10 V
					21 9 4 E
Polwarth	8 0 0			10 13 4	14 5 6
Greenlaw	30 0 0	20 13 4 V	5 6 8 V	5 6 8 V	12 2 9 V
					36 8 0 E

Table 76 (*cont.*)

Parish	*Antiqua Taxatio*	Baiamund's roll – first year of assessment	Baiamund's roll – second year of assessment (a)	Baiamund's roll – second year of assessment (b)	Bishop Halton
Gordon	20 0 0				26 0 0
Hallyburton	2 13 4				
Hume	16 0 0				27 11 8
Stitchill	23 6 8	6 13 4 V	3 6 8 V	3 6 8 V	10 0 0 V
					26 13 4 E
Ednam	36 13 4	6 13 4 V		20 0 0 V	8 0 0 V
					38 0 0 E
Eccles	66 13 4				
Smailholm	30 0 0	26 13 4 E			26 13 4
Makerstoun	13 6 8				6 0 0 V
					20 0 0 E
Mertoun	26 13 4				38 0 0
Earlston	40 0 0	13 6 8 V	6 13 4 V	6 13 4 V	13 6 8 V
					38 0 0 E
Legerwood	26 13 4	16 13 4 V	8 6 8 V	8 0 0 V	16 0 0 V
Lauder	60 0 0				68 1 2 E
Wedale	46 13 4		20 0 0 V	13 6 8 V	9 13 4 V
Channelkirk	26 13 4	16 13 4 V	3 6 8 V	3 6 8 V	10 0 0 V
					30 0 0 E

Notes: The symbols £ s. d. are omitted. E stands for ecclesia – either the whole church or the Rector's portion. V stands for the vicarage. Obviously such a Table involves simplifications. Occasionally land and chapels or rights moved between parishes.

been suggested in terms of monetary deflation, but this is not supported by the prices evidence advanced here.[9] The answer more probably lies in the ravages of war and plague, compounded by certain administrative and political factors tending towards underassessment. The new assessment was carried out in considerable haste, and in some areas encountered stiff resistance. Contributions had been levied for several years since the king's return in 1357 before the 1366 parliament[10] in addition

[9] See Mayhew, 'Alexander III', and above, p. 18. The detailed consideration of post-Plague prices, shows clearly that although some prices may have fallen below their pre-Plague high, they did not fall below thirteenth-century levels. Moreover, other prices – e.g. wheat – rose after the Plague. It should be conceded, however, that the available prices do not usually relate to the regions with the most startling fall in value, namely the north and west.

[10] For contributions from Coldingham in 1361–2, 1364–5, 1365–6, and 1366–7, see Raine (ed.), *Correspondence*. However, Stevenson's contrary argument is that these earlier taxations would have provided the basis for an accurate assessment in 1366.

to heavy royal customs levies, and it seems possible that tax payer resistance may have contributed to the lowering of assessments.[11]

A consideration of the sole surviving set of sheriffs' accounts for the period (rendered 1358/9) throws some light, both on the effect of war and plague, and on the administrative weakness and confusion consequent upon David II's years of exile. These accounts are full of references to royal lands no longer returning income to the crown, not only as a result of royal grants, which could be revoked, but also because of unauthorized assumptions of power by local magnates and prelates stepping into the vacuum caused by David's exile. Although we may presume that much progress had been made by 1366 in the process of re-establishing full royal authority in the regions, it is possible that a more rigorous tax assessment might have been carried out by a more firmly established king.

Much royal land, however, yielded no income to the crown because it was *vasta*. Such land may on occasion have been ravaged in war, but it is by no means restricted to areas of warfare. There is no doubt that war could have a devastating impact on agricultural income,[12] but such effects were usually relatively short term. War could prevent cultivation in a given area for a year or so, but farming and habitation were normally quick to re-establish themselves once the troops had passed on.[13] Yet the *Exchequer Roll* accounts rendered in 1358/9 reveal a pattern of much more enduring devastation. From Banff, Perth, Fife, Kinghorn, Peebles, Roxburgh, Clackmannan, Stirling, Kinross, Ayr, Kincardine, and Forfar we hear of lands, fishings, ferries, and brewhouses vacant, or let short term (in assedacione) rather than at the previous assize rent or on longer-term farm.[14] Occasionally a new tenant is found, but only at a reduced rent.[15] On other occasions men owing fines cannot be located,[16] and incidental feudal dues cannot be col-

[11] Is it even possible that the new lower assessment was a government concession in the face of rising hostility? Yet if that were the case, it was imperfectly understood in the north and west where any assessment was resisted.

[12] A bovate on the Coldingham manor of Swinton worth 6s. 8d. before the battle of Falkirk was worth half that afterwards. About a century later, the Coldingham assize rents 1399–1400 were low, 'et non plus, quia tenentes ibidem non potuerunt bona sua et catalla quovismodo possidere, nec terras suas pacifice gaudere, causa guerrae, sed sunt vasta': Raine (ed.), *Correspondence*. For the devastating effects of war on trade, see Alexander Stevenson, 'Trade between Scotland and the Low Countries in the Late Middle Ages' (unpublished PhD thesis, University of Aberdeen, 1982).

[13] Froissart's remarks about the speed with which humble Scottish dwellings could be rebuilt are well known. Aberdeen, sacked by the English in 1336, was clearly back to normal by the early 1340s.

[14] *ER* I. 548–9, 554, 556–7, 565–8, 571–4, 576, 580, 584, 586.

[15] *ER* I. 548, 554, 560, 564.

[16] *ER* I. 559, 593.

lected.[17] In these accounts we see the economic consequences of that fundamental alteration in the ratio between land and labour which was the lasting legacy of the Black Death.

Scottish historians have perhaps been unduly impressed by the reticence of the chroniclers on the subject of the Black Death in Scotland,[18] but no one doubts that the Plague struck Scotland hard. Bower and the canons of St Andrews knew that, and comparison with Scandinavia and upland England make it inconceivable that Scotland should have escaped. Grant, who cited evidence suggesting a less severe impact in Scotland than elsewhere, concluded, 'Although Scotland may have escaped relatively lightly, plague still appears to have been the worst disaster suffered by the people of Scotland in recorded history.'[19]

The accounts of Coldingham Priory, though missing for some crucial years, span the period 1342 to 1375, and provide much indirect evidence of the consequences of the demographic collapse. Nevertheless, there is only one explicit reference in the sacristan's account for 1362–3 thus: 'Item in pecunia soluta diversis hominibus pro emendacione bladi destructi per animalia sacristae in tempore pestilenciae, infra territorium de Coldingham, xxvj s. iij d. ob.'[20] These same animals may have been those mortuary beasts sold later, which increased the sacrist's cash receipts to unusual heights in that grim year.

On the other hand, the general Coldingham Priory accounts make no mention of plague, and a cursory reading seems to suggest mounting cash receipts and untroubled prosperity. More careful scrutiny, however, reveals many features common to English manorial accounts of this period. Demesne ploughed acreage drops sharply after the Plague, and to the extent that cash receipts hold up, it is usually a result of stock sales, significant borrowing, and the carrying over of mounting arrears totals. As in England, the accounts often record anticipated income, but allow the accountant significant sums for rents which did not in fact materialize. Thus, in the final surviving account of this period, 1374–5, arrears of £80 and assize rents of £118 were off-set by £131 'debitis de tenentibus baroniae de Coldingham, quorum nomina patent

[17] *ER* I. 554, 573.

[18] Nicholson, *Scotland: The Later Middle Ages*, p. 149 and Grant, *Independence and Nationhood*, p. 74, both comment on the lack of interest in this subject shown by Fordun and Wyntoun.

[19] Grant, *Independence and Nationhood* p. 75. See also Audrey-Beth Fitch, 'Assumptions about Plague in Late Medieval Scotland', *American–Canadian Journal of Scottish Studies*, II (1987), 30–40, which argues that plague, especially pneumonic plague, struck Scotland very hard.

[20] Raine (ed.), *Correspondence*, p. xli.

in quadam cedula liberata super compotum'.[21] Thus we may conclude that the huge collapse in values indicated by the 1366 *Verus Valor* may reflect the ravages of war, some erosion in royal authority, a degree of tax payer resistance, but above all a dramatic fall in land values as a result of the demographic catastrophe.

The evidence of prices in the immediate aftermath of the Plague is at best thin. However, from the late fourteenth century it becomes increasingly plentiful, and the dramatically enhanced prices of later medieval Scotland are very clear. In large part these high prices are attributable to currency devaluation, but even expressed in sterling-equivalent terms, some prices – especially cereal – are still very high. A brief consideration of the economy, sector by sector, may help to explain this phenomenon.

In the 1360s the wool trade was still strong, and customs receipts and mint output were correspondingly high. Those left alive in Scotland, as in England, enjoyed something of an Indian summer. From the 1370s, however, the later medieval European economic climate turned first autumnal, and then wintry. Recent analysis of Scottish trade in the later middle ages has revealed a picture of deficit and overall decline.[22] The decline in the value of Scots wool exports from the late fourteenth century revealed by the surviving customs accounts is clear.[23] The evidence for deficit, however, is less certain, though Scotland's fourteenth-century dependence on imported manufactures[24] and grain is well established. Despite the introduction of duty payable on imported English goods, and on bullion exported, we do not know enough about Scottish imports compared with the customs figures for exports to give us even an approximate balance of trade. The shortage of bullion unquestionably felt in Scotland may imply a trade deficit, but it should be recalled that all Europe suffered from bullion scarcity at this time.

[21] Since Raine did not publish this *cedula*, we may presume it did not survive.

[22] Stevenson, 'Trade between Scotland and the Low Countries'; Stevenson, 'Trade with the South'; *Stevenson, Scottish Historical Atlas,* II.

[23] It may, however, be appropriate to enter a small caveat about the customs figures. Ditchburn, 'Trade with Northern Europe', p. 167, has found evidence of Scottish merchants handling cloth in Danzig in 1444 which did not appear in the Scots customs accounts. He interprets this as re-exported English cloth, but this incident may serve to remind us that all James I's new customs duties lapsed in the 1440s; I am grateful to A. Stevenson for this point. Cf. Leslie J. Macfarlane, *William Elphinstone and the Kingdom of Scotland 1431–1514* (Aberdeen, 1985), p. 151, where he notes evidence for evasion of English customs on a very substantial scale. See also *ER* III.219 for unsuccessful evasion of the custom on wool in Scotland 1390–1. Whatever the true explanation for the cloth in Danzig, with a value of over £4,500 it was clearly an awful lot of cloth.

[24] Froissart, cited by Stevenson, 'Trade with the South', p. 189.

In short, the case for a deficit in Scottish trade seems to be based chiefly on the clear evidence of a decline in exports.

Stevenson has performed a great service in charting this decline in the volume of Scottish exports. His figures show a dramatic fall in wool exports. In the late fifteenth century they stood at only about a quarter of the early fourteenth-century levels. Figures for cloth exports survive in a usable series from the 1460s, though duty on exported cloth was first ordered in 1398,[25] and Grant has suggested that 'quite a respectable Scottish cloth industry' may have existed in the fourteenth century.[26] It is possible to convert the cloth export figures to get some idea of the quantities of wool being exported in this finished form.[27] Table 77 converts Stevenson's cloth export figures to a rough wool equivalent and adds them to Stevenson's wool export figures. However, the result is still not particularly impressive. Even with the cloth addition, later fifteenth-century figures hardly reach the earlier fifteenth-century levels achieved by wool alone, while these figures in turn fall well below the fourteenth-century levels. Moreover, as we have seen, some unknown quantity of cloth was also being made in Scotland at these earlier dates. Thus it seems clear that Scottish cloth exports do not make good the decline in Scottish wool exports, as happened to a considerable extent in England.

The performance of other commodities is not quite as bad as that of wool exports. The decline in the export of woolfells and hides was nothing like as steep as that for wool, and other new exports, notably salmon, had an important contribution to make. If 100 lasts of salmon were exported per year, a fairly normal sum in the period 1470–1540,[28] that would earn about £2,250 p.a. for the Scottish balance of payments.[29] And yet the dominance of the Scottish wool trade was such that the serious decline in this sector must have gravely weakened Scottish later medieval exports.

To some extent, however, some such decline was to be expected. Overall demand in Europe may be presumed to have fallen as a conse-

[25] Nicholson, *Scotland: The Later Middle Ages*, p. 265. Stevenson informs me that the legislation passed by parliament was not then actually enforced.

[26] Grant, *Independence and Nationhood*, p. 79.

[27] The *Coventry Leet Book* tells us that in 1451 at least 30 lb of woollen yarn was required for one dozen of cloth (i.e. half a cloth of assize), cited by E.M. Carus-Wilson, *Medieval Merchant Venturers* (London, 1967), p. 250 n. 2. Dr Carus-Wilson herself uses a figure of 81 lb to a whole cloth, so 30 lb for a dozen is likely to be a minimum.

[28] Stevenson, *Scottish Historical Atlas* II.

[29] Assuming 45s. a barrel and 10 barrels to a last, (there may actually have been 12 barrels to the last). Moreover, Aberdeen burghers enjoyed partial exemption from the duty on exported salmon, and since Aberdeen was by far the most important centre of salmon export in Scotland we may be confident that export levels exceeded those indicated by the duty paid.

Table 77. *Scottish wool exports (after Stevenson)*

Date	Wool	Wool in cloth[a]	Total
1327–33	867		867
1361–70	761		761
1371–80	857		857
1381–90	608		608
1391–1400	623		623
1401–11	321		321
1412–22	357		357
1424–35	540		540
1445–9	398		398
1450–9	216		216
1460–9	309	45	354
1470–9	274	58	332
1480–9	200	42	242
1490–9	215	80	295
1500–9	236	80	316
1510–19	191	59	250
1520–9	124	88	212
1530–9	219	119	338

[a]Calculated from Stevenson's figures on the basis of 30 lb of wool to a dozen of cloth. 360 lb to a sack of wool. Stevenson gives 187.58 kg to a sack after 1426 (perhaps taking the reform of that year a little too literally) 100 dozen of cloth thus contain 1563 kg of wool.

quence of low late-medieval population levels, and the collapse of the Flemish cloth trade was particularly marked.[30] Thus a decline in the volume of Scottish exports was inevitable and need not necessarily imply a Scottish trade deficit. A weakened Scottish currency should also have discouraged imports. It remains to be asked, should the very process of debasement in Scotland be seen as evidence of an enfeebled trading position? Or, to put it another way, was debasement a symptom of decline or a cure for it ?

It is true that fifteenth-century Scotland was chronically short of bullion, but this was a condition common to the whole of Europe at this time.[31] Currency depreciation occurred in France and Flanders, as well as Scotland; it even happened in England, though only to a limited degree. Everywhere in Europe bullion rose in value in the later middle

[30] John H. Munro, 'Monetary contraction and industrial change in the late-medieval Low Countries, 1335–1500', in N.J. Mayhew (ed.), *Coinage in the Low Countries* (Oxford, BAR, 1979), Table 12, p. 151.

[31] J. Day 'The Great Bullion Famine of the Fifteenth Century', *Past and Present*, 79 (1978).

ages, reflecting declining mined output and the constant flow through Venice and Genoa to the East to pay for spices and silks.[32]

In the present state of our knowledge we can hardly even guess at the size of Scotland's currency in the fifteenth century. It had certainly shrunk below fourteenth-century levels, and it certainly grew again in the sixteenth century before the influx from the Americas after 1540, but whether the dip in the fifteenth century betokened a balance of trade deficit, settled by exported bullion, or merely reflected the scarcity of silver and gold common to all Europe remains a difficult question. Stevenson and Ditchburn, who have studied Scots trade more closely than anyone, were both convinced about a Scottish trade deficit,[33] but it is worth considering for a moment how a medieval trade deficit might have worked. In the absence of huge reserves of international capital characteristic of the modern world, medieval Scotland could only have financed a balance of payments deficit by the export of bullion; and since Scotland was never totally stripped of coin it seems clear that trade deficits could only have been of moderate size or short duration or both. An unhealthy balance of payments could have constrained the money supply and depressed the economy but again such a chronic rather than acute problem would be difficult to distinguish from money supply problems occasioned by international bullion scarcity.

Turning to the domestic situation, there are some reasons for thinking that later medieval Scotland may not have been quite as depressed as is sometimes assumed. The price evidence summarized in Chapter 1 demonstrates that even after due allowance has been made for the effects of devaluation, currency-adjusted prices still indicate fairly healthy levels of demand for most commodities except livestock. The contrast between steadily rising prices in Scotland and the stagnation apparent in England raises the possibility that rising Scottish prices may not only be a symptom of growth there but also an active cause of it.

Even a pessimistic view of Scotland's export performance has the corollary that local crafts may have benefited if the Scots were unable to afford imports.[34] This, of course, is exactly how a devaluation is theoretically meant to work. Moreover, the financial position of the

[32] Frederick Lane, 'Exportations venitiennes d'or et d'argent de 1200 à 1450', J. Day (ed.), in *Etudes d'Histoire Monétaires* (Lille, 1984). F.C. Lane and R.C. Mueller, *Money and Banking in Medieval and Renaissance Venice*, I (Baltimore, 1985). Louise Buenger Robbert, 'Monetary Flows – Venice 1150–1400' in J.F. Richards (ed.), *Precious Metals in the Later Medieval and Early Modern Worlds* (Durham, N. C., 1983).

[33] Ditchburn, 'Trade with Northern Europe', p. 176, Stevenson, 'Trade with the South', p. 198.

[34] Stevenson, 'Trade with the South', p. 202.

Scots monarchy seems to have been fundamentally healthy. The treasure amassed by James III before Sauchieburn in 1488 suggests that whatever his other problems illiquidity was not one of them.[35] Although income from customs receipts became less vital to the royal finances, and direct taxation was never a favoured Scottish option, the royal position was safeguarded by increasingly successful accumulation and exploitation of crown lands.[36] This process reached its peak during the reign of James IV, whose annual income seems to have much more than doubled in the course of the reign.[37] Apart from the sale of feudal casualties, the chief source of this enhanced income seems to have been a fuller appreciation of rising land values. A detailed assessment of royal wealth in the fifteenth and sixteenth centuries remains to be made. Various figures have been advanced for the income of James III, IV, and V, but these figures are not usually directly comparable with one another. Even when the complexities of gross and net income in the treasurer's and comptroller's accounts have been mastered, varying royal policy for income generation and expenditure make the royal finances an uncertain guide to the prosperity of the nation.

In contrast, the church's wealth may provide a more reliable, though still very approximate, indication of the state of later medieval Scottish agriculture. It has been estimated that the church as a whole received an income of some £300,000 to £400,000 p.a. at the time of the Reformation. On the basis of the lower figure, and converting to sterling this compares reasonably with the English figure of £310,000 sterling for the *Valor Ecclesiasticus* of 1535. Thinking only in the broadest terms, and this sort of calculation can hardly be made in any other way, it looks as if the Scottish church at least maintained the 1:5 relationship to English church wealth indicated by the *Taxatio* of 1291. If this was the case, it was a considerable achievement, given the success of the English wool and cloth trades in the later middle ages. In the absence of such consistently profitable exports, Scottish agriculture was perhaps more domestically orientated, but it seems to have been no less profitable for all that. However, it may even be that the Scottish church enjoyed an income some 33% higher than this if the higher estimate were

[35] J.M. Brown (ed.), *Scottish Society in the Fifteenth Century* (London, 1977), p. 36. *TA* I.79–87 and 166ff for royal treasure 1488. Alexander Suthyrland of Dunbeath's will 1456 equally does not suggest liquidity problems. As well as a large number of debts owing to him, he had £480 cash in hand. I am grateful to Dr Barbara Crawford for this reference. *Bannatyne Miscellany*, III.

[36] Athol Murray, 'Crown Lands 1424–1542' in McNeill and Nicholson (eds.), *An Historical Atlas of Scotland*, pp. 72–3.

[37] Macfarlane, *William Elphinstone*, pp. 413–16.

accurate. On this basis the income of the Scottish church seems to have grown very significantly more than English church income grew.[38]

Nevertheless, both church and crown seem to have experienced financial problems as their costs rose with inflation faster than their income; both resorted to feuing to raise cash. The granting of feu-farm charters conveying permanent tenancies on fixed conditions raised cash in the short term because they usually involved substantial down payments, and increased annual rents and dues. Thus James IV feued Ettrick forest converting rents of £525 p.a. before 1501 to £2,672 thereafter.[39] But the development of feuing is not only important for the history of church and crown finances. It shows us that old rents had become dramatically detached from the real value of the lands, and that there was no shortage of men who were happy to invest very considerable sums in Scottish agriculture. The high price of cereals probably did much to stimulate this investment in farming. Moreover, although nobles and lairds may have been prominent in feuing crown lands, Nicholson has shown that these classes often sold on their purchases, while merchant classes were more likely to retain their acquisitions.[40] Still more significantly, recent analysis of feued kirk lands reveals very substantial investment by men below laird status.[41] It appears that the financial position of both crown and church was founded on an agricultural society sufficiently prosperous to have generated a body of men with both the will and the means to invest further in land. Further research is revealing patterns of rural lending in which it is often the laird who borrows from his tenants.[42] The discovery of this sub-laird group with capital at their disposal in turn raises considerations of the terms on which land had been held before the feuing revolution. Could it be that the traditional short Scottish tacks had not after all produced John Major's class of down-trodden farmers deterred from investment and improvement by the ever-present fear of eviction? This is certainly the conclusion reached by Margaret Sanderson, and by Lythe.[43] The

[38] G.Donaldson, *Accounts of the Collectors of Thirds of Benefices 1561–72*, SHS (Edinburgh, 1949), and later, his *Scotland: James V to James VII* (Edinburgh, 1965), pp. 132–3. Donaldson's larger estimate presumably corrects the lower figure in the light of further work.

[39] Wormald, *Court, Kirk and Community*, p. 53. In the context of inflation, however, these new rents and payments rapidly became as modest as those they replaced.

[40] Ibid., pp. 48ff, and Ranald Nicholson, 'Feudal Developments in Late Medieval Scotland', *Juridical Review* (April 1973), part i, 1–21.

[41] Margaret Sanderson, *Scottish Rural Society in the Sixteenth Century* (Edinburgh, 1982).

[42] I am most grateful to Dr Margaret Sanderson for information about this aspect of her current research.

[43] In his 1993 Rhind Lectures Dr Mark Dilworth also questioned the more pessimistic interpretations of Major's comment.

length of fifteenth-century tacks seems to have varied considerably, there being no shortage of longer leases for terms of years or for life, as well as shorter leases.[44] Moreover, even when tacks came to an end they were often renewed in favour of existing tenants or their heirs, and when they were not renewed it seems often to have been the tenant's decision to move. Tenants do not appear to have been often evicted against their will. The simple arithmetic of the late medieval supply of labour and tenants set against the available land insured tenant security, so far as they wished it, more effectively than legal arrangements could have done.

For the same reasons it is difficult to believe that later medieval Scottish rents are likely to have kept pace with inflation. Unfortunately, little evidence on this point is available. For the crown lands, Murray found rents were rarely increased, except for James IV's onslaught early in the 1500s, and tenants enjoyed a good deal of security.[45] For the nobility the Dalkeith rental of 1373 may be compared with an undated Dalkeith rental *c.* 1450 or earlier in the Scottish Record Office.[46] Equally Strathearn rent rolls of the 1380s and 1440s survive in the *Exchequer Rolls*. These sources, together with information gleaned from scattered unpublished Retours have led Grant to believe that though rents may have risen some 50% between about 1366 and 1424, they seem then to have remained quite static till the last quarter of the fifteenth century when they started to move upward again.[47]

If rents did move as slowly as this, they will not have kept up with inflation. Dr Macfarlane has associated 'the widespread fall in land values' with a general crisis in the affairs of landowners who became increasingly litigious, and yet also lawless, as a result.[48] Rising prices combined with more slowly moving rents could have brought about an important, and for some painful, redistribution of wealth in later medieval Scotland. If, as we have seen, short tacks did not enable landlords to protect their rents adequately from inflation because of the simple difficulty of finding tenants at any price, old rents will quickly have become cheap. If tenant farmers saw their rents lagging behind the

[44] For nineteen year tacks of Arbroath lands, see Sanderson, *Rural Society*, p. 49.
[45] Murray, 'Crown Lands', pp. 72–3.
[46] *Registrum Honoris de Morton*, ed. C. Innes, Bannatyne Club (Edinburgh, 1853) SRO GD150/100A.
[47] A.Grant, 'The Higher Nobility in Scotland and their Estates, c.1371–1424' (unpublished DPhil thesis, Oxford, 1975). I am most grateful to Dr Grant for his advice on these points.
[48] Macfarlane, *William Elphinstone*, pp. 100–1. Strictly speaking it was the rents which were falling in real terms; the true value of the land reflected in rising prices as properly understood by the farmers themselves was actually rising.

prices they were able to get for their produce, it is no wonder they were both willing and able to put down large sums to feu their land.

Of course, this rather simplistic analysis requires a good deal of qualification. In the late fourteenth century it may have taken the tenantry a good deal of time to appreciate the strength of their position, while in the course of the sixteenth century rising population may have again begun to weaken the tenants' bargaining power. To some extent rents, wholly or partly, in kind will have provided a measure of protection to landlords. Similarly, the value of church teinds will have risen with prices.[49] However, the church was not always the beneficiary, since teinds were sometimes leased to local gentry on very long tacks.[50] Occasionally, more lowly tenants – husbandmen – were obliged to sell goods to the landlord at a fixed price, in which case such tenants suffered from inflation. In theory, such tenants may have been protected to some extent by the rising prices they could get for their other goods sold on the open market, but such protection was dependent on access to markets. In the remoter regions prices may well have moved upward more slowly than our calculations suggest.

Wage-earners will also have gained some measure of protection from inflation through wages in food or other goods. Unfortunately, we have almost no data on wages to work with. We may presume that money wages were less 'sticky' than rents, but more so than prices. If this were the case, the overall shortage of late-medieval labour will gradually have operated in the workers' favour. In short, even contracts or relationships expressed in kind will have reflected the improved bargaining position of labour after the Plague, but those expressed in money terms will have been affected both by inflation and by the shortage of labour and tenants. Thus debasement forced the renegotiation of all deals, introducing a degree of flexibility to all social and commercial relations which must have seemed quite alien to medieval man. Simultaneously, the fall in population weakened the position of landowners. Given the grotesquely ill-distributed pattern of wealth in medieval society, it is difficult to regard this redistribution as anything

[49] Sanderson, *Cardinal of Scotland*, p. 25, notes 'Some people were prepared to pay enormous duty for a tack of teinds', citing £80 p. a. for the Garvoch, Kincardineshire, teinds, and £1,000 p. a. for the Glamis teinds, both from the Arbroath *Liber* II. Hannay noted that the teinds of Kinkell in Aberdeenshire were worth some 700 merks *c.*1515 (*ALCPA*, p. lvii).

[50] The provost of Trinity College sought a legal reduction in the nineteen-year tack held by Sir Walter Scott of Branxholm, the college and the provost being greatly hurt by the outdated, low valuation of the teinds. Despite various lines of argument, the Lords found for Scott. *ALCPA*, p. 519. On other occasions also the Lords, and James V himself, argued in favour of nineteen-year tacks despite the efforts of churchmen to have them overturned. Ibid, p. lvii.

but beneficial. Resources were effortlessly redirected away from landowning consumers and towards landholding producers.

In England, of course, population had also fallen dramatically, but money had held its value and fifteenth-century prices had remained stable, even stagnant. In consequence, wages rose sharply but producers received no help from rising prices. Rents were stagnant also, but concessions were only wrung from landowners with difficulty. Often land was left uncultivated as landowners held out for outdated rents, while farmers hesitated to commit themselves when the prices they received were so low. In an essentially stable and conservative society, the difference between rent reductions which had to be won from powerful landlords who could well afford to leave land unlet if they chose, and 'real' rent reductions which would occur automatically through inflation, cannot be overstated. At the same time, while rising prices stimulated Scots production, English farmers faced static profits. A clearer illustration of the benefits of moderate inflation would be hard to find.

Debasement and inflation will also have contributed to the prosperity of Scottish merchants. The high rates of customs levied on exports in the fourteenth century were gradually eroded by inflation. James I recognized this effect of devaluation, and tried to collect customs at old money rates while meeting his own obligations in devalued money,[51] but such a palpably dishonest scheme was doomed to failure, and probably won him nothing but unpopularity. As the money value of exports rose the old frozen customs charges came to represent a dwindling proportion of the profit.[52] It seems likely that some English wool came north to be exported from Scotland to take advantage of these lower rates.[53] Moreover, as we have seen, merchants also benefited from devaluation since their domestically incurred costs were met in devalued local money while profits were earned in international hard currency. Thus, whatever the deficiencies of Scottish cloth or salt may have been, Scots merchants were able to market it abroad at the lowest prices.[54] With these advantages it is not surprising that some Scots merchants made fortunes, incurring the wrath of the poet Dunbar in the process, and such merchant prosperity may cast further doubt on the idea of a sustained Scottish trade deficit. Indeed, although Scotland did pass

[51] Mayhew, 'Contemporary Valuation'.

[52] Perhaps for this reason fifteenth-century customs charges were usually fixed as a proportion of the value of the goods rather than at so much per unit of goods.

[53] Stevenson, 'Trade with the South', p. 193, cites evidence from *ER*, for the period 1363–79.

[54] Lythe on salt in 'Economic Life', p. 78; Mayhew on Scottish black, above, pp. 353–4.

bullionist laws designed to limit imports and build up currency reserves, Aberdeen was probably not alone among Scottish burghs in understanding the need to encourage the import of capital goods such as salt and iron. Faced with a European recession, the greater danger was not deficit but economic depression. In general, then, and taking due account of the European economic climate as a whole, it is arguable that perhaps the Scots trading performance in the later middle ages was not as bad as has sometimes been suggested.

Recent assessments of Scottish fifteenth-century building have also taken a rather optimistic view. Lythe noted important fifteenth-century work at Lincluden, Roslin, Crossraguel, Elgin, Dunkeld, Linlithgow, and Craigmillar,[55] to which Stell added Cambuskenneth, St Andrews, Jedburgh, Melrose, and Glasgow.[56] Bridge building projects on the rivers Garnock, Bladenock, Dee, and Tay were clearly important investments in infra-structure.[57] Domestic buildings also provoked some favourable comment, while sizeable church projects illustrated burghal pride.[58] The range of late-medieval building has even provoked the observation that building perhaps implied 'a slightly more widespread distribution of wealth'.[59] The point is not that Scotland's building achievement was any more impressive than that in England, but that the Scots economy was capable of such investment without the support of the strong wool and cloth exports which made such a huge contribution to England's wealth.

Similarly, later medieval Scottish diet has also been found to exhibit signs of prosperity similar to those found in England. Dyer has noted a rise in meat eating in England in the later middle ages.[60] The increased quantity of meat eaten by English peasants was found by him to be part of a general improvement in diet including also increased quantities of cereals and ale. For Scotland Gibson and Smout have identified a clear shift away from the animal-based protein prominent in later medieval Scottish food, towards an increasingly cereal-based diet from the 1550s when life was becoming increasingly harsh for many.[61] Gibson and Smout were in no doubt that a rise or fall in meat eating in

[55] Lythe, 'Economic Life', p. 74.
[56] G. Stell, 'Architecture: The Changing Needs of Society', in J.M. Brown (ed.), *Scottish Society in the Fifteenth Century* (London, 1977), pp. 116–21.
[57] Ibid., p. 134. Though Macfarlane, *William Elphinstone*, has shown what a long-drawn-out business such investment might be.
[58] Stell, 'Architecture' pp. 161–2, and for churches at Aberdeen, Dundee, St Vigeans, Cupar, Perth, Stirling, Linlithgow, Edinburgh, Haddington, Dysart, Kilkenny, and Falkirk, see pp. 165–6.
[59] Ibid., p. 183.
[60] Dyer, *Standards of Living*, p. 159.
[61] Gibson and Smout, 'Scottish Food and Scottish History'.

Scotland indicates a rise or fall in the general standard of living. By this token the later middle ages was clearly a period of some prosperity in Scotland.

This attempt to re-evaluate the fifteenth-century Scottish economy in a more favourable light may be necessary to correct an earlier, and excessively gloomy, view, but it should not be allowed to get out of hand. Even though individual consumption may have risen, low levels of population and real monetary shortages, both evident right across Europe, meant that overall production levels seldom reached levels common before the Black Death. Piracy and political troubles frequently afflicted trade, and intermittent bursts of disease kept population levels low. Indeed, it has wisely been observed that any epoch which depended for its prosperity on the repeated extinction of large numbers of its people through disease can hardly be regarded as a golden age. Nevertheless, it does seem that the later-medieval Scots economy enjoyed some success, and that some of that success may have been aided by devaluation and inflation. Scotland seems to have been right to adopt currency devaluation broadly in line with much of continental Europe, while England's excessively hard money policy may well have inhibited later medieval growth there. Whether this interpretation finds favour or not, it is hoped that the collection of price data offered here, together with the studies of currency and weights and measures, will prove a useful tool for historians, and perhaps encourage further work on the medieval economic and social history of Scotland.

Glossary of unusual terms

This Glossary is in two parts. Part One contains brief notes on unusual terms which may not be immediately familiar to readers who, like the authors, are not Scottish. For an authoritative key to the Scots language researchers should contact the *Dictionary of the Older Scottish Tongue*, senior editor Marace Dareau (University of Edinburgh), while *The Concise Scots Dictionary*, editor-in-chief Mairi Robinson (Aberdeen, 1985), provides an invaluable one-volume guide.

Part Two was compiled with special reference to the problems presented by weights and measures. Much detailed and technical evidence on this topic is presented here, and this part of the Glossary thus serves as an important appendix to Chapter 3.

PART ONE

BAWBEE

A Scottish coin of debased silver worth 6d. Scots introduced in 1538. It derived its name from Alexander Orok of Sillebawby, master of the mint at the time.

BAXTER

A baker.

BERE

A Scottish variety of barley, also found as bear.

BLACK MONEY

Heavily debased coin often almost entirely of copper, lacking silver content.

BILLON

Debased coin usually of less than 50% silver. Such alloyed silver was often especially appropriate for small denominations which might otherwise have become impossibly tiny.

BOUK

Animal carcase.

CHARITY

Generous measure used in selling, as a sweetener to the buyer.

COCKET

A customs seal for goods on which duty had been paid.

COCKET LOAF

A specially fermented English bread of well-sieved wheat flour, corresponding to the quachet loaf in Scotland.

CRAKNEL

An expensive type of bread.

CURROCH

A small boat made of tanned and tarred hide stretched over a wooden frame.

DEMY

A Scottish gold coin introduced by James I.

DINMONT

A castrated sheep between its first and second shearing.

FERM

Like the English equivalent 'farm', the term originally applied to the letting of land at a fixed rent. It was often used to indicate either the fixed rent or the cost of land so let.

FEU

A feudal tenure of land. In later medieval Scotland tenants often acquired heritable possession of rented land by means of a large lump-sum payment and agreeing to pay an increased annual rent thereafter. Over time, even the enhanced rents came to seem modest. Feuing thus brought short-term benefits to the landowner, and long-term rewards to the tenant who effectively became the new owner.

FLESHER

Butcher and fishmonger.

FORESTALL

Illegal purchase, either before or outside the market, disrupting supply, and selling on at an unjustified profit.

FOWAT

An expensive type of bread.

GIMMER

A ewe between its first and second shearing.

GRASSUM

An entry fine paid in kind or money on taking up a lease or feu.

GROAT

A silver coin initially (mid-fourteenth century) worth 4d. sterling.

GROOT

A Flemish denomination originally corresponding to the English and Scottish groat. The groot became the foundation of the monetary system of Flanders and the Burgundian Netherlands, so money groot (pl. groten) came to mean the currency of that region in whatever denomination.

HOG

A sheep from its weaning to first shearing.

HUCKSTER

Small-scale retail trader, sometimes of a somewhat disreputable kind.

LION

A Scottish gold coin first introduced under Robert III.

LITSTER

A dyer.

MAIL

Rent.

MART

An ox or cow intended for slaughter and consumption as, usually salted, meat. Derived from the customary slaughter of such beasts around Martinmas (11 November).

MERK

A Scottish mark, being two-thirds of a pound, whether of weight or, more often, of money of account. In the latter case the merk was worth 13s. 4d. (or 160d.) Scots.

NOBLE

A gold coin introduced by Edward III in England and David II in Scotland. In the mid-fourteenth century both versions were worth 6s. 8d. or 80d.

NOLT

A young ox or steer.

PLACK

A billon coin introduced in Scotland by James III.

PYNOR

A docker or shore porter.

QUACHET

A specially fermented loaf of well-sieved wheat flour, corresponding to the English cocket loaf.

REGRATING

Retailing at an unjustifiable profit.

RIDER

A gold coin introduced in Scotland by James III.

RYAL

An English gold coin introduced by Edward IV, and also known as a rose noble. In Scotland Mary and James VI struck large silver ryals from 1565.

SIMNEL

A high quality bread of fine flour superior to the wastel loaf (see below).

STIRK

Young bullock, or rarely heifer, after weaning, usually intended for slaughter aged two or three.

STRAIK

The difference between a heaped and a flattened measure of grain.

TAP

Retail, usually in small amounts.

TEIND

A tenth of the produce of a parish surrendered to support the church and its rector, corresponding to the English tithe. The rectorial teinds were often appropriated by the institutions holding the gift of the living, who instead installed a vicar on a reduced stipend, diverting the rest of the parish teind to other purposes. See Ian B. Cowan, 'Appropriation of Parish Churches', in McNeill and Nicholson (eds.), *An Historical Atlas of Scotland*, pp. 37–8, and *The Parishes of Medieval Scotland*, Scottish Record Society, Old Series (Edinburgh, 1967).

TUP

A ram.

UNICORN

A Scottish gold coin introduced by James III.

WASTEL

A white loaf of well-sifted wheat flour.

WEDDER

A wether, a castrated sheep.

PART TWO

BARREL

A container, used especially for fish, and also for ale, beer, wine, grain, flour, iron, coal, salt, and butter. For salmon it was also a measure of capacity.

(a) For ale and beer: there is evidence in the *Treasurer's Accounts* for 1513 for both 10 and 12 gallon barrels of ale: *TA* IV.463, 464, and, possibly, 471 (10 gallons); *TA* IV.485, 487, 491, 493 (12 gallons; barrels are said to be new salmon barrels); *TA* IV.499, 500, 501 (12 gallons). *TA* VI.156 (Temptalloune, 1532), is for a purchase of 5 gallon barrels of ale. Evidence from the Household Book of James V gives barrels of 9.5 gallons for beer: HBJV, pp. 148, 151, 154, and (assuming use of long hundred) Appendix, p. 30.

(b) For herring: our evidence about the size of the herring barrel is sparse, and also inconsistent; calculations are further complicated by the possibility of the use of long hundreds for counting herring. The Household Book of James V suggests that barrels of herring of the assize of Glasgow might contain 435/520, 570/680, or 748/896 and barrels of the assize of Leith 868/1040 or 866.67/1040 (HBJV, pp. 44, 52, 56, 64, 139, and Appendix, p. 8).

(c) For salmon: the salmon barrel was a subject for both royal and burghal legislation because it was necessary to establish a proper standard for exported salmon. It was ordained in 1487 that the barrel of salmon should keep to the measure of 14 gallons; and in 1489 that the Hamburg barrel should measure 14 gallons (*APS* II. 178–9 and 213). At Aberdeen the capacity of the Hamburg barrel was set at 13¾ gallons of water in 1479 but at 12 gallons or thereby in 1511, a capacity which was still in force in 1521 (ACR VI.598, IX.1, and X.281–2). By 1527 the right measure of Aberdeen barrels was 11½, 11¾, or 12 gallons (ACR, XII i.180). See above, pp. 103–7, for a discussion of the legislation concerning salmon barrels in Aberdeen. Although the Aberdeen measure was apparently slightly smaller than the standard prescribed by royal government, in fact royal legislation about salmon barrels speaks of the old assize or bind of Aberdeen as being definitive: see *APS* II.119 and 237. The fact that 12 gallon barrels of ale in the *Treasurer's Accounts* were said to be salmon barrels would suggest that the government had by the sixteenth century accepted a capacity less than the 14 gallons stipulated as the standard in 1487 and 1489.

Barrels for salmon are described variously from the fifteenth century as large, small, Hamburg, or herring, but it is interesting to note from the salmon series that by the end of the century, and thereafter, they are generally undistinguished. As salmon grew in importance as an export, and as a source of customs revenue, it became necessary to know the size of the barrels in which it was packed, but once a standard barrel was established, the need to describe it lessened. It was the Hamburg barrel which seems to have emerged as the definitive measure. In James III's parliament in June 1478 it was ordained, because of complaints by foreigners and other purchasers of salmon about the 'mynising' (shrinking) of the vessels and barrels in which it was packed, that in future all salmon should be packed in barrels of the measure of Hamburg after the old assize of Aberdeen (*APS* II.119). Moreover, the royal legislation of 1489 and the Aberdeen legislation of 1479 were for the Hamburg barrel. Barrels so described are, furthermore, found more frequently, and also later than other types. It is possible that the large barrel was equivalent to the Hamburg barrel and the small barrel to the herring barrel. For example, at Aberdeen in 1427–8 Pelygrin Grellus was paid for 13 lasts and 2 Hamburg barrels of salmon and for 11 lasts and 11 small barrels of salmon; he was then paid the custom of 13 lasts, and 2 Hamburg barrels and of 11 lasts, 11 herring barrels of salmon (*ER* IV.443–4 and 445); *ER* IV.479 (Aberdeen, 1428–9): large barrel used synonymously with Hamburg barrel. Hamburg barrels and small barrels are, moreover, clearly distinguished from each other in the records (*ER* IV.475, V.105, and ACR V i.241). There is a little evidence from the Household Book of James V about the actual number of salmon and grilse in the barrel (HBJV, pp. 126, 221, and Appendix, p. 26). Grilse were in the later middle ages apparently less valuable than the mature salmon (as is shown in the case between Baudy and Reaucht at Aberdeen in 1538: see 'Appendix of documents', no. III), so it was necessary to explain clearly what relative quantities of grilse and salmon were actually being purchased.

(d) For grain: *ER* II.454 (queen's clerk of liverance, 1374–5): 1 chaldron, 11 bolls wheat flour (adeps frumenti) contained in 12 barrels, suggesting each barrel contained 2¼ bolls; ACR VIII.1020 (Aberdeen, 1509): a barrel in which Orkney bere was sent to ?'Pettorthy', measured with an Edinburgh firlot and peck, was found to contain 3 firlots and ¼ peck of the just measure of Edinburgh; ACR XIV.612–13 (Aberdeen, 1535): claim for 6 barrels full of bere, each containing 3½ firlots, intermeddled with in 1529. There is no real evidence, however, to suggest there was a standard grain barrel.

(e) For butter: ACR VI.844 (Aberdeen, 1484): barrel of salted butter weighing 100/120 pounds. If there were 16 pounds to the stone (see below, under stone), the barrel would have weighed either 6 stone 4 pounds or 7 stone 8 pounds. Evidence from the *Treasurer's Accounts* for 1513 gives barrels of butter containing 12 stones (*TA* IV.489) and 10 stones (*TA* IV.492, 496).

(f) For other commodities: *ER* II.449 (clerk of liverance, 1374): barrel of mustard containing 9 gallons; ACR II.33 (Aberdeen, 1409): barrel of olive oil clearly containing 10 gallons; *TA* IV.492 (treasurer, 1513): 2 barrels candle containing 20 stones at 5s. 4d. per stone came to total cost of £5 6s. 8d., so each barrel would have contained 10 stones.

BATUM

A capacity measure for grain, found in the Dunkeld accounts in the sixteenth century. The evidence of explicit unit prices shows consistently that there were 16 bata to the boll: esp. SHS 2,10.90, 97–8, 104, 109, 247, 262. The batum seems therefore to have been a local equivalent of the peck, although the peck is also met in these records.

BOLL

A measure of capacity for grain and other dry products.

APS I.674 (Assisa Regis David): 'De bolla . // Item bolla debet continere in se sextarium videlicet . xij . lagenas seruicie . Et bolla ex profunditate debet esse . ix . pollicium . In latitudine superiori debet esse . xxiiij . pollices cum spissitudine ligni vtriusque partis . In rotunditate superiori debet esse . lxxij . pollicium in medio ligni vtriusque partis superioris . // In rotundine inferiori debet esse . lxxj . pollicium .' The Scots text reads: 'Of the boll . Item the boll sall contene a sexterne videlicet . xij gallonis of aile and it sould haue in deipnes ix inches and in wydenes abone xxiiij inches by the thicknes of the trie and in the roundnes and circumference abone lxxij inches and in the roundnes at the boddom lxxi inches .'

See above, pp. 86–8, for our reconciliation of this with the boll capacity calculated from what is said in the assize about the gallon.

APS II.12 (assize of James I, 1426): 'ITEM the boll sal contene in breid xxix Inchys withtin the burdis and abufe xxvij Inche and a half evin oure thort ande in deipnes' xix Inchys . . . Ande the boll contenande four ferlotis weyis viij [xx] and iiij pundis.'

See above, pp. 86–7, for a discussion of this legislation as it relates to the boll.

The legislative evidence of a 4 firlot boll is confirmed abundantly by the evidence of explicit unit prices, and this is the assumption on which we have worked.

On the relationship of the boll to the bushel and the quarter: SSG, p. 896, states the boll varied from the old boll of 6 bushels to the new boll of 2; *ER* I.356 (Kirkcudbright, 1330–1): 2 bushels meal said to make 8 bolls; *DHS* II.321 (Berwick, 1298): 29 quarters, 2 bolls coal used over two years and fourteen weeks at rate of 1 boll per week; *ALA* I.81–2 ('Corswod', 1479): quarter of oats priced at 8s. and in same entry 2 bolls of oats consistently priced at 4s. The last two examples suggest 4 bolls = 1 quarter. See further under chaldron.

See above, p. 99, for local variations in the size of the boll.

BUSHEL

A measure of capacity for grain and other dry products, and found in the English rather than the Scots records. We have assumed 4 pecks = 1 bushel. See further under boll, chaldron, and quarter.

BUTT (other forms: boit, bota, bote)

A container for wine, particularly the choicer types. It is not clear if it had a standard capacity. *TA* IV.470 (treasurer, Forth, 1513): 1 'boit' of Malvesey of 40 gallons.

CADE

A measure, or at least a container, found for herring and wine.

(a) For herring: Rogers, *A History of Agriculture and Prices in England*, I, p. 610, states that the cade contained between 500 and 600 herring; SSG, p. 899, citing 'Promptorium Parvulorum', p. 57 n. 4, says a cade contained 600 herrings by the long hundred (i.e. 720).

(b) For wine: *ER* IV.564 (Perth, 1433–4): 23 gallons Rhenish in 1 cade.

CASLAMUS

A measure of capacity or a weight for cheese and meal, found at Tarbert; used for what appear to be wages paid in kind. *MLWL* says the word may mean a basket. It is, perhaps, related to the later castlaw, q.v. Simpson, 'Scots "Trone" Weight', suggests the weight of both caslamus and castlaw was closely equivalent to that of the codrus, q.v.

CASTLAW

A measure for cheese and meal, found as render in kind in south and north Kintyre in the sixteenth century. *ER* XII.586 speaks of a castlaw of small measure.

CELDRA = CHALDRON

CHALDRON

A measure for grain and other dry products. Evidence from explicit unit prices shows consistently that there were generally 16 bolls to the chaldron, but we have also found evidence of a 14 boll (heaped) chaldron in the thirteenth century. Certain grains (malt, oats, and provender) appear to have been measured using heaped bolls of which 14 were equivalent to 16 unheaped: e.g. malt and oats, *ER* I.42, 48; *CDS* III.327, 377. For provender, see *ER* I.42 (Edinburgh, 1288–9): 'quatuordecim bolle cumulate numerantur pro qualibet celdra, vel sexdecim bolle sine cumulo', and *ER* I.48 (Linlithgow, *c.* 1288): ref. to unheaped chaldron. It may have been this practice of heaping bolls which was the origin of the larger firlot for barley, oats, and malt which was approved in 1618: see above, p. 109.

There is also evidence in the fifteenth and sixteenth centuries of a 17 boll chaldron. *ALC* I.119, 1489: 20 chaldrons of victual, bere and meal, each containing 17 bolls; ACR XII ii.536 (Aberdeen, 1529): obligation to deliver 1 chaldron of bere, that is, 17 bolls for the chaldron in 'Fingask'. It is possible that these 17 boll chaldrons included charity at 1 boll per chaldron: see above, pp. 107–9, for a discussion of charity.

On the relationship between the chaldron and the quarter, there is considerable evidence to show there were 4 quarters to the chaldron: *DHS* I.209–10 (Berwick, 1290–1): 3 chaldrons wheat said to contain 12 quarters by the English measure; *DHS* II.319 (Berwick, 1298): 30 chaldrons coal said to contain 120 quarters; *DHS* II.321 (Berwick, 1298): 29 quarters 2 bolls said to have been used over two years and fourteen weeks at the rate of 1 boll per week (i.e. 118 bolls used, so this would suggest 4 bolls to the quarter); *CDS* II, no. 1608, p. 423 (south of Forth, 1302–3): 13 chaldrons, 1 quarter, 2 bushels oatmeal at 13s. 4d. the chaldron cost £8 17s. 6d. (the ratio of chaldrons to quarters in this instance is confirmed by the fact that oatmeal is priced consistently in this document at 13s. 4d. the chaldron and in one instance at 3s.4d. the quarter); SS 12.xliv–xlv (Coldingham, 1363–4): 1 chaldron, 1 boll oats at 15d. the boll, that is, 2 quarters, 1 boll for sowing and 2 quarters for provender; SS 12.xlvii (Coldingham, 1364–5): 3½ quarters, ½ boll oats and peas at 16d. the boll cost 18s. 11½d. This does not yield an exact 4 quarter chaldron, but the inexactitude is probably the result of rounding off.

There is, however, some evidence that there were more than 4 quarters to the chaldron: *DHS* I.212: 52 chaldrons oats by Scots measure; Scots measure exceeds English for oats so that 4 quarters oats equals at least 5 quarters by English measure (may suggest 5 English quarters equivalent to the chaldron); *DHS* II.326 (burgess of Berwick, *c.* 1298): 20 quarters Poitou salt at 16s. 8d. per chaldron cost £4 (so 1 chaldron = 4.17 quarters); PRO E101/22/40 (extracted, but this price not included, in *CDS* III, no. 1382, p. 252 (constable of Roxburgh, 1340–2): 20 quarters, 2½ bushels malt by English measure containing 4 chaldrons and 1 boll, at 26s. 8d. the chaldron cost 108s. 4d. (suggests 5 English quarters = 1 chaldron, and also that 2.5 bushels = 1 boll).

See also under quarter.

The chaldron was used widely to describe large quantities of grain and other dry products but there was no royal legislation to determine its dimensions. It seems therefore to have existed solely as a multiple of the boll.

CHOPPIN (Latin chopinum, copina)

A liquid measure.

ER VI.501–2 (Aberdeen, 1458–9): 7 gallons, 1 quarter, and 1 choppin Rhenish at 8s. gallon cost 58s. 6d. If 1 quarter = ¼ gallon then this suggests 16 choppins made a gallon. There would, therefore, have been 2 choppins to the pint. The choppin is mentioned, but not defined, in the legislation of 1426: *APS* II.12.

CLOVE (other forms 'clowf', 'clof'; Latin clavus)

A unit of weight for iron, wool, and other products. Its name suggests it may have been the same thing as the nail, q.v. 'Ayr Burgh Accounts', ed. Pryde, p. 144 n. 5: the clove was a weight of 7–8 lb.

CODRUS

A measure for cheese, found at Tarbert. It seems to have been used particularly for wages paid in kind. *MLWL* says it was a Scots weight of cheese; G.W.S. Barrow, *Kingship and Unity: Scotland 1000–1306* (London, 1981), p. 173, states that the 'cudthrom' was the Gaelic equivalent of the petra. The codrus may have been equivalent to the 'cudthrom'. We have not, however, converted prices by the codrus to prices per stone. See also Simpson, 'Scots "Trone" Weight'.

COGALL (other form 'tonegall')

Barrow, *Scotland 1000–1306*, p. 173, says the 'cogall' was a wooden vessel into which the cheese was put; *MLWL* says it was a Scots measure of cheese. *ER* I.50 (Forfar, two years to 1290): rent in cheese from Forfar, Glamis, Kingaltenyn, measured in 'tonegall'. After entry for Glamis: 'Et sciendum est quod quelibet tonegall valet vj petras.' We have assumed this is correct. See also Simpson, 'Scots "Trone" Weight'.

DICKER (Latin dacra)

A measure of quantity, used particularly for hides.

ER I.xcviii, says the dicker contained 10 or 12 hides; SSG, p. 909, says the 'dakyr' or dicker (Latin decuria) meant ten, and was a term used in reckoning hides; *MLWL* says the dacra and variants meaning dicker was a measure of 10 hides and also finds it used as a measure of horseshoes, knives, and iron.

Hanham, 'A Medieval Scots Merchant's Handbook', 117: 'Here begynnys the Reknyng of the hidis that ar salde be the last ore be the dacer ['dicker']. And the dacer contenys x hidis, and xx dacer makis the last, and thay ar sald be the li. gr. And the last contenys ij ^{c} hydis.'

Calculations of the size of the last and the dicker as based on customs levies would also show that the dicker was generally reckoned at 10 hides, and this is the assumption on which we have worked. E.g. *ER* II.90 (Edinburgh, 1361–2): 22s. 2½d. custom from 7 dickers, 4 hides at 3s. dicker, and see also the references cited below under the last for hides. Calculations based on the price evidence, especially on explicit unit prices, confirm a 10 hide dicker. E.g. SHS 2,10.3–4 (bishop of Dunkeld's merchant, 1509): 9 dickers, 3 hides at 6s. each, total price £27 18s.; *ER* XIV.118 (receiver of king's possessions, 1515): 141/161 hides at 50s. dicker, total value £40 5s., from 141/161 marts; *ER* XIV. 217 (comptroller, Ross, 1515–16): 68 hides at 50s. dicker sold for £17; *ER* XIV.284 (comptroller, 1516–17): sale of 4 dickers of hides from 40 marts; *ER* XIV.347 (comptroller, 1517–18): 8 dickers, 3 hides at 50s. dicker sold for £20 15s., and this sale is followed by an entry for the intestines of 83 marts; *ER* XV.197 (comptroller, 1524–5): 26 dickers, 6 hides at 50s. dicker sold for £66 10s.; *ER* XV.377–8 (comptroller, 1526–7): 15 dickers, 9 hides at 50s. dicker sold for £39 15s. (these were from 139/159 marts bought for the household); *ER* XVI.131 (comptroller, 1530–1): 3 dickers, 6 hides from 36 marts at 50s. dicker sold for £9. See also *ER* I.184 and 191 (clerk of liverance, 1328–9): sale of 'decem et septem coriorum et unius corii' issuing from so many marts killed at Berwick at the time of the wedding; but it is clear on p. 191 that 171 marts were killed: 'dacrarum' omitted? Also ACR XI.24–5, 33–4, 50, and 61: dicker of hides owing becomes 10 hides.

See also under last.

DUODENUM

A linear measure for canvas (i.e. a dozen ells) which could also mean a dozen generally. SSG, p. 912, states that the duodenum contained a dozen ells and this is the assumption on which we have worked.

There is also evidence of a baker's dozen for bread. E.g. SHS 3,49.64 (Aberdeen, 1399). Named bakers obliged under penalty to sell no more than 13 loaves per dozen. In fact selling 13 loaves per dozen seems on another occasion to have been an offence: see ibid., pp. 138–9.

ELL

A linear measure for cloth, found throughout the canvas series.

APS I.673 (Assisa Regis David): 'Vlna Regis Dauid debet continere in se . xxxvij . pollices mensuratas cum pollice trium hominum . scilicet ex magno .

ex medio . et paruo . Et ex medio pollice hominis debet stare . aut ex longitudine trium granorum boni ordei sine caudis . Pollex autem debet mensurari ad radicem vnguis pollicis .' The Scots version of this chapter renders the medium-sized man's thumb as that 'of a man of messurabill statur' and 'of a medilkin-man'. James I ratified David's 37 inch ell in his statute of 1426: *APS* II.12.

There does not seem to have been any particular change in the ell over time, but there is explicit reference in the records to the ell of Scottish measure. *TA* II.234 (treasurer, purchase in Flanders, 1504): 24 Flemish ells of grey damask ('gray dames') equivalent to 18 Scots ells, so the Flemish ell was only three-quarters of the size of the Scots ell in this instance.

FIRLOT

A measure of capacity for grain and other dry products.

APS II.12 (assize of James I, 1426): 'ITEM the mesoure of the ferlote is this It sal contene in breid evin ourethort' xvj Inchys vndir and abon'e within the burdis and in deipnes' vj Inche the thiknes' of bath the burdis sal contene ane Inche and a halfe the half ferlote and the peke thare eftir folowande as efferis . . . The ferlote sal contene twa galon'is ande a pynte Ande Ilk pynt sal contene be wecht of cleir wattir of tay xlj vnce that is for to say ij pundis and ix vnce troyis . . . Swa weyis the ferlote xlj pundis.'

See above, pp. 88–90, for a reconciliation of the conflicting parts of this assize in relation to the firlot.

Evidence based on explicit unit prices shows clearly there were 4 pecks to the firlot.

FOTHER (occurs as 'lie fidderis' for lead in *ER* XVI.66)

A unit of quantity.

ER VI.164 (sheriff of Stirling, 1455–6): 'j plastrato feni dicto j fudyr'; there is another similar entry.

ACR VI.316 (Aberdeen, 1474): 3 fothers lead each containing 6 score (120) stones.

GALLON (Latin lagena; occurs in one instance as dailloune – for beer)

A measure of capacity for liquids.

APS I.674 (Assisa Regis David): 'De quantitate lagene . // Item lagena debet esse sex pollicium et dimidii in profunditate . In latitudine inferiori debet esse . viij . pollicium et dimidii . cum spissitudine ligni vtriusque partis . In rotunditate superiori debet esse . xxvij . pollicium et dimidii . In rotunditate inferiori debet esse . xxiij . pollicium .' The Scots text reads: 'Of the gallon . Item the galloun suld be sax inches and ane half in deipnes and in breid of the boddom viij inches and a half with the thicknes of the trie on baith the sides and in rowndnes abone xxvij inches and a half and in rowndnes below xxiij inches . Item the gallon aw to conteyn . xij . pundis of watir that is for to say iiij pundis of salt watir of the see / iiij pundis of standande watir and iiij pundis of rynnand watir .'

APS II.12 (assize of James I, 1426): 'Ande Ilk pynt sal contene be wecht of cleir wattir of tay xlj vnce that is for to say ij pundis and ix vnce troyis Swa weyis the galone xx punde and viij vnce.' This suggests there were to be 8 pints to the gallon. The old gallon was said to have weighed 10 lb Troy and 4 oz of divers waters; 2½ gallons and a choppin of the old measure were said to be equivalent to 41 lb. See above, pp. 86–7, 90–2, 97 for a discussion of medieval Scottish legislation on the gallon.

Evidence in the form of explicit prices per pint from the Household Book of James V confirms there were 8 pints to the gallon.

On the number of choppins to the gallon: *ER* VI.501–2 (Aberdeen, 1458–9): 7 gallons, 1 quart, 1 choppin Rhenish at 8s. the gallon came to a total of 58s. 6d., suggesting there were 16 choppins to the gallon. This is the assumption on which we have worked. See also R.E. Zupko, 'The Weights and Measures of Scotland before the Union', *SHR*, 56 (1977), 127.

HOGSHEAD

A container, found for herring and wine. We are not certain of its capacity, though for England, Connor, *The Weights and Measures of England*, p. 171, suggests ¼ of a tun. See also under vas.

HUDE

A measure found occasionally at Aberdeen, for wheat (ACR VII.950); it was doubtless used for other grains too. *CDS* says this is a Dutch measure of dry capacity.

LONG AND SHORT HUNDRED

A hundred was sometimes reckoned to be six instead of five score. It is possible to tell that it is being used, from calculations based on unit prices compared with total price, or when a numerical quantity given in figures distinguishes a hundred from five score. Peter Gouldesbrough, 'The Long Hundred in the Exchequer Rolls', *SHR* 46 (1967), 79–82, postulates a general use of the long hundred in that source for non-monetary items. We have assumed a long hundred for certain commodities found in particular sources when it is clear that the long hundred was the norm for that commodity in that source.

Hanham, 'A Medieval Scots Merchant's Handbook', 116 and 117, tells us that 'woll skyns ['fells'], schorlingis [Flemish *schoorlinc*, skin from a sheep killed soon after shearing], & hogrell ['lamb-skins']' were reckoned by the short hundred, but that there were certain skins reckoned by the long hundred. This fits in with evidence from Aberdeen: ACR XVI.586–7 (Aberdeen, 1540): 210 wool and slaughter skins according to Scots reckoning said to be equivalent to 250 (2 hundred and a half hundred) by Flemish reckoning, suggesting use of the long hundred by Scots and the short by Flemings.

There is also evidence of the existence of a kind of hundredweight. ACR XIV.546 and 547 (Aberdeen, 1535): receipt acknowledged by skipper of ship of Dieppe of 2 hundred and a half hundred of salt of the measure of 'Burvage'

(? Bruges); skipper admitted loss of 4 bolls and that he had not delivered above 18 score bolls and 3 'moye' extending to 50 bolls (total delivery therefore 410 bolls). Judgement that 48.5 bolls wanting (so total consignment in bolls should have been 458.5; thus the hundred of salt of the measure of 'Burvage' was equivalent to 183.4 bolls). On same day and in connection with this case it was proven by eight men that every hundred of salt of 'Burvage' extended to 9 score and 5 bolls (185 bolls) of 'our' measure. Discrepancy between this statement and the result of calculations based on the actual consignment may be due to the 4 bolls said to have been lost. If these are added on then the discrepancy disappears.

ACR XI.270 refers to a 'hundred' of wool. See also under moye.

The Scots merchant's handbook also speaks of goods bought by the hundred: 'Here begynnys the Reknyng of it that is boght be the li. inglis and be the honder ['by the £ esterlin and by the hundred']. Thre pondis ynglis makis the li. gr. and v ^{xx} of eln ['ells'] makis the C.' (Hanham, 'A Medieval Scots Merchant's Handbook', 117–118; as explained by the editor, 110, the statement refers to the Flemish pound esterlin, not the English pound sterling). The 'C' here referred to was a hundred ells, so the commodity will have been cloth in various forms. In the same way, the 'C canues' was a short hundred of ells of canvas, and the 'C yrne' a short hundred of pounds of iron, as can be deduced from the relationship between the ell and the hundred prices given in the handbook, due allowances being made for rounding off: see also under the piece for salmon. See also Julian Goodare, 'The Long Hundred in Medieval and Early Modern Scotland', *PSAS*, 123 (1993), 395–418.

LAST

A measure of quantity, used with different meanings for ale and beer, grain, hides, and fish.

(a) For herring: *ER* I.293 (chamberlain, 1329–30): (herring) 'Et sic debet dimidiam lastam et v^{m}, que sunt j lasta.' This suggests that the last was equivalent to 10,000 herring, or 12,000 if the 'v^{m}' was made up of long hundreds. Another pointer is a comparison of the unit prices for herring (*ER* I.494), which come from the account of the provost of Crail, 1341–2. A last of herring cost 20s. 10d.; and 4,000/4,800 cost 8s. 4d. which would produce the same last price if there were 10,000/12,000 herring to the last. This evidence strengthens the rather equivocal results based on calculations from breakdowns of charge and discharge in *Exchequer Rolls* accounts, which are difficult to make because we do not always know when the long hundred was being used. We have assumed there were 10,000/12,000 herring to the last.

As will be seen in the herring series, accountants did not always convert numerical quantities into numbers of lasts. This may have been because fish measured by the last had undergone a stage of processing which the fish measured numerically had not.

Rogers, *A History of Agriculture and Prices in England*, I, pp. 608–9, says the last was equivalent to 12,000 herring. Rogers assumes a constant use of the long hundred and we have done the same when comparing our series with his.

There were 12 barrels to the last of herring, as is clear from explicit unit prices: *ER* XIV.370, XV.57, 59–60, 178, 294, 467, 552, XVI.62, 140.

(b) For salmon: there is clear evidence that there were 12 barrels of salmon to the last, from calculations based on explicit unit prices (e.g. *ER* IV.443–4, XIV.455–6, and *TA* IV.492), and on charge and discharge of salmon quantities (e.g. *ER* VI.531, VII.135, VIII.86–7, 149, 411, 580–1). See also ACR VI.717 (Aberdeen, 1482) and *ER* VI.317: freight of 1 last and 7 Hamburg barrels salted salmon, at 2s. barrel, cost 38s.; ACR XI.621 (Aberdeen, 1525): 6 barrels of salmon clearly synonymous with half a last; ACR XII ii.724 (Aberdeen, 1529): new salmon barrels at 2s. each came to total cost of £3 12s. for three lasts; ACR XVI.245 (Aberdeen, 1539): obligation by three men to pay 2 lasts salmon between them; each is to pay 8 barrels.

(c) For hides: *ER* I.201 (clerk of kitchen, 1328–9): 'Et de iiij lastis, iij dacris et ij coriorum, prouenientium de sexcentis quinquies viginti et duodecim martis.' If the dicker contained 10 hides (see above) then 800 hides were here equivalent to 4 lasts so the last contained 200 hides.

The rate at which customs were levied sometimes shows there were 20 dickers to the last and also 10 hides to the dicker, although calculations rarely yield precise results; see esp. *ER* II.8–9, 21, 89, 202, 232, 233–4, 275, 276. Cf. *ER* I.xcviii and note, where it is stated that at the time of Assisa de Tolloneis (which is of uncertain date) there were only 8 dickers to the last. This seems to be based on the fact that custom on hides was set in that document at 8d. per last and at 1d. per dicker (Assisa de Tolloneis, *APS*, p. 668). However, it is clear from the assize of tolls that custom was often levied at a relatively higher rate on smaller quantities of goods; the relation between the rates of custom to be charged on different quantities does not therefore reflect the relation between the quantities themselves.

Hanham, 'A Medieval Scots Merchant's Handbook', 117, says there were 20 dickers or 200 hides to the last (the text is quoted above, under dicker).

(d) For wool: Assisa de Tolloneis, *APS*, p. 668: 'De vna lasta lane videlicet de . x . saccis qui simul habuerit . viij . d'.' (Scots text: 'of a last of wol that is to say for ten sekkys gaddryt togyddyr aucht peniis .'). Calculations based on customs levied on wool confirm there were 10 sacks to the last and, though not always precisely, 24 stones to the sack: see esp. *ER* I.529, II.8, 11, 13, 15–16, 17, 18, 20, 21, 22, 89, 91, 93, 94, 95, 119, 127, 186, 187, 193, 194, 199–200, 202, 231–2, 233, 236, 237, 239, 267, 274, 275–6.

See further under sack.

(e) For grain: ACR VII.135 (Aberdeen, 1489): master of Stralsund ship and certain merchants of Haddington and Leith declared publicly on 26 August that the Stralsund last of rye extended to 28 bolls of Scots water mett; the entry is marginated as being a statute concerning the Stralsund last.

ACR V i.435 (Aberdeen, 1461): 2 lasts of barrels of oatmeal equivalent to 24 barrels; ACR V i.512 (Aberdeen, 1464): claim for 6d. per barrel amounts to 30s. for 5 lasts of 'beir'; cf. ACR V ii.700 (Aberdeen, 1445): cargo of ship whose master was from Danzig included 10½ lasts of barrels of meal, 16 barrels for the last. ACR IV.498 (Aberdeen, 1447) refers to a Prussian last of wheat which was to be delivered by Scots measure.

(f) For ale: there is evidence in the *Treasurer's Accounts* that the last of ale contained 12 barrels, each barrel containing 12 gallons: *TA* IV.485, 500, and 501. The last would therefore have contained 144 gallons. There is, however, also evidence that the last of ale contained 120 gallons (*TA* IV.484 and 485); this was doubtless because the ale was stored in 10 gallon barrels which are also met in the *Treasurer's Accounts* (see above, under barrel); the fact that the last of ale was a fixed number of barrels rather than a fixed number of gallons is also clear from HBJV, p. 151, which shows (though the gallon total is slightly inaccurate) that there were 12 barrels of 9½ gallons to the last.

In general, the last was a fixed multiple of smaller units, regardless of the capacity of those smaller units.

LOAD (other forms laid, leyd; Latin onus, sarcina)

A unit found in the coal series. Coal prices by the load are found regularly from the end of the fifteenth century, in the *Treasurer's Accounts* and the Dunkeld accounts; the load is also found in fifteenth-century *Exchequer Roll* material, although *Exchequer Roll* coal prices are more often expressed in chaldrons and bolls. The frequency of the use of the load by the sixteenth century would suggest that it may have been a known quantity, although its actual size is not clear to us.

The load is also found for salt (*ALC* I.*90) and for malt (*ALCPA*, pp. 184 and 366–7: in the latter it is clear that the size should in principle vary according to the price of bere).

LUMP

A quantity or a weight of iron, found occasionally in the Dunkeld accounts: SHS 2,10.93, 110. See also Rogers, *A History of Agriculture and Prices in England*, I, p. 472.

MEASE

A measure of herrings.

ER I.162 (Ayr, 1328–9): 14,960/17,940 herring at 4s. per mease came to a total of 119s. 7d., suggesting that the mease was equivalent to approximately 500 fish, or 600 by the long hundred. See also SSG, p. 935, s.v. Mayse. We have assumed there were 500/600 herring to the mease.

MEIL

A measure found at Aberdeen, for malt, in 1486 (ACR VI.239).

MOYE (Latin modius)

A measure found for salt and for grain. See *MLWL*, s.v. modius. *APS* I.324 (Assise Regis David, cap. xxxi): Latin modius is rendered as boll in the Scots text.

(a) For salt: ACR XIV.546 (Aberdeen, 1535): 3 moye of salt said to extend to 50 bolls (see under hundred for more details about this case), so 1 moye would have been equivalent to 16.67 bolls; ACR XVI. 855 (Aberdeen, 1541): 5 August: complaint by merchants against French skipper, who received 12 moye of their salt which he was to have transported from Dieppe to Aberdeen. Merchants claimed loss of 8 'mett' ' salt of each moye through leakage: he received 48 'mett' ' for each moye and delivered only 36 'mett' ' for each moye in Aberdeen.

The 'moury', a French measure found for salt at Aberdeen in 1505 (ACR VIII.495), may have been a variant form of 'moye'.

(b) For grain: the modius, found as a grain measure in the Dunkeld accounts, was a local equivalent of the firlot, in that explicit unit prices consistently show there were 4 modia to the boll: SHS 2,10.109, 121, 225, 231, 240. It was also used on one occasion in these accounts for coal (SHS 2,10.283).

MUTCHKIN

A measure of capacity for liquids. It occurs only once in our series (SHS 2,10.233), although it is mentioned in the 1426 legislation dealing with the gallon.

NAIL

A weight of wool, apparently containing 6 pounds Bruges weight: see under sack and also under clove.

OUNCE

A unit of weight. The assize of bread was expressed in terms of the number of ounces to be contained in the half penny, penny, and two penny loaf.

APS I.673 (assize of King David): 'De pondere uncie . //Item vncea continebat in se tempore Regis Dauid . xx . d' . sterlingorum . Nunc autem vncea debet continere in se . xxj . d' . sterlingorum . quia noua moneta nunc in tantum minuitur .' The Scots text reads: 'Of the wecht of the unce . The unce contenit in King Dauidis time xx gude and sufficient sterling penijs and now it sall wey . xxi . penijs for the demynicioune of the mone .' See above, p. 114 for the dating of these statements and their implications for the coinage.

PECK

A measure of capacity for grains and dry products. See further under firlot. We have assumed there were 4 pecks to the firlot, as is shown consistently in evidence from explicit unit prices.

PIECE (Latin pecia)

A measure of quantity, bearing relation to weight; sometimes used to mean the individual item or piece; see *MLWL*, s.v. pecia.

(a) For wax: *ER* I.119 (chamberlain, 1328): 'xiij peciis cere, continentibus ducentas petras . . . '; so 1 piece would contain 15.39 or 18.46 stones; ACR X.279 (Aberdeen, 1521): 'pece' of wax containing 2 'leis' ' pounds. The evidence is too scant to make any assumptions about the relationship between the piece and the stone or the pound; in any case the piece does not seem to have been a weight. See also under stone, for wax.

(b) For iron: the piece implied iron in its partially wrought state. An example of the confusion which can be caused by this is in *ER* VI.308 (king's burgh loans, 1457): 8,000/9,600 pounds iron 'precium centinarii quadraginta unus grossi, continentibus ducentas et decem et octo pecias ferri vangarum grecilium et decem et octo pecias ferri vangarum latarum ferri'. Vanga = spade, shovel.

Rogers says there were 25 pieces of iron to the hundred of 108 pounds, so the piece would have weighed 4.32 pounds: Rogers, *A History of Agriculture and Prices in England*, I, pp. 170 and 471–2.

(c) For steel: *DHS* II.321 (Berwick, 1298): 120 pieces containing 4 shaves.

(d) For cloth: the evidence suggests the piece of cloth often contained between 22 and about 27 ells: *ER* II.439–40 (clerk of the wardrobe, 1373–4): 16 pieces wide coloured Ypres cloth, containing 357¾ or 417¾ ells (suggesting 22.36 or 26.11 ells per piece); 2 pieces narrow coloured Ypres cloth, each piece containing 26 ells; 6 pieces containing 27 ells of silk cloth; 1 piece taffeta containing 95 ells; *ER* II.465–6 (clerk of the wardrobe, 1374–5): 12 pieces, 4¾ ells wide Ypres cloth, containing 276¾ or 316¾ ells (suggesting 22.67 or 26 ells per piece); 1 piece, 8¼ ells 'Arcte' Ypres cloth, containing 32¼ ells (suggesting 24 ells to the piece); 5½ pieces, 1½ ells 'cortrikys et communis' containing 124½ or 144½ ells (suggesting 22.36 or 26 ells per piece); *ER* II.546–7 (clerk of the wardrobe, 1377–8): 7½ pieces containing 184¾ or 204¾ ells wide Ypres cloth (suggesting 24.63 or 27.3 ells per piece); 2½ pieces containing 68 ells 'cortrikis' (suggesting 27.2 ells per piece). Calculations based on charge and discharge of various kinds of cloth in the accounts suggest 12, 16, 23½, 24, and 25 ells to the piece: *ER* I.142, 229, 242, 294–5, 383. Cf. ACR IV.287 (Aberdeen, 1442): 'quedam pecia quinque ulnarum panni viridi'.

(d) For salmon: *ER* I.66 (Perth, 1327–8): 364 salmon making 430 pecie.

PINT

APS II.12 (assize of James I, 1426): 'Ande Ilk pynt sal contene be wecht of cleir watter of tay xlj vnce that is for to say ij pundis and ix vnce troyis.' See above, pp. 90, and 93–6, for a discussion of the size of the pint.

PIPE

A measure of capacity, or a container, for liquids, used especially for wine. Coal, honey, salmon (see *ER* VI.504), and wheatmeal could also be contained in pipes.

(a) For wine: Rogers says there were 126 gallons to the pipe (*A History of Agriculture and Prices in England*, I, p. 619). *ER* VI.308 (king's burgh loans, 1457): 1 pipe Rhenish wine containing 9 sesters and 12 quarters, suggesting a pipe of 111 gallons (see under boll); the entry is given in Flemish money.

(b) For ale: *TA* IV.459, 462, 470 (1512, 1513): pipes containing 36 gallons; *TA* IV.467 (1513): pipes of 38 gallons.

We have not made any assumptions about the actual size of the pipe as the evidence is too scant. See also under tun.

PISA, PEISE

A measure of weight.

See *MLWL*, s.v. pensa, which, in its various forms, is translated as 'wey'. Rogers, *A History of Agriculture and Prices in England*, I, p. 404, suggests the pisa and the wey were synonymous when used for cheese. We have not, however, made any assumptions about the pisa.

The peise, paise, pace, etc., was the standard weight on which the assize of bread was based; those who failed to bake bread of the required weight were said to have broken the 'peise'.

POKE (Latin poca)

A container, found especially for wool, skins, and woad (see 'Appendix of documents', no. III).

(a) For wool: *ER* IV.276 (Edinburgh, 1416–17): 'poca' of unweighed wool estimated at 8 stones; ACR VII.520 (Veere, 1492): poke of wool said to weigh 4 weys, 4 nails; ACR XI.145 and 164 (Aberdeen, 1522): claim made 28 July for 65 francs for 60 stones wool; claim (which perhaps refers to same goods) made ?9 September for 65 francs, 6s. 4d. for a poke of wool, suggesting if so that the poke was equivalent to 60 stones; ACR IX.40 (Aberdeen, 1511): poke containing 55 stones; ACR X.24 (Aberdeen, 1518): poke of 'foull' wool containing 1,022/1,222 pounds; if there were 16 pounds to the stone (see below under stone) the poke would have contained 63.88/76.38 stones; ACR XI.634 (Aberdeen, 1525): poke containing 'ix ᶜ xxiiij ij' pounds; if this implies about 926/1,106 pounds and there were 16 such pounds to the stone there would have been 57.88/69.13 stones to the poke; ACR XIV.587 (Aberdeen, 1535): poke of lambswool containing 55 Scots stones. There is therefore some consistency in the evidence to suggest a poke commonly contained between 55 and 77 stones of wool. But it is more likely that a poke was simply not an established or standard unit of weight, but rather a mode of carrying wool.

(b) For skins: ACR VIII.1072 (Aberdeen, 1510): poke of skins containing 20 score (400).

PONDUS

A unit of weight. It is found in the fourteenth-century accounts from Tarbert as a weight of cheese and meal.

MLWL finds pondus used in the thirteenth and fourteenth centuries to denote a wey; Rogers, *A History of Agriculture and Prices in England*, I, p. 404, finds the word occasionally used as a synonym for pisa, with cheese. It also seems to have been used generally to denote 'weight'.

ER I.53 (Tarbert, 1325–6): 'Et de iiij li. xvjs., per nonaginta sex pondera casei, recepta de balliuis de Kentire, de pondere eiusdem loci, computando pro quolibet pondere duodecim denarios.'

ER VII.152 (Haddington, 1461–2): 'pro novem ponderibus salis continentibus unam celdram undecim bollas'; in this instance the pondus would have contained 3 bolls.

POUND (Latin libra)

A unit of weight for iron, cheese, candle, tallow, coal, wool, wax, and butter.

APS I.673 (Assisa Regis David): 'De pondere libre . //Item libra debet ponderare . xxv . s'. hoc erat in illo tempore assise pretacte . [Nunc autem libra ponderabit] . xxvj . s' . et . iij . d' . quoniam in tantum nunc minuitur noua moneta ab antiqua tunc vsitata . Item libra debet ponderare . xv . vncias .' The Scots text reads: 'Of the wecht of the pund . Item the pund in King Dauidis dayis weyit xxv . schillingis . Now the pund aw to wey in siluer xxvi schillingis and iij sterling penijs and that for the mynoratioun of the peny that is in the tym now . Item the pund sould wey . xv . vncis .' See above, p. 114, for a discussion of dating of this and its implications for coinage.

APS II.12 (assize of James I, 1426): 'Ilk troyis punde to conten' xvj vnce.' See further under stone and above, p. 88.

APS II.226 (parliament of James IV, 1491): statute and ordinance that old statutes and ordinances concerning 'mett' ', and measures, customs, and other matters be kept 'and specialy of wechtis als' wele of wax as spice and xvj vnce In the pund'.'

PUNCHEON

A measure for liquids and also flour.

(a) The puncheon is met frequently as a container for wine in the sixteenth century. See further under tun.

(b) For ale: *TA* IV.470 and 474 (treasurer, 1513): 'puncions' of ale containing 18 gallons (there is also an ambiguous entry on p. 470, for 2 puncheons of ale containing 36 gallons; it is not clear whether each of them contained 36 or whether the total of the two was 36); *TA* VI.164 (Glasgow, 1533): ale purchased to fill 18 puncheons, each puncheon containing 16 gallons; explicit unit price 12d. per gallon, total cost £14 8s.

(c) For flour: ACR VII.1030 (Aberdeen, 1500): deposition by two witnesses that buyer had 3 'puntionis terceanse[?]' flour measured, sold to him by townsman of Dieppe, which contained 7 bolls, 1 peck flour of measure of said burgh.

QUARTER

(a) A measure of capacity for grain and dry products, and found as such in the English rather than the Scottish records. There were 32 pecks or 8 bushels to the quarter. We have converted our prices given in chaldrons and bolls into quarter prices in our comparative tables on the basis that there were 4 quarters to the chaldron. Evidence from Berwick in 1340 may suggest the existence of a Scots quarter: see *CDS* III.245, no. 1338: claim that merchants supplying the king sell at so much per quarter by English measure while merchants around sell at a different price per quarter by Scots measure. The Scots quarter prices are lower than the English; but the writer may have converted the unit used into a quarter in order to draw attention to the dearness of grain being bought for the king.

See further under chaldron.

(b) We also meet the term 'petty quarter' in the Aberdeen records, for salt (see ACR IV.170, VIII.119, IX.224–5, XII i.27); also ACR IV.413 (Aberdeen, 1445): case between shipmaster of Sluys and his steersman over 'twa petty quarterez and sex meet' ' of salt claimed by steersman for his 'furyng'; and for wheat: e.g. ACR V i.592 and 626 (Aberdeen, 1467 and 1468).

(c) Quarter in the sense of a fourth part of another unit is also met; where it is clear from the context what that other unit was, we have calculated our unit prices on this basis. We also find the quarter used as a measure in its own right, particularly in the sense of a quart, for liquids: e.g. ACR VII.723 (Aberdeen, 1496): 29 quarters 'maluasie' at 14d. per pint came to a total of £3 7s. 8d., so there were 2 pints to the quarter. We also meet 'quarters' of canvas, iron, wool, and bitumen.

'QW'

Possibly a container for wine; it occurs only once in the series: see *ALC* I.97.

RODA

A measure of capacity for wine. *MLWL* says the 'rood' was a measure of (Rhenish) wine; Dutch *roede*. The rood was also a measure of land.

'RODD' '

A quantity of iron. It seems to have been a large one, because at Aberdeen in 1401 sales of iron by 'whole rods' seem to have been regarded as bulk sales, and were in consequence to be made cheaply: see ACR I.197, and above, p. 69.

RUBBOUR

A container for ale and for wine, especially the choicer sorts.

(a) For ale: SHS 2, 10.205 (Perth, 1506–7): 8 'rubbouris', 34 gallons ale at 12d. the gallon bought for 47s. 4d. If the 'rubbouris' were priced in proportion to the gallons this suggests there were 1.67 gallons in each.

(b) For wine: *TA* IV.474 (Forth, 1513): 1 'rowbour' each of Malvesy and Muscaldy, each containing 5 gallons; HBJV, p. 87 (household, 1525): 2 'lez Roubbouris' claret containing 7 gallons, 1 quart, at 12d. per pint came to total of 58s. suggesting that each contained 29 pints.

In general the 'rubbour' seems to have varied in size; and that it was a general term meaning a vessel is also suggested in *ER* VI. 501–2, where there is a purchase of 7 gallons, 1 quart, and 1 choppin of Rhenish, while the cost of its carriage and mending of 'lez rubbouris' is recorded as 12s. 6d.

SACK

A measure of quantity for wool.

Calculations based on customs levies confirm albeit approximately that there were 24 stones of wool to the sack: see esp. *ER* II.11, 88, 89, 119–20, 236, and 274–5, and the references cited above, under last. Royal customs seem often to have been charged at a slightly higher rate on the odd stones, which explains the entries suggesting a smaller number of stones to the sack.

Calculations based on wool sales at Coldingham Priory, however, suggest a larger number of stones to the sack. This will most probably have been because the accounts were rendered at Durham Cathedral Priory which operated on the English system (see below). CS 1344–5ii (Coldingham, 1344–5): 3 sacks less 1½ stones wool at 73s. 4d. per sack sold for £10 15s. 4d., suggesting 25 stones to the sack; SS 12.1 (Coldingham, 1365–6): 3 sacks, 11 stones wool at 63s. 4d. per sack, with 100/120 lambs at 5½d. each, priced at £13 10s. 8d. (if long hundred for lambs, this suggests 27.14 stones per sack; if short hundred, 20 stones per sack); SS 12.lii (Coldingham, 1366–7): 3 sacks, 3 stones wool at 72s. per sack, with 105/125 lambs at 6d. each, priced at £14 6s. 6½d. (if long hundred for lambs, this suggests 26.88 stones per sack; if short hundred, 11.97 stones per sack); SS 12.lvii (Coldingham, 1367–8): 3 sacks, 6 stones wool at £4 4s. per sack and 69 lambs at 6d. each priced at £15 7s. 6d. (this suggests 24 stones to the sack). The inexactitudes of this evidence are probably due to rounding off.

Evidence from the later fifteenth century confirms there were supposed to be 24 stones to the Scottish sack of wool: *ALA* I.131 (?Kirkpatrick, Dumfriesshire, 1489): 1 sack teind wool extending to 24 stone; *ALA* I.137 (1490): payment ordered of sack of wool of 24 stones weight, sufficient merchant ware; *ALC* I.175 (1491): payment ordered of 2 sacks wool 'forest fyne gude merchand gude without cot and ter' Ilke sek contenand xxiiij stane'. Further, ACR IV.127 (Aberdeen, 1438): 'sacculus' (small sack) of wool said to weigh 2 weys Flemish weight. If the wey was 12 stones (see below) this again suggests a sack of 24 stones, though it was a small sack and there is the added complication of the Flemish weys.

See also *ER* IV.78 (Edinburgh, 1408–9) where the breakdown into stones and sacks of 23 sacks with which the accountants did not charge themselves produces a clear 24 stone sack. Simpson, 'Scots "Trone" Weight', points out that the David assize set the wool sack at 360 pounds. Grant, *Independence and Nationhood*, p. 70, bases his calculations of Scotland's wool exports on a 360 pound sack (equivalent to 24 stones of 15 pounds each). Hanham, 'A Medieval Scots Merchant's Handbook', 115, confirms a 360 pound sack and it is encouraging that this is based on units other than the stone: 'This is the Reknyng of the Scotis woll . . . Item vj lib. of woll mak the nayle and xxx nayle makis the walle & ij walle makis the sec.' The editor states, p. 110, that this was the Bruges (or Middelburgh) wool sack and that the pounds were Bruges weight.

While it seems clear that the standard wool sack which merchants were accustomed to contained 24 stones, there is evidence from sixteenth-century Aberdeen of a much larger sack: ACR XII i.72 (Aberdeen, 1526): acknowledgement of sale of 2 sacks wool containing or which should have contained 142/162 stones, with obligation to pay to purchaser any shortfall on production of weigh masters' certification as to amount of shortfall (suggests 71 or 81 stones per sack); ACR XII i.76 (Aberdeen, 1526): acquittance of vendor of sack of wool sold containing 88 stones, and of any shortfall of said 88 stones.

The English wool sack appears to have contained 26 stones, and each stone probably 14 pounds. Thus, although the Scots sack contained only 24 stones, it was almost exactly the same weight as the English sack, if the Scots stone for wool contained 15 rather than 14 pounds (see under stone). See esp. T.H. Lloyd, *The English Wool Trade in the Middle Ages* (Cambridge, 1977), pp. 1–3; Rogers, *A History of Agriculture and Prices in England*, I, pp. 367–8; and E. Power, *The Wool Trade in English Medieval History*, Ford Lectures (Oxford, 1941), p. 23. Cf. *CDS* III. 277, no. 1518 note, where it is said the Berwick weight of wool exceeded the English by 20 pounds per sack.

If the English sack weighed 364 pounds and the Scots 360 the difference between them was negligible and we have not converted our figures to take account of it. If there was variation in weight in English wool sacks, the same was doubtless true in Scotland. In comparing our Scots wool prices with our English ones, we have taken the figures from Rogers and Lloyd and have converted them on the basis of a 26 stone sack.

SARPLIER

A quantity of wool.

MLWL, s.v. sarpellarium, says the sarplier was a wrapper for wool or a bale; SSG, that sarpelers, etc., were sacks made of coarse canvas or woolsacks. It seems that while sarpliers began, like sacks, as a convenient way of packing wool the sarplier did not become a standard weight as the sack did. In general the sarplier seems to have weighed more than the sack.

ER IV.248 (Aberdeen, 1415–16): 8 sarpliers wool, of which two said to weigh 2 sacks and 15 stone, suggesting one would have weighed 1 sack and 7½ stone; *ER* IV.321 (Edinburgh, 1418–20): in an interrogation by auditors into a quantity of wool, fells, and hides, 24 lasts of sarpliers were estimated by auditors at 30 lasts of sacks.

The Aberdeen evidence suggests considerable variety in the size of the sarplier: ACR IV.418 (Aberdeen, 1445): sarplier of wool containing 50 stones; ACR VII.165–6 (Aberdeen, 1490): sarplier of wool containing 6 weys 'with the mair' (and more): three entries; see also pp. 173–4; ACR VIII.812 (Aberdeen, 1508): allegation that sarplier of wool contained 88 stones.

Nicholson, *Scotland: The Later Middle Ages*, p. 433, says the sarplier was equivalent to half a sack for staple wares.

The sarplier was also used for wool fells: e.g. ACR IV.174 (Aberdeen, 1439): claim concerning a sarplier of fells 'ad summam quadringentarum pellium et ultra'.

SEAM

A quantity, found in the coal series.

MLWL, s.v. sagma, finds sagma and summa and variants used to mean 'seam' or horse-load; see also SSG, s.v. seme, seym, and summa.

SESTER

APS I.674 (assize of King David): '//Item bolla debet continere in se sextarium vi[delicet] . xij . lagenas seruicie .' See above, p. 86, for the dimensions of the boll as given in David's assize.

APS I.676 (assize of wine according to David I): 'Item sextarium debet continere tres lagenas .'

APS II.12 (assize of James I, 1426): 'The ald boll first maid be king Dauid contenit a sextern' the sextern' contenit xij galon'is of the ald met.'

STERLING

The name given to the English currency which then consisted exclusively of sterling pennies. Grierson dates the earliest use of the term *c.* 1080 (P. Grierson, 'Sterling', in R.M.H. Dolley (ed.), *Anglo-Saxon Coins: Studies Presented to F.M. Stenton on the Occasion of his Seventieth Birthday* (London, 1961), pp. 267–8). The system of weights was also based on the sterling penny, at least in 'King David's' day.

APS I.674 (assize of King David): 'De pondere sterlingi . //Item sterlingus debet ponderare . xxxij . grana boni et rotundi frumenti .' The Scots text reads: 'Of the wecht of the sterling . King David ordanyt at the sterlyng suld wey xxxij cornys of gude and round quhete.'

STIC

(a) Another way of saying the piece, i.e. the individual item. See, for examples, Hanham, 'A Medieval Scots Merchant's Handbook', 116 and 117.

(b) A container or cask for wine.

STONE (Latin petra and also (far more rarely) lapis)

A unit of weight, found for a wide range of commodities.

Rogers says ruefully: 'Of all ancient weights the most ambiguous and puzzling is the petra' (Rogers, *A History of Agriculture and Prices in England*, I, p. 169). Although the weight of the petra varied, from commodity to commodity and also over time, it is clear it was intended as a fixed unit, which is not true of all the weights and measures we are here attempting to quantify.

APS I.673 (Assisa Regis David): 'De pondere petre . //Item lapis ad lanam et ad alias res ponderandas debet ponderare . xv . libras . Item vaga debet continere . xij . petras cuius pondus continet . viij libras.' The Scots text reads: 'Of the wecht of the stane . Item the stane for weying of woll and uther geir aw to wey . xv . pund . Item the stane of wax aw to conteyne . viij . pund . Item the vaw aw to conteyn . xij . stan .' Only the Latin text explicitly associates the wey with an 8 pound stone, and only the Scots associates the 8 pound stone with wax.

APS II.10 (parliament of James I, 1426): 'ITEM the king and the parliament has ordanit that thare be maid a stane for gudis saulde and bocht be wecht the quhilk sall wey xv lele troyis pundis Ande at the stane be diuidyt in xvj lele scottis pundis'; *APS* II.12 (assize of James I, 1426): 'ITEM thai ordanit ande statute the stane to wey Irne woll ande vthir merchandice to conten' xvj pundis troyis Ilk troyis punde to conten' xvj vnce Ande that stane to be devidit in half stane quarter half quarter punde half punde and all vthir smallar wechtys.' See above, pp. 88, and 92–5 for a discussion of the new system of weights introduced in 1426.

It seems that the number of pounds to the stone varied from commodity to commodity and from place to place, and that there were, as is clear from the assize of David I, two distinctly different stones. James V may have been trying to establish a single stone in his statute of 1541 (*APS* II.376), in which he forbade any burgh to have one weight to buy with and a different one to sell with, stipulating that all burghs should have 'ane vniuersale wecht of the stane' for buying and selling everything in future.

a) For wax: wax was weighed by the stone of 8 pounds, as is evidenced by calculations based on accountants' breakdowns in their charge and discharges in *ER* I.232, 243–4, and 256 (see also *ER* I.220, 290 where calculations based on explicit unit prices suggest a stone of 8.29 pounds and 8.31 pounds). An 8 pound stone is confirmed by ACR VII.22–3 (Aberdeen, 1487): deposition that defendant should pay plaintiff 13s. 4d. for each stone of wax proved by plaintiff to have been received by defendant; judgement that plaintiff should prove how many pounds the 'pece' of wax delivered to defendant contained; thereafter defendant to pay plaintiff 20d. for each pound received. If as seems highly probable the judgement was made in accordance with the deposition then there were 8 pounds to the stone of wax in this instance, although a complicating factor here is that the claim seems to have been for Flemish pounds: see ACR VII.21.

Use of a Prussian stone for wax at Aberdeen: ACR VI.585–6, 595.

The existence in Scotland of a stone specifically for wax is further suggested in ACR X.339 (Aberdeen, 1521): 2 'leis' ' pounds of wax which extended to 4 stones Scots weight of the wax stones of the said 'rovme' (realm).

We have assumed there were 8 pounds to the stone when calculating unit prices for wax and in the comparative tables.

(b) For iron: *CDS* II.389, no. 1500 (Berwick, 1304): 124/144 stones weighing 15 pounds; SS 12.xlviii (Coldingham, 1364–5): 18 stones, 19 pounds at 15½d. per stone came to total price of 24s. 10d. Implies stone of 15½ pounds despite the fact that 19 pounds is given as a fraction of the stone in the entry itself.

Note: both entries predate the 1426 legislation for a 16 pound stone. Moreover, conversion may have been made into English measures for accounting purposes. We have not made conversions from a larger Scots stone to a smaller one for cheese or for iron, because the difference between them for these commodities is difficult to quantify. Much would depend on the weight of the pounds which made up the stone and this again cannot be quantified for different commodities.

The evidence of explicit unit prices for iron in the *Treasurer's Accounts* in the sixteenth century in many cases produces a clear 16 pound stone (*TA* V.327, VI.303, 349, VII.491, 496, 502, VIII.128) but sometimes gives a 15 pound stone (*TA* V.222, VII.496), and stones varying between about 15¼ pounds and about 17½ pounds (*TA* V.267, 322, VI.349, VII.212, 351, 360, VIII.120, 128).

(c) For lead: *CDS* III.261, no. 1434 (Berwick, 1344): 720 stones lead at 16 pounds per stone, Scots weight. See note above for iron. For early seventeenth-century evidence of a 20 pound stone for lead, see Simpson, 'Scots "Trone" Weight'.

(d) For metal utensils: *ER* VII.149 (Edinburgh, 1461–2): 'Et pro duabus parvis duodenis perapsidum et totidem discorum et quatuor chargeouris, ponderantibus sex petras septem libras cum dimedia ponderis de troye, precium libre sexdecim denarii.' Total price £6 16s. 9d., so this would suggest there were 15.84 pounds to the stone.

(e) For wool: the English stone for wool varied, but generally weighed 14 pounds of 15 ounces each: Rogers, *A History of Agriculture and Prices in England*, I, pp. 367–8, and Lloyd, *The English Wool Trade*, pp. 1–3. See further under sack for the comparability of English and Scottish wool measures.

(f) For grain: it is interesting to see that valuations of meal were given in stones in royal assessments on the inner Hebrides in 1541: *ER* XVII.529, 625.

(g) For butter: calculations based on the breakdowns of charge and discharge in the Household Book of James V suggest the stone of butter contained 16 pounds: HBJV, pp. 13 and 154.

(h) For candle: *TA* IV.509, where calculations suggest a 16 pound stone.

TERSAN (other forms 'teirsan', 'tersing')

This term occurs as a measure for wine, ale, and flour, or at least as a container, in the sixteenth century. See C. Du F. Du Cange, *Glossarium mediae et infirmae Latinitatis*, ed. G.A.L. Henschel (Paris, 7 vols., 1840–50), s.v. tercellum, terceneria, and tertia, 6; *MLWL*, s.v. tertia. Its name implies it may have meant a third part of another measure (?possibly the tun).

TA IV.469 and 470 (treasurer, 1513): 'tersan', 'teirsanis' of ale containing 24 gallons; that it was indeed some sort of container for ale is clear at p. 470, where the cost of empty 'teirsans' was 2s. apiece.

See also under puncheon.

THOUSAND

Apart from its use as a numerical quantity, found especially for herring, the thousand was a weight used for iron.

ACR VII.1011 (Aberdeen, 1500): payment to be made of 5 'stiks' of iron, corresponding to the weight of the thousand; *TA* IV.481 (treasurer, 1513): 8 thousands of iron, each extending to 6½ weys.

TRONE WEIGHT (other form 'tron')

A system of weight larger than ordinary commercial or merchant weight, it is first defined in the seventeenth century, but seems to have been customarily employed for some commodities earlier than that (Simpson, 'Scots "Trone" Weight').

TUN (other form 'twn'; Latin doleum)

A measure of capacity for liquids (especially wine) and other products, e.g. grain.

(a) For wine: *ER* II.C: states that there were two pipes to the tun; Rogers, *A History of Agriculture and Prices in England,* I, p. 619, says the tun contained 252 gallons and the pipe 126. There is some evidence in our records to suggest there were 2 pipes to the tun, as implied by Rogers, though it is by no means as conclusive as we should like. See *ER* I.224 (chamberlain, 1328–9): breakdown of charge and discharge suggests, though not unequivocally, that 1 pipe was equivalent to half a tun; *TA* I.391 (treasurer, 1498): 1 tun, 2 pipes wine at £12 per tun purchased for £24, suggesting 2 pipes were equivalent to 1 tun. It should be stressed that each measure seems to have existed independently of the other as a vessel for carrying wine and that conversions between them were rarely made; another of the rare examples of conversions between the two is at *ER* II.454 (queen's clerk of liverance, 1374–5): purchase of 4 tuns, 1 pipe, 92¼ gallons wine, whereof 2 pipes were Rhenish; wine bought by the gallon was 'venalis'. We have assumed 2 pipes equal 1 tun.

On the relationship between the tun and the puncheon: SHS 2,10.7 (Dunkeld, 1509): purchase of 1 tun of wine, that is, 1 pipe, 1 puncheon claret, 1 puncheon Gascon wine; *ER* XIV.200 (Edinburgh, 1516): 13½ tuns, 1 puncheon claret and Beaune at £20 the tun bought for £277 10s. If the puncheon was priced proportionately this suggests there were 2.67 puncheons to the tun; HBJV, p. 85 (?Edinburgh, 1525): 2 tuns, 4 puncheons of claret at £6 15s. the puncheon bought for £74 5s., suggesting 3½ puncheons to the tun; HBJV, p. 88 (?Edinburgh, 1526): 3 tuns, 2 puncheons of claret and white at £21 the tun bought for £78 10s., suggesting if the puncheons were priced proportionately 2.71 puncheons to the tun; HBJV, p. 88 (?Edinburgh, 1526): 2 tuns, 3 puncheons claret and white at £4 5s. the puncheon bought for £46 15s., suggesting if the tuns were priced proportionately to the puncheons 4 puncheons to the tun; *TA* VII.40 (treasurer, Rouen, 1536–8): purchase of 2 tuns white wine, containing 8 puncheons; and of 8 tuns claret, containing 24 puncheons, suggesting there were respectively 4 puncheons or 3 to the tun. The tun could therefore contain anything from 2⅔ to 4 puncheons. It seems clear that the tun, the pipe, and the puncheon were all containers for wine, with only an incidental relationship to one another.

We have not converted prices per gallon into prices per tun, pipe, or puncheon, since wine bought by the gallon was usually being retailed, whereas wine bought by the tun, pipe, or puncheon was being bought in bulk.

Hanham, 'A Medieval Scots Merchant's Handbook', 119: 'Here begynnys the Reknyng of the wyne. It is till ['to'] vndyrstand that xvj stope ['stoop'] makis a cester [Flemish *sester*], and xxij cester makis a ton of wyne.' The writer goes on to give per pint prices when the tun is at a given amount, and although he does not explicitly state the number of pints to the tun it can be inferred it contained 704 pints. These were, however, doubtless quite different from Scottish pints of which (after 1426) 8 made a Scots gallon.

(b) For ale: *TA* IV.495, 497, 498, 499 (treasurer, 1513): tuns of ale containing 72 gallons.

(c) For other goods: peas: *ER* I.200 (clerk of kitchen, 1328–9): 2 tuns peas, each containing 13 bolls; woad: ACR V i.83 (Aberdeen, 1450): at least 16 bolls, 1 firlot in 1 tun.

VAS (other form 'vasa')

A container for wine. It does not seem to have had the status of a measure, but was rather a generic term denoting a vessel. See *ER* II.449 (1½ tuns, 12 gallons Rhenish contained in 1 'vas'), *ER* III.654 (of ten tuns wine purchased, one was spilt 'per fracturam vasis'), and ACR IV.172 ('vasa' of 'bastard' wine called a hogshead).

WEIGH/WEY (other forms 'wall' and 'waw')

A unit of weight, found for iron, wax, and wool. See above, under stone.

(a) For wax: the assize of King David said that the wey ought to contain 12 stones, apparently those of 8 pounds, giving a 96 pound wey. Hanham, 'A Medieval Scots Merchant's Handbook', 119 : 'Here begynnys the Reknyngis of the wax . . . vj li. makis the nayle, & thretty nayle makis the walle ['weigh'].' The editor states, p. 110, that these were pounds of Bruges, which may explain the discrepancy between this and the evidence in David's assize.

(b) For wool: Assisa de Tolloneis, p. 668: 'of a waw of wol that is to say half a sek twa peniis .'

Evidence from the *Exchequer Rolls* and the *Treasurer's Accounts* from the end of the fifteenth century and in the early sixteenth shows a clear 12 stone wey. *ER* IX.218–19 (Edinburgh, 1482–3): purchase recorded in Latin account of 108/128 dozen stones iron; royal warrant, in Scots, gives 108/128 weys; *TA* V.55 (treasurer, 1515): 12 stone 'makand ane wall of irne'. Further confirmation of this relationship is from explicit unit prices in *TA* I.284 (which also confirms a 16 pound stone), 349, 384, 391, II.82, 271, IV.45, although when pounds as well as stones are involved rounding off often takes place (e.g. *TA* I.335, III.136, IV.278, V.68, VII.487). *TA* I.291 produces a wey of 191.08 pounds; II.270 produces a 192 pound wey (both also suggesting therefore a stone of 16 pounds); cf. II.89 which produces a 162 pound wey.

'WIDDE' (other forms 'vidde', 'wedy', 'wethy', 'wyddy', etc.)

A quantity or a weight of iron.

Select bibliography

LIST OF MANUSCRIPTS

PUBLIC RECORD OFFICE, CHANCERY LANE

E 101 (Exchequer, Wardrobe)/9/12; E 101/19/21, 27; E 101/22/40; E 101/98/33; E 101/365/9; E 101/366/1; E 101/482/28. Details of editions and extractions made from these MSS in *DHS* and *CDS* are listed below.

DURHAM, DEAN AND CHAPTER ARCHIVES

Accounts and *status* of obedientiaries in Durham Cathedral Priory: Almoner, 1338–48; Bursar, 1278–1350; Cellarer, *c.*1300–49; Chamberlain, 1334–50; Hostiller, 1302–50; Sacrist, 1318–50

Accounts and *status* of cells: Coldingham Prior, 1342–50; Coldingham Sacrist, 1311–45; Finchale, 1303–49; Holy Isle, 1308–48; Jarrow, 1303–48; Wearmouth, ?1321–50.

Accounts of Durham's Scottish Proctor: 1325–39. The accounts of the proctor are edited in the volume of edited Coldingham accounts. See the list of printed primary sources (under Raine) for the editions of accounts of Durham cells and for editions and extractions of obedientiary accounts.

ABERDEEN, TOWN HOUSE

Aberdeen Council Registers: vols. I–II, IV–XVI, 1398–1414, 1434–1541.

Dean of Guild Accounts: 1452–3 (in Guildry Accounts, 1453–1650) and 1470–1 (Acc. 1000/7; photocopy from Gordon of Gordonstoun MSS in Yale University Library).

PRINTED PRIMARY SOURCES

Aberdeen *Extracts from the Council Register of the Burgh of Aberdeen*, I; *1398–1570*, ed. J. Stuart, Spalding Club 12 (Aberdeen, 1844).

Aberdeen *Early Records of the Burgh of Aberdeen, 1317, 1398–1407*, ed. W.C. Dickinson, *SHS*, 3rd ser., 49 (1957).

Aberdeenshire *Illustrations of the Topography and Antiquities of the Shires of Aberdeen and Banff*, Spalding Club, 9 (Aberdeen, 1843).

P.J. Anderson (ed.), *Charters and Other Writs illustrating the History of the Royal Burgh of Aberdeen* (Aberdeen, 1890).
'Articuli Inquirendi in Itinere Camerarii', in *Ancient Laws*, pp. 114–26.
'Assise Willelmi Regis', in *Ancient Laws*, pp. 60–2.
'Ayr Burgh Accounts, 1428–9', ed. G.S. Pryde, *SHR* 31 (1952).
Bain, Joseph (ed.), *Calendar of Documents relating to Scotland Preserved in Her Majesty's Public Record Office, London* (Edinburgh, 4 vols., 1881–8). Grant G. Simpson and James D. Galbraith (eds.), *Calendar of Documents relating to Scotland Preserved in the Public Record Office and the British Library*, V (supplementary AD 1108–1516), SRO (Edinburgh, 1986).
Bannatyne Miscellany, III, ed. David Laing (Edinburgh, 1855).
Bower, Walter, *Scotichronicon*, general editor D.E.R. Watt, VIII ed. D.E.R. Watt (Aberdeen, 1987).
Cochran-Patrick, R.W. (ed.), *Records of the Coinage of Scotland* (Edinburgh, 2 vols., 1876).
Early Records relating to Mining in Scotland (Edinburgh, 1878).
Dickinson, W. Croft (ed.), *The Sheriff Court Book of Fife 1515–22*, *SHS* 3rd ser., 12 (1928), p. 321.
Dickson, Thomas (ed. of I) and Paul, Sir James Balfour (ed. of II–VII), *Compota Thesaurariorum regum Scotorum. Accounts of the Lord High Treasurer of Scotland*, I–VII, 1473–1541 (HMSO, Edinburgh, 1877–1907).
Dunkeld *Rentale Dunkeldense, Being Accounts of the Bishopric* (A.D. 1505–1517), with Myln's, 'Lives of the Bishops' (A.D. 1483–1517), trs. and ed. Robert K. Hannay, with a note on the cathedral church by E.C. Eeles, *SHS* 2nd ser. 10 (1915).
Edinburgh *Extracts from the Records of the Burgh of Edinburgh.* A.D. 1403–1528, ed. Sir James D. Marwick, *SBRS*, 2 (1869).
Fowler, Canon (ed.), *Extracts from the Account Rolls of the Abbey of Durham*, SS, 99, 100, and 103, (London, 1899–1901).
'Fragmenta Collecta', in *Ancient Laws*, pp. 160–86.
Hannay, R.K. (ed.), *Acts of the Lords of Council in Public Affairs 1501–1554* (Edinburgh, 1932).
Historical Manuscripts Commission, 12th Report, Appendix, Part 8: MSS of the Duke of Athol, K.T., and of the Earl of Home, HMSO (Edinburgh, 1891).
Innes, Cosmo (ed.), *Ancient Laws and Customs of the Burghs of Scotland I* A.D. 1124–1424, SBRS (1868).
'Leges Burgorum', in *Ancient Laws*, pp. 4–58.
MacKenzie, J.H. and J. and Graham, R. (eds.), 'Excerpta e libris domicitii domini Jacobi Quinti Regis Scotorum. MDXXV–MDXXXIII', Bannatyne Club, 54 (Edinburgh, 1836).
'Modus Procedendi in Itinere Camerarii', in *Ancient Laws*, pp. 132–54.
Moray *Registrum Episcopatus Moraviensis*, ed. C. Innes, Bannatyne Club (Edinburgh, 1837).
Morton *Registrum Honoris de Morton*, ed. C. Innes, Bannatyne Club (Edinburgh, 1853).
Murray, Sir Thomas of Glendook, *The Laws and Acts of Parliament Made by King James the First, Second, Third, Fourth, Fifth, Queen Mary, King James*

the Sixth, King Charles the First, King Charles the Second . . . Kings and Queen of Scotland (Edinburgh, 1681).

Oschinsky, Dorothea (ed.), *Walter of Henley and Other Treatises on Estate Management and Accounting* (Oxford, 1971).

Raine, James, *The History and Antiquities of North Durham* (London, 1852).

Raine, James (ed.), *The Charters of Endowment, Inventories and Account Rolls of the Priory of Finchale*, SS 6 (London, 1837).

Correspondence, Inventories, Account Rolls and Law Proceedings of the Priory of Coldingham SS 12 (London, 1841).

The Inventories and Account Rolls of the Benedictine Houses or Cells of Jarrow and Monk-Wearmouth, SS 29 (London, 1854).

Regiam Majestatem, Sir John Skene (Edinburgh, 1609).

Registrum secreti sigilli Scotorum: the Register of the Privy Seal of Scotland, ed. M.Livingstone (1908-)

St Andrews *Rentale Sancti Andree, Being the Chamberlain and Granitar Accounts of the Archbishopric in the Time of Cardinal Betoun, 1538–1546*, ed. Robert K. Hannay, *SHS*, 2nd ser. 4 (1913).

'Statuta Gilde', in *Ancient Laws*, pp. 64–88.

Stevenson, Joseph (ed.), *Documents Illustrative of the History of Scotland from the Death of King Alexander the Third to the Accession of Robert Bruce, 1286–1306* (HMSO, Edinburgh, 2 vols., 1870).

Stuart, John, and others, *Rotuli Scaccarii regum Scotorum. The Exchequer Rolls of Scotland*, I–XVII, 1264–1542 (HMSO, Edinburgh, 1878–97).

Sylloge of Coins of the British Isles, XXXV: *Scottish Coins*, J.D. Bateson and N.J. Mayhew (Oxford, 1987).

Thompson, W.N., and Tout, T.F. (eds.), *Register of John de Halton*, Canterbury and York Society (London, 1913).

Thomson, Thomas (ed.), *The Acts of the Lords Auditors of Causes and Complaints*, Record Commission (Edinburgh, 1839).

Acta Dominorum Concilii: The Acts of the Lords of Council in Civil Causes, Record Commission (Edinburgh, 1839).

Thomson, T., and Innes, C. (eds.), *Acts of the Parliaments of Scotland*, I–V (Edinburgh, 1814–75).

SECONDARY WORKS

Balfour, Sir James, *Practicks: Or, a System of the More Ancient Law of Scotland* (Edinburgh, 1754).

Barrow, G.W.S., *Kingship and Unity: Scotland 1000–1306* (London, 1981).

'The Sources for the History of the Highlands in the Middle Ages', in Loraine Maclean (ed.), *The Middle Ages in the Highlands* (Inverness 1981).

Bateson, J.D., 'Roman and Medieval Coins Found in Scotland, to 1987', *PSAS*, 119 (1989), 165–88.

Braudel, F., *The Structures of Everyday Life* (London, 1981).

Bridbury, A.R., *England and the Salt Trade in the Later Middle Ages* (Oxford, 1955).

Burns, E., *The Coinage of Scotland*, (Edinburgh, 3 vols., 1887).
Burrell, L., 'The Standards of Scotland', *Monthly Review of the Institute of Weights and Measures Administration*, 69 (March, 1961), 49–60.
Challis, C.E., 'Debasement: The Scottish Experience in the Fifteenth and Sixteenth Centuries', in *Coinage in Medieval Scotland*.
Challis, C.E. (ed.), *New History of the Royal Mint* (Cambridge, 1992).
Connor, R.D., *The Weights and Measures of England* (London, 1987).
Connor, R.D., and Simpson, A.D.C., *The Weights and Measures of Scotland*, forthcoming, to be published by HMSO with the National Museums of Scotland.
Dickinson, W.C., 'A Chamberlain's Ayre in Aberdeen, 1399 x 1400', *SHR*, 33 (1954), 27–36.
Ditchburn, David, 'Trade with Northern Europe, 1297–1540', in *SMT*.
Duncan, A.A.M., *Scotland: The Making of the Kingdom* (Edinburgh, 1975).
Dyer, Christopher, *Standards of Living in the Later Middle Ages: Social Change in England c. 1200–1520* (Cambridge, 1989).
Enno Van Gelder. H., and Hoc, Marcel, *Les Monnaies des Pays-Bas Bourgignons et Espagnols 1434–1713* (Amsterdam, 1960).
Farmer, D.L., 'Some Price Fluctuations in Angevin England', *EcHR*, 2nd ser. 9 (1956), 34–43.
'Some Grain Price Movements in Thirteenth-Century England', *EcHR*, 2nd ser. 10 (1957), 207–20.
'Some Livestock Price Movements in Thirteenth-Century England', *EcHR*, 2nd ser. 22 (1969), 1–16.
in *Agrarian History of England and Wales*, II, ed. H.E. Hallam (Cambridge, 1988), and III, ed. Edward Miller (Cambridge, 1991).
Gibson, Alexander and Smout, Christopher, 'Scottish Food and Scottish History, 1500–1800', in R.A. Houston and I.D. Whyte (eds.), *Scottish Society 1500–1800* (Cambridge, 1989), pp. 59–84.
Prices, Food and Wages in Scotland, 1550–1780 (Cambridge, 1994).
Gilbert, John M., 'The Usual Money of Scotland and Exchange Rates against Foreign Coin', in *Coinage in Medieval Scotland*, pp. 131–54.
Grant, A., 'The Higher Nobility in Scotland and their Estates, c. 1371–1424' (unpublished DPhil. thesis, Oxford, 1975).
Independence and Nationhood: Scotland 1306–1469 (London, 1984).
Grierson, P., *Dark Age Numismatics* (London, 1979).
Hanham, Alison, 'A Medieval Scots Merchant's Handbook', *SHR*, 50 (1971), 107–20.
Harvey, Barbara, *Living and Dying in England 1100–1540: The Monastic Experience* (Oxford, 1993).
Heath, Peter, 'North Sea Fishing in the Fifteenth Century: The Scarborough Fleet', *Northern History*, 3 (1968), 53–69.
Henderson, J.M., *Scottish Reckonings of Time, Money, Weights and Measures*, Historical Association of Scotland, New Series, 4 (Edinburgh, 1926).
Holmes, N., 'A Fifteenth-Century Coin Hoard from Leith', *BNJ*, 53 (1983), 78–107.
James, Margery K., 'The Fluctuations of the Anglo-Gascon Wine Trade during the Fourteenth Century', *EcHR*, 2nd ser. 4 (1951), 170–96 in E.M. Carus-Wilson (ed.), *Essays in Economic History*, II (London, 1962).

Keene, D., 'A New Study of London before the Great Fire', *Urban History Yearbook* (1984).

Survey of Medieval Winchester (Oxford 1985) I.

Kennedy, William, *Annals of Aberdeen, from the Reign of King William the Lion* (London, 2 vols., 1818).

Latham, R.E. *Revised Medieval Latin Word-List from British and Irish Sources* (London, 1965).

Lloyd, T.H., *The Movement of Wool Prices in Medieval England* (*EcHR* Supplement, no. 6, 1973).

The English Wool Trade in the Middle Ages (Cambridge, 1977).

Lynch, Michael, 'The Social and Economic Structure of the Larger Towns, 1450–1600', in *SMT*.

Lynch, M., Spearman, M., and Stell, G. (eds.), *The Scottish Medieval Town* (Edinburgh, 1988).

Lythe, S.G.E., 'Economic Life', in J.M. Brown (ed.), *Scottish Society in the Fifteenth Century* (London, 1977).

Macdougall, Norman, *James III: A Political Study* (Edinburgh, 1982).

Macfarlane, Leslie J., *William Elphinstone and the Kingdom of Scotland 1431–1514* (Aberdeen, 1985).

McNeill, P., and Nicholson, R. (eds.), *An Historical Atlas of Scotland c.400–c.1600* (St Andrews, 1975).

Macqueen, H., and Windram, William J., 'Laws and Courts in the Burghs', in *SMT*.

Mayhew, N.J., 'Money in Scotland in the Thirteenth Century', in *Coinage in Medieval Scotland*.

Sterling Imitations of Edwardian Type (Oxford, 1983).

'The Contemporary Valuation of the Fleur-de-Lis Groats of James I and James II', *BNJ*, 58 (1988), 130–2.

'Alexander III – A Silver Age? An Essay in Scottish Medieval Economic History', in Norman H. Reid (ed.), *Scotland in the Reign of Alexander III 1249–1286* (Edinburgh, 1990).

'From Regional to Central Minting, 1158–1464', in C.E. Challis (ed.), *A New History of the Royal Mint* (Cambridge, 1992).

Metcalf, D.M., 'The Evidence of Scottish Coin Hoards for Monetary History, 1100–1600', in *Coinage in Medieval Scotland*.

'The Quality of Scottish Sterling Silver, 1136–1280', in *Coinage in Medieval Scotland*.

Metcalf, D.M. (ed.), *Coinage in Medieval Scotland (1100–1600)*, BAR, 45 (Oxford, 1977).

Miller, E., 'The Fortunes of the English Textile Industry in the Thirteenth Century', *EcHR*, 2nd ser. 18 (1965), 64–82.

Murray, Athol, 'The Exchequer and Crown Revenue of Scotland 1437–1542' (unpublished PhD thesis, University of Edinburgh, 1961).

'Crown Lands 1424–1542' in P. McNeill and R. Nicholson (eds.), *An Historical Atlas of Scotland c.400–c.1600* (St Andrews, 1975).

'Foreign Trade and Scottish Ports 1471 and 1542' in P. McNiell and R. Nicholson (eds.), *An Historical Atlas of Scotland c.400–c.1600* (St Andrews, 1975).

Murray, J.E.L., 'The Early Unicorns and the Heavy Groats of James III and James IV', *BNJ*, 40 (1971), 62–96.
'The Black Money of James III', in *Coinage in Medieval Scotland*.
'The Organisation and Work of the Scottish Mint 1358–1603', in *Coinage in Medieval Scotland*.
Murray, J.E.L. and Cowell, M.R., 'Some Placks and Base Groats of James III of Scotland', in D.M. Metcalf and W.A. Oddy (eds.), *Metallurgy in Numismatics* (London, 1980).
Nicholson, Ranald, *Scotland: The Later Middle Ages* (Edinburgh, 1974 and 1978).
'Scottish Monetary problems in the Fourteenth and Fifteenth Centuries', in *Coinage in Medieval Scotland*.
Nightingale, Pamela, 'The Evolution of Weight Standards and the Creation of New Monetary and Commercial Links in Northern Europe from the Tenth Century to the Twelfth Century', *EcHR*, 2nd ser. 38 (1985), 192–209.
Power, E., *The Wool Trade in English Medieval History*, Ford Lectures (Oxford, 1941).
Rogers, J.E. Thorold, *A History of Agriculture and Prices in England, 1259–1793* (Oxford, 7 vols., 1866–1902).
Six Centuries of Work and Wages: The History of English Labour (Oxford, 1890).
Ross, A.S.C., 'The Assize of Bread', *EcHR*, 2nd ser. 9 (1956), 332–42.
Sanderson, Margaret, *Scottish Rural Society in the Sixteenth Century* (Edinburgh, 1982).
Cardinal of Scotland: David Beaton c.1494–1546 (Edinburgh, 1986).
Saul, A., 'The Herring Industry at Gt Yarmouth', *Norfolk Archaeology*, 38 (1981), 40–1.
Simpson, A.D.C., 'Grain Packing in Early standard Capacity Measures: Evidence from the Scottish Dry Capacity Standards', *Annals of Science*, 49 (1992), 337–50.
'Scots "Trone Weight": Preliminary Observations on the Origin of Scotland's Early Market Weights', *Northern Studies*, 29 (1992), 62–81.
Smith, Adam, *The Wealth of Nations* (London, 1977).
Spufford, P., *Money and its Use in Medieval Europe* (Cambridge, 1988).
Stevenson, Alexander, 'Trade between Scotland and the Low Countries in the Late Middle Ages' (unpublished PhD thesis, University of Aberdeen, 1982).
in *Scottish Historical Atlas*, II, forthcoming.
'Trade with the South, 1070–1513', in *SMT*.
Stevenson, R.B.K., 'The Bawbee Issues of James V and Mary', *BNJ*, 59 (1989), 120–56.
Stewart, Ian, 'Some Scottish Ceremonial Coins', *PSAS*, 98 (1964–6), 254–75.
The Scottish Coinage (London, 1967).
'Scottish Mints', in R.A.G. Carson (ed.), *Mints, Dies and Currency* (London, 1971).
Stell, G., 'Architecture: The Changing Needs of Society' in J.M. Brown (ed.), *Scottish Society in the Fifteenth Century* (London, 1977).
Swinton, Lord John, *A Proposal for the Uniformity of Weights and Measures in Scotland* (Edinburgh, 1779).

Symms, Peter, 'Market regulation in the Early 16th-Century Burgh', *PSAS* 118 (1988), 277–87.

Titow, J.Z., *English Rural Society, 1200–1350* (London, 1969).

Torrie, Elizabeth P.D., 'The Guild in Fifteenth-Century Dunfirmline', in *SMT*.

Walton, Penelope, 'Textiles', in John Blair and Nigel Ramsey (eds.), *English Medieval Industries* (London, 1991).

Whittington, G., and Edwards, K.J., 'The Cultivation and Utilisation of Hemp in Scotland', *Scottish Geographical Magazine*, 106 (1990), 167–73.

'Palynological Evidence for the Growing of Cannabis Sativa L. (Hemp) in Medieval and Historical Scotland', *Trans. Inst. Br. Geog.* (1990), 60–9.

Wormald, Jenny, *Court, Kirk and Community: Scotland 1470–1625* (London, 1981).

Zupko, R.E., 'The Weights and Measures of Scotland before the Union', *SHR*, 56 (1977), 119–45.

Index

Since the arrangement of the book is essentially thematic, the index is summary rather than exhaustive. In addition the reader is referred to the Glossary especially for weights and measures, and of course to the table of Contents, and the lists of Figures and Tables. Place-names in the price lists have not been indexed.